Introduction to
Third World Politics

CONTRIBUTORS

Ervand Abrahamian
BARUCH COLLEGE

Merilee S. Grindle
JOHN F. KENNEDY SCHOOL OF GOVERNMENT,
HARVARD UNIVERSITY

Richard A. Joseph
EMORY UNIVERSITY

William A. Joseph
WELLESLEY COLLEGE

Mark Kesselman
COLUMBIA UNIVERSITY

Darren Kew
TUFTS UNIVERSITY

Atul Kohli
PRINCETON UNIVERSITY

Joel Krieger
WELLESLEY COLLEGE

Peter Lewis
AMERICAN UNIVERSITY

Al Montero
CARLETON COLLEGE

Scott D. Taylor
SMITH COLLEGE

Introduction to Third World Politics

SECOND EDITION

GENERAL EDITORS

William A. Joseph
WELLESLEY COLLEGE

Mark Kesselman
COLUMBIA UNIVERSITY

Joel Krieger
WELLESLEY COLLEGE

Houghton Mifflin Company

Boston   New York

To our children, who are growing up in a complex and exhilarating world:
WAJ—for Abigail, Hannah, and Rebecca
MK—for Ishan and Javed
JK—for Nathan

Sponsoring Editor: Melissa Mashburn
Basic Book Editor: Jennifer Sutherland
Editorial Associate: Vikram Mukhija
Project Editor: Gabrielle Stone
Assistant Manufacturing Coordinator: Andrea Wagner
Senior Marketing Manager: Sandra McGuire

Printed in the U.S.A.

Library of Congress Catalog Card Number: 99-71975

ISBN: 0-395-93705-1

2 3 4 5 6 7 8 9-DC-03 02 01 00 99

BRIEF CONTENTS

CONTENTS

3 India   83

Atul Kohli

4 Mexico   129

Merilee S. Grindle

5 Brazil   177

Al Montero

6 Nigeria   233

Richard A. Joseph, Peter Lewis, Darren Kew, and Scott D. Taylor

7 Iran   295

Ervand Abrahamian

These are exciting yet daunting times to teach about politics in the Third World. For decades, most of the countries of Africa, Asia, and Latin America seemed trapped in a vicious cycle of dictatorship and underdevelopment. But the recent spread of democracy and the improved economic prospects in many less developed nations have challenged scholars and teachers to think anew about the Third World, and—as discussed in Chapter 1 of this volume—have even called into question the continuing validity of the term "Third World." *Introduction to Third World Politics* deals with a subject matter whose intellectual, as well as political and economic boundaries are very much in flux.

Introduction to Third World Politics is an extensively revamped version of *Third World Politics at the Crossroads* (1996). We were very gratified by the enthusiastic response to the high level of scholarship, the wealth of information, and the innovative themes in the first edition. We were also pleased to receive many excellent suggestions for changes from reviewers and instructors who assigned the book. In response to many of these suggestions—and to the dramatic changes in the study of Third World politics—we decided that an uncommonly thorough revision was needed.

The book's new title signifies the sweeping nature of the revision. Although we have retained the theoretical framework of *Third World Politics at the Crossroads* and provide coverage of the same countries (Brazil, China, India, Iran, Mexico, and Nigeria), we have also made some very important changes. Every chapter has been carefully rewritten to make the book accessible to students with little or no background in political science. We have used simple, sprightly prose and have maximized symmetry among the chapters in order to facilitate comparison. We have also updated the material on each of the countries to take account of major events and regime changes that have occurred since 1996. (Even as we write, Nigeria has held competitive presidential elections and appears to be in transition from military dictatorship to democracy—a moving target for authors and editors, but that's just what makes the study of Third World politics so exciting!)

We have written this book to help students analyze the problems confronting six important and diverse countries in the Third World and to equip them with an understanding of where these countries may be headed politically. We have kept in mind the needs of instructors for clear and readable prose, for comparative analysis focused on countries and

political systems, for comprehensive treatment of institutions, political behavior, political economy, and the policy-making process.

A chapter is devoted to each country, and each country chapter consists of five sections. Section 1 treats the historic formation of the modern state and includes a new discussion of the geographic setting. Section 2 describes the political economy of past and current national development. Section 3 outlines the major institutions of governance and policy-making. Section 4 explains the widely varying processes of representation, participation, and contestation. Finally, Section 5 reflects on the major issues that confront the country and are likely to shape its future.

Introduction to Third World Politics emphasizes patterns of state formation, political economy, domestic politics, and the politics of collective identities within the context of the international political and economic systems. A distinctive feature of the book is the use of four comparative themes to frame the presentation of each country's politics. We explain the themes in Chapter 1 and present an intriguing "puzzle" for each to stimulate student thinking. These themes—treated in each country study—focus attention on the continuities and contrasts among the six countries:

- **The Democratic Idea** explores the challenges posed by citizens' demands for greater control and participation in both democracies and non-democracies.

- **Governing the Economy** analyzes state strategies for promoting economic development and stresses the effects of economic globalization on domestic politics.

- **A World of States** highlights the importance of state formation and the interstate system for political development.

- **The Politics of Collective Identities** considers the political consequences of race, ethnicity, gender, religion, and nationality and their complex interplay with class-based politics.

Through our four themes, the methods of comparative analysis come alive as students examine similarities and differences among countries and within and between political systems. This thematic approach facilitates timely and comprehensive analysis of political challenges and changing agendas within countries.

Introduction to Third World Politics strikes a balance between the richness of national political development and a more general comparative analysis. Chapter 1 explains the comparative method, explores the uses and limitations of the concept of the "Third World," describes core features of political institutions and processes in developing countries, and analyzes the four key themes of the book. Each country study presents a clear and thorough treatment of political institutions and their relation to socioeconomic, cultural, and transnational influences.

Several special features assist in the teaching and learning process. At the beginning of each chapter, students will find a page of basic demographic, social, economic, and political information to aid in comparing countries. Throughout the chapters a wide array of maps, tables, charts, photographs, and political cartoons enliven the text and present key information in clear and graphic ways. Each country study includes four to six boxes that highlight interesting and provocative aspects of politics—for example, the biography of an important political leader, institutional intricacies, or unconventional forms of participation. Key terms are set in boldface when first introduced and are defined in the Glossary at the end of the book. Students will find that the Glossary defines many key concepts that are used broadly in the analysis of Third World and comparative politics.

In *Introduction to Third World Politics,* we combine an innovative thematic approach and comprehensive coverage of political institutions and processes. We hope that it serves as a stimulating and accessible introduction to the study of Third World politics for your students.

One final note: The country chapters in this volume are drawn from our text, *Introduction to Comparative Politics: Political Challenges and Changing Agendas* (Houghton Mifflin, © 2000), which also includes chapters on Britain, France, Germany, Russia, and the United States. The Preface and Chapter 1 of this book are also adapted from the larger text, with some important modifications specific to the study of Third World politics.

We are grateful for the advice and critical comments of many colleagues, including Amrita Basu. We also want to thank Shylashri Shankar, Elora Shehabuddin and Rani Tudor for their assistance in preparing the chapter on India and Andre Leroux, for his help with Mexico and to Maria do Carmo Campello de Souza for her contribution to the first edition. We are especially indebted to those who critiqued the first edition or reviewed portions of the second edition manuscript:

Daniel P. Franklin, Georgia State University; **Margaret Keck,** Johns Hopkins University; **Nikki Keddie,** University of California, Los Angeles; **Peter R. Kingstone,** University of Vermont; **Stephen Manning,** University of Detroit, Mercy; **Jennie Purnell,** Boston College.

Finally, our thanks to the talented and professional staff at Houghton Mifflin, especially Melissa Mashburn, sponsoring editor; Jennifer Sutherland, development editor; Gabrielle Stone, project editor; Vikram Mukhija, editorial associate, and Sandra McGuire, marketing manager.

W. A. J.

M. K.

J. K.

Introduction to
Third World Politics

CHAPTER 1

Introducing Third World Politics

William A. Joseph, Mark Kesselman,
and Joel Krieger

Section ❶ The Global Challenge of Comparative Politics

At the turn of the twentieth century, politics throughout the world are more unsettled than many would have predicted a decade ago. Then, a host of developments heralded a dramatic shift in historic epochs and created the sense that a more harmonious, democratic, and prosperous order might be dawning. The revolutions of 1989 in eastern and central Europe marked the disintegration of much of the communist world. When the Berlin Wall—which divided East and West in both physical and symbolic terms—was dismantled brick by brick beginning in November 1989, the architecture of Europe was forever altered. Within a year, Germany was unified after nearly a half-century of **Cold War** division, and by the end of 1991 the Soviet Union, once a formidable superpower, had collapsed into fifteen troubled republics, including a much humbled Russia.

Recent years have also witnessed a flood of history-making events in the developing, or **Third World**, nations of Asia, Africa, and Latin America. To cite just a few examples: China, long one of the world's poorest countries, has become one of the world's most dynamic economies. In the mid-1990s, Nelson Mandela was transformed from prisoner to president of a newly democratic South Africa, and an awkward handshake between the Palestinian leader Yasir Arafat and the Israeli prime minister Yitzhak Rabin inspired hope for a new era in the Middle East. Latin America has changed from being a region dominated by harsh military regimes to one in which nearly every country is either a democracy or can be said to be moving toward democratization.

Today we know that this shift in historical epochs not only created exciting opportunities for human progress but also increased the risks of instability and conflict, particularly in the Third World. As we have painfully learned in recent years, freedom, peace, and a reasonable standard of living cannot be built on hopes alone. In the developing countries, economic scarcity, widespread poverty, and extreme inequality make it especially hard to turn such dreams into reality. Toppling dictatorial regimes often proves less difficult than building new democracies. In many Third World nations, the rush to democracy has awakened new and restless constituencies with demands that cannot easily be met by the government or the economy. Even in a relatively long-established Third World democracy like India, religious divisions frequently explode into communal violence that not only threatens the social order but also shakes the foundations of the country's democratic political system.

An Uncertain World Order

Post–Cold War political changes and the transformation of the global balance of power have produced new forms of international cooperation and competition— as well as new sources of international tension and violence. The grim but predictable bipolar world of superpower rivalry between the United States and the Soviet Union, reinforced by the North Atlantic Treaty Organization (NATO) and Warsaw Treaty Organization (Warsaw Pact) alliances, has been replaced by the uncertainties of a more fragmented map of global power. Increasing economic, religious, and ethnic divisions create tensions in every corner of the globe.

The harsh consequences of these tensions are evident in newspaper headlines and heartrending stories on television news. Consider one of the major sources of conflict in the post–Cold War world—a wave of violent religious and ethnic conflict. No region of the world is a sanctuary. In Africa members of the Hutu majority in Rwanda slaughtered hundreds of thousands of the Tutsi minority. In Asia religious and ethnic minorities in India and Indonesia were savagely attacked and massacred. Europe was also the setting for an onslaught on religious and ethnic groups. In the Balkans leaders of the Serb majority in Yugoslavia expelled from their homes and butchered hundreds of thousands of Muslims and ethnic Albanians. The 1990s saw the creation of a new term, *ethnic cleansing*, to describe the elimination of minorities within a territory. But the phrase does not convey the inhumanity of the process. In brief, what is certainly one of the most violent centuries in world history ended no more respectful of human rights and human life than when it began.

The end of Cold War divisions has also failed to eliminate other massive problems. Consider the issue of economics. Although a major cause of the demise of communism in the Soviet Union and its allies in East-Central Europe was that capitalist countries vastly outperformed the communist bloc, the triumph of capitalism and expansion of markets have not ushered in economic progress for many people throughout the world. Quite the contrary. For example, the globalization of trade, investment, and communications has destroyed many traditional communities and damaged the natural environment. During the 1970s and 1980s the rapidly developing countries in East and Southeast Asia were held up as an economic miracle. However, these same countries became an economic nightmare in the late 1990s, as financial crises produced economic recession and sharply reduced living standards for many of their citizens.

These international changes have had a far-reaching effect on the countries of Asia, Africa, and Latin America. During the Cold War, the rivalry between the Soviet Union and the United States was often fought and contained in the Third World at a safe distance from the superpowers, as in the Vietnam War or conflicts in the Middle East and Central America. This situation was certainly politically destabilizing for and caused much human suffering in the Third World. But the superpower standoff also gave the developing nations some bargaining power when it came to securing economic or military aid, as the United States and the Soviet Union wooed allies among the developing nations.

The end of the Cold War has meant an end to such strategic leverage for the Third World. Indeed, the collapse of communism has diverted economic resources away from the Third World as the developed nations and international organizations channel more funds to help the struggling democracies and market economies of Russia, other Soviet successor states (such as Ukraine), and Eastern Europe. On the other hand, one reason democracy has recently been able to spread throughout much of the Third World is that dictators can no longer rely on their superpower patrons to keep them in power for strategic reasons.

In short, both the national and international contexts of politics in the Third World changed profoundly in the last decades of the twentieth century. Yet (as we discuss in more detail later) there remain very important continuities in the domestic and global situations of the developing nations of Asia, Africa, and Latin America that continue to distinguish them in major ways from the world's economically richer and politically more powerful countries.

Making Sense of Turbulent Times

It is not surprising that in the flash of newspaper headlines and television sound bites, these upheavals and changes may make politics look chaotic beyond comprehension. Although the study of comparative politics can help us understand current events in a rapidly changing world, it involves much more than snapshot analysis or Monday morning quarterbacking. *Introduction to Third World Politics* describes and analyzes in detail the government and politics of six countries (China, India, Mexico, Brazil, Nigeria, and Iran) and identifies common themes in their political development that explain longer-term causes of both changes and continuities in the Third World. This book provides cross-national comparisons and explanations based on four themes that we believe are central for understanding politics in today's world. The four key themes are these:

- *The Democratic Idea:* the pressures for more democracy and the challenges of democratization
- *Governing the Economy:* the role of the state in economic management
- *A World of States:* the interaction of states within the international order
- *The Politics of Collective Identities:* the political impact of diverse attachments and sources of group identity, including class, **gender**, **ethnicity**, and religion

We also expect that these four themes will be useful for analyzing where the countries discussed in this book may be heading politically in the twenty-first century. Moreover, the themes illustrate how comparative politics can serve as a valuable tool for making political sense of even the most tumultuous times. The contemporary period presents an extraordinary challenge to those who study comparative politics in general and Third World politics in particular. But the study of comparative politics also provides a unique opportunity for understanding this uncertain era.

In order to appreciate the complexity of politics and political transitions in the Third World and elsewhere, we must look beyond our own national perspectives. Today, business and trade, information technology, mass communications and culture, immigration and travel—as well as politics—forge deep connections among people worldwide. It is particularly urgent that we adopt a truly global perspective as we explore the politics of different countries and their growing interdependence.

There is an added benefit: by comparing political institutions, values, and processes across countries, the student of comparative politics acquires useful analytical skills. After you study comparative politics, you begin to think like a comparativist. As comparison becomes almost automatic, you look at the politics of your own country differently, with a wider focus and new insights.

The contemporary Third World provides a fascinating laboratory for the study of comparative politics and gives unusual significance to the subject. We hope that you share our sense of excitement and join us in the challenging effort to understand the complex and ever-shifting terrain of politics in the Third World. We begin by first exploring what comparative politics actually compares and how comparative study enhances our understanding of politics generally.

Section ❷   What—and How—Comparative Politics Compares

To compare and contrast is one of the most common human exercises, whether in the classroom study of literature or politics or animal behavior—or in selecting dorm rooms or listing your favorite movies. In the observation of politics, the use of comparisons is very old, dating at least from Aristotle, the Greek philosopher. Aristotle categorized Athenian city-states in the fifth century B.C. according to their form of political rule: rule by a single individual, rule by a few, or rule by all citizens. He added a normative dimension (a claim about how societies *should* be ruled) by distinguishing ("contrasting") good and corrupt versions of each type. The modern study of comparative politics refines and systematizes the age-old practice of evaluating some feature of X by comparing it to the same feature of Y in order to learn more about it than isolated study would permit.

The term **comparative politics** refers to a field within the academic study of politics (that is, political science) as well as to a method or approach to the study of politics.[1] The subject matter of comparative politics is the domestic politics of countries or peoples. This book focuses on the comparative study of several Third World countries, whereas other comparative politics books might focus, for example, on the industrial democracies of Western Europe. Within the discipline of political science, comparative politics is one of four areas of specialization. In addition to comparative politics, most political science (or government) departments in U.S. colleges and universities include courses and academic specialists in three other fields—political theory, international relations, and U.S. politics.

The comparative approach relies principally on analysis designed to identify the similarities and differences between countries by focusing on selected institutions and processes. Students of comparative politics (we call ourselves **comparativists**) believe that we cannot make reliable statements about most political observations by looking at only one case. We often hear statements such as, "The United States has the best health care system in the world." Comparativists immediately wonder what kinds of health care systems exist in other countries, what they cost and how they are financed, who is covered by health insurance, and so on. Besides, what does *best* mean when it comes to health care systems? Is it the one that provides the widest access? the one that is the most technologically advanced? the one that is the most cost-effective? the one that produces the healthiest population? We wouldn't announce the "best movie" or the "best car" without considering other alternatives or deciding what specific factors enter into our judgment.

Comparativists often analyze political institutions or processes by looking at two or more cases deliberately selected for their mix of common and contrasting features. The analysis involves comparing similar aspects of politics in more than one country. For example, a comparativist might ask what explains the vastly different political roles of the military in India and Nigeria (both former British colonies)? One of the strengths of democracy in India is that the Indian military has never intervened in politics, whereas the Nigerian military has done so frequently and with disastrous political and economic consequences for the country. Some comparative political studies take a thematic approach and draw on many different countries to analyze broad issues, such as what causes revolutions.[2]

Levels of Analysis

Comparisons can be very useful for political analysis at several different levels. Political scientists often compare developments in different cities, regions, provinces, or states. Comparative analysis can also focus on specific institutions and processes in different countries, such as the legislature, executive, political parties, social movements, or court systems. The organization of *Introduction to Third World Politics* reflects our belief that the best way to begin the study of comparative politics is with countries. Countries, which are also sometimes referred to as **nation-states**, comprise distinct, politically defined territories that encompass political institutions, cultures, economies, and ethnic and other social identities.

Although often highly divided internally, countries have historically been the most important source of a people's collective political identity, and they are the major arena for organized political action in the modern world. Therefore, countries are the natural unit of analysis for most domestic political variables and processes. These include

- **political institutions** (the formal and informal rules and structured relationships that organize power and resources in society)
- **political culture** (attitudes, beliefs, and symbols that influence political behavior)
- **political development** (the stages of change in the structures of government)

Within a given country, the state is almost always the most powerful cluster of institutions. But just what is the state? The way the term is used in comparative politics is probably unfamiliar to many students. In the United States, it usually refers to the states in the federal system—Texas, California, and so on. But in comparative politics, the **state** refers to a country's key political institutions that are responsible for making, implementing, enforcing, and adjudicating important policies in that country. The most important state institution is the national **executive**, usually the president and/or prime minister and the **cabinet**. In some cases, the most powerful individual may be a Communist Party leader (as in China), the head of the military government (as in Nigeria until 1999), or the supreme religious leader (as in Iran's Islamic Republic). Other important state institutions include the legislature, administrative **bureaucracy**, courts, army, and police. In casual usage, the terms *state* and *government* are sometimes used interchangeably. However, in comparative politics, *government* often does not refer to the permanent administrative or bureaucratic agencies but to the key officials and offices whose fates are linked by election or appointment to the president or prime minister and who direct major administrative agencies. The use of the term *government* in comparative politics, as in the phrase, "the government of Prime Minister Vajpayee of India," is very similar to the term *administration* in U.S. politics.

States claim, usually with considerable success, the right to issue rules—notably, laws, administrative regulations, and court decisions—that are binding for people within the country. Even democratic states, in which top officials are chosen by procedures that permit all citizens to participate, can survive only if they can preserve enforcement (or coercive) powers both internally and with regard to other states that may pose challenges. A number of countries have highly repressive states whose political survival depends largely on military and police powers. But even in such states, long-term stability requires that the ruling regime have some measure of political **legitimacy**; that is, a significant segment of the citizenry must believe that the state acts with some moral authority. Political legitimacy is greatly affected by the state's ability to "deliver the goods" through satisfactory economic performance and an acceptable distribution of economic resources. Moreover, in the contemporary period, legitimacy seems to require that states represent themselves as democratic in some fashion, whether or not they are in fact. Thus, *Introduction to Third World Politics* looks closely at both the state's role in governing the economy and the pressures exerted on states to develop and extend democratic participation.

The fact that states are the fundamental objects of analysis in comparative politics does not mean that all states are the same. Indeed, the organization of state institutions varies widely, and these differences have a powerful impact on political and social life. Hence, each country study in this book devotes considerable attention to variations within the Third World in institutions of governance, participation, and representation, and their political implications. Each country study begins with an analysis of how the institutional organization and political procedures of the state have evolved historically. This process of **state formation** fundamentally influences how and why Third World states differ politically.

Causal Theories

Because countries are the basic building blocks in politics and because states are the most significant political organizations and actors, these two are the critical units for comparative analysis. The comparativist looks at similarities and differences among countries or states and tries to develop causal theories—hypotheses that can be expressed formally in a causal mode: "If X happens, then Y will be the result." Such theories include factors (the independent variables, symbolized by X) that are believed to influence some outcome, and the outcome (the dependent variable, symbolized by Y) that is to be explained. For example, it is commonly argued that if a country's economic pie shrinks, conflict among groups for resources will intensify. This hypothesis suggests what is called an inverse correlation between variables: as X varies in one direction, Y varies in the opposite direction. As the total national economic product (X) decreases, political and social conflict over economic shares (Y) increases. This was the case in Iran, for instance, when economic problems caused by sharply declining oil revenues fed the social discontent that led to the Islamic Revolution of 1979.

It is important to recognize the limits on just how "scientific" political science—and thus comparative politics—can be. In laboratory sciences such as physics or chemistry (often called natural sciences), experimental techniques can be applied to isolate the contribution of distinct factors to a particular outcome. It is possible to change the value or magnitude of a factor—for example, the force applied to an object—and measure how the outcome has consequently changed. However, like other social scientists, political scientists and comparativists rarely have the opportunity to apply such experimental techniques.

In the real world of politics, unlike in a laboratory, variables cannot easily be isolated or manipulated. Some political scientists employ techniques that attempt to identify the specific causal weight of a variable in explaining a political outcome. But it is very difficult to measure precisely how, for example, a person's ethnicity, gender, or income influences her or his choice when casting a ballot. Nor can we ever know for sure what exact mix of factors—conflicts among elites, popular ideological appeals, the weakness of the state, the organizational capacity of rebel leaders, or the discontent of the masses—precipitates a successful revolution.

Despite these difficulties and limitations, the study of comparative politics involves the search for just the right balance in an explanation between the specifics of individual cases and universal patterns. One common goal of comparativists is to develop what is called **middle-level theory**. Such a theory explains phenomena found in a limited range of cases, which in comparative politics means a specific set of countries with the same or similar characteristics, political institutions, or processes. If we study only individual countries without any comparative framework, then comparative politics would become merely the study of a series of isolated cases. It would be impossible to recognize what is most significant in the collage of political characteristics we find in the world's many countries. As a result, the understanding of patterns of similarity and difference among countries would be lost, along with an important tool for evaluating what is and what is not unique about a country's political life.

If we go to the other extreme and try to make universal claims that something is always true in all countries, we would either have to stretch the truth or ignore the interesting differences and patterns of variation. For the political world is incredibly complex, shaped by an extraordinary array of factors and an almost endless interplay of variables. Indeed, after a brief period in the 1950s and 1960s when many comparativists tried—and failed—to develop a "grand theory" that would apply to all countries, most comparativists see the attempt to develop middle-level theory as the most promising.

For example, comparativists have worked hard to analyze the efforts in many countries to replace (or attempt to replace) authoritarian forms of government, such as military **dictatorships** and one-party states, with more participatory and democratic regimes. In studying democratic transitions, comparativists do not treat each national case as unique or try to construct a universal pattern that ignores all differences. Applying middle-level theory, we identify the influence on the new regime's political stability of specific variables such as institutional legacies, political culture, levels of economic development, the nature of the regime before the transition, and the degree of ethnic conflict

or homogeneity. Comparativists have been able to identify patterns in the emergence and consolidation of democratic regimes in southern Europe in the 1970s (Greece, Portugal, and Spain) and have compared them to developments in Latin America, Asia, and Africa since the 1980s, and in eastern and central Europe since the revolutions of 1989. Thus, in this text we can study the transition from military rule to democracy in Brazil and progress toward democratization in Mexico and Nigeria knowing that both fit within a broader comparative framework.

The study of comparative politics has many challenges, including the complexity of the subject matter, the fast pace of change in the contemporary world, and the impossibility of manipulating variables or replicating conditions. What can we expect when the whole political world is our laboratory? When we put the method of comparative politics to the test and develop a set of themes derived from middle-level theory, we discover that it is possible to find explanations and discern patterns that make sense of a vast range of political developments in the Third World.

Section ❸ The Third World in a World in Transition

Most textbooks and courses in comparative politics have traditionally distinguished between industrial (and primarily Western) democracies—the First World; communist states as the Second World; and poor countries in Asia, Africa, and Latin America that had recently gained independence as the Third World. This categorization was based, in part, on distinctive economic features that helped characterize different political systems. Economic organization and performance both affected and reflected the realities of politics in these different political systems: the capitalist (or market) economies and high standard of living in North America, Western Europe, Japan, and a few other countries; the socialist (or planned) economies of countries ruled by a Communist Party, such as the Soviet Union and China; and the low level of economic development and widespread poverty characteristic of the Third World.

Democracy was another dividing line in this way of looking at the nations of the world. The capitalist

industrialized countries were not only wealthy but also stable and democratic; communist systems were unquestionably dictatorial; and Third World nations had a despotic leader, one-party rule, a military regime, or—at best—democracy marred by high levels of social and political violence.

One of the consequences of the many profound changes of recent decades is that these economic and political differences among types of countries are no longer so clear. For one thing, sharp differences in growth rates among developing countries in recent years make it difficult to generalize with confidence about the Third World. Furthermore, scores of developing countries have become democratic in the past two decades. From Argentina to Zimbabwe, countries that were formerly undemocratic have adopted democratic institutions. Linked to the swelling of the ranks of democratic countries in the Third World has been the near-disappearance of countries in the Second World. Beginning in 1989, the collapse of communism

This cartoon captures some of the dramatic trends and tensions in comparative politics during the last decades of the twentieth century. It depicts a triumphant and rich, but economically fragile, First World (the industrial democracies), a defeated Second World (the Soviet bloc and most former Communist-ruled countries) led to ruin by misguided policies (that's Stalin's head being cut off), and a deprived and neglected Third World. The venomous snake of nationalism threatens all parts of the world with ethnic, religious, and other types of communal conflict.
Source: ©1991 WittyWorld International Cartoon Magazine. Reprinted with permission.

in the former Soviet Union and East-Central Europe set off a revolutionary change in world politics. Only a handful of countries—China, Cuba, Vietnam, Laos, and the Democratic People's Republic of Korea (North Korea)—are now ruled by Communist Parties and declare an allegiance to communist ideology. It follows that "Second World" is no longer a useful category by which to classify countries.

These recent economic and political trends challenge and complicate the way that comparativists categorize the world's countries. But we believe that "Third World" remains a valid and useful concept and that the countries included in this text continue to share many distinct characteristics that allow us to identify them as part of the Third World.

The Meaning of *Third World*

The term *Third World* was coined by French authors in the 1950s to draw attention to the plight of the world's poorer nations, which they believed to be as important as the headline-grabbing Cold War and its superpower adversaries. To make their point, they adapted terminology from the French Revolution of the eighteenth century. In the mid-twentieth century, a long-neglected and oppressed *Third* World was struggling against the *First* World (the industrial democracies) and the *Second* World (the Soviet Union and other communist countries) for recognition and power just as the *Third* Estate of the common people in France had struggled against the privileged and powerful clergy (the *First* Estate) and the nobility (the *Second* Estate) in the 1780s.

Some people have criticized the label as suggesting a numerical order in which the Third World ranked behind the First World and the Second World in a cultural sense. But its creators intended the term *Third World* to embody the struggle of poor nations for empowerment in the international system and a fairer share of global wealth. For many, the term remains a powerful symbol of common purpose and determination and is still widely used to describe the developing countries of Asia, Africa, and Latin America.[3]

When reading about the Third World, you also may encounter the term *South* as a way of referring collectively to developing nations in contrast to the developed nations of the *North*. Like Third World, *South* has achieved a certain symbolic importance by conveying the fact that there are enormous differences between the richer and poorer nations of the world. Granted, *South* is geographically somewhat misleading, since there are developed nations in the southern hemisphere (like Australia) and less developed nations in the northern part of the globe (like Afghanistan).

The terms *Third World* and *South* are applied to countries that are economically poorer than the developed industrial democracies, and we will use other terms, such as *developing* and *less developed*, interchangeably with *Third World*. But it is very important to recognize that these countries (which contain about 85 percent of the world's population) are very

Table 1

Diversity in the Third World				
Country	Location	Political System	Economy	Selected Comparative Themes
Brazil	South America	Recently established multiparty democracy	Capitalist, upper-middle income	Transition from military rule to democracy; the politics of economic crisis
China	East Asia	Communist party-state	Socialist, low income with high growth	Why Communist power survives
India	South Asia	Established competitive democracy	Mixed, low income with moderate growth	Democracy, poverty, and religious conflict
Iran	Middle East	Islamic Republic; theocracy	Lower-middle income, heavily dependent on a single export (oil)	Rise and spread of Islamic populism
Mexico	Northern Central America	Single-party dominant democracy	Capitalist, upper-middle income	Peasant rebellion, political violence, and democratization
Nigeria	West Africa	Former military regime in very early stages of democratic transition	Low income, heavily dependent on a single export (oil)	Transition from military rule to democracy; politics in a multiethnic state

diverse geographically, economically, politically, and culturally. Some observers have asserted that there is such great diversity in the Third World that the concept is outdated because it implies too much similarity in the challenges facing the developing nations and too much unity in their international policies. They point to the enormous differences in levels of economic development among countries usually considered part of the Third World. They question whether a country like Bangladesh, with its extreme poverty and overwhelmingly rural population, has much in common with the economically booming and highly urbanized **newly industrializing countries** (NICs), such as the Republic of Korea (South Korea), which are often considered to be part of the Third World. Others argue not for abandoning the term *Third World*, but for taking account of such differences by adding the concept of "Fourth World" to refer to very poor countries with deteriorating economies.

This book acknowledges the rich diversity of the Third World. In fact, the countries to be studied were chosen, in part, to reflect this variety as well as to illustrate important issues in the study of comparative politics. Table 1 indicates some of the important differences that mark the developing nations studied in this text.

The Development Gap

If there are such extensive differences among developing nations, what gives coherence to the concept of "Third World"? Simply put, Third World nations are poorer, their peoples have a lower standard of living, and their economies are not as modernized as the industrialized countries. In other words, they are less developed. A few examples should make the realities of this development gap between the Third World and the industrialized countries clearer.

The World Bank, a major international organization that provides financial assistance to the Third World, divides developing countries according to their annual **gross national product** (GNP) per capita (in other words, the total output of the economy divided by the total population) into three groups: low income (US$785 or less), lower-middle income (US$786–$3125), and upper-middle income (average US$3126–$9655). By contrast, the industrialized (high income) countries have an average GNP per capita of over US$25,000 per year.

Generally speaking, a country's GNP per capita reflects both its level of modernization and its relative power in the international economic system. But GNP per capita figures also reflect the ability of a country to meet the material needs of its people. Thus, lower

Global Connection: *How Is Development Measured?*

One frequently used measure of a country's level of economic development is its gross national product (GNP) per capita. This figure is an estimate of a country's total economic output (including income earned from abroad) divided by its total population. Such estimates are made in a country's own currency, such as pesos in Mexico or rubles in Russia.

In order to make comparisons of GNP per capita across countries, it is necessary to convert them to a common currency, usually the U.S. dollar. This is done using official international currency exchange rates, which, for example, would tell you how many pesos or rubles it takes to buy one U.S. dollar. But many economists believe that an estimate of GNP per capita in dollars based on official exchange rates doesn't give a very accurate sense of the real standards of living in different countries because it doesn't tell what goods and services (such as housing, food, and transportation) people can actually buy with their local currencies.

An alternative and increasingly popular means of comparing per capita GNP levels and levels of economic development across countries is to use exchange rates based on purchasing power parity (PPP). PPP-based exchange rates take into account the actual cost of living in a particular country by figuring what it costs to buy the same bundle of goods in different countries; for example, how many pesos does it actually take to buy a certain amount of food in Mexico or how many rubles to pay for housing in Russia? Many analysts think that PPP provides a more reliable (and revealing) tool for comparing standards of living among countries.

The data boxes that are part of each country unit in this text give both GNP per capita at official exchange rates and using purchasing power parity. The differences between the two calculations can be quite dramatic, especially for developing countries. For example, China's 1997 GNP per capita according to conventional methods was calculated to be only US$860, whereas its PPP-based GNP per capita in the same year was estimated at US$3570.

Because income comparisons based on either GNP per capita or purchasing power parity do not provide a complete picture of a country's level of development, the United Nations has introduced another concept that is useful in making socioeconomic comparisons among nations: the Human Development Index (HDI). Based on a formula that takes into account the three factors of *longevity* (life expectancy at birth), *knowledge* (literacy and average years of schooling), and *income* (according to PPP), the UN assigns each country of the world for which there are enough data a Human Development Index decimal number between 0 and 1; the closer a country is to 1, the better its level of human development.

Out of 174 countries ranked according to HDI by the United Nations in 1998, Canada (1) was at the top and Sierra Leone (174) was ranked last. Among the countries included in this book, Mexico (49) and Brazil (62) scored as having "high human development"; Iran (78) and China (106) had "medium human development"; and India (139) and Nigeria (142) had "low human development."

---

average standards of living and greater poverty also distinguish less developed from more developed nations.

The stark contrasts in the statistics used to measure a country's overall **physical quality of life** (PQLI) give some sense of what such poverty means in terms of people's lives:

- **Life expectancy** in the low-income countries averages only 59 years; in the middle-income developing countries it is about 69, and in the high-income developed countries a person can expect to live 78 years on average. In the poorest countries, such as Afghanistan, life expectancy is only about 45; in Sierra Leone it is 37.

- The **infant mortality rate** (how many children die between birth and age one) in low-income countries is 80 per 1000 live births, and in the very poorest countries it reaches well over 100 per 1000; in the middle-income countries the average infant mortality rate is 35 per 1000; in the world's richest countries, the infant mortality rate is only 6 per 1000 live births.

- **Illiteracy** among adults (people over fifteen who cannot read or write) averages 47 percent in the low-income countries (up to 70–80 percent in some) and 19 percent in the middle-income countries. In the developed countries, illiteracy is generally well under 5 percent.

It is important to recognize that there are vast differences in the PQLI statistics among Third World countries that have similar levels of GNP per capita. For example, China, India, and Nigeria are all ranked as low-income countries by the World Bank with roughly comparable levels of GNP per capita (US$860, $390, and $260, respectively), but China's life expectancy of 69 is considerably higher than India's (62) and Nigeria's (31). China also has much lower levels of infant mortality and illiteracy than do India and Nigeria. The case studies in this book analyze how such differences reflect important contrasts in the historical experiences and government policies of various nations.

The use of national averages tends to mask class, gender, and racial inequalities *within* countries. Although this is true in all countries, developing or developed, the disparities are particularly acute in the Third World. For example, in the West African nation of Burkina Faso the overall literacy rate is 19 percent, but among women it is an even more dismal 9 percent (for males it is about 30 percent). Some people have even suggested that poor women in low-income countries (the Fourth World) should be called the Fifth World because they are, indeed, the poorest of the poor.

Some developing nations have achieved significant progress over the last few decades. A few, such as China, have experienced tremendous economic growth, and infant mortality rates in the low-income countries as a whole have dropped by more than 30 percent since 1980. Similar trends are apparent in the other figures that are used to measure poverty in the less developed countries.

Nevertheless, many developing countries still have very low and sometimes even negative economic growth rates. Others may be experiencing increases in production but their swelling populations are swallowing up the gains of increased output, making real economic expansion impossible. The economy of Honduras, for example, grew by an average of 3.4 percent per year in the period 1990–1997, but its population grew by 3.0 percent per year during the same period. The result? Per capita income in Honduras hardly grew at all. Thus, the enormous socioeconomic gap that separates most of the Third World and the industrialized nations (which have very low population growth rates) is at best closing very slowly—and, in some cases, is even widening—and remains one of the most important ways of categorizing the world's countries (see Figure 1 on p. 13).

Third World States

There are many types of political systems in the Third World. As Table 1 on p. 10 indicates, the countries studied in this book include an established, highly competitive democracy (India), a single-party donant democracy that has only very recently begun to permit real political competition (Mexico), a new democracy (Brazil), an authoritarian military regime (Nigeria) that is in the early stages of democratization, a Communist party-state (China), and a theocracy (Iran), in which supreme political power is held by the religious elite. Analyzing the differences among these varied types of political systems is one of the most important and interesting tasks in the study of comparative politics. But it is also important to note some of the political characteristics shared by Third World countries that distinguish them politically from the industrialized nations.

First, politics and government in Third World countries are shaped by the basic facts of scarce economic resources, extensive poverty and inequality, and a relatively weak position in the international system. Political leaders in less developed countries simply have fewer options available for resolving problems or responding to demands from various groups for a bigger piece of the national economic pie. Economic conflicts therefore are more likely to lead to violence or repression in Third World states; for example, peasants may rebel in their quest for more land, or the government may violently suppress labor unions striking for higher wages. Corruption—a recurrent theme in the case studies in this book—is a very serious problem in much of the Third World because officials personally profit from the state's

Figure 1

The Development Gap

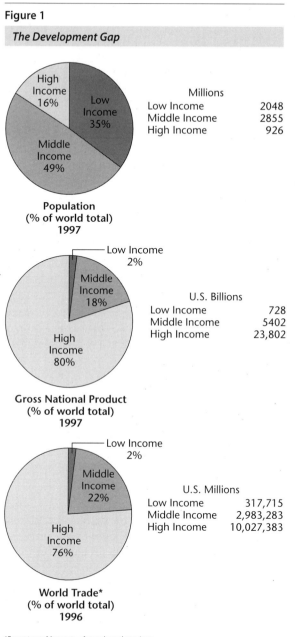

	Millions
Low Income	2048
Middle Income	2855
High Income	926

Population
(% of world total)
1997

	U.S. Billions
Low Income	728
Middle Income	5402
High Income	23,802

Gross National Product
(% of world total)
1997

	U.S. Millions
Low Income	317,715
Middle Income	2,983,283
High Income	10,027,383

World Trade*
(% of world total)
1996

*Exports and imports of goods and services

These charts show just how unequally the world's wealth is divided between the developed (high-income) and developing (middle- and low-income) countries.
Source: World Development Report 1998.

control over the limited economic opportunities. Resistance to democratization in the Third World has often come—as it also did during earlier stages in the political development of Europe and North America—from elites who fear that greater popular control of government will jeopardize their economic privileges as well as their political power.

Second, the political legitimacy of many Third World states is very weak. Most citizens do not have much faith in their political leaders or perhaps even in the very nature of the political system of their country. They may obey the law, they may even vote. But they do not see the government as being very relevant to their lives or as being able to do anything about their most serious concerns; they may even regard the national government as having a negative impact on their lives. Membership in a religious or ethnic group is often a more important source of political identity in the Third World than formal citizenship in a particular country. For example, many Tibetans feel only loosely (and perhaps negatively) connected to the Chinese government even though Tibet is part of the People's Republic of China.

There are various causes of weak state legitimacy in the Third World. The government may be seen as favoring one ethnic, religious, or economic group or even actively discriminating against some groups. Economic failure, political repression, extreme corruption, and military defeat may cause people to lose faith in the government. New democracies—which are now quite common in the Third World—simply have not had enough time to establish legitimacy in the eyes of their citizens. Whatever the cause, states with weak legitimacy are prone to political violence, radical and sudden changes (such as a military **coup d'état**), and government paralysis.

Third, the effective power of governments in the less developed countries is often very limited. The state may have little ability to exert its authority much beyond the capital city and a few large urban centers. In the rural areas and small towns where much or most of the population lives, political life is frequently based more on the relationship between powerful and usually wealthy individuals ("patrons") and those they control ("clients") by dispensing favors or instilling fear. In much of the Third World, the formal aspects of government such as laws, parties, and elections are less important than the nonformal **patron-client politics** and other types of personal relationships.

There are significant variations in how governments in the developing countries face the political struggle over scarce resources, weak legitimacy, and the influence of patron-client politics. But, to one degree or another, they all experience these problems in ways that make the Third World state a distinctive and important entity in the study of comparative politics.

Section ❹   Third World Politics: Themes for Analysis

This section describes four themes that help organize the information on political institutions, processes, conflicts, policy, and changes in the six countries discussed in *Introduction to Third World Politics*. These themes help explain continuities and contrasts among countries and demonstrate what patterns apply to a group of countries—and why—and what patterns are specific to a particular country. We also suggest a way that each theme highlights some puzzle in the study of Third World politics.

Before we introduce the themes, a couple of warnings are necessary. First, our four themes cannot possibly capture the infinitely varied experience of politics throughout the Third World. Our framework provides a guide to understanding many features of contemporary Third World politics. But we urge students (and rely on instructors) to challenge and expand on our interpretations. Second, we want to note that a textbook builds from existing theory but does not construct or test new hypotheses. That task is the goal of original scholarly studies. The themes are intended to distill some of the most significant findings in the field of contemporary comparative politics. Finally, the four themes are treated in the six case studies in different orders and with varying degrees of depth depending on their role in influencing the state formation and contemporary politics of the particular country.

Theme 1: The Democratic Idea

Our comparative case studies reveal the strong appeal of the democratic idea, which we define as the claim by citizens that they should, in some way, exercise substantial control over the decisions made by their states and governments. Nevertheless, the cases also show that there is still a lot of **authoritarianism** in the Third World; that is, there remain many states based on arbitrary and unchecked political power in which citizens cannot freely choose their leaders, openly oppose the government, or question the decisions of rulers.

But as authoritarian rulers have recently learned in Brazil, Nigeria, and China, once persistent and widespread pressures for democratic participation develop, they are hard (although not impossible) to resist. A good indication of the near-universal appeal of the democratic idea is that even authoritarian regimes proclaim their attachment to democracy—usually asserting that they embody a superior form to that prevailing elsewhere. For example, leaders of the People's Republic of China claim that their brand of "socialist democracy" represents the interests of the vast majority of citizens more effectively than do the "bourgeois democracies" of capitalist societies.

Second, the case studies draw attention to diverse sources of support for democracy. Democracy has proved appealing for many reasons. In some historical settings, it may represent a standoff or equilibrium among political contenders for power, in which no one group can gain sufficient strength to control outcomes alone.[4] Democracy may appeal to citizens in authoritarian settings because democratic regimes often rank among the world's most stable, affluent, and cohesive countries. Another important pressure for democracy is born of the human desire for dignity and equality. Even when dictatorial regimes appear to benefit their countries—for example, by promoting economic development or nationalist goals—citizens are still likely to demand democracy. Although authoritarian governments can suppress demands for democratic participation, the domestic and (in recent years) international costs of doing so are high.

Third, several of the country studies illustrate the potential fragility of democratic transitions. The fact that popular movements or leaders of moderate factions displace authoritarian regimes and then hold elections does not mean that democratic institutions will prevail or endure: a wide gulf exists between a transition to democracy and the consolidation of democracy. Historically, powerful groups have often opposed democratic institutions because they fear that democracy will threaten their privileges. On the other hand, disadvantaged groups may oppose the democratic process because they see it as unresponsive to their deeply felt grievances. As a result, reversals of democratic regimes have occurred in the past and will doubtless occur in the future. The case studies do not support a philosophy of history or theory of political development that identifies a single (democratic) end point toward which all Third World countries will eventually converge. One important work, published in the early phase of the most recent democratic wave, captured the tenuous process of democratization in its title: *Transitions from Authoritarian Rule: Tentative Conclusions about Uncertain Democracies.*[5] Some suggest that it is far easier for a country to hold its first democratic election than its second. Hence, the fact that the democratic idea is powerful does not mean that all countries will adopt or preserve democratic institutions.

A puzzle: democracy and stability. Comparativists have debated intensely whether democratic institutions contribute to political stability or, on the contrary, to political disorder. On the one hand, democracy by its very nature permits political opposition: one of its defining characteristics is competition for high political office. Political life in democracies is turbulent and unpredictable. On the other hand, the fact that political opposition and competition are legitimate in democracies appears to deepen support for the state even among opponents of a particular government. History reveals far more cases of durable democratic regimes than durable authoritarian regimes in the modern world. In the country-by-country studies, look for the stabilizing and destabilizing consequences of recent democratic transitions in Brazil and Mexico, the pressures (or lack of pressures) for democratization in China, Iran, and Nigeria, and the challenges faced by even India's decades-old democracy.

Theme 2: Governing the Economy

The success of states in maintaining their authority and sovereign control is greatly affected by their ability to assure an adequate volume of goods and services to their populations. Certainly, the inadequate performance of the Soviet economic system was an important reason for the rejection of communism and the disintegration of the Soviet Union. In contrast, the success of China's Communist Party in promoting economic development is one of the major factors in explaining why communist rule has survived in that country.

How a country "governs the economy"[6]—how it organizes production and intervenes to manage the economy—is one of the key elements in its overall pattern of political as well as economic development. It is very important to analyze, for example, how countries differ in the balance between agricultural and industrial production in their economies, how successful they are in competing with other countries that offer similar products in international markets, and the relative importance of market forces versus government control of the economy.

An important goal of all countries in the contemporary world is to achieve durable economic development. In fact, effective economic performance is near the top of every state's political agenda and is an especially urgent issue in the Third World, where the extent of poverty and inequality is more extreme than in the developed nations. The term **political economy** refers to how governments affect economic performance—and how economic performance in turn affects a country's political processes. We accord great importance to political economy in this book because we believe that politics in all countries are deeply influenced by the relationship between government and the economy, in both domestic and international dimensions.

A puzzle: What is the relationship between economic development and political democracy? There are several aspects of this relationship that you should ponder while reading this book.

First, what special burdens do the difficult economic conditions typical of the Third World impose on a country that is trying to establish or sustain democracy? Many social scientists have argued that for democracy to take root and flourish a certain level of economic development—one characterized, for example, by a decent average standard of living, extensive urbanization, a large middle class, and high literacy rates—is necessary. Yet, democratization in the Third World has recently spread to some of the world's poorest countries (such as Haiti and Nepal), which do not meet any of these socioeconomic prerequisites. What chance does democracy have to flourish in such circumstances? In this book, Brazil is the clearest case of a Third World country in transition from authoritarianism to democracy. In some ways, including its level of industrialization, Brazil is a relatively well-off Third World nation; but in other ways, such as the extreme inequality of its income distribution and the severe poverty of a great many of its citizens, Brazil is very much part of the Third World. Its struggle to establish democracy must be understood within the context of the special economic challenges it faces as a Third World nation. Do these challenges make it harder for Brazil to build the kind of basic national consensus and spirit of compromise on which a healthy democracy depends?

Second, can democratic governments in the Third World adequately address the serious economic problems that plague the less developed nations? As the case of India shows, it is possible to have democracy without development—or at least, with only very limited development. Democracy may give the poor a voice in government, but it can also allow the economic elite to use their political power to block needed changes (such as land reform). Economic failure was one of the principal causes of the collapse of communist and other dictatorial regimes in recent decades. The political fate of the new democracies of the Third World will also depend largely on their economic records. You might also ask why some Third World authoritarian states (like China) are able to promote effective economic development, whereas others (like Nigeria) have much poorer economic records.

Finally, in what ways, and with what effects, do economic development and modernization create pressures for democratization in the Third World? Social scientists have observed that as an economy and society become more modern and complex, as incomes and educational levels rise, and as a country becomes more connected economically and in other ways to the outside world, the pressures on a state to democratize tend to grow. These pressures may come from within the government itself, from the society below, or from abroad. Some of the most successful cases of economic growth in the Third World in recent years, such as South Korea and China, have been achieved under harsh authoritarian regimes (development without democracy). But in such cases (as discussed in some detail in the China case study in this book), successful economic development generates powerful pressures for political change that confront an authoritarian government with fundamental dilemmas and challenges.

Theme 3: A World of States

The theme that we call "a world of states" reflects the fact that, since the beginning of the modern era about five hundred years ago, states have been the primary actors on the world stage. Although international organizations play a crucial role, for the most part it is the rulers of states who send armies to conquer other states and territories. It is the legal codes of states that make it possible for businesses to operate within their borders and beyond. And it is states that regulate the movement of people across borders through immigration law. While courses in international relations focus primarily on interaction among states, courses in comparative politics stress what goes on within a country's borders. In *Introduction to Third World Politics* we emphasize one key feature of the international arena: the impact on a state's domestic political institutions and processes of its relative success or failure in competing economically and politically with other states.

No state, even a powerful one such as the United States, is unaffected by influences originating outside its borders. Today, a host of processes associated with **globalization** underscore the heightened importance of various cross-national influences. A wide array of international organizations and treaties, including the United Nations, the European Union, the World Trade Organization, the North American Free Trade Agreement, Mercosur (the "Southern Common Market" made up of Argentina, Brazil, Paraguay, and Uruguay) and countless others, challenge the sovereign control of national governments. Transnational corporations, international banks, and currency traders in New York, London, Frankfurt, and Tokyo affect countries and people throughout the world. A country's political borders do not protect its citizens from environmental pollution or infectious diseases that come from abroad. More broadly, developments linked to technology transfer, the growth of an international information society, immigration, and cultural diffusion have a varying but undeniable impact on the domestic politics of all countries. For example, thanks to the global diffusion of radio, television, and the Internet, people everywhere are remarkably well informed about international developments. This knowledge may fuel popular local demands that governments intervene in faraway Bosnia, Rwanda, or elsewhere. And this global awareness may make citizens more ready to hold their own government to internationally recognized standards of human rights.

As we begin a new millennium, nation-states are experiencing intense pressures from an expanding and increasingly complex mix of external influences. In all countries, politics and policy-making are being shaped by influences from beyond their borders. But international political and economic influences do not have the *same* impact in all countries; nor do all states equally shape the institutional form and policy of international organizations in which they participate. It is likely that the more advantaged a state is, as measured by its level of economic development, military power, and resource base, the more it will shape global influences. The policies of less advantaged countries are more extensively molded by other states, by international organizations, and by broader international constraints. One feature that typifies all the countries included in this volume (though not to the same degree) is a weak or subordinate position in the international system. How this relative weakness in the global order shapes the domestic political and economic situations of Third World states is one of the major questions addressed in our case studies.

The theme we identify as a world of states includes a second important focus: similarities and contrasts among countries in state formation. We study the ways that states have developed historically, diverse patterns in the organization of political institutions, the processes—and limits—of democratization, the ability of the state to control social groups in society and sustain power, and the state's economic management strategies and capacities. We observe the linkage between state formation and the position of states in the international order. For example, why did China and India, both of which mark the formation of their modern states in the late 1940s, take such divergent paths? What have been the outcomes of these different paths in terms of the political and economic development of each country? For Third World countries it is particularly important to note how the experiences of colonialism and imperialism shaped the formation of the state. For example, in India the British established a professional civil service staffed by Indians to help run the colony, a legacy that greatly influenced the shape of independent India's government and that has contributed to the durability of Indian democracy. By contrast, in Iran, Britain and the United States supported a despotic monarchy because it protected Western oil interests; the end result was the revolution that produced that country's contemporary Islamic Republic.

One point at which the themes of "a world of states" and "governing the economy" intersect is in the trend toward **economic liberalization** throughout the Third World. Most developing countries are taking steps to reduce the state's role in regulating the economy and are increasing the nation's involvement in the international economy by expanding exports and seeking foreign investment. The collapse of communism and the discrediting of the socialist model of extensive government control of the economy have vastly increased the global economic influence of the world's great capitalist powers, including the United States, Japan, and Germany. Furthermore, the World Bank and the International Monetary Fund (another major source of economic aid and advice for developing countries) are taking the lead—sometimes quite forcefully—in steering developing countries toward economic liberalization. Some observers see the emphasis on free markets and international competition that are at the heart of economic liberalization as a blueprint for development and modernization. Others see the pressures on developing countries to liberalize their economies as an example of **neoimperialism**, in which the powerful capitalist countries are once again dictating policies to the Third World. In either case, the trend toward economic liberalization, which, in one way or another, affects every country discussed in this book, demonstrates how a state's approach to governing its economy is strongly shaped by its position in the world of states.

A puzzle: To what extent do states remain the basic building blocks of political life? Increasingly the politics and policies of states are shaped by external actors as well as by the more impersonal forces of globalization. At the same time, many states face increasingly restive constituencies who challenge the power and legitimacy of central states. In reading our six country case studies, try to assess what impact pressures from above and below—and from outside and inside—have had on the role of the state in carrying out its basic functions and in sustaining the political attachments of its citizens. Are states losing their ability to control policy and secure political outcomes? Consider the dilemma of the contemporary Mexican state: It is facing pressures from the World Bank and International Monetary Fund to privatize more of its economy and cut government in exchange for urgently needed debt relief. Such measures, in the short run at least, often jeopardize the poor and increase inequality. At the same time, Mexico is facing demands from impoverished and rebellious peasants in the southern state of Chiapas for greater economic and social justice. How can the Mexican state—or other Third World states—respond effectively to such seemingly contradictory pressures without alienating constituencies (such as, in this case, powerful international organizations or the peasant masses) whose displeasure with the government could have profound consequences for political stability and economic development?

Theme 4: The Politics of Collective Identities

How do individuals understand who they are in political terms, and on what basis do groups of people come together to advance common political aims? In other words, what are the sources of collective political identity? At one point, social scientists thought they knew. Observers argued that the age-old loyalties of ethnicity, religious affiliation, race, gender, and locality were being dissolved and displaced by economic, political, and cultural modernization.

Comparativists thought that **social class**—solidarities based on the shared experience of work or, more broadly, economic position—had become the most important source of collective identities. They believed that most of the time groups would pragmatically pursue their interests in ways that were not politically destabilizing.[7] We now know that the formation of group attachments and interplay of politically relevant collective identities are far more complex and uncertain.

In industrial democracies such as the United States, the importance of identities based on class membership has declined, although class and material sources of collective political identity remain significant in political competition and economic organization. But in much of the Third World, class remains a very important source of identity and political conflict because of the extreme socioeconomic inequalities and barriers to social mobility that are found in these countries. And contrary to earlier predictions, in many developed and developing countries nonclass identities have assumed growing, not diminishing, significance. These affiliations develop from a sense of belonging to particular groups based on language, religion, ethnicity, race, nationality, or gender. Such conflicts are often particularly intense in postcolonial countries, such as Nigeria, where the colonists drew borders with little regard to preexisting collective identities. This process of state formation by the imposition of external power sowed the seeds for future ethnic conflict in Nigeria and elsewhere, and threatens the survival and prospects for democracy of many postcolonial countries.

The politics of collective political identities involves struggles to define which groups are full participants in the political community and which are marginalized or even ostracized. It also involves a constant tug-of-war over the relative power and influence, both symbolic and substantive, among groups. Issues of inclusion and priority remain pivotal in many countries, and they may never be resolved. In addition, questions of representation are very hard to resolve—Who is included in an ethnic minority community, for example, or who speaks for the community or negotiates with a governmental authority on its behalf? One reason why conflict around this question can be so intense in the Third World is that political leaders in the state and in opposition movements often seek to mobilize support by sharpening ethnic, religious, racial, or regional rivalries.

A puzzle: collective identities and distributional politics. Once identity demands are placed on the political agenda, can governments resolve them by distributing resources in ways that redress the grievances of the minority or politically weaker identity groups? Collective identities operate both at the level of symbols, attitudes, values, and beliefs and at the level of material resources. However, the contrast between material- and nonmaterial-based identities and demands should not be exaggerated. In practice, most groups are animated both by feelings of attachment and solidarity and by the desire to obtain material benefits and political influence for their members. But the analytical distinction between material and nonmaterial demands remains useful, and it is worth considering whether the nonmaterial aspects of the politics of collective identities make political disputes over ethnicity or religion or language or nationality especially divisive and difficult to resolve.

In a situation of extreme economic scarcity, as is found in much of the Third World, it may prove impossible to reach any compromise among groups with conflicting material demands. But if an adequate level of resources is available, such conflicts may be easier to resolve because groups can negotiate at least a minimally satisfying share of resources. The process of determining who gets what or how resources are distributed is called **distributional politics**. However, the demands of ethnic, religious, and nationalist movements may be difficult to satisfy by a distributional style of politics. The distributional style may be quite ineffective when, for example, a religious group (such as Hindu extremists in India or Islamic radicals in Iran) demands that its religious values be imposed on the whole society. In such cases, political conflict tends to move from the distributive realm to a cultural realm, where compromises cannot be achieved by dividing the pie of material resources. The country studies examine a wide range of conflicts involving collective identities. It is interesting (and possibly troubling) to ponder whether and under what conditions they are subject to the normal give-and-take of political bargaining.

These four themes—the democratic idea, governing the economy, a world of states, and the politics of collective identities—form the analytic scaffold of this text. We hope that they will provide you with some important insights about Third World politics that will help guide you through the individual case studies.

Section ⑤ Organization of the Text

The core of this book consists of case studies of six countries selected for their significance in terms of our comparative themes and to provide a reasonable cross-section of types of political systems and geographic regions in the Third World. Although each of the country studies makes some important comparative references, they are primarily intended to provide detailed descriptions and analyses of the politics of individual countries. At the same time, the country studies have common section and subsection headings to help you make comparisons and explore similar themes across the various cases. The following are brief summaries of the main issues and questions covered in the country studies.

Section 1: The Making of the Modern State

This section provides an overview of the forces that have shaped the particular character of the state. We believe that an understanding of the contemporary politics of any country requires some familiarity with the historical process by which its current political system was formed. "Politics in Action" uses a specific event to illustrate an important political moment in the country's recent history and to highlight some of the critical political issues it faces. "Geographic Setting" locates the country in its regional context and discusses the political implications of its geographic setting. "Critical Junctures" looks at some of the major stages and decisive turning points in state development. This discussion should give you an idea of how the country arrived at its present political order and a sense of how relations between state and society have developed over time. "Themes and Implications" shows how the past pattern of state development continues to shape the country's current political agenda. "Historical Junctures and Political Themes" applies the text's core themes to the making of the modern state: How was the country's political development affected by its place in the world of states? What are the political implications of the state's approach to economic management? What has been the country's experience with the democratic idea? What are the important bases of collective identities in the country, and how do these relate to the people's image of themselves as citizens of the state? "Implications for Comparative Politics" discusses the broader significance of the country for the study of comparative politics.

Section 2: Political Economy and Development

This section traces the country's recent and contemporary economic development. It explores the issues raised by the core theme of "governing the economy" and analyzes how economic development has affected political change. The placement of this section near the beginning of the country study reflects our belief that an understanding of a state's economic situation is essential for analyzing its politics. "State and Economy" discusses the basic organization of the country's economy, with an emphasis on the role of the state in managing economic life and on the relationship between the government and other economic actors. This section also analyzes the state's social welfare policies, such as health care, housing, and pension programs. "Society and Economy" examines the social and political implications of the country's economic situation. It asks who benefits from economic change and looks at how economic development creates or reinforces class, ethnic, gender, regional, or ideological cleavages in society. "The International Political Economy" considers the country's global role: How have patterns of trade and foreign investment changed over time? What is the coun-

try's relationship to regional and international organizations? To what degree has the country been able to influence multilateral policies? How have international economic issues affected the domestic political agenda?

Section 3: Governance and Policy-Making

Here we describe the state's major policy-making institutions and procedures. "Organization of the State" lays out the fundamental principles—as reflected in the country's constitution, its official ideology, and its historical experience—on which the political system and the distribution of political power are based. It also sketches the basic structure of the state, including the relationship between different levels and branches of government. "The Executive" encompasses whatever key offices (for example, presidents, prime ministers, Communist Party leaders) are at the top of the political system, focusing on those who have the most power, how they are selected, and how they use their power to make policy. It looks at the national bureaucracy and its relationship to the chief executive(s) and the governing party and its role in the policy-making. "Other State Institutions" generally includes the military, the judiciary and the legal system, state-run corporations, and subnational government. "The Policy-Making Process" summarizes how state policy gets made and implemented. It describes the roles of formal institutions and procedures as well as nonformal aspects of policy-making, such as patron-client relations and interest group activity.

Section 4: Representation and Participation

The relationship between the state and the society it governs is the topic of Section 4. How do different groups in society organize to further their political interests, how do they participate and get represented in the political system, and how do they influence policy-making? Given the importance of the U.S. Congress in policy-making, American readers might expect to find the principal discussion of "The Legislature" in "Governance and Policy-Making" rather than in "Representation and Participation." But the United States is rather exceptional in having a legislature that is very nearly a co-equal branch of government with the executive in the policy process. In most political systems, the executive dominates the policy process, even when it is ultimately responsible to the legislature, as in a parliamentary system. In most countries other than the United States, the legislature functions primarily to represent and provide a forum for the political expression of various interests in government; it is only secondarily (and in some cases, such as China, only marginally) a policy-making body. Therefore, although this section does describe and assess the legislature's role in policy-making, its primary focus is on how the legislature represents or fails to represent different interests in society. "Political Parties and the Party System" describes the overall organization of the party system and reviews the major party or parties. "Elections" discusses the election process and recent trends in electoral behavior. It also considers the significance (or lack of significance) of elections as a vehicle for citizen participation in politics and in bringing about changes in the government. "Political Culture, Citizenship, and Identity" examines how people perceive themselves as members of the political community: the nature and source of political values and attitudes, who is considered a citizen of the state, and how different groups in society understand their relationship to the state. The topics covered may include political aspects of the educational system, the media, religion, and ethnicity. "Interests, Social Movements, and Protest" discusses how various groups pursue their political interests outside the party system. When do they use formal organizations (such as unions) or launch movements (such as "green" environmental movements)? What is the relationship between the state and such organizations and movements? When and how do citizens engage in acts of protest that may take them beyond the boundaries of the law? And how does the state respond to such protests?

Section 5: Politics in Transition

In Section 5, each country study returns to the book's focus on the major challenges that are reshaping our world and the study of Third World politics. "Political Challenges and Changing Agendas" returns to the four

themes, lays out the major unresolved issues facing the country, and assesses which are most likely to dominate in the near future. "Politics in Comparative Perspective" highlights what the case study tells us about politics in other countries that have similar political systems or that face similar kinds of political challenges.

It is quite a challenge to understand politics in the contemporary world. We hope that the timely information and thematic focus of this book will prepare and inspire you to explore further the endlessly fascinating terrain of politics in the Third World.

Key Terms

Cold War	dictatorships
Third World	newly industrializing
gender	countries
ethnicity	gross national product
comparative politics	physical quality of life
comparativists	life expectancy
nation-states	infant mortality rate
political institutions	illiteracy
political culture	coup d'état
political development	patron-client politics
state	authoritarianism
executive	political economy
cabinet	globalization
bureaucracy	economic liberalization
legitimacy	neo-imperialism
state formation	social class
middle-level theory	distributional politics

Suggested Readings

Anderson, Benedict. *Imagined Communities: Reflections on the Origins and Spread of Nationalism*. Rev. ed. London: Verso, 1991.

Cammack, Paul. *Capitalism and Democracy in the Third World: the Doctrine for Political Development*. London: Leicester University Press, 1997.

Connor, Walker. *Ethnonationalism: The Quest for Understanding*. Princeton, N.J.: Princeton University Press, 1994.

Diamond, Larry, and Marc F. Plattner, eds. *The Global Resurgence of Democracy*. 2d ed. Baltimore: Johns Hopkins University Press, 1996.

Evans, Peter. *Embedded Autonomy: States and Industrial*

Transformation. Princeton, N.J.: Princeton University Press, 1995.

Greenfield, Liah. *Nationalism: Five Roads to Modernity*. Cambridge, Mass.: Harvard University Press, 1992.

Grindle, Merilee S. *Challenging the State: Crisis and Innovation in Latin America and Africa*. New York: Cambridge University Press, 1996.

Hall, Peter A. *Governing the Economy: The Politics of State Intervention in Britain and France*. New York: Oxford University Press, 1986.

Haynes, Jeffrey. *Democracy and Civil Society in the Third World: Politics and New Political Movements*. Malden, Mass.: Blackwell, 1997.

Huntington, Samuel P. *The Third Wave: Democratization in the Late Twentieth Century*. Norman: University of Oklahoma Press, 1991.

Inglehart, Ronald. *Modernization and Postmodernization: Cultural, Economic, and Political Change in 43 Societies*. Princeton, N.J.: Princeton University Press, 1997.

Isbister, John. *Promises Not Kept: The Betrayal of Social Change in the Third World*. 4th ed. West Hartford, Conn.: Kumarian Press, 1998.

Marx, Anthony. *Making Race and Nation: A Comparison of the United States, South Africa, and Brazil*. New York: Cambridge University Press, 1998.

Mason, Michael. *Development and Disorder: A History of the Third World since 1945*. Hanover, N.H.: University Press of New England, 1997.

Migdal, Joel S., Atul Kohli, and Vivienne Shue, eds. *State Power and Social Forces: Domination and Transformation in the Third World*. New York: Cambridge University Press, 1994.

Pickney, Robert. *Democracy in the Third World*. Boulder, Colo.: Lynne Rienner, 1994.

Seligson, Mitchell A., and John T. Passé-Smith. *Development and Underdevelopment: The Political Economy of Inequality*. 2d ed. Boulder, Colo.: Lynne Rienner, 1998.

Smith, Brian C. *Understanding Third World Politics: Theories of Political Change and Development*. Bloomington: Indiana University Press, 1996.

Waylen, Georgina. *Gender in Third World Politics*. Boulder, Colo.: Lynne Rienner, 1996.

Woo-Cummings, Meredith, ed. *The Developmental State*. Ithaca, N.Y.: Cornell University Press, 1999.

Endnotes

[1] See Philippe Schmitter, "Comparative Politics," in *The Oxford Companion to Politics of the World*, ed. Joel Krieger (New York: Oxford University Press, 1993), 171–177. This essay provides a comprehensive and insightful discussion of the methods of comparative politics and its evolution, and several elements of the discussion here are drawn from it.

[2] See, for example, Theda Skocpol, *Social Revolutions in the Modern World* (Cambridge: Cambridge University Press, 1994).

[3] See, for example, Vicky Randall and Robin Theobald, *Political Change and Underdevelopment: A Critical Introduction to Third World Politics*, 2d ed. (Durham, N.C.: Duke University Press, 1998); and Nelly P. Stromquist, ed., *Women in the Third World: An Encyclopedia of Contemporary Issues*. (New York: Garland, 1998).

[4] This view has been developed well by Adam Przeworski, *Democracy and the Market: Political and Economic Reforms in Eastern Europe and Latin America* (Cambridge: Cambridge University Press, 1991).

[5] Guillermo O'Donnell, Philippe Schmitter, and Laurence Whitehead, eds. *Transitions from Authoritarian Rule: Tentative Conclusions about Uncertain Democracies* (Baltimore: Johns Hopkins University Press, 1986).

[6] This term is borrowed from Peter A. Hall, *Governing the Economy: the Politics of State Intervention in Britain and France* (New York: Oxford University Press, 1986).

[7] For a survey of political science literature on this question, see Mark Kesselman, "The Conflictual Evolution of American Political Science: From Apologetic Pluralism to Trilateralism and Marxism," in *Public Values and Private Power in American Democracy*, ed. J. David Greenstone (Chicago: University of Chicago Press, 1982), 34–67.

CHAPTER 2
China

William A. Joseph

People's Republic of China

Land and Population

Capital	Beijing
Total Area (square miles)	3,696,100 (slightly larger than the U.S.)
Population	1.2 billion
Annual Average Population Growth Rate (1990–1997)	1.1%
Urban Population	32%
Ethnic Composition	Han (Chinese) 92%
	Other 8%
Major Languages	Chinese (various dialects)
Religious Affiliation	Officially atheist, though many people practice traditional folk and other religions
	Taoist, Buddhist, Muslim 2%–3%
	Christian 1.0%

Economy

Domestic Currency	Renminbi ("people's currency"), also called yuan
Total GNP (US$)	$1.055 trillion
GNP per capita (US$)	$860
GNP per capita at purchasing power parity (US$)	$3570
GNP average annual growth rate (1996–1997)	8.9%
GNP per capita average annual growth rate	1996–1997 7.8%
	1980–1995 8.6%
	1965–1980 4.1%
Income Gap:	Richest 20% of population
GDP per capita (US$)	$5114
	Poorest 20% of population
	$772
Structure of Production (% of GDP)	Agriculture 18.7%
	Industry 49.2%
	Services 32.1%
Labor Force Distribution (% of total)	Agriculture 72%
	Industry 15%
	Services 13%
Exports as % of GDP	21%
Imports as % of GDP	19%

Society

Life Expectancy	Female	71.3
	Male	67.3
Doctors per 100,000 people		115
Infant Mortality per 1000 live births		38
Adult Literacy	Female	72.7%
	Male	89.9%
Access to Information and Communications (per 1000 people)	Radios	185
	Televisions	247
	Telephone Lines	34
	Personal Computers	2.1

Women in Government and Economy

Seats in national legislature held by women	21.8%
Women at ministerial level	6.0%
Women as % of total labor force	45.0%
Female business administrators and managers	11.6%
Female professional and technical workers	45.1%
1998 Human Development Index ranking (out of 174 countries, 1 = highest)	106

These data do not include Hong Kong.

Political Organization

Political System   Communist party-state; officially, a people's democratic dictatorship.

Regime History   Established in 1949 after the victory of the Chinese Communist Party (CCP) in the Chinese civil war.

Administrative Structure   Unitary system with 22 provinces, 5 autonomous regions, 4 centrally administered municipalities, and 1 Special Adminstrative Region (Hong Kong).

Executive   Premier (head of government) and president (head of state) formally elected by legislature, but only with approval of CCP leadership; the head of the CCP, the general secretary, is in effect the country's chief executive.

Legislature   Unicameral National People's Congress; delegates elected indirectly from lower-level people's congresses for five-year terms. Largely a "rubber stamp" body for Communist Party policies, although in recent years has become somewhat more assertive.

Judiciary   A nationwide system of people's courts, which is constitutionally independent but, in fact, largely under the control of the CCP; a Supreme People's Court supervises the country's judicial system and is formally responsible to the National People's Congress, which also elects the court's president.

Party System   A one-party system, although in addition to the ruling Chinese Communist Party, there are eight politically insignificant "democratic" parties.

Politics in Action

In June 1998, U.S. President Bill Clinton was greeted by China's president and Communist Party leader, Jiang Zemin, in Tiananmen Square in Beijing. Clinton was the first U.S. president to visit the People's Republic of China (PRC) since Chinese troops had used brutal force to remove pro-democracy demonstrators from that same square nearly a decade earlier. Some Americans and human rights groups were highly critical of Clinton's decision to be received just steps from where hundreds of civilians were massacred on the orders of China's leaders.

The 1989 demonstrations had begun in April when university students gathered in Tiananmen ("Gate of Heavenly Peace") to protest widespread official corruption and to demand that the Chinese Communist Party (CCP) allow more democracy in China. The protesters had been emboldened by the fact that the Chinese people had, for the past decade, been experiencing greater economic freedom than at any time since the Communists had come to power in 1949. The students now wanted to extend the process of reform into the realm of government and politics.

Throughout that spring, the demonstrations grew, and at one point more than a million people from all walks of life gathered in and around Tiananmen. For several months, the CCP, constrained by internal divisions about how to handle the protests and intensive international media coverage, did little other than engage in some threatening rhetoric to dissuade the demonstrators.

But China's leaders ran out of patience and the troops were ordered in during the very early morning hours of June 4. One protester who survived the assault described what happened when he and others joined hands on the outskirts of the square to form a human barricade to halt the army's advance:

> Then, without warning, the troops opened fire on us. People cursed, screamed and ran. In no time, seventy or eighty people had collapsed all around me. Blood spattered all over, staining my clothes.[1]

Student demonstrators erected a statue called the "Goddess of Democracy" in Beijing's Tiananmen Square in late May 1989 to symbolize their demands for greater political freedom in China. In the background is an official portrait of former Chinese Communist Party leader, Mao Zedong. Chinese troops toppled and destroyed the statue after they occupied the square on June 4, 1989, a process that also resulted in the death of many protesters.
Source: AP/Wide World Photos.

By the time dawn broke in Beijing, Tiananmen Square had indeed been cleared, but with a death toll that has still not been revealed. In the days that followed, thousands of Chinese citizens were arrested for their role in the demonstrations in Beijing and other cities, and

25

there were several well-publicized executions of people charged with sabotage during the protests.

The order to move with deadly force against the students and their supporters was made by a handful of party elders, including Deng Xiaoping, who at that time was China's most powerful leader and the mastermind of the country's remarkable record of economic reform and success. The massacre was meant to send an unmistakable message that no political challenge to the Chinese Communist Party would be tolerated and all necessary means would be used to suppress any opposition.

The crushing of the Tiananmen demonstrations was one of the late twentieth century's most tragic political events, and it still casts a dark shadow over China's domestic politics as well as over U.S.-China relations. At a joint press conference with Jiang Zemin during the 1998 summit, President Clinton raised the issue of Tiananmen, saying that "the American people believe that the use of force and the tragic loss of life was wrong." Jiang Zemin's response made it clear that the Chinese Communist Party had not changed its views: "With regard to the political disturbances [in 1989]," Jiang said, "had the Chinese government not taken the resolute measures then we could not have enjoyed the stability that we are enjoying today."[2]

The People's Republic of China is one of only a few countries in the world that is still a **Communist party-state**, a political system in which the ruling Communist Party holds a monopoly on political power, claims the right to lead or control all government and social institutions, and proclaims allegiance (at least officially) to the ideology of **Marxism-Leninism**. China has experienced many changes since the Tiananmen tragedy, including further economic and social liberalization and even some political relaxation. But the CCP maintains a tight grip on power and rejects any meaningful movement toward democracy.

The rift between an oppressive party-state and an increasingly assertive society, which led to the shedding of blood in Tiananmen in 1989, remains deep and ominous. Yet, as the Chinese economy and society have become freer and more open to the outside world, the pressures for political change have also grown stronger.

Official attitudes about the Tiananmen demonstrations are one barometer of the potential for political change in China. As long as the Chinese authorities continue to insist that the protests were a "counter-revolutionary rebellion," the prospects for democratization will remain dim. But a willingness on the part of the CCP to set the historical record straight—or even to provide an honest accounting of how many people were killed—would be a significant political change that could be a step on the road to democracy.

Geographic Setting

The People's Republic of China is located in the eastern part of mainland Asia at the heart of one of the world's most strategically important and volatile regions. It shares land borders with more than a dozen countries, including Russia, India, Pakistan, Vietnam, and the Democratic People's Republic of Korea (North Korea) and is a relatively short distance by sea from Japan, the Philippines, and Indonesia. China, which had largely assumed its present geographic identity by the eighteenth century, is slightly bigger than the United States in land area, making it the third largest country in the world, after Russia and Canada.

The PRC is bounded on all sides by imposing physical barriers: the sea to the east, mountains to the north, south, and west (including the world's largest, Mt. Everest), deserts, vast grasslands, and dense forests in various parts of the north, and tropical rain forests to the south. In traditional times, these barriers isolated China from extensive contact with other peoples and contributed to the country's sense of itself as the "Middle Kingdom" (which is how the Chinese word for China, *zhongguo*, is translated) that lay not only at the physical but also at the political and moral center of its known world.

Administratively, the PRC is made up of twenty-two provinces, five **autonomous regions**, and four centrally administered cities (including the capital, Beijing), and one Special Administrative Region (Hong Kong). The sparsely populated but territorially vast western part of the country is mostly mountains, deserts, and high plateaus. The northeast, which is much like the U.S. plains states in terms of weather and topography, is both a wheat-growing area and China's industrial heartland. Southern China has a much warmer, and in places even semitropical climate, which allows year-round agriculture and intensive rice cultivation. The country is very rich in natural resources, particularly coal and petroleum (including significant, but untapped on- and off-shore reserves) and is considered to have the world's greatest potential for hydroelectric power.

Although China and the United States are roughly equal in geographic size, China's population of 1.2 billion—by far the world's largest—is five times greater. But only about 10 percent of China's land is usable for agriculture. From a global perspective, China has a little over 20 percent of the world's population but only 7 percent of the world's arable land. The precarious balance between people and the land needed to feed them has been a dilemma for China for centuries and remains one of the government's major concerns.

Industrialization and urbanization have expanded significantly in recent years. The PRC now has more than thirty cities of a million or more—the three largest being Shanghai (14 million), Beijing (12.5 million), and Tianjin (9.5 million). In 1997 the former British colony of Hong Kong, one of the world's great commercial centers (population 6.1 million), became part of the People's Republic of China. Nevertheless, about 70 percent of China's people still live and work in rural areas. The countryside has played—and continues to play—a very important role in China's political development.

Background: *A Very Brief Chinese Lesson*

Chinese is spoken by more people than any other language in the world. Yet Chinese really comprises many dialects, some of which are so different from one another that they are mutually incomprehensible and are often considered separate languages. Two of the major Chinese dialects are Mandarin, which is the form of Chinese spoken mainly in the northern part of the country, and Cantonese, which is spoken in the south.

But people who speak different Chinese dialects share the same written language. In other words, Mandarin and Cantonese speakers cannot understand each other in face-to-face conversations or over the telephone, but they can communicate by letter. This is because written Chinese is made up of characters rather than phonetic letters. These characters, which have evolved over time from symbolic pictures, depict meanings more than sounds, so that speakers of various Chinese dialects may pronounce the same character very differently. There are more than 40,000 different Chinese characters, although basic literacy requires knowledge of about 4000 because most of the characters are ancient and have fallen out of common usage.

Chinese does not have an alphabet; both the meaning and the pronunciation of Chinese characters can only be learned by memorization. Like many of the world's other languages—including Arabic, Greek, Hebrew, Japanese, and Russian—that do not use the Roman alphabet on which English is based, Chinese characters must be romanized, or transliterated, if English speakers are to have any idea of how to pronounce them. The most common way of romanizing Chinese is the *pinyin* ("spell sounds") system used in the People's Republic of China and by the United Nations. But because linguists have differed about how best to approximate distinctive Chinese sounds using Roman letters, there are still several alternative methods of romanizing Chinese.

This book and most other English-language publications now use the *pinyin* romanization for Chinese names, places, and phrases. In most cases, a word in *pinyin* is pronounced as it looks. However, there are a few letters that appear in Chinese words in this chapter for which a pronunciation guide may be helpful:

- *z* is pronouced "dz" (e.g., President Jiang Zemin)
- *x* is pronounced "sh" (e.g., Deng Xiaoping)
- *q* is pronounced "ch" (e.g., Emperor Qin)
- *zh* is pronounced "j" (e.g., Zhongguo, the Chinese word for China)

One other important point: In China (as in Japan and Korea), the family name, or surname (for instance, Deng), comes *before* the personal, or given, name (for instance, Xiaoping). Some people interpret this as a reflection of the priority given to the family or the group over the individual in East Asian culture.

China's population is highly concentrated along the eastern seaboard and in the most agriculturally fertile areas around the country's three great rivers, the Yellow River, the Yangzi (Yangtze) and the West River. The vast majority (92 percent) of China's citizens are ethnically Chinese (referred to as the Han people, after one of China's earliest dynasties). The remaining 8 percent is made up of more than fifty ethnic minorities, who differ from the Han in several major ways, including race, language, culture, and religion. Most of these minority peoples live in the country's geopolitically vital border regions, including Tibet. This makes the often uneasy and sometimes hostile relationship between China's minority peoples and the central government in Beijing a critical issue in Chinese politics today.

Critical Junctures

The People's Republic of China was founded in 1949. But understanding the critical junctures in the making of the modern Chinese state requires that we go back much further into China's political history. Broadly considered, that history can be divided into three periods: the imperial period (221 B.C.–A.D. 1911), during which China was ruled by a series of dynasties and emperors; the relatively brief and unstable republican period (1912–1949), when a weak central government was plagued by civil war and foreign invasion; and the communist period that takes us from the military and political triumph of the Chinese Communist Party and the founding of the People's Republic of China in 1949 to the present.

From Empire to Republic (221 B.C.–A.D. 1911)

Modern China is heir to one of the world's oldest cultural and political traditions. The roots of Chinese culture date back more than 4,000 years, and the Chinese empire first took political shape in 221 B.C., when a number of small kingdoms were unified under the Emperor Qin, who laid the foundation of an imperial system that lasted for more than twenty centuries until its overthrow in 1911. During those many centuries, China was ruled by more than a dozen different dynasties and experienced extensive geographic expansion and dramatic political, economic, social, and cultural development. Nevertheless, many of the core features of the imperial system remained remarkably consistent over time.

There are several reasons why the Chinese empire survived for such a long time. First, imperial China developed a sophisticated and effective system of national government long before the strong monarchical states of Europe took form in the seventeenth century. At the pinnacle of this government was an all-powerful emperor and a small group of advisers and ministers in the capital. But the most distinctive feature of the Chinese political tradition was the civil service branch made up of scholar-officials (mandarins) chosen through a rigorous and highly selective examination process and stationed throughout the empire.

Second, the traditional Chinese economy was a source of great strength to the empire. Chinese farmers pioneered some of the premodern world's most productive agricultural techniques, including irrigation and multicropping. Commerce, transport, and handicraft industries were also highly developed for the times. Urbanization expanded in China much sooner than it did in Europe, and Westerners, like Marco Polo, who journeyed to China as early as the thirteenth century were amazed by the grandeur of the Middle Kingdom's cities.

Third, the structure of traditional Chinese society, especially in the million or more small villages that were its foundation, gave the imperial system great staying power. The vast majority of the population was made up of peasants who were subordinated to a tiny landlord class that dominated life on the local level. The most powerful of the landlord families— the gentry—had close ties to the imperial civil service

and helped the imperial officials extend their reach down to the very basic level of Chinese society by carrying out many government functions, such as collecting taxes.

Fourth, the traditional order was supported by the enduring influence in Chinese society of **Confucianism**. This philosophy, based on the teachings of Confucius (c. 551–479 B.C.), stresses the importance of the group over the individual, deference to one's elders and superiors, and the need to maintain social harmony. Confucianism did contain a teaching—the "Mandate of Heaven"—that an unjust ruler could be overthrown by the people, and Chinese history is full of rebellions against emperors who were judged to have lost the heavenly mandate. Nevertheless, Confucianism was basically a conservative philosophy that justified and preserved an autocratic state, a patriarchal culture, and a stratified society.

Finally, the Chinese imperial system endured because, throughout most of its history, China was the dominant political, military, and cultural force in its known world. Foreign influences or peoples that could not be repelled, such as Buddhism from India or invaders from Mongolia (who conquered China in 1279), were absorbed, or sinicized, by Chinese culture. China's power and relative geographic isolation contributed to a pervasive feeling among the Chinese that all non-Chinese were barbarians and that the Middle Kingdom could meet any challenge from outside without altering its basic way of life.

But in the late eighteenth and early nineteenth centuries, China experienced a population explosion and economic stagnation, along with a significant rise in official corruption and exploitation of the peasants by both landlords and the government. Social unrest culminated in the Taiping Rebellion (1850–1864), a massive revolt that took 20 million lives and nearly toppled the dynasty.

In the meantime, the West, which had surged far ahead of China in industrial development and military technology, was pressing China to expand its trade. China showed little interest in such overtures and tried to limit the activities of Westerners in China. But Europe, most notably Britain, in the midst of its era of mercantile and colonial expansion, used its military supremacy to compel China to engage in "free" trade with the West. China's efforts to stop Britain from selling opium in China led to military conflict between the two countries. After suffering a humiliating defeat in the Opium War (1839–1842), China was literally forced to open its borders to foreign merchants, missionaries, and diplomats on terms dictated by Britain and other Western powers. China lost control of significant pieces of its territory to foreigners (including Hong Kong) and important sectors of the Chinese economy fell into foreign hands.

There were many efforts to revive or reform the dynasty in the late nineteenth and early twentieth centuries. But political power in China remained largely in the hands of staunch conservatives who resisted change. As a result, when change came, it came in the form of a revolution in 1911, which brought an end to the 2000-year-old imperial system.

Warlords, Nationalists, and Communists (1912–1949)

The Republic of China was founded on January 1, 1912, with Dr. Sun Yat-sen, then China's best-known revolutionary and founder of its first political party, as president. However, the Western-educated Sun was not able to hold onto power, and China soon fell into a lengthy period of conflict and disintegration. Although the republic continued to exist in name, different parts of the country were controlled by military leaders known as warlords. Sun set about organizing another revolution to defeat the warlords and reunify the country under his Nationalist Party (the *Guomindang*).

In 1921 the Chinese Communist Party (CCP) was established by a few intellectuals who had become disenchanted with the derailing of the republican movement and with continuing foreign intervention in China's government and economy. They had been inspired by the Bolshevik triumph in Russia in 1917 and by the anti-imperialism of the newly founded Soviet Union to look for more radical solutions to China's problems. In 1924 the small Communist Party, acting on Soviet advice, joined with Sun Yat-sen's Nationalists to fight the warlords. After some initial successes, this alliance came to a tragic end in 1927 when Chiang Kai-shek, a military leader who had become the head of the Nationalist Party after Sun's death in 1925, turned against his coalition part-

---

Critical Junctures in Modern China's Political Development

1911   Revolution led by Sun Yat-sen overthrows 2000-year-old imperial system and establishes the Republic of China.

1912   Sun Yat-sen founds the Nationalist Party (*Guomindang*) to oppose warlords who have seized power in the new republic.

1921   Chinese Communist Party (CCP) founded.

1927   Civil war between Nationalists (led by Chiang Kai-shek) and Communists begins.

1934   Mao Zedong becomes leader of the CCP.

1937   Japan invades China, marking the start of World War II in Asia.

1949   Chinese Communists win the civil war and establish the People's Republic of China.

1958–1960   Great Leap Forward

1966–1976   Great Proletarian Cultural Revolution

1976   Mao Zedong dies.

1978   Deng Xiaoping becomes China's paramount leader and launches economic reforms.

1989   Tiananmen massacre; Deng promotes Jiang Zemin to become head of the Chinese Communist Party.

1997   Deng Xiaoping dies.

---

ners and ordered a bloody suppression that nearly wiped out the Communists. Chiang then proceeded to unify the Republic of China under his personal rule largely by striking an accommodation with some of the country's most powerful remaining warlords.

Ironically, the defeat of the CCP created the conditions for the eventual triumph of the man who would lead the party to nationwide victory. Mao Zedong, who had been one of the junior founders of the Communist Party, strongly advocated paying more attention to China's suffering peasants as a potential source of support. "In a very short time," he wrote in 1927, "several hundred million peasants will rise like a mighty storm, like a hurricane, a force so swift and violent that no power, however great, will be able to hold it back."[3] Mao's views grew out of his own peasant background and his investigations of spontaneous peasant uprisings against oppressive rural conditions.

However, his assessment was at odds with the orthodox Marxist-Leninist belief that a Communist-led revolution in China had to be based in the cities and rely on the support of the country's then minuscule industrial **proletariat**.

But after the suppression of the CCP by the Nationalists, the Communists had no choice but to retreat to the countryside, where Mao's strategy of peasant revolution gradually gained support in the party. In 1934–1935 the party undertook its fabled Long March, an epic journey of 6000 miles through some of China's roughest terrain, to escape attacks by Chiang's forces. At the end of the Long March, the CCP established a base in Yanan, a remote rural area in northwestern China.

In Yanan, Mao consolidated his political and ideological leadership of the Chinese Communist Party (through sometimes repressive means) and was elected party chairman in 1943, a position he held until his death in 1976. He also guided the effort to generate peasant support for the Communists through policies such as land reform and party-led quasi-democratic self-government, in which peasants were given a direct role in running village affairs.[4] At the same time, the Republic of China, under Chiang Kai-shek, became a right-wing dictatorship closely allied with big business, foreign interests, and the rural elite. Although the Nationalists did have some success in promoting economic modernization, the **legitimacy** of Chiang's government was severely undermined by corruption, mismanagement, and repression.

The course of the Chinese civil war between Nationalists and Communists was profoundly shaped by the Japanese invasion of China in 1937. Japan's assault pushed the Nationalist government deep into China's southwest and effectively eliminated it as an active combatant against Japanese aggression. In contrast, the CCP base in Yanan was on the front line against Japan's troops in northern China, and Mao and the Communists successfully mobilized the peasants to use **guerrilla warfare** to fight the invaders. By the end of World War II in 1945, the CCP had vastly expanded its membership and controlled much of the countryside in north China, while the Nationalists were isolated and unpopular with many Chinese.

The civil war resumed in earnest shortly after the Japanese surrender. Without any significant support from the Soviet Union, Communist forces won a decisive and surprisingly quick victory over the U.S.-backed Nationalists, who were forced to retreat to the island of Taiwan, 90 miles off the Chinese coast. On October 1, 1949, Mao Zedong stood on a rostrum in Tiananmen near the entrance to the former imperial palace in Beijing and declared the founding of the People's Republic of China.

Mao in Power (1949–1976)

The Chinese Communist Party came to power on the crest of an enormous wave of popular support because of its members' reputation as social reformers and patriotic fighters. In the early years of its rule, the CCP achieved some notable successes in rebuilding China's war-torn economy and restoring political order. Although most foreign-owned firms and many large businesses were taken over by the government, the PRC's economy in the early 1950s was a mix of state and private ownership. The CCP established firm control over China's new political system, but meaningful participation by noncommunists was also allowed.

Chairman Mao and the CCP also quickly turned their attention to some of the country's most glaring social problems. For instance, a massive **land reform** campaign redistributed property from the rich to the poor and increased productivity in the countryside. Highly successful drives eliminated opium addiction and prostitution from the cities, and a national law greatly enhanced the legal status of women in the family and allowed many women to free themselves from unhappy arranged marriages. Although the CCP did not hesitate to use violence to achieve its objectives and silence opponents, the party gained considerable legitimacy because of its popular and successful policies during these years.

In 1953–1957, the PRC implemented the first of its Soviet-style five-year plans. The complete **nationalization** of industry and **collectivization** of agriculture carried out as part of this plan were decisive steps away from the mixed state-private economy and toward **socialism**.

But Mao was particularly troubled by the persistence of inequalities in China, especially those caused by the First Five-Year Plan's emphasis on industrial and urban development and relative neglect of the countryside. In response, he launched the **Great Leap Forward** (1958–1960), a utopian effort to accelerate the country's economic development while making China into a radically egalitarian communist society. The Great Leap's objectives were to be reached by relying on the sheer labor and willpower of workers, peasants, and party activists rather than on the bureaucrats and intellectuals who had previously guided economic policy. Industry and agriculture were reorganized in ways that assumed people would work harder for communist goals than for monetary rewards.

The Great Leap was a great flop and turned into "one of the most extreme, bizarre, and eventually catastrophic episodes in twentieth-century political history."[5] In the rural areas, irrational policies, wasted resources, poor management, and the lack of labor incentives combined with bad weather to produce a famine that claimed between 20 and 30 million lives. An industrial depression soon followed the collapse of agriculture, causing a terrible setback to China's economic development.

In the early 1960s, Mao took a less active role in day-to-day decision-making. Two of China's other top leaders at the time, Liu Shaoqi and Deng Xiaoping, took charge of efforts to revive the economy using policies that combined the careful planning of the First Five-Year Plan with some market-oriented policies to stimulate production, particularly in agriculture.

This strategy revived the Chinese economy, but once again Mao found himself profoundly unhappy with the consequences of China's development. By the mid-1960s the chairman had concluded that the policies of Liu and Deng had led to a resurgence of bureaucratism and inequality that were threatening his revolutionary goals for China.

The result was the **Great Proletarian Cultural Revolution** (1966–1976), an ideological crusade launched by Mao to jolt China back toward his vision of socialism. Like the Great Leap Forward, the Cultural Revolution was a campaign of mass mobilization and utopian idealism, but its methods were much more violent and its main objective was the political purification of the party and the nation through class struggle, not accelerated economic development. Using his unmatched political clout

and **charisma**, Mao put together a potent coalition of radical party leaders, loyal military officers, and student and worker rebels to purge anyone thought to be guilty of revisionism, that is, betrayal of his version of Marxism-Leninism known as Mao Zedong Thought.

In the movement's first phase (1966–1969), 20 million or so high school and college students responded to Mao's pronouncement, "It is right to rebel!" by forming organizations called the Red Guards. They went on a rampage across the country, destroying countless priceless historical artifacts considered to be remnants of the imperial or capitalist past and, most tragically, harassing, torturing, and killing people accused of being class enemies. The Red Guards' reign of terror particularly targeted intellectuals, officials, and their families.

During the next phase of the Cultural Revolution (1969–1971), Mao used the People's Liberation Army (PLA) to restore political order. The army stopped the violence of the Red Guards, and millions of the young rebels were sent for several years to live and work in the countryside, where they were supposed to be reeducated by the peasants. The military's influence in politics was ended after some of its leaders allegedly attempted an abortive coup to seize power from Mao.

The final phase of the Cultural Revolution (1972–1976) involved intense conflict between radical leaders, who wanted the CCP to continue its emphasis on class struggle, and a more moderate group, who believed that the country needed to focus on economic development. These factions were locked in a dispute over who would succeed Mao as party chairman. Mao died in September 1976, and a month later the power struggle was settled when a coalition of the moderate leaders masterminded the arrest of their radical rivals, the so-called Gang of Four, which included Mao's wife and a leading radical, Jiang Qing.

The arrest of the Gang (who were sentenced to long prison terms) and the subsequent removal from power of many of their followers marked the end of the decade-long Cultural Revolution. Mao's last effort to steer China toward his vision of a communist utopia had claimed at least a half million lives, brought the nation to the brink of civil war, and led to a period of prolonged economic stagnation.

Deng Xiaoping and the Transformation of Chinese Communism (1976 to the Present)

China's first post-Mao leaders restored to office many of the veteran officials who had been purged by the radicals, including Deng Xiaoping. By 1978, Deng had clearly become the most powerful member of the CCP leadership. He remained so for nearly two decades even though he never occupied the formal top positions in either the party or the government, making sure instead that those posts were held by loyal lieutenants. Deng achieved this preeminence by skillful political maneuvering, through his close personal connections to many key party and military figures, and because he was widely regarded as the leader best able to repair the damage done to China by the Cultural Revolution.

Deng lost little time in using his newly consolidated political power to put China on a path of dramatic economic reform that transformed the nation. Deng's reforms were a profound break with the Maoist past. State control of the economy was significantly reduced, and market forces were allowed to play an increasingly important role. Agriculture was decollectivized and the management of farm production was turned over to individual families. Private businesses were encouraged in both city and countryside. The Chinese economy was opened to unprecedented levels of foreign investment and international trade soared.

On the cultural front, Chinese artists and writers saw the shackles of party dogma that had bound them for decades greatly loosened. Deng took major steps to revitalize China's government by bringing in younger, better-educated officials.

The results of Deng's initiatives were, by any measure, astounding. After decades of stagnation, the Chinese economy experienced unprecedented growth throughout the 1980s. The winds of freedom and openness seemed to be blowing through every sector of life in China. Deng was named *Time* magazine's "Man of the Year" in 1979 and 1986 in recognition of the boldness and success of his efforts to change China (see Figure 1).

These charts show dramatically how the Chinese economy has been transformed by the market reforms that were first introduced by Deng Xiaoping in 1978.

Figure 1

The Economic Transformation of Post-Mao China

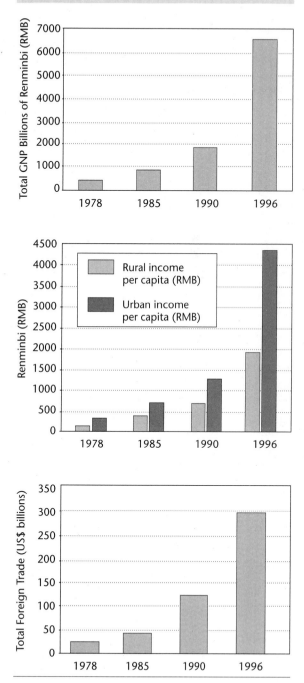

Source: China Statistical Yearbook 1997 (Beijing: China Statistical Publishing House, 1998).

FREE
MARKETS
NOT
PEOPLE!

DENG

WASSERMAN
©'92 BOSTON GLOBE
DIST. BY L.A. TIMES SYNDICATE

This cartoon captures the contradiction between economic reform and political repression that characterized China under the leadership of Deng Xiaoping. *Source:* © 1992, *The Boston Globe.* Distributed by Los Angeles Times Syndicate. Reprinted with permission.

Then came June 4, 1989, and the massacre near Tiananmen Square. There were a number of reasons why large-scale demonstrations erupted in Beijing and several other Chinese cities that spring, including discontent over skyrocketing inflation and widespread official corruption as well as a desire, especially among students and intellectuals, for more democracy. The brutal crushing of the Tiananmen protests was a shocking reminder that, for all the economic changes that had taken place under Deng Xiaoping, politics in China were to remain subject to strict regulation by the CCP.

Following the Tiananmen crackdown, China went through a few years of intensified political repression and economic retrenchment. But in early 1992, Deng Xiaoping took some bold steps to accelerate the reform of the economy. He did so largely because he hoped it would help the PRC avoid a collapse of the communist system such as had occurred just the year before in the Soviet Union. Since then, the Chinese economy has continued to become both more marketized and more internationalized and has continued its record of spectacular growth and modernization.

Another important consequence of the 1989 Tiananmen crisis was the replacement as head of the Chinese Communist Party of one Deng protégé, Zhao Ziyang, by another, Jiang Zemin. Zhao was ousted because he was considered too sympathetic to the student demonstrators, while Jiang was promoted from his previous post as CCP chief in Shanghai because of his firm but relatively bloodless handling of similar protests in that city. Although Deng remained the power behind the throne for several years, he gradually turned over greater authority to Jiang, who in addition to his positions as general secretary of the CCP and chair of the powerful Central Military Commission became president of the People's Republic of China in 1993. When Deng Xiaoping died in February 1997, Jiang was fairly secure in his position as China's top leader. By the time he hosted President Bill Clinton at the Beijing summit in June 1998, Jiang Zemin had proven himself to be a capable leader committed to continuing, even deepening, the process of economic reform begun by Deng Xiaoping. Despite some signs of political relaxation in the late 1990s, Jiang also appeared determined to maintain the rule of the Chinese Communist Party. Dissidents who even indirectly challenged the authority of the CCP were sentenced to harsh prison terms, and writers considered too critical of party policy were silenced.

It will take several years before it is clear what, if any, special mark Jiang Zemin will make on Chinese politics. But he does represent a new kind of leader for the PRC. Unlike Deng or Mao, Jiang Zemin is not a professional revolutionary. Although they turned out to have very different ideas about how China should develop, Deng and Mao both made their whole careers in the inner sanctums of the Chinese Communist Party. In contrast, Jiang, although a member of the party since 1946, was trained as an engineer and served as a technical expert and bureaucrat in factories and government ministries before becoming mayor (and later party leader) of Shanghai in 1985. In this sense, the passing of power from Deng Xiaoping to Jiang Zemin in 1997 was a critical juncture in the political history of the People's Republic of China.

Themes and Implications

Historical Junctures and Political Themes

The World of States.   The making of the modern Chinese state has been profoundly influenced at several critical points by China's encounters with other countries. The end of the Middle Kingdom's relative isolation from the non-Asian world and the conflict with the militarily superior West in the nineteenth century was a major factor in the collapse of the imperial system in 1911. Anger over European and U.S. treatment of China, admiration for the Russian revolution, and the invasion of China by Japan in the 1930s all played a role in propelling the Chinese Communist Party to power in 1949.

American hostility to the new Communist regime in Beijing helped push the People's Republic of China into an alliance with the Soviet Union and follow the Soviet model of development in the early 1950s. But Mao's disapproval of the direction in which Soviet Communist leaders were taking their country greatly influenced his decisions to launch both the Great Leap Forward in 1958 and the Cultural Revolution in 1966. In the early 1970s, Mao approved the beginnings of **détente** with the United States in response to what he saw as a growing and more immediate threat to China from the Soviet Union. The relationship between China and the United States deepened throughout the 1970s and paved the way for the marketization and globalization of the Chinese economy under Deng Xiaoping.

When the People's Republic was founded, China was in a relatively weak position in the international system. For more than a century, its destiny had been shaped by incursions and influences from abroad that it could do little to control. Mao made many tragic and terrible blunders, but one of his great achievements was to build a strong state able to affirm and defend its sovereignty. China's international stature has increased as its economic and military power have grown in recent decades. Though still a poor country by many per capita measures, the sheer size of its economy makes the PRC an economic powerhouse whose import and export policies have an important impact on many other countries. China is a nuclear power with the world's largest conventional military force; it is an active and influential member of nearly all international organizations, including the United Nations, where it sits as one of the five permanent members of the Security Council. Clearly, China has become one of the major players on the global scene.

Governing the Economy.   Economic issues were central to the revolutionary process that led to the founding of the People's Republic. The Western powers were primarily motivated by the lure of the China market in their aggressive policies toward the Chinese empire in the nineteenth century. Chiang Kai-shek's Nationalist government lost popular support partly because of its mismanagement of the economy and inability to control corruption. Mass poverty and terrible inequality fueled the Chinese revolution and led millions of peasants and workers to back the Communist Party in the civil war.

The history of the PRC is largely the story of experimentation with a series of very different economic systems: a Soviet-style planning system in the early 1950s; the radical egalitarianism of the Maoist model; and Deng Xiaoping's market-oriented policies. Ideological disputes within the CCP over which of these development strategies China should follow were the main cause of the ferocious political struggles, such as the Cultural Revolution, that have so often wracked the country. Deng's bold reforms were, in large measure, motivated by his hope that improved living standards would restore the legitimacy of the CCP, which had been badly tarnished by the economic failings of the Maoist era. The remarkable successes of those reforms have helped sustain the CCP in power at a time when most other communist regimes have disappeared. Continuing China's economic progress will be one of the most important challenges facing Jiang Zemin and China's other leaders.

The Democratic Idea.   Jiang and the CCP also face major political challenges, especially the challenge of the democratic idea, which has had a troubled history in twentieth-century China. The revolution of 1911, which overthrew the imperial system and established the Republic of China under Sun Yat-sen, was the culmination of the first effort to establish a Chinese government in which citizens would have more say. But the combination of warlordism, civil war, world war, and Chiang Kai-shek's sharp turn toward dictatorship undermined any real progress toward democracy. Any hope that the democratic idea might take root in the early years of Communist rule in China was violently dispelled by the building of a one-party Communist state and Mao's unrelenting campaigns against alleged enemies of his revolution. The Deng Xiaoping era brought much greater economic, social, and cultural freedom for the Chinese people, but time and again the CCP acted to strangle the stirrings of the democratic idea, most brutally in Tiananmen Square in 1989.

The Politics of Collective Identity.   Because of its long history and high degree of cultural homogeneity, China has a very strong sense of national identity. Memories of past humiliations and suffering at the hands of foreigners still influence the international relations of the PRC. For example, Beijing's insistence that Britain return Hong Kong to Chinese control in 1997 was largely fueled by the desire to redress what it saw as one of the most blatant injustices of China's defeat in the Opium War of the mid-nineteenth century. And China believes that Japan should apologize more fully for atrocities committed by the Japanese army during World War II before the two Asian powers can have completely cordial diplomatic relations. As faith in **communism** has weakened, party leaders have increasingly turned to nationalism as a means to rally the Chinese people behind their government.

China's cultural homogeneity has also saved it from the kind of ethnic or religious violence that has plagued so many countries in the modern world. The exception to this has been in the border regions of the country, where there is a large concentration of minority peoples, particularly in Tibet and the Muslim areas of China's northwest (see Section 4).

China did experience a particularly vicious and destructive kind of identity politics during the Maoist era. Although landlords and capitalists had lost their private property and economic power by the mid-1950s, Mao continued to promote class struggle that pitted workers, peasants, and loyal party activists against "capitalist roaders" and other alleged counter-revolutionaries. When he took over in the late 1970s, Deng Xiaoping called for an end to such divisive class struggles and proclaimed an era of social harmony in which the whole nation could concentrate its energies on the overarching goals of modernization and economic development. But Deng's reforms led to new (or renewed) cleavages in Chinese society, including glaring inequalities between those who have profited handsomely from the marketization of the economy and those who have done less well or even been disadvantaged by the changes. These inequalities could become the basis of class, regional, or other kinds of identity-based conflicts that severely test the economic and political management skills of China's leaders.

Implications for Comparative Politics

For the student of comparative politics, China is a particularly important and interesting case. First, the PRC can be compared with other Communist party-states with which it shares or has shared many political and ideological features. From this perspective, China raises intriguing questions. Why has China's Communist party-state so far proven more durable than that of the Soviet Union and nearly all other similar regimes? By what combination of reform and repression has the Chinese Communist Party held onto power? What signs are there that it is likely to continue to be able to do so for the foreseeable future? What signs suggest that Communist rule in China may be coming to an end? Studying Chinese politics is important for understanding the past, present, and future of a type of political system—the Communist party-state—that has had a major impact on the modern world.

Second, China can fruitfully be compared with other developing nations that face similar economic and political challenges. Although the PRC is still very

Table 1

China's Development in Comparative Perspective					
	Purchasing Power Parity GNP per Capita (US$)	GNP Growth Rate (%)	Life Expectancy at Birth (years)	Infant Mortality (per 1000 live births)	Adult Literacy (%)
China	3570	8.9	69	38	82
Brazil	6240	2.4	67	44	83
India	1650	5.0	62	73	52
Iran	5530	3.2	70	32	72
Mexico	3680	8.0	72	27	90
Nigeria	880	4.2	51	114	57

Note: All figures are for 1995–1997.

Sources: World Bank; United Nations.

much part of the Third World as measured by the average standard of living of its population, its record of growth in the 1980s and 1990s has been far better than most of the world's other developing countries. Furthermore, educational and health levels of the Chinese people are quite good when compared with many other countries at a similar level of economic development, for example, India and Nigeria (see Table 1). How has China achieved such relative success in its quest for economic development? On the other hand, while most of the Third World has gone through a wave of democratization in recent decades, China remains a one-party dictatorship. How and why has China resisted the wave of democracy? What does the experience of other developing countries say about how economic modernization might influence the prospects for democracy in China?

Napoleon Bonaparte, emperor of France in the early nineteenth century, is said to have remarked, "Let China sleep. For when China wakes, it will shake the world."[6] China has awakened, and given its geographic size, vast resources, huge population, surging economic strength, and formidable military might, the People's Republic will certainly be among the world's great powers in the future.

Section ❷ Political Economy and Development

The growth of China's economy since Deng Xiaoping began his market-oriented reforms in the late 1970s has been called "one of the century's greatest economic miracles," which has, in turn, led to "one of the biggest improvements in human welfare anywhere at any time."[7] Such superlatives seem justified in describing overall economic growth rates that have averaged about 10 percent per year for nearly two decades while most of the world's other economies were growing much more slowly. During the same period, the average income of the Chinese people quadrupled, and although there are still many very poor people in China, more than 200 million have been lifted from living in absolute poverty to a level where they have a minimally adequate supply of food, clothing, and shelter.

China's economic miracle has involved much more than growth in gross domestic product and personal income. There has also been a profound transformation of the very nature of economic life in the PRC from what it had been during the Maoist era.

State and Economy

The Maoist Economy

When the CCP came to power in 1949, the Chinese economy was suffering from the devastating effects of more than a hundred years of rebellion, invasion, civil war, and bad government. The first urgent task of China's new Communist rulers was the stabilization and revival of the economy. Although a lot of property was seized from wealthy landowners, rich industrialists, and foreign companies, much private ownership and many aspects of capitalism were allowed to continue in order to gain support for the government and get the economy going again.

Once production had been restored, the party turned its attention to building socialism in China by following the Soviet model of economic development. The essence of this model was a **command economy**, in which the state owns or controls most economic resources and economic activity is driven by government planning and commands rather than by market forces.

The command economy in China was at its height during the First Five-Year Plan of 1953–1957, when the government took control of the production and distribution of nearly all goods and services. The First Five-Year Plan yielded some impressive economic results, but it also created huge bureaucracies and new inequalities, especially between the heavily favored industrial cities and the investment-starved rural areas. These trends led Mao and his radical supporters to try to build a distinctive Chinese road to socialism that would be less bureaucratic and more egalitarian than the Soviet model. Both the Great Leap Forward and the Cultural Revolution embodied this Maoist approach to economic development.

In the Great Leap, more than a million backyard furnaces were set up throughout the country to prove that steel could be produced by peasants in every village, not just in a few huge modern factories in the cities. In the Cultural Revolution, highly participatory revolutionary committees, controlled by workers and party activists, replaced the Soviet-style system of letting managers run industrial enterprises. Both of these Maoist experiments were less than successful. The backyard furnaces yielded great quantities of useless steel and squandered precious resources, while the revolutionary committees led many factories to pay more attention to politics than production.

The economic legacy of Maoism is a mixed one. One the one hand, Mao's utopian experiments had very serious negative effects on the ability of the PRC to embark on a path of sustained economic development. The relentless suppression of any kind of economic activity thought to be a "capitalist weed" and the denial of opportunities to accumulate personal wealth meant that most people had little incentive to work hard. Furthermore, for all of its radical rhetoric, the Maoist strategy of development never really broke decisively with many of the basic precepts of the command system, including government domination of the economy. Bureaucratic interference, poor management, and ill-conceived projects led to wasted resources of truly staggering proportions. Overall, China's economic growth rates, especially in agriculture, barely kept pace with population increases during the Mao years, with the result that the standard of living for most Chinese rose very little between the late 1950s and Mao's death in 1976.

On the other hand, under Mao, the PRC "did accomplish, in however flawed a fashion, the initial phase of industrialization of the Chinese economy, creating a substantial industrial and technological base that simply had not existed before."[8] The state, as part of its socialist commitment to promote equality and reduce poverty, also assigned a high priority to building schools and medical clinics throughout the country. By the end of the Mao era, the people of China were much healthier and more literate than they had been in the early 1950s, and they were doing considerably better in terms of health and education than were people in most other developing countries, where government took little initiative to address such issues.

China Goes to Market

After he came to power in 1978, Deng Xiaoping took China in a direction far different from Mao's and any that had ever been followed by a Communist party-state anywhere. By the early 1960s, Deng had come to the conclusion that China needed less politics and ideology and more economic development. Deng's pragmatic views on how to promote development were captured in his famous 1962 statement, "It doesn't matter whether a cat is white or black, as long as it catches mice."[9] He meant that China should not be overly concerned about whether a particular policy was socialist or capitalist if it in fact helped the economy. Of course, Deng also believed that the economic cat should be kept on the party's political leash.

Deng knew that drastic action was needed to get the Chinese economy moving after the Cultural Revolution and to adapt China's socialist system to the realities of an increasingly interdependent and competitive modern world. He spearheaded a program of far-reaching reforms that, in the course of less than a decade, literally remade the Chinese economy, touched nearly every aspect of life in the PRC, and redefined the very nature of socialism in China. Deng referred to his economic reform program as China's second revolution, comparing it in importance to the first revolution, which had brought the Communists to power in 1949.[10] The upshot of these reforms was to greatly reduce (though not eliminate) the role of government commands while allowing market mechanisms to operate in increasingly large areas of the economy. Under Deng's leadership, China moved toward a mixed economic system that was based partly on socialist planning and partly on the capitalist free market.

Deng declared that the PRC had a socialist market economy. This may sound like a contradiction in terms, since a market economy is usually associated with capitalism. The idea of a socialist market economy can be seen as mere ideological window-dressing to allow the introduction of capitalism into a country still ruled by the Communist Party. But from the official CCP perspective, the term conveys the facts that China's economy now combines elements of both socialism and capitalism and also (in theory at least) that the market remains subordinate to government planning and party leadership, which will prevent too much capitalist-like exploitation and inequality.

Deng's reforms involved a significant degree of **decentralization** in the economy. Authority for making economic decisions passed from bureaucrats to individual families, factory managers, and private entrepreneurs, all of them presumably motivated by the desire to make more money. Most prices are set according to supply and demand, as in a capitalist economy, rather than by administrative decree, and in many sectors of

the economy decisions about what to produce and how to produce it are no longer dictated by the state.

The Chinese government now encourages private and foreign ownership of factories and businesses. In many areas of the economy, government monopolies have given way to fierce competition between state-owned and non-state-owned firms. For example, the government-run national airline, which was the country's only airline until 1985, now competes with more than two dozen foreign and domestic carriers. Several government-approved stock markets, which sell shares in enterprises to private individuals, have been established, and many more unauthorized ones have sprung up around the country.

There are still more than 100,000 state-owned enterprises, which employ more than 100 million workers. These enterprises produce a large share of China's total industrial output and continue to dominate critical sectors of the economy, such as the production of steel and petroleum. But the role of the state sector is diminishing as private industries and so-called collective enterprises (which are usually run by combinations of local governments and private entrepreneurs) are expanding at a much faster rate (see Figure 2 on page 502). Even the government firms have been made more responsive to market forces. Under the command economy, state-owned industries had to turn over all profits to the government and were bailed out by state banks if they ran into financial difficulty, so there was little incentive to work hard or operate efficiently. Now a company pays a set tax on any profits, with the remainder available to be used as bonuses for the workers and managers and for investment in the factory.

Nevertheless, the majority of state-owned enterprises are still overstaffed and inefficiently run firms with outdated machinery. They remain a huge drain on the country's banking system and hinder modernization of key sectors of the Chinese economy. Threats to shut down the worst of them have never been seriously implemented because of the government's fear of the political consequences of tens of millions of unemployed workers. In late 1997, President Jiang Zemin made state-enterprise reform one of the government's top priorities. He unveiled plans to move ahead with bankruptcies of unprofitable firms and partially privatize what remains of the government-run sector of the economy.

These charts show how the share of China's total industrial output that comes from state-owned enterprises has declined sharply since Deng Xiaoping began to reform the PRC economy in 1978. The category "Collective" consists mostly of rural township and village enterprises (TVEs), which are owned by local governments but operate according to the market rather than by state planning. "Private" refers to industries owned by individuals, and "Other" includes foreign-owned enterprises and various kinds of mixed ownership.

Figure 2

China's Industrial Output by Ownership Type

1978

1985

1990

1997

Source: China Statistical Yearbook 1997.

The economic results of China's move to the market have been phenomenal. As noted, the PRC has become one of the fastest-growing economies in the world and is likely to remain so for some time, given the financial crisis that struck much of the rest of East Asia in the late 1990s. China's gross national product (GNP) per capita (that is, the total output of the economy divided by the total population) grew at an average rate of 8.6 percent per year from 1980 to 1995. By way of comparison, the per capita GNP of the United States grew at only 1.5 percent per year during the same period, India's at 3.2 percent, and Brazil's at –0.4 percent. A booming economy and rapidly rising

incomes unleashed a consumer revolution in the PRC. To cite just one example, in the late 1970s, hardly anyone owned a television; now more than 90 percent of urban households have a color TV and nearly as many rural families have at least a black-and-white set.

The success of the reforms can be attributed largely to the reduction of bureaucratic and political interference in the economy and to the increased motivation to work hard created by the enormous expansion of opportunities for individuals, families, and businesses to earn, keep, and spend money.

Still, the PRC economy is only half-reformed. Central planning has been refined, not abandoned, and

This picture, taken in Shanghai in the early 1990s, graphically captures how the modern and the traditional exist side-by-side in China. It also shows how the market-style reforms introduced by Deng Xiaoping have greatly increased disparities in wealth, a problem that could lead to growing social and political tensions in the future. *Source:* Dan Habib/Impact Visuals.

national and local bureaucrats still exercise a great deal of control over the production and distribution of goods, resources, and services. The extent of private property is still restricted, while unproductive state enterprises continue to exert a considerable drag on key economic sectors. And even though the market reforms have gained substantial momentum that would be very hard to reverse, the Communist Party continues to wield the power to decide what direction economic reforms will take and whether they will continue. In other words, bureaucracy, politics, and ideology continue to tilt the balance of economic power in China decisively toward the party-state.

Remaking the Chinese Countryside

The economic changes in China have been particularly striking in the countryside, where over 900 million people still live and work.

One of the first major efforts launched by the CCP after it came to power in 1949 was a land reform campaign that confiscated the property of landlords and redistributed it as private holdings to the poorer peasants. But by the mid-1950s, as part of the transition to socialism, China's peasants had been reorganized into collective farms made up of about 250 families each. The land now belonged to the collective, and production and labor were directed by local officials working in coordination with the state plan. Individuals were paid according to how much they worked on the collective land, while most crops and other farm products had to be sold to the state at low fixed prices. During the Great Leap Forward, the collective farms were merged into gigantic **people's communes** with several thousand families. Although the size of the communes was scaled back following failure of the Leap, the commune system remained as the foundation of the rural economy throughout the rest of the Maoist period.

The system of collectivized agriculture proved to be one of the weakest links in China's command economy. The communes were able to deliver improved social services to the people in the country-side, and they undertook some large-scale construction projects (especially irrigation) that were of great benefit to rural areas. But many of the communes were poorly managed, and peasants often saw little reason to work hard, since much of the fruits of their labor went into the communal pot or to the state. Agricultural production and rural living standards were essentially stagnant from 1957 to 1977.

The first changes in the organization of agriculture in post-Mao China came from the spontaneous actions of local leaders who were looking for ways to boost production. They moved to curtail the powers of the commune and to allow peasants more leeway in planting and selling their crops. In the early 1980s, Deng Xiaoping used his newly won political power to support this trend and moved to "bury the Maoist model once and for all" in the countryside by the "massive dismemberment of the basic features of the former collectivized system."[11] The communes were replaced by a **household responsibility system**, which is still in effect today. In this system, farmland is contracted out to individual families who take full charge of the production and marketing of crops—functions that were previously tightly controlled by the commune. After paying government taxes and contract fees to the village, which still owns the land, the family is largely free to consume or sell what it produces. Families can now sign contracts for thirty years or more, but there has been no move to privatize agriculture fully by actually selling the land to individual families.

The freeing of the rural economy from the constraints of the communal system led to a sharp increase in agricultural productivity. In the 1980s agricultural production grew at the rate of about 6 percent a year, but it slowed considerably in the 1990s. This growth has greatly improved the living standards of China's rural families and provided the raw materials needed to support the country's efforts to modernize industrial production and feed the growing urban population.

But nothing has contributed more to the remaking of the Chinese countryside than the spread of a rural industrial and commercial revolution that, in speed and scope, is unprecedented in the history of the modern world. Although the foundations of rural industrialization were laid during the Maoist period, **township and village enterprises** (TVEs) expanded enormously under Deng's reforms. These rural factories and businesses, which vary greatly in size, are generally owned and run by local government and private entrepreneurs. Although they are called collective enterprises, TVEs operate outside of the state plan, make their own decisions about all aspects of the business process, and are responsible for their profits and losses. TVEs are the fastest-growing sector of the Chinese economy, produce 80 percent of the nation's clothes, and account for about 40 percent of China's total industrial output. They can be found in nearly every part of the country and employ over 130 million people. Although many people have moved from the countryside to the cities in search of better economic opportunities, the number of migrants would be much higher if the TVEs had not been able to absorb so much surplus rural labor.

The transformation of the Chinese countryside has not been without serious problems. Local officials who run TVEs "often behave more like business tycoons than public servants" and pay more attention to making money for themselves than to their civic duties.[12] Peasants have protested, sometimes violently, against high taxes, corrupt local officials, and delays in payments for agricultural products purchased by the government. There have also been concerns about China's ability to produce enough food to feed its big population. Now that the state no longer commands farmers to give priority to the production of grain and other essential foods, they often choose to raise more lucrative cash crops such as flowers and vegetables. In fact, China has recently had to import fairly large quantities of grain.

The social services safety net provided for China's rural dwellers by the communes has all but disappeared with the return to household-based farming. Many rural clinics and schools closed once government financial support was eliminated. The availability of health care, educational opportunities, disability pay, and retirement funds now depends on the relative wealth of families and villages, which has led to very large gaps between the prosperous and the poor areas of the country. Economic factors, such as the need for larger families in situations where income is dependent on household labor, have also contributed

Current Challenges: *China's One-Child Policy*

While he was in power, Mao Zedong did not see a reduction of China's population growth rate as an important national priority. On the contrary, he viewed vast amounts of human labor and the revolutionary enthusiasm of the masses as precious national resources. As a result, little was done to promote family planning in China during most of the Maoist era.

By the early 1970s, China's population had reached over 800 million, and because of greatly improved health conditions, it was growing at about 2.8 percent per year. This meant that the number of people in China would double in just twenty-five years, which would put a great strain on the country's resources. Cutting the birthrate came to be seen as a major prerequisite to modernization and economic development. Under Deng Xiaoping, the Chinese government implemented a stringent population control policy that has used various means to encourage or even force couples to have only a single child. These means have included intensive media campaigns lauding the virtues and benefits of small families, the monitoring of contraceptive use and women's fertility cycles by workplace medics or local doctors, positive incentives such as more land or preferred housing for couples with only one child, and negative sanctions such as fines or demotions for those who violate the policy.

The one-child campaign, the growing and modernizing economy, and a comparatively strong record in improving education and employment opportunities for women all played a role in the reduction of the population growth rate to 0.9 percent per year in the late 1990s. This figure is very low for a country at China's level of economic development. India, for example, has also had some success in promoting family planning, but its annual population growth rate is 1.6 percent, while Nigeria's is 2.9 percent. These might not seem like big differences, but consider this: At these respective growth rates, it will take seventy-eight years for China's population to double, whereas India's population will double in forty-four years and Nigeria's in twenty-four years.

There have, however, been some very serious problems with China's population policy. The compulsory, intrusive nature of China's family-planning program and the extensive use of abortion as a major means of birth control has led to some international criticism, criticism that Beijing has rejected as interference in its domestic affairs.

Farmers have evaded the one-child policy—for example, by not registering births—because the return to household-based agriculture has made the quantity of labor an important ingredient in family income. The still widespread belief that male children will contribute more to the family economically and that a male heir is necessary to carry on the family line causes some rural families to take drastic steps to make sure that they have a son. Female infanticide and the abandonment of female babies have increased dramatically, and the availability of ultrasound technology has led to a large number of sex-selective abortions of female fetuses. As a result, China has an unusual gender balance: Normally, 105 boys are born for every 100 girls, but in some parts of China the ratio is as high as 117 boys for every 100 girls. As a result, there are tens of thousands of "missing girls" in China's under-30 population.

In response to rural resistance and international pressures, the Chinese government has relaxed its population policies somewhat. Rural couples are now often allowed to have two children. In the cities, where there has been more voluntary compliance with the policy because of higher incomes and limited living space, the one-child policy is still basically in effect.

---

to peasant efforts to circumvent China's controversial one-child population control policy.

The Political Impact of Economic Reform

Efforts to transform the economy through market-style policies have had an important impact on China's domestic politics. First, both Deng Xiaoping and Jiang Zemin have faced opposition from other party leaders who believe that China has moved too fast and too far toward a market economy. The strongest opposition has come from "conservatives" in the Communist Party who do not want the party-state to give up so much control over the economy or society. There has also been "leftist" opposition from those who believe that the party is paying too little attention to politics and ideology, and has strayed too far from its socialist commitment to equality. Both conservatives and leftists blame the appearance of democratic ideas on the spread of capitalist influences at home and from abroad. Deng Xiaoping was able to beat back such challenges, and Jiang Zemin's emergence as Deng's clear successor put power in the hands of a leader strongly committed to continuing economic reform. But a major economic setback or widespread political turmoil could lead to a resurgence of antireform elements in the party.

Second, the decentralization of economic decision-making, which was such an important factor in the success of Deng's reforms, has greatly increased the autonomy of provincial and local governments. Some observers have even spoken of the appearance of "economic warlordism" in China as regions compete with one another by erecting tariff and other trade barriers between provinces. Some local governments defy or ignore the central government by, for example, evading taxes or undertaking massive construction projects without consulting Beijing. Such seepage of economic and political power from the central to the local levels poses serious questions about the ability of the national government to maintain control in the country.

Finally, China's economic transformation has brought far-reaching social change to the country, creating new pressures on the political system and new challenges to the Communist Party. The party wants the Chinese people to believe that economic growth depends on the political stability that only continuing party leadership can provide. CCP leaders hope that growing prosperity will leave most people satisfied with the Communist Party and reduce demands for political change. But economic reform has created many groups—entrepreneurs, professionals, middle-class consumers, the hundreds of thousands of Chinese students who have studied abroad—that must be allowed free rein if the party wants to sustain the economic boom. In time, these and other emerging groups are likely to press their claims for a more independent political voice and confront the regime with some fundamental questions about the nature of Communist power in China. Another challenge to the party may come from Hong Kong, the former British colony that became a Special Administrative Region of the People's Republic of China in July 1997.

China's government wants to take full advantage of Hong Kong's economic dynamism but is more wary of the free press, independent judiciary, and respect for civil liberties that developed under British rule.

Society and Economy

Market reform and modernization of the Chinese economy has created a more diverse and open society. People are much freer to choose careers, travel about the country (or even abroad), practice their religious beliefs, buy private homes, join nonpolitical associations, and engage in a wide range of other activities that were prohibited or severely restricted during the Maoist era. But economic change has also caused serious social problems. There has been a sharp increase in crime, prostitution, and drug use; although such problems are still far less prevalent in China than in many other countries, they are serious enough to be a growing concern for national and local authorities.

Economic reform has also brought significant changes in China's basic system of social welfare. The Maoist economy was characterized by what was called the **iron rice bowl**. As in other command economies such as the Soviet Union, this meant that employment, a certain standard of living (albeit, a low one), and basic cradle-to-grave benefits were guaranteed to most of the urban and rural labor force. In the cities the workplace was more than just a place to work and earn a salary; it also provided its employees with housing, health care, daycare, and other services.

China's economic reformers believe that such guarantees led to poor work motivation and excessive costs for the government and enterprises, and have implemented policies designed to break the iron rice bowl. Income and employment are now no longer guaranteed but are more directly tied to individual effort. Workers in state enterprises still have rather generous health and pension plans, but employees in the rapidly expanding semiprivate and private sectors usually have few benefits.

The breaking of the iron rice bowl has increased productivity and motivated people to work harder in order to earn more money. But it has also led to a dramatic increase in unemployment, which is estimated to be as high as 20 percent of the total labor force. Labor unrest, including strikes, slowdowns,

Current Challenges: Hong Kong—From China to Britain and Back Again

Hong Kong became a British colony in three stages during the nineteenth century as a result of what the Chinese call the "unequal treaties" imposed under military and diplomatic pressure from the West. Two parts of Hong Kong were ceded permanently to Britain in 1842 and 1860, respectively, but the largest part of the tiny territory was given to Britain with a ninety-nine year lease in 1898. It was the anticipated expiration of that lease that set in motion negotiations between London and Beijing in the 1980s over the future status of Hong Kong. In December 1984 a joint declaration was signed by the two countries in which Britain agreed to return all of Hong Kong to Chinese sovereignty on July 1, 1997. On that date, Hong Kong became a Special Administrative Region (SAR) of the People's Republic of China.

Britain ruled Hong Kong in a traditional, if benevolent, colonial fashion. A governor sent from London presided over a colonial administration in which foreigners rather than the local people exercised most of the power. There was a free press, a fair and effective legal system, and other important features of a democratic system. In the last years of British rule, there were efforts to appoint more Hong Kong Chinese to higher administrative positions and expand the scope of elections in choosing some members of the colony's executive and representative bodies. The British, who controlled Hong Kong for over a century, were criticized for taking steps toward democratization only on the eve of their departure from the colony. They allowed only a small number of Hong Kong residents to emigrate to the United Kingdom before the start of Chinese rule.

Hong Kong flourished economically under the free-market policies of the British and became one of the world's great centers of international trade and finance. Hong Kong has the highest standard of living in Asia outside of Japan and Singapore. At the same time, Hong Kong is characterized by extremes of wealth and poverty. China pledged to preserve Hong Kong's capitalist system for at least fifty years after 1997. Because of the growing integration of the economies of Hong Kong and southern China, the PRC has a strong motivation not to do anything that might destroy the area's economic dynamism.

Although the PRC took over full control of Hong Kong's foreign policy and has stationed some troops of the People's Liberation Army in Hong Kong, Beijing has generally fulfilled its promise that the Special Administrative Region will have a high degree of political as well as economic autonomy. Civil liberties, the independence of the judiciary, and freedom of the press have been maintained.

However, the PRC has made sure that it keeps a grip on political power in Hong Kong. The SAR is headed by a chief executive, Tung Chee-hwa, a very wealthy businessman appointed by the PRC, and PRC-approved civil servants wield enormous authority in the government. China dissolved the legislature that had been elected prior to the start of Chinese rule and replaced it with a body filled with pro-Beijing members. In May 1998 democratic parties critical or at least skeptical of the Chinese Communist Party won nearly three-quarters of the twenty legislative seats up for election, although the remainder of the sixty-member legislature is chosen by an indirect process that strongly favors pro-China candidates. All in all, the SAR government is responsible to Beijing and ultimately subject to its authority, leading some residents and politicians who favor democracy in Hong Kong to worry that British colonialism has only been replaced by Chinese authoritarianism.

Hong Kong

Land Area (sq. miles)	401.5 (about six times the size of Washington, D.C.)
Population	6.5 million
Ethnic Composition	Chinese, 95%; other, 5%
GNP (US$)	$164 billion
GNP per capita (US$)	$26,000
Life Expectancy	Male, 76; Female, 82
Infant Mortality (per 1000 live births)	5
Literacy	93%

demonstrations, and sit-ins, was on the rise in the late 1990s. In the past the CCP has not dealt gently with protesting workers: the army was ordered to crush the 1989 Tiananmen demonstrations partly because party leaders were alarmed by the large number of workers who had joined the protests under the banner of an unauthorized union. If inefficient state-owned firms are shut down or downsized as the current leadership has promised, another 30 million workers could lose their jobs. The best hope for dealing with this situation is if the economy continues to grow fast enough to create jobs for displaced workers. Otherwise unemployment and labor unrest could be a political time bomb for the Communist party-state.

Market reforms have also opened China's cities to a flood of rural migrants. After the agricultural communes were disbanded in the early 1980s, many of the peasants who were not needed in the fields found work in the rapidly expanding township and village enterprises. But many others, no longer constrained by the strict limits on internal population movement enforced in the Mao era, headed to the urban areas to look for jobs. The more than 100 million people who make up this so-called floating population are mostly employed in very low-paying temporary jobs such as unskilled construction work—that is when they can find any work at all. These migrants are putting increased pressure on urban housing and social services, and their presence in Chinese cities could become politically destabilizing if they find their aspirations thwarted by a stalled economy or if they are treated too roughly or unfairly by local governments, who often see them as intruders.

China's economic boom has also created enormous opportunities for corruption. In a country in transition from a command to a market economy, officials still control many resources and still have power over many economic transactions from which there are large profits to be made. Bribes are common in the heavily bureaucratized and highly personalized system. Because the rule of law is often weaker than personal connections (called *guanxi* in Chinese), nepotism and cronyism are rampant. In a major speech in the fall of 1997, President Jiang Zemin acknowledged, "The fight against corruption is a grave political struggle vital to the very existence of the Party and the state. . . . If corruption cannot be punished effectively, our Party will lose the support and confidence of the people."[13] The government has repeatedly launched well-publicized campaigns against official graft. Thousands of officials have been fired or jailed including the former mayor of Beijing, and some people have even been executed for particularly massive embezzlement. But this has done little to stem the widespread feeling that the use of official power for private economic gain pervades the political system from top to bottom.

The benefits of economic growth have spread throughout most of China. But there has also been a growth in various kinds of inequality—a contradiction for a country led by a Communist Party that still claims to believe in socialist ideals. Maoist China was never as egalitarian as its rhetoric led many people to believe, but various policies did limit the extent of inequality between people and parts of the country. China's market reforms and economic boom have created sharp class differences, generally benefited people who live in the cities more than those in the countryside, and caused a widening gap between the richer coastal regions and poorer inland areas.

Gender inequalities also appear to have increased in some ways since the 1980s. The situation of women in China has improved enormously since 1949 in terms of social status, legal rights, employment, and education. Women have also benefited from the improved living standards and expanded economic opportunities that the reforms have brought. But the trend toward marketization has not benefited men and women equally. In the countryside, only male heads of households may sign contracts for land, and therefore men dominate household economic life. This is true despite the fact that farm labor has become increasingly feminized as many men move to jobs in rural industry or migrate to the cities. Economic and cultural pressures have also led to an alarming suicide rate (the world's highest) among rural women. Although nine out of ten urban Chinese women work (giving China one of the highest female urban labor participation rates in the world), the market reforms have "strengthened and in some cases reconstructed the sexual division of labor, keeping urban women in a transient, lower-paid, and subordinate position in the workforce."[14] Sixty percent of China's unemployed—and 70 percent of its illiterates—are women.

Finally, the momentous economic changes in China have had serious environmental consequences. China's environment suffered greatly under the old command system, but ecological damage has gotten worse in the profit-at-any-cost atmosphere of the market reforms. Industrial expansion is fueled primarily by the use of highly polluting coal, which has made the air in China's cities and even many rural areas among the dirtiest in the world. Soil erosion, the loss of arable land, and deforestation are serious problems for the countryside. The dumping of garbage and toxic wastes goes virtually unregulated, and it is estimated that 80 percent of China's rivers are badly polluted. The government has enacted some policies to protect the environment and increase environmental spending. However, "as is the case in most developing countries, the quest for economic development has superseded concern over environmental pollution."[15]

Dealing with some of the negative social consequences of China's market reforms and economic growth is one of the main challenges facing the government of the PRC. The ability of labor, women's, or environmental movements to get these social issues on the political agenda remains limited by the party's tight control of political life and restrictions on the formation of autonomous interest groups in China (see Section 4).

China and the International Political Economy

Deng Xiaoping's program for transforming the Chinese economy rested on two pillars: the market-oriented reform of the domestic economy and the policy of opening China to the outside world. The extensive internationalization of the Chinese economy that has taken place in recent decades contrasts sharply with the semi-isolationist policy of economic self-reliance pursued by Mao Zedong.

In 1978, when Deng came to power, China was not a major trading nation. Total foreign trade was about US$20 billion (about 10 percent of GDP), and foreign investment in China was minuscule, as the stagnant economy and heavy-handed bureaucracy were not attractive to potential investors from abroad.

In the early 1980s, China embarked on a strategy of using trade as an important component of its drive for economic development, following in some ways the model of export-led growth pioneered by Japan and newly industrializing countries such as the Republic of Korea (South Korea). The essence of this model is to use low-wage domestic labor to produce goods that are in demand internationally and then to use the earnings from the sale of those goods to finance the modernization of the economy.

In 1997 foreign trade totaled more than US$300 billion (about 40 percent of GDP), making China the tenth largest trading nation in the world. China exports mainly clothing, fabrics, shoes, toys, and some light industrial goods, and imports mostly machinery, technology, and raw materials needed to support modernization. Despite having large domestic sources of petroleum and significant untapped reserves, China became a net importer of oil for the first time in 1993 because of the huge energy demands of its economic boom.

Most of China's trade is in East Asia, particularly with Japan, South Korea, and Taiwan. The financial crisis that hit that part of the world in the late 1990s caused a sharp drop in the rate of growth of Chinese exports (from 27 percent in 1997 to 0.5 percent in 1998) and raised concerns about the long-run viability of economic development that is so heavily dependent on foreign trade.

The United States has become one of the PRC's major trading partners (12 percent of imports and 17 percent of exports in 1995), and by the late 1990s the U.S. trade deficit with China had reached over US$50 billion per year, the second highest after Japan's. The growing trade imbalance increased tensions in U.S.-China relations, especially over the issue of restricted access to China's domestic market for U.S. goods and the violation of U.S. copyrights by Chinese firms that produce compact discs, video recordings, and computer software.

Foreign investment in China has also skyrocketed. Since 1978 about US$180 billion in foreign capital has been invested in or pledged to 240,000 different PRC enterprises. These enterprises range from small factories producing toys and clothing for export to large firms producing goods and services for the Chinese market, like Coca-Cola, Jeeps, and McDonalds.

Many of these foreign ventures are located in Special Economic Zones (SEZs) set aside by the government to attract overseas investors through incentives such as tax breaks, modern infrastructure, and the promise of less bureaucratic red tape. The SEZs are even more free-wheeling and faster-growing than the Chinese economy as a whole and have also become hotbeds of speculation, corruption, and crime. The largest SEZ, Shenzhen (near Hong Kong), has been

Current Challenges: *The Republic of China on Taiwan*

Despite the founding of the People's Republic of China on the Chinese mainland in October 1949, the Republic of China (ROC) under Chiang Kai-shek and the Nationalist Party continued to function on Taiwan. The Chinese Communists would very likely have taken over Taiwan at the end of the civil war if the United States had not intervened to protect the island. The U.S. government, alarmed by the outbreak of the Korean War in 1950, saw the defense of the Nationalist government on Taiwan as part of the effort to stop the further expansion of communism in Asia.

When Chiang Kai-shek and his supporters fled to Taiwan in 1949, the island was already firmly under the control of Nationalists, who had killed or arrested many of their opponents on Taiwan in the aftermath of a popular uprising in February 1947. The harsh dictatorship imposed by Chiang's Nationalists deepened the sharp divide between the "mainlanders," who had come over to escape the Communists, and the native Taiwanese majority, whose ancestors had first settled on the island centuries before and who spoke a distinctive Chinese dialect.

Economically, Taiwan prospered under Chiang Kai-shek's rule. With large amounts of U.S. aid and advice, the Nationalist government sponsored a highly successful and peaceful program of land reform and rural development, attracted extensive foreign investment, and encouraged an export-led strategy of economic growth that made Taiwan a model newly industrializing country by the 1970s. The government also invested heavily in the modernization of Taiwan's roads and ports, and promoted policies that have given the island health and education levels that are among the best in the world and a standard of living that is among the highest in Asia.

Political change, however, came slowly to Taiwan. After his death in 1975, Chiang Kai-shek was succeeded as president by his son, Chiang Ching-kuo, who most people expected would continue the repressive political policies of his father. Instead, the younger Chiang permitted some opposition and dissent, and gave important government and party positions previously dominated by mainlanders to Taiwanese. When he died in 1988, the presidency of the republic passed to the Taiwanese vice president, Lee Teng-hui, who also became head of the Nationalist Party. Under President Lee, Taiwan continued to make great progress toward democratization. The laws used to imprison dissidents were revoked, the media are free of all censorship, and there are open multiparty elections for all local and islandwide positions. In presidential elections in 1996, Lee Teng-hui won 54 percent of the vote in a hotly contested four-way race, reflecting both the new openness of the political system and the credit that Taiwan's voters give the Nationalist Party for the island's progress.

The most contentious political issue in Taiwan is whether the island should continue to aspire to reunification with the mainland or declare its independence as a separate Republic of Taiwan. Advocating Taiwanese independence used to be a treasonous act, often resulting in a long prison term. The fact that this issue can now be openly debated shows that Taiwan's political transformation in recent decades has been as dramatic as its economic development.

Since the early 1980s, Taiwan and the People's Republic of China have developed extensive, if indirect, economic relations with each other, and millions of people from Taiwan have gone to the mainland to do business, visit relatives, or just sightsee. The governments of the PRC and ROC, though still technically in a state of war with each other, have engaged in some negotiations about possible reunification, but the two sides remain far apart because of their vastly differing political, economic, and social systems.

Taiwan

Land Area (sq. miles)	13,895 (about one-third the size of Virginia)
Population	22 million
Ethnic Composition	Taiwanese 84%, mainland Chinese 14%, aborigine 2%
GDP (US$)	$315 billion
GDP per capita (US$)	$14,700
Life Expectancy	Male, 74; Female, 81
Infant Mortality (per 1000 live births)	7
Literacy	86%

transformed in less than twenty years from a nondescript border town of 70,000 people into China's most modern city, with a population of over 2 million.

The growing economic integration of southern China, including Hong Kong, and Taiwan has led to the emergence of what is called Greater China. In this informal, emerging economic community, China provides inexpensive labor while Hong Kong and Taiwan provide capital, know-how, and technology. Extensive investment has also poured into the region from the far-flung community of overseas Chinese, who live in North America, Western Europe, and elsewhere. Many observers believe that Greater China is well on its way to becoming a powerhouse in the world economy.

China has emerged from the relative isolation of the Cultural Revolution period to become an active and important player in international politics. In 1971 the People's Republic took over China's seat in the United Nations. Prior to that, the UN, acting in accordance with the wishes and veto power of the United States, had recognized the Nationalist-led Republic of China as the legitimate government of all of China, even though it controlled only the island of Taiwan after 1949. The PRC is one of the five permanent members of the UN Security Council, and it acts there (and in the General Assembly and other UN-affiliated organizations) in a manner that reflects its dual status as both a major power and a developing nation.

In many international forums, the PRC serves as a strong advocate of what it sees as Third World interests. At the 1992 United Nations Conference on the Environment and Development in Rio de Janeiro, China took the position that the developed nations bore the "main responsibility for global environmental degradation" and that since the Industrial Revolution they "have exploited the environment without heeding the consequences of their actions."[16] The PRC argued that it was unfair to ask the world's poorer nations to sacrifice economic growth for environmental reasons and called on the developed nations to take the lead in making the sacrifices necessary to halt pollution.

Human rights became a sore point in relations between China and the United States after the Tiananmen massacre, when some members of the U.S. Congress wanted to impose restrictions on U.S.-China trade because of political repression in China. They argued that the United States should revoke China's most-favored-nation (MFN) status, an agreement between trading partners that guarantees each will extend to the other the same favorable terms (for instance, low tariffs on imports) that it grants to any other country. However, many Americans believed that restrictions on U.S.-China trade would harm U.S. business and consumer interests, dampen Chinese economic growth, and hurt those in China, such as private entrepreneurs, who might become a force for democratization in the future. This was the position adopted by both the Bush and Clinton administrations, and China's MFN status has been repeatedly renewed since Tiananmen, with only minor and easily fulfilled human rights conditions attached.

In response, China has challenged Western nations on the issue of human rights. The PRC vehemently rejects foreign criticism of its human rights record. It sees such criticism as interference in China's internal affairs, based on a narrow and ethnocentric definition of rights. A view of rights that stresses individual liberties above all else, they argue, is inappropriate to cultures like China's, which emphasize social needs and responsibilities. China contends that the "right to subsistence" as measured by economic growth and decent health and education standards, is the most basic human right and that on this score the PRC has done remarkably well compared to many nations. It points to homelessness, a high crime rate, and racism in the United States as human rights violations that invalidate U.S. criticism of the policies of other nations.

The sale of weapons by China to other Third World nations has also become a point of contention in China's relations with the United States and other developed countries. The PRC has become a major international weapons dealer in the post–Cold War era, though it still ranks well behind Russia, the United States, Britain, and France in terms of total arms sales. China has been criticized for selling weapons to countries involved in conflicts with the West, such as Iran and Iraq, and for providing advanced missile technology to potential nuclear powers like Pakistan. China argues that the West's position on international arms sales is self-serving, although the PRC has agreed to abide by international conventions regulating weapons transfers.

China has an important but somewhat contradictory position in the international system. On the one hand, its low level of economic and technological development compared to the industrialized countries makes it very much a part of the Third World. On the other hand, the total output and rapid expansion of its economy, its vast resource base (including its population), and its military strength make the PRC a superpower—or at least a potential superpower—among nations. In the years ahead, China is certain to become an even more active participant on the world scene. At the same time, international influences are likely to play an increasingly important role in China's economic and political development.

Section ❸   Governance and Policy-Making

The People's Republic of China is one of the world's few remaining Communist party-states, and by far the most important in terms of size and power. The basic political organization of the PRC, like that of the Soviet Union before its collapse in 1991, reflects the defining characteristics of this very distinctive type of system. These include Communist domination of all government and social institutions, the existence of an official state ideology, and the repression of any opposition to the party. The Chinese Communist Party claims that only it can govern in the best interests of the entire nation and therefore has a right to exercise the "leading role" throughout Chinese society. Although China has moved sharply toward a market economy in recent decades, the CCP still asserts that it is building socialism with the ultimate objective of creating an egalitarian and classless communist society.

Organization of the State

"The force at the core leading our cause forward is the Chinese Communist Party," observed Mao Zedong in a speech given in 1954 at the opening session of China's legislature, the National People's Congress, which according to the constitution adopted at that meeting, was the "highest organ of state power" in the People's Republic.[17] Mao's statement was a blunt reminder that the party was in charge of the national legislature and all other government organizations.

This same line was the very first entry in "The Little Red Book," the bible of Mao quotes used by the Red Guards who ransacked the country in the name of ideological purity during the Cultural Revolution. Although many party members became targets of the Cultural Revolution, the prominence of this quotation reflected the fact that, even at the height of the move-

ment's near anarchy, Mao and his supporters never intended to call into question the primacy of Communist Party rule in China.

Similarly, Deng Xiaoping, despite embracing extensive economic liberalization, remained unshakably committed to the preservation of Communist rule in China after he came to power in 1978. In a speech in 1979 (a decade before Tiananmen), Deng rejected calls for more democracy and clearly spelled out his views on the role of the CCP in the Chinese political system:

> In the China of today we can never dispense with leadership by the Party and extol the spontaneity of the masses. Party leadership, of course, is not infallible and the problem of how the Party can maintain close links with the masses and exercise correct and effective leadership is still one that we must seriously study and try to solve. But this can never be made a pretext for demanding the weakening or liquidation of the Party's leadership.[18]

Despite the many fundamental changes that have taken place since the Maoist era, "Party leadership" remains an unchangeable principle of political life in China, and the nation's rulers still claim allegiance to communist ideology. Any analysis of governance and policy-making in China must begin with the ideology and power of the Communist Party.

Communist ideology in China is referred to as Marxism-Leninism–Mao Zedong Thought. The core of this ideology is said to be based on universal truths in the works of the founding fathers of communism, including Marx's critique of capitalism and his definitions of socialism and communism and Lenin's theories on party organization and leadership. Mao's contributions to the ideology come from his adaptation of Marxism-Leninism to China's particular historical circumstances, including its economic underdevelopment and largely peasant society. In 1997 the CCP added Deng Xiaoping Theory to its official ideology to reflect the late leader's role in justifying a self-proclaimed socialist country's use of market forces to promote economic development.

Most people in China have lost faith in communist ideology because of the Communist Party's erratic and repressive leadership over the last several decades. Many party members (about 58 million as of 1998) join more for career advancement than because of ideological commitment. There are also numerous other sources of beliefs and values in society, such as the family and religion. But Marxism-Leninism–Mao Zedong Thought–Deng Xiaoping Theory provides the framework for governance and policy-making and sets the boundaries for what, in the party's view, is permissible in politics.

The underlying political and ideological principles of party-state organization are clearly laid out in China's current constitution.[19] The preamble refers explicitly to "the leadership of the Communist Party of China and the guidance of Marxism-Leninism–Mao Zedong Thought." Article 1 defines the PRC as "a socialist state under the people's democratic dictatorship" and declares that "disruption of the socialist system by any organization or individual is prohibited." Such provisions imply that the Chinese "people"— implicitly defined as those who support socialism— enjoy democratic rights and privileges; but the Chinese constitution also gives the CCP the authority to exercise dictatorship over any person or organization that it believes is opposed to socialism and the party.

The People's Republic of China has had several governing documents since its founding in 1949, including four very different constitutions (1954, 1975, 1978, and 1982). These documents have only marginally had the force of law. Rather, constitutional change (from amendments to total replacement) has reflected the shifting political winds in China. The character and content of the document in force at any given time bears the ideological stamp of the prevailing party leadership. For example, in 1993 the current PRC constitution (adopted in 1982) was amended to replace references to the superiority of central planning and state ownership with phrases more consistent with economic reform, including the statement (Article 15) that China "practices a socialist market economy."

The constitution of the People's Republic specifies the structures and powers of subnational levels of government, including the country's provinces, autonomous regions, and centrally administered cities. But China is not a federal system (like Brazil, Germany, India, Nigeria, and the United States), in which subnational governments have considerable policy-making autonomy. Provincial and local authorities operate "under the unified leadership of the central authorities" (Article 3), which makes China a **unitary state** (like Britain, France, and Japan), in which the national government exercises a high degree of control over other levels of government.

The Executive

The government of the People's Republic of China is organizationally and functionally distinct from the Chinese Communist Party. For example, the PRC executive consists of both a premier (prime minister) and a president, whereas the CCP is headed by a general secretary. But there is no alternation of parties in power in China, and the Communist Party controls all government organizations and personnel. Therefore real executive power in the Chinese political system lies in the top leaders and organizations of the CCP. The government essentially acts as the administrative agency for carrying out and enforcing policies made by the party. Nevertheless, to fully understand governance and policy-making in China, it is necessary to look at both the Chinese Communist Party and the government of the People's Republic of China and the relationship between the two.

The Chinese Communist Party

The constitution of the Chinese Communist Party (which is a separate document from the constitution of the PRC) specifies in great detail local and national party structures and functions, the distribution of authority among party organizations, the requirements for joining the party, the behavior expected of members, and procedures for dealing with infractions of

Table 2

Who's Who in Beijing: China's Top Party and State Leaders Since 1949

Leader	Highest Position Held	Comment
Mao Zedong (1893–1976)	CCP Chairman (1943–1976) PRC President (1949–1959) Military Commission Chair (1949–1976)	Became effective leader of the CCP in 1934–1935 during the Long March. Formally elected Chairman of the Politburo in 1943.
Liu Shaoqi (1898–1969)	PRC President[a] (1959–1968) CCP Vice Chairman (1949–1968)	Purged as a "capitalist roader" during the Cultural Revolution. Died in prison.
Zhou Enlai (1898–1976)	PRC Premier (1949–1976) PRC Foreign Minister (1949–1958)	Longtime Mao ally, but a moderating influence during the Cultural Revolution. Architect of détente with U.S. in early 1970s.
Lin Biao (1907–1971)	CCP Vice Chairman (1958–1971) PRC Vice Premier (1954–1971) PRC Defense Minister (1959–1971)	One of Mao's strongest supporters in the Cultural Revolution. Allegedly killed in plane crash after failure of attempted coup against Mao.
Hua Guofeng (1920–)	PRC Premier (1976–1980) CCP Chairman (1976–1981) Military Commission Chair (1976–1981)	Became CCP Chairman after Mao's death and purge of Gang of Four. Removed from power by Deng Xiaoping, who saw him as too much of a Maoist.
Deng Xiaoping (1904–1997)	PRC Vice Premier (1952–1966;1973–1976; 1977–1980) CCP Vice Chairman (1975–1976; 1977–1987) Military Commission Chair (1981–1989)	Purged twice during Cultural Revolution. Retired from all official posts by 1989, but remained China's most powerful leader for most of the 1990s.
Hu Yaobang (1915–1989)	CCP Chairman[b] (1981–1982) CCP General Secretary[b] (1982–1987)	Protégé of Deng. Ousted for favoring too much political reform. His death in 1989 helped touch off the Tiananmen demonstrations.
Zhao Ziyang (1919–)	PRC Premier (1980–1988) CCP General Secretary (1987–1989)	Another Deng protégé. Ousted for being too sympathetic to pro-democracy demonstrators during Tiananmen crisis.
Li Xiannian (1909–1992)	PRC President (1983–1988)	Veteran party leader rewarded with ceremonial post at end of career. Became PRC's first president since 1968.
Yang Shangkun (1907–1998)	PRC President (1988–1993)	Veteran military officer and Deng supporter.
Jiang Zemin (1926–)	CCP General Secretary (1989–) PRC President (1993–) Military Commission Chair (1989–)	Former Shanghai mayor and party leader promoted by Deng as a safe choice to carry out his policies after Tiananmen crisis. Consolidated his own power after Deng's death in 1997.
Li Peng (1928–)	PRC Premier (1988–1998) Chair, National People's Congress (1998–)	One of China's most conservative leaders. Widely held responsible for Tiananmen crackdown.
Zhu Rongji (1928–)	PRC Premier (1998–)	Committed reformer credited with effective management of the Chinese economy.

[a]The position of PRC president was vacant from 1968 to 1983.
[b]The position of CCP chairman was abolished in 1982 and replaced by the general secretary as the party's top position.
Note: All the listed leaders were also members of the Standing Committee of the CCP Politburo, the party's most powerful decision-making body.

party rules. But such details do not negate the fact that individual power, factional maneuvering, and personal connections are ultimately more important than formal constitutional arrangements for understanding how the party works.

For example, Deng Xiaoping, who was indisputably the most powerful individual in China from 1978 until he became physically incapacitated before his death in 1997, never occupied any of the top executive offices in the party or the government (see Table 2 on page 514). His highest formal positions during these years were vice chairman of the CCP (1977–1987), vice premier of the People's Republic (1977–1980), and chairman of the party's military commission (1978–1989), a post that made him the commander in chief of China's armed forces. By the early 1990s, Deng had resigned from all his formal positions other than that of president of China's bridge association, reflecting his continuing enjoyment of a card game he learned while a student in France in the 1920s. Although he no longer played an active role in day-to-day governance, he was still consulted about important policy matters, and no major decision was made without his approval. In the Chinese media, he was regularly referred to as China's "paramount leader" and the "chief architect" of the nation's economic boom. The sources of Deng's immense power came from informal factors, such as his seniority as one of the founding leaders of the regime, his deep personal connections to other influential political and military leaders, and his longtime advocacy of now widely supported ideas about how China should develop into a strong and modern nation.

By the late 1990s, most of the elderly men (including Deng) who had wielded great informal authority in post-Mao China were dead. Despite the persisting strong influence of personal ties in Chinese politics, the formal structures of power have assumed greater importance for understanding who has the power and how decisions are made.

According to the CCP constitution, the "highest leading bodies" of the party are the National Party Congress and the Central Committee (see Figure 3). But its infrequent meetings (every five years) and large size (more than 2000 delegates) means that the role of the Congress in the party is more symbolic than

Figure 3

Organization of the Chinese Communist Party

*Indicates full and alternate members

Numbers in parentheses refer to the number of members as of the late 1990s.

substantive. The essential function of the National Party Congress is to approve decisions already made by the top leaders and provide a showcase for the party's current policies. For example, the party congress that convened in the fall of 1997 was a highly orchestrated validation of Jiang Zemin's consolidation of power as Deng Xiaoping's successor.

The Central Committee is the next level up in the pyramid of party power. It has about 190 full and 150 alternate members (consisting of party leaders from around the country) and meets annually for about a week. It is elected by the National Party Congress by secret ballot, and there is some choice of candidates. Contending party factions may jockey to win seats, but the overall composition of the Central Committee is closely controlled by the top leaders to ensure compliance with their policies. The Central Committee elected in late 1997 continued a trend toward promoting younger and better-educated party members who are strong supporters of economic reform.

The Central Committee directs party affairs when the National Party Congress is not in session, but its size and relatively short and infrequent meetings (called plenums) greatly limit its effectiveness. However, Central Committee plenums and occasional informal work conferences do represent significant gatherings of the party elite, which can be a very important arena of political maneuvering and decision-making.

The most powerful political organizations in the Communist party-state are the two small "executive" bodies at the very top of the CCP's structure: the Politburo (or Political Bureau) and its even more exclusive Standing Committee. These bodies are elected by the Central Committee from among its own members under carefully controlled conditions. In the late 1990s, the Politburo had twenty-four members (including two alternates) and the Standing Committee—the formal apex of power in the CCP—had seven. Each member of the Standing Committee has executive responsibility for a particular area of policy, for example, economic affairs, national security, and foreign policy. People who study Chinese politics scrutinize the membership of the Politburo and Standing Committee for clues about leadership priorities, the balance of power among party factions, and the relative influence of different groups in policy-making.

The Politburo and Standing Committee are not responsible to the Central Committee or any other institution in any meaningful sense. The workings of these organizations are shrouded in secrecy. Their meetings are rarely announced and most of their work goes on, and many of the top leaders live, in a high-security compound adjacent to the former imperial palace near Tiananmen Square in Beijing. Their most important meetings are held every year in August, when they gather in exclusive villas at the seashore.

Power in the Chinese Communist Party is highly concentrated in the hands of the few individuals who control the highest party organizations and have little accountability to the general party membership. Prior to 1982 the top position in the party was the chairman of the Politburo's Standing Committee, which was occupied by Mao Zedong (hence, Chairman Mao) for more than three decades until his death in 1976. The title of chairman was abolished in 1982 to symbolize a break with Mao's highly personalistic and often arbitrary style of leadership. Since then the party's chief executive has been the general secretary, who presides over the Politburo and the Standing Committee, a position which has been held since 1989 by Jiang Zemin. Although Jiang emerged in the early post-Deng era as China's most powerful individual, he does not have the personal clout or charisma of either Deng or Mao and therefore governs as part of a collective leadership that includes his fellow members on the Standing Committee and Politburo.

Two other party organizations deserve brief mention. The Secretariat (currently seven members) manages the day-to-day work of the Politburo and Standing Committee and coordinates the party's complex and far-flung structure. The Secretariat has considerable authority in organizational and personnel matters but is not a center of political or policy-making power, although it is important that anyone who aspires to the top leadership of the party have strong supporters on the Secretariat.

The Central Commission for Discipline Inspection is responsible for monitoring the compliance of party members with the CCP constitution and other rules. It has the power to investigate and recommend punishment (including expulsion from the party) for violations of party discipline, and it may turn its findings over to judicial authorities if it thinks criminal proceedings are warranted. The commission has been used as a vehicle against thousands of party members accused of corruption, but it has also been used to enforce adherence to the party line and to punish, for example, those who supported the Tiananmen demonstrations.

Below the national level, the CCP has a hierarchy of local party organizations in provinces, cities, and counties, each headed by a party committee. There are also more than 3 million primary party organizations, called branches and cells, which are found in workplaces, schools, urban neighborhoods, rural towns, villages, and army units. Local and primary organizations extend party control throughout Chinese society and are designed to ensure the subordination of each level of party organization to the next-higher level and ultimately to the central party authorities in Beijing.

The National Government

Government authority in China is formally vested in a system of people's congresses, which begins with a National People's Congress at the top and continues in hierarchically arranged levels down through provincial people's congresses, municipal people's congresses, rural township people's congresses, and so on (see Figure 4). In theory, these congresses (the legislative branch) are empowered to supervise the work of the "people's governments" (the executive branch) at the various levels of the system, but in reality, government executives (such as cabinet ministers, provincial governors, and mayors) are ultimately subject to party authority rather than to the people's congresses. Unlike the parallel system of *party* congresses, the *people's* congresses are supposed to represent *all* of the citizens at the relevant level, not just the minority who are members of the CCP. Like the party congresses, the people's congresses play a politically limited, but symbolically important, role in policy-making.

The National People's Congress elects the president and vice president of China. But there is only one candidate, chosen by the Communist Party, for each office. The president's term is concurrent with that of the congress (five years), and he is limited to two

Figure 4

Organization of the Government of the People's Republic of China

consecutive terms. Citizens must be forty-five or older to be eligible to serve as president. The position is largely ceremonial, though a senior party leader has always held it. As China's head of state, the president is important in greeting and negotiating with other world leaders. Jiang Zemin, who is also the general secretary of the CCP, was elected to a second term as China's president in 1998.

The premier is the head of the government and has considerable authority over the bureaucracy and policy implementation. The premier is formally appointed by the president with the approval of the National People's Congress. But, in reality, the Communist Party decides who will serve as premier, and that post has always been held by a member of the party's most powerful body, the Standing Committee. Like the president, the premier may serve only two five-year terms. Zhu Rongji, who became the PRC's premier in 1998, is a strong supporter of market reform and is widely credited with having dealt successfully with a number of serious economic problems (including skyrocketing inflation) that China faced in the mid-1990s while he was the vice-premier in charge of the economy.

The Bureaucracy

The premier directs the State Council, constitutionally "the highest organ of state administration" (Article 85). The State Council, which, in theory, is appointed by the National People's Congress, functions like the cabinet in a parliamentary system and is made up of the premier, the vice-premiers, the heads of government ministries or their equivalents, a secretary-general (who manages the day-to-day work of the council), and a few other top officials called state councillors.

The size of the State Council varies as ministries and commissions are created, merged, or disbanded to meet changing policy needs. At times, it has included more than one hundred ministerial-level officials, but in the late 1990s there were forty ministries and commissions (with plans to cut the number to twenty-nine), reflecting the decreased role of central planning and the administrative streamlining undertaken to make the government more efficient. The ministers and councillors run either functionally specific departments, such as the Ministry of Public Health, or organizations with more comprehensive responsibilities, such as the powerful State Economic and Trade Commission. Beneath the State Council is an array of support staffs, research offices, and other bureaucratic agencies charged with policy implementation.

Government administration in the PRC is based on the principle of **dual rule**, which was adapted from the Soviet political system. Dual rule means that government organizations below the national level are under both the *vertical* supervision of the next higher level of government and the *horizontal* supervision of the Communist Party at their own level. For example, the organization in charge of education in one of China's provinces would be subject to both administrative supervision by the Ministry of Education in Beijing and to political control by the province's CCP committee. Such a system leads to complex and sometimes conflicting lines of authority within the Chinese bureaucracy. It also reinforces two key aspects of governance and policy-making in the PRC: centralization and party domination.

Since the 1980s government administration in China has become increasingly decentralized as the role of central planning has been reduced and more power has been given to provincial and local authorities, particularly in economic matters. Efforts have also been made to reduce party interference in administrative work. For example, the top party leader in a province (the party secretary) is no longer allowed to serve simultaneously as the province's governor, its chief administrator (although the governor is always a CCP member). Despite such reforms, government administration remains a top-down system that is subordinate to the power of the Communist Party.

China's bureaucracy is immense in size and expansive in the scope of its reach throughout the country. The total number of **cadres**—people in positions of authority who are paid by the government or party—in the PRC is in the range of 30 million. Of these, around 8 million work directly for the government or the CCP. The remainder occupy key posts in economic enterprises (e.g., factory directors); schools (e.g., principals); and scientific, cultural, and other state-run institutions. Not all party members are cadres; in fact, most party members are just "ordinary" workers, farmers, teachers, and so on. And not all cadres are party members, though party cadres ultimately have power over nonparty cadres.

During the Maoist years, cadre recruitment and promotion standards often gave strong preference to people with good ideological credentials ("reds") over those who may have been more professionally qualified ("experts"), which seriously compromised the ability of the bureaucracy to do its job well. The balance has now clearly shifted to the experts, and there is much greater emphasis on having better-educated and more technically proficient personnel staffing the government bureaucracy. Economic reform has made a technocratically oriented bureaucracy an essential part of the policy process in China. In 1998 the government also announced plans to cut the number of cadres directly on the state payroll in half (to 4 million) in order to promote efficiency and save money.

One of the most important administrative reforms of the post-Mao era—and one that is quite unprecedented in a Communist party-state—has been the implementation of measures to limit how long officials can stay in their jobs. Depending on their position, both government and party cadres must now retire between the ages of 60 and 70. A two-term limit has been set for all officials. In 1998, Premier Li Peng became the first top leader of the People's Republic to leave office at the end of a constitutionally specified term limit. But exceptions are still sometimes made for core leaders such as Jiang Zemin (born in 1926), who has nonetheless pledged to retire at the end of his current terms as president and General Secretary in 2003.

Other State Institutions

The Military and the Police

China's People's Liberation Army (PLA), which encompasses all of the country's ground, air, and naval armed services, is the world's largest military force, with about 3 million active personnel, although plans were announced in 1998 to cut this by a half million. The PLA also has a formal reserve of another million or so and a backup people's militia of around 12 million, which could be mobilized in the event of war, although the level of training and weaponry available to the militia are generally minimal. There is a draft in China, and Article 55 of the constitution says, "It is the honorable duty of citizens of the People's Republic of China to perform military service and join the militia in accordance with the law."

The Chinese military is, in fact, small in relation to China's total population. In the mid-1990s the PRC had 2.4 military personnel per 1000 population, far less than the U.S. ratio of 6.2 per 1000. China said that it spent US$10 billion on defense in 1998, which would be only about 4 percent of U.S. military spending in that year. Many analysts think that the PRC vastly understates its defense budget and estimate that it is really closer to three times the official figures; still, China devotes a much smaller part of its annual government spending to defense than does the United States.

The military has never held formal political power in the PRC, but it has been a very important influence on politics and policy. Ever since the days of the revolution and the civil war, there have been close ties between the political and military leaders of the CCP, with many top leaders (such as Mao and Deng) serving in both political and military capacities. One of the most famous quotes from Chairman Mao's writings, "Political power grows out of the barrel of a gun," conveyed his belief that the party needed strong military backing in order to win and keep power. However, the often overlooked second half of the quote, "Our principle is that the party commands the gun, and the gun must never be allowed to command the party,"[20] made the equally important point that the military had to be kept under civilian (that is, CCP) control. Although there have been a few periods when the role of the military in Chinese politics appeared to be particularly strong (such as during the Cultural Revolution), the party has always been able to keep the "gun" under its firm command.

The PLA assumed a prominent political role during the Tiananmen crisis in 1989, when the army was ordered to recapture the square from the demonstrators and did so with brutal force. While some senior PLA officers opposed the intervention, in the end they ordered the troops in because the Chinese military "is a disciplined, professional army that takes orders from the Party leadership."[21] The massacre greatly harmed the image of the PLA in the eyes of the Chinese public, who previously had a high regard for the military because of its incorruptibility and record of dedicated service to the nation.

The PLA continues to play an important, if muted, role in Chinese politics. Military support remains a crucial factor in the factional struggles that still figure prominently in inner-party politics. Deng Xiaoping's long-standing personal ties to many very senior PLA officers were critical to his success in defeating the efforts of conservative party leaders to slow down economic reform. Jiang Zemin, who has no such ties and lacks any military experience, has paid close attention to building political bridges to the PLA by supporting increased defense spending (13 percent in 1998) and promoting generals who are loyal to him. Although there are no military officers on the party's most elite body, the Standing Committee, two out of the twenty-four members of the Politburo are generals and PLA representatives make up over 20 percent of the full members of the Central Committee.

Chinese Communist leaders have long been divided over the issue of what kind of armed forces the People's Republic of China needed. Mao was a strong advocate of equality between rank-and-file soldiers and officers, the use of guerrilla tactics ("people's war") even in modern warfare, the importance of ideological education within the military, and of the extensive use of the PLA in nonmilitary tasks such as the construction of public works projects and the training of citizen paramedics ("barefoot doctors"). Some of China's foremost military leaders believed just as strongly that the PLA ought to emphasize the discipline, professionalism, and modernization needed to defend the nation. Under Deng Xiaoping and Jiang Zemin, the military leadership has been able to keep politics and ideology in the armed forces to a minimum and focus on making the PLA an effective, modern fighting force. But the PLA remains not only an institution committed to the national defense but also an instrument for keeping the CCP in power.

The key organizations in charge of the Chinese armed forces are the party's Military Affairs Commission and state's Central Military Commission. On paper, these appear to be two distinct organizations, but, in fact, they overlap entirely in membership and function. The chair of the state Military Commission is "elected" by the National People's Congress and is, in effect, the commander in chief of the PLA. This position is always held by a top party leader, for example, by Deng Xiaoping from 1977 to 1989 and since then by Jiang Zemin. The Communist Party extends its control of the PLA through a system of party committees and political officers who are attached to all military units.

Beginning in the 1980s, the PLA climbed on the economic reform bandwagon in order to supplement its official budget by converting a number of its military factories to the production of consumer goods such as refrigerators and motorcycles; running hotels and even discos; and opening up some of its secret facilities to foreign tourists. At one point it was estimated that the PLA was running more than 15,000 nonmilitary enterprises at home and abroad with over US$10 billion in revenues. In 1998 the government, concerned about both corruption and the need for the military to concentrate on its defense responsibilities, ordered the PLA to sell off many of its commercial ventures.

China's police apparatus consists of several different organizations. The Ministry of State Security is responsible for combating espionage and gathering intelligence both at home and abroad. The Ministry of Public Security is responsible for the maintenance of law and order, the investigation of crimes, and the surveillance of Chinese citizens and foreigners in China suspected of being a threat to the state. A one-million strong "People's Armed Police" guards public officials and buildings and is used to quell serious public disturbances, including worker or peasant unrest. The local branches of these various security organizations are under the command of central authorities in Beijing. So, in effect, China has a national police force stationed throughout the country. There are also local police forces, but they do little more than supervise traffic.

Public security bureaus have the authority to detain indefinitely people suspected of committing a crime without making a formal charge and can use administrative sanctions, that is, penalties imposed outside the court system, to levy fines or sentence detainees to up to three years in reformatories or prisons or to be supervised under a kind of house arrest. For people convicted of serious crimes, including political ones, the Ministry of Public Security maintains an extensive system of labor reform camps. These camps, noted for their harsh conditions and remote locations, are estimated to have millions of prisoners. They have become a contentious issue in

U.S.-China relations because of claims that they use political prisoners as slave labor to produce millions of dollars worth of products (such as toys) that are then exported to U.S. and other foreign markets. China has agreed to curtail the export of prison-produced goods, but it maintains that productive work by prison inmates (common in many countries, including the United States) helps to rehabilitate prisoners and is an important and legitimate part of the penal system.

The Judiciary

China has a four-tiered "people's court" system reaching from a Supreme People's Court down through higher, intermediate, and basic people's courts located at the various administrative levels of the state. The Supreme People's Court supervises the work of lower courts and the application of the country's laws, but it hears few cases and does not exercise judicial review over government policies. A nationwide organization called the "people's procuratorate" serves in the courts as both public prosecutor and public defender and also has investigatory functions in criminal cases. Citizen mediation committees based in urban neighborhoods and rural villages also play an important role in the judicial process by settling a large majority of civil cases out of court.

China's judicial system came under attack as a bastion of elitism and revisionism during the Cultural Revolution. The formal legal system pretty much ceased to operate during that period, and many of its functions were taken over by political or police organizations, which often acted arbitrarily in making arrests or administering punishments.

In recent decades, the legal system of the PRC has been revitalized. More than 100,000 judges and lawyers have been trained (some have even been sent abroad for legal education), and legal advisory offices have been established throughout the country to provide citizens and organizations with advice and assistance in dealing with the courts. Many laws and regulations have been enacted, including new criminal and civil codes, in the effort to regularize the legal system. In 1997 the government revoked a vaguely worded law against "counterrevolutionary crimes," which had given the authorities broad powers to detain political dissidents.

In recent years, there has been an enormous surge in the number of lawsuits filed (and often won) by people against businesses, local officials, and government agencies. Chinese courts can provide a real avenue of redress to the public for a wide range of nonpolitical grievances, including loss of property, consumer fraud, and even unjust detention by the police.

The criminal justice system works swiftly and harshly. Great faith is placed in the ability of an official investigation to find the facts of a case, and the outcome of cases that actually do come to trial is pretty much predetermined. In 1997 there was a conviction rate of 99.65 percent for all criminal cases that came to trial. Prison terms are long and subject only to cursory appeal. A variety of offenses in addition to murder—including, in some cases, rape and particularly serious cases of embezzlement and other "economic crimes"—are subject to capital punishment, which is carried out within days of sentencing. Hundreds, perhaps thousands, of people have been executed during the periodic government-sponsored anticrime campaigns, and China has been harshly criticized by human rights organizations such as Amnesty International for its extensive use of the death penalty.

Although the Chinese constitution speaks of judicial independence, China's courts and other legal bodies remain under rigorous party control. The appointment of judicial personnel is subject to party approval, and the CCP can and does bend the law to serve its interests. Recent legal reforms in China have been undertaken because China's leaders know that economic development requires detailed laws, professional judicial personnel, predictable legal processes, and binding documents such as contracts. Like other government institutions, the judicial system is meant to serve—or at least not challenge—the rule of the Communist Party. The scope of legality—the areas of society regulated by the legal system rather than by the whims of officials or personal connections—has widened greatly in the post-Mao era. China has, by and large, become a country where there is rule *by* law, in which the CCP uses the law to carry out its policies and enforce its rule. But it is still far from having established the rule *of* law, in which everyone, including the CCP, is accountable and subject to the law.

Subnational Government

There are four main layers of formal state structure beneath the central government in China: provinces (and autonomous regions), cities, counties, and rural towns. Each of these levels has a representative local people's congress that meets infrequently and briefly, and plays a limited role in managing local affairs.

Day-to-day administration at each subnational level is carried out by a local people's government, which consists of an executive (for instance, a provincial governor or city mayor), various functional bureaus, and judicial organs. According to China's constitution, the work of a local government is to be supervised by the local people's congress. But, in fact, the principle of dual rule makes local officials accountable more to higher levels of state administration and party organizations than to the local congresses.

Economic reform has led to a decentralization of decision-making. Provinces, cities, counties, and towns are now encouraged to take more initiative in promoting economic development in their areas. As a result, local governments are becoming increasingly vigorous in pursuing their own interests. Nevertheless, the central government still retains the power to intervene in local affairs when and where it wants. This power of the central authorities derives not only from their ability to set binding national priorities but also from their control over the military and the police, critical energy sources, and the construction of major infrastructure projects.

Beneath the formal layers of state administration are China's 900,000 rural villages, which are home to the large majority of the country's population. These villages are technically self-governing and are not formally responsible to a higher level of state authority. In recent years, village leaders and representative assemblies have been directly and competitively elected by local residents (see Section 4), which has brought an important degree of democracy to village government. Nevertheless, the most powerful person in Chinese villages is still the local Communist Party leader, who remains responsible to and under the supervision of higher-level CCP organizations.

The Policy-Making Process

At the height of Mao's power, many analysts described the policy process in China as a Mao-in-command system, in which the Chairman and a few of his closest associates made all major decisions and passed them along to be implemented by obedient party and government cadres. The Cultural Revolution led many scholars to conclude that policy-making in China was best understood as a result of factional and ideological struggles within the Chinese political elite. More recently, emphasis has shifted to analyzing the importance of bureaucratic actors and institutions in the policy process. Policy-making in the PRC is still seen as being very undemocratic. But rather than portraying it as simply a matter of the top party leaders' issuing orders, a new model of "fragmented authoritarianism" sees policy outcomes as the result of conflict, competition, and bargaining among party and government organizations at various levels of the system.[22]

Nevertheless, control of the policy process at all levels still rests with the Chinese Communist Party. The Communist Party makes policy and the government bureaucracy (headed by the premier and the State Council) implements it. Government policies and laws in China are formally enacted and in some ways significantly shaped by nonparty bodies such as the State Council and the National People's Congress. But the key decisions behind those policies and laws are made only by the Communist Party. Furthermore, public debate, media scrutiny, and the influence of organized interest groups play almost no role in the policy process in the Communist party-state.

The CCP uses a weblike system of organizational controls to make sure that the government bureaucracy complies with the party's will. For example, almost all key government officials are also party members and therefore subject to party discipline. The CCP also exercises control over the policy process through party organizations that parallel government agencies at all levels of the system. For example, each provincial government works under the watchful eye of a provincial party committee. In addition, through its committees, branches, and cells, the CCP maintains an effective presence inside every government organization.

Another means by which the Chinese Communist Party exercises control over the policy process is through the use of a cadre list, or as it was known in the Soviet Union, the ***nomenklatura*** system. The cadre list covers millions of positions in the government and elsewhere (including newspapers, hospitals, banks, and trade unions). Any personnel decision involving appointment, promotion, transfer, or dismissal that affects a position on this list must be approved by the party's organization department, whether or not the official involved is a party member. In recent years, the growth of nonstate sectors of the economy and administrative streamlining have led to a reduction in the number of positions directly subject to party approval. Nevertheless, the cadre list is still one of the major instruments by which the CCP tries to "ensure that leading institutions throughout the country will exercise only the autonomy granted to them by the party."[23]

Through these various mechanisms, the Chinese Communist Party not only supervises but has often taken over the work of the government. In recent years, there has been much talk about drawing a sharper distinction between party and government functions and bringing more nonparty experts into the policy loop. While some limited action has been taken, party domination remains a central feature of the policy process in China.

No account of policy-making or implementation in China is complete without noting the importance of *guanxi* ("connections"), the personal relationships and mutual obligations based on family, friendship, school, military, professional, or other ties. The notion of *guanxi* has its roots in Confucian culture and has long been an important part of political, social, and economic life in China. *Guanxi* still count mightily in the highly personalized world of elite politics within the CCP where policy is made. They are also basic facts of life within the Chinese bureaucracy, where personal ties are often the key to getting things done. Depending on how they are used, *guanxi* can either help cut red tape and increase efficiency or bolster organizational rigidity and feed corruption.

In sum, the power of the Communist Party—particularly the nearly unchecked power of the top twenty-five or thirty leaders—is at the heart of governance and policy-making in China. Party domination, however, does not mean that the system "operates in a monolithic way"; in fact, the system "wriggles with politics"[24] of many kinds, formal and informal. In order to get a complete picture of the policy process in China, it is important to look at how various influences, including ideology, factional struggles, bureaucratic interests, and personal connections shape the decisions made by the Communist Party leadership.

Section ❹ Representation and Participation

The Chinese Communist Party describes the government of the People's Republic as a **socialist democracy**, which it claims is superior to democracy in a capitalist country. From the CCP's point of view, the unequal division of private property and wealth profoundly influences politics in a capitalist country like the United States. The government of China under the leadership of the CCP, the argument goes, serves all the people, not just the privileged few. The official CCP view is that the party "has no interests of its own and rules solely in the interests of the nation and the people. It follows that rule by the party's leaders is rule in the people's interest and by definition democratic."[25] Unlike the social democracy of some Western European

political parties, such as the British Labour Party and the French Socialist Party, which is rooted in a commitment to competitive politics and political pluralism, China's socialist democracy is based on the unchallengeable leadership of the Chinese Communist Party.

Representation and participation play important roles in China's socialist democracy. There are legislative bodies, elections, and organizations like labor unions and student associations, all of which are meant to provide citizens with ways of influencing public policy-making and the selection of government leaders. But such mechanisms of popular input are strictly controlled by the CCP and are bound by the party's continuing insistence that all politics and policies in the country uphold the Four Cardinal Principles first laid down by Deng Xiaoping in 1979: the socialist road, the people's democratic dictatorship, the leadership of the Communist Party, and the ideology of Marxism-Leninism–Mao Zedong Thought. In essence, then, representation other than that guided by the CCP is regarded as unnecessary or marginal. Participation other than that sanctioned by and supportive of the party is seen as subversive.

The Legislature

Legislatures in Communist party-states have often been described as "rubber stamp" bodies. This implies that their main function is to give policies made by the party the appearance of being approved by representatives of the people. They may have some influence in important, though routine, state business (such as the formulation of the national budget), but such legislatures have very little substantive power when it comes to critical issues and in no way provide a check on the authority of the party.

The label "rubber stamp" may be a bit extreme to describe China's legislature, the National People's Congress (NPC), but it does convey the fact that the CCP closely monitors every aspect of the NPC's operations to ensure that it is in compliance with party policy. Nevertheless, the NPC is a very visible part of the Chinese political system, and it is important to understand its structure and function and to gauge whether the legislature could become an active force for democratization in China.

The Chinese constitution grants the National People's Congress (see Figure 4) the power to enact and amend the country's laws, approve and monitor the state budget, and declare and end war. It is also empowered to elect (and recall) the president and vice president of the PRC, the chair of the Central Military Commission (the commander in chief of the armed forces), the head of China's Supreme Court, and the Procurator-General (something like the U.S. Attorney General). It also has final approval over the selection of the premier and members of the State Council. These powers make China's legislature the most powerful branch of the government, with supervisory authority over the executive and judicial branches. The official Chinese view is that this is a very

democratic system because it vests supreme power in the branch of government most closely connected to the people, but in fact these powers are exercised only in the manner allowed by the Communist Party.

The National People's Congress is a unicameral legislature. It is elected for a five-year term and meets annually for only about two weeks. Deputies to the NPC are not full-time legislators but remain in their regular jobs and home areas except for the brief time when the Congress is in session. One of their responsibilities is to make regular "inspection tours" of their local areas. The Chinese government sees this as another advantage of the system because it allows deputies to stay in touch with their constituents and keeps them from becoming professional politicians.

The precise size of the NPC is set by law prior to each five-year electoral cycle. The NPC that was elected to serve from 1998 to 2002 consisted of just under 3000 deputies, which makes it the largest legislative body in the world. All the delegates, except those who represent the People's Liberation Army, are chosen on a geographic basis from China's various provinces, autonomous regions, and major municipalities. About 70 percent of the deputies elected to the currently serving congress are members of the Chinese Communist Party, with the others either belonging to one of China's few noncommunist political parties or having no party affiliation.

Rather than emphasizing the party affiliation of NPC deputies, the Chinese government stresses their occupational and social backgrounds in order to show that the legislature represents people from all walks of life. For example, workers and farmers made up about 20 percent of the deputies elected in 1998; intellectuals and professionals made up another 20 percent; government and party cadres accounted for a little more than a third; and the remainder consisted of representatives of other occupational categories, such as military personnel and entrepreneurs. Women made up 22 percent of the deputies. The average age of the deputies was 52 years, and 81 percent had at least a college education. The constitution guarantees that all minority groups have representation in the National People's Congress, and about 14 percent of the deputies elected in 1998 were ethnic minorities.

The annual sessions of the NPC are hailed with great fanfare in the Chinese press as an example of

Current Challenges: **The Three Gorges Dam**

The Three Gorges dam, which is being built on the Yangzi (Yangtze) River in China's Hubei province, will be the largest dam (over 600 feet high) and hydroelectric generating plant (84 billion kilowatt-hours per year) in the world when it is completed in the year 2009. The current budget for the project is US$11 billion, but some estimates that take inflation into account foresee huge cost overruns and put the total at around $70 billion.

Proponents of the dam argue that the project is needed to meet the huge energy demands of economic development in central and southwestern China, and that hydroelectric power is much preferable to the polluting coal that is currently China's major energy source. It will also make it possible for large ships to navigate the Yangzi deep into China's interior, and thus help promote domestic commerce and foreign trade. They also say that the dam will help to control the river's periodic lethal floods, which have killed more than 300,000 people in this century alone. In the summer of 1998 about 2,000 people died, 14 million were made homeless, and another 240 million people (one-quarter of China's population) in the Yangzi river basin were affected directly or indirectly by severe flooding.

Opponents of the Three Gorges dam see the project as an environmental, human, and political nightmare. The dam will submerge some of China's most stunning scenery, along with thousands of hectares of fertile cropland, rice paddies, and orchards. Many experts also believe that it will threaten several endangered species, including the rare Chinese river dolphin. Hundreds of historical sites will be inundated, some containing artifacts more than 10,000 years old. More than 1.3 million people will have to be relocated from the villages and towns that will end up under the 400-mile-long artificial lake (longer than Lake Superior) created by the dam. Although the Chinese government is compensating and assisting those who need to move, critics of the project say that most of those who relocate will probably, in the long run, be poorer than before they moved. There are also serious questions about the dam's safety in the earthquake-prone region, about whether the project's energy output will ever justify the huge cost, and even about whether it will solve or make worse the flooding situation along the Yangzi.

Opponents of Three Gorges also point out the completely undemocratic way in which the project was planned and implemented. The Chinese government, and especially former Premier Li Peng (who is a Soviet-trained hydroelectric engineer), has made the Three Gorges project into a symbol of Chinese modernization and nationalism, and the authorities have attempted to silence people who have spoken out against the dam. Critics of the project have been purged from their party and state offices, and others have been forced into exile. The media are allowed to carry only positive assessments of the project. A collection of essays by scientists, journalists, and intellectuals opposed to the dam was banned in China shortly after its publication in 1989. Citizen-based environmental groups are only now beginning to emerge in China but do not dare to seriously challenge a state-backed megaproject such as the Three Gorges dam.

The fact that even under such repressive circumstances one-third of the National People's Congress voted against the final authorization for the Three Gorges project in 1992 or abstained from voting shows just how much doubt about the dam there must be in China. But, given the current political situation, there is little reason to believe that such doubt can be expressed in open public debate or could deter the Chinese government from moving ahead with the project.

---

socialist democracy at work. During these sessions, deputies discuss and decide on legislation introduced by the premier and the State Council. Deputies may also make motions and suggestions to the congress, which are sometimes enacted into law. In recent years, important legislation has included major criminal and civil law statutes, laws governing foreign investment in China, and environmental regulations.

Most of the work of the NPC is routine, such as attending committee meetings or listening to long reports by officials. Legislation and other motions are generally passed by an overwhelming majority. But some debate and dissent do occur. For example, in 1992 about a third of the NPC deputies either voted against construction of the ecologically controversial Three Gorges dam project or abstained from voting. On rare occasions, government legislative initiatives have even been defeated. But all NPC proceedings are subject to party scrutiny. The congress never debates politically sensitive issues, and deputies, even though their right to speak and vote freely is protected by constitutional immunity, would be in serious political jeopardy if their actions were seen as a challenge to the principle of party leadership.

The CCP monitors the elections process to make sure that no outright dissidents are elected as NPC deputies, and the most important leadership positions in the NPC are on the CCP's cadre list, which means that they can only be filled by people who have the party's approval. The party's top bodies decide behind closed doors who will get which government position. This is followed by a more or less pro forma nomination and election process within the NPC, although some deputies do vote against or abstain from voting for party-endorsed nominees. For example, in 1998, 11 percent of the deputies did not vote for the official (and only) nominee to become chair of the congress (equivalent perhaps to the U.S. Speaker of the House of Representatives), Li Peng, the former premier whom many people despise because of his key role in the decision to crush the 1989 Tiananmen demonstrations. Such protest votes may signal a somewhat more independent attitude on the part of some NPC deputies, but they do not yet add up to meaningful opposition to party-designated candidates.

Still, as economics has replaced ideology as the main priority of China's leaders, the NPC has become a much more important and lively part of the Chinese political system than it was during the Mao era. Many NPC deputies are now chosen because of their ability to contribute to China's modernization rather than simply on the basis of political loyalty; therefore, some of them have become a bit more assertive in expressing their opinions on various issues.

Political Parties and the Party System

China is often called a one-party system because the country's politics are so thoroughly dominated by the Chinese Communist Party. In fact, China has eight political parties in addition to the CCP, but these parties neither challenge the basic policies of the CCP nor play a significant part in running the government.

The Chinese Communist Party

At the time of the National Party Congress in 1997, the CCP had about 58 million members. The party has grown steadily since it came to power in 1949, when it had just under 4.5 million members.

The Chinese Communist Party is the largest political party in the world in terms of total formal membership. But, as with all other former and current ruling communist parties, its members make up only a small minority of the country's population. CCP members are now only about 5 percent of China's population, or about 8 percent of those over eighteen, the minimum age for joining the party.

From the viewpoint of the CCP, the small percentage of Communists in Chinese society reflects the vanguard status and role of the party. Only those who are judged to be fully committed to the ideals of communism and who are willing to devote a great deal of time and energy to party affairs may join, and the process is long and arduous. Those admitted swear allegiance to the party and vow to "fight for communism throughout my life, be ready at all times to sacrifice my all for the party and the people, and never betray the people" (Article 6 of the CCP constitution).

The economic reforms begun by Deng Xiaoping paved the way for a milestone transition in the backgrounds of party members. During the Maoist era, "revolutionary cadres," whose careers depended on political loyalty and ideological purity, led the CCP at all levels; recruitment strongly favored the working classes and discriminated against intellectuals and other professionals. The CCP is now increasingly led by "party technocrats," people with higher-level technical training who have made their careers by climbing the ladder of the party-state bureaucracy. For example, all seven members of the party's current Standing Committee have academic and professional backgrounds in technical fields, and five of them (including General Secretary–President Jiang Zemin and Premier Zhu Rongji) were trained as engineers.

The social composition of the CCP's membership has also changed considerably in recent decades. In the mid-1950s peasants made up nearly 70 percent of party membership, and although they are still the largest single group in the party, less than 40 percent of party members now come from the peasantry. Factory workers account for less than 20 percent of party membership. The fastest growing membership category consists of officials, intellectuals, technicians, and other professionals, who together constitute about 30 percent of party membership. The remainder is made up of various groups, including military personnel, retired persons, and service workers. Women make up less than 20 percent of the CCP as a whole and only 4 percent of the Central Committee elected in 1998. One of the two alternate members of the Politburo is a woman (Wu Yi, who is also a senior government official and former minister of foreign trade). There are no female full members of the Politburo or its Standing Committee. The only woman ever to be a member of one of these elite bodies was Jiang Qing, the wife of Chairman Mao Zedong, who rose to power during the Cultural Revolution and was purged shortly after Mao's death in 1976.

Despite the party's tarnished image since Tiananmen and what many Chinese feel is the increasing irrelevance of communist ideology to their lives and the nation's future, the party's Youth League membership grew by 10.5 million between 1993 and 1998 (to a total of 68 million) and the CCP recruits between 1 and 2 million new members each year. Some join because they believe in communist ideals, but most are probably motivated more by opportunism than by idealism. Party membership provides unparalleled access to influence and resources, especially given the current quasi-market nature of China's economy, and being a party member is still a prerequisite for advancement in many careers in China.

China's Noncommunist Parties

The eight noncommunist political parties in the PRC are referred to as the democratic parties, a designation meant to signify the role they play in representing different interests in the political process and to lend some credibility to China's claim that it is a kind of democracy. Each democratic party draws its membership from a particular group in Chinese society. For example, the China Democratic League consists mostly of intellectuals, whereas the China Democratic National Construction Association draws members mainly from the business world.

The democratic parties have a total membership of less than half a million and operate within what the preamble to the PRC constitution calls "a system of multiparty cooperation and political consultation under the leadership of the Communist Party." The noncommunist parties do not contest for power or challenge CCP policy. Their function is to provide advice to the CCP and generate support within their particular constituencies for CCP policies. Individual members of the parties may assume important government positions. But organizationally these parties are relatively insignificant and function as little more than "a loyal non-opposition."[26]

The main forum through which the noncommunist parties express their views on national policy is the Chinese People's Political Consultative Conference (CPPCC). This body meets in full session once a year for about two weeks at the same time as the National People's Congress (NPC), which CPPCC members attend as nonvoting deputies. Most of the leading figures in the 1998 CPPCC (approximately 2100 from various spheres of national life, such as education, business and the arts) were noncommunists. But all the delegates were chosen through a process supervised by the CCP, and a high-ranking party leader heads the CPPCC itself. CPPCC delegates sometimes speak out about national problems like corruption or the environment, but they do not express serious dissent from the party line on any matter. The severe prison sentences given to the activists who tried to establish a new, independent China Democratic Party in 1998 showed just how determined China's leaders are to prevent the formation of any political organization not subservient to the CCP.

Elections

Elections in the PRC are basically mechanisms to give the party-state greater legitimacy by allowing large numbers of citizens to participate in the political process under very controlled circumstances. The CCP has what amounts to effective veto power over all candidates for office. It controls the commissions that run elections, and it reviews draft lists of proposed candidates to weed out those it finds politically objectionable. But the CCP rarely has to exercise its veto power over nominations or elections because very few people dare to oppose the party openly.

China has both direct and indirect elections. In direct elections, all eligible citizens vote for candidates for offices in a particular government body. For example, all the voters in a rural county would vote for the deputies to serve at the county-level people's congress. In indirect elections, higher-level bodies are elected by lower-level bodies rather than by the voters at large. For example, deputies to the National People's Congress are elected by the provincial-level people's congresses, which, in turn, have been elected by county- or city-level people's congresses. All elections above the county level are indirect; there are no direct elections at the provincial or national levels.

Turnout for direct elections is heavy, usually over 90 percent of the eligible electorate. All citizens over the age of eighteen have the right to vote, except those who (as the Chinese constitution puts it) have been "deprived of political rights according to law" (Article 34). This latter category may include the mentally ill, convicted criminals, and political prisoners.

For several decades after the founding of the PRC only one candidate stood for each office, so the only choice facing voters was to approve or abstain. Since the early 1980s many direct and indirect elections have had multiple candidates for each slot, with the winner chosen by secret ballot. The nomination process has also become more open. Any group of more than ten voters can nominate candidates for an election. Most candidates in direct elections are now nominated by the voters, and there have been a significant number of cases where independent candidates have defeated official nominees, though even independent candidates are basically approved by the CCP.

The most significant progress toward true democratic representation and participation in China has occurred in the rural villages. Laws implemented since the late 1980s have provided for directly elected village representative assemblies and the election, rather than the appointment from above, of village officials. These are, for the most part, multicandidate, secret-ballot elections, though still carried out under the watchful eye of the CCP. The village assemblies are usually made up of one representative from every ten or so households and meet at least once every few months. Although the local Communist Party committee is still the most powerful organization in China's villages, these assemblies do have considerable authority over local economic matters and exercise some supervision over local officials. The direct election of local leaders has also given village people the opportunity to oust corrupt or ineffective officials. By 1999 about 60 percent of China's villages had held such contests, and there were some very tentative experiments to expand democratic elections in a few rural townships, the lowest formal level of state government in China.

Recent electoral reform has certainly increased popular representation and participation in China's government. But elections in the PRC still do not give citizens a means by which they can exercise effective control over the party officials and organizations that have the real power in China's political system. The CCP has repeatedly rejected calls from both domestic and foreign critics for freer and more extensive elections. They argue that multiparty elections would not work well in China because of the country's low level of educational and economic development and its relatively poor communications system. They also express the fear that more democracy might plunge the country into chaos, perhaps even civil war. Obviously, they also have reason to be apprehensive about the consequences of truly democratic elections for the party's hold on power. In a major speech in December 1998 marking twenty years of economic reform, President Jiang Zemin stated bluntly, "The model of the West's political system should not be copied." He vowed that China would adhere to a system of socialist democracy in which "the Communist Party, being the ruling party . . . , leads and supports the people in controlling and exercising the power to manage the country."[27]

Political Culture, Citizenship, and Identity

From Communism to Consumerism

Since the PRC's founding in 1949 its official political culture has been based on communist ideology, and the party-state has made extensive efforts to make people's political attitudes and behavior conform to the currently prevailing version of Marxism-Leninism. But this ideology has gone through severe crises and profound changes during the turbulent decades of Communist rule, which has left its future in China seriously in doubt.

During the Maoist era, Mao Zedong Thought was hailed as holding the answer to all of China's problems in domestic and foreign policy. By the mid-1970s, however, the debacles of the Mao years had greatly tarnished the appeal of communism in China.

After Deng Xiaoping came to power in 1978, he set about trying not only to restore the legitimacy of the Communist Party through economic reforms but also to revive communist ideology. As a first step, Mao's contributions to China and Mao Zedong Thought were reevaluated. There was no complete repudiation of Mao as there had been of Stalin in the Soviet Union in the 1950s, but Mao was judged to have made serious mistakes as well as great contributions. Those parts of Mao Zedong Thought, such as his views on the importance of maintaining a close relationship between communist officials and the people (the "mass line"), were considered useful in maintaining Communist rule. Parts considered outmoded or counterproductive, such as the emphasis on class struggle, were jettisoned.

Toward the end of 1997 the CCP amended the party constitution to add "Deng Xiaoping Theory" to its official ideology. Deng's theories, which are often referred to under the rubric of "Building Socialism with Chinese characteristics," emphasized that China is a relatively poor country in the "primary stage of socialism" and therefore must use any means possible—even capitalist ones—to develop the economy. But Deng, like Mao, believed that only the Communist Party can lead China in this quest for development. In essence, Deng Xiaoping Theory is an ideological rationale for the combination of economic liberalization and party dictatorship that characterizes contemporary China.

The CCP still tries to keep communist ideology viable and visible by continued efforts to influence public opinion and socialization—for instance, by controlling the media and overseeing the educational system. Although China's media are much livelier and more open than during the Maoist period, there is no true freedom of the press. Reduced political control of the media has, to a large extent, meant only the freedom to publish more entertainment news, human interest stories, and local coverage. Media sources that stray beyond the proscribed boundaries are shut down; television and radio are entirely state-controlled. Internet access is growing fast in the PRC, especially among university students and intellectuals. The government, worried about the potentially subversive influence of e-mail and Web pages from abroad, has found it difficult to control the flow of electronic information as tightly as it would like, although, in another sign of the times, the government of the PRC has set up its own Internet site (http://www.chinanews.org).

Schools are one of the main institutions through which all states instill political values in their citizens. Educational opportunities have expanded enormously in China since 1949. Today, primary school enrollment is close to 100 percent of the age-eligible (6–11) population, which helps to explain why China has such a high literacy rate (80 percent) for such a relatively poor country. However, enrollment rates drop sharply after primary school. Only about half of those between the ages of 12 and 17 are in secondary school (compared to about 90 percent in the United States), and only about 2 percent of the age-eligible population is in some type of college (compared to about 75 percent in the U.S.). Obviously, China is going to have to expand secondary and college education if its goals for economic modernization are to be met. At the same time, a more educated population could pose a potential threat to a regime intent on maintaining tight political control over its citizens.

In Mao's China, students at all levels spent a considerable amount of time studying politics and working in fields or factories, and teaching materials were often overlaid with a heavy dose of political propaganda. Today politics is a minor part of the curriculum as students are urged to gain the skills and knowledge they need to further their own careers and help China modernize. Yet schools are by no means centers of critical or independent thinking, and teachers and students are still closely monitored for political reliability. More than 80 percent of China's youth between the ages of 7 and 14 belongs to the Young Pioneers, an organization designed to promote good social behavior, patriotism, and loyalty to the party among school children. However, the party's efforts to keep socialist values alive in China do not appear to be meeting with much success, and public confidence in the party and in communist ideology is very low.

Alternative sources of socialization are growing in importance, although these do not often take expressly political forms because of the threat of repression. In the countryside, there has been a resurgence of traditional customs and organizations. Peasants have replaced portraits of Mao and other Communist heroes with statues of folk gods and ancestor worship tablets, and the influence of extended kinship groups such as clans often outweighs the formal authority of the party in the villages. In the cities, popular culture, including gigantic rock concerts, shapes youth attitudes much more profoundly than do party messages about socialism. Throughout China, consumerism and the desire for economic gain rather than communist ideals of self-sacrifice and the common good, provide the principal motivation for much personal and social behavior. And religions of various kinds, once ferociously repressed by the Maoist party-state, are attracting an increasing (though still small) number of Chinese adherents. Buddhist temples, Christian churches, and other places of worship operate more freely than they have in decades. However, the Chinese Catholic Church is prohibited from recognizing the authority of the Vatican, and clergy of any religion who are considered to be a political threat are still imprisoned.

Citizenship and National Identity

The PRC constitution grants citizens extensive rights, including political rights, such as freedom of speech and assembly, and economic rights, such as the right to work and the right to health care and education. The constitution also proclaims, "Women in the People's Republic of China enjoy equal rights with men in all spheres of life, political, economic, cultural and social, including family life" (Article 48).

The constitution also specifies the duties of China's citizens, including the duty to work, perform military service, pay taxes, and practice family planning. In addition, there are more general duties, such as "the duty to safeguard the security, honor and

interests of the motherland" (Article 54). Such duties are vague enough to allow the authorities great leeway in interpretation and enforcement.

There is even an article in the Chinese constitution that has been cited by party leaders as giving precedence to the duties expected of citizens over those articles that grant them rights such as freedom of speech and assembly. Article 51 states that in exercising their freedoms and rights, citizens of the PRC "may not infringe upon the interests of the state, of society and of the collective, or upon the lawful freedoms and rights of other citizens." This provision gives the party-state constitutional grounds for suppressing dissent and opposition.

China in the late 1990s was going through a profound and uncertain transformation in its national identity. CCP leaders realize that most citizens view communist ideology as irrelevant to their lives. Therefore the CCP has turned increasingly to nationalism to rally the country. The official media now put considerable emphasis on the greatness and antiquity of Chinese culture, with the not-so-subtle message that it is time for the Chinese nation to reclaim its rightful place in the world order. The government also does all it can to get political capital out of China's recent economic progress, its impressive performances in international sports competitions, and the return of Hong Kong to Chinese sovereignty in 1997. Some observers have expressed concern that such officially promoted nationalist sentiments could lead to a more aggressive foreign and military policy, particularly toward areas such as the potentially oil-rich South China Sea, where the PRC's historical territorial claims conflict with those of other countries like Vietnam and the Philippines.

China's Non-Chinese Citizens

China's ethnic minorities number more than 90 million, or about 8 percent of the total population of the PRC. There are fifty-five officially recognized minority groups in China, ranging in size from over 15 million (the Zhuang of southwest China) to about 2000 (the Lloba in the far west of the country). There are about 20 million Muslims spread among several different ethnic groups. Most of these minorities have come under the rule of China through the territorial expansion of the Chinese state over many centuries rather than through migration into China.

China's minority peoples are highly concentrated in the five autonomous regions of Guangxi, Inner Mongolia, Ningxia, Tibet, and Xinjiang, although only in the latter two do minority groups actually outnumber ethnic Chinese. These five regions are sparsely populated, yet they occupy about 60 percent of the total land area of the PRC. Some of these minority areas are resource-rich, and most are located in strategic border areas of the country, including the borders with Vietnam, India, and Russia.

The Chinese constitution grants autonomous areas the right of self-government in certain matters, such as cultural affairs, but their autonomy is, in fact, very limited, and the minority regions are kept firmly under the control of the national government. Minority peoples are given more latitude to develop their local economies as they see fit, religious freedom is generally respected, and the use of minority languages in the media and literature is encouraged, as is bilingual education. In order to keep the already small minority populations from dwindling further, China's stringent family planning policy is applied much more loosely among minorities, who are often allowed to have two or more children per couple rather than the one child that is the prescribed limit for most Chinese.

The constitution also specifies that chairs of people's congresses and the administrative heads of autonomous areas must be members of the minority nationalities in that area. There has also been a concerted effort to recruit and promote minority cadres to run local governments in autonomous areas.

The impact of these positive political trends is, however, tempered by the fact that there are very few minorities in the upper echelons of the party and military leadership. Furthermore, even in minority areas, the most powerful individual, the head of the regional or local Communist Party, is likely to be Chinese. Also despite significant progress in modernizing the economies of the minority regions, these areas remain among the poorest in China.

The most extensive ethnic conflict in China has occurred in Tibet, which has been under what is essentially Chinese military occupation since the early 1950s. There has also been increasing unrest in areas where some of China's 20 million Muslims live.

Several clashes with Islamic separatists have caused the Chinese government to worry that pan-Islamic sentiments and activities may spread to western China from Afghanistan, Pakistan, and the Central Asian states that were once part of the former Soviet Union.

China's minority population is relatively small and geographically isolated, and where ethnic unrest has occurred, it has been limited, sporadic, and easily quelled. Therefore, the PRC has not had the kind of intense identity-based conflict experienced by countries with more pervasive religious and ethnic differences, such as India and Nigeria. But it is very likely that in the future both domestic and international forces will cause identity issues to become more visible and volatile on China's national political agenda.

Interests, Social Movements, and Protest

The formal structures of the Chinese political system are designed more to extend state control of political life than to facilitate citizen participation in politics. Therefore, people make extensive use of their personal connections based on kinship, friendship, and other ties (*guanxi*) to help ease their contacts with the bureaucrats and party officials who wield such enormous power over so many aspects of their lives. Patron-client politics is also pervasive at the local level in China, as it is in many developing countries where ordinary people have little access to the official channels of power. For example, a village leader (the patron) may help farmers (the clients) avoid paying some taxes by reporting false production statistics in exchange for their support to keep him in office. Such clientelism can be an important way for local communities to resist state policies that they see as harmful to their interests.

Organized interest groups and social movements that are truly independent of party-state authority are not permitted to influence the political process in any significant way. Rather, the party-state tries to preempt the formation of autonomous groups and movements through the use of official "mass organizations." These organizations provide a means for interest groups to express their views on policy matters within strict limits. The charters of these organizations place them explicitly under the leadership of the CCP; however, they appear to be gaining influence

Current Challenges: *Tibet and China*

Tibet is located in the far west of China on the border with India, Burma, Nepal, and Bhutan. It is a large area (about 470,000 square miles, which is nearly 13 percent of China's total area) and is ringed by some of the world's highest mountains, including the Himalayas and Mt. Everest. Tibet has a population of only about 2 million people, 95 percent of whom are Tibetans, who are ethnically, linguistically, and culturally distinct from the Chinese. Another 2.5 million ethnic Tibetans live elsewhere in China, mostly in provinces near Tibet.

In the thirteenth century, Tibet became a theocracy in which absolute power was held by a Buddhist priest, called the Dalai Lama, who ruled the country with the help of other clergy and the aristocracy. Traditional Tibetan society was sharply divided between the tiny ruling class and the common people, most of whom were serfs living and working under difficult and often brutal conditions.

Tibet became subordinate to China in the early eighteenth century, although the Dalai Lama and other Tibetan officials continued to govern the country. After the collapse of China's imperial system in 1911, Tibet achieved de facto independence. However, Britain, which saw Tibet in the context of its extensive colonial rule in South Asia, exercised considerable influence in Tibetan affairs.

Shortly after coming to power, the Chinese Communists made known their intention to end foreign intervention in Tibet, which they, like previous Chinese governments, considered to be part of China. In 1951 the Dalai Lama, rather than face a full-scale military assault, agreed to the peaceful incorporation of Tibet into the People's Republic of China. Although some Chinese troops and officials were sent to Tibet, the Dalai Lama remained in a position of symbolic authority for much of the

1950s. In 1959 a widespread revolt against Chinese rule led to the invasion of Tibet by the People's Liberation Army; the Dalai Lama and over 50,000 of his supporters fled to exile in India, and Chinese rule was even more firmly established. In 1965 the Tibetan Autonomous Region was officially formed, but Chinese political and military officials have kept a firm grip on power in Tibet.

During the Maoist era, traditional Tibetan culture was suppressed by the Chinese authorities. Since the late 1970s, Buddhist temples and monasteries have been allowed to reopen and Tibetans have gained a significant degree of cultural freedom; the Chinese government has also increased its investment in Tibet's economic development. However, China still considers talk of Tibetan political independence to be treason, and Chinese troops have violently crushed several anti-China demonstrations in Lhasa, the capital of Tibet.

The current Dalai Lama is very active internationally in promoting the cause of independence for Tibet. In 1989 he was awarded the Nobel Peace Prize, and in 1991 he met at the White House with President George Bush and addressed the U.S. Congress, much to the displeasure of the Chinese government. In 1997 the Dalai Lama met with President Bill Clinton, and in 1999 the U.S. State Department appointed a special Coordinator for Tibetan Issues, which China saw as further proof of U.S. support for Tibetan independence. There have been some inconclusive talks between the Dalai Lama and Chinese officials about the conditions under which he might return to Tibet in some capacity. But the two sides appear far from any agreement, and tensions between Tibetans and Chinese in Tibet remain high and potentially explosive.

---

in the policy process as China's leadership tries to enlist broad support for its development goals.

China has many mass organizations formed around social or occupational categories, with a total membership in the hundreds of millions. Two of the most important mass organizations are the All-China Federation of Trade Unions, to which most Chinese factory workers belong, and the All-China Women's Federation, which is the only national organization representing the interests of women in general. Both of these federations are top-down, party-controlled organizations, and neither constitute an independent political voice for the groups they are supposed to represent. But they do sometimes act as an effective lobby in promoting the nonpolitical interests of their constituencies. For example, the Trade Union

Federation has pushed for legislation to reduce the standard work week from six to five days, while the Women's Federation has become a strong advocate for women on issues ranging from domestic violence to economic rights.

The reform era has led to the spread of **non-governmental organizations** (NGOs) less directly subordinate to the CCP than the traditional mass organizations. There is an enormous variety of such NGOs, including environmental organizations, charitable foundations, and professional associations such as the China Political Science Association and the All-China Women's Entrepreneurs Association. These nongovernmental organizations have considerable latitude to operate within their functional areas of expertise without direct party interference if they steer clear of politics and don't challenge official policies. For example, environmental groups cannot openly oppose the Three Gorges project. All NGOs are supposed to register with the government, and organizations that would represent interests that the party-state does not recognize as legitimate, such as human rights or homosexuality, would not be given official permission to operate. In recent years, however, many thousands of unofficial grassroots organizations have formed to represent the interests of their members, but they run the risk of being shut down if they do anything to displease the authorities.

The various government bodies and other organizations discussed in this section should not be dismissed as entirely irrelevant to politics and policy-making in the PRC. Although they remain subordinate to the CCP, the National People's Congress, the Chinese People's Political Consultative Conference, the democratic parties, the mass organizations, and the NGOs do "provide important access points between the Party and the organized masses, which allow the voicing of special interests in ways that do not threaten Party hegemony and yet pressure the shaping of policy."[28]

Mechanisms of Social Control

While China has certainly loosened up politically since the days of Mao Zedong, the party's control mechanisms still penetrate to the basic levels of society and serve the CCP's aim of preventing the formation of groups or movements that could challenge its authority. In the rural areas, the small-scale, close-knit nature of the village facilitates control by the local party and security organizations. But the major means of control used by the party-state in urban China, called the unit (or *danwei*) system, is more complex. In the cities, almost everyone belongs to a unit, usually their place of work.

The unit is the center of economic, social, and political life for most urban residents. People depend on their units for jobs, income, and promotion, and larger units (like state-owned industries) may also provide housing, medical clinics, cafeterias, daycare centers, recreational facilities, and the like. The unit is also the citizen's basic point of contact with the formal political system. People vote in their workplace. If they belong to the party, they vote through the CCP branch in their unit; if there is a national campaign in progress, it is publicized through the unit. For example, compliance with the national family-planning policy is usually monitored through a woman's work unit.

The unit holds meetings to discuss the official line on important policies or events. The personnel departments of units also keep a political dossier on every employee. The dossier contains a detailed record of the political activities and attitudes of the employee and his or her immediate family members, and if a person changes jobs, the dossier moves, too. In these and other ways, the unit acts as a check on political dissidents.

Residents' committees are another instrument of control in every urban neighborhood. These citizen organizations, which are often staffed by retired persons, housewives, or others not attached to a work unit, effectively extend the unofficial reach of the party-state down to the most basic level of urban society. The committees address neighborhood concerns like crime prevention and sanitation, but they also keep a semi-official eye on who is doing what in the neighborhood. Suspicious doings are reported to the Public Security Bureau for further investigation. Foreign journalists in China have often found it difficult to meet with Chinese citizens in their homes because of the surveillance of the residents' committees.

As Chinese society continues to change because of the impact of economic reform, these control mechanisms are weakening. The growth of private and semi-private enterprises, increasing labor and residential mobility, and new forms of association (such as discos and coffeehouses) and communication (for example, cell phones, e-mail, fax machines, and TV satellite dishes) are just some of the factors that are making it much harder for the party-state to monitor citizens as closely as it has in the past.

Protest and the Party-State

The Tiananmen massacre of 1989 showed the limits of protest in China. The leadership was particularly alarmed at signs that a number of grassroots organizations, such as the Beijing Federation of Autonomous Student Unions and the Beijing Workers' Autonomous Union, were emerging from the protests. The success of Solidarity, the independent Polish workers' movement, in challenging the power of the communist party in Poland in the 1980s was much in the minds of China's leaders as they watched the Tiananmen protests unfold. Massive repression was their way of letting it be known that the "Polish disease" would not be allowed to spread to China and that neither open political protest nor the formation of autonomous interest groups would be tolerated.

There have been no significant political demonstrations in China since 1989, and pro-democracy groups have been driven deep underground. Known dissidents are continuously watched, harassed, imprisoned—and recently and more benevolently—expelled from the country.

But repression has not put an end to all forms of protest in the PRC. As mentioned previously, ethnic protests occur sporadically on China's periphery. Labor unrest has also been growing, with reports of thousands of strikes and other actions in recent years.

There have been large demonstrations at state-owned factories, where workers are angry about the ending of the iron rice bowl system of lifetime employment and guaranteed salaries. Workers at some foreign-owned enterprises have gone on strike to protest unsafe working conditions or low wages. Such actions have remained limited in scope and duration, so the government has usually not cracked down on the protesters and has, on occasion, actually pressured the employers to meet the workers' demands.

There have also been significant protests in China's countryside, especially in poorer inland provinces. Farmers have attacked local officials and rioted over high taxes and extralegal fees, corruption, and the government's failure to pay on time for agricultural products purchased by the state. These protests have remain localized and have focused on farmers' immediate material concerns, not on grand-scale issues like democracy. Nevertheless, if the countryside is left too far behind in the process of economic development, rural discontent could spread and translate into more generalized anger against the regime.

The political situation in China at the beginning of the twenty-first century presents a rather contradictory picture. Although people are freer in many ways than they have been in decades, repression can still be intense, and open political dissent is almost nonexistent. But there are many signs that the Chinese Communist Party is losing some of its ability to control the movements and associations of its citizens and can no longer easily limit access to information and ideas from abroad. Some forms of protest also appear to be increasing and, in some places, may come to pose a serious challenge to the authority of the party-state.

Section ❺   Chinese Politics in Transition

Political Challenges and Changing Agendas

Scenes from the Chinese Countryside

The economic and political circumstances of China's vast rural population differ dramatically depending on where in the countryside you look.[29]

Daqiuzhuang, Hebei Province   This village is perhaps the most prosperous place in all of China, with a per capita income (US$24,000 in the mid-1990s) nearly equal to that of the United States. Many villagers drive Mercedes-Benzes and other luxury cars, and all live in modern brick two-story houses—an unheard-of level of comfort for most Chinese. Although it is clearly still a rural area, the source of the village's wealth is industry, not agriculture. It has more than two hundred enterprises and tens of millions of dollars' worth of foreign investment. In addition to the 4000 or so now-rich native residents, many of whom hold managerial positions, there are several thousand less well-off—some would say exploited—workers from elsewhere in China who provide most of the labor for the factories. Although several of its former leaders were jailed on corruption and other criminal charges in 1993, the economic fortunes of Daqiuzhuang have continued to soar.

Qibailong, Guangxi Zhuang Autonomous Region This rural town is located in one of the areas known as China's Third World, where persistent poverty rather than growing prosperity is still the common lot in life. There are no luxury cars here; most peasant families have a total income of less than US$50 a year. Many of the children are hungry and half-naked, and most of the houses are little more than poorly constructed huts. Education, professional health care, and other social services are minimal or nonexistent. There is no industry, and the land barely supports those who work it. Tens of millions of Chinese peasants in villages like Qibailong remain mired in poverty and have benefited little from the country's economic boom.

Daolin, Hunan Province In January 1999 thousands of angry farmers marched on the township government headquarters to protest excessive taxes and the gross corruption of local officials. One farmer was killed and dozens injured when the police used clubs and tear gas to disperse the crowd. Shortly afterwards, nine people suspected of being ringleaders of the protests were arrested. The demonstrations had been spurred by a grassroots organization called Volunteers for Publicity of Policies and Regulations, formed to bring attention to local violations of a national law that limits taxes on farmers to 5 percent of their income. In many parts of rural China, villagers are subject to a wide range of arbitrary fees; there are charges for slaughtering pigs, for sending kids to school, for permits to get married or to have a baby, for registering land, and for outhouse renovations—to name just a few. As a result of such local fees, Daolin's farmers were paying double the legal tax rate—which for people with an annual per capita income of only US$170 was quite a burden. And people were even more furious because the extra fees often went to support the "wining and dining" of township bureaucrats rather than for worthy local projects.

Beiwang, Hebei Province This village of 2500 people recently elected its first representative assembly to supervise the work of local government officials. One of the first decisions made by the forty representatives was to reassign the contracts for tending the village's 3000 pear trees. After the rural communes were disbanded in the 1980s, each of the five hundred or so families in the village was given six trees to look after under the new household responsibility system. The assembly, however, decided that it would be better to reassign the trees to a very small number of families who would care for them in a more efficient and productive manner. The local Communist Party branch objected to this on the grounds that the village might lose much of the revenue that it earned from signing contracts with many households, which was used to pay for various public works projects such as road maintenance. The party was probably also concerned about the ideological implications of a less egalitarian distribution of the village's trees and the income derived from them. Nevertheless, assembly representatives were able to generate strong support from their constituents for their proposal, and the party branch allowed the trees to be recontracted to just eleven households. In a short time, pear production zoomed. The new system proved to be economically beneficial not only to the few families who looked after the trees but also to the village as a whole because of the government's share of the increased profits.

The varied scenes just described make several important points about Chinese politics today. First, they remind us of the central role that China's rural areas will play in the nation's future. Most Chinese still live in the countryside, and China's political and economic fate will be greatly influenced by what goes on there.

These scenes also reflect the diversity of the Chinese countryside: prosperity and poverty, mass protests and peaceful politics. It is very hard to generalize about such a vast and varied nation by looking at what is going on in only one small part of the country.

Although China has become more industrialized and urbanized in recent decades, most Chinese people still live in rural areas, and many of them still earn their living through fairly traditional agricultural labor. In general, rural incomes are less than half those of the urban areas. *Source:* AP/Wide World Photos.

The scene from Beiwang reminds us that in China, as in other countries, not all politics involves matters of national or international significance. For many, perhaps most, Chinese, who looks after the village pear trees matters more than what goes on in the inner sanctums of the Communist Party or the outcomes of U.S.-China presidential summits. The victory of the Beiwang representative assembly on the pear tree issue shows that sometimes, even in a one-party state, the people prevail against the government and democracy works on the local level—as long as the basic principle of party leadership is not challenged.

The Qibailong and Daolin scenes reflect the trouble that is brewing in parts of the Chinese countryside. No one would deny the astonishing improvement in living standards throughout most of rural China brought about since the 1980s by decollectivization and industrialization. But huge pockets of severe poverty persist, especially in inland regions like Guangxi that are far removed from the more prosperous coastal regions. Most of rural China falls somewhere between the conspicuous wealth of Daqiuzhuang and the extreme poverty of Qibailong. In the in-between areas like Daolin the combination of new hopes brought about by economic improvements and the anger caused by blatant corruption, growing inequalities, stagnating incomes, and other frustrations may prove to be politically explosive. Economic reform has yielded a better life and higher hopes for most of China's peasants. The CCP now faces the challenge of having to satisfy those hopes or risk the wrath of a social group that for decades has been the bedrock of the party's support.

Economic Management and Political Legitimacy

The problems of China's rural areas are part of a larger challenge facing the country's leadership, namely, how to sustain and effectively manage the economic growth on which the CCP's legitimacy as China's ruling party is now largely based. The party is gambling that solid economic performance will literally buy it legitimacy in the eyes of the Chinese people and that most people will care little about democracy if their material lives continue to improve.

A serious economic crisis could raise questions about the future viability of communist rule in China. If the economy were to falter in a way that gravely affected the livelihood or dashed the expectations of a large segment of the population, the potential for social unrest and political upheaval would increase immeasurably. The party would be left with nothing but sheer coercion to sustain itself in power.

Despite the overall success of reform, the CCP faces a number of challenges in governing the economy that will affect the party's political fortunes. Failure to keep inequality under control, especially between city and countryside, or to continue providing opportunities for advancement for the less well-off could become a source of social instability and a liability for a political party that still espouses a commitment to socialist goals. The considerable autonomy gained by provinces and localities as a result of the decentralization of economic decision-making has fostered a growing regionalism that poses a potentially serious threat to the political control of the central government. Corruption, which affects the lives of most people more directly than does political repression, has become so blatant and widespread that it is probably the single most corrosive force eating away at the legitimacy of the Chinese Communist Party.

The reforms begun by Deng Xiaoping have unquestionably spurred national economic growth and improved the material well-being of most Chinese. However, there are deep doubts about the ability of the CCP to continue to manage the economy effectively because of its reluctance to make even more fundamental changes, such as extending the market reforms to sectors of the economy that remain under state control, like banking and the production of steel and oil. However, it is in just such crucial areas of the economy that the Chinese Communist Party has found it most difficult to pull back. This difficulty stems partly from entrenched bureaucratic interests in government ministries that do not want to give up control of their bailiwicks. It also comes from the political opposition of ideological conservatives in the party leadership who are very reluctant to allow the dismantling of the last strongholds of the socialist command economy. Even those committed to reform are fearful of the political consequences of laying off millions of workers from state-owned factories. But if China's leaders choose not to make these hard policy choices, the country is unlikely to be able to sustain its remarkable economic growth, which could have even more severe repercussions for the CCP's ability to continue governing the country.

China and the Democratic Idea

China in the 1990s evolved toward a system of what has been called Market-Leninism, a combination of increasing economic openness and continuing political rigidity under the leadership of a ruling party that adheres to a remodeled version of communist ideology.[30] The major political challenges now facing the CCP and the country emerge from the sharpening contradictions and tensions of this hybrid system.

In the short run, the CCP's gamble that the country's economic boom would divert the attention of most Chinese from politics to profits has paid off. Continuing repression has also contributed to political calm in China since the Tiananmen crisis. However, as the people of China become more secure economically, better educated, and more aware of the outside world through access to modern media and telecommunications, they are likely to become politically less quiescent. Specific groups created or influenced by the course of economic development could become the source of pressures for political change. The rapidly expanding class of private entrepreneurs may want political clout to match their economic wealth; the intellectuals and specialists whose knowledge and skills are needed for the country's modernization drive may become more outspoken about the lack of political freedom; and the many Chinese citizens who travel or study abroad may find the political gap between China and the world's growing number of democracies to be increasingly intolerable. As China becomes more integrated with the global economy, the pressures from abroad for political change will also increase.

Maoist policies successfully eliminated any sphere of independent activity in China that might pose a challenge to the CCP's political domination. But economic reform and modernization over the last few decades in the PRC has led to the growth of **civil society**—a sphere of public life and citizen association truly autonomous from party-state control, which, if allowed to thrive and expand, could provide fertile soil for future democratization. The development of such a civil society, for example, among workers in Poland and intellectuals in Czechoslovakia, played an important role in the collapse of communism in East-Central Europe in the late 1980s by weakening the critical underpinnings of party-state control of society.

The Tiananmen demonstrations of 1989 reflected the stirrings of civil society in post-Mao China. One of the most remarkable things about Tiananmen was the way in which divergent groups, including students, workers, journalists, and entrepreneurs, joined the demonstrations to express their various dissatisfactions with the Communist Party. The viciousness of the Tiananmen crackdown revealed the CCP's determination to crush civil society before it could seriously challenge Communist authority.

But civil society in China has begun to stir again. Continuing economic modernization and social liberalization have led to the appearance of a multitude of unregistered grassroots organizations, such as those representing the interests of rural migrants in some of China's cities, which have become "a boiling pot [that's] difficult for Beijing to keep the lid on."[31] Similarly, a surprisingly wide-ranging discussion about the merits of democracy that took place in academic journals and conferences in the late 1990s was a sign that intellectuals were once more testing the waters of what was possible to advocate in the way of fundamental political reform. And in the spring of 1999, more than 10,000 Chinese followers of a charismatic martial arts and meditation master staged a peaceful protest in front of Communist Party headquarters in Beijing against government efforts to stifle their movement.

At some point, the leaders of the Chinese Communist Party will face the fundamental dilemma of whether to accommodate or—as they have done so often in the past—repress organizations and ideas that grow outside of its control. On the one hand, accommodation would require making some very basic changes in the Chinese political system, namely, less party control and more meaningful citizen representation and participation. The party would have to modify or abandon its claim to an exclusive "leading role" in Chinese society, something that no communist party has been able to do and still retain power. On the other hand, continued repression would strike at the heart of some of the groups and processes that are vital to the country's economic dynamism. This would have terrible costs for China and could also spell political trouble for the CCP.

The Future of Democracy

There are reasons to be both optimistic and pessimistic about the future of the democratic idea in China.[32] On the negative side, China's long history of bureaucratic and authoritarian rule in both traditional

and modern forms and the hierarchical values of still-influential Confucian culture seem to be mighty counterweights to democracy. And even though its political legitimacy may be weak and some aspects of its social control have broken down, the coercive power of China's Communist party-state remains formidable.

China's status as a developing nation with a low general standard of living, large areas of extreme poverty, and poor communications also imposes some impediments to democratization. Neither are all segments of the population equally receptive to calls for democracy. The appeal of democratic values is most apparent among intellectuals and urban residents, who still constitute a minority of the population. A large majority of the Chinese people are likely apathetic about national politics (preferring to focus on their immediate economic concerns) or fearful of the violence and chaos that radical political change might unleash.

On the positive side, the impressive successes of democratization in Taiwan in the 1990s, including free and fair multiparty elections from the local level up to the presidency, strongly suggests that the values, institutions, and process of democracy are not incompatible with Chinese culture. And, though it is still a relatively poor, developing country, China has a higher literacy rate, more extensive industrialization and urbanization, and less inequality (though there are some worrisome trends here) than most countries at its level of economic development—all of which are conditions widely seen by social scientists as favorable to democracy.

Despite the CCP's continuing tight hold on power, there have been a number of significant political changes in China under Deng Xiaoping and Jiang Zemin that could be planting the seeds of democracy. They are the decentralization of political and economic power to local governments; the setting of a mandatory retirement age and term limits for all officials; the coming to power of younger, better educated, and more worldly leaders; the increasingly important role of the National People's Congress in the policy-making process; the introduction of competitive elections in rural villages; the spread of semiautonomous nongovernmental organizations; the strengthening and partial depoliticization of the legal system; tolerance of a much wider range of artistic, cultural, and religious expression; and the important freedom (unheard of in the Mao era) for individuals to be apolitical.

Furthermore, the spread of democracy around the globe in the last decades of the twentieth century has created an international trend that will be increasingly difficult for China's leaders to resist. The PRC has become a major player in the world of states, and its government must be more responsive to international opinion in order to continue the country's deepening integration with the global economy and growing diplomatic stature.

But the future of the democratic idea in China is far from certain, and bleaker outcomes are also possible. There are still very powerful hard-liners in the CCP who could come to power, particularly if the economy falters, and who could reimpose ideological orthodoxy and resist efforts to weaken the party's control of political life. A serious foreign policy crisis or an outbreak of widespread social disorder could provoke a military coup in the name of national security.

There are also circumstances that could lead China to experience various kinds of identity-based and other conflicts that would undermine the prospects for democracy. The sharp class differences that have emerged along with growing national prosperity have the potential to spill into political violence, especially if groups such as impoverished farmers or urban migrants lose hope that their rising expectations for a better life will be met. Serious disputes within the leadership or between the party and the people over the nation's future could lead to civil war, while economic troubles might propel a splintering of China into regional blocs only nominally loyal to Beijing. If the central government should be paralyzed by a power struggle or seriously weakened for any other reason, separatist movements in Tibet and other minority areas could gain momentum and alter the political map of the PRC. But the unifying power of Chinese culture makes it unlikely that China will experience the kind of extreme national fragmentation that occurred in the former Soviet Union or ethnic warfare like that in the former Yugoslavia.

Chinese Politics in Comparative Perspective

As mentioned in Section 1, it is particularly useful to compare politics in China with the politics of other nations from two perspectives. First, the People's Republic of China can be compared with other communist party-states with which it shares or has shared many political characteristics. Second, China can be compared with other Third World nations that face similar challenges of economic and political development.

China as a Communist Party-State

Why has the Chinese Communist party-state so far proven more durable than other regimes of its type? The PRC's successful economic restructuring and the rising living standard of most Chinese people have saved the CCP from the kinds of economic crises that greatly weakened other communist systems.

The nature of the revolution that first brought the CCP to power also provides some clues about why communism has survived in China. The Chinese Communists came to power through an indigenous revolution and did not depend on foreign support for their victory. This is very different from the situation in most of East-Central Europe, where the Soviet Red Army helped to install and maintain communist regimes, which never quite shed the image of having been imposed from the outside. Furthermore, because of their success as social reformers and patriotic fighters against the Japanese, the Chinese Communists were able to build a much larger and broader base of support, especially among the peasantry, than the Soviet Communists, who came to power much more quickly through a rapid, largely urban revolution. Therefore, even though repression and corruption may be harming the popularity of the CCP, among some segments of the population the party still has a deep reservoir of historical legitimacy.

But China also has many things in common with other communist party-states, including the basic features of what is often called its totalitarian political system. **Totalitarianism** (a term also applied to fascist regimes such as Nazi Germany) describes a system in which the ruling party prohibits all forms of meaningful political opposition and dissent, insists on obedience to a single state-determined ideology, and enforces its rule through coercion and terror. Such regimes also seek to bring all spheres of public activity (including the economy and culture) and many spheres of its citizens' private lives under the *total* control of the party-state in the effort to modernize the country and, indeed, to transform human nature.

Totalitarian systems like those in China under Mao and in the Soviet Union under Stalin are different in several important ways from authoritarian dictatorships like the military governments that have ruled Nigeria and Brazil. Both totalitarian and authoritarian regimes suppress opposition and dissent, often quite brutally, but authoritarian governments do not attempt to control or penetrate society in as thorough a manner as do totalitarian states. Authoritarian governments generally allow a large "zone of indifference" in society where citizens are free to pursue their interests (such as in religion or the arts) without state interference as long as they steer clear of sensitive political issues.

The case of China sheds interesting comparative light on the nature of change in totalitarian systems. Partly because of their inflexibility, totalitarian regimes in Russia and Eastern Europe collapsed quickly and thoroughly, to be replaced by democracies—or at least efforts to democratize. The CCP appears to be trying to save Communist rule in China by abandoning or at least moderating some of its totalitarian features.

In order to promote economic development, the CCP has relaxed its grip on many areas of life, resulting in a relatively large apolitical "zone of indifference." The PRC under Deng Xiaoping evolved from Maoist totalitarianism toward a less intrusive, but still dictatorial, "consultative authoritarian regime" that "increasingly recognizes the need to obtain information, advice, and support from key sectors of the population, but insists on suppressing dissent . . . and maintaining ultimate political power in the hands of the Party."[33] Thus, China may be going through a type of post-totalitarian transition that is characterized by bold economic reforms but leads to another form of dictatorship rather than to democracy.

China as a Third World State

The record of Communist rule in China raises important issues about the role of the state in economic development. It also raises interesting comparative questions about the complex relationship between economic and political change in the Third World.

When the Chinese Communist Party came to power in 1949, China was a desperately poor country, with an economy devastated by a century of civil strife and world war. The nation had also been torn apart politically and socially, and was in a weak and subordinate position in the post–World War II international order. Measured against this starting point, the People's Republic of China has made remarkable progress in improving its citizens' living standards and quality of life. The Communist Party has also enhanced China's global role and international prestige. It has built a strong state that not only has the capacity to control and repress its people but can also carry out most of the necessary functions of a modern government from running schools to delivering the mail.

Why has China been more successful than many other developing nations in meeting some of the major challenges of development? Many Third World states serve narrow class or foreign interests more than the national interest, and corrupt political leaders are a drain on development rather than a stimulus. The result is that governments of Third World countries often become defenders of a status quo built on extensive poverty and inequality rather than agents of needed fundamental change.

In contrast, the PRC's rulers have been quite successful in creating what social scientists call a **developmental state**, in which political leaders effectively use government power and public policy to promote economic growth. The Chinese Communist Party has not hesitated to use force to achieve its ends, but it has also been unflinching in pursuit of China's national development and unafraid to undertake radical change to do so. The Chinese developmental state under Deng Xiaoping and now Jiang Zemin certainly has serious economic and social problems, but the policies of market reform and opening the country to the international market made China one of the world's great economic success stories in the last decades of the twentieth century.

While much of the Third World seems to be heading toward democracy without development (or at least very slow development), China seems to be following the reverse course of very fast development without democracy. There is a sharp and disturbing contrast between the harsh political rule of the CCP and its remarkable accomplishments in improving the material lives of the Chinese people. This contrast is at the heart of what one journalist has called the "riddle of China" today. The government of the PRC, he notes, "fights leprosy as aggressively as it attacks dissent. It inoculates infants with the same fervor with which it arrests its critics. Partly as a result, a baby born in Shanghai now has a longer life expectancy than a baby born in New York City."[34] This "riddle" makes it difficult to settle on a clear evaluation of the overall record of Communist rule in China today. It also makes it hard to predict the future of the Chinese Communist Party, since the regime's economic achievements could provide it with a source of legitimacy and support that may help keep the CCP in power despite its serious political shortcomings.

The CCP's tough stance on political reform is, in part, based on its desire for self-preservation. But in keeping firm control on political life while allowing the country to open up in other important ways, the Chinese Communist Party also believes it is wisely following the model of development pioneered by the newly industrializing countries (NICs) of East Asia such as South Korea, Taiwan, and Singapore.

The lesson that the CCP draws from the NICs' experiences is that only a strong government can provide the political stability and social peace required for rapid economic growth. According to this view, democracy—with its open debates about national priorities, political parties contesting for power, and interest groups squabbling over how to divide the economic pie—is a recipe for chaos, particularly in a huge and relatively poor country. Chinese leaders point out that democracy has not often been conducive to successful economic development in the Third World. In India, for example, a democratic but weak government has been unable to respond effectively to internal ethnic strife and has been thwarted by entrenched interests in its efforts to alleviate poverty.

But another of the lessons from the East Asian NICs, one that most Chinese leaders have been reluctant to acknowledge so far, is that economic development, social modernization, and global integration also create powerful pressures for political change from below and abroad. In both Taiwan and South Korea, authoritarian governments that had presided over economic miracles in the 1960s and 1970s were forced to give way to democratic forces in the 1980s and 1990s. The dynamic expansion and transformation of the Chinese economy suggest that the PRC is in the early stages of a period of growth and modernization that may eventually lead it to NIC status.

However, in terms of the extent of industrialization, per capita income, and the strength of the middle and professional classes, China's economic development is still far below the level at which democracy succeeded in Taiwan and South Korea. It is also important to remember that "authoritarian governments in East Asia pursued market-driven economic growth for decades without relaxing their hold on political power."[35] Nevertheless, economic reform in China has already created groups and processes, interests and ideas that are likely to become sources of pressure for more and faster political change; and the experience of the NICs and other developing countries suggests that such pressures are likely to intensify as the economy and society continue to modernize. Therefore, at some point in the not-too-distant future, the Chinese Communist Party may again face the challenge of the democratic idea. How China's new generation of leaders responds to this challenge is perhaps the most important and uncertain question about Chinese politics as we enter the twenty-first century.

Key Terms

Communist party-state
Marxism-Leninism
autonomous regions
Confucianism
proletariat
legitimacy
guerrilla warfare
land reform
nationalization
collectivization
socialism
Great Leap Forward
Great Proletarian
  Cultural Revolution
charisma
détente
communism
command economy

decentralization
people's communes
household responsibility
  system
township and village
  enterprises
iron rice bowl
guanxi
unitary state
dual rule
cadres
nomenklatura
socialist democracy
nongovernmental
  organizations
danwei
civil society
totalitarianism
developmental state

Suggested Readings

Baum, Richard. *Burying Mao: Chinese Politics in the Era of Deng Xiaoping*. Princeton, N.J.: Princeton University Press, 1994.

Blecher, Marc J. *China Against the Tides: Restructuring Through Revolution, Radicalism, and Reform*. London: Pinter, 1997.

Brugger, Bill, and Stephen Reglar. *Politics, Economy, and Society in Contemporary China*. Stanford, Calif.: Stanford University Press, 1994.

Calhoun, Craig. *Neither Gods Nor Emperors: Students and the Struggle for Democracy in China*. Berkeley: University of California Press, 1994.

Chang, Jung. *Wild Swans: Three Daughters of China*. New York: Simon and Schuster, 1991.

Davin, Dalia. *Mao Zedong*. Herndon, Va.: International Publishers Marketing, 1998.

Fairbank, John King, and Merle Goldman. *China: A New History*. Cambridge, Mass.: Harvard University Press, 1998.

Gao Yuan. *Born Red: A Chronicle of the Cultural Revolution*. Stanford, Calif.: Stanford University Press, 1987.

Gilley, Bruce. *Tiger on the Brink: Jiang Zemin and China's New Elite*. Berkeley: University of California Press, 1998.

Gilmartin, Christina, Gail Hershatter, Lisa Rofel, and Tyrene White, eds. *Engendering China: Women, Culture, and the State*. Cambridge, Mass.: Harvard University Press, 1994.

Goldman, Merle. *Sowing the Seeds of Democracy in China: Political Reform in the Deng Xiaoping Era*. Cambridge, Mass.: Harvard University Press, 1994.

Goodman, David S.G., and Gerald Segal, eds. *China Rising: Nationalism and Interdependence*. London: Routledge, 1997.

Harding, Harry. *China's Second Revolution: Reform after Mao*. Washington, D.C.: Brookings Institution, 1987.

Joseph, William A., ed. *China Briefing: The Contradictions of Change*. Armonk, N.Y.: M. E. Sharpe, 1997.

Kristof, Nicolas D., and Sheryl WuDunn. *China Wakes: The Struggle for the Soul of a Rising Power*. New York: Time Books, 1994.

Lieberthal, Kenneth. *Governing China: From Revolution Through Reform*. New York: Norton, 1995.

MacFarquhar, Roderick, ed. *The Politics of China, 1949–1989*. Cambridge: Cambridge University Press, 1993.

Mackerras, Colin. *China's Minorities: Integration and Modernization in the Twentieth Century*. New York: Oxford University Press, 1994.

Meisner, Maurice. *Mao's China and After: A History of the People's Republic*. 3d ed. New York: Free Press, 1999.

Nathan, Andrew J., and Robert S. Ross *The Great Wall and the Empty Fortress: China's Search for Security*. New York: Norton, 1997.

Naughton, Barry. *Growing Out of the Plan: Chinese Economic Reform, 1978–1993*. Cambridge: Cambridge University Press, 1995.

Oi, Jean. *Rural China Takes Off: The Institutional Foundations of Economic Reform*. Berkeley: University of California Press, 1999.

Perry, Elizabeth J. *Shanghai on Strike: The Politics of Chinese Labor*. Stanford, Calif.: Stanford University Press, 1995

Schell, Orville. *Mandate of Heaven: A New Generation of Entrepreneurs, Dissidents, Bohemians, and Technocrats Lay Claim to China's Future*. New York: Simon and Schuster, 1994.

Schell, Orville, and David Shambaugh, eds. *The China Reader: The Reform Era*. New York: Vintage Books, 1999.

Shambaugh, David, ed. *Deng Xiaoping: Portrait of a Chinese Statesman*. New York: Oxford University Press, 1995.

Spence, Jonathan D., and Annping Chin. *The Chinese Century: A Photographic History of the Last Hundred Years*. New York: Random House, 1996.

Starr, John Bryan. *Understanding China: A Guide to China's Economy, History, and Political Structure*. New York: Hill and Wang, 1997.

White, Gordon. *Riding the Tiger: The Politics of Economic Reform in Post-Mao China*. Stanford, Calif.: Stanford University Press, 1993.

Zweig, David. *Freeing China's Farmers: Rural Restructuring in the Reform Era*. Armonk, NY: M. E. Sharpe, 1997.

Endnotes

[1] Wu Ming (pseud.), "I Witnessed the Beijing Massacre," cited in Timothy Brook, *Quelling the People: The Military Suppression of the Beijing Democracy Movement* (New York: Oxford University Press, 1992), 129.

[2] *New York Times*, June 28, 1998.

[3] Mao Zedong, "Report on an Investigation of the Peasant Movement in Hunan," March 1927, in *Selected Readings from the Works of Mao Tsetung* (Beijing: Foreign Languages Press, 1971), 24.

[4] Brantly Womack, "The Party and the People: Revolutionary and Post-Revolutionary Politics in China and Vietnam," *World Politics* 39, no. 4 (July 1987): 479–507.

[5] David Bachman, *Bureaucracy, Economy, and Leadership in China: The Institutional Origins of the Great Leap Forward* (Cambridge: Cambridge University Press, 1991), 2.

[6] See, for example, "When China Wakes," *The Economist*, November 28, 1992; and Nicholas D. Kristof and Sheryl WuDunn, *China Wakes: The Struggle for the Soul of a Rising Power* (New York: Time Books, 1994).

[7] "When China Wakes," *The Economist*, November 28, 1992, pp. 3, 15.

[8] Barry Naughton, "The Pattern and Legacy of Economic Growth in the Mao Era," in *Perspectives on Modern China: Four Anniversaries*, ed. Kenneth Lieberthal, et al., (Armonk, N.Y.: M. E. Sharpe, 1991), 250.

[9] Deng Xiaoping first expressed his "cat theory" in 1962 in a speech entitled "Restore Agricultural Production" in the aftermath of the failure and famine of the Great Leap Forward. In the original speech, he actually quoted an old peasant proverb that refers to a "yellow cat or a black cat," but it is most often rendered "white cat or black cat." See *Selected Works of Deng Xiaoping (1938–1965)* (Beijing: Foreign Languages Press, 1992), 293.

[10] Deng Xiaoping, "Reform Is China's Second Revolution," March 28, 1985, in *Selected Works of Deng Xiaoping (1982–1992)* (Beijing: Foreign Languages Press, 1994), 119–120.

[11] Kathleen Hartford, "Socialist Agriculture Is Dead; Long Live Socialist Agriculture! Organizational Transformation in Rural China," in *The Political Economy of Reform in Post-Mao China*, ed. Elizabeth J. Perry and Christine P. W. Wong. Harvard Contemporary China Series Vol. 2. (Cambridge, Mass.: Council on East Asian Studies, Harvard University, 1985), 55.

[12] Christine P. W. Wong, "China's Economy: The Limits of Gradualist Reform," in *China Briefing, 1994*, ed. William A. Joseph (Boulder, Colo.: Westview Press), 50.

[13] Jiang Zemin, "Hold High the Great Banner of Deng Xiaoping Theory for an All-round Advancement of the Cause of Building Socialism with Chinese Characteristics to the 21st Century," *Beijing Review*, 40, no. 40 (October 6–12, 1997): 32.

[14] Emily Honig and Gail Herschatter, *Personal Voices: Chinese Women in the 1980s* (Stanford, Calif.: Stanford University Press, 1988), 337.

[15] Baruch Boxer, "China's Environment: Issues and Economic Implications," in Joint Economic Committee of Congress, *China's Economic Dilemmas in the 1990s: The Problems of Reform, Modernization, and Interdependence*, vol. 1 (Washington, D.C.: Government Printing Office, 1991), 306–307.

[16] "Environment and Development: A World Issue," *Beijing Review* 35, no. 23 (June 8–14, 1992): 20.

[17] Mao Zedong, "Strive to Build a Great Socialist Country," September 15, 1954, in *Selected Works of Mao Tsetung*, vol. 5 (Beijing: Foreign Languages Press, 1977), 149.

[18] "Uphold the Four Cardinal Principles," March 30, 1979, in *Selected Works of Deng Xiaoping (1977–1982)*, (Beijing: Foreign Languages Press, 1984), 178.

[19] The full text of the constitution of the People's Republic of China can be found in James C. F. Wang, *Contemporary Chinese Politics: An Introduction*, 6th ed. (Upper Saddle River, N.J.: Prentice Hall, 1999), 373–398. A text of the constitution of the Chinese Communist Party can also be found in Wang, 399–424.

[20] Mao Zedong, "Problems of War and Strategy," November 6, 1938, in *Selected Works of Mao Tsetung*, vol. 2 (Beijing: Foreign Languages Press, 1972), 224.

[21] Ellis Joffe, "The Chinese Army: Coping with the Consequences of Tiananmen," in *China Briefing, 1991*, ed. William A. Joseph (Boulder, Colo.: Westview Press, 1992), 42.

[22] Kenneth Lieberthal and David Michael Lampton, eds., *Bureaucracy, Politics, and Decision-Making in Post-Mao China* (Berkeley: University of California Press, 1992).

[23] John P. Burns, *The Chinese Communist Party's Nomenklatura System: A Documentary Study of Party Control of Leadership Selection, 1979–1984* (Armonk, N.Y.: M. E. Sharpe, 1989), ix–x.

[24] Gordon White, *Riding the Tiger: The Politics of Economic Reform in Post-Mao China* (Palo Alto, Calif.: Stanford University Press, 1993), 20.

[25] Andrew J. Nathan, *Chinese Democracy* (Berkeley: University of California Press, 1985), 124.

[26] James D. Seymour, *China's Satellite Parties* (Armonk, N.Y.: M. E. Sharpe, 1987), 87.

[27] BBC Summary of World Broadcasts, December 21, 1998, FE/3415/G; a summary of Jiang's speech is reported in *New York Times*, December 19, 1998, p. A6.

[28] James R. Townsend and Brantly Womack, *Politics in China*, 3d ed. (Boston: Little, Brown, 1986), 271.

[29] The following scenes are extrapolated from Nicholas D. Kristof and Sheryl WuDunn, *China Wakes: The Struggle for the Soul of a Rising Power* (New York: Times Books, 1994); Andrew Higgens, "Corrupt Village Regains Its Glory," *The Guardian* (London), November 24, 1995, p. 15; Agence France Presse English Wire Service, "Peasants Surviving on Less than 20 Dollars a Year," China News Digest–Global (on-line service), February 19, 1994; Erik Eckholm, "Heated Protests by Its Farmers Trouble Beijing," *New York Times*, February 1, 1999, pp. A1, A12; Susan V. Lawrence, "Democracy, Chinese-Style: Village Representative Assemblies," *Australian Journal of Chinese Affairs*, no. 32 (July 1994): 61–68.

[30] Nicholas D. Kristof, "China Sees 'Market-Leninism' as Way to Future," *New York Times*, September 6, 1993, pp. 1, 5.

[31] Jude Howell, cited in Matt Forney, "Voice of the People," *Far Eastern Economic Review*, May 7, 1998, p. 10.

[32] Many of the points in this section are based on Martin King Whyte, "Prospects for Democratization in China," *Problems of Communism* (May–June 1992): 58–69; Michel Oksenberg, "Will China Democratize? Confronting a Classic Dilemma," *Journal of Democracy* 9, no. 1 (January 1998), 27–34; and Minxin Pei, "Is China Democratizing?" *Foreign Affairs* 77, no. 1 (January–February 1998), 68–82.

[33] Harry Harding, *China's Second Revolution: Reform after Mao* (Washington, D.C.: Brookings Institution, 1987), 200.

[34] Nicholas D. Kristof, "Riddle of China: Repression as Standard of Living Soars," *New York Times*, September 7, 1993, pp. A1, A10.

[35] Nicholas Lardy, "Is China Different? The Fate of Its Economic Reform," in *The Crisis of Leninism and the Decline of the Left*, ed. Daniel Chirot (Seattle: University of Washington Press, 1991), 147.

CHAPTER 3

India

Atul Kohli

Republic of India

Land and Population

Capital New Delhi

Total Area (square miles) 1,222,559 (slightly more than one-third the size of the U.S.)

Population 961 million

Annual Average Population Growth Rate (1990–1997) 1.8%

Urban Population (% of total) 27%

Major Languages*

Hindi	38.77%
Telugu	7.96%
Bengali	7.56%
Marathi	7.28%
Tamil	6.56%
Other	31.87%

*Hindi is the main language, but English is the most important language for political, commercial, and other national level communication.

Religious Affiliation

Hindu	80.3%
Muslim	11.0%
Christian	3.7%
Sikh	2.0%
Buddhist and other	3.0%

Economy

Domestic Currency Rupee

Total GNP (US$) $373.9 billion

GNP per capita (US$) $390

GNP per capita at purchasing power parity (US$) $1650

GNP average annual growth rate (1996–1997) 5.0%

GNP per capita average annual growth rate

1996–1997	3.2%
1980–1995	3.2%
1965–1980	1.5%

Income Gap:
GDP per capita (US$)

Richest 20% of population	$4288
Poorest 20% of population	$907

Structure of Production (% of GDP)

Agriculture	29%
Industry	29%
Services	41%

Labor Force Distribution (% of total)

Agriculture	64%
Industry	16%
Services	20%

Exports as % of GDP 12%

Imports as % of GDP 15%

Electricity Consumption per capita (kwh) 448

CO_2 Emissions per capita (metric tons) 1

Society

Life Expectancy

Female	61.8
Male	61.4

Doctors per 100,000 people 48

Infant Mortality (per 1000 live births) 73

Adult Literacy

Female	37.7%
Male	65.5%

Access to Information and Communications (per 1000 people)

Radios	81
Televisions	61
Telephone Lines	13
Personal Computers	1.2

Women in Government and Economy

Women in Parliament	2.6%
Women at ministerial level	4.0%
Women as % of total labor force	31.0%
Female business administrators and managers	2.0%
Female professional and technical workers	21.0%

1998 Human Development Index ranking (out of 174 countries; 1 = highest) 139

Political Organization

Political System Parliamentary democracy and a federal republic.

Regime History Current government formed by the Bharatiya Janata Party (BJP), under the leadership of Atal Behari Vajpayee.

Administrative Structure Federal, with 26 state governments.

Executive Prime minister, leader of the party with the most seats in the parliament.

Legislature Bicameral, upper house elected indirectly and without much substantial power; lower house, the main house, with members elected from single-member districts, winner-take-all.

Judiciary Independent constitutional court with appointed judges.

Party System Multiparty system. Congress Party is dominant; major opposition parties include Bharatiya Janata Party (BJP), Janata Party, and the Communist Party of India, Marxist (CPM).

Politics in Action

On December 6, 1992, thousands of Hindus, encouraged by a leading opposition party, the Bharatiya Janata Party (BJP), stormed and destroyed an Islamic mosque in Ayodhya, India.

In May 1998, the BJP-led coalition government proclaimed that India was a nuclear power, since it had successfully detonated five underground nuclear explosions.

The tense, tumultuous, and bloody trek from Ayodhya to the nuclear bomb highlights the turbulent nature of Indian democracy at the end of the twentieth century. The Ayodhya incident was triggered by the electoral mobilization strategies of the Bharatiya Janata Party (BJP—Indian People's Party), a religious, nationalist party that had been courting the electoral and political support of **Hindus**, India's largest religious group at over 80 percent of the country's population. BJP leaders argued that the Islamic mosque at Ayodhya, a place of worship for India's **Muslims**, who constitute nearly 11 percent of India's population, had been built on the site that the BJP claimed was the birthplace of the Hindu god Rama. They wanted to replace the mosque with a Hindu temple. When the ruling party of that time, India's main centrist party, the Indian National Congress (or Congress Party), refused to allow demolition of the mosque, the BJP mobilized Hindus, including unemployed youth and small traders throughout India, in political protest. The political use of religious symbols touched a raw nerve in a multiethnic society in which religious conflict has a long history and in which stories and memories of communal hostility and suspicion are ever-present. After all, Indian independence in 1947 was achieved in an atmosphere of sectarian violence accompanying the dismemberment of the country into India and Pakistan. The ambivalent attitude of the Congress-led national government of that time in 1992 toward the growing Hindu mobilization highlights the challenge faced by Indian politics today. On the one hand, the government needed to protect India's minorities and maintain law and order, but on the other hand, the Congress Party was afraid of alienating the Hindu majority group, whose electoral support was crucial for winning future elections. As the national government hesitated, thousands of Hindus raged out of control and demolished the mosque at Ayodhya.

A crowd of Hindu fundamentalists listens to speeches by leaders around a disputed mosque in Ayodhya, a town in northern India, on December 6, 1992. The mosque was later torn down by belligerent volunteers, precipitating a major political crisis. *Source:* Reuters/Bettmann.

The BJP's political mobilization using religious divisions was quite successful, culminating in its emergence as India's ruling party in March 1998 parlimentary elections. Shortly afterwards, in fulfillment of one of the BJP's electoral promises, the BJP-led coalition government gate-crashed the nuclear club, triggering a nuclear arms race in South Asia. Though the Indian government cited regional threats from China and Pakistan as the key reason, the decision to become a nuclear state can also be traced directly to the evolution of domestic politics of democracy in India since the late 1980s. The electoral mobilization along ethnic lines (religious, language, or caste) interacted with demands by the mobilized groups for more influence in an atmosphere of economic turmoil and poverty. The nuclear detonations provided a ready tool for mobilizing Indians under the slogan of national pride and turned popular attention away from the domestic woes of poverty and crises of government. By the end of May, India's archenemy and neighbor, Pakistan, had responded by testing its own bomb. Swift worldwide condemnation followed as economic and technology sanctions were imposed on both countries as punishment for the explosions. Over the course of 1998 tensions were managed through diplomatic channels organized by the United States and other Western powers.

The two incidents thus capture three important themes in contemporary Indian politics. First, political struggles in a relatively poor democracy are especially likely to be contentious. Given the multicultural nature of India, many of these struggles readily become ethnic conflicts; the lines of conflict are sometimes defined along religious affiliations, at other times, along language, caste, or territorial attachments. Second, attempts to satisfy the demands of the mobilized groups could lead to nationalistic and sometimes dangerous results, as witnessed by the decision to become overtly nuclear. And third, although growing conflicts often push Indian politics to the brink, for over half a century India's democracy has managed to somehow pull back, absorb the crises, and muddle through, albeit with a strained democratic system. The central dilemma for India is how a democratic government can simultaneously accommodate the demands of its diverse social groups and create a wealthier, egalitarian, and stable society.

Geographic Setting

India is a large, populous, and geographically and culturally diverse country. Its large size, at approximately 2,000 miles (3,200 kilometers) in both length and width, is rivaled in Asia only by China. And its rich geographic setting includes three diverse

Indian nuclear test, May 1998. *Source:* Baldev/ Sygma.

topographical zones (the mountainous northern zone, the basin formed by the Ganges river, and the peninsula of southern India) and a variety of climates (mountain climate in the northern mountain range; dry, hot weather in the arid, northern plateau; and subtropical climate in the south). Along with its neighbors Pakistan and Bangladesh, the region is physically isolated from the rest of Asia by the Himalayas to the north and the Indian Ocean to the east, south, and west. The northwest frontier is the

only permeable frontier, and it is the route successive series of invaders and migrants have used to enter this region.

With a population of over 900 million (nearly the population of all African and Latin American countries combined), India is the second most populous country in the world, after its neighbor China. It is the world's largest democracy and the oldest democracy among the developing countries of Asia, Africa, and Latin America. India has functioned as a democracy with full adult suffrage since the late 1940s, when it emerged as a sovereign nation-state following the end of British colonial rule. The durability of Indian democracy is especially intriguing considering the diversity of Indian society. Some fourteen major languages and numerous dialects are spoken in India. Although Hinduism is the religion of four out of five Indians, people subscribing to nearly every one of the world's great religions live in India. These include many different ethnic groups, such as different, regionally concentrated tribal groups, as well as different religious minority groups such as Muslims, **Sikhs**, Jains, Buddhists and Christians. Furthermore, Indian society, especially the Hindu society, is divided into a myriad of castes. Although these are mainly occupation groups, they also tend to be closed social groups in the sense that people are born into, marry, and die within their caste.

Critical Junctures

India is among the most ancient civilizations of the world, dating back to the third millennium B.C. The Indian subcontinent, comprising Pakistan, India, and Bangladesh, has witnessed the rise and fall of many civilizations and empires. Only the most recent legacies that have shaped present-day politics are reviewed here. Of these, four are especially significant. First is the impact of nearly two hundred years of British colonial rule on the subcontinent from the mid-eighteenth to the mid-twentieth century, from which India and Pakistan emerged as sovereign states in 1947. Independent India inherited a relatively stagnant economy and a nationalist movement committed to bringing prosperity to a new nation. Second is the Nehru era (1947–1964), during which India developed a democratic and federal system of government and a planned economy. Third is the era of Indira Gandhi (1966–1984), under whom democratic politics became more populist and turbulent; her left-leaning rhetoric also failed to relieve India's considerable poverty. And fourth, in the 1990s, is the rise of opposition parties, most notably the BJP, more fragmented and fragile government coalitions, and the change in India's international role through its emergence as a nuclear power.

The Colonial Legacy (1757–1947)

Motivated by a combination of economic and political interests, the British started making inroads into the Indian subcontinent in the late seventeenth and early eighteenth centuries. Since 1526 large sections of the subcontinent had been ruled by the Mughal dynasty, who hailed from Central Asia and were Muslim by religion. As the power of the Mughal emperors declined in the eighteenth century, lesser princely contenders vied with one another for supremacy. In this environment the British East India Company—a large English trading organization with commercial interests in India and strong backing for its ventures from the British Crown—was able to play off one Indian prince against another, forming alliances with some, subduing others, and thus managing to enhance its control by a policy of divide and rule.

This informal empire was replaced in the mid-nineteenth century with a more formal one. After a major revolt by an alliance of Indian princes against growing British power—an incident known in Indian history as the Sepoy Rebellion or the Mutiny of 1857—the British Crown assumed the direct control of India. British rule over India from 1857 to 1947 left important legacies for the future of Indian politics. Like other colonies, India contributed to Britain's Industrial Revolution because it was a source of cheap raw materials and provided an outlet for both British manufactured goods and investment. Colonial rule in India also provided a model for subsequent British colonial ventures, for example, in Nigeria.

In order to consolidate their political and economic hold over India, the British entered into alliances with India's traditional ruling groups and eventually helped form a modern central government. The British created three main varieties of ruling arrangements within India. First, numerous small- to medium-sized states—as many as five hundred—covering an area equal to two-fifths of the subcontinent, continued to be ruled through the colonial period by traditional Indian princes, the **Maharajas**. In exchange for accepting British rule, these Indian princely states were allowed a relatively free hand within their realms. Second, in other parts of India, British indirect rule penetrated more deeply than in the princely states, for example, in the Bengal area (currently Bihar, West Bengal, and Bangladesh). In these regions, the British transformed traditional Indian elites, who controlled much agricultural land, into legal landlords, the **zamindars**, in exchange for periodic payments to the colonial administration. Third, the British established direct rule in other parts of India, for example, in Bombay and the Madras presidencies (large areas around the cities of the same name), where British civil servants were directly responsible for collecting land taxes and for adjudicating law and order.

Although British rule in India took on a variety of forms, it seldom reached very deep into Indian society, especially in rural areas, which were organized into many relatively self-sufficient villages. Within villages, social life was further divided into religiously sanctioned caste groups, with some landowning castes dominating many other castes lower in the ritual hierarchy and occupational and income scales.

A semblance of coherence to British rule in India was achieved through the creation of a central government that could impose control over these various territories and indigenous authority structures. The British thus helped create an all-India civil service, police force, and army. Although at first only British nationals could serve in these institutions,

with the introduction of modern educational institutions some educated Indians were incorporated into these government services. Unlike in some other colonies, especially those in Africa, the British in India helped create a relatively effective state structure. When India emerged from British rule in 1947, the new Indian state inherited, maintained, and expanded these colonial institutions. Since the civil, police, and armed services in contemporary India continue to be organized along the principles established by the British colonialists in the last century, it is fair to suggest that the roots of the modern Indian state can be traced back to their colonial origins.

The Nationalist Movement (1885–1947)

With the growth of commerce, education, and urban life, groups of urban, educated Indian elites, often of high caste origin, emerged as the new Indian "middle classes." They both observed and closely interacted with their colonial rulers and often felt slighted by their treatment as second-class citizens. Among these were early Hindu nationalists who believed that a reformed Hinduism could provide a basis for a new, modern India. Others were attracted to British liberal ideas and invoked these to seek greater equality with the British.

The two centuries of British colonial rule witnessed growing intellectual and cultural ferment in India. The British colonial rulers and traditional Indian elites had become allies of sorts, squeezing from the poor Indian peasantry resources that were simultaneously used to maintain the colonial bureaucratic state and to support the conspicuous life-styles of a parasitic landlord class. It was not long before Indian nationalists sought to oppose these arrangements, by founding the Indian National Congress (INC) in 1885. Its aim was to right the racial, cultural, and political wrongs of colonial rule.

In its early years, the INC was mainly a collection of Indian urban elites who periodically met and sent petitions to India's British rulers, invoking liberal principles of political equality and requesting greater Indian involvement in higher political offices. The British largely ignored these requests, and over time the requests turned into demands, pushing some angry

Leaders: *Mohandas Gandhi*

Born in 1869 in western India, Mohandas Gandhi studied law in London for two years and worked in Durban, South Africa, as a lawyer and an activist for twenty-one years before returning home to join the Indian nationalist movement. His work among the different communities in South Africa helped him to develop the political strategies of nonviolence, or *satyagraha* ("grasp of truth"). On his arrival in India in 1915, he set about transforming the Indian National Congress into a mass party by reaching out to the urban and rural poor, non-Hindu religious groups, and the scheduled castes, whom he called *Harijans*, or Children of God.

Following the British massacre of unarmed civilians gathered in protest in the Punjab (at the Jallianwala Bagh, a location well known in Indian history) in April 1919, Gandhi and Jawaharlal Nehru proposed a noncooperation movement. This required a boycott of British legal and educational institutions as well as British merchandise, for which were substituted indigenous, or *swadeshi*, varieties. (The image of Gandhi weaving his own cloth is familiar to many.) Gandhi believed that mass civil disobedience could succeed only if people were truly committed; the involvement of some Congress workers in a violent incident in 1922 greatly disturbed him, causing him to call off the noncooperation movement.

Gandhi was strongly opposed to the partition of India along religious lines in 1947, but because he had resigned from the Congress in 1934, his protests went unheard. Nevertheless, he dominated India's nationalist movement for more than two decades until he was assassinated in January 1948, five short months after India achieved its goal of self-rule, or *swaraj*. He is often referred to as the Mahatma, or "great soul."

Mahatma Gandhi, the leader of India's independence movement as he appeared at the head of a 200-mile march, staged in defiance of the statute establishing a government salt monopoly by the British colonial government in 1930. *Source:* UPI/Bettmann.

Indian elites into militancy and others into the nonviolent mobilization of the Indian masses.

World War I was an important turning point for Indian nationalists. After the war, as great European empires disintegrated, creating new sovereign states in Europe and the Middle East, the principle of self-determination for people who considered themselves a nation gained international respectability. The Russian revolution of 1917 also encouraged Indian nationalists because they interpreted it as a successful rising against imperialism.

The man most responsible for helping transform the INC from a narrow, elitist club to a mass nationalist movement was Mohandas Karamchand Gandhi, called Mahatma ("great soul") by his followers, one of the most influential and admirable leaders of the twentieth century. After becoming the leader of the INC in the 1920s, Gandhi successfully mobilized the Indian middle classes, as well as a segment of the Indian peasantry, into an anti-British movement that came to demand full sovereignty for India.

Three characteristics of the nationalist movement greatly influenced state-building and democracy in India. First, within what is now modern India, the INC succeeded in bringing together a wide variety of Indians in a relatively cohesive nationalist movement. Indians of different economic classes, castes, and ethnic backgrounds came to share some core political values. Because the INC became a powerful political organization committed to establishing an Indian nation, many conflicts could play themselves out within the INC as long as they did not threaten the cause of the Indian nation. The INC thus came to embody the principle of "unity within diversity," a principle that served India well in creating and maintaining a relatively stable political system.

Second, although a variety of Indians in their encounter with the British discovered what they had in common with each other—that is, their Indianness—they also recognized their differences, especially their different languages and their different gods. Even Hindus, India's majority population, are a highly diverse lot. There is no organized church in Hinduism; Hindus worship a variety of deities; and they are divided among themselves along different castes. As leaders of the INC sought to unite Indians against the British, some Indian groups became suspicious of other Indian groups. With much to gain by emphasizing the divisions among Indians, whenever the opportunity arose the British favored one group over another, thus contributing to growing divisiveness.

The most serious conflict was between Hindus and Muslims. A segment of the Indian Muslim elite refused to accept the leadership of Gandhi and the INC, demanded separate political rights for Muslims, and when the INC refused, demanded a separate Muslim state. The eventual division of the Indian subcontinent into the two states of India and Pakistan, and subsequent Hindu-Muslim hostilities within India (including those in the Indian state of Kashmir today), originated in the discovery of these differences.

And third, although the INC opposed British rule in India, it did so in a manner that was consistent with democratic norms. Many of the INC's prominent leaders, like Jawaharlal Nehru, were educated in England and were committed democrats. Gandhi's mobilizational style was also largely nonviolent. Moreover, the INC participated in limited elections allowed by the British, ran democratic governments with limited powers in various British Indian provinces, and elected its own leaders through internal elections within the INC. These pre-independence democratic tendencies were valuable assets for the subsequent success of democracy in India.

During the 1920s and 1930s, Gandhi, Nehru, and other leaders of the INC were increasingly successful in mobilizing Indians in an anti-British nationalist movement for India's independence. The more successful the movement became, the more the British had to either repress the INC or make concessions, and they tried both. However, World War II consumed Britain's energies so that the government could not simultaneously deal with a major European war and insurgent colonies. In order to gain Indian support for its war efforts, the British promised Indians greater independence following the war.

The Nehru Era (1947–1964)

India became a sovereign state in August 1947, when the British, weakened from World War II, decided to withdraw from the subcontinent. The resulting division of the subcontinent into two sovereign states—the Muslim state of Pakistan and the secular state of India—was a turbulent, bloody affair. Millions of Muslims rushed from India to Pakistan, and millions of Hindus fled the other way; over 10 million people migrated and nearly half a million died in communal violence. The euphoria of independence in India was thus tempered by the human tragedy that accompanied the subcontinent's partition.

Within India, Nehru, who was initially favored by Gandhi, emerged as the leader of the new nation. Soon thereafter Gandhi, who opposed the partition and later ardently defended Muslims within India, was assassinated by a Hindu fanatic. Nehru had become the uncontested leader of a new India, a position he maintained until his death in 1964. The years of Nehru's rule shaped the dominant patterns of India's future development.

Nehru's India had inherited an ambiguous legacy from the British rule: a relatively strong central government and a weak economy. Nehru, as a committed nationalist and social democrat, sought to strengthen India's independence and national power, on the one hand, and to improve its economy and the lives of the Indian poor, on the other. Nehru used the governmental machinery that India had inherited to accomplish these tasks.

At independence, India was confronted with major political problems, including a massive inflow of refugees, war with Pakistan over the disputed state of Kashmir, and the attempt to consolidate numerous Indian princely estates into a coherent national state. Concerned about India's capacity to deal with such problems, Nehru and other leaders, especially Vallabhai Patel, came to depend on and further strengthened the civil, police, and armed services that were a legacy of colonial rule. The strong state apparatuses facilitated India's political stability but also had other, less positive, long-term consequences. Most important, the new Indian state came to resemble the old British Indian state that Nehru and others had so vociferously opposed. The colonial state's tendency to favor traditional Indian elites, extract resources from Indian society, and maintain order within it was carried over into the post-independence era.

After independence, India adopted a democratic constitution and established a British-style democracy with full adult suffrage. Since political power now required winning elections, the INC had to transform itself from an opposition movement into a political party, the Congress Party. This it did quite successfully, by establishing a nationwide patronage system. Another important change in the decade following independence was the linguistic reorganization of states. As in the United States, the Indian constitution defines India as a federal system. The contentious political issue in the 1950s was the criterion by which Indian political groups could demand a state within the federal union. With Indians divided by the languages they speak, one obvious way to create a federal system was around language groups. Hindi is the most common indigenous language of India; however, most of India's Hindi speakers are concentrated in the north-central part of the country.

Those living in the south, east, and parts of the west are generally non-Hindi speakers. Concerned about domination by Hindi-speakers, many of these non-Hindi groups demanded a reorganization of the Indian union into linguistically defined states. Initially, Nehru resisted this demand, worried that linguistic states within a federation could turn secessionist and demand a sovereign country of their own. As demands for linguistic states mounted, especially from southern Indian groups, Nehru compromised in 1956, and the new Indian union was organized around fourteen linguistically defined states. Following subsequent changes, there are now twenty-three major states within India.

Major political changes instituted during the Nehru era put India firmly on a stable, democratic road. The powerful groups in the society—elite bureaucrats; wealthy landowners; entrepreneurs; and leaders of well-organized ethnic movements—were accommodated within the new system. However, the poor and the unorganized did not fare as well. While Nehru and the Congress Party continued to maintain a pro-poor, socialist rhetoric, their capacity to deliver on their promises was limited. This was not a serious political liability in the 1950s because the poor masses, mired in a centuries-old caste hierarchy, could not readily challenge elitist rule. Only in a few literate states such as Kerala were the poor organized, and they elected a communist state government.

Another legacy of the Nehru era is noteworthy. Jawaharlal Nehru was an internationalist who wanted India to play a global role. However, as Nehru was consolidating power in India, the Cold War was unfolding between the Soviet Union and the United States. Together with postcolonial leaders of Asia and Africa, Nehru initiated what became known as the nonaligned movement, which united those countries wishing to maintain a healthy distance from the two superpowers. India and many other developing countries viewed both Western capitalism and Soviet communism with suspicion. Under Nehru, India played a leadership role among other nonaligned developing countries while pursuing mixed economic policies at home that were neither fully capitalist nor fully socialist (see Section 2).

Leaders: *The Nehru-Gandhi Dynasty*

Jawaharlal Nehru

Jawaharlal Nehru was a staunch believer in liberal democratic principles. Along with Gandhi and others he was at the forefront of India's nationalist movement against the British. When India became independent in 1947, Nehru became prime minister as head of the Congress Party and retained that position until his death in 1964. During this period, he established India as a socialist, democratic, and secular state—in theory if not always in practice. On the international front, he helped found the nonaligned movement, a forum for expressing the interests and aspirations of developing countries that did not want to team with the United States or the Soviet Union during the Cold War.

Nehru attempted to set India on a rapid road to industrialization by establishing heavy industry. His efforts to effect redistribution of wealth through land reform were combined with an equally strong commitment to democratic and individual rights, such as the right to private property. Upon his death, India inherited a stable polity, a functioning democracy, and an economy characterized by a large public sector and an intricate pattern of state control over the private sector.

Indira Gandhi

Indira Gandhi became prime minister shortly after the death of her father, Jawaharlal Nehru, and dominated the Indian political scene until her assassination in 1984. Her years in power strengthened India's international position, but her domestic policies weakened the organizational structure of the Congress Party. Her tendencies toward centralization and the personalization of authority within Congress and the concomitant use of populist rhetoric in electoral campaigns contributed to the erosion of the Congress Party. By presenting the regional conflict in the Punjab and problems with Pakistan as Hindu-Sikh and Hindu-Muslim problems, respectively, she contributed to further erosion of the party's secular base and to rising religious factionalism. Her decision to send troops into the holiest of the holy Sikh temples in Amritsar deeply alienated Sikhs, a small but important religious group in India. The ensuing bloodshed culminated in her assassination by one of her Sikh bodyguards in 1984. Her assassination ushered in a new generation of the Nehru-Gandhi dynasty, as her son Rajiv Gandhi served as prime minister until 1989.

The Indira Gandhi Era (1966–1984)

When Nehru died in 1964, the Congress Party was divided over the choice of a successor and hurriedly selected mild-mannered Lal Bahadur Shastri to be prime minister. When he died of a heart attack in 1966, the party elites found a compromise candidate in Nehru's daughter, Indira Gandhi. Two reasons favored her choice: (1) as Nehru's daughter, she would be helpful in elections; and (2) she was perceived by the Congress Party leaders as a weak woman who could be manipulated by competing factions within the party. They were right about the first point, but decisively wrong about the second.

As prime minister from 1966 to 1984, except for the brief period from 1977 to 1980, Indira Gandhi left several long-term legacies for contemporary Indian politics. First, Indian politics became not only more personal and populist but also more nationalist.

To bolster her popularity Indira Gandhi deliberately reignited Indian nationalism. During the late 1960s the Bengali-speaking eastern half of Pakistan, which was separated from its western half by nearly 1,000 miles of Indian territory, demanded sovereignty. As violence escalated within Pakistan and refugees from East Pakistan began pouring into India, Gandhi ordered Indian forces to intervene on the side of East Pakistan, which led to the creation of the sovereign state of Bangladesh. Because the United States sided with Pakistan in that conflict (and the Soviet Union backed India), Indira Gandhi was able to mobilize Indian nationalist sentiment against both Pakistan and the United States. This war-related victory added to her popularity. After losses in the 1967 national elections weakened many established Congress Party leaders, Indira Gandhi moved swiftly to consolidate her position. She pushed out the Congress Party leaders who opposed her, replaced them with those loyal to her, and created a new Congress Party in her own image. Subsequently, she depicted the old Congress elite as having stood for the status quo and having prevented her from helping the poor and implementing progressive policies. Gandhi's populist rhetoric won her immense popularity among India's poor. By 1971 she dominated Indian politics as much as Mahatma Gandhi or her father ever had, until her assassination in 1984.

A second legacy of Indira Gandhi's rule was the introduction of a top-down quality to India's political system. During the Nehru era, local elites had helped select higher political officeholders, but in the 1970s Gandhi appointed these same officeholders at both the national and regional levels. Although this strategy helped her consolidate her power rapidly, it led to such negative consequences for governing as growing centralization of decision-making in the nation's capital, Delhi, and the erosion of the legitimacy of local leaders.

A third important legacy of Indira Gandhi's rule was her failure to translate populist rhetoric into real gains for India's poor. She was neither able to redistribute agricultural land from large landowners to those who worked the land nor able to generate employment, provide welfare, or improve access to education and health for the really poor. The reasons for these failures are complex and controversial. Some analysts argue that she was never sincere in her commitment to the poor and that her populism was mainly a strategy for enhancing electoral popularity. But even if she had wanted to improve the lot of India's poor, she would have encountered many obstacles, given India's enormous numbers of poor, especially in relation to its wealth.

During Indira Gandhi's tenure, Indian politics became more and more turbulent. And this is a fourth legacy of her rule, with long-term significance. As her popularity soared, so did the opposition to her. The old Congress elite formed into a loosely knit but coherent opposition. They denounced Gandhi's populist political style, arguing that her government was corrupt and that India needed a total revolution to oust her from power and cleanse the government. This opposition, led by a credible follower of Mahatma Gandhi, Jai Prakash Narain, began organizing mass demonstrations and strikes to press its case. During 1974 the political situation in India became volatile, with the

opposition organizing general strikes and Indira Gandhi threatening massive state repression. When Narain called on the Indian armed forces to mutiny, Gandhi declared a national Emergency, suspended many democratic rights, and arrested most of the opposition leaders. This **Emergency** lasted nearly two years, the only period since 1947 when India was not a full democracy.

When the prime minister rescinded the Emergency and called for new national elections in 1977, she was rudely surprised. She was voted out of office, and for the first time since independence, a non-Congress government came to power. Various groups that had opposed Indira Gandhi joined together in a loosely and hastily organized party (the Janata Party) and won power. The party won because Indira Gandhi's authoritarian measures during the Emergency were unpopular but also because the Janata Party temporarily united India's fragmented opposition groups (a united opposition has a better chance of winning in India's electoral system). However, the Janata Party was a loose coalition, and soon after the elections top Janata leaders started bickering for positions. Factionalism at the top became so unwieldy that the Janata government collapsed, providing a new opportunity for Indira Gandhi to return to power in the 1980 parliamentary elections.

To summarize, a personal and populist political style, a more and more centralized, top-down political system, failure to implement antipoverty policies, and growing political turbulence were the most important legacies of Indira Gandhi's rule in the 1970s. Although much of this continued after she regained power in 1980, she slowly introduced two important sets of changes that have also had long-term significance. The first of these was in the realm of the economy. During the 1970s, India's industrial establishment grew relatively slowly for several reasons: the government was spending too much public money buying political support and not enough on investment; incomes of the poor were not improving and therefore demand for new products was limited; and excessive rules and regulations were counterproductive, both for domestic entrepreneurs and for integrating India into the world economy. With few means to rechannel government spending or to improve the spending capacity of the poor, Indira Gandhi started liberalizing the rules that governed India's economy.

The second important change concerns the strategy used to mobilize support for elections. Because poverty was not diminishing, it was clear that continuing appeals to poverty alleviation would not provide a successful electoral strategy. Moreover, economic policy was moving toward liberalization, whereas rapid progress toward poverty alleviation would have required greater government involvement. With the loss of populist promises as a strategy to win support, the prime minister needed a new appeal—at this point, religion returned to Indian politics. Since the 1950s, Nehru and Indira Gandhi had argued for socialism and secularism. In the early 1980s, however, Gandhi started experimenting with a different theme: using religious appeals to mobilize India's majority religious group, the Hindus. By introducing religion into politics the Congress Party itself sowed the seeds that grew into rising support for religious parties such as the BJP and thereby accelerated its own fall. Thus, religious conflicts reentered Indian politics in the early 1980s, as illustrated by the growing conflict between the Sikh religious minority, based in the Punjab, and the national government. During this conflict, Indian security forces attacked Sikh militants hiding inside the holiest of the Sikh shrines, the Golden Temple in the city of Amritsar. The resulting alienation of Sikhs from Indira Gandhi peaked with her assassination by one of her Sikh bodyguards in 1984.

India since Indira Gandhi (1984 to the Present)

With the death of Indira Gandhi, the tradition of powerful and populist prime ministers came to an end. Indian politics has been facing a crisis of governance because of three factors, all introduced during the Indira Gandhi era.

First, increasing factionalism and disintegration within the Congress Party; second, a similar scenario at the level of the central government because of the inability of other parties to fill the vacuum; and third, the rise of ethnic mobilization electoral strategies. Since 1984 only two governments, both Congress-led, have lasted their full terms, one led by Rajiv Gandhi from 1984 to 1989, and the second by Narasimha Rao from 1991 to 1996. Rao rode to victory on a sympathy vote in the aftermath of Rajiv Gandhi's assassination. The Congress Party split in May 1995 added to the

Table 1

Prime Ministers of India, 1947–1998		
	Years in Office	*Party*
Jawaharlal Nehru	1947–1964	Congress
Lal Bahadur Shastri	1964–1966	Congress
Indira Gandhi	1966–1977	Congress
Morarji Desai	1977–1979	Janata
Charan Singh	1979–1980	Janata
Indira Gandhi	1980–1984	Congress
Rajiv Gandhi	1984–1989	Congress
V. P. Singh	1989–1990	Janata
Chandra Shekhar	1990–1991	Janata (Socialist)
Narasimha Rao	1991–1996	Congress
Atal Bihari Vajpayee	1996 (13 days)	BJP & allies
H. D. Deve Gowda	1996–1997	United Front
I. K. Gujral	1997–1998	United Front
Atal Bihari Vajpayee	1998–1999	BJP & allies

corrosion of party structures and vitality, a process set in motion by Indira Gandhi.

Second, at the level of the central government, the tendency for Indian elections to produce unstable and short-lived coalitions under leaders with little personal power or charisma has increased since 1996. The other parties have been able to fill the vacuum left by the Congress Party. Governments have alternated between the Congress, Janata, United Front, and BJP parties (see Table 1). The Congress Party's decline underlines deeper changes in Indian politics, namely, the decline of anticolonial nationalism, on the one hand, and the spread of power to many underprivileged groups, on the other. The United Front coalition represents mainly India's middle and lower castes. The BJP, by contrast, seeks to create a Hindu nationalist majority. None of these have come close to capturing a majority of the seats. The coalition governments from 1996 to 1998 were led by weak leaders of small parties and were provided with external support by the fractured Congress Party. The BJP government that came to power in 1998 was also a coalition; it lasted for only about a year.

Third, the religious factionalism that had been set in motion by Indira Gandhi's appeal to Hindus peaked during the Ayodhya episode, culminating in the victory of the BJP for a brief period in 1996 and again in 1998. Electoral mobilization strategies divided the country along ethnic lines and contributed to conflictual relationships in government and society. The BJP government initially appeared fragmented and weak as it sought to rule with a coalition of smaller, ideologically diverse parties. Even the brief nationalist resurgence among the populace, in the aftermath of the nuclear bomb testing in 1998, was not enough to unify the various religious, caste, and ethnic groups. In the late 1990s, mismanagement of the economy generated a popular backlash against the BJP. In elections held in November 1998 for seats in four state government assemblies, the BJP performed very badly, losing to the Congress Party in three states and to a regional party in the fourth state. Prior to the elections, soaring inflation had made basic commodities unaffordable to India's poor masses. The BJP government finally collapsed in April–May 1999 due to infighting among its coalition partners.

Whether any party or charismatic leader capable of unifying the country across the salient cleavages will emerge remains to be seen. (Attempts by Rajiv Gandhi's Italian-born widow, Sonia Gandhi, to knit together warring factions within the Congress Party bore fruit in the form of victory for the Congress Party in three states in the November 1998 elections.) Thus politics in India at the end of the 1990s is characterized by governments of precarious coalitions, weakened political institutions, and considerable political activism along ethnic lines. These developments have generated policies that range from limited action on the economic front to nationalist outbursts on the military front.

Themes and Implications

Historical Junctures and Political Themes

India in a World of States.   India's domestic troubles both reflect and influence its changing status in the world of states. In an increasingly interdependent global political and economic system, the arrival of India as a nuclear power signaled the dawn of a new era, where simmering historical tensions over territories (such as Kashmir) will need to be managed very carefully. Today, India shares its borders with two nuclear powers, China and Pakistan, and has engaged

in wars as well as periodic border skirmishes with them. With the end of the Cold War and the birth of a multipolar world, managing regional tensions poses problems. India and Pakistan have fought two wars, and tensions between them have been continually exploited by their politicians during domestic political crises. The challenge facing the Indian state is how to prevent domestic pressures from being translated into international belligerence. How will India's new role as a declared nuclear power change its international standing and influence its political and economic development? A very positive development in this regard was that India's and Pakistan's prime ministers made historic visits to each other's country in 1999. Nevertheless, shortly thereafter the two countries were again engaged in military conflict over Kashmir.

Governing the economy.   The second theme is particularly important for India if it wants to fulfill its national and domestic ambitions. The historical junctures reveal a series of policies in the economic sphere that shifted from being protectionist to slowly and tentatively liberalizing the economy. Indian policy-makers initially sought economic self-sufficiency through a policy of state-led industrialization focused on meeting the needs of its large internal market. This economic strategy had mixed results and did little to alleviate the country's terrible poverty. Like many other developing nations, India is having to adjust its economic strategy to meet the demands of increasingly competitive and interdependent global markets. But in a global environment that requires taking quick decisions and grasping ephemeral opportunities, the halting steps taken by Indian economic liberalizers have fallen short of expectations. How can India prevent its liberalization policy from being held hostage by entrenched elites? How can the policy-makers simultaneously provide for social benefits through well-aimed schemes that avoid clientalism and patronage, and pursue economic reforms? Will liberalization of India's state-controlled economy provide a basis for increased wealth in that poor country? These are among the most serious challenges that face Indian leaders and observers who are concerned about the future of this continent-sized, poor democracy.

The Democratic Idea.   The democratic idea has been sustained in India for over half a century, barring a short period of authoritarianism in 1977–1979. India can boast of a vibrant and vigilant civil society, periodic elections, unfettered media, and relatively autonomous courts and bureaucracy. However, these institutions have been corroded over the years as a result of frequent interference from political leaders. Democracy in India has become increasingly participatory, as an elitist style gave way to a populist one under Indira Gandhi. Because the institutional capacity to implement antipoverty policies was missing, Indira Gandhi's radical posturing brought turbulence to Indian democracy, damaged the economy, and never provided real benefits to the poor. Since the late 1980s ethnic tensions have been exacerbated by electoral strategies deployed by most political parties. The challenge faced by India is how to balance an increasingly divided society with the demands of social, economic, and political citizenship demanded by democracy. Contemporary Indian politics poses major questions. For example, what political strategies can help create a successful and durable formula for appealing to a dominant identity and thereby winning elections? Has the appeal to religion provided such a formula? Then, if appeals to the dominant religion provide electoral dividends, what are the implications for India's religious minorities? Can India's democracy cope with numerous religious and other identity-based political conflicts especially when they turn violent? In recent years, brutal attacks have been directed against Muslims, Sikhs, and Christians. In other words, democracy and identity politics have become intricately linked, often in destructive fashion, in contemporary Indian politics.

The Politics of Collective Identity.   That there are intense conflicts around the issue of collective identity is not surprising in multicultural India. What is alarming is how mobilization of the electorate on ethnic grounds could corrode democratic values. Democracy, by its nature, provides a level playing field for a tussle between different interests and identities. But the victory of a Hindu nationalist party deepened regional and religious divisions and fundamentally changed the nature of Indian democracy. Thus India faces the challenge of reconciling domestic electoral strategies of ethnic mobilization to capture power with the demands of moderation demanded in the exercise of such power; and the challenge of coping with demands of multiethnic and multiclass groups and sustaining economic growth.

Implications for Comparative Politics

In this section, we examine some of the exceptional political features of the Indian state and discuss their significance for comparative politics.

First, India is poor and multiethnic, yet it is a democracy. Most Indians value their citizenship rights and, in spite of poverty and illiteracy, exercise them with vigor. In the face of expectations of modernization theorists who posited that democracy and economic growth were usually found together, India stands out as an exception. Indian history shows that at independence, the country was struggling to tackle problems of nation-building, poverty, poor human development indicators, and managing a transition to democracy. Against all odds, the country became and remains today a thriving and vibrant democracy, an achievement that seems even more striking when compared to the authoritarian fate of other newly independent British colonies in Asia and Africa.

Second, unlike other multiethnic states such as Yugoslavia or the former Soviet Union, which disintegrated with the advent of democracy, the Indian state has managed to remain cohesive and stable, albeit with a few frayed edges in Punjab, Kashmir, and Assam. Indian politics thus offers a case study of the tempering influence of democracy on ethnic cleavages. Contrast the exclusionist rhetoric of Hindu nationalism during the BJP's tenure as an opposition party with its rhetoric as India's ruling party. In an attempt to stabilize a fractious multiparty coalition government, the BJP was forced to put contentious religious issues such as the conflict at Ayodhya on a back burner.

Third, as home to nearly a billion people with diverse cultural, religious, and linguistic ties, Indian democracy offers an arena for testing and studying various theories and dilemmas of comparative politics. For instance, one dilemma in comparative politics is how multiethnic democracies can develop a coherent institutional system that gives representation to diverse interests without degenerating into authoritarianism or total collapse. The history of the

Congress Party until the Indira Gandhi era offers an example of how one party successfully managed to unite diverse and multiple ethnic identities under one umbrella.

Fourth, theorists dealing with recent transitions to democracy in Latin America and Eastern Europe have puzzled over the question of what constitutes a consolidated democracy and how one achieves such consolidation. Here, a comparison of India with Pakistan, which became authoritarian for much of its fifty-year existence, would help us evaluate the role of historical junctures, leaders, and their interaction with institutions. Moreover, the Indian experience with authoritarianism during the Emergency era in the late 1970s, and the resurgence of democratic norms when Indira Gandhi was voted out by an angry populace, shows the importance of democratic procedures such as elections in consolidating democracy. Indian politics shows that the practice of democratic procedures leads to the imbibing of democratic norms by people over a period of time.

Fifth, comparativists have focused on the dilemma of whether democracy and social equity can be achieved simultaneously in poor countries. The case of Kerala, a state in southern India, shows that such simultaneity is possible. Kerala's life expectancy of 72 years and infant mortality rate of 17 per 1,000 live births is on a par with several developed countries.

Thus, the preceding discussion of critical junctures in Indian history highlights the central challenge of contemporary Indian politics: how to establish a coherent, legitimate government while using the power of this government to facilitate economic growth and equitable distribution. The former requires forming durable electoral coalitions without exacerbating political passions and ethnic conflicts. The latter, in turn, requires careful implementation of policies that simultaneously help entrepreneurs produce goods and ensure a fair distribution of the growth in production. How India is coping with these contemporary challenges is discussed in subsequent sections.

Section ❷   Political Economy and Development

India at the time of independence was largely a poor, agricultural economy. Although it still has a very large agricultural sector and considerable poverty continues, India today also has a fairly substantial industrial base and a vibrant middle class. Since the introduction of economic liberalization policies under Narasimha Rao's Congress government in 1991, all Indian governments have listed the liberalization of India's economy as one of their priorities. Before discussing what liberalization entails, why it has become a main priority, and some of its implications for Indian politics, it is important to review the development of the Indian political economy.

State and Economy

The Economy under British Rule

The Indian economy during British rule remained inefficient and largely stagnant. The British did not colonize India to develop its economy; instead they ruled India for their own economic and political interests. An example of this is that their control enabled the British to sell their relatively cheap manufactured goods to Indians, with significant long-term economic consequences: indigenous manufacturing, especially of textiles, and a whole generation of Indian artisans were ruined by the forced opening of the Indian market to British goods. Another example is the agricultural sector. During the colonial period the Indian economy was largely agricultural, with hundreds of millions of poor peasants, living in thousands of small villages, tilling the land with primitive technology and producing at a fairly low level. The British, along with Indian landlords, extracted extensive resources from Indian agriculture, mainly in the form of land revenues, land taxes, and tributes from Indian princes. However, they only reinvested a small portion of this surplus into improving agricultural production. Most resources were squandered through conspicuous consumption by Indian princes and landlords or used to run the expensive colonial government. The result of this mismanagement of resources was that Indian agricultural productivity—that is, the amount of wheat, rice, or other products produced from one unit of land—mostly stagnated in the first half of the twentieth century. Agricultural productivity in India was considerably lower in 1950 than in Japan or even China.

Some industry developed under colonial rule, but its scope was limited. The British wanted to sell their own manufactured goods to India in exchange for Indian raw materials, and because the British economy was more advanced, it was difficult for Indians to establish manufacturing enterprises that could compete successfully. The British did not provide any real protection to Indian industry, and in any case most Indians were too poor to generate a substantial demand for industrial products. These factors made it difficult for Indians to enter manufacturing as viable competitors. The Indian economy at independence from Britain in 1947 was thus relatively stagnant, especially in agriculture, but also in industry.

The Economy after Independence

One of the central tasks facing Indian leaders after 1947 was to stimulate the growth of the sluggish economy. During Nehru's rule India adopted a model of development largely based on private property, although government ownership of firms and government guidance to private economic activity were considerable. Nehru created a powerful planning commission that, following the Soviet model, made five-year plans for the Indian economy, outlining the activities in which government investment would be concentrated. Unlike the plans in communist party-states, the Indian plans also indicated priority areas for private entrepreneurs, who remained a powerful force in the Indian economy.

The Indian government also levied high tariffs on imports, arguing that new Indian industries, so long disadvantaged under colonial rule, required protection from foreign competitors. The government tightly regulated the start-up and expansion of private industries under the presumption that the government was a better safeguard of the public interest than private entrepreneurs. This government-planned private economy achieved mixed results. It helped India create an impressive industrial base but did not do much to help the poor; and even the protected industries turned out to be quite inefficient by global standards.

Nationalist in temperament, Nehru and the Congress Party leaders were suspicious of involving foreign investors in India's economic development. If Indian investors were to be encouraged, however, they needed support from the government and protection from the more advanced foreign competitors. Indian government thus undertook a series of coordinated economic activities. It made significant public-sector investments to create such heavy industries as steel and cement; it protected Indian entrepreneurs from foreign competition; where possible, it further subsidized these producers; and finally, it created elaborate rules and regulations controlling the activities of private producers. As a result, India developed a substantial industrial base over the next few decades.

To improve India's agriculture, the Congress leaders promised to redistribute land from landowners to tenants. Their rationale was that such a move would simultaneously weaken the former supporters of colonial government and improve the incentives of those who till the land to increase production. Although some of the largest landowners were indeed eliminated in the early 1950s, poor tenants and agricultural laborers received very little land. Unlike the communist government in China, India's nationalist government had neither the will nor the capacity to undertake radical property redistribution. Instead, most of the land remained in the hands of medium- to large-sized landowners. Many of these became part of the Congress machine in the countryside. This development further weakened the Congress Party's capacity to side with the rural poor and diluted its socialist commitments to the point of ineffectiveness.

The failure of land reforms led to a new agricultural strategy in the late 1960s known as the **green revolution**. Instead of addressing land redistribution, this strategy sought to provide those who owned land with improved seeds and access to subsidized fertilizer. However, because irrigation was essential for this strategy to succeed, and because irrigation was only assured to larger farmers in some parts of India, the success of the green revolution was uneven. Production increased sharply in some parts of India, such as the Punjab, but in other regions the poorer farmers often got left behind. Nevertheless, India grows enough food to feed its population, even exporting some, and has avoided the worst scenarios of mass starvation and famines.

Between 1950 and 1980 the Indian government facilitated what is best described as **state-led economic development**. This development policy consisted of an expansion of the public sector, protection of the domestic sector from foreign competition, and rules and regulations to control private-sector activity—a policy most closely resembling the one followed by Brazil. The nationalist rulers hoped to strengthen India's international position by promoting self-sufficient industrialization. To a great extent the Indian government succeeded in achieving this goal. Even though it is a poor country, by 1980, India was a major industrial power that produced its own steel, airplanes, automobiles, chemicals, military hardware, and most consumer goods. On the agricultural side, although land reforms failed, a revised agricultural strategy improved food production.

This pattern of state-led development insulated the Indian economy from the dynamics of the global economy while allying the Indian state with its business and landowning classes. The strategy resulted in modest economic growth, not as impressive as that achieved in Brazil, Mexico, or the Republic of Korea (South Korea) but better than the performance of such African countries as Nigeria. The main beneficiaries of this economic growth were business classes, medium and large landowning farmers, and political and bureaucratic elites. A substantial urban middle class also developed during this phase.

There were also problems related to state-led development. First, given the lack of competition, much of this industry was inefficient by global standards. Second, the elaborate rules and regulations controlling private economic activity encouraged corruption, as entrepreneurs bribed bureaucrats to get around the rules. And third, the focus on heavy industry directed a substantial portion of new investment into buying machinery rather than creating jobs. In addition, poor tenant farmers and landless laborers failed to gain much from this pattern of growth. As a result, a large proportion of India's population—as much as 40 percent—did not share in the fruits of this growth. Also, since population continued to increase, the number of very poor people increased substantially during these decades.

A number of global and national changes moved India toward **economic liberalization**. Throughout the 1980s socialist models of development came under attack globally; India did not escape this worldwide trend. Within India, the political and economic elites were increasingly dissatisfied with India's relatively sluggish economic performance, especially in comparison to dynamic East Asian economies. For example, while India's economy during the 1970s grew at the rate of 3.4 percent per year, South Korea's grew at 9.6 percent. These new elites, less nationalist and socialist than their 1950s counterparts, interpreted India's slow economic growth as a product of too many governmental controls and of India's relative insulation from the global economy. India's business and industrial classes had grown during the intervening decades; now they increasingly found government intervention in the economy more of a hindrance than a help. Last, the elites were realizing that increased production would have to be sold to buyers abroad because India's poor did not have enough income to consume the new products.

Since 1984, but especially since 1991, Indian governments have been more or less committed to the liberalization of India's economy. Liberalization has both a domestic and an international component. The government has sought to dismantle its own controls over private-sector economic activities, especially in industry, and to improve the economic performance of the relatively large public sector. With respect to the global economy, the attempt was made to attract more foreign investment and to buy and sell more products from other countries, especially Western countries.

India's economy did relatively well during the 1980s—growing at nearly 5 percent per year—especially in comparison to the dismal performance of many debt-ridden Latin American and African economies, such as Brazil and Nigeria. Some of this improved performance resulted from the economic liberalization that integrated India more and more into the global economy. However, a large part of it was based on increased borrowing from abroad, which followed a shift away from a fairly conservative fiscal policy. An expansionary fiscal policy, largely funded by foreign loans, was harmful because India's exports to other countries did not grow very rapidly. For example, India's exports during the 1980s grew at approximately 6 percent per year in comparison to 12 percent per year for both South Korea and China. As a result, the need to pay back foreign loans put enormous pressure on the government toward the end of the decade. India was forced to borrow even more foreign currencies from such international agencies as the International Monetary Fund (IMF), which generally lend money only on condition that a government dismantles protectionist barriers and other forms of economic regulation. The Indian government entered into an agreement with the IMF in 1991 to further liberalize India's economy. This external pressure was the last of the forces that propelled India to shift its economic direction.

Despite these external and internal changes, the Indian government's efforts to liberalize the economy have not been consistent, perhaps because it is difficult to make sharp policy changes in India's large, cumbersome democracy. India's leaders are often worried about the impact these policy changes will have on their future electoral prospects. For example, the liberalization package involved reduction in government spending, but many groups in society who benefit from government spending reacted negatively to this planned reduction. So when Rao's government sought to reduce subsidies on fertilizer in 1992, farmers across India protested and the government made a hurried policy retreat. Other policy changes also affect specific groups adversely. Organized Indian labor, for example, reacted negatively to government plans to improve the efficiency of the public sector through privatization and increased private-sector competition, an effort likely to involve significant layoffs. In 1998 government efforts to increase private-sector participation in the insurance industry led to heavy protests by labor unions, thereby slowing down the process. This reaction has made the Indian government hesitant to sell public-sector companies to private buyers and has resulted in a slow privatization process, especially when compared to countries in Latin America or Eastern Europe. Even Indian business continued to resist certain aspects of the government's economic program, especially those parts aimed at encouraging foreign investors and foreign goods that Indian industrialists find threatening.

The liberalization program affects India's industry more directly than its agriculture. During the 1990s, India's agricultural production made steady and modest progress. Weather patterns, especially the timeliness of seasonal rains (the monsoons), continue to have significant bearing on Indian agriculture. Government policy also matters but has been of secondary importance. Agricultural production in India is dominated by medium- and small-sized peasant farmers. (Even the largest landowners in India are small by global standards; anyone who owns 40 to 50 acres of land is considered a large landowner.) The majority of the land is cultivated by farmers owning between 5 and 30 acres of land. Medium-sized and even some small farmers tend to use tenants or hired laborers to till the land. Scattered across different regions of India, millions of these peasant farmers are themselves divided by language and local culture, and even within the same region, they often belong to different castes, live in dispersed villages, and lack frequent communication with each other. As a result, India's peasant farmers cannot be readily organized as a distinct and cohesive national-level political force. When their political presence is felt at the national level, it is through indirect means. More often, landowning agriculturalists tend to be a powerful political force in state and local governments.

As a result of the green revolution, the largest landowning peasant farmers have become quite well-off in some states of India, notably the Punjab and Haryana. Increased wealth has also enabled these peasant farmers to become a political force. When the national government attempts to implement policies that may affect these groups adversely—as, for example, the removal of fertilizer subsidies—they express their opposition through mass protests and demonstrations. In this way, although they are not a well-organized political force, these peasant farmers can block the implementation of liberalizing policies that entail curtailing public expenditures. Moreover, because of their large numbers, most political leaders must consider the interests of these well-off peasants to attract their electoral support.

Below the national level, landowning peasant farmers play an influential political role in most Indian states, especially in the green revolution states. In some other states, the landowning peasant status tends to overlap with caste status; for example, in parts of Uttar Pradesh and Bihar, medium-sized agriculturalists are often members of the "backward castes," or a caste status that is intermediate, somewhere between the high-caste Brahmins and the lowly scheduled castes. This overlap between middle-level economic and middle-level caste positions strengthens the identity of members of this group, who often vote as a bloc and thus become a significant political force. For example, in the state elections held in Uttar Pradesh in 1993, the backward castes in alliance with the scheduled castes elected a state-level government from their numbers and thus temporarily displaced Brahmins and other elite castes from ruling positions.

Within India, governmental and bureaucratic elites, the business and industrial classes, and large and medium sized landowning farmers are generally the privileged groups. Considering that India is a very poor country, many of these privileged groups are not that affluent by global standards. Moreover, these groups constitute India's ruling strata, and although there are differences and conflicts among them, for most purposes they manage to work together. They share many more interests and views with each other than they do with the bottom half of India's poor, the lower caste groups.

However, the BJP government that came to power in 1998 based much of its campaign on nationalist rhetoric. It gained support from those groups that feared liberalization, such as powerful Indian businesses whose monopolies were being threatened as well as public-sector employees who feared losing their jobs as a consequence of privatization. Once the BJP gained power, this rhetoric was toned down, though the extent of its commitment to liberalization still remains to be seen.

Social Welfare Policy

India's poor are a diverse, heterogeneous, and enormous social group constituting more than one-third of the population. Since independence, the percentage of poor has decreased from nearly two-thirds of the population to one-third. However, because of India's rapid population growth, this advance has not been sufficient to reduce the absolute number of poor, which increased from around 200 million in the 1950s to about 350 million by the late 1990s. The large number of poor has given India the sad distinction of having the largest concentration of poor people in the world. While nearly two-thirds of the Indian population live in rural areas, over three-fourths of the poor live in these areas. Moreover, though urban poverty only accounts for one-fourth of the poor population, the number of poor urban people, over 70 million, is staggering.

The truly poor of India tend to be the illiterate, women and children, and members of scheduled castes and tribes. They are often peasant farmers who own little land, agricultural tenants, landless laborers in villages, and those without regular jobs in cities who eke out a living on society's margins, often huddled into shantytowns or living on the streets of cities like Calcutta or Bombay. Although most of these poor remain politically unorganized, their political weight is felt in several ways. First, their sizable numbers impel many Indian politicians to adopt populist or socialist electoral platforms. Second, because many of the poor share a lower-caste status (especially within specific states), their group identity and united electoral behavior can have considerable impact on electoral outcomes. In some states, such as West Bengal and Kerala, there is a long history of radical politics; the poor in these states are well organized by communist or socialist parties, and they have periodically helped elect left-leaning governments. Third, the anger and frustration of the poor probably provides the raw material for many contemporary "movements of rage" within India. Although it is difficult to illustrate exactly how poverty leads the poor to participate in demonstrations, riots, or religious and other ethnic movements, the fact is that the participants in many incidents of political violence are the young and the poor.

The last point to be made in this discussion of the state and economy concerns government policies aimed at improving the lot of the poor. Over the years, Indian governments have tried different programs aimed at poverty alleviation, some of which have been successful, although most have not. Given the breadth of poverty in India, it is nearly impossible for any government to attempt a comprehensive welfare program. Redistribution of agricultural land to the poor was attempted but was mostly a failure compared to results in countries like China, where radical land redistribution was a key component of a successful assault on poverty. As a communist dictatorship, however, China could use government coercion to implement property redistribution. In some Indian states, such as West Bengal and Kerala, elected communist governments have also had some success in land redistribution. Overall, however, land reforms have proved to be nearly impossible in India's democracy.

India has very few Western-style welfare programs such as unemployment insurance, comprehensive public health programs, or guaranteed primary education. Some of these programs exist on paper but not in practice. The size of the welfare problem is considerable and would tax the resources of any government. No Indian government has ever attempted to provide universal primary education, although there has been considerable pressure from both Western and Indian observers to do so.

The one set of welfare-enhancing programs that has had modest success in India is public employment programs. These programs enable the national and state governments to allocate a portion of the public budget to such projects as the construction of roads or bridges, or the cleaning of agricultural waterways. Because the poor in villages are often unemployed for nearly half the year when there are no agriculture-related jobs, public employment programs become their off-season source of employment and income. Many surveys have demonstrated that such programs do help the poor, though the impact is not sufficient to improve their living conditions beyond the short run and the programs usually fail to reach the poorest. In the 1990s, however, under the impact of liberalization policies, government budgets came under considerable pressure, creating a squeeze on public investments, especially in such areas as public employment.

Society and Economy

Wealth and income present intense contrasts in Indian society. At the top are a small number of the incredibly affluent who have made their fortunes in basic business and industry. The personal wealth of the wealthiest of these—for example, Ambanis, Tatas, and Birlas, three of India's largest business houses—rivals the wealth of the richest business executives around the world. Below them, a much larger group, nearly 100 million Indians, are relatively well-off and have

the same standard of living as middle classes in many developed countries. By contrast, India's lower middle classes, some 500 million Indians, are mainly small farmers or urban workers, relatively poor by global standards; they barely eke out a living. And finally, at the bottom of the class structure are about 300 million people who are extremely poor and are concentrated mostly in India's thousands of villages as landless laborers or as the urban unemployed in shabby city slums.

Another aspect of Indian diversity is the contrast between primitive and sophisticated technologies of production. Low levels of literacy, poverty, and primitive technology characterize a good part of India's rural society. At the other end of the spectrum, India has a very sophisticated, technologically developed industrial sector that produces a variety of consumer products, military technologies, nuclear energy, and computers. For instance, the recent nuclear explosions were the culmination of years of scientific preparation.

So far the focus of this section has been on the state, social classes, and economy of India. In addition, the following issues need to be discussed to understand India's political economy: the growing size of the population; the status of women and children; the role of caste; and the role of intellectuals and the media in public life.

India's large population continues to grow at a relatively rapid pace. For better or for worse, it has been forecast that by 2005, India will become the largest country in the world, surpassing China. This suggests that India's population is growing at a faster rate than that of China. Since India already has more labor than it can use productively, rapid population growth hinders economic growth. Simply put, the more people there are, the more mouths there are to feed, and the more food and economic products must be produced to maintain people's standard of living, not to mention improve it.

Why should India's population continue to grow at such a rapid pace? The underlying causes are complex. The comparison with China again helps. The communist-led government of China has pursued very strict birth control policies—one child per family—since the late 1970s. In part, coercion was used to implement these policies, which did succeed in bringing down birthrates. India's democratic government, by contrast, has found it difficult to implement population control. Rates of population growth in some Indian states have slowed. For example, by 1995 the national rate of population growth was around 2 percent per year, while the rate in Kerala was 1.4 percent, close to that of China in the early 1990s. This statistic has important implications; it suggests that government coercion is not necessary to control population growth rates. What helped Kerala was one of the highest literacy rates, especially female literacy rates, in India. Whereas the national average female literacy rate in India is around 37 percent (the rate for males is around 65 percent), Kerala's female literacy rate is 87 percent. Since literate women are more likely to marry later, have more options in the workforce, have greater power in personal relationships, and use birth control, female literacy may be responsible for decreasing population growth in states like Kerala. If true, an important policy implication is that the education of women plays a significant role in bringing down the rates of population growth in countries like India.

India is one of the few countries in the world that has a lower percentage of females than males. This statistic is representative of the status of women in India. Despite the facts that India had a female prime minister, that about 10 percent of parliament members are women compared to just over 5 percent of the U.S. Congress, and that women have entered most professional jobs, the plight of the majority of Indian women is a dismal one. Indian society favors boys over girls, as evidenced in all social indicators from lower female literacy and nutrition rates to lower survival of female versus male infants. The favoring of males over females is reinforced through traditions, including the dowry system (the Hindu custom of giving the groom and his family a dowry, some form of assets, at the time of a daughter's wedding). These traditions, deeply rooted and slow to change, confine the majority of Indian women, particularly poor women, to a life of fewer opportunities than those available to men.

India also has the world's largest population of child labor. Children are employed widely, not only in agricultural labor but also in such urban enterprises as match-making and rug-weaving factories and selling tea or sweets at train stations. This is a problem, not only because children often work long hours under difficult conditions and at low wages, but because it deprives a segment of the population of an opportunity to develop through education and thus advance upward. The issue of child labor is closely related to India's failure to provide universal primary education. If school-age children were required to be in school, they could not be readily employed as full-time laborers. Many Indian elites argue that in their poor country, compulsory primary education is an unaffordable luxury. However, this argument is not very persuasive; many poor African countries have higher rates of primary school enrollments than does India. The more likely obstacle to universal primary education is India's caste system. Many upper-caste elites do not see lower-caste children as potentially their equals, and do not consider the issue of educating lower-caste children a priority. The deep-rooted cultural inequalities of India thus lock children into wage labor and out of schools. Child labor is directly linked to poverty and survival, since many poor families see larger numbers of children as a form of insurance. Yet, for most poor families, a larger family also means not being able to invest in each child's education and depending on their children's labor for survival. Thus child labor and poverty reinforce each other.

Caste issues pervade many other aspects of India's political and economic life. Not only does caste affect nearly all aspects of social life—social interactions, marriages, choice of occupation, social status, and political behavior—but it influences India's economy as well. First, by assigning people to specific occupations, it impedes the free movement of labor and talent. Although the link between caste and occupation has been weakening in India, especially in urban areas, it is nevertheless a very important principle on which employment is organized. And to the extent that caste inhibits the free movement of labor, it is an economic deficit for Indian society. Second, in the political arena, caste is a powerful force around which political groups and voting blocs coalesce. Although this is discussed in detail in Section 4, two side effects of this general tendency need to be mentioned here. Because caste is usually a local category, to a large extent Indian politics takes on a local and segmented quality. Related to this, caste cuts across class, making

Institutional Intricacies: *The Caste System*

Originally derived from the Portuguese word *castas*, today the word *caste* inevitably evokes images of a rigid hierarchy that characterizes Indian society. In reality, however, castes are less immutable and timeless categories than suggested by the popular image.

Historically, the **caste system** compartmentalized and ranked the Hindu population of the Indian subcontinent through rules governing various aspects of daily life, such as eating, marriage, and prayer. Sanctioned by religion, the hierarchy of caste is based on a conception of the world as divided into realms of purity and impurity. Each hereditary and endogamous group (that is, a group into which one is born and within which one marries) constitutes a *jati*, which is itself organized by *varna*, or shades of color. The four main varna are the **Brahmin**, or priestly, caste; the *Kshatriya*, or warrior

and royal, caste; the *Vaishyas*, or trading, caste; and the *Shudra*, or artisan, caste. Each of these *varna* is divided into many *jatis* that often approximate occupational groups (such as potters, barbers, and carpenters). Those who were not considered to be members of organized Hindu society—because they lived in forests and on hills rather than in towns and villages, or were involved in "unclean" occupations such as sweepers and leather workers—were labeled **untouchables**, outcastes, or **scheduled castes**.

Because each *jati* is often concentrated in a particular region, it is sometimes possible to change one's *varna* when one moves to a different part of the country by changing one's name or adopting the social customs of higher castes, for example, giving up eating meat. Some flexibility within the rigidity of the system has contributed to its survival across the centuries.

---

it difficult for labor, business, and other economic classes in India to act in a politically cohesive manner. Third, Indian government often uses caste as a basis for **reservations**, the Indian version of affirmative action. The government reserves some jobs, admissions into universities, and similar privileges for members of specific underprivileged castes. This has become a highly contentious issue in Indian politics. And last, those who suffer the most in India's caste system are those at the bottom of the caste hierarchy, namely, the untouchables. Nearly 10 percent of India's population, or some 90 million people, is categorized by the Indian census as belonging to the scheduled castes. Notwithstanding considerable government efforts, the social stigma suffered by members of this group runs deep in India. Because many untouchables are also poor, they suffer doubly: poverty and social ostracism lead to a lack of dignity.

A variety of social injustices abound in India's political economy. Nevertheless, it is important to note that there is widespread recognition of these injustices within India and that they are widely discussed and debated. India is a free and democratic country with a lively public culture. Although it is plagued by poverty, India has a significant middle class, many members of which are highly educated

and politically active. India's media, especially its newspapers and magazines, are as free as any in the world. They endlessly debate what is wrong with India and its politicians, and thus maintain the pressure for public action. This combination of a vocal intellectual stratum and a free press is a cherished one in India's democracy; its role, as well as the potential for the organization of the poor, sustains hope that pressures to address challenging social problems will be maintained within India.

India and the International Political Economy

After a prolonged colonial experience, nationalist India in the 1950s shunned economic links with the outside world. Although India pursued an active foreign policy as a leader of the **nonaligned bloc**, it was defensive in its economic contacts. A prolonged and successful nationalist movement helps explain both the urge within India to play a global political role and the urge to protect its economy from foreign influence. As mentioned earlier, India's political and economic elites favored protectionism in trade and sought to limit foreign investment. Although three decades of this policy helped generate an industrial base and domestic capitalism within India, at the same time several new problems arose. The subsequent efforts to liberalize and reintegrate the Indian economy into the world economy were in part aimed at dealing with such nagging problems. And these efforts have also run into some obstacles.

During the three decades of relatively autarkic development, powerful groups emerged that now have vested interests in maintaining the old order. To illustrate, many bureaucrats abused the system of government controls over private economic activities by accepting bribes to issue government licenses to start private businesses. Indian industry was often relatively inefficient because neither cheaper foreign goods nor foreign investors were readily allowed into India. Moreover, organized labor, especially in government-controlled factories, had a stake in maintaining inefficient factories because they offered a greater number of jobs. These well-entrenched groups resisted liberalization and threatened to throw their political weight behind opposition parties, making the ruling government hesitant to undertake any decisive policy shift.

The other significant component of India's performance in the international political economy concerns its regional context. India is a giant among the South Asian countries of Pakistan, Bangladesh, Sri Lanka, Nepal, and Bhutan, though its northern neighbor is an even bigger and more powerful giant, the People's Republic of China. Since 1947, India has experienced a fair amount of regional conflict: a war with China in 1962; three wars with Pakistan, the last of which was fought in 1971 and precipitated the break-up of Pakistan into the two states of Pakistan and Bangladesh; a military intervention into strife-torn Sri

Figure 1

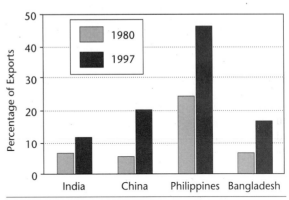

Exports of India and Its Trading Partners, 1980 and 1997

Source: *World Development Report 1998/99* (Washington D.C.: World Bank, 1998).

Lanka in the 1980s; and on-and-off troubled relations with Nepal. The net effect is that India has not developed extensive economic interactions with its neighbors. Figure 1 compares exports as a percent of GNP for India and its major trading partners; India's export quantity and rate of growth are relatively low. As nations increasingly look to their neighbors for trade and investment, the pressure on India and its neighbors to put aside their mutual conflicts for increased economic contact is likely to grow. Some move in this direction was already evident in the first half of the 1990s, especially toward China, but there is still a long way to go before South Asia develops an integrated zone of economic activity.

Section ❸ Governance and Policy-Making

During the last decades of the twentieth century, some of India's essential political institutions, such as political parties, the federal system, the bureaucracy, and the judiciary, did not function very effectively, partly because of the demands from India's diverse political groups. However, this ineffectiveness also resulted from the actions of India's top political leaders who, when threatened, sought to block access that challengers might have to powerful positions. This is one reason why India's important political party, the Congress, stopped conducting internal party elections for selecting party officers. Also, leaders below the national level, especially at the state level, tend now to be appointed from above rather than elected from below. Loyal rather than competent party members have similarly been favored for appointments in the bureaucracy and the judiciary. Such developments have contributed to the growing ineffectiveness of some of India's most important political institutions, further complicating the task of governing India's complex society.

Organization of the State

India is a democratic republic with a parliamentary and a federal system of government. The constitution adopted in 1950 created this system, and although there have been many profound changes since then in the distribution and the use of power, the basic character of India's political system has remained unchanged. Moreover, for much of this period India has been a stable, democratic country with universal suffrage and periodic elections at all levels—local, provincial, and national. This continuity and democratic stability are remarkable among developing countries. Note the contrast with such other countries as Brazil and Nigeria. To simplify a complex reality, the main explanation for this stability is that Indian democracy has accommodated many new power challenges while successfully repressing the most difficult ones. India's democratic institutions, though always under pressure, have achieved considerable resilience and established their authority to mobilize sufficient coercion to contain the most serious political threats.

India's constitution is a lengthy and, in contrast to the British one on which it is modeled, a written document that is periodically amended by legislation. Among its special features, three are worth noting. First, unlike many constitutions, the Indian constitution directs the Indian government to promote social and economic equality and justice. The constitution thus goes beyond stipulating formal procedures of decision-making and allocating powers among political institutions, and outlines the goals of politics and of the state. Although the impact of these constitutional provisions on government policies is limited, the provisions ensure that issues of welfare and social justice cannot be ignored. Second, the Indian constitution, similar to the U.S. constitution, provides for freedom of religion and makes India a secular state. This was an especially controversial issue in Indian politics

during the late 1990s because the ruling BJP was committed to establishing Hinduism as a state-sanctioned religion. And third, the Indian constitution allows for the temporary suspension of many democratic rights under conditions of emergency. These provisions were used, somewhat understandably, during wars with Pakistan or China. But they were also invoked, more disturbingly, to deal with internal political threats, most dramatically during the national Emergency from 1975 to 1977, when a politically vulnerable Indira Gandhi suspended many democratic rights and imprisoned her leading political opponents.

India's federal system of twenty-six states and several other special political units is relatively centralized. The central government controls the most essential government functions such as defense, foreign policy, taxation and public expenditures, and economic planning, especially industrial planning. State governments formally control such policy areas as agriculture, education, and law and order within the states. Because they are heavily dependent on the central government for funds in these policy areas, however, the power of the states is limited.

India's social, economic, and political diversity provides a challenging context within which to comprehend the functioning of Indian democracy. India is a parliamentary democracy designed on the British model. The parliament—in India known as the **Lok Sabha**, or House of the People—is the most significant political body. The leader of the political party with the most seats in the *Lok Sabha* becomes the prime minister, who nominates a cabinet, mostly from the ranks of the other elected members to parliament. The prime minister and the cabinet, along with permanent civil servants, control much of the government's daily functioning. The prime minister is the linchpin of the system because effective power is concentrated in that office, where most of the country's important policies originate. By contrast, the office of the president is largely ceremonial. In periodic national elections, 544 members of the *Lok Sabha*, the lower house of the bicameral parliament, are elected. The *Lok Sabha* is much more politically significant than the **Rajya Sabha**, the upper house. The prime minister governs with the help of the cabinet, which periodically meets to discuss important issues, including any new legislation that is likely to be initiated.

Individually, these cabinet members are the heads of various ministries—for example, Foreign Affairs or Industry—that direct the daily work of the government and make up the permanent bureaucracy.

The Executive

The President and the Prime Minister

The president is the official head of the state and is elected indirectly every five years by an electoral college, using a complex formula that ultimately involves elected representatives from both the national and state governments. In most circumstances, the president acts on the advice of the prime minister and is thus not a very powerful political figure in India. The presidency is a ceremonial office, symbolizing the unity of the country, and is supposedly above partisan politics. Under exceptional circumstances, however, especially when the selection of a prime minister becomes a complex issue, the president can play an important political role. For example, in the 1998 election there was a "hung parliament" with no party gaining a clear majority. The president then requested the party with the largest percentage of votes, the BJP, to show that it could muster enough allies to form a government.

The prime minister and the cabinet are the most powerful political figures in India. Because they represent the majority party in parliament, the passage of a bill is not always as complicated a process as it can be in a presidential system, especially one with a divided government. The prime minister and the cabinet also head various ministries, so that after legislation is passed, they oversee its implementation. In practice, the permanent bureaucracy, especially the senior and middle-level bureaucrats, are truly responsible for policy implementation. Nevertheless, as in most parliamentary systems, such as those in Britain, Germany, and Japan, there is considerable overlap in India between the executive and the legislative branches of the government, creating a greater degree of centralization of power than at first seems evident.

The issue of who will become the prime minister has been a rather dramatic and initially infrequent issue in India's political life. Between 1947 and 1984, except for a few brief interludes, India had only two

prime ministers: Nehru and Indira Gandhi (see Table 1). This is nearly unique among democracies; it underlines the powerful hold that the Nehru-Gandhi family had on India's political imagination, including the imagination of poor, illiterate Indians. Since then, however, there has been a more rapid turnover. Rajiv Gandhi, Indira Gandhi's son, succeeded his mother after her assassination in 1984. When he lost power four years later, there were two attempts to form non-Congress governments under the leadership of V. P. Singh and Chandra Shekhar. Factionalism within the loose coalitions that constituted these non-Congress governments broke out, however, and curtailed these attempts. As Rajiv Gandhi campaigned in a bid to return to power, he too was assassinated. Subsequently, the Congress Party returned to power in 1990 with Narasimha Rao as prime minister. While this Congress victory lasted six years, it was followed by a thirteen-day BJP government under the prime ministership of A. B. Vajpayee and two short-lived United Front prime ministerships under H. D. Deve Gowda and I. K. Gujral. In 1998 the BJP returned to power, with Vajpayee again prime minister. The BJP government's term in office again turned out to be short-lived because of internal factionalism.

The method of selecting a prime minister in India is fairly complex. The original choice of Nehru was a natural one, given his prominent position in the nationalist movement. The choice of Indira Gandhi was less obvious. She was chosen to head the Congress Party by a group of prominent, second-tier party leaders. Her choice reflected several considerations, the most important of which was her national name recognition and its ability to attract the popular vote. Although the process of passing power from a father to a daughter may appear rather feudal—to some extent it is—there is valid electoral rationale for such a choice in India. A similar logic prevailed when Rajiv Gandhi was chosen by party elites to succeed his mother. Rajiv Gandhi benefited from the wave of sympathy generated by his mother's assassination, and he led the Congress Party back to power in 1984 with a handsome electoral majority.

Following Rajiv Gandhi's assassination, the Nehru-Gandhi family line appeared to have reached an end, since Rajiv Gandhi was married to an Italian, Sonia Gandhi, and their children were too young to enter politics. In 1991, Narasimha Rao was brought back as an "elder statesman," nonthreatening and acceptable to competing factions within the Congress Party. He was the first prime minister from the south of India; all the previous heads of state had been from the north. Both subsequent United Front prime ministers, Gowda and Gujral, were compromise candidates who lacked the personality and power to manage their disparate coalitions. In 1998 the Congress Party attempted to resurrect its fortunes by choosing Sonia Gandhi to head their party. This effort appeared quixotic initially. However, the BJP's nationalist appeal faded in 1998 as bread-and-butter issues became politically salient. The Sonia Gandhi–led Congress stepped into this vacuum, opening the possibility that the political rule of the Nehru-Gandhi family may continue.

The Cabinet

The prime minister chooses the cabinet, mostly from among the party's elected members to parliament. Seniority, competence, and personal loyalty are the top criteria that any prime minister takes into account when choosing the cabinet ministers. Regional and caste representation at the highest level of government must also be considered. During Indira Gandhi's rule, personal loyalty was critical in the choice of senior ministers. Rajiv Gandhi, by contrast, put a high premium on competence, which unfortunately he equated with youth and technical skills at the expense of political experience. Since Vajpayee was able to form a government only with the help of many smaller parties, the heads of these parties had to be accommodated, producing an eclectic, disparate cabinet. Given his party's narrow power base, Vajpayee was less free than his Congress Party predecessors to select a personally loyal cabinet. Rather, he needed to include all those with power in one region or another of India, while taking into account issues of competence and the demand for representation by different castes, as well as ensuring that potential challengers are either coopted or kept at bay.

The Bureaucracy

The prime minister and cabinet ministers run the government in close collaboration with senior civil servants. Each senior minister oversees what is often a sprawling bureaucracy, staffed by some very competent, overworked, senior civil servants and by many not so competent, underworked, lowly bureaucrats, well known for taking long tea breaks while they stare at stacks of unopened files.

Because political leaders come and go, whereas senior civil servants stay, many civil servants possess a storehouse of knowledge and expertise that makes them very powerful. The higher-level civil servants in India reach their positions after considerable experience within the government. They enter the service, formally known as the **Indian Administrative Service** (IAS), at a relatively young age, usually in their early twenties, by passing a very competitive general exam. Some of India's most talented young men and women were attracted to the IAS during the 1950s and the 1960s, reflecting the prestige that service in national government used to enjoy in Indian society. This attraction of the IAS has declined, however, and many talented young people now also go into engineering or business administration, or if possible, leave the country for better opportunities abroad. Government services have become tainted as areas of corruption have developed and the level of professionalism within the IAS has eroded, mainly because politicians prefer loyalty over merit and seniority when making promotions. Nevertheless, the IAS continues to recruit very talented young people, many of whom mature into dedicated senior civil servants and who still constitute the backbone of the Indian government.

The IAS produces India's elite bureaucrats, those who occupy a critical but relatively thin layer at the top of India's sprawling bureaucracy. The competence of these elite bureaucrats is a central reason why India is moderately well governed. Below the IAS, unfortunately, the level of talent and professionalism drops rather sharply. Within each ministry at the national level, and in many parallel substructures at the state level, the bureaucracy in India is infamous for corruption and inefficiency. These problems contribute to the gap that exists in India between good policies made at the top and their poor implementation at the local level.

Other State Institutions

The Military and the Police

The Indian military, with more than a million well-trained and armed people, is a highly professional organization that enjoys the respect of Indian society. Unlike the militaries in many other developing countries—say, Brazil and Nigeria—the Indian military has never intervened directly in politics. This has to do with the fact that India is a relatively well-functioning democracy, and with the character of the Indian military. Over the years the continuity of constitutional, electoral politics and a relatively apolitical military have come to reinforce and strengthen each other. Civilian politicians provide ample resources to the armed forces and, for the most part, let them function as a professional organization. The armed forces, in turn, obey the orders of democratically elected leaders, and although they lobby to preserve their own interests, for the most part they stay out of the normal tumble of democratic politics.

Since the 1970s two factors have weakened this well-institutionalized separation of politics and military. First, during Indira Gandhi's rule, loyalty to political leaders became the key criterion for securing top military jobs. This policy tended to politicize the military and narrow the separation between politics and military. Second, there were growing political problems in India, especially regional and ethnic demands for secession (see Section 4). As these demands became more intense in some states, notably in Kashmir, and as those making the demands armed themselves, occasionally with the help of India's often hostile neighbor Pakistan, the Indian government called in the armed forces. However, soldiers are not trained to resolve political problems; rather, they are trained to use force to secure compliance from reluctant political actors. As a result, not only have democratic norms and human rights been violated in India, but the distance between politics and the military has narrowed further.

A similar trend toward politicization and deprofessionalization has occurred in India's sprawling police services, but with a difference. The Indian police organization was never as professionalized as the Indian armed forces, and the police services in India come under the jurisdiction, not of the central government, but of various state governments. Because state governments are generally less well run than the national government, the cumulative impact is that the Indian police are no longer apolitical civil servants. State-level politicians regularly interfere in police personnel issues, and police officers in turn regularly oblige the politicians who help them. The problem is especially serious at lower levels, where police officials interact with members of society. The image of the average police officer in most of India is not positive. The police are rightly viewed as easily bribed and often allied with criminals or politicians. In some states, such as Bihar and Uttar Pradesh, police often take sides in local conflicts instead of acting as neutral arbiters or enforcers of laws. Thus they tilt the power balance in favor of dominant social groups such as landowners or upper castes or the majority religious community, the Hindus.

In addition to the regular armed forces and the state-level police forces, there are paramilitary forces of nearly half a million men. These troops are organized under various names and are controlled by the national government. As Indian politics became more turbulent in the 1980s, these paramilitary forces steadily increased; their expansion reflects the Indian government's growing concern with maintaining internal law and order. But because the national government calls on the regular armed forces only as a last resort in the management of internal conflicts and because the state-level police forces are not very reliable, these paramilitary forces are viewed as a way to maintain order, albeit a very expensive solution. A large, sprawling, and relatively ineffective police service continues to remain a problematic presence in Indian society. Also, as terrorists or "freedom fighters" have become better armed, especially in Kashmir, paramilitary forces have proven inadequate to contain them.

The Judiciary

An independent judiciary is another component of India's state system. But unlike in Britain where the judiciary's role is limited by parliamentary sovereignty, Indian courts are haunted by a fundamental contradiction embedded in the Indian Constitution

Institutional Intricacies: *The Executive Versus the Judiciary*

Over the years, the Supreme Court has clashed head-to-head with the parliament as a result of the contradiction between principles of parliamentary sovereignty and judicial review that is embedded in India's constitution. For instance, during the early years of independence, the courts overturned state government laws to redistribute land from landlords (zamindars), saying that the laws violated the zamindars' fundamental rights. In retaliation, the parliament passed the first of a series of amendments to the constitution to protect the executive's authority to promote land redistribution. But matters did not end there. The Supreme Court responded by passing a judgment stating that the parliament did not have the power to abrogate the fundamental rights. In 1970 the court also invalidated the bank nationalization bill and a presidential order abolishing privy purses (including titles and privileges of former rulers of India's princely states).

In retaliation, the parliament passed a series of amendments that undercut the Supreme Court's rulings, thus moving the power balance toward parliamentary sovereignty. The Supreme Court responded that the court still reserved for itself the discretion to reject any constitutional amendments passed by parliament on the grounds that the amendments could not change the constitution's "basic structure". During the Emergency period, the parliament passed yet another amendment that limited the Supreme Court's judicial review to procedural issues. The Janata government in the post–Emergency era, however, reversed these changes, thus reintroducing the tension between the executive and judiciary.

Since the 1980s the courts have increasingly functioned as a bulwark for citizens by protecting their civil liberties from state coercion. For instance, since 1993 it has enforced a policy of compensating victims of violence while in police custody. In 1985, the Supreme Court upheld a verdict finding two people guilty of dowry murder and sentenced them to life imprisonment. In the mid-1980s the Supreme Court clashed with parliament on its interpretation of personal law, now referred to as the Shah Bano case. In India, in keeping with a secular ethos, personal law falls under the purview of religion, although an individual can choose secular alternatives. However, this recourse is circumscribed: a woman married under religious law cannot seek divorce or alimony under secular law. Neither Muslim nor Hindu personal law entitles women to alimony. The British colonial government had passed a law entitling destitute divorced women to maintenance by their husbands. Shah Bano, a destitute 75-year-old woman abandoned and later divorced by her husband, filed for maintenance under this law. The Supreme Court upheld Shah Bano's right to maintenance on the grounds that secular laws transcended personal law (religious law). The parliament, succumbing to pressures from religious leaders, passed a bill excluding Muslim women from the purview of secular laws.

The battle between the executive and the judiciary has taken a toll on the autonomy of the courts. The judiciary has been affected by the general malaise of institutional decay that has affected Indian politics over the years. The backlog of cases has grown phenomenally, while expeditious judgment of cases has declined dramatically.

---

between the principles of parliamentary sovereignty and judicial review. Over the years, the judiciary and the parliament have clashed, with the former trying to preserve the constitution's basic structure and the latter asserting its rights to amend the constitution. The judiciary comprises an apex court at the national level, high courts in states, and lower courts in districts.

The apex institution is the Supreme Court, comprising a chief justice and seventeen other judges, appointed by the president, but as in most matters of political significance in India, only on the advice of the prime minister. Once appointed, the judges cannot be removed from the bench until retirement at age sixty-five. The caseload on the Supreme Court, as on much of the Indian legal system, is extremely heavy, with a significant backlog. The main political role of the Supreme Court is to ensure that legislation conforms with the intent of the constitution. Because the Indian constitution is very detailed, the need for interpretation is not as great as in many other countries.

Nevertheless, there are real conflicts, both within the constitution and in India's political landscape, that often need to be adjudicated by the Supreme Court.

For example, the constitution simultaneously protects private property and urges the government to pursue social justice. Indian leaders have often promulgated socialist legislation such as requiring the redistribution of agricultural land. Legislation of this nature is necessarily considered by the Supreme Court because it potentially violates the right to private property. Many Supreme Court cases have involved the conflict between socialistically inclined legislation and basic constitutional rights. Cases involving other politically significant issues—for instance, rights of religious minorities such as Muslims and the rights of women in society—also periodically reach the Supreme Court for decisions.

Like many other Indian political institutions, the Supreme Court lost much of its autonomy in the 1980s and 1990s. The process began during Indira Gandhi's rule when she argued that the court was too conservative and an obstacle to her socialist program. To remedy this shortcoming, she appointed many pliant judges, including the chief justice. The Supreme Court itself more or less complied with her wishes during the two years of Emergency (1975–1977), when the political and civil rights of many Indians were violated. Unfortunately, this episode cost the Supreme Court considerable prestige as a neutral arbiter in India's state system. No such dramatic instance of a politicized Supreme Court has recurred since the late 1970s. Nevertheless, India's highest court, although still a political institution of some significance, is by no means as independent an institution as the founders of India's state system may have intended. However, that the Supreme Court still functions as a bulwark of sorts for citizens against state invasiveness is evident from many landmark judgments in defense of civil rights.

Subnational Government

Under its federal system, the balance of power between the central and state governments in India varies according to time and place. In general, the more popular the central government and the prime minister, the more the states feel obligated to the central government. During Nehru's, and especially during Indira Gandhi's rule, the states were often quite constrained. By contrast, a weaker central government, as for example the BJP-led alliance that took office in 1998, enlarges the room for state governments to maneuver. When state governments are run by political parties other than the national ruling party—and this is often true in contemporary India—there is considerable scope for central-state conflict. For example, a popular communist government in West Bengal has often disagreed with the national government in New Delhi, charging it with discriminatory treatment in the allocation of finances and other centrally controlled resources.

Below the national government, many different parties govern India's twenty-six states. The federal system allows for this political diversity, though not without political conflict between the central and state governments. Political power at state levels is held by the leader of the party with a majority of parliament seats. These leaders formulate policies that are implemented by a permanent bureaucracy. The quality of government below the national level is often poor, contributing to flaring regional and ethnic conflicts.

While the political parties at the national and the state levels may differ, the formal structure of the state governments parallels that of the national government. The chief minister of each state heads the state government; the office of the chief minister of a state thus parallels the office of the prime minister nationally. The chief minister is the leader of the majority party (or the party with most seats) in the lower house of the state legislature. As the prime minister does, the chief minister appoints cabinet ministers who head various ministries staffed by a state-level, permanent bureaucracy. In lieu of a president, each state has a governor, appointed by the national president. The governors, like the president, are supposed to serve on the advice of the chief minister, but in practice, they often become politically powerful, especially in states where the national government is at odds with the state government or where state governments are unstable. The governors can dismiss elected state governments and proclaim temporary presidential rule if they determine state governments to be ineffective. When this happens, the elected government is dissolved and the state is governed from New Delhi until fresh elections are called and a new government is elected. Although intended to be a sensible constitutional option, this provision has unfortunately often been used by an intrusive national government to achieve political ends in one state or another. For example, following the Ayodhya incident described in Section 1, the Supreme Court ruled that the BJP had acted illegally, a decision that allowed Narasimha Rao to dismiss four state governments governed by the BJP. When new elections were held in these four states in November 1993, the BJP returned to power in only one of the four states, contributing to long-term acrimony between the BJP and the Congress Party.

The power struggle between the central government and the states is an ongoing one. With many Indian states inhabited by people who share different histories and cultures, including language, and with political parties in power in the national government that differ from those in the states, the central-state conflicts become multidimensional, couched in the rhetoric of relative jurisdictions but fueled by substantial political and ethnic conflicts. Note that despite the formal division of power between the central and state governments, India's central government is really quite powerful.

Below state governments are district, city, and village governments. In 1992 the government added an amendment to the constitution that created the legal framework for all states to implement the Panchayat Raj (local self-government) Institutions, though models were allowed to differ between states. The primary role of the **panchayats** was envisioned as being in the areas of development, planning, and implementation of programs for economic development and social justice. While it is still too early to judge the effectiveness of these institutions, the establishment of the panchayats was an attempt to create greater local involvement in government and a direct effort to improve the quality of local governance. Given India's size, it is not surprising that the specific forms, quality of personnel, and effectiveness of these local governments vary greatly. Usually, however, most local governments have both elected and bureaucratic personnel. None of these subgovernments is a policy-making body; instead, policy is made at the national and state levels and these lower levels are responsible for implementation. Thus considerable resources pass

through these institutions, and even though local governments seldom enjoy formal discretion over how these resources are allocated, there is ample room for misuse. Local political elites, bureaucrats, and other local "big men" often collude as they decide the location of projects, who gets a contract, or who gets jobs on public projects, ensuring themselves a healthy share of the public money. This is why many local governments in India tend to be corrupt and ineffective. There are some exceptions. In the state of West Bengal, a reform-oriented, leftist government helped improve the functioning of local governments. But for the most part, local governments in India languish and waste resources. City streets are not kept clean; potholes do not get filled; irrigation canals do not get desilted; wells are located in the backyards of village "big men"; and rural schools are so poorly built that they leak as soon as the monsoons start.

The Policy-Making Process

Major policies in India are made at the highest level of government, in New Delhi, the nation's capital. As mentioned earlier, the prime minister and the senior cabinet ministers are generally responsible for initiating new policies and related legislation. Behind the scenes, senior civil servants in each ministry, as well as in such specific cross-ministry offices as the prime minister's secretariat or the planning commission, play a critical role in identifying problems, synthesizing available data, and presenting alternative solutions and their implications to political leaders. After decisions have been made at the highest level, many of them require new legislation. Since the prime minister usually has a clear majority in the parliament, passage of most legislation is assured in India, except in extremely controversial areas. Rather, the real policy drama in India occurs during the early process, when major bills are under consideration, and then during the process of implementation. To understand these processes, one must understand how interests get organized and find representation.

Examples of several specific policies will help clarify these issues. First, consider economic liberalization policies. These policies represented a major economic change, and they were decided at the highest level of government, involving only a handful of senior ministers and bureaucrats. To reach these decisions, however, a fairly complex set of political activities took place. For example, the decision-makers needed to consult some of the most important interest groups, such as associations of Indian businessmen or representatives of multinational organizations like the World Bank or the IMF. Others, including those who might be adversely affected, needed to be heard; organized labor, for example, might call a one-day general strike (it actually did) to warn the government that any attempt to privatize the public sector would meet considerable resistance. Newspapers, magazines, and intellectuals also expressed their support or opposition publicly. Then political parties got into the act. Members of the ruling party, the Congress in this case, did not necessarily support the political thinking of their own leaders at the early stage; rather, they worried about the political implications of policies, both for intraparty power struggles and for future elections. Opposition parties, in turn, worried about the interests of their constituencies and adopted a more or less principled stand toward the new policies under consideration—that is, for, against, or somewhere in between. All of these pulls and pushes modified the policy that the government eventually adopted.

After policies have been adopted, their implementation is far from assured. Again, continuing with the liberalization example, some aspects of the new policy package proved easier to implement than others. Changing the exchange rate (the value of the Indian rupee in relation to such currencies as the U.S. dollar) was relatively easy to implement because both the policy decision and its implementation require the actions of only a handful of politicians and bureaucrats. By contrast, the attempts to simplify the procedures for Indian or foreign business executives to create new business enterprises proved more complicated. Implementation of such policies involves layers of bureaucrats, most of whom at one time benefited from the control they exercised over entrepreneurs. When forced to relinquish this control, many of them dragged their feet and, where possible, sabotaged the newly simplified procedures.

Another example is the policies aimed at improving the standard of living for the Indian poor. Since the 1960s the national government has attempted to redistribute agricultural land and provide public works programs to help India's rural poor. The national government set the broad outlines for land reforms and allocated funds for public works programs; but because both of these measures primarily influence rural and agricultural life within the jurisdiction of state governments, further refinement of these policies, as well as their implementation, was left to the states. State governments vary, both in terms of the class coalitions and political parties that rule within them and in terms of the quality of their bureaucracies. The result is that the implementation of antipoverty policies within India has been quite uneven.

Land redistribution involves taking land from well-off, powerful landlords and redistributing it to poor tenants or agricultural laborers. This is a highly controversial process, requiring some combination of forceful actions by state governments and the organization of the poor beneficiaries. Generally, attempts at land redistribution have been relatively unsuccessful in most Indian states because the interests of landowning classes are well-represented and state-level bureaucrats often have close links to these landowning groups. Partial exceptions to these trends are found in the states of Kerala and West Bengal, where communist state governments and the well-organized poor have made some progress in land reform.

Attempts to generate extra employment for the rural poor through public works projects (such as road construction and canal cleaning) have been somewhat more successful than land redistribution policies because they do not involve any direct confiscation of property. The main issues in the implementation of these policies are the quality of projects chosen, whether they target the poor, and how honestly they are completed. Because the quality of local governments in implementing national policies varies, although rarely is it very high, considerable resources assigned to poverty alleviation programs have been wasted. Public works policies have been most effectively implemented in the states of Maharashtra and West Bengal, where there is considerable political pressure from caste or class politics, and in some southern states, where the quality of local bureaucracy is somewhat better.

To review, the policy-making process in India, though relatively centralized, takes into account various interests and frequently produces well-developed policies. By contrast, the process of implementation is quite decentralized and relatively ineffective. What often start out as sound policy ideas and positive inten- tions do not always come to fruition, both because policies are diluted as they get redefined at the state level and because of lackluster implementation.

Section ④ Representation and Participation

Over the years, India has become a participatory democracy, as previously excluded social groups such as the poor, the landless, and backward castes entered the political arena and used their influence to shape the political process. In the early years of independence, the Congress Party mobilized most groups. However, in recent years there has been a proliferation of political parties that have appealed to the Indian masses on ethnic grounds (particularly caste and religion), a trend initiated by Indira Gandhi. Simultaneously, the adoption of the democratic idea in the institutional sphere led to an explosion of social movements in civil society. Poor women have marched on the streets of Andhra Pradesh demanding prohibition of the sale of liquor (because of the economic toll it inflicts and its role in domestic violence), while in Maharashtra poor tribals have protested their displacement by the construction of large dams. The democratic idea is so insidious that today thousands of nongovernmental organizations function in the country representing causes ranging from welfare issues to environment to human rights. Some social movements have transformed themselves into political parties, while others have remained defiant of the system.

The Legislature

A good place to begin the discussion of representation and participation in a democracy is with the legislature, one arena in which diverse groups seek representation. As mentioned in Section 3, the Indian parliament consists of a two-house legislature, the *Rajya Sabha* and the *Lok Sabha*. The *Lok Sabha* at the national level and the various legislative assemblies at the state level provide such arenas in India. With considerable overlap between the executive and the legislative branches of government, legislative bodies do not have a direct or significant role in policy-making.

Nevertheless, election to a legislature is still much sought after in India, for two reasons. First, because a prime minister or a chief minister of a state needs the support of a majority in the legislature to acquire and maintain a position of leadership, legislatures hold a significant place in the pyramid of power. Second, those who become members of this power structure, although unable to influence policies directly, achieve considerable status, personal access to resources, and influence over allocations of government monies and contracts within their constituencies.

Elections to the *Lok Sabha* are supposed to be held at least every five years but, as in other parliamentary systems, the prime minister may choose to call elections earlier. India is currently divided into 544 electoral districts of roughly equal population, each of which elects and sends one representative to the national parliament. Those who contest elections generally contest them as nominees of one of the major political parties; that is, they contest them on a party ticket, with the support of one of the parties. Elections in India are won or lost mainly by parties, especially by party leaders, so most legislators are beholden to party leaders for securing a party ticket. Success in elections, therefore, does not depend on an independent power base but on a party whose leader—or, occasionally, whose programs—appeals to the populace. When these victorious legislators reach the *Lok Sabha*, they often fall in line with the goals of the party leadership, especially if the leadership is strong (in other words, has proven its capacity to appeal to voters).

The main business of the *Lok Sabha* is to pass new legislation as well as to debate the pros and cons of government actions. Most new legislation is introduced by the government, although there are opportunities for independent members to introduce bills. After the political and bureaucratic elite introduce new legislation, as in most parliamentary systems, the new bills are formally announced and then assigned to parliamentary committees for detailed study and discussion. The committees report the bills back to the *Lok Sabha* for debate, amendments, and preliminary votes. Then the bills go to the *Rajya Sabha*, the upper house. Most members of the *Rajya Sabha* are elected indirectly by state legislatures. This is not a very powerful body in India; it mostly accepts bills that have been passed by the *Lok Sabha*. After any final modifications by the *Rajya Sabha*, the bills come back for a third reading, after which they are finally voted on in both houses and eventually forwarded to the president for approval.

To understand why the *Lok Sabha* in India does not play a significant independent role in policy-making, keep in mind that (1) new legislation is generally introduced by a small group of government leaders; (2) most legislators, especially those belonging to the Congress Party, feel politically beholden to party leaders; and (3) all parties use party whips to ensure voting along party lines. One unfortunate implication of parliament's relative ineffectiveness is that its social composition does not have direct policy consequences. In other words, whether members of parliament are business executives or workers, men or women, members of upper or lower castes, is not likely to lead to dramatic policy shifts within India. The policy-making process is relatively centralized, and various interest groups influence it through channels other than the legislature. Nevertheless, dramatic shifts in social composition are bound to influence policy, and even if marginal shifts have little impact on policy, many groups in society derive satisfaction from having one of their own in the parliament.

The typical member of parliament in India tends to be a male university graduate between forty and sixty years of age. Over the years, there have been changes in the social composition along some criteria but not others. For example, an average legislator in the 1950s was likely to be a man of urban background, often a lawyer and a member of the higher castes. However, nearly half the members of parliament now come from rural areas, and many have agricultural backgrounds. Members of the middle castes (the so-called backward castes) are also well represented today. These changes reflect some of the broad shifts in the distribution of power in Indian society. By contrast, the proportion of women and of poor, lower-caste individuals in the parliament remains low.

Political Parties and the Party System

Political parties and elections are areas where much of the real drama of Indian politics occurs. Parties in control of a majority of seats in the national or state parliaments form the national or state governments and control government resources. Parties thus devote substantial political energy to contesting and winning elections. Since independence, the party system has evolved from one dominated by the Congress Party to one in which the party's role has been significantly challenged (see Table 2).

What began as nearly a one-party system has evolved into a real multiparty system, with three main

Table 2

Major Party Election Results

	1991		1996		1998	
	% of Popular Vote	Seats	% of Popular Vote	Seats	% of Popular Vote	Seats
Congress (I)	37.3	225	29	143	25.4	140
BJP & Allies	19.9	119	24	193	36.2	250
Janata	10.8	55	Joined with United Front		Joined with United Front	
United Front	—	—	31	180	20.9	98
Communists[a]	—	48	Joined with United Front		Joined with United Front	

[a] Includes both the CPM and the CPI.

Source: *India Today,* July 15, 1991, 40–55, *Economic Times* Web site; and *India Today,* March 16, 1998.

political tendencies: centrist, center-left and center-right. Within this framework there are at least four potentially significant national parties and many regional parties competing for power. The four parties with significant national presence are the Congress (I); the Janata Party; the BJP; and the Communist Party of India (Marxist), or the CPM. Whereas the CPM is a left-leaning party and the BJP is a religious, right-leaning one, both Congress (I) and the Janata are more or less centrist parties. During the 1996 elections the Janata Party joined forces with the CPM and other smaller parties to form the United Front and has been able to form two short-lived left-leaning governments.

The Congress Party

The Congress (I), usually referred to as the Congress, was India's premier political party until the 1990s. Many aspects of the Congress have already been discussed because it is impossible to analyze Indian politics without referring to the role of the Congress Party. To briefly summarize, the Indian National Congress, under the leadership of Mahatma Gandhi, Nehru, and others, spearheaded India's nationalist movement during the 1920s and 1930s. After independence, the Congress Party needed the electoral support of a majority of Indians, most of whom were poor, low-caste village dwellers. Because they were new to the democratic system, most of these underprivileged, uneducated poor citizens tended in the early years to follow the political lead of village "big men"—local influential people in villages and often men of high caste and means. The Congress Party thus built its electoral network by establishing a patronage system with such "big men" across India; the "big men" would mobilize electoral support for the Congress Party during elections and, once in power, the Congress Party would channel government resources to them further enhancing their local position and assuring their support. This patronage system (some call it machine politics) worked quite well for the Congress Party for nearly two decades. Even when electorally successful, however, this strategy bequeathed internal contradictions to the INC. The great, pro-poor Congress Party of India, with a socialist shell, came to be internally dominated by high-caste, wealthy Indians.

By the early 1950s, with Nehru at its helm, Congress was the unquestioned ruling party of India. Over the years, especially since the mid-1960s, this hegemony came to be challenged. By the time Indira Gandhi assumed power in 1966, India's old Congress Party had begun to lose its political sway and anti-colonial nationalism was fading. The spread of democratic politics had mobilized many poor, lower-caste citizens who depended less and less on village "big men" for political guidance. As a result, numerous regional parties started challenging Congress's monopoly on power. Weather-related food shortages in the mid-1960s also hurt the Congress Party in the 1967 elections.

Indira Gandhi sought to reverse the decline in Congress's electoral popularity through mobilizing India's vast majority, the poor, by promising "alleviation of poverty" as the core of her political program. This promise struck a popular chord, propelling Indira Gandhi to the top of India's political pyramid. Her personal success, however, came at a cost to the Congress Party. The old Congress split into two parties, with one branch, the Congress (O), dying and leaving the other, Congress (I)—the "I" standing for Indira—to inherit the position of the old undivided Congress. Nevertheless, the Congress Party formed the governments from independence to 1989, with only one interlude during which the Janata Party formed the government, during 1977–1980. Since 1989 the government has been formed by the Janata (1989–1991), the United Front (1996–1998), and the BJP (1998), with Congress heading the government from 1991 to 1996.

Prior to Indira Gandhi's prime ministership, rank-and-file party members elected the lowest-level Congress Party officers, who in turn elected the officers at higher levels of the party organization, up to the position of the party leader, who was the prime minister. In effect, the prime minister was elected from below and by the party. Indira Gandhi reversed this bottom-up party structure. She gained immense personal popularity by populist appeals to the masses and subsequently created a top-down party in which party officers were appointed by the leaders. With some modifications, including some limited internal party elections, this is basically how the contemporary Congress Party is organized. The top-down structure enables the leaders to control the party, but it is a major liability when grassroots support is necessary. As the nation's oldest party, the Congress continues to attract substantial electoral support. However, if this support ever declined sharply, most likely the party rank-and-file would demand its reorganization.

Whereas Congress during the 1970s had a left-of-center, pro-poor political platform, beginning in 1984 it moved toward the ideological center under Rajiv Gandhi. (See Section 2 for the reasons behind this shift.) Today the current Congress Party tilts to right-of-center, championing issues of economic efficiency, business interests, and limited government spending over the rights of the poor and the working people, and over social questions of health, education, and welfare.

As a nationalist party, the Congress Party is intimately associated with the stability of the Indian nation and the state in Indian political culture. Irrespective of its economic program, therefore, the Congress has always attracted support from diverse social groups: rich and poor, upper and lower castes, Hindus and Muslims, northerners and southerners. Nevertheless, elections in the 1990s indicate that the Congress has lost some of its traditional constituencies among the poor, lower castes, and such minorities as Muslims.

The Janata Party

The Janata Party, India's other centrist party, formed short-lived national governments in 1977, 1989, and together with other parties through the United Front in 1996 and 1997. The Janata Party, however, is not so much a political party as an umbrella for various parties and factions who move in and out depending on political circumstances. The Janata Party was created in 1977 when several smaller parties, who opposed Indira Gandhi's Emergency, hurriedly united to contest her and, much to their own surprise, won the national elections. This loose coalition lasted only for a little over two years, when conflicting leadership ambitions tore apart the fragile veneer of a party.

During the late 1980s the Janata Party enjoyed another brief term as a national government under the leadership of a breakaway Congress leader, V. P. Singh, who championed himself as an honest native son battling the corrupt and Westernized Rajiv Gandhi. Gandhi had been tainted by the Bofors scandal, so-called because the Swedish arms manufacturing company Bofors apparently bribed senior Congress officials in Rajiv Gandhi's government to obtain a lucrative arms contract. With these appeals, the Janata Party won enough seats in the national parliament to form a minority government in 1989. Once again factionalism overwhelmed any attempt at a stable government, and this second attempt with a non–Congress-led government collapsed after a little over two years. This brought about national elections in 1991; Rajiv Gandhi was assassinated during a campaign rally and Narasimha Rao was elected. Since then, the Janata Party has been able to survive only under the umbrella of the United Front, which is a collection of smaller parties, including the CPM.

The Janata Party has a very weak organizational structure and lacks a distinctive, coherent political platform. To distinguish itself from the Congress, it claims that it is more Gandhian—a reference to the decentralized, village-oriented vision of Mahatma Gandhi for modern India—more rural-oriented, and less pro-Brahmin. Although most of its efforts at political self-definition have not been very successful, while in power V. P. Singh undertook one major policy initiative that identified the Janata Party with a progressive cause. This was the acceptance of the Mandal Commission's recommendations that India's backward castes—generally, the middle, rural castes who constitute a near majority in the Indian countryside—be provided substantial reservations (or reserved access) in government jobs and educational institutions. The acceptance of this recommendation produced a nationwide outburst of riots and violence, led by members of upper castes who felt threatened. The uproar eventually contributed to the downfall of V. P. Singh's government. Nevertheless, the acceptance of "Mandal" by V. P. Singh associated the Janata Party with the interests of the backward castes. How strongly backward castes will continue to identify with the Janata in the future is unknown. For now, the Janata Party is viewed, especially in north-central India, as a party of small, rural agriculturalists who generally fall somewhere in the middle of the rigid caste hierarchy between Brahmins and the untouchables.

The Bharatiya Janata Party

The major new political party in contemporary India is the Bharatiya Janata party (BJP). Although formally constituted only in the early 1980s, the party is a direct descendant of the Jana Sangh party that entered the Indian political scene in 1951. The BJP is a right-leaning, Hindu-nationalist party, the first major party to mobilize explicitly on the basis of religious identity; it is also exclusionary in its appeals to Hindu identity that vilify Muslims. In comparison to both the Congress and the Janata, the BJP is better organized; it has disciplined party members, who after a prolonged apprenticeship become party cadres, and the authority lines within the party are relatively clear and well respected.

The party is closely affiliated with many related political organizations, the most significant of which is the Rashtriya Sevak Sangh (Association for National Service), the RSS. Most BJP leaders were at one time members of the RSS, which recruits young people (especially educated youth in urban areas) and involves them in a fairly disciplined set of cultural activities, including the study of a chauvinistic reinterpretation of India's "great Hindu past." These young people, uniformed in khaki shorts and shirts, can often be seen in Indian cities doing group exercises in the mornings and evenings and singing songs glorifying India's Sanskritic civilization (Sanskrit is the classical language in which some of the ancient Hindu scriptures are written). Recalling the pursuits of right-wing fascist groups of interwar Europe, the activities of these youth groups—seemingly no more than an appeal to cultural pride—dismay many non-Hindu minorities and Indian liberals, who fear the havoc that cultural pride can produce, as for example in Nazi Germany.

Those traditionally attracted to the Jana Sangh and the BJP were mainly urban, lower-middle-class groups, especially small traders and commercial groups. As long as this was its main source of support, the BJP remained a minor actor on the Indian political scene. Since the mid-1980s, however, the BJP appreciably widened its base of support by appealing to Hindu nationalism, especially in north-central India. The decline in the Congress Party's popularity created a vacuum that the BJP was well positioned to fill.

Moreover, the BJP found in Indian Muslims a convenient scapegoat for the frustrations of various social groups and successfully mobilized Hindus in an attempt to create a religiously oriented political force where none had existed before. The electoral success of the BJP in 1989 and 1991 and its formation of the government in 1998 underscore the party's rapid rise to power. BJP's early efforts resulted in its ruling four states from 1991 to 1993, though it lost power in three of the four in 1993. However, during the 1998 parliamentary elections the BJP scored a major success by being the party with the largest number of seats and thus being able to head the national government. There are many poor or otherwise frustrated social groups in India whose anger is available for political mobilization. Whether the BJP will succeed in continuing to tap this anger in the longer term cannot be predicted. What can be said is that democracy and large pockets of social frustration provide a combustible mix that will continue to generate unexpected outcomes in Indian politics.

The Communist Party

The fourth major political party is the Communist Party of India (Marxist), or CPM. The CPM is an offshoot of the Communist Party of India (CPI), which was formed during the colonial period and has existed nearly as long as the Congress Party. Though the contemporary CPM has a national presence—that is, it nearly always elects representatives to the *Lok Sabha*—its political base is concentrated in two of India's states, West Bengal and Kerala. These states have often been ruled by the CPM, and they often elect *Lok Sabha* members who run on a CPM ticket.

The CPM is a disciplined party, with party cadres and a hierarchical authority structure. Other than its name and internal organization, however, there is nothing communist about the CPM; rather it is a social democratic party like the British Labour Party or the German Social Democratic Party. The CPM accepts the framework of democracy, regularly participates in elections, and often wins them in West Bengal and Kerala. In these two states, the CPM enjoys the support of the lower-middle and lower classes, both factory workers and poorer peasants. Within the national parliament, CPM members often strongly criticize government policies that are likely to hurt the poor. On occasion the CPM joins with other parties against the BJP, as it did in the 1996 elections by joining the United Front. Where the CPM runs state governments, for example in West Bengal and Kerala, it has provided a relatively honest and stable administration. It has also pursued a moderate but effective reform program, ensuring the rights of agricultural tenants (such as preventing their evictions), providing services to those living in shantytowns, and encouraging public investments in rural areas.

Elections

The four major parties, along with several other minor parties, periodically compete for the votes of the Indian electorate. Elections in India are a colossal event. Nearly 500 million people are eligible to vote and close to 300 million actually do so. The turnout rate in the 1990s has been over 60 percent, considerably higher than in the United States. The level of technology used both in campaigning and in the conduct of elections is fairly low. Television plays an increasingly important

Village women wait in line to get voting slips at a polling station in a village in India's Orissa state, March 7, 1995. *Source:* Reuters/Bettmann.

role, but much campaigning still involves face-to-face contact between politicians and the electorate. Senior leaders fly around the country, making speeches to millions of potential supporters at political rallies held in tiny villages and district towns. Lesser politicians and thousands of their party supporters travel the dusty streets, blaring music and political messages from loudspeakers mounted on their vehicles.

Given the high rate of illiteracy, pictures of party symbols are critical: for example, a hand for the Congress (I); a lotus for the BJP; a hammer and sickle for the CPM. The way many voters signify their vote for a candidate in the polling booth is to put their thumb mark on one of these symbols. During the campaign, therefore, party representatives work very hard to associate certain individuals and election platforms with specific symbols. A typical election slogan, for example, is, "Vote for the hammer and sickle because they stand for the rights of the working people."

India's electoral system, like the British system, is a first-past-the-post system. A number of candidates compete in an electoral district; the candidate who has the most votes wins. For example, if the Congress candidate wins the most votes, say 35 percent of the vote from a district, and the candidates of other parties split the remaining votes, the Congress candidate is victorious. This system privileges the major political parties. It also generates considerable pressure for opposition parties to collaborate as a single voice against the government. In practice, however, given the differences between opposition parties and the considerable clash of leadership ambitions, many parties compete, enabling the candidates of the larger party to squeeze by as winners.

Political Culture, Citizenship, and Identity

The only generalization that can be made about Indian political culture is that, in such a large and culturally diverse country, no single set of cultural traits is shared by the entire population. Nevertheless, three important tendencies—or habits of mind, produced by repeated practice—are worth noting. These political cultural traits reflect India's hybrid political style, as a rigid, hierarchical, and village-oriented old civilization adapts itself to modern socioeconomic changes, especially to democratic politics.

The members of India's political elite often have difficulty working and cooperating with each other, so a factionalized elite is a well-known characteristic of Indian politics. The roots of such behavior are complex, reflecting India's fragmented social structure; this style of politics by now seems deeply ingrained in India. Although some important exceptions exist, generally the personal political ambitions of Indian leaders prevent them from pursuing such collective goals as forming cohesive political parties, running a stable government, or focusing on problems of national development. In contrast to many East Asian countries, where the norms of consensus are powerful and political negotiation is often conducted behind closed doors, politics in India veer toward the other extreme, with open disagreements and conflicts the norm.

India's political and public spheres of activity are not sharply divided from personal and private spheres of activity. India is not unique in this; it is an issue in most developing countries and, in some respects, given its long history of a nationalist movement and its well-established civil service, India has a much better developed sense of the public sphere than, say, many African countries. Nevertheless, the idea that a public office is not a legitimate means for personal enrichment or for furthering the interests of family members or of personal associates is not yet fully accepted in India. One important result is a fairly widespread misuse of public resources for personal gain, or more directly, widespread corruption in political life.

The third political cultural tendency that deserves mention concerns fragmentation of political life in India. Indian society is highly segmented. Different regions have different languages and cultures; within regions, villages are poorly connected with each other; and within villages, different castes often live in isolation from one another. As this segmented and localized society has been drawn into democratic politics, the results have often been unexpected. For example, there is an expectation in democratic politics that those sharing similar interests will unite politically to pursue collective interests. Following this logic, one might expect the poor in India to come together politically to make collective demands on the state. However, the habits of mind in India have inhibited any such group formation based on class. Instead, politics is often fragmented along caste lines, but even caste grievances tend to remain local rather than accumulate nationally or even regionally. Some observers of India find this segmented quality of Indian politics a blessing because it localizes problems, facilitating political stability, but others find it a curse because it stymies the possibility of pursuing reforms to improve the lot of the poorest members of Indian society.

Democracy is relatively well established in India. Most Indians value their citizenship rights and, in spite of poverty and illiteracy, exercise them with vigor. One of the four core themes of this book is the power of the democratic idea. This can certainly be applied to India. However, the spread of democratic politics can simultaneously fuel political conflicts. In India, the spread of democracy is undermining many of India's political givens, including some of the most rigid hierarchies, and has begun to produce new political patterns.

The most significant of these recent developments concerns identity politics, whereby the dynamics of democratic politics mobilizes latent identities to produce powerful collective identities. Region, language, religion, and caste all help Indians define who they are and, as a result, help them categorize "we" and "they" in political associations and conflicts. Such differences have generated political cleavages in India, underlining the importance and yet the malleability of collective identities, for example, the Hindu-Muslim conflict at the time of independence. Some of these identity conflicts remained dormant when Nehru's secular nationalism and Indira Gandhi's poor-versus-rich cleavage defined the core political issues. In the 1980s and 1990s, however, with the relative decline of the Congress Party, and with developments in communications and transportation making people more aware of each other's differences, identity-based political conflicts have mushroomed in India. Two of the more significant conflicts deserve mention.

First, caste conflicts, though usually confined to local and regional politics, have taken on a national dimension in recent years, for example, the acceptance of the Mandal Commission recommendations by the former prime minister V. P. Singh. These recommendations were meant to benefit India's backward castes, who are numerically significant and who tend to be rural agriculturalists by occupation and somewhere in the middle of the caste hierarchy. Groups of backward castes had made a political mark in many states, but prior to "Mandal," they were seldom a cohesive factor in national politics. In all probability, V. P. Singh, by approving the Mandal recommendations, hoped to create a powerful support base out of these disparate groups. However, the move backfired. The threatened upper castes reacted sharply with demonstrations, riots, and political violence. Not only did this disruption contribute to the downfall of V. P. Singh's government but it also converted the conflict between castes from a local and regional issue to a divisive national issue.

The second identity-based political conflict that has reemerged in recent years has pitched Indian Hindus and Muslims against each other. Tensions between these religious communities go back several centuries to when Muslim rulers from Central Asia established the Moghul dynasty in India. Stories and memories of the relative greatness of one community over the other, or of atrocities and injustices unleashed on one community by the other, abound in India's popular culture. For the most part, these legends fan low-level, latent hostilities that do not prevent peaceful coexistence. However, political circumstances, especially political machinations by ambitious leaders, can unleash these latent tendencies and instigate overt conflict. This is what has happened since the mid-1980s as the BJP has whipped up anti-Muslim sentiments in an effort to unite disparate Hindu groups into a political force. The resulting victimization of Muslims in acts of political violence, including destruction of life, property, and places of worship, illustrates the dangers of identity-based political passions.

Interests, Social Movements, and Protest

India's democracy is an active one. At any time, numerous groups are demanding a greater share of wealth, status, or power from a state or the national government. How business and other elite groups influence government has been discussed. In addition, organized labor is politically active in India, but labor unions are politically fragmented. Instead of the familiar model of one factory/one union, within one factory in India competing unions can be organized by different political parties. Above the factory level,

several labor organizations compete for labor's support. While unions can bring considerable pressure to bear on both management and politicians, for the most part they are not well-organized on the national level. The government generally stays out of labor-management conflicts. India's industrial relations are thus closer to the pluralist model practiced in Anglo-American countries than to the corporatist model, say, of Mexico. The political energies of unions are channeled into frequent local battles involving strikes, demonstrations, and a peculiarly Indian protest technique called *gherao*, "encirclement." Labor groups using *gherao* will encircle a member of management and not let him go—sometimes for days—until management meets their demands. Labor politics in India is thus active but not coherent.

Except for big business groups and unionized labor, many demand groups unite for a specific purpose and then disband. For example, the better-off peasantry periodically organize at the state or national level to demand higher support prices for agricultural products or increased subsidies for inputs such as fertilizer. Groups formed around caste and religion are also very active in Indian politics. Such political activities demonstrate the health of Indian democracy but highlight a central tension in it: How can government simultaneously accommodate multiple demands and yet facilitate a coherent program for national development?

There are several active women's movements in India, especially in urban areas but also in rural settings. They bring together educated, middle-class women and, at other times, poor women. The movements composed of middle-class women tend to be more durable because they usually aim to alter deeply held attitudes, whereas others are likely to raise a protest against an immediate specific injustice like a rape or a dowry death (a murder or suicide because of a perceived inadequate marriage dowry) or against the unrestricted sale of alcohol, which is viewed as responsible for alcoholism among husbands.

A number of environmental movements also exist. These are often led by educated, urban environmentalists who mobilize victims of development projects. For example, the movement against deforestation, called the Chipko movement, has been fairly successful. Also, a very large project sponsored by the World Bank—construction of a dam over the river

Narmada—aroused protestors, who said the construction would cause environmental problems, including the displacement of thousands of families. The protest was sufficient to cause the World Bank to rescind its support, but the Indian government is still pursuing the project.

A variety of poor people's movements flourish. Most tend to be local and short-lived, but they can mobilize quickly and have considerable political impact. For example, a variety of "tribal" groups, often ethnically distinct, live in remote areas, tend to be very poor, and are categorized as tribals because the government chooses to label them as such. Many of these groups organize political protest, demanding a greater share of public resources, preservation of the meager resources they control, or the like. India's untouchable castes also organize politically to protest caste injustices. In some states, like Bihar, such movements have become very violent, with various caste groups arming themselves in private armies. At times, issues of caste, tribe, and poverty overlap to produce a highly volatile mix. In the southern state of Andhra Pradesh, for example, poor tribals have been organized by armed revolutionaries who hang village landlords and other perceived exploiters to achieve a measure of local justice. Even though such protests are violently suppressed by police intervention, their proliferation illustrates the considerable activism and dissatisfaction in India's political society.

To review, political participation in India has over the years broadened in scope and deepened in intensity. As more groups demand a share of power, it can be suggested that forces of democratization in India have spread wide and deep. A single-party system dominated by the Congress Party has slowly been supplanted by a multiparty system of parties on the left and the right. Similarly, old hierarchies of caste have eroded in Indian society; upper castes cannot readily control the political behavior of those below them. The result is that many groups in society increasingly feel empowered and hope to translate this new consciousness and sense of efficacy into material gains by influencing government policies. The challenge for any government in India is how to respond to these growing demands; the dilemma is how to promote economic efficiency and growth while channeling resources to these newly empowered groups.

Section ⑤   Indian Politics in Transition

Between 1996 and 1998 India had four national governments (see Table 1). All were minority governments, requiring a variety of coalition arrangements to survive. The BJP government that came to power in 1998 lost a vote of confidence in the *Lok Sabha* in May 1999. The government resigned, necessitating yet another election. As these developments demonstrate, India desperately needs a stable, majority government to meet its enduring challenges.

Political Challenges and Changing Agendas

Because India is a large developing country and a democracy, a study of Indian politics sheds light on more general issues of comparative politics. In this chapter, India's development has been examined in light of four comparative themes. As a large country with a legitimate government and sizable armed forces, India is not readily influenced by external forces. For example, India tested nuclear bombs in 1998 and successfully withstood international condemnation and sanctions. However, in an increasingly interdependent global economic context, as seen in the 1997 East Asian economic crisis, India is no longer invulnerable to global pressures. An examination of the sequence of events in the aftermath of the nuclear tests in India will clarify the interdependent dynamic of the world of states.

The nuclear tests of May 1998 opened a Pandora's box of intensified geopolitical rivalry in Asia and the risk of future copycat attempts in other volatile regions of the world. The focus of international (particularly U.S.) diplomacy shifted from punitive economic and technological sanctions to seeking a universal nonproliferation agreement. India cannot ignore its dependence on other states for economic and technological support, and the rest of the world cannot ignore the implications of India's nuclear outing. The Vajpayee and the Clinton administrations engaged in several rounds of delicate arms control talks; efforts were made to persuade India to sign the Comprehensive Test Ban Treaty (CTBT) and the Nuclear Non-Proliferation Treaty (NPT) in exchange for completely lifting U.S. sanctions. India opposed the NPT on the grounds that it was unfair to non-nuclear countries because it did not establish a procedure for eventual phaseout of nuclear weapons by the nuclear powers. The United States also urged India to exercise restraint on its nuclear weapons and missiles programs, while New Delhi insisted on its right to minimum nuclear deterrence. In late 1998, India announced its intention to sign the Comprehensive Test Ban Treaty if talks with the United States ended successfully and also signaled its willingness to join other nuclear control groups.

Thus one major political challenge for India is how to negotiate with the rest of the world, particularly the United States, on its emergence as a nuclear weapons state. How will India combine its new nuclear power status with responsible use of such weapons? How will it negotiate with its nuclear neighbors, Pakistan and China, to ensure that South Asia does not set off a nuclear disaster? In February 1999, during a historic visit to Pakistan by the Indian prime minister, both countries agreed to continue their declared nuclear moratoriums on further nuclear tests. How India confronts challenges on the nuclear front is closely tied to its success on the economic front and management of rising ethnic tensions.

Comparativists debate how well an economy is governed. India's economic experience is neither a clear success nor a clear failure. If many African countries have done rather poorly economically and many East Asian countries (prior to 1997) have had dramatic successes, India falls somewhere in the middle. Three conditions may explain this outcome. First may be the nature and the quality of the government for promoting economic growth. In this, India has been fortunate to have enjoyed relatively good government since independence: its democratic system is mostly open and stable; its most powerful political leaders are public-spirited; and its upper bureaucracy is well trained and competent. These positive attributes truly stand out when India is compared to such African countries as Nigeria. The second condition concerns India's strategy for economic development. As noted previously, India in the 1950s chose to insulate its economy from global forces, limiting the role of trade and foreign investment and emphasizing the role of government in promoting self-sufficiency in heavy industry and in agriculture. The positive impact of this strategy was that India now produces enough food to feed its large and growing population while it simultaneously produces a vast range of industrial goods. This strategy, however, was not without costs. The protective atmosphere reduced competition to the extent that most of India's manufactured goods are produced rather inefficiently by global standards. The additional economic growth that might have come from competing effectively in the global markets and by selling its products abroad was sacrificed. India also gave up another area of potential economic growth by discouraging foreign investment. And last, during the phase of protective industrialization, India did little to alleviate its staggering poverty: land redistribution failed, job creation by heavy industries was minimal, and investment in the education and health of the poor was minuscule in relation to the magnitude of the problem. The poor also became a drag on economic growth because they were unable to buy goods and stimulate demand for increased production and because an uneducated and unhealthy labor force is not a productive labor force.

A stable government and an emphasis on self-sufficiency have promoted modest economic growth in India; higher rates of growth, however, have been difficult to achieve without greater links to the outside world and with the staggering numbers of poor people. This leads to the third condition regarding India's middling political economy: it concerns the emerging trends. India's continuing economic weakness has made it more vulnerable to global forces. The country's economic crisis in the early 1990s during the Gulf War exposed its vulnerability and prompted a shift toward a more open economy. This trend reflects a growing confidence and an awareness that sustained higher rates of growth necessitate such a shift. Meanwhile, the continuation of staggering levels of poverty in India is a disturbing problem. If India is to achieve sustained levels of high economic growth, the

Indian government must address the issues of literacy, health, and welfare for the poor, enabling them to join the economy as truly productive participants. The challenge faced by Indian politicians is to reconcile the demands of promoting an efficient economy with those of winning elections. The latter involves encouraging an expansion of government programs and subsidies to discontented groups, while the former calls for austerity. Restricting government's role conflicts with implementing distributive or populist programs; opening the national economy to foreign economic actors and products is likely to aggravate nationalist sentiments.

Some comparative scholars suggest that the widespread desire of citizens to exercise some control over their government is a potent force encouraging democracy. This assumption is clearly illustrated in Indian political trends. Even though democracy was introduced to India by its elites, the democratic tendency has permeated society, helping democracy put down firm roots in India. A clear example supporting this view was India's experience with Emergency rule, when Indira Gandhi curtailed democratic freedoms from 1975 to 1977. In the next election, in 1977, Indian citizens decisively voted Indira Gandhi out of power, registering their preference for democratic rule. Moreover, although India is challenged with numerous strains and stresses, no widespread antidemocratic movement exists. On the contrary, most Indians value democracy and use its institutions to advance their claims, at times even excessively.

India also provides a rich case for studying a fourth area of comparative interest, namely, the growing political impact of ethnic identities. Mobilized ethnic groups seeking access to state power and state-controlled economic resources are a basic component of the contemporary Indian political scene. Caste, language, and religion all provide identities around which political mobilization can be galvanized. Identification with a group, in turn, is further heightened by the democratic context, in which parties and leaders freely choose to manipulate such symbols. When studying Indian politics, it is difficult to separate interest- and identity-based politics. For example, caste struggles in India are simultaneously struggles for identity, for power, and for wealth. Identity politics in India is likely to be characterized by two trends: considerable political

ferment, with a variety of dissatisfied groups making demands on parties and governments; and pressure on political parties to broaden their electoral appeal to disadvantaged groups, especially those belonging to the middle and lower strata, many of whom are very poor. India's political leaders will thus continue to experience pressures to expand their support base by promising economic improvements or by manipulating nationalist symbols. Under what conditions will such political forces engage in constructive rather than destructive actions? Will democracy succeed in merely tempering the effect of such forces, or will it in the long run promote a positive channelling of identity politics?

Indian Politics in Comparative Perspective

By the twenty-first century, India will surpass China as the most populous country in the world. How such a country is governed will remain an issue of considerable significance, not only for the billion people residing within India's boundaries but also for India's neighbors and the world. A democratic and prosperous India could be a stabilizing force. A turbulent India, driven by ethnic and class turmoil, and with a collapsing authority structure, could have profound negative consequences, not just for Indians, but globally. In this concluding section, we first examine the implications of the study of India for comparative politics, and then assess how Indian politics and its economy will influence developments in a regional and global context.

Comparativists debate whether democracy or authoritarianism is better for economic growth. In the past, India did not compare well with the success stories of East Asian and Chinese authoritarian-led countries. The collapse in the late 1990s of several East Asian economies and the subsequent rise of instability within those societies makes a study of Indian democracy more relevant to understanding the institutional and cultural factors underpinning economic stability in the long run.

Another theme has been to assess the implications of establishing democracy in multiethnic societies. The rising tide of nationalism and the break-up of the Soviet Union and Yugoslavia, among others, has prompted closer examination of how and why India continues to exist as a cohesive entity. By studying India's history, particularly the post-1947 period, comparativists could explore questions of how cleavages of caste, religion, and language in India balance one another and cancel the most destructive elements in each.

Comparativists have also puzzled about the conditions under which multiple and contradictory interests could be harnessed within a democratic setup to generate positive economic and distributional outcomes. Here, the variable performance of the different regions in India could serve as a laboratory. For instance, two communist-ruled states, Kerala and West Bengal, have (to a certain extent) engaged in land redistribution policies. An examination of factors such as the role of the mobilizing parties and the interaction between the landless poor and the entrenched landed elite could provide answers. Another question engaging comparativists is whether success in providing education and welfare inevitably leads to success in the economic sphere. Again, the case of Kerala provides pointers for further research. Kerala scores high on human development indicators such as literacy and health, but paradoxically the state has not performed well on the economic front.

What are the international and domestic challenges faced by India at the dawn of the twenty-first century? How will India cope with its new-found status as a nuclear power? How can India prevent further escalation of conflict in the region that could end in a nuclear conflagration? A worst-case scenario would be a conventional war with Pakistan that could escalate into a nuclear war. Domestically, both countries are currently wracked with ethnic tensions and weak central governments. In an attempt to hold on to power, the leaders of each country could try to divert attention toward a national security threat from its neighbor, a ploy that has been used effectively in the past by politicians in both countries. The past history of three wars between India and Pakistan, the simmering tensions over Kashmir, and the fear of a decisive first strike could prompt a nuclear strike. The challenge for India is to establish a stable relationship with its nuclear neighbors, Pakistan and China, that would eschew proliferation of its nuclear and ballistic missiles arsenals and engage in constructive diplomatic and economic cooperation. India's history of wars with both countries is not an encouraging starting point, but the engagement of Western powers in generating a dialogue between these countries is a portent for the future. The visit to Pakistan by the Indian prime minister in 1999, the first visit in ten years and only the third ever, provides grounds for optimism. Whether such overtures will result in fruitful negotiations on Kashmir and on economic cooperation in the region remains to be seen. Answers to these questions depend heavily on developments in the sphere of domestic politics.

The history of fifty years of democracy in India has been a double-edged sword. Winning elections involves attracting votes. While avoiding authoritarianism, the practice of democracy, particularly electoral politics, has worsened ethnic animosities between Hindus and Muslims, upper caste and lower caste, and north and south. With the spread of democracy, many dissatisfied groups are finding their voices and becoming politically mobilized. The challenge for Indian politics is how to repair the divide within a democratic framework. The results of the November 1998 elections to the state government assemblies provides a more optimistic scenario. Despite the BJP-led central government's nuclear achievements, voters opted for the Congress party in three of the four states, and for a regional party in the fourth state. Current voter emphasis on good governance and sound economic management rather than on religious or nationalistic issues might transform electoral platforms in the twenty-first century. In any case, Indian politics will continue to tread a shaky path, as witnessed by the intensification of communal tensions marked by the macabre killing of a Christian missionary and his two young sons in Orissa in January 1999 by Hindu fundamentalists, as well as other attacks on Christians in scattered regions. Will India be able to manage its domestic tensions and enlarge social, political, and economic rights for its citizens?

Another challenge for India is how to combine its global ambitions of becoming a strong power with its program for economic liberalization. The increasing interdependence of global economies as manifested in global effects of the 1997 East Asian crisis and the dependence of developing countries on investor confidence and external aid should not be underestimated. While India was protected from the East Asian debacle because of the partially closed nature of its economy, the country nevertheless suffered economic blows in the aftermath of becoming nuclear in the form of frozen aid programs worth billions. In addition, a decrease in foreign direct investment followed from the loss of investor confidence as a result of the downgrading of India's credit rating. The economic woes engendered by the sanctions were accentuated by the BJP government's lack of progress on the economic liberalization front. Instead of opening up sectors such as insurance and consumer goods in an attempt to further integrate the Indian economy with the rest of the world, the BJP has so far continued to champion the protection of Indian businesses from global competitors. The Indian case embodies the tensions inherent in combining democracy with economic liberalization. Political parties in India face pressures to expand their support base by promoting contradictory economic improvements or by manipulating nationalist symbols. But simultaneously, these promises clash with the task of economic liberalization. The challenge faced by governments in India is how to combine the task of economic liberalization with the conflicting demands of electoral politics. Can India afford to take halting steps toward transformation of its economy? If the economic problems are not addressed swiftly and effectively, the world will be confronted by an India that is poor, ethnically mobilized, and controlling a formidable nuclear arsenal. This would compromise not just the regional but also global security.

How India reconciles its national political ambitions, domestic political demands for greater economic redistribution, and global pressures for an efficient economy will affect India's influence on regional and global trends. Will India be able to capitalize on some of its positive achievements such as the long-standing democratic ethos framed by functioning institutions, a vibrant civil society and media, and a growing middle class imbued with the desire to succeed economically? Or will India be chained down by increasingly belligerent ethnic cleavages resulting in, at best, inaction on all fronts and, at worst, total disintegration of the country? If the Congress Party is able to remobilize its old "umbrella party" constituency (such as Muslims, backward castes, and others) under Sonia Gandhi, we might see a return to the era of one-party rule in India. However, if current trends are any indication, the stage seems set for a scenario of two-party rule, with

either a BJP-led or a Congress-led coalition ruling at the center. There also seems to be some room for optimism with regard to voter needs and interests on the international and domestic fronts. For instance, during the February 1999 Vajpayee visit to Pakistan, some public opinion polls showed that an overwhelming number of people in India and Pakistan wanted improved relations between the two countries. On the domestic side, the preoccupation of voters with economic management, law and order, and other governance issues was evident from the results of the 1998 assembly elections. Of course, balancing the demands of simultaneously achieving equity and efficiency generates its own problems. The study and understanding of evolving political trends in India will remain matters of continuing significance.

Key Terms

Hindus	caste system
Muslims	Brahmin
Sikhs	untouchables
Maharajas	scheduled castes
zamindars	nonaligned bloc
Emergency	*Lok Sabha*
green revolution	*Rajya Sabha*
state-led economic development	Indian Administrative Service
economic liberalization	panchayats
reservations	

Suggested Readings

Bardhan, Pranab. *The Political Economy of Development in India.* New Delhi: Oxford University Press, 1984.

Bayly, C. A. *The New Cambridge History of India: Indian Society and the Making of the British Empire.* Vol. 2, no. 1. Cambridge: Cambridge University Press, 1988.

Brass, Paul R. *The New Cambridge History of India: The Politics of India Since Independence.* Vol. 4, no. 1. Cambridge: Cambridge University Press, 1990.

Carras, Mary C. *Indira Gandhi: In the Crucible of Leadership.* Boston: Beacon Press, 1979.

Chatterjee, Partha, ed. *State Politics in India.* Themes in Politics Series. Vol. 1. New Delhi: Oxford University Press, 1997.

Cohen, Stephen P. *The Indian Army: Its Contribution to the Development of a Nation.* Berkeley: University of California Press, 1971.

Dreze and Sen Amartya, eds. *Economic Development and Social Opportunity.* New Delhi: Oxford University Press, 1995.

Frankel, Francine. *India's Political Economy, 1947–1977.* Princeton, N.J.: Princeton University Press, 1978.

Gopal, Sarvepalli. *Jawaharlal Nehru: A Biography.* Vols. 2 and 3. New Delhi: Oxford University Press, 1984.

Graham, Bruce. *Hindu Nationalism and Indian Politics.* Cambridge: Cambridge University Press, 1990.

Hardgrave, Robert L., Jr., and Stanley A. Kochanek. *India: Government and Politics in a Developing Nation.* 4th ed. New York: Harcourt Brace Jovanovich, 1986.

Jaffrelot, Christophe. *The Hindu Nationalist Movement and Indian Politics, 1925 to the 1990s: Strategies on Identity Building, Implantation and Mobilization.* New York: Columbia University Press, 1996.

Jalan, Bimal. *India's Economic Crisis: The Way Ahead.* New Delhi: Oxford University Press, 1991.

Kohli, Atul. *The State and Poverty in India: The Politics of Reform.* Cambridge: Cambridge University Press, 1987.

——. *Democracy and Discontent: India's Growing Crisis of Governability.* Cambridge: Cambridge University Press, 1991.

Misra, B. B. *Government and Bureaucracy in India: 1947–1976.* New Delhi: Oxford University Press, 1986.

Nayar, Baldev Raj. *India's Mixed Economy.* Bombay: Popular Prakashan, 1989.

Rothermund, Dietmar. *An Economic History of India: From Pre-Colonial Times to 1986.* London: Croom Helm, 1988.

Rudolph, Lloyd, and Susanne Rudolph. *In Pursuit of Lakshmi: The Political Economy of the Indian State.* Chicago: Chicago University Press, 1987.

Sarkar, Sumit. *Modern India: 1885 to 1947.* Madras: Macmillan, 1983.

Weiner, Myron. *The Indian Paradox: Essays in Indian Politics.* New Delhi: Sage Publications, 1989.

——. *The Child and the State in India.* Princeton, N.J.: Princeton University Press, 1992.

CHAPTER 4

Mexico

Merilee S. Grindle

United Mexican States

Land and Population

Capital	Mexico City
Total Area (square miles)	756,066 (about three times the size of Texas)
Population	98.5 million
Annual Average Population Growth Rate (1990–1997)	1.8%
Urban Population	74%
Ethnic Composition	Mestizo (Amerindian-Spanish) 60%
	Amerindian 30%
	White 9%
	Other 1%
Major Languages	Spanish 94.1%
	Indigenous Languages 5.9%
	Other languages not significant
Religious Affiliation	Roman Catholic 89%
	Protestant 6%
	Other and none 5%

Economy

Domestic Currency	Peso
Total GNP (US$)	$348.6 billion
GNP per capita (US$)	$3680
GNP per capita at purchasing power parity (US$)	$8120
GNP average annual growth rate (1996–1997)	8%
GNP per capita average annual growth rate	1996–1997 6.2%
	1980–1995 −0.9%
	1965–1980 3.6%
Income Gap: GDP per capita (US$)	Richest 20% of population $19,383
	Poorest 20% of population $1437
Structure of Production (% of GDP)	Agriculture 8%
	Industry 26%
	Services 67%
Labor Force Distribution (% of total)	Agriculture 28%
	Industry 24%
	Services 48%
Exports as % of GDP	25%
Imports as % of GDP	22%
Electricity Consumption per capita (kwh)	1646

CO_2 Emissions per capita (metric tons)		3.9

Society

Life Expectancy	Female	75.1
	Male	69.2
Doctors per 100,000 people		107
Infant Mortality per 1000 live births		27
Adult Literacy	Female	87.4%
	Male	91.8%
Access to Information and Communications (per 1000 population)	Radios	263
	Televisions	192
	Telephone Lines	96
	Personal Computers	26

Women in Government and Economy

Seats in Parliament held by Women	17.4% (upper house)
	11.8% (lower house)
Women at ministerial level	14.0%
Women as % of total labor force	32.0%
Female business administrators and managers	20.0%
Female professional and technical workers	45.0%
1998 Human Development Index ranking (out of 174 countries, 1 = highest)	49

Political Organization

Political System   Federal republic.

Regime History   Current form of government since 1917.

Administrative Structure   Federal with 31 states and a federal district.

Executive   President, elected by direct election with a six-year term of office; reelection not permitted.

Legislature   Bicameral; upper and lower house elections held every three years. There are 128 senators, 4 from each state, elected for six years to serve in the upper house. Three senators from each state are elected by simple majority vote, the fourth is assigned to the largest minority party. Five hundred deputies are elected every three years to serve in the lower house: 300 are elected by simple majority, 200 by proportional representation.

Judiciary   Independent Supreme Court with 21 justices and 5 auxiliary judges.

Party System   Multiparty system, with the Institutional Revolutionary Party (PRI) dominating elections after 1929; other important parties are the National Action Party (PAN) and the Democratic Revolutionary Party (PRD).

Section ❶ The Making of the Modern Mexican State

Politics in Action

On March 23, 1994, presidential candidate Luis Donaldo Colosio finished a campaign speech in the northern border city of Tijuana. Then, as he struggled through the noisy crowd greeting his supporters, an unknown assailant approached quickly, drew a gun, and shot Colosio in the head and torso. The candidate for Mexico's highest office died a few hours later.

The assassination of Colosio, the candidate of the Institutional Revolutionary Party (PRI, pronounced "pree"), which had governed the country without interruption since 1929, shocked Mexico's 90 million citizens and shook its political elite deeply. Not since 1923, when a military revolt threatened presidential elections, had there been such uncertainty about who would lead the government for the next six years. Not since 1928, when president-elect Alvaro Obregón was assassinated, had a politician bound for the highest office met with violent death. Not since 1929, when the PRI was founded, had there been such fear that the political elite was so divided that overt violence, not accommodation and compromise, might be used to resolve disputes.

President Carlos Salinas de Gortari moved quickly to appoint a new candidate. He chose Ernesto Zedillo, Colosio's campaign manager, one-time Minister of Education, and former Minister of Planning and Budgeting, who had never held an elected office. Zedillo was another economic planner in a line of U.S.-educated technocrats who had governed the PRI (and therefore the nation) since 1982, seeking to reform the party from within. Many Mexicans were convinced that the assassination was part of a conspiracy involving party "dinosaurs," political hard-liners who opposed any kind of democratic transformation.

Although the self-confessed "lone gunman" was jailed, the ensuing investigation raised concerns about a possible conspiracy involving party and law enforcement officials as well as drug cartels. Rumors circulated about a cover-up scandal. Eventually, skepticism about the integrity of the inquiry was so great that President Salinas called for a new investigation.

At this point, little remains known about what exactly happened in Tijuana and why.

Despite the public's widespread disillusionment with the political system, Ernesto Zedillo easily won election in August 1994. Many Mexicans feared the prospect of violence and instability caused by political change more than they feared politics as usual. It is a sentiment eloquently expressed in Mexico with a saying, "Better to have the bad that you know than the good that you don't." Some citizens, having spent all their lives under the PRI, remembered the party's triumphs of decades past and continued to support it with a sense of national pride.

Yet great changes were already under way. Increasingly during the 1980s and 1990s, many Mexicans openly questioned the right of the PRI to monopolize political power. They organized to press for fairer elections and more responsive public officials. They demanded the right of opposition parties to compete for power on an equal basis with the PRI. They argued that the president had too much power and that the PRI was riddled with corruption.

At the same time, the government introduced major policy changes that affected virtually every aspect of the country's economy. Reformers wanted Mexico to have a market-oriented economic system to replace one in which the state played a major role in guiding the process of development. They wanted to see the country's industry and agriculture thrive in a competitive global market. However, the new policies, together with a series of economic crises, affected many people adversely. Incomes fell, businesses went bankrupt, jobs were lost, and government services were cut back.

Political and economic dissatisfaction surge today in part because of painful inequalities among social classes in the country. For elites, the opportunities of globalization have provided unprecedented wealth and a cosmopolitan life-style that spans the continent. At the same time, indicators of malnutrition are rising in the general population. The public education and health systems struggle with minimal resources to meet the demands of the poor. In the countryside,

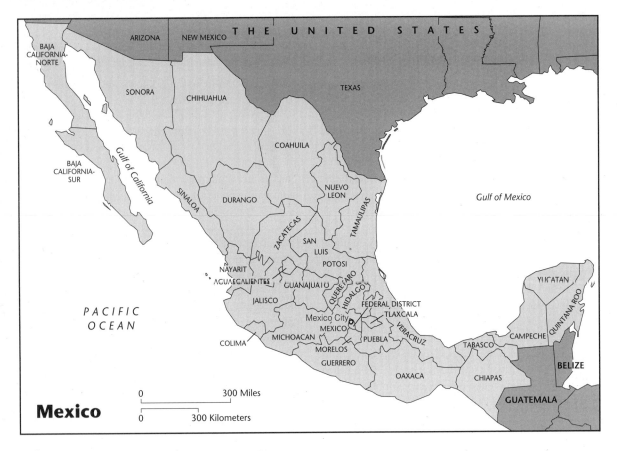

THE UNITED STATES

ARIZONA | NEW MEXICO | TEXAS

BAJA CALIFORNIA-NORTE

SONORA

CHIHUAHUA

COAHUILA

Gulf of California

BAJA CALIFORNIA-SUR

NUEVO LEON

Gulf of Mexico

SINALOA

DURANGO

ZACATECAS

TAMAULIPAS

SAN LUIS POTOSI

NAYARIT

AGUASCALIENTES

GUANAJUATO

QUERETARO

HIDALGO

YUCATAN

PACIFIC OCEAN

JALISCO

FEDERAL DISTRICT

TLAXCALA

Mexico City

MEXICO

VERACRUZ

QUINTANA ROO

COLIMA

MICHOACAN

PUEBLA

CAMPECHE

MORELOS

TABASCO

GUERRERO

BELIZE

OAXACA

CHIAPAS

GUATEMALA

Mexico

0   300 Miles

0   300 Kilometers

modern commercial farmers prosper as the country's large peasant population faces increasing poverty. Many citizens feel that the government must become more representative and responsive to their needs, and that an overhaul of the political system is essential.

As a result, the assassination of Colosio drew attention to ongoing and interrelated challenges of Mexico's development:

- Would a country with a long tradition of authoritarian government be able to move toward the more open and democratic political system being demanded by its citizens?
- Would a country that had long sought economic development through government activism and the growth of a domestic market be able to compete effectively in a competitive and market-driven global economy?

- Would a country long noted for severe inequalities between the rich and the poor be capable of providing better living standards for its growing population?

Geographic Setting

Mexico is one of the most geographically diverse countries in the world, encompassing snow-capped volcanoes, coastal plains, high plateaus, fertile valleys, rain forest, and desert within an area slightly less than three times the size of Texas. To the north, it shares a 2000-mile-long border with the United States; to the south, a 600-mile-long border with Guatemala and a 160-mile-long border with Belize.

Two imposing mountain ranges run the length of Mexico, the Sierra Madre Occidental to the west and the Sierra Madre Oriental to the east. As a result, the country is noted for its peaks, plateaus, and valleys that produce an astonishing number of microclimates and a rich diversity of plants and animals. Mexico's varied geography has historically made communication and transportation between regions difficult, and infrastructure expensive. The mountainous areas tend to limit large-scale commercial agriculture to irrigated fields in the northern part of the country, while the central and southern regions produce a wide variety of crops on small farms. Soil erosion and desertification are major problems because of the steep terrain and unpredictable rainfall in many areas. The country is rich in oil, silver, and other natural resources but has long struggled to manage those resources wisely.

The human landscape is equally dramatic. With over 98.5 million inhabitants, Mexico is among the world's ten most populated countries—the second-largest nation in Latin America after Portuguese-speaking Brazil, and the largest Spanish-speaking nation in the world. Sixty percent of the population are *mestizos*, or people of mixed Amerindian and Spanish descent. Another thirty percent are all or mostly **Amerindian**, while the rest are Caucasian or have other backgrounds. Official figures report that about 8 percent of the population speaks an indigenous language, the largest **indigenous groups** being the various Maya in the south and Náhuatl in the central regions, with well over a million speakers each. Other important groups like the Zapotec, Mixtec, Otomi, Purépecha, and the Tarahumara number in the tens of thousands. However, there are dozens and perhaps hundreds of smaller linguistic and social groups throughout the country. Although Mexicans pride themselves on their Amerindian heritage, problems of racism and classism run deep, and there is a great deal of ambivalence about issues of "Indian-ness."

Mexico was transformed from a largely rural to a largely urban country in the second half of the twentieth century, with approximately 74 percent of the population now living in urban areas. Meanwhile, Mexico City has become one of the world's largest cities with about 18 million inhabitants. Population growth has slowed to about 1.8 percent, but society continues to adjust to the baby boom of the 1970s and early 1980s as these 15–30-year-olds enter a competitive job market and form families during a housing crunch.

Migration both within and beyond Mexico's borders has become a major issue. Greater economic opportunities in the industrial cities of the north lead many men and women to seek work there in the *maquiladoras*, or assembly industries. Border cities like Tijuana and Cuidad Juárez have experienced tremendous growth in the last fifteen years. Many job-seekers continue on to the United States, lured by a larger job market and higher wages. The problem repeats itself in reverse on Mexico's southern border, with many thousands of Central Americans looking for better prospects in Mexico and beyond.

Critical Junctures

Mexicans are deeply affected by the legacies of their collective past, particularly the central formative event in the country's modern history, the Revolution of 1910. Mexico experienced the first great social

Critical Junctures in Mexico's Political Development

1810–1821	War of independence from Spain.
1876–1911	Dictatorship of Porfirio Díaz.
1910–1921	Mexican Revolution.
1917	Mexican Constitution.
1929	Plutarco Elías Calles founds PRI.
1934–1940	Presidency of Lázaro Cárdenas; entrenchment of corporatist state.
1968	Massacre of Tlaltelolco; 200 students are killed.
1978–1982	State-led development reaches peak with petroleum boom and bust.
1982	Market reformers come to power in PRI.
1988	Carlos Salinas elected amid charges of fraud.
1989	First governorship won by an opposition party.
1994	NAFTA goes into effect; uprising in Chiapas; Colosio assassinated.
1996	Four largest political parties agree on electoral reform.
1997	Opposition parties advance nationwide; PRI loses absolute majority in congress for first time in its history.

Global Connection: **Conquest or Encounter?**

The year 1519, when the Spanish conqueror Hernán Cortés arrived on the shores of the Yucatán Peninsula, is often considered the starting point of Mexican political history. But the Spanish explorers did not set off across an uninhabited land waiting to be excavated for gold and silver. Instead, the land that was to become New Spain and then Mexico was home to extensive and complex indigenous civilizations that were advanced in agriculture, architecture, and political and economic organization—civilizations that were already over a thousand years old. The Mayans of the Yucatán and the Toltecs of the central highlands had reached high levels of development long before the arrival of the Europeans. By 1519 diverse groups had fallen under the power of the militaristic Aztec Empire, which extended throughout what is today central and southern Mexico.

The encounter between the Europeans and these indigenous civilizations was marked by bloodshed and violence. The great Aztec city of Tenochtitlán—the site of Mexico City today—was captured and largely destroyed by the Spanish conquerors in 1521. Cortés and the colonial masters who came after him subjected indigenous groups to forced labor, robbed them of gold, silver, and land, and introduced flora and fauna from Europe that destroyed long-existing aqueducts and irrigation systems. They also brought alien forms of property rights and authority relationships, a religion that viewed indigenous practices as the devil's work, and an economy based on mining and cattle—all of which soon overwhelmed existing structures of social and economic organization. Within a century,

wars, savage exploitation at the hands of the Spaniards, and the introduction of European diseases reduced the indigenous population from an estimated 25 million to 1 million or less. The Indian population took three hundred years just to stop decreasing after the disaster of the Conquest.

Even so, the Spanish never constituted more than a small percentage of the total population, and massive racial mixing between the Indians, Europeans, and to a lesser extent Africans, produced a new *raza*, or *mestizo* race. This unique process remains at once a source of pride and conflict for Mexicans today. What does it mean to be Mexican? Is one the conquered or the conqueror? While celebrating Amerindian achievements in food, culture, the arts, and ancient civilization, middle-class Mexico has the contradictory sense that to be "Indian" nowadays is to be against progress, backwards, even barbaric. Many Amerindians are stigmatized by mainstream society if they speak a native dialect. But perhaps the situation is changing, with the upsurge of indigenist movements from both the grassroots and the international level striving to promote ethnic pride, defend rights, and foster the teaching of Indian languages.

The collision of two worlds resonates in current national philosophical and political debates. Is Mexico a Western society? Is it colonial or modern? Third or First World? South or North? Is the United States an ally or a conqueror? Perhaps most important, many Mexicans at once welcome and fear full integration into the global economy, asking themselves: Is globalization the new Conquest?

revolution of the twentieth century, a conflict that lasted for more than a decade and claimed the lives of as many as 2 million people. Some died in violent confrontations, but the majority lost their lives through the massive destruction, dislocation, and famine caused by the shifting and sporadic nature of the conflict. The revolution was fought by a variety of forces for a variety of reasons, which made the consolidation of power that followed as significant as the revolution itself. The institutions and symbols of the current political regime emerged from these complex conflicts.

Independence and Instability (1810–1876)

Spain ruled Mexico for three centuries, administering a vast economic, political, and religious empire in the interests of the imperial country, its kings, and its representatives in North America. Colonial policy was designed to extract wealth from New Spain and to limit the possibilities for Spaniards in the New World to benefit from agriculture, commerce, or industry without at the same time benefiting Spain. It was also designed to ensure commitment to the Roman Catholic religion.

In 1810, however, a parish priest in central Mexico named Miguel Hidalgo issued a rallying cry to a group assembled in a parish church in the town of Dolores. He called for an end to Spanish misrule. At the head of a motley band of rebels, he began the first of a series of wars of independence that pitted rebels against the Spanish crown for eleven years. Despite the fact that independence from Spain was recognized in 1821, Mexico struggled to create a stable and legitimate government for decades thereafter.

Liberals and conservatives, federalists and centralists, those who sought to expand the power of the church and those who sought to curtail it, and those who wanted a republic and those who wanted a monarchy were all engaged in the battle for Mexico's soul during the nineteenth century. Between 1833 and 1855, thirty-six presidential administrations came to power. During this disorganized period, Mexico lost half its territory to the United States.

Mexico's northern territory of Texas proclaimed and then won independence in a war ending in 1836. The Lone Star Republic was annexed to the United States by Congress in 1845, and claims on Mexican territory north of the Rio Grande were increasingly heard from Washington. On the basis of a very dubious claim that Mexico had invaded U.S. territory, the United States declared war on its southern neighbor. The war was first fought along what was later to become the border between the two countries and then, in 1847, the U.S. army invaded the port city of Veracruz. Causing considerable loss of civilian lives, this army marched toward Mexico City and the final battle at Chapultepec Castle. An 1848 treaty gave the United States title to what later became the states of Texas, New Mexico, Utah, Nevada, Arizona, California, and part of Colorado for about $18 million, leaving a legacy of deep resentment about U.S. imperialism.

Throughout this period, liberals and conservatives continued their struggle to resolve issues of political and economic order and, in particular, the power of the Catholic Church. The constitution of 1857 incorporated many of the goals of the liberals, such as republican government, a bill of rights, abolition of slavery, and limitations on the economic and political power of the church. Benito Juárez, who occupied the presidency on three separate occasions, continues to be revered in Mexico today as an early proponent of open and republican government.

The constitution of 1857 did not guarantee stability, however. In 1861, Spain, Great Britain, and France occupied the coastal town of Veracruz to collect customs claims from the government, providing the French army an opportunity to march on Mexico City and establish the government of Emperor Maximilian and Empress Carlota (1864–1867). Conservatives and Catholic loyalists welcomed this respite from the liberals. But Juárez was back in office in 1867, spearheading reforms in economic, social, and political arenas as well as building up the institutions of a new national government.

Over the next few years, a popular retired general named Porfirio Díaz became increasingly dissatisfied with the tedious new rule of law and criticized what he saw to be a "lot of politics" and "little action." After several failed attempts to win and then take the presidency, he finally succeeded in 1876. His dictatorship lasted thirty-four years and was at first welcomed by many because it brought sustained stability to the country.

The Porfiriato (1876–1911)

When Díaz took power, Mexico had been experiencing decades of political and economic turmoil. Díaz imposed a highly centralized authoritarian system to create political order and economic progress. In time, he relied increasingly on a small clique of advisers, known as *científicos* (scientists), who wanted to adopt European technologies and values to modernize the country, forcefully if necessary. Deeply disdainful of the vast majority of the country's population, Díaz and the *científicos* encouraged foreign investment and amassed huge fortunes, which they used to support lavish life-styles and to copy the latest European styles. During this period, known as the Porfiriato, this small elite monopolized political power and reserved lucrative economic investments for themselves and their allies. Economic and political opportunities were closed off for new generations of middle- and upper-class Mexicans, who became increasingly sensitive to the greed of the Porfirians and their own lack of opportunities.

In 1914, Pancho Villa (right) met with Emiliano Zapata in Mexico City to discuss the revolution and their separate goals for its outcome. *Source:* Freck/Odyssey, Chicago.

The Revolution of 1910 and the Sonoran Dynasty (1910–1934)

In 1910 conflict broke out as a new generation of reformers sought to end the dictatorship. Díaz had pledged himself to an open election for president, and in 1910, Francisco I. Madero, a landowner from the northern state of Coahuila, presented himself as a candidate. The slogan "Effective Suffrage, No Reelection" summed up the reformers' goals in creating opportunities for a new class of politically ambitious citizens to move into positions of power. When this opposition swelled, Díaz decided against having an election and tried to clamp down. But it was too late. Madero—who was later assassinated—became president of a distintegrating country.

At the same time that middle-class reformers struggled to displace Díaz, a peasant revolt that focused on land claims erupted in the central and southern states of the country. This revolt had roots in legislation that made it easy for wealthy landowners and ranchers to claim the lands of peasant villagers. Encouraged by the weakening of the old regime and driven to desperation by increasing landlessness, villagers armed themselves and joined forces under a variety of local leaders. The most famous of these

was Emiliano Zapata, who amassed a peasant army from Morelos, a state in southern Mexico. Peasant battalions swept through the countryside and grew in numbers; women as well as men flocked to fight under Zapata and other revolutionary leaders. Zapata's Plan de Ayala, first announced in 1911 and agreed to at a national meeting of revolutionary leaders in 1915, became the cornerstone of the radical agrarian reform that would be incorporated into the constitution of 1917.

In the northern part of the country, Francisco (Pancho) Villa rallied his own army of workers, small farmers, and ranch hands. He presented a major challenge to the national army, now under the leadership of Venustiano Carranza, who had inherited Madero's middle-class reformist movement and eventually became president. Villa's forces recognized no law but that of their chief and combined military maneuvers with banditry, looting, and warlordism in the territories under their control.

The constitution of 1917 was forged out of this diverse and often conflicting set of interests. It established a formal set of political institutions and guaranteed a range of progressive social and economic rights to citizens—agrarian reform, social security, the right to organize in unions, a minimum wage, an eight-hour work day, profit sharing for workers, and universal secular education. One thing it did not do, it should be noted, is provide suffrage for women, which was granted for local elections in 1953 and for national elections in 1958. In an effort to limit the power of foreign investors, the constitution declared that only Mexican citizens or the government could own land or rights to water and other natural resources. It also contained numerous articles that severely limited the power of the Roman Catholic Church, long a target of liberals who wanted Mexico to be a secular state. The signing of the document signaled the formal end of the revolution and the intent of the contending parties to form a new political regime. Despite such noble sentiments, violence continued as competing leaders sought to assert power and displace their rivals. Political assassinations were common through the 1920s, as were regional skirmishes among local warlords. Zapata, Villa, Carranza, and General Obregón were all assassinated, the last two while president.

Despite this violence, power was gradually consolidated in the hands of a group of revolutionary leaders from the north of the country. Known as the Sonoran Dynasty, after their home state of Sonora, these leaders were committed to a capitalist model of economic development. During the 1920s they skillfully outmaneuvered those who wished to see a socialist economy rise from the ashes of civil war. Eventually, one of the Sonorans—Plutarco Elías Calles—emerged as the *jefe máximo*, or supreme leader. Elected president in 1924, Calles managed to select and dominate his presidential successors from 1929 to 1934. The consolidation of power under his control was accompanied by extreme **anticlericalism**, which eventually resulted in warfare between conservative leaders of the Catholic Church and their followers, and the government.

In 1929, Calles brought together many of the most powerful contenders for leadership, including many regional warlords, to create a political party. The bargain he offered was simple. Contenders for power would accommodate each others' interests in the expectation of even greater power and spoils. Despite name changes in 1939 and 1946, the party they created exists to this day—the PRI. For the next sixty-five years, Calles's bargain was effective in ensuring a tradition of nonviolent conflict resolution among elites and the uninterrupted rule of the PRI in national politics.

Although the revolution was complex and the interests contending for power in its aftermath were numerous, there were five clear results of this protracted conflict. First, the power of traditional rural landowners was undercut. In the years after the revolution, wealthy elites would again emerge in rural areas, but they would never again be so powerful in national politics, nor could their power be so unchecked in local areas. Second, the power of the Catholic Church at the national level was firmly destroyed. While the church remained important in many parts of the country, it no longer participated openly in national political debates. Third, the power of foreign investors was severely limited; prior to the revolution, foreign investors owned much of the country's land as well as many of its railroads, mines, and factories. Henceforth, a clear sense of Mexican nationalism would shape economic policy-making.

Fourth, a new political elite consolidated power and agreed to resolve conflicts through accommodation and bargaining rather than violence. And fifth, the new constitution and the new party laid the basis for a strong central government that could assert its power over the agricultural, industrial, and social development of the country. Modern Mexican government and the country's economic development were profoundly affected by these accomplishments.

Lázaro Cárdenas, Agrarian Reform, and the Workers (1934–1940)

In 1934, Plutarco Calles handpicked Lázaro Cárdenas, a revolutionary general and state governor, as his successor to the presidency. He fully anticipated that Cárdenas would go along with Calles's behind-the-scenes management of the country and continue the economic policies of the postrevolutionary coalition. To his great surprise, Cárdenas executed a virtual coup that established his own supremacy and sent Calles packing to the United States for an "extended vacation."[1] Even more unexpectedly, Cárdenas mobilized peasants and workers in pursuit of the more radical goals of the 1910 revolution. He encouraged peasant syndicates' to petition for land and claim rights promised in the constitution of 1917. He eventually superintended the distribution of more than 17 million hectares of land (1 hectare = 2.471 acres). Most of these lands were distributed in the form of *ejidos* (collective land grants) to peasant groups who would be responsible for them. *Ejidatarios* (members of the *ejido*) became one of the most enduring bases of support for the government because of the redistribution of lands that was so forcefully pursued in the 1930s. Cárdenas also encouraged workers to form unions and demand higher wages and better working conditions. He established his nationalist credentials when he nationalized the petroleum industry in 1938, wresting it from U.S. and British investors.

During the Cárdenas years from 1934 to 1940, the bulk of the Mexican population was incorporated into the political system. Organizations of peasants, workers, middle-class groups, and the military were added to the party, and the voices of the poor majority were heard within the councils of government, reducing the risk that they would become radicalized outside them.

Mexican presidential candidates are expected to campaign hard, traveling to remote locations, making rousing campaign speeches, and meeting with citizens of humble origins. Here, presidential candidate Ernesto Zedillo is on the campaign trail in 1994. *Source:* AP/Wide World Photos.

In addition, the Cárdenas years witnessed a great expansion of the role of the state as the government set up a powerful investment bank to encourage industrialization, provided credit to agriculture, and invested in infrastructure.

Lázaro Cárdenas continues to be a national hero to Mexicans, who look back on his presidency as a period when government was clearly committed to improving the welfare of the country's poor. His other legacy was to institutionalize patterns of political succession and presidential behavior that continue to set standards for Mexico's leaders. He campaigned extensively, even though he was not seriously challenged by other candidates, and his campaign travel took him to remote villages and regions, where he listened to the demands and complaints of humble people. Cárdenas served a single six-year term, called a *sexenio*, and relinquished full political power to the new president, Manuel Avila Camacho. Cárdenas's conduct in office created hallowed traditions that subsequent PRI presidents have all observed.

The Politics of Development (1940–1994)

Although Cárdenas had directed a radical reshuffling of political power in the country, his successors were able to use the institutions he created to counteract his

reforms. Ambitious local and regional party leaders and leaders of peasants' and workers' groups began to use their organizations as pawns in exchange for political favors. Gradually, the PRI developed a huge patronage machine, providing union and *ejido* leaders with jobs, opportunities for corruption, land, and other benefits in return for delivering their followers' political support. Extensive chains of personal relationships based on the exchange of favors allowed the party to amass far-reaching political control and limit opportunities for organizing independently of the PRI. These exchange relationships, known as **clientelism**, became the cement that built loyalty to the PRI and the political system.

This kind of political control translated into the capacity of post-Cárdenas presidents to reorient the country's development away from the egalitarian social goals of the 1930s toward a development strategy in which the state actively encouraged industrialization and the accumulation of wealth. Initially, industrialization created jobs and made available a wide range of basic consumer goods to Mexico's burgeoning population. Growth rates were high during the 1940s, 1950s, and 1960s, and Mexicans flocked to the cities to take advantage of the jobs created in the manufacturing and construction industries. By the 1960s, however, industrial development policies were no longer generating rapid growth and could not keep pace with the rapidly rising demand for jobs.

The country's economy was in deep crisis by the mid-1970s. Just as policymakers began to take actions to correct the problems, however, vast new amounts of oil were discovered in the Gulf of Mexico. Soon, rapid economic growth was refueled by extensive public investment programs in virtually every sector of the economy. Based on the promise of petroleum wealth, the government and private businesses borrowed huge amounts of capital from foreign lenders who were, of course, eager to do business with a country that had so much oil. Unfortunately for Mexico, however, international petroleum prices plunged sharply in 1981. Almost overnight, there was no more credit to be had and much less money from petroleum to pay for economic expansion or the interest on the debts incurred in preceding years. Mexico plunged into a deep economic crisis that affected many countries around the world.

In fact, this crisis helped two presidents, Miguel de la Madrid (1982–1988) and Carlos Salinas (1988–1994), introduce the first major reversal of the country's development strategy since the 1940s. New policies were put in place to limit the government's role in the economy and to make it easier for Mexican producers to export their goods. This period clearly marked the beginning of a new effort to become more important in international economic affairs. In 1993, by signing the North American Free Trade Agreement (NAFTA), which commits Mexico, the United States, and Canada to eliminating trade barriers among them, Mexico's policymakers signaled the extent to which they envisioned the future prosperity of their country as tied to that of its two neighbors to the north. Efforts to increase trade and investment to Latin American, European, and Asian countries also emphasized Mexico's new commitment to competitiveness in a global economy. The economic reforms of the 1980s and 1990s were a turning point for the country's development, even though they left unresolved issues of democratic and social reform, and meant that Mexico's future development would be closely tied to conditions in the international economy. A major economic crisis at the end of 1994, in which billions of dollars of foreign investment fled the country, was indicative of this new international vulnerability. The administraton of Ernesto Zedillo (1994–2000) struggled to recover from this crisis.

Rifts and Openings (1994 to the Present)

For the Mexican government, 1994 was not an auspicious year. On January 1 a guerrilla movement called the Zapatista National Liberation Front (EZLN) seized four towns in the southern state of Chiapas. The group demanded land, democracy, indigenous rights, and an immediate repeal of NAFTA. Many citizens throughout the country openly supported the aims of the rebels, pointing out that the movement brought to light the reality of two very different Mexicos: those Mexicans who marched forward confidently into the twenty-first century with wealth and influence; and those who were getting left behind because of poverty and repression. The government and the military were criticized for inaction and human rights abuse in the state.

Following close on the heels of the rebellion came the Colosio assassination in March. The murder opened wide rifts within the PRI and unleashed a flood of speculation and distrust among the citizenry. Fear of violence helped provide the PRI with strong support in the August 1994 elections, although the secretary-general of the PRI, José Francisco Ruiz Massieu, was assassinated the following month. But the year's crowning inglorious event came in the form of economic meltdown in December, just three weeks after Zedillo took office. A severely overvalued peso led to a currency crisis and devaluation. This, coupled with tremendous government debt from the year's rampant public spending to soothe Chiapas and other impoverished areas, led to a financial emergency, loss of confidence, and massive amounts of money leaving the country. The peso lost half of its value against the dollar within a few short days, and the government lacked the funds to pay its obligations. Suddenly, Mexico's status among nations seemed dubious once more, and the country felt betrayed by outgoing President Salinas, convinced that he had patched together a shaky house of cards only long enough to get himself out of office.

The economy shrank by 6.2 percent in 1995, inflation soared, taxes rose while wages were frozen, and the bank system collapsed. The United States orchestrated a 50-billion-dollar bailout, $20 billion of

Citizen Action: *Rebellion in Chiapas*

In the months after January 1994 indigenous women set out daily for the tourist-laden zones of central Mexico City to sell handmade dolls. These dolls, dressed in brightly colored costumes, also sported black ski masks. They represented a symbolic connection to the rebels of the Zapatista National Liberation Front (EZLN) in the southern state of Chiapas, who wore ski masks to avoid identification by the government. Images of the ideological leader and public spokesman of the Zapatista movement, Subcomandante Marcos, also appeared throughout the country, and people of diverse ethnic, class, and political backgrounds began expressing support for the goals of the rebels.

The rebellion by some 2000 members of the EZLN broke out on January 1, 1994, the day that NAFTA went into effect. The Zapatista army captured four towns in the state of Chiapas, including the city of San Cristobal de las Casas, a popular tourist destination. The EZLN demanded "jobs, land, housing, food, health, education, independence, freedom, democracy, justice and peace."* The peasant army also called on the government to repeal NAFTA. These demands and the progress of the rebellion were immediately transmitted throughout Mexico and around the globe by domestic and international media as camera crews and reporters flocked to this remote, poverty-stricken state.

The EZLN's call for an end to exploitation at the hands of voracious landowners and corrupt bosses of the PRI, as well as for social services and citizenship rights, resonated deeply throughout the country. Soon, a broad spectrum of local, regional, professional, and human rights groups took up the banner of the Chiapas rebels and called on the government to open the political system to more just and democratic elections, decision-making processes, and policies. By calling in the army to suppress armed peasants, most of whom were Mayan Indians, and to retake the four towns by force, the government only increased sympathy for the marginalized, impoverished indigenous groups. The Chiapas rebellion symbolized for many the reality of Mexico's political, economic, and social inequalities.

The Zapatistas were not seeking to overthrow the Mexican political system. They believed, however, that the system created and maintained by the PRI had become very much like the dictatorship of Porfirio Díaz, toppled in the Revolution of 1910. They were united in their demand that indigenous groups throughout Mexico be granted fair treatment and the means to escape their poverty and powerlessness. They resorted to violence because they believed the government would not otherwise pay attention to their demands.

The Zapatista rebellion presented a major challenge to Mexico's image of political stability. It had a profound effect on the election of 1994, as competing political parties and candidates sought to identify with rebel demands for indigenous rights, economic justice, and honest elections. The rebels rejected a peace treaty that would have promoted the electoral fortunes of the PRI, arguing instead for increased space for political debate and dialogue. The government spent over $200 million on social programs and infrastructure projects in the state in the months leading up to the election, a 44 percent increase over what had been budgeted. Just weeks before the elections, however, the EZLN hosted a National Democratic Convention of a large number of groups committed to pressuring the government for fundamental political reform.

The rebels insisted that economic assistance alone would not solve the problems in the southern part of the country. They pointed to the deeper causes of injustice—namely, concentration of wealth in the hands of a brutal local elite and monopolization of power by a government that valued stability and compromise with local elites above all else.

In the aftermath of the rebellion, Mexican officials sought to erase the impression that the insurgency was an Indian uprising. They pointed out that many indigenous groups rejected the EZLN. Yet major indigenous organizations across Mexico and elsewhere in Latin America expressed solidarity with the Chiapas rebels and with the decision to take up arms. While some argued that the Chiapas rebellion was a local phenomenon and an isolated set of incidents, others predicted the spread of the Mexican example of armed uprisings by indigenous groups. The roots of such insurrections are in economic and social exploitation, they argued, not in specific ethnic identities. A stalemate still existed five years later: talks broke down, foreign observers were expelled, and accusations of human rights violations by the government were on the rise.

---

*As cited in Neil Harvey, *Rebellion in Chiapas: Rural Reforms, Campesino Radicalism, and the Limits to Salinismo* (San Diego: Center for U.S.-Mexican Studies, University of California, 1994), 1.

which came directly from the U.S. Treasury. Faced with limited options, Zedillo implemented a severe and unpopular economic austerity program, which restored financial stability over the next two years.

In the meantime, a second guerilla movement came to light, called the Popular Revolutionary Army (EPR), which was far more mysterious, less ideological, and more committed to violence than the Zapatistas. Considered terrorist by the government, the movement claimed to have operatives throughout the country and took responsibility for several destructive actions. Also in 1996, Raúl Salinas, brother of the former president, was indicted on charges of masterminding the murder of Ruiz Massieu as well as illicit enrichment and money-laundering.

These shocks provoked widespread disillusionment and frustration with the political system. Many citizens, especially in urban areas, decided that there was no longer any reason to support the PRI. Since 1994 opposition parties have become much more organized, experienced at governance, and effective at challenging the PRI nationwide. Buoyed by a 1996 electoral reform agreed upon by the four largest parties (PRI, PAN, PRD, and PT [Partido del Trabajo—Worker's Party]), important gains were made by the opposition in the July 1997 elections. For the first time in modern Mexican history, the PRI lost its absolute majority in the Chamber of Deputies. Since then, the congress has shown increasing dynamism as a counterbalance to the presidency, blocking executive decisions, demanding unrestricted information, and initiating new legislation. In addition, opposition parties have won important governorships and mayorships; it is estimated that more than half of Mexico is now governed by the opposition on the state or local level.

Mexicans seem to have increasing faith in the electoral process, but the biggest test of all remains: the presidency. Many citizens believe that Mexico will not be a truly democratic country until an opposition candidate sits in the presidential palace.

Themes and Implications

Historical Junctures and Political Themes

The modern Mexican state emerged out of a popular revolution that proclaimed goals of democratic government, social justice, and nationalism. In the chaotic years after the revolution, the state created conditions for political and social peace. By incorporating peasants and workers into party and government institutions and providing benefits to low-income groups during the 1930s, it became widely accepted as legitimate. In encouraging considerable economic growth in the years after 1940, it also encouraged belief in its ability to provide material improvements in the quality of life of large portions of the population. These factors worked together to create a strong state capable of guiding economic and political life in the country.

In its external relations, Mexico has always prided itself on ideological independence from the world's "great powers." Its large population, cultural richness, political stability, and front-line position in regard to the United States has prompted Mexico to consider itself a natural leader of Latin America and the developing world in general. However, the reforms of the 1980s and 1990s, especially NAFTA, have caused great concern among many citizens, who perceive that the government is accepting a position of political, cultural, and economic subordination to the United States.

Mexico has enjoyed considerable economic advancement since the 1940s, although a number of other developing countries have been equally or more successful in generating sustained economic growth and improving standards of living. In the 1990s it acquired aspirations to be considered one of the newly industrializing countries of the world, similar in stature to countries such as South Korea, Malaysia, and Taiwan. It was certainly facing up to many of the problems of the more advanced industrial nations—trying to achieve international competitiveness for its products, dealing with problems of air and water pollution, and managing the growth of its megacities. The decision to promote a free-trade agreement with its northern neighbors clearly indicated the government's recognition of the need to secure Mexico a place in the global economy.

However, the crises of 1994 and 1995 shook Mexico's confidence in its ability to achieve this goal on its own terms and highlighted conflict between a market-oriented development strategy and the country's philosophical tradition of a strong and protective state. The larger questions of whether a new development strategy can generate growth, whether Mexican products can find profitable markets overseas, whether investors can create extensive job opportunities for millions of unemployed and part-time workers, and whether the country can maintain the confidence of those investors over the longer term continue to challenge the country.

In many ways, the Revolution of 1910 could be interpreted as a struggle between collective identities that had remained latent during the Porfiriato. Its resolution, through the creation of the PRI and the notion of a strong state, represented the victory of the *mestizos* as a group, curtailing the colonial power of the Roman Catholic Church and Western-style elites as well as resubmerging the demands of justice and autonomy for the indigenous poor. The PRI was very successful at replacing the traditional politics of collective identities with the politics of a **corporatist state**, meaning that interest groups became an institutionalized part of state structure.

Despite the fact that many citizens remained marginal to full participation in the country's economic, political, and social life, most Mexicans agreed, at least until the 1980s, that the state was legitimate and nationalist. This does not mean that Mexican society was unorganized or passive. Indeed, many Mexicans were actively involved in local community organizations, religious activities, unions, and public interest groups. But traditionally, the scope for challenging the government, for insisting on basic civil rights, or for demanding an open and responsive government was very limited. Nor did Mexico's strong state mean that the government was openly repressive or brutal. On the contrary, officials in the government and the party generally worked hard to find ways to resolve conflicts peacefully, and they maintained the belief that the state represents the aspirations of all Mexicans. In fact, most Mexicans pursued their daily lives without feeling directly threatened by the power of the state. The norm in Mexico's state-society relationship has been peaceful resolution of conflict and behind-the-scenes accommodation of conflicting interests.

With frustrations mounting in the 1980s and 1990s because of economic crises and the incapacity of government to respond to civilian demands, the traditional politics of collective identities began to strongly surface once more. Ethnic groups, religious groups, community movements, private business, and regionalism have all emerged as important forces, and it remains to be seen how the current transformation of the Mexican political scene will accommodate them.

The revolution resolved the conflict between the democratic idea and Mexico's centralized, authoritarian tradition in much the same way it dealt with the conflict among collective identities: through corporativism. The country opted not for true democracy but for representation through government-mediated organizations within a corporatist state. This development increased state power in relation to civil society. The state took the lead in defining goals for the country's development and, through the school system, the party, and the media, inculcated a broad sense of its legitimate right to set such goals. In addition, the state had extensive resources at its disposal to control or co-opt dissent and to purchase political loyalty. The PRI was an essential channel through which material goods, jobs, the distribution of land, and the allocation of development projects flowed to increase popular support for the system or to buy off opposition to it. Citizens wishing to have greater input into national decision-making faced an uphill battle.

By the 1980s, however, cracks began to appear in the traditional ways in which Mexican citizens interacted with the government. As the PRI began to lose its capacity to control political activities, and as civic groups increasingly insisted on their right to remain independent from the PRI and the government, the terms for the state-society relationship were clearly in need of redefinition. Through the formation of private interest groups and organized social movements, civil society increasingly pressured government to be more responsive, fair, democratic, and effective. The administration of President Zedillo signaled its willingness to cede political power to successful opposition parties in fair elections, with the electoral reform of 1996 and the elections of 1997 being particularly significant steps in the emergence of a true multiparty system. As more citizens found themselves governed by different parties, they seemed to gain confidence that democracy can succeed in Mexico. Of course, many groups benefit from the corporatist system and do not want it to change. Mexico's future stability depends on how well the government can accommodate these conflicting interests while, at the same time, transforming political institutions and providing economic opportunities to a largely poor population.

Implications for Comparative Politics

The Mexican political system is unique among developing countries in the extent to which it has managed to institutionalize and maintain civilian political authority for a very long time. In a world of developing nations, wracked by political turmoil, military coups, and regime changes, this regime has established enduring institutions of governance and conditions for political stability. Other countries have sought to emulate the Mexican model of stability based on an alliance between a dominant party and a strong development-oriented state, but rarely have governments had the legitimacy to appropriate all facets of social life as in Mexico. The regime's revolutionary heritage as well as its ability to maintain a sense of national identity are important factors in accounting for its political continuity.

Currently, Mexico represents a nation attempting to undergo significant political change without violence, to transform itself from a corporatist state to a truly democratic one for the first time in its long history. At the same time, it struggles to resolve the conflicts of development through an integration with its North American neighbors that it hopes will improve the quality of life of its citizens.

Section ❷   Political Economy and Development

Mexico has been categorized as a relatively prosperous developing country, along with countries such as Argentina, Portugal, South Korea, and Venezuela.[2] It has made significant strides in industrialization, which accounts for about 26 percent of the country's gross domestic product (GDP). Agriculture contributes about 8 percent to GDP, and services contribute some 67 percent. This structure is very similar to the economic profiles of Brazil, New Zealand, and Hungary. But, unlike those countries, Mexico is oil-rich. The government-owned petroleum industry is a ready source of revenue and foreign exchange, but it is also extremely vulnerable to changes in international oil prices.

Mexico's industrial and petroleum-based economy means a higher per capita income than in most other developing countries. If income were spread evenly among all Mexicans, each would receive $3680 annually—far more than the per capita incomes of India ($390), China ($860), and Nigeria ($269) but considerably less than those of Britain ($20,710), France ($26,052), and Germany ($28,260).[3] Of course, income is not spread evenly. Mexico suffers from great inequalities in how wealth is distributed, and poverty continues to be a grim reality for millions of Mexicans. The way Mexico promotes economic growth and industrialization is important in explaining why widespread poverty has persisted and why political power has not been more equitably distributed.

State and Economy

During the years of the Porfiriato (1876–1911), the country began to produce some textiles, footwear, glassware, paper, beer, tiles, furniture, and other simple products. At that time, however, policymakers were convinced that Mexico could grow rich by exporting its raw materials to more economically advanced countries. Their efforts to attract domestic and international investment encouraged a major boom in the production and export of products such as henequin (for making rope), coffee, cacao (cocoa beans), cattle, silver, and gold. Soon, the country had become so attractive to foreign investors that large amounts of land, the country's petroleum, its railroad network, and its mining wealth were largely controlled by foreigners. Nationalist reaction against the power of these foreign interests played a significant role in the tensions that produced the Revolution of 1910.

In the new Mexican state, this nationalism combined with a sense of social justice inspired by popular revolutionary leaders such as Zapata. Mexicans widely shared the idea that the state had the responsibility to generate wealth for all its citizens. In addition, it was thought that only the state was powerful enough to mobilize the resources and stimulate the development necessary to overcome the destruction of the revolution. As a result, the country adopted a strategy in which the government guided the process of industrial and agricultural development and set the political conditions for its success. Often referred to as **state capitalism**, this development strategy relied heavily on government actions to encourage private investment and to lower risks for private entrepreneurs.

In the twenty years following the revolution, many of those concerned about the country's development became convinced that economic growth would not occur unless Mexico could industrialize more fully. They argued that reliance on exports of agricultural products, minerals, and petroleum—called the agro-export model—forced the country to import manufactured goods which, over the long term, would always cost more than what was earned from exports. Critics of the agro-export model of development also argued that prices of primary products shifted greatly from one year to the next. Countries that produced them were doomed to repeat boom/bust cycles as their domestic economies reflected sharp fluctuations in international prices for the goods they exported. Mexico, they believed, should begin to manufacture the goods that it was currently importing.

Import Substitution and Its Consequences

Between 1940 and 1982, Mexico pursued a form of state capitalism and a model of industrialization known as import substitution, or **import substituting industrialization** (ISI). Like Brazil and other Latin American countries during the period, the government promoted industrialization by encouraging domestic and international investment, providing credit and tax incentives to industrialists, maintaining low rates of inflation, and keeping wage demands low through subsidized transportation, housing, and health care for workers. It also fostered industrialization by establishing state-owned steel mills, electric power generators, ports, and petroleum production. Between 1940 and 1970, over 40 percent of all fixed capital investment came from the government. These policies had considerable success. Initially, the country produced mainly simple products like shoes, clothing, and

processed foods. But by the 1960s and 1970s it was also producing consumer durables (refrigerators, automobiles, trucks), intermediate goods (steel, petrochemicals, and other products used in the manufacturing process), and capital goods (heavy machinery to produce manufactures).

Mexican agriculture was also affected by this drive to industrialize. With the massive agrarian reform of the 1930s (see Section 1), the *ejido* had become an important structure in the rural economy, accounting for half the cultivated area of the country and 51 percent of the value of agricultural production by 1940. After Cárdenas left office, however, government policymakers moved rapidly away from the economic development of the *ejidos*. They became committed instead to developing a strong, entrepreneurial private sector in agriculture. For them, "the development of private agriculture would be the 'foundation of industrial greatness.'"[4] They wanted agriculture to provide foodstuffs for the growing cities, raw materials for industry, and foreign exchange from exports. To encourage these goals, the government invested in transportation networks, irrigation projects, and agricultural storage facilities. It provided extension services and invested in research. It encouraged imports of technology to improve output and mechanize production. Since policymakers believed that modern commercial farmers would respond more to these investments and services than would peasants on small plots of land, the government provided most of its assistance to large landowners.

The government's encouragement of industry and agriculture set the country on a three-decade path of sustained growth. Between 1940 and 1950, gross domestic product grew at an annual average of 6.7 percent, while manufacturing increased at an average of 8.1 percent. In the following two decades, GDP growth rates remained impressive and manufacturing growth continued to outpace overall growth in the economy. In the 1950s manufacturing achieved an average of 7.3 percent growth annually; in the 1960s, 10.1 percent annually. Agricultural production grew rapidly as new areas were brought under cultivation and green revolution technology (scientifically improved seeds, fertilizers, and pesticides) was extensively adopted on large farms. These were years of great optimism as foreign investment increased, the

Table 1

Mexican Development, 1940–1990						
	1940	*1950*	*1960*	*1970*	*1980*	*1990*
Population (thousands)	19,815	26,282	38,020	52,771	70,416	88,598
Life expectancy[a] (years)	—	51.6	58.6	62.6	67.4	68.9
Infant mortality[a] (per 1,000 live births)	—	—	86.3	70.9	49.9	42.6
Illiteracy (% of population age 15 and over)	—	42.5	34.5	25.0	16.0	12.7
Urban population (% of total)	—	—	50.7	59.0	66.4	72.6
Economically active population in agriculture (% of total)	—	58.3	55.1	44.0	36.6	22.0

	1940–1950	*1950–1960*	*1960–1970*	*1970–1980*	*1980–1990*
GDP growth rate (average annual percent)	6.7	5.8	7.6	6.7	1.6
Per capita GDP growth rate	—	—	3.7	3.7	−0.7

[a]Five-year average.

Sources: *Statistical Abstract for Latin America* (United Nations, Economic Commission for Latin America); Roger Hansen, *The Politics of Mexican Development* (Baltimore, Md.: Johns Hopkins University Press, 1971); *Statistical Bulletin of the OAS.*

middle class grew larger, and indicators for health and welfare steadily improved. Between 1940 and 1970, Mexico City grew from a modest-sized city of a million and a half people to a major metropolis of over 8 million inhabitants. Even the poorest Mexicans believed that their lives were improving. Table 1 presents data that summarize a number of advancements during this period. So impressive was Mexico's economic performance that it was referred to internationally as the Mexican Miracle, paralleling Germany's *Wirtschaftswunder* and Japan's Economic Miracle.

U.S. private investment was an important source of capital for the country's effort to industrialize; in the twenty years after 1950, it grew at an average of over 11 percent a year. In 1962 the United States accounted for 85 percent of all foreign investment in Mexico. Moreover, two-thirds of Mexico's imports typically came from the United States, while it regularly sent two-thirds of its exports there. Mexican policymakers increasingly saw the closeness and size of

the U.S. economy as a significant threat, and many policy initiatives—restricting foreign investment in industries considered important to national development and seeking to diversify trade relationships with other countries, for example—were undertaken to lessen the country's dependence on the United States.

While the government took the lead in encouraging industrialization, it was not long before a group of domestic entrepreneurs developed a special relationship with the state. Government policies protected their products through high tariffs or special licensing requirements, limiting imports of competing goods. Business elites in Mexico received subsidized credit to invest in equipment and plants; they benefited from cheap, subsidized energy; and they rarely had to pay taxes. Additionally, inflation was kept in check and the government helped ensure a supply of cheap labor by providing workers' housing, transportation, and medical coverage.

Through the impact of such policies, an elite of protected businesses emerged as powerful players in national politics. In the 1940s and 1950s they strengthened a set of industry-related interest groups that worked to promote and sustain favorable policies. With this organizational base, groups like the chambers of industry, commerce, and banking began to play increasingly important roles in government policymaking. They were able to veto efforts by the government to cut back on their benefits and to lobby for even more advantages. The government remained the source of most policy initiatives, but generally it was not able to move far in the face of opposition from those who benefited most from its policies. Perhaps just as important, business elites became adept at sidestepping government regulations, paying bribes to acquire licenses, credit, permits, and exemptions, and working out deals with officials on a one-to-one basis.

Workers also became more important players in national politics. As mentioned in Section 1, widespread unionization occurred under President Cárdenas, and workers won many rights that had been promised in the constitution of 1917. Cárdenas organized the unions into the National Confederation of Workers, the CTM, which became the most powerful official voice of organized labor within the PRI. The policy changes initiated in the 1940s, however, made the unions more dependent on the government for benefits and protection; the government also limited the right to strike. Wage standards were set through active annual negotiation between the CTM and the government, with employer groups largely sitting on the sidelines. Despite the fact that unions were closely controlled, organized workers continued to be an elite within the country's working classes. Union membership meant job security and important benefits such as housing subsidies and health care for families. These factors helped compensate for the lack of democracy within the labor movement. Moreover, labor leaders had privileged access to the country's political leadership and benefited personally from their control over jobs, contracts, and working conditions. In return, they guaranteed labor peace.[5]

In agriculture, those who benefited from government policies and services were primarily farmers who had enough land and economic resources to irrigate and mechanize and who had the capacity to make technological improvements in their farming methods and crops. By the 1950s a group of large, commercially oriented farmers had emerged to dominate the agricultural economy.[6] They, like their urban counterparts in business, became rich and powerful. Industrialization also created a powerful class of government officials. Many abused their power to dispense jobs, licenses, and permits for a variety of activities, public works projects, and government investments by selling such favors in return for *mordidas* (bites, or bribes) or political support. They also became firm supporters of the continuation of government policies that provided them with special advantages.

There were significant costs to this pattern of economic and political development. Most important, government policies eventually limited the potential for further growth.[7] Industrialists who received extensive subsidies and benefits from government had few incentives to produce efficiently. High tariffs kept out foreign competition, further reducing incentives for efficiency or quality in production. Importing technology to support industrialization eventually became a drain on the country's foreign exchange. In addition, the costs of providing benefits to workers increased beyond the capacity of the government to generate revenue, especially because tax rates were kept extremely low as a further incentive to investors. Mexico's tax rates, in fact, were among the lowest in the world, and opportunities to avoid payment were extensive. Eventually, the ISI strategy became less effective in generating new jobs as industrialists moved from investing in labor-intensive industries such as processed foods and textiles to capital-intensive industries such as automobiles, refrigerators, and heavy equipment. As a result, cities began to fill up with underemployed and unemployed workers.

Moreover, as the economy grew, and with it the power of industrial, agricultural, and urban interests, many were left behind. The ranks of the urban poor grew steadily, particularly from the 1960s on. Mexico developed a sizable **informal sector**—workers who produced or sold goods and services at the margin of the economic system and who faced extreme insecurity. By 1970 a large proportion of Mexico City's population was living in inner-city tenements or squatter settlements surrounding the city.[8]

Also left behind in the country's development after 1940 were the country's peasant farmers. Their lands were often the least fertile, plot sizes were minuscule, and access to markets was impeded by poor transportation and exploitive middlemen who trucked products to markets for exorbitant fees. The 1940s and 1950s were important years for increasing the gap between commercial agriculture, largely centered in the north and northwestern regions of the country, where much of Mexico's political elite originated, and subsistence agriculture, largely made up of small private farmers and *ejidatarios* who lived in central and southern parts of the country. Farming in the *ejido* communities, where land was held communally, was particularly difficult. Because *ejido* land could not be sold or (until the early 1980s) rented, *ejidatarios* could not borrow money from private banks because they had nothing to pledge as collateral if they defaulted on their payments. Government banks provided credit, but usually only to those who had political connections. The government invested little in small infrastructure projects throughout the 1960s, and because the *ejidatarios* did not have individual title to their land, they had little incentive to provide their own infrastructure. Agricultural research and extension focused on the large-farm sector. Since prices for basic foodstuffs were controlled, the *ejidos* saw little advantage to investing in farming. Not surprisingly, the *ejido* sector consistently reported low productivity.

Increasing disparities in rural and urban incomes, coupled with high population growth rates, contributed to the emergence of rural guerrilla movements and student protests in the mid- and late 1960s. The government was particularly alarmed in 1968, when a student movement openly challenged the government on the eve of the Olympic games being hosted by Mexico City. Moreover, by the early 1970s, it was becoming evident that the size of the population, growing at a rate of some 3.5 percent a year, and the structure of income distribution were impeding further industrial development. The domestic market was limited by poverty; many Mexicans could not afford the sophisticated manufactured products the country would need to produce in order to keep growing under the import substitution model.

Mexican governments hoped that industrialization would free the economy from excessive dependence on the industrialized world, and particularly on the United States, making the country less subject to abrupt swings in the prices for primary commodities. Industrialization, however, highlighted new vulnerabilities. Advanced manufacturing processes required ever more foreign investment and imported technology. Concern grew about powerful multinational companies, which had invested heavily in the country in the 1960s, and so did the need to spend scarce foreign exchange for foreign technology. By the late 1960s the country was unable to meet domestic demand for basic foodstuffs and was forced to import increasingly large quantities of food, costing the government precious foreign exchange that it could have used for better purposes. By the 1970s some policymakers had become convinced that industrialization had actually *increased* the country's dependence on advanced industrial countries and particularly on the United States.

Sowing the Oil and Reaping a Crisis

In the early 1970s, Mexico faced the threat of social crisis brought on by rural poverty, chaotic urbanization, high population growth, and the questioning of political legitimacy. The government responded by increasing investment in infrastructure and public industry, regulating the flow of foreign capital, and increasing social spending. The government was spending much more than it generated, causing the public internal debt to grow rapidly and requiring heavy borrowing abroad. Between 1971 and 1976 inflation rose from an annual average of 5.3 percent to almost 16 percent and the foreign debt more than tripled. In response to mounting evidence that current policies could not be sustained, the government devalued the peso in 1976 and signed a stabilization agreement with the International Monetary Fund (IMF) to reduce government spending, increase tax collection, and control inflation. Little progress was made in changing the existing set of policies, however, because just as the seriousness of the economic situation was being recognized, vast new finds of oil were reported.

Between 1978 and 1982, Mexico was transformed into a major oil exporter. As international oil prices rose rapidly—from US$13.30 per barrel in 1978 to $33.20 per barrel in 1981—so did the country's fortunes, along with those of other oil-rich countries such as Nigeria, Iran, Indonesia, and Venezuela. The administration of President José López Portillo

(1976–1982) embarked on a policy to "sow the oil" in the economy and "administer the abundance," with vast investment projects in virtually all sectors and major new initiatives to reduce poverty and deal with declining agricultural productivity. Oil revenues paid for much of this expansion, but the foreign debt also mounted as both public and private sectors borrowed heavily to finance investments and lavish consumer spending. Mexico, like many other countries, was able to borrow extensively because international financial markets were flush with so-called **petrodollars**, money not only generated but also anticipated by the oil boom.

In 1982, Mexico's foreign debt was US$86 billion and the exchange rate was seriously overvalued, making the peso and Mexican products more expensive on the world market. Oil accounted for 77.2 percent of the country's exports, causing the economy to be extremely vulnerable to changes in oil prices. And change they did. In 1983 global overproduction brought the international price for Mexican petroleum down to $26.3 a barrel. Revenues from exports declined dramatically. At the same time, the United States tightened its monetary policy, and access to foreign credit dried up. Wealthy Mexicans responded by sending vast amounts of capital out of the country just as the country's international creditors were demanding repayment on their loans. In August 1982 the government announced that the country could not pay the interest on its foreign debt, triggering a crisis that reverberated around the world.

The impact of these conditions on the Mexican economy was devastating. GDP growth in 1982 was –0.6 percent and fell to –4.2 percent the following year. New policy measures were put in place by the administration of Miguel de la Madrid (1982–1988) to deal with the economic crisis, but they were repeatedly overtaken by escalating inflation, financial-sector panic, depleted foreign reserves, severe trade imbalances, and debt renegotiations. In 1986 petroleum prices dropped to $12 a barrel.

The economic crisis had several important implications for structures of power and privilege in Mexico. First, faith in the import substitution policy was destroyed. The crisis convinced even the most diehard believer that import substitution created inefficiencies in production, failed to generate sufficient

employment, cost the government far too much in subsidies, and increased dependency on industrialized countries. By the mid-1980s, few policymakers or informed citizens argued strongly for the traditional highly interventionist state or for its protectionist and social welfare role.

In addition, the power of interest groups and their ability to influence government policy declined. Prolonged economic crisis hit the business sector particularly hard. When the economy stagnated, declined, and failed to recover rapidly, private debts could not be repaid, inflation and unemployment reduced demand, government subsidies were repeatedly cut back, and most public investment plans were put on hold. The inevitable result was the failure of many Mexican companies. Bankruptcy and recession exacted their toll on the fortunes of even large entrepreneurs. As economic hardship affected their members, traditional business organizations lost their ability to put strong pressure on the government.

Similarly, the country's relatively privileged unions lost much of their bargaining power with government over the issues of wages and protection. Union leaders emphasized the need for peace and order to help the nation get through tough times, while inflation and job loss focused many of the country's workers on putting food on the table. A shift in employment from the formal to the informal sector further fragmented what had once been the most powerful sector of the PRI. Cuts in government subsidies for public transportation, food, electricity, and gasoline created new hardships for workers. The combination of these factors weakened the capacity of labor to resist policy changes that affected the benefits they received.

New voices emerged to demand that the government alter its policies. During the recession years of the 1980s, wages lost between 40 and 50 percent of their value, increasingly large numbers of people became unemployed, inflation cut deeply into middle-class incomes, and budgets for health and education services were severely cut back. Mexico's citizens demanded that the government do something to address the hardship. During the 1980s a wide variety of interests began to organize outside the PRI. Massive earthquakes in Mexico City in September 1985 proved to be a watershed for Mexican society. Severely disappointed by the government's failure to respond to the problems created by death, destruction, disorientation, and homelessness, hundreds of communities organized rescue efforts, soup kitchens, shelter, and rehabilitation initiatives. A surging sense of political empowerment developed, as groups long accustomed to dependence on government learned that they could solve their problems better without government than with it.[9]

In addition, the PRI was challenged by the increased popularity of opposition political parties, one of them headed by Cuauhtémoc Cárdenas, the son of the country's most revered president, Lázaro Cárdenas. The elections of 1988 became a focus for protest against the economic dislocation caused by the crisis and the political powerlessness that most citizens felt. Carlos Salinas, the PRI candidate, received a bare majority of 50.7 percent, but opposition parties claimed widespread electoral fraud.

New Strategies and Emerging Democratic Institutions

Demands on the Salinas administration to deal with the economic and political crisis were extensive. At the same time, the weakening of the old centers of political power provided it with a major opportunity to reorient the country's strategy for economic development. The government took advantage of this opportunity. Between 1988 and 1994, the dependent relationship between industry and government was weakened when new free-market policies were put in place. Decreasing regulation was an important part of this restructuring of state-economy relationships. Deregulation gave the private sector more freedom to pursue economic activities and less reason to seek special favors from government. A number of large government industries, such as the telephone company, the banking sector, the national airlines, and steel and sugar mills, were reorganized and sold to private investors. A constitutional revision made it possible for *ejidatarios* to become owners of individual plots of land; this made them less dependent on government but more vulnerable to losing their land. In addition, financial-sector reform, such as changing laws about banking and establishing a stock exchange, encouraged the emergence of new banks and brokerage and insurance firms.

Salinas pursued, and Zedillo continued, an overhaul of the federal system and the way government agencies work together. Called the New Federalism, it is an attempt to give power and budgetary responsibilities to state and local governments, which are historically very weak in Mexico. Beginning with pilot programs in education and health, the presidents hoped through this decentralization to make government more responsive to citizens and more effective. In addition, federal agencies began to be broken down into regional bureaus, which work more closely with lower levels of government. In the past, nearly all important government functions were carried out by federal government offices located in Mexico City. Additionally, the central bank became independent from the government in 1994, though exchange rates are still determined by the Finance Ministry.

Among the most far-reaching initiatives carried out by the Salinas administration was the North American Free Trade Agreement (NAFTA) with Canada and the United States. This agreement created the basis for gradual introduction of free trade among the three countries. These changes were a major reversal of import substitution and economic intervention that had marked government policies in the past. However, the liberalization of the Mexican economy and opening up its markets to foreign competition increased the vulnerability of the country to changes in international economic conditions. These factors, as well as mismanaged economic policies, led to a major economic crisis for the country at the end of 1994 and profound recession in 1995. Since then, exports have increased tremendously because of the cheapness of the peso internationally, government finances look steady, and GDP has risen by 5.2 percent in 1996, 7 percent in 1997, and over 4 percent in 1998. Foreign investment has also recuperated, reaching record levels in 1997.[10]

In political matters, a series of electoral reforms culminated in 1996 with the creation of an independent election board composed of private citizens, as well as constitutional amendments regarding campaign fairness. Election funds are mostly public, with private expenditures limited. There are also procedures for auditing the political parties. As mentioned previously, elections have become much more hotly contested.

Leaders: *Carlos Salinas de Gortari*

No other man in the modern era of Mexico has inspired as much hope or hatred as former president Carlos Salinas de Gortari (1988–1994). Born in Mexico City in 1948 to a politically prominent family, he attended the National Autonomous University and later earned a Ph.D. in political economy from Harvard University. During his *sexenio*, Mexico aspired to leave behind the twin phantoms of backwardness and unrealized economic potential to join the ranks of developed nations.

He originally rose to prominence after 1982 during a terrible economic crisis that gave market reformers a chance to control the PRI. Called technocrats for their advanced degrees and detached attitude toward traditional politics, this group began to deregulate the economy and weaken powerful interest groups. At the end of the *sexenio*, the outgoing president, Miguel de la Madrid, thought that Minister of Budgeting and Planning Salinas would be the most likely to continue these changes. He appointed him the PRI's candidate for president.

But years of crisis had left the country tired and bitter, and the presidential race was tight. The PRI emerged from a mysterious computer failure on election night with a tight victory. The popular opposition candidate, Cuauhtémoc Cárdenas, claimed that only blatant fraud had prevented him from winning, and many observers agreed.

But once he became president, Salinas worked hard to regain legitimacy. He created a new Ministry for Social Development and implemented a Solidarity program that directed vast resources to infrastructure projects in local communities. Some citizens complained that it was controlled by PRI groups and used for political ends, but most praised the program. Salinas began to talk about the power that Mexico had to take charge of its own development and destiny.

He confronted opponents forcefully, jailing corrupt union bosses and smothering the opposition. His government undertook sweeping administrative reforms and privatized numerous state-owned industries, and the economy began to improve markedly in the early 1990s. He also projected a strong international presence and gained worldwide recognition, promoting his administration's environmental efforts at the Earth Summit in Rio de Janeiro in 1992, for example.

Perhaps most important, he spoke of Mexico as a great nation, ready to take its place at the table of advanced industrial society. New currency was issued, without the "zeros" of past inflation. Instead of three thousand pesos equaling one U.S. dollar, three pesos equaled one dollar. With a strong currency, controlled inflation, and increasing free trade, Mexicans had more purchasing power than ever before. But his greatest project was NAFTA. Salinas promoted a free-trade agreement with the United States more than any other single person, and his negotiations were so successful that Canada decided to join. The culmination of his efforts went into effect on January 1, 1994, the same day that everything began to unravel.

With an uprising in Chiapas, the assassinations of Colosio and Ruiz Massieu, widespread spending by the PRI, rumors of rampant drug mafias, and increasing suspicions falling on him and his associates, Salinas left office. No sooner had he done so than the currency collapsed and the country entered a sudden and sharp state of economic emergency. Overnight, he became a popular villian. Masks of his face, some with diabolical horns, sold on street corners. Shortly thereafter, his brother was found to have millions of dollars in Swiss banks and was indicted in the murder of Ruiz Massieu. After a widely ridiculed hunger strike to protest the accusations against him, Carlos Salinas left the country in unofficial exile. Since then, the PRI itself has declared him an outcast.

However, although he left office at the end of 1994, Salinas continues to cast a long shadow over Mexican politics. Newspaper articles report his activities and movements (first in Ireland, then in Cuba), and speculate on his motives. In response, he says that the future will vindicate him and his policies, and that he would like to return to Mexico.

Society and Economy

Mexico's economic development has had a significant impact on social conditions in the country. Overall, the standard of living has improved markedly since the 1940s. Rates of infant mortality, literacy, and life expectancy have steadily improved. Provision of health and education services expanded until government cutbacks on social expenditures in the early 1980s. Among the most important consequences of economic growth was the development of a large middle class, most of whom live in Mexico's numerous large cities. By the 1980s a third or more of Mexican households could claim a middle-class life-style, that is, steady income, secure food and shelter, access to decent education and health services, a car, some disposable income and savings, and some security that their children would be able to experience happy and healthy lives.

These achievements reflect well on the ability of the economy to increase social well-being in the country. However, the impressive economic growth through the early 1970s and between 1978 and 1982 could have produced greater social progress. In terms of standard indicators of social development—infant mortality, literacy, and life expectancy—Mexico fell behind a number of Latin American countries that grew less rapidly but provided more effectively for their populations. Costa Rica, Colombia, Argentina, Chile, and Uruguay had less overall growth but greater social development in the period after 1940. These countries paid more attention to the distribution of the benefits of growth than did Mexico. Moreover, in its pursuit of rapid industrialization, Mexico City has become one of the most congested and polluted cities in the world. In some rural areas, oil exploitation has left devastating environmental damage, destroying the life-styles and opportunities of *ejidatarios* and small farmers.

Mexico's economic development has also resulted in a widening gap between the wealthy and the poor and among different regions in the country. Although the poor are better off than they were in the early days of the country's drive toward industrialization, they are worse off when compared to middle- and upper-income groups. In 1950 the bottom 40 percent of the country's households accounted for about 14 percent of total personal income, while the top 30 percent had 60 percent of total income.[11] In 1992, it is estimated, the bottom 40 percent accounted for about 11 percent of income, while the top 30 percent shared 69 percent.[12] As in the United States, the rich are growing richer and the poor are growing poorer.

Among the poorest are those in rural areas who have little or no access to productive land and those in urban areas who do not have steady jobs. Harsh conditions in the countryside have fueled a half-century of migration to the cities. Nevertheless, some 23 million Mexicans continue to live in rural areas, many of them in deep poverty. Many of them work for substandard wages and migrate seasonally to search for jobs in order to sustain their families. Traditionally, those who crossed the border to the United States, legally and illegally, in search of jobs came from depressed rural areas. Increasingly, however, they come from urban areas.

Among those rural inhabitants with access to land, almost half have five hectares (1 hectare = 2.471 acres) or less. Almost all of this land is unirrigated and dependent on erratic rainfall. The land is often bleached of nutrients as a result of centuries of cultivation, population pressure, and erosion. Many families have land that is insufficient to provide even for their subsistence. The crops grown on such farms, primarily corn and beans, are poor people's crops and do not bring high prices in the markets. To improve production, peasant farmers would have to buy fertilizer, improved seeds, and insecticides, and they would have to find ways to irrigate their plots. But they generally have no money to purchase these supplies or invest in irrigation. In many areas, farm production provides as few as twenty to one hundred days of employment each year. Not surprisingly, underemployment is high in rural Mexico, as are rates of seasonal migration. It is also not surprising to learn that the incidence of disease, malnutrition, and illiteracy is much higher in Mexico's rural areas than in urban areas. When the rebels in Chiapas called for jobs, land, education, and health facilities, they were clearly reflecting the realities of life in much of the country.

Poverty has a regional dimension in Mexico. The northern areas of the country are significantly better off than the southern and central areas. Much of the regional distribution of poverty is related to conditions

A farmer with a hat labeled "rural misery" hangs his overalls on a cactus: "Welcome, Mr. President." Among those who have benefited least from the government's development policies are the rural poor. *Source: Ausencias y Presencias Gente de Ayer y Hoy en su Tinta: Problematica Politica, Social, Vista por un Cartoonista Potosino* by Luis Chessal, Unversidad Autonoma de San Luis Potosi, Mexico, 1984.

turing and assembly plants, called *maquiladoras*, has provided numerous jobs, particularly for young women who are seeking some escape from the burdens of rural life or the constraints of traditional family life.

In the southern and central regions of the country, however, the population is denser, the land poorer, and the number of *ejidatarios* eking out subsistence is greater. Transportation is often difficult, and during parts of the year, some areas may even be inaccessible because of heavy rains and flooding. In addition, most of Mexico's remaining indigenous groups live in the southern regions, often in very remote areas where they have been forgotten by government programs and exploited by regional bosses for generations. The conditions that spurred the Chiapas rebellion are found throughout the southern states.

The economic crisis of the 1980s had an impact on social conditions in the country. Wages declined by about half and unemployment soared as businesses collapsed and the government laid off workers in public offices. The informal sector expanded rapidly. Here, people eke out a living by hawking chewing gum, umbrellas, sponges, candy, shoelaces, mirrors, and a variety of other items in the street, jumping in front of cars at stoplights to wash windshields and sell newspapers, producing and repairing cheap consumer goods such as shoes and clothing, and selling services on a daily or hourly basis. While the informal sector provides important goods and services, conditions of work are often dangerous and insecurity about where the next peso will come from is endemic.

The economic crisis of the 1980s also reduced the quality and availability of social services. Expenditures on education and health declined after 1982 as the government imposed austerity measures. Salaries of primary school teachers declined by 34 percent between 1983 and 1988, and many worked second and even third jobs in order to make ends meet. Per capita health expenditures declined from a high of about 150 pesos in 1980 to under 90 pesos in 1990. Hospitals, clinics, and schools were left in disrepair, and obtaining equipment and supplies became almost impossible. Although indicators of mortality did not rise during this troubled decade, the incidence of diseases associated with poverty—malnutrition, cholera, anemia, and dysentery—increased. The diet

in the agricultural sector. In the north, large commercial farms grow fruits, vegetables, and grains for export using modern technologies. The U.S. border, the principal destination of agricultural products, is close at hand, and transportation networks are extensive and generally in good condition. Moreover, industrial cities such as Monterrey and Tijuana provide steady jobs for skilled and unskilled labor. Along the border, a rapidly growing band of manufacof most Mexicans became less rich in protein as they ate less meat and drank less milk. The crisis began to ease in the early 1990s, however, and many came to believe that conditions would improve for the poor. The government began investing in social services. Then, in late 1994, a new economic crisis emerged, marking 1995 with rapidly rising levels of unemployment and austerity measures that severely limited investments.

Although macroeconomic indicators have rebounded since then and large businesses look to grow, wages remain low for the majority of workers while taxes have increased. Subsidies on basic goods like tortillas, water, and gas have been lowered or eliminated, making the cost of living rise steeply for the poor and the working class.

Mexico and the International Political Economy

The crisis that began in 1982 clearly indicated that a policy of encouraging more Mexican exports and opening markets to foreign goods was essential. In the years after 1982 the government relaxed restrictions on the ability of foreigners to own property, reduced and eliminated tariffs, and did away with most of the import licenses. Foreign investment was courted in the hope of increasing the manufacture of goods for export. The government also introduced a series of incentives to encourage the private sector to produce goods for export. In 1986, Mexico joined the General Agreement on Tariffs and Trade (GATT), a multilateral agreement that attempts to promote freer trade among countries.

The government's effort to pursue a more outward-oriented development strategy culminated in the ratification of NAFTA in 1993, with gradual implementation beginning on January 1, 1994. This agreement is important to Mexico. In 1996, 83.9 percent of the country's exports were sent to the United States and 75.5 percent of its imports came from that country. The next most active trading country with Mexico was Japan, which received only 1.7 percent of its exports and accounted for only 4.6 percent of its imports.[13] Access to the U.S. market is thus essential to Mexico and to domestic and foreign investors. NAFTA

signaled a new period in U.S.-Mexican relations by making closer integration of the two economies a certainty. To date, trade between Mexico, Canada, and the United States has increased along with foreign direct investment.

Additionally, NAFTA contains two "parallel agreements" regarding the environment and labor that were negotiated in order to pass the treaty in the U.S. Congress. These documents created trinational institutions to cooperate and mediate on these issues to prevent potentially damaging side effects from the free trade. They have not been terribly active, however, and it is unknown what positive effect, if any, they are having.

NAFTA also entails risks for Mexico. Domestic producers worry about competition from U.S. firms. Farmers worry that Mexican crops cannot compete effectively with those grown in the United States; for example, peasant producers of corn and beans have been hard hit by lower-priced U.S.-grown grains. In addition, many people believe that embracing free trade with Canada and the United States indicated a loss of sovereignty and that Mexico's economic situation would now be much more vulnerable to the ebb and flow of economic conditions in the U.S. economy.

The incorporation of Mexico into NAFTA introduced novelties in economic and political relationships. During negotiations, new international political alliances developed. Environmental groups from the United States sought support in Mexico and Canada for fighting the agreement, and labor groups also looked across both borders for allies in opposing new trade relations. Environmental and labor groups united around concerns that Mexico would not enforce environmental protection and fair labor legislation. Some business interests allied across countries in supporting the agreement, anticipating opportunities for larger markets, cheaper labor, or richer sources of raw materials. For Mexico, which has traditionally feared the power of the United States in its domestic affairs, internationalization of political and economic relationships poses particularly difficult problems of adjustment.

On the other hand, the United States, newly aware of the importance of the Mexican economy to its own economic growth and concerned about instability on its southern border, hammered together a US$50 billion economic assistance program composed of U.S., European, and IMF commitments to support its neighbor when crisis struck in 1994. The Mexican government imposed a new stabilization package that contained austerity measures, higher interest rates, and limits on wages. By 1998, Mexico had remarkably paid off all of its obligations to the United States. When a similar crisis affected the economies of many Asian countries in 1997 and then spread throughout the globe, Mexico may have been partly shielded by its close relationship with the U.S. economy, which was enjoying a period of peak performance.

Socially, the expansion of modern means of communication has stripped Mexico of some of the secrecy that traditionally surrounded government decision-making, electoral processes, and efforts to deal with political dissent. More than before, the 1980s and 1990s focused international attention on the country. The Internet and e-mail, along with lower international telephone rates, have all played strong roles in increasing information flow across borders. The government could no longer respond to events such as the peasant rebellion in Chiapas, alleged electoral fraud, or the management of exchange rates without considering how such actions would be perceived in Tokyo, Frankfurt, Ottawa, London, or Washington.

Section ❸   Governance and Policy-Making

Mexico is a federal republic, though the state and local governments have held few resources and a limited sphere of action when compared with the national level. The nation's government can be characterized as a strong presidential system. Historically, the executive branch was the only true operative branch of government, while the legislative and judiciary followed the executive's lead and were considered "rubber stamp" bodies. Like Japan, India, and Sweden at different moments, Mexico has had a predominant party, the PRI, in power for an extended period of time. Though it has always been nominally democratic, Mexico has often been characterized as authoritarian and corporatist. Interestingly enough, all of these characterizations have been changing since the end of the 1980s, with great efforts being made by the government and civil society to reinvigorate the nation's laws and institutions and make the country fully democratic in practice.

Organization of the State

According to the supreme law of the land, the constitution of 1917, Mexico's political institutions resemble those of the United States. There are three branches of government, and a set of checks and balances limits the power of each. The congress is composed of the Senate and the Chamber of Deputies. One hundred twenty-eight senators are elected, four from each of the country's thirty-one states and an additional four from the federal district (capital). Five hundred deputies are elected from 300 electoral districts, 300 by simple majority vote and 200 by proportional representation. States and local governments are also elected. The president, governors, and senators are elected for six years, and deputies and municipal officials are elected for three.

In practice, the Mexican system is very different from that of the United States. The constitution is a very long document that is easily amended, especially when compared to that of the United States. It lays out the structure of government and guarantees a wide range of human rights, including familiar ones such as freedom of speech and protection of the law, but also economic and social rights such as the right to a job and the right to health care. The political system is highly centralized and presidentialist. It is making a series of pragmatic adjustments to pressures for greater democracy and electoral honesty, but it still has a way to go before it is fully democratic. Its policy-making processes are also very distinct from those in the United States, even though the constitutional arrangement of powers is superficially similar.

The Executive

The President and the Cabinet

"The political sun rises and sets every six years on the presidency."[14] This statement by an observer of

Mexican politics suggests the importance of the presidency to the political system. In residence at Los Pinos, the Mexican presidency is the central institution in a centralized system of governance and policy-making. In the past, the incumbent president always selected who would run as the PRI's next presidential candidate, appointed officials to all positions of power in the government and the PRI, and often named the PRI candidates, who almost automatically won elections as governors, senators, deputies, and local officials. The president continues to set the broad outlines of policy for the administration and has numerous resources to ensure that those policy preferences are adopted. Until the mid-1970s, Mexican presidents were considered above criticism in national politics and revered as symbols of national progress and well-being. While economic and political events of the 1980s and 1990s diminished presidential prestige, the extent of presidential power remains impressive.

Mexican presidents have a set of formal powers that allows them to initiate legislation, lead in foreign policy, create government agencies, make policy by decree or through administrative regulations and procedures, and appoint a wide range of public officials. More important, informal powers provide them with the capacity to centralize control in the executive. As head of the PRI, the president manages a vast patronage machine for filling positions at all levels of government and the party, and initiates legislation and policies that were, until recently, routinely approved by the congress.

To date, the PRI presidential candidate has always been male and almost always a member of the outgoing president's cabinet. In past years, several had been Minister of the Interior, the person responsible for maintaining law and order. This was true of Miguel Alemán (1946–1952), Adolfo Ruiz Cortines (1952–1958), Gustavo Díaz Ordaz (1964–1970), and Luis Echeverría (1970–1976). With the expansion of the government's role in economic development, candidates in the 1970s and 1980s were selected from the ministries that manage the economy. José López Portillo (1976–1982) had been Minister of Finance, and Miguel de la Madrid (1982–1988) and Carlos Salinas (1988–1994) had served as Minister of Budgeting and Planning. The selection of Luis Donaldo Colosio, who had been Minister of Social

Development and Welfare, was thought by political observers to signal renewed concern with problems of social development. When Colosio was assassinated, the selection of Ernesto Zedillo, who had first been Minister of Budgeting and Planning and then Minister of Education, was interpreted as an ongoing concern with social problems of the country and as an effort to maintain the policies of economic liberalization that Salinas had introduced.

Candidates since the mid-1970s have spent more of their careers in Mexico City and have tended to be trained in economics and public management rather than in the traditional field of law. Presidents since López Portillo have had postgraduate training at elite institutions in the United States. Miguel de la Madrid held a master's degree in public administration from Harvard; Carlos Salinas received a Ph.D. degree in political economy and government from Harvard; Luis Colosio studied for a Ph.D. degree in economics from the University of Pennsylvania; and Ernesto Zedillo had a Ph.D. degree in economics from Yale. Some have argued that because of their urban and elite backgrounds recent presidents have lost touch not only with the masses but also with the traditional politicians of the PRI, who have their roots in regional, labor, or rural politics. By the 1980s a topic of great debate in political circles was the extent to which a divide between *políticos* and *técnicos* (technocrats) had emerged within the national political elite. Among the old guard of the PRI, there was open skepticism about the ability of young technocrats like Carlos Salinas and Ernesto Zedillo to manage political conditions in the country. During the presidential campaign of 1994, considerable efforts were made to stress the more humble beginnings of Colosio and Zedillo and the fact that they had had to work hard to get an education.

Once elected, the president moves quickly to name a cabinet. Generally, he selects as his closest advisers those with whom he has worked over the years as he has risen to political prominence. He may also use cabinet posts to make certain he has a broad coalition of support; in this regard, he may appoint people with close ties to the labor movement, or to business interests, or to some of the regional strongholds of the party. Only in rare exceptions have they not been active members of the PRI. Few women have been selected for ministry-level posts—there are a handful of examples in recent administrations—and thus far only in those agencies that have limited influence over decision-making, like Tourism, Ecology, and Foreign Relations.

The president fills numerous high-level positions, which allows him to provide policy direction and keep tabs on what is occurring throughout the government and the party. The president uses his appointment power to build a team of like-minded officials in the government and ensure their loyalty to him. In turn, high-level appointees fill many jobs in their organizations. Like the president, they use this patronage power to put together personally loyal teams of officials whose career advancement is tied to their own political fate. These officials, in turn, build their own teams, and so on down through middle levels in the bureaucracy.

The beginning of each administration is therefore characterized by extensive turnover of positions, although many of the newly appointed officials served in other positions in prior administrations. This giant patronage system has the potential to be extremely inefficient. Indeed, little happens in government in the year prior to an election as officials bide their time or jockey for positions in the next administration, or in the year following an election as newly appointed officials learn the ropes and assemble their teams. Nevertheless, when a president has set clear goals and expects high performance from his personally chosen officials, these people in turn must expect good performance from their staffs if they are to produce for the president. In many situations, then, the patronage system results in the potential for increased presidential leadership and effective performance, at least at high levels in government. Many middle- and high-level officials hope that their performance will be noticed by their minister, especially if that person has the potential to be selected as the PRI's presidential candidate. If this should happen, they could expect to be appointed to a higher-level office in the next administration. This system, however, assumes that the PRI will continue to win elections.

Mexican presidents, though powerful, are not omnipotent. They, must, for example, abide by a deeply held constitutional norm—fully adhered to since 1940—to step down at the end of their term, and they must honor the political norm to step out of the political limelight to allow the successor to assume full presidential leadership. In addition, several factors tend to limit the extent of presidential discretion. Mexican presidents in the past have always been "creatures of the system," selected because they have proved themselves adept at understanding and playing by the existing rules. Through their careers in politics or government, they became familiar with the range of interest groups in the country and demonstrated a willingness to compromise on policy and political issues so that these interests would not unduly challenge the government. They also proved themselves to be skillful in the fierce bureaucratic politics that surround career advancement and in guessing about who the next PRI candidate for president was likely to be. In addition, presidents must demonstrate their loyalty to the myths and symbols of Mexican nationalism, such as the indigenous roots of much of its culture, the agrarian origins of the revolution, commitment to social justice, and sovereignty in international affairs. If, in the future, Mexico should elect a president who is not from the PRI, an important question will be whether these traditions will continue to hold true.

In the 1990s, President Zedillo relinquished a number of the traditional powers of the presidency, favoring instead a larger role for checks and balances in government. He announced, for example, that he would not select his PRI successor. In doing so, however, he created considerable conflict and tension as other institutions had to take on unaccustomed roles and as politicians sought to fill the void left by the "abandonment" of presidential power.

The Bureaucracy

Mexico's executive branch is large and powerful. Almost a million and a half people work in the federal bureaucracy, most of them in Mexico City. An additional million work in the national education system, and yet another million work for the large number of state-owned industries and semiautonomous agencies of the government. State and local governments employ over 600,000 people. Pay scales are usually low, and in the past the number of people filling lower-level positions such as drivers and messengers and clerical and maintenance jobs far exceeded the demand for them. In the 1980s austerity measures cut down on some of this overstaffing.

Officials at lower levels in the bureaucracy are unionized and protected by legislation that gives them job security and a range of benefits. At middle and upper levels, most officials are called confidence employees; that is, they serve as long as their bosses have confidence in them. These are the officials who are personally appointed by their superiors at the outset of an administration. Their modest salaries are compensated for by the prospect of career mobility and by the significant power that they can have over public events. For aspiring young professionals, a career in government is often attractive because of the challenge of dealing with important problems on a daily basis and being part of the process of finding solutions. Some employees also benefit from opportunities to take bribes or use insider information to promote private business deals.

The Para-Statal Sector

The **para-statal sector**—composed of semiautonomous or autonomous government agencies, many of which produce goods and services—has been extremely large and powerful in Mexico. Because the government provided significant support for the development of the economy as part of its post-1940 development strategy, it engaged in numerous activities that in other countries are carried out by the private sector. Thus, until the Salinas administration (1988–1994), the country's largest steel mill was state-owned, as were the largest fertilizer producer, sugar mills, and airlines. In addition, the national electricity board still produces energy and supplies at subsidized prices to industries. The petroleum company, PEMEX, grew to enormous proportions in the 1970s and 1980s under the impact of the oil boom. NAFIN, a state investment corporation, provides a significant percentage of all investment capital in the country. At one point, a state marketing board called CONASUPO was responsible for the importation and purchase of the country's supply of basic staples, and in the 1970s it played a major role in distributing food, credit, and farm implements in rural areas.

The para-statal sector was significantly trimmed by the economic policy reforms of the 1980s and 1990s. In 1970 there were 391 para-statal organizations in Mexico. By 1982 their number had grown to 1155, in part because of the expansion of government activities under presidents Echeverría and López Portillo and in part because of the nationalization of private banks in 1982. In the 1980s and 1990s concerted efforts were made to privatize many of these industries, including the telephone company, the national airline, and the nationalized banks. By 1994 only 215 state-owned industries remained and efforts continued to sell or liquidate many of them.

Other State Institutions

The Military

Mexico is one of only a few countries in the developing world that have successfully depoliticized the military. Much of the credit for this process belongs to Plutarco Calles, Lázaro Cárdenas, and subsequent presidents who introduced the rotation of regional commands so that generals could not build up regional bases of power. In addition, postrevolutionary leaders made an implicit bargain with the military leaders by providing them with opportunities to engage in business so that they did not look to political power as a way of gaining economic power. After 1946 the military no longer had institutional representation within the PRI and became marginalized from the centers of power.

The military has been called in from time to time to deal with domestic unrest—in rural areas in the 1960s, in Mexico City and other cities to repress student protest movements in 1968, in 1988 in the arrest of a powerful labor leader, in 1989 to break a labor strike, in 1990 to deal with protest over electoral fraud, in Chiapas beginning in late 1994, and to manage the Mexico City police in 1997. The military was also called in to deal with the aftermath of the earthquake in Mexico City in 1985, but its inadequate response to the emergency did little to enhance its reputation in the eyes of the public. In recent years, the military has been heavily involved in efforts to combat drug trafficking, and rumors abound about deals struck between military officials and drug barons. Such fears were confirmed when General Jesus Gutierrez Rebollo, the head of the anti-drug task force, was arrested in February 1997 on accusations of protecting a drug lord.

Whenever the military is called in to resolve domestic conflicts, some Mexicans become concerned that the institution is becoming politicized and may come to play a larger role in political decision-making. From time to time, rumors of preparations for a coup are heard, as during financial panics in the 1980s and in the aftermath of Colosio's assassination. Thus far, such fears have not been realized, and many believe that as long as civilian administrations are able to maintain the country's tradition of stability, the military will not intervene directly in politics.

The Judiciary

Unlike Anglo-American law systems, Mexico's law derives from the Roman/Napoleonic tradition and is highly formalized and explicit. The constitution of 1917 is a lengthy document that has been amended many times and contains references to a wide range of civil rights, including, for example, items as broad as the right to a healthy environment. Regulatory agencies can also create rules and regulations regarding material under their jurisdiction; this is considered administrative law. Because Mexican law tends to be explicit and definable, and because there are no punitive damages, there are few lawsuits. One important exception to this is the *amparo*, whereby citizens may ask for a writ of protection claiming that their constitutional rights have been violated by specific government actions or laws. Each citizen who wants an *amparo* must present a separate case.

There are federal and state courts in Mexico. The federal system is composed of the Supreme Court, which decides the most important cases in the country; circuit courts, which take cases on appeal; and district courts, which is where all cases enter the system. Supreme Court justices are nominated by the president and approved by the Senate. Since most of the important laws in Mexico are federal, state courts have played a subordinate role. However, this is changing. As Mexican states become more independent from the federal government, state law has been experiencing tremendous growth. In addition, there are many important specialized federal courts, such as labor courts, military courts, and electoral courts.

Like other political institutions in Mexico, the judiciary was for many decades politically, though not constitutionally, subordinate in the presidential system. The courts occasionally slowed the actions of government by issuing *amparos*; however, in almost every case in which the power of government or the president was at stake, the courts ruled on the side of the government. The administration of Ernesto Zedillo has tried to change this by emphasizing the rule of law over that of powerful individuals. Increasing interest in human rights issues by citizens' groups and the media has added pressure to the courts to play a stronger role in protecting basic freedoms. Citizens and the government are increasingly resorting to the courts as a primary weapon against sticky problems like corruption and police abuse. President Zedillo's refusal to interfere with the courts' judgments has also strengthened the judiciary.

Subnational Government

As with many other aspects of the Mexican political system, regional and local government in Mexico is quite different from what is described in the constitution. Mexico has a federal system, and each state has its own constitution, executive, unicameral legislature, and judiciary. Municipalities (equivalent to U.S. counties) are governed by popularly elected mayors and councils. But state and municipal governments are poor and are subordinate to Mexico City economically and politically. Most of the funds they command are transferred to them from the central government, and they have little legal or administrative capacity to raise their own revenue.

States and localities suffer greatly from the lack of well-trained and well-paid public officials. As at the national level, many jobs are distributed as political patronage, but even officials who are motivated to be responsive to local needs are generally ill-equipped to do so. Several presidents have sought to decentralize public-sector activities to the state level, but most such initiatives have sought to decentralize central government functions rather than delegate powers to subordinate levels of government. For example, in the early 1970s regional headquarters of the national Ministry of Agriculture were established in the states rather than improving the capacities and responsibilities of the state-level ministries of agriculture. A similar effort to decentralize the Ministry of Health was undertaken in the early 1980s. In a break with this tradition, the Salinas administration delegated powers over education to state ministries of education. Interestingly, many governors resisted this initiative because it meant that they would have to deal with the powerful teachers' union and because they lacked the administrative capacity to handle such a large and complex responsibility. They were also worried that they would be unable to acquire the budgetary resources necessary to carry out their new responsibilities.

There are exceptions to this picture of regional and local government impoverishment and lack of capacity. State governments in the north of the country, such as Nuevo Leon, have been more responsive to local needs and better able to administer public services. In such states, local municipalities have become famous for the extent to which they differ from the norm in most of Mexico. Monterrey, in Nuevo Leon, for example, has a reputation for efficient and forward-looking city government. Much of this local capacity can be credited to a regional political tradition that has stressed independence from—and even hostility to—Mexico City and the PRI. In these cases entrepreneurial groups and private citizens have often invested time and resources in local government.

Until 1988 all governors were from the PRI, although many believe that only electoral fraud kept two governorships out of the hands of an opposition party in 1986. Finally, in 1989, a non-PRI governor assumed power in Baja California Norte—an important first. As of February 1999 opposition parties had won seven more gubernatorial elections, some in large and important states. Also, municipalities have increasingly been the focus of authentic party competition. As opposition parties came to control these levels of government, they were challenged to improve services such as police protection, garbage collection, sanitation, and education. PRI-dominated governments have also tried to improve their performance because they are threatened by the possibility of losing elections.

The Policy-Making Process

The Mexican system is enormously dependent on the quality of its leadership and presidential understanding of how economic and social policies can affect the development of the country. As indicated throughout this chapter, the *sexenio* is an extremely important fact of political life in Mexico. New presidents introduce extensive change in positions within the government and the PRI. They are able to bring in "their" people who, in turn, build teams of "their" people within ministries, agencies, and party networks. This generally provides the president with a group of high- and middle-level officials who share a general orientation toward public policy and who are highly motivated to carry out his goals. They also believe that, in doing so, they enhance their chances for upward political mobility. In such a context, it is likely for changes in public policies to be introduced every six years, creating innovation, discontinuity, or both.

Policy initiative is routinely taken by the central ministries in direct response to the president's policy priorities. Ministries headed by the most likely presidential candidates and staffed by people closest to the president are the ones that respond with greatest zeal to the president's lead. Ministries awarded to groups or interests that are important to the PRI's coalition may be more resistant to presidential preferences that might have negative consequences for those interests.

Once the newly appointed officials are in office, the president is in a position to set and carry out important policy measures. Together with the bureaucracy, the president is the focal point of policy formulation and political management. Until 1997 the legislature always had a PRI majority and acted as a "rubber stamp" body on presidentially sponsored legislation. Since then, the congress has proven to be a more active policymaker, blocking legislation, forcing its negotiation, and introducing its own bills.

The extent of change is usually limited by the resources the government has and by elite support for such changes. Presidential skills in negotiating, managing the opposition, using the media to acquire public support, and maneuvering within the bureaucracy can be important for ensuring that his program is fully endorsed. Under extraordinary conditions such as the deep and sustained economic and political crisis faced by Carlos Salinas, it is even possible to reverse national development strategies. Ernesto Zedillo's administration was marked by considerable conflict with disaffected elements in the PRI and many questioned the president's political skills and ability to build support for his agenda.

Significant limits on presidential power also occur when policy is being implemented. In fact, in areas as diverse as the regulation of working conditions, antipollution laws, tax collection, election monitoring, and health care in remote rural areas, Mexico has extremely advanced legislation on the books. Yet the persistence of unsafe factory conditions, pollution in Mexico City, tax evasion, election fraud, and poor health care suggests that legislation is not translated into practice. At times, policies are not implemented because public officials at the lower levels disagree with the policies or make deals with affected interests so they can benefit personally. This is the case, for example, with taxes that remain uncollected because individuals or corporations bribe officials to overlook them. In other cases, lower-level officials may lack the capacity or skills to implement some policies, such as those directed toward improving education or rural development services. For whatever reasons, Mexican presidents cannot always deliver on their intentions. Traditionally, they have been above criticism when this has occurred because of the willingness of Mexican citizens to blame lower-level officials for such "slippage." However, exempting the president from responsibility for what does or does not occur during his watch became much less common in the 1980s and 1990s.

Section ❹   Representation and Participation

How do citizen interests get represented in Mexican politics, given the high degree of centralization, presidentialism, and, until recently, PRI domination? Is it possible for ordinary citizens to make demands on government and to influence public policy? In fact, Mexico achieved more than seventy years of relatively peaceful political interactions in part because the political system offered some channels for representation and participation. Through its long history, the political system emphasized compromise among contending elites, behind-the-scenes conflict resolution, and distribution of political rewards to those willing to play by the formal and informal rules of the game. It has also responded, if reluctantly and defensively, to demands for change.

Often, citizens are best able to interact with the government through a variety of informal means rather than through the formal processes of elections, campaigns, and interest-group lobbying. Interacting with government through the personal and informal mechanisms of clientelism usually means that the government retains the upper hand in deciding which interests to respond to and which to ignore. For many interests, this has meant "incorporation without power."[15] Increasingly, however, Mexican citizens are organizing to alter this situation.

The Legislature

Students in the United States are frequently asked to study complex charts explaining how a bill becomes a law, because the formal process of lawmaking affects the content of legislation. In Mexico, while there are formal rules that prescribe such a process, studying them would not be useful for understanding how the legislature worked for most of its history. Mexico's two-chamber legislature—the Senate and the Chamber of Deputies—was dominated by the PRI for almost sixty years. Because of the overwhelming presence of this political party, opposition to presidential initiatives was rarely heard. To the extent that representatives did not agree with policies they were asked to approve, they counted on the fact that policy implementation was flexible and allowed for after-the-fact bending of the rules or disregard of measures that were harmful to important interests.

The PRI's grip on the legislature was broken in 1988. The growing strength of opposition parties, combined with legislation that provided for greater representation of minority parties in the congress, led to the election of 240 opposition deputies that year. After that, when presidential legislation was sent to the chamber, the opposition challenged the tradition of legislative passivity and insisted on real debate about issues. Because the Salinas administration introduced major reforms, some of which required constitutional amendments in order to be implemented, some initiatives were not brought to congress, slowing down the reform process. In other cases, the president pursued policy initiatives through decree laws and administrative measures rather than submitting them to the legislature where they might be questioned. The two-thirds PRI majority was returned in 1991—amid allegations of voter fraud—and presidentialism was reasserted. Nevertheless, the strong presence of opposition parties continued to encourage debate as the PRI delegates were challenged to defend proposed legislation. The 1994 elections returned a clear PRI majority of 300 deputies and 64 senators, but in 1997, the PRI lost this majority when 261 deputies (of a total of 500) and 51 senators (of a total of 128) were elected from opposition parties. For the first time in its history, the PRI did not have an absolute majority in the Chamber of Deputies.

Because important policy decisions were not made—only approved—in congress until 1997, interest groups did not pay much attention to the deputies or senators or to the process of legislation. Groups wishing to influence policy preferred to focus their attentions on the president and the executive branch.

As a genuine multiparty system begins to emerge, the Mexican congress has become a more important forum for a variety of political voices and points of view. PRI candidates are facing more competitive elections in many locales, and the number of "safe seats" for party stalwarts is declining. As the congress increases in importance as a place where legislation is debated and shaped, interest groups will begin to pay it greater attention and focus more of their lobbying activities on it.

Representation in congress seems to have diversified somewhat since the end of the 1980s. In 1998 women held 14.2 percent of all seats which, though paltry, compared favorably with 11.2 percent in the United States.[16] Some representatives also emerged from the ranks of community activists who had participated in activities such as the urban popular movements.

Political Parties and the Party System

The PRI

Mexico's Institutional Revolutionary Party, the PRI, was founded by a coalition of political elites who agreed that it was preferable to work out their conflicts within an overarching structure of compromise than to continue to resort to violence. In the 1930s the PRI incorporated a wide array of popular interests,

becoming a mass-based party that drew support from all classes in the population. Its principal activities were—and continue to be—generating support for the government, organizing the electorate to vote for its candidates, and distributing jobs and development resources in return for loyalty to the system.

Until the 1990s party organization was based largely on the corporate representation of class interests. Labor was represented within party councils by the National Confederation of Labor (CTM), which includes industry-based unions at local, regional, and national levels. Peasants were represented by the National Confederation of Peasants (CNC), an organization of *ejido* and peasant unions and regional syndicates. The so-called popular sector, comprising small businesses, community-based groups, and public employees, had less internal cohesion but was represented by the National Confederation of Popular Organizations (CNOP). Of the three, the CTM was consistently the best organized and most powerful.

Within these corporate structures, the PRI functioned through extended networks that distributed public resources—particularly jobs, land, development projects, and access to public services—to lower-level activists who controlled votes at the local level. This informal clientelist organization forms multiple chains of patron-client interaction that culminate at the highest level of political decision-making within the PRI and the office of the president. In this system, those with ambitions to public office or to positions within the PRI put together networks of supporters from above (patrons), to whom they deliver votes, and supporters from below (clients), who trade allegiance for access to public resources. Traditionally, the PRI's strongest support has come from the countryside, where *ejidatarios* and other peasants have been the most grateful for and dependent on rewards of land or jobs. As the country has become more urbanized, the support base provided by rural communities has remained important to the PRI but less so in terms of overall electoral support.

For well over half a century, this system worked extremely well. PRI candidates won by overwhelming majorities until the 1980s (see Figure 1 on p. 410). Of course, electoral fraud and the ability to distribute government largesse are central explanations for these numbers, but they also attest to an extremely

Figure 1

PRI Support in Congressional Elections, 1946–1997

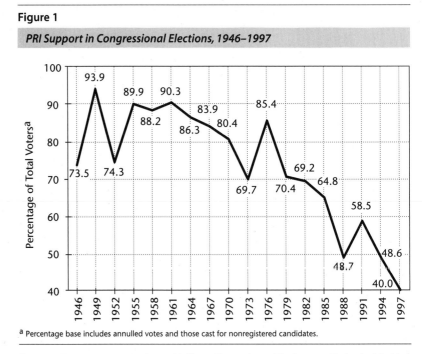

[a] Percentage base includes annulled votes and those cast for nonregistered candidates.

Source: For 1946–1988: Juan Molinar Horcasitas, *El tiempo de la legitimidad: Elecciones, autoritarismo y democracia en México* (México, D.F.: Cal y Arena, 1991). For 1991: Secretaría Nacional de Estudios, Partido Acción Nacional, *Análisis del Proceso Federal Electoral 1994*, 1995. For 1994: Instituto Federal Electoral, *Estadística de las Elecciones Federales de 1994, Compendio de Resultados*, México, D.F., 1995. For 1997: http://www.ife.org.mx/wwworge/tablas/mrent.htm.

well-organized party. Although the PRI became much weaker in the 1980s and 1990s, it was still the only political party that could boast a network of constituency organizations in virtually every village and urban community in the country. Through the patron-client networks, it continues to provide means for people of humble origin, especially those living far from the center of political power, to interact with the political system in ways that allow them some access to benefits, however meager. Its vast political machinery also allows it to monitor events, even in remote areas.

Within the PRI, power was centralized, and the sector organizations (the CTM, the CNC, and the CNOP) responded primarily to elites at the top of the political pyramid rather than to member interests. Over time, the corporate interest-group organizations, particularly the CTM and the CNC, became widely

identified with corruption, bossism, centralized control, and lack of effective participation. By the 1980s the PRI was facing increasing difficulties because of the way in which such characteristics limited effective representation of interests. New generations of voters were less beholden to patronage-style politics and much more willing to question the party's dominance. When the administrations of de la Madrid, Salinas, and Zedillo imposed harsh austerity measures, the PRI was held responsible for the resulting losses in incomes and benefits. Simultaneously, as the government cut back sharply on public-sector jobs and services, the PRI had far fewer resources to distribute to maintain its traditional bases of support. Moreover, it began to suffer from increasing internal dissension between the old guard and those who wanted to reform the party. In the aftermath of the election of

Table 2

Voting in Presidential Elections, 1934–1994

Year	Votes for PRI Candidate[a] %	Votes for PAN Candidate %	Votes for All Others[b] %	Turnout (% Voters Among Eligible Adults)[c]
1934	98.2	—	1.8	53.6
1940	93.9	—	6.1	57.5
1946	77.9	—	22.1	42.6
1952	74.3	7.8	17.9	57.9
1958	90.4	9.4	0.2	49.4
1964	88.8	11.1	0.1	54.1
1970	83.3	13.9	1.4	63.9
1976[d]	93.6	—	1.2	29.6
1982	71.0	15.7	9.4	66.1
1988	50.7	16.8	32.5[e]	49.4[f]
1994	50.1	26.7	23.2	77.16

[a]From 1958 through 1982, includes votes cast for the Partido Popular Socialista (PPS) and the Partido Auténtico de la Revolutión Mexicana (PARM), both of which regularly endorsed the PRI's presidential candidate. In 1988, they supported opposition candidate Cuauhtémoc Cárdenas.
[b]Excludes annulled votes; includes votes for candidates of nonregistered parties.
[c]Eligible population base for 1934 through 1952 includes all males ages 20 and over (legal voting age: 21 years). Both men and women ages 20 and over are included in the base for 1958 and 1964 (women received the franchise in 1958). The base for 1970–1988 includes all males and females ages 18 and over (the legal voting age was lowered to 18, effective 1970).
[d]The PRI candidate, José López Portillo, ran virtually unopposed because the PAN failed to nominate a candidate. The only other significant candidate was Valentín Campa, representing the Communist Party, which was not legally registered to participate in the 1976 election. More than 5 percent of the votes were annulled.
[e]Includes 31.1 percent officially tabulated for Cuauhtémoc Cárdenas.
[f]Estimated using data from the Federal Electoral Commission. However, the commission itself has released two different figures for the number of eligible voters in 1988. Using the commission's larger estimate of eligible population, the turnout would be 44.9 percent.

Source: From *Comparative Politics Today: A World View*, 4th ed. by Gabriel Almond and G. Bingham Powell, Jr. Copyright ©1988. Reprinted by permission of Addison-Wesley Educational Publishers, Inc. For 1994, Insituto Federal Electoral, *Estadística de las Elecciones Federales de 1994, Compendio de Resultados*, México, D.F., 1995.

1994, these tensions resulted in open conflict between the modernizers and the so-called dinosaurs. Most significantly, many of the groups that became politically active during the 1980s fiercely resisted traditional methods of control used by the party.

Until the elections of 1988, there was no question that the PRI candidate would be elected president. Victories recording 85–95 percent of the total vote for the PRI were the norm (see Table 2 above). In 1988 and in 1994, however, PRI candidates were challenged by parties to the right and left, and outcomes were hotly

contested by the opposition, which claimed fraudulent electoral practices. In 1994, Zedillo won primarily because the opposition was not well organized and failed to present a program beyond opposition to the PRI. Presidents Salinas and Zedillo also distanced themselves from the party during their administrations, giving the first clear signals in PRI history that there was a distinction between the party and the government.

As the PRI faced greater competition from other parties and continued to suffer from declining popularity, efforts were made to restructure and reform it. The

Table 3

Support for the PRI by Type of Congressional District (percentage of total vote)								
Districts	*1979*	*1982*	*1985*	*1988*	*1991*	*1994*	*1997*	*Average 1979–1997*
Federal District (Mexico City)	46.7	48.3	42.6	27.3	46.2	39.5	23.1	39.1[a]
Other Urban[b]	53.4	56.2	51.1	34.3				
Mixed[c]	67.9	66.2	59.2	46.4				
Rural[d]	83.5	80.9	77.3	61.3				

[a]Average for the 1979–1997 period.
[b]Urban districts are those in which 90 percent or more of the population lives in communities of 50,000 or more inhabitants. Total number: 40 in the Federal District and 56 in other urban areas.
[c]Districts in which more than 50 percent but less than 90 percent of the population live in communities of 50,000 or more inhabitants. Total number: 44.
[d]Districts in which less than 50 percent of the population live in communities of 50,000 inhabitants. Total number: 160.

Sources: For 1979–1988: Juan Molinar Horcasitas, *El tiempo de la legitimidad*; *Comparative Politics Today: A World View*, 4th ed. by Gabriel Almond and G. Bingham Powell, Jr. Copyright © 1988. Reprinted by permission of Addison-Wesley Educational Publishers, Inc. For 1991, Eduardo Castellanos Hernández, *Formas de Gobierno y Sistemas Electorales en México*. Published by Centro de Investigación Científica "Ing. Jorge L. Tamayo", A. C., 1995. For 1994, Instituto Federal Electoral, *Estadística de las Elecciones Federales de 1994, Compendio de Resultados*, México, D.F., 1995. For 1997, http://www.ife.org.mx/wwworge/tablas/mrent.htm.

CNOP was replaced by the UNE (Citizens in Movement), which sought to incorporate a wide array of non-class-based citizen and neighborhood movements. In 1990 membership rules were altered to allow individuals and groups not identified with its corporate-sector organizations to join. In addition, regional party organizations gained representation at the national level. Party conventions were introduced in an effort to democratize the internal workings of the party, while some states and localities began to hold primaries to select PRI candidates—a significant departure from the old system of selection by party bosses. Efforts were made to undercut regional bosses who had been closely allied with the patron-client system of the past. To give the appearance of a modern party system, electoral reforms introduced by the López Portillo, de la Madrid, Salinas, and Zedillo administrations made it easier for opposition parties to contest elections and win seats in the legislature. In 1990 an electoral commission was created to regulate campaigns and elections, and in 1996 it became fully independent from the government. Parties receive funding from government and have assured access to the media.

The PRI continues to face a difficult future. The Mexican electorate is now predominantly urban. Voters are younger, better educated, and more middle-class than in the days of the PRI's greatest success—the 1940s, 1950s, and 1960s. In 1990 only 27 percent of the population lived in rural areas, while 32 percent of the population lived in cities of 1 million or more; 25 percent of the population lived in Mexico City, which has become one of the world's largest megacities. The 1988 elections demonstrated the relevance of these demographic conditions for the PRI when only 27.3 percent of the population of Mexico City voted for the PRI candidate and only 34.3 percent of the population in other urban areas supported him. While rural support for the party had remained strong, it had also clearly diminished since the 1970s (see Table 3).

The PAN

Several opposition parties compete in elections. The National Action Party, or PAN, is among the oldest. Founded in 1939 to represent business interests opposed to the centralization and anticlericalism of the PRI, its strength is centered in northern states where the tradition of resistance to Mexico City is strong. The PAN has traditionally campaigned on a platform endorsing greater regional autonomy, less government intervention in the economy, reduced regulation of business, clean and fair elections, rapprochement with the Catholic Church, and support for private and religious education.

In the past, the PAN was usually able to elect 9–10 percent of all deputies to the national congress and to capture control of a few municipal governments. Then, in the early 1980s, and especially after President López Portillo nationalized the banks, opposition to centralism and statism grew more popular. The PAN began to develop greater capacity to contest elections at higher levels of government. In particular, the party gained popularity among urban middle-class voters, won elections in several provincial cities, and came close to winning governorships in two states. In 1988 it captured 16.8 percent of the vote for president, 101 Chamber of Deputies seats, and one Senate seat. The following year, it won the governorship of the state of Baja California Norte. For the first time since the PRI was founded, the dominant party did not control all governorships in the country. In the 1994 elections, PAN's candidate, Diego Fernández de Cevallos, garnered 26 percent of the presidential vote and the party won 119 seats in the Chamber of Deputies and 25 in the Senate. In 1997 it managed to win 121 seats in the Chamber and 33 in the Senate. In closely watched elections during the administration of Ernesto Zedillo, the PAN won the governorships of several large and important states. It is widely recognized for its organizational effectiveness, and its strong base of support in the north of the country.

The PRD

Another significant challenge has come from the Democratic Revolutionary Party, or PRD, a populist and nationalist alternative to the PRI. Its candidate in the 1988 and 1994 elections was Cuauhtémoc Cárdenas, the son of Mexico's most famous and revered president. He was a PRI insider until party leaders virtually ejected him for demanding internal reform of the party and a platform emphasizing social justice. In the 1988 elections Cárdenas was officially credited with winning 31.1 percent of the vote, and the party captured 139 seats in the Chamber of Deputies. He benefited from massive political defection from the PRI and garnered support from workers disaffected with the boss-dominated unions as well as peasants who remembered his father's concern for

agrarian reform and investment in the poor. Mexico City gave him 50.4 percent of the vote, which also represented some middle-class support.

Even while the votes were being counted, the party began to denounce widespread electoral fraud and claim that Cárdenas would have won an honest election. The PRD challenged a number of vote counts in the courts and walked out of Salinas' inaugural speech. Considerable public opinion supported the party's challenge. In the aftermath of the 1988 elections, then, it seemed that the PRD was a strong contender to become Mexico's second most powerful party. It was expected to have a real chance in future years to challenge the PRI's "right" to the presidency.

However, in the years leading up to the 1994 elections, the party was plagued by internal divisions over its platform, leadership, organizational structure, and election strategy. By 1994 it still lagged far behind the PRI in establishing and maintaining the local constituency organizations needed to mobilize votes and monitor the election process. In addition, the PRD found it difficult to define an appropriate left-of-center alternative to the market-oriented policies carried out by the government. While the claims that such policies ignored the need for social justice were popular, policies to respond to poverty that did not imply a return to unpopular government intervention were difficult to devise. In the aftermath of the Colosio assassination, citizens also became more alarmed about violence, and some were concerned that the level of political rivalry represented by the PRD threatened the country's long-term political stability. In the 1994 elections Cárdenas won only 17 percent of the votes; the PRD elected 71 deputies and 8 senators.

But thanks to the government's continued unpopular economic policies and the leadership of a successful grassroots mobilizer named Andres Manuel Lopez Obrador, who was elected to head the party in 1996, the PRD began to stage a remarkable turnaround. Factional bickering was controlled and organizational discipline increased. In addition, the PRD proved successful in moving beyond its regional stronghold and established itself as a truly national party. In 1997 the party increased its share of seats to 125 in the Chamber of Deputies and 13 in the Senate. Most important, Cárdenas became the first popularly elected mayor of Mexico City. This provided him and the party with a critically important opportunity to demonstrate their ability to govern, not to mention a potential platform for the presidential elections of 2000. By February 1999, the PRD had managed to shed some of its reputation as a "one-horse show" and had won two governorships, with the PRI under question for fraud in a third.

Elections

Each of these three political parties draws voters from a wide and overlapping spectrum of the electorate. Nevertheless, a typical voter for the PRI is likely to be from a rural area or small town, to have less education, and to be older and poorer than voters for the other parties. A typical voter for the PAN is likely to be from a northern state, to live in an urban area, to be a middle-class professional, to have a comfortable life-style, and to have a high school or even a university education. A typical voter for the PRD is likely to be young, to be a political activist, to have an elementary or high school education, to live in one of the central states, and to live in a small town or an urban area.

As we have seen, the support base for the PRI is the most vulnerable to economic changes occurring in the country. Voting for opposition parties is an urban phenomenon, and Mexico continues to urbanize at the rate of 3 percent per year. This means that, in order to stay competitive, the PRI will have to garner more support from urban areas. It must also be able to appeal to younger voters, especially the large numbers who are attracted to the PRD and the PAN. The cost of acquiring such support, however, may be willingness to democratize its internal decision-making processes and to desist from blatant acts of electoral fraud.

Elections are becoming more competitive in Mexico. The government is also under tremendous pressure to make them fairer. In the 1990s, laws to limit campaign spending and campaign contributions and to mandate greater media coverage of opposition parties and candidates were part of the response to the demand to "level the playing field" between the PRI and the other parties. Voter registration was reformed to ensure that fraud would be more detectable. Election monitoring was also strengthened and another reform increased the chances for opposition parties to win representation in the Senate. In the 1994 elections, however, citizens continued to be skeptical about the honesty of elections. An opinion poll carried out during the first week of June 1994 indicated that only 50.4 percent of respondents were "confident that the upcoming presidential election [would] be clean."[17] In fact, the elections were credited with having been among the fairest in history, and midterm and subsequent congressional elections reinforced the impression that electoral fraud is on the wane in many areas. Some state and local elections continue to be questioned, especially in rural areas in the south, where local PRI bosses remain powerful. For example, many citizens could not believe that the PRI had swept the 1997 congressional elections in the state of Chiapas, where opposition to the government is so strong that it generated a guerrilla movement.

Political Culture, Citizenship, and Identity

Most citizens in Mexico demonstrate overall commitment to the system while expressing considerable criticism—and often cynicism—about how it works and how equitable it is. A survey of almost any *ejido*, for example, will uncover lengthy local histories of how *ejidatarios* have been mistreated, "given the runaround" by bureaucratic organizations, and cheated by local, regional, and national leaders of the CNC, the PRI, and government agencies. The survey will reveal deep commitment to the country's heroes, the president, and the institutions of government along with anger, distrust, frustration, and biting jokes told at the expense of the rich and powerful.

Most Mexicans have a deep familiarity with how the political system works and the ways in which they might be able to extract benefits from it. They understand the informal rules of the game in Mexican politics that have helped keep the system in place despite extensive inequalities in economic and political power.

Clientelism, or the exchange of favors among people of different status or degrees of power, extends from the very top of the political system to the most remote and poverty-stricken villages. It is a form of participation in the sense that many people, even the poorest, are able to interact with public officials and get something out of the political system. This kind of participation emphasizes how limited resources, such as access to health care, can be distributed in a way that provides maximum political payoff. This informal system is a fundamental reason why many Mexicans continue to vote for the PRI.

However, new ways of interacting with government are emerging, and they coexist along with the clientelistic style of the past. An increasing number of citizens are seeking to negotiate with the government on the basis of citizenship rights, not relationships. The movements that emerged in the 1980s sought to form broad but loose coalitions with other organizations and attempted to identify and work with reform-oriented public officials. Their suspicion of traditional political organizations such as the PRI or the CNC and the CTM also carried over to suspicion of close alliances with the PAN and the PRD.

As politics and elections become more open and competitive, the roles of public opinion and the mass media are also becoming more important. In the past, public opinion polling was often contaminated by the dominance of the PRI, and some polling organizations were even subsidized by the party or the government. Increasingly, however, even the PRI and the government are interested in objective information and analysis of public opinion. These data have influenced the content and timing of government decisions and the development of strategies in election campaigns. In 1994 politicians, citizens, and political activists closely followed the popularity polls for the three major candidates for president, and party officials monitored how the image of their contender could be molded to capture higher voter approval ratings.

Since extensive public opinion polling is comparatively new in Mexico, it is difficult to assess how attitudes toward the regime have changed over time. Surveys taken in the 1980s and 1990s indicate that confidence in the regime fell extensively during the 1980s but rebounded somewhat in the 1990s. Fewer Mexicans claim a party preference today than in the past, and the percentage of citizens who identify with the PRI has fallen sharply. According to one analyst, "The average Mexican regards participation in electoral campaigns, attendance at rallies, voting, and affiliation with political parties as ritualistic activities. He or she believes that engaging in such activities may be necessary to extract benefits from the system, but they have little effect on the shape of public policy or the selection of public officials."[18]

The media play an important role in public opinion formation in Mexico. In the past, it was not easy for newspapers, magazines, or radio and television stations to be openly opposed to the government. For many years, the government used access to newsprint, which it controlled, to reward sympathetic news coverage and penalize coverage it considered hostile. In addition, the government subsidized the salaries of some reporters, and politically ambitious public and PRI officials paid stipends to those who covered their activities sympathetically. A considerable amount of the revenue of newspapers and other media organizations came from advertising placed by the government. Each of these mechanisms was used to encourage positive reporting of government activities, strong endorsement of presidential initiatives, and quashing of stories that reflected ill on the party or the government, all without resorting to outright government control of the media.

As with other aspects of Mexican politics, the media are also in a period of transition, enjoying a "spring" of greater independence and diversity of opinion. There are currently several major television networks in the country, and many citizens have access to CNN and other global networks. The number of newspapers is expanding, as is their circulation, and news magazines such as *Nexos* and *Proceso* play the same role in Mexico that *Time* and *Newsweek* do in the United States. Citizens in Mexico today clearly hear a much wider range of opinion and much greater reporting of opposition to government and the PRI than at any time previously.

Interests, Social Movements, and Protest

As has been noted, clientelism is a way for individuals to acquire benefits from a system that is controlled from the top. The Mexican system also responds to broader groups of citizens through pragmatic **accommodation** to their interests. This is one important reason why political tensions among major interests have rarely escalated into the kind of serious conflict that can threaten stability. Where open conflict has occurred, it has generally been met with efforts to find some kind of compromise solution, even in cases in which the government has repressed opposition. Accommodation serves to respond to interests as diverse as business, labor, and rebellious students.

Accommodation has been particularly apparent in response to the interests of business. Mexico's development strategy encouraged the growth of wealthy elites in commerce, finance, industry, and agriculture (see Section 2). Although these elites were the primary beneficiaries of the country's development, they were never incorporated into the PRI. Instead, they represent themselves through a set of business-focused interest groups and through personal relationships with influential officials. Through these networks, business organizations and individuals have long sought policies that are favorable to their interests.

Labor has been similarly accommodated within the system. Wage levels for unionized workers grew fairly consistently between 1940 and 1982, when the economic crisis caused a significant drop in wages. At the same time, labor interests were attended to in terms of concrete benefits and limitations on the rights of employers to discipline or dismiss workers. Labor union leaders controlled their rank-and-file in the interest of their own power to negotiate with government but, at the same time, they sought benefits for workers who continued to provide support for the PRI. The power of the union bosses is declining, in part because the unions are weaker than in the past, and in part because union members are demanding greater democratization.

Accommodation is often coupled with **co-optation** as a means of incorporating dissidents into the system so that they do not threaten its continuity. In 1968, for example, students protesting against authoritarianism and the failure to address poverty and inequity challenged the government just prior to the opening of the Olympic games. The government responded with force—in one instance killing several hundred students in Mexico City—sparking even greater animosity. When Luis Echeverría became president in 1970, he recruited large numbers of the student activists into his administration. He also dramatically increased spending on social services, putting many of the young people to work in expanding antipoverty programs in the countryside and in urban slums. Through these actions, a generation of political and social activists was incorporated into the

system and there was some accommodation to their concerns.

Despite the strong and controlling role of the PRI in Mexico's political history, the country also has a tradition of civic organizations that operate at community and local levels with considerable independence from politics. Local village improvement societies, religious organizations, sports clubs, and parents' organizations are widespread. Many of their activities are not explicitly political, although they may have political implications in that they encourage individuals to work together to find solutions to problems or organize around common interests. Other organizational experiences are more explicitly political. The student movement of 1968 provided evidence that civic society in Mexico had the potential to contest the power of the state. The emergence of independent unionism in the 1970s was another indication of renewed willingness to question the right of the state to stifle the voices of dissent and the emergence of demands for greater equity and participation.

The economic crisis of 1982 combined with this civic tradition to heighten demands for assistance from the government. In October 1983 as many as 2 million people participated in a civic strike to call attention to the crisis and demand a forceful government response. A less successful strike in June 1984 made the same point to the government. In urban areas, citizen groups demanded land rights in squatter settlements, as well as housing, infrastructure, and urban services, as rights of citizenship rather than as a reward for loyalty to the PRI. In the aftermath of the 1985 earthquake, citizen groups became especially dynamic in demanding that government respond to the needs of citizens without reference to their history of party loyalty. Residents of Mexico City demanded that the government let them decide how to rebuild and relocate their neighborhoods and choose who would serve as mayor and represent them.[19] Many also became active in groups that share concerns about quality-of-life issues such as clean air and safe neighborhoods.

In rural areas, peasant organizations also demanded greater independence from government and the leaders of the PRI and the CNC in the 1980s.[20] In addition to greater access to land, they also

Citizen Action: **Urban Popular Movements**

In October 1968 hundreds of students and working-class people took to the streets of Mexico City to protest high unemployment and the authoritarianism of the government. What began as a peaceful rally in Tlatelolco Plaza ended in a tragedy when government troops opened fire on the crowd and killed an estimated two hundred people.

The political activism of the students heralded the birth of urban popular movements in Mexico. The massacre in Tlatelolco became a symbol of a government that was unwilling or unable to respond to citizen demands for economic and political equity. The protest movements sparked by the events of 1968 sought to transcend class boundaries and unite voices around a range of urban issues, from housing shortages to inadequate urban services to lack of land to government centralization in decision-making. Such social movements forged new channels for poor and middle-class urban residents to express their needs. They also generated forums for demanding democratic government that the traditional political system was not providing. In May 1980 the first national congress of urban movements was held in Monterrey in northern Mexico.

Urban popular movements, referring to activities of low- and modest-income (popular) groups, gained renewed vitality in the 1980s. When the economic crisis resulted in drastic reductions of social welfare spending and city services, working- and middle-class neighborhoods forged new coalitions and greatly expanded the national discussion of urban problems. The Mexico City earthquake of 1985 encouraged the formation of unprecedented numbers of grassroots movements in response to the slow and poorly managed relief efforts of the government. Turning to each other, earthquake victims organized to provide shelter, food, and relocation. The elections of 1988 and 1994 provided these groups with significant opportunities to press parties and candidates to respond to their needs. They insisted on their rights to organize and protest without fear of repression or co-optation by the government or the PRI. As the opposition parties expanded rapidly, some leaders of urban movements enrolled as candidates.

Urban popular movements bring citizens together around needs and ideals that cut across class boundaries. Neighborhood improvement, the environment, local self-government, economic development, feminism, and professional identity have been among the factors that have forged links among these groups. As such identities have been strengthened, the need of the political system to negotiate and bargain with a more independent citizenry has increased. Urban popular movements have helped transform political culture on the most local level—one reason the PRI has become less certain that it can maintain its hold on political power in the future.

demanded better prices for the crops they produced, access to markets and credit, development of better infrastructure, and the provision of better education and health services. They began to form alliances with other groups. For example, in the Yucatán peninsula in the late 1970s and 1980s, PEMEX's exploration and production of oil caused massive ecological damage and was carried out with complete disregard for the rights of local *ejidatarios*. Environmental groups joined peasant organizations and student activists in protesting against PEMEX. Since 1994 the rebels in Chiapas have become a focal point for broad alliances of those concerned about the rights of indigenous groups (ethnic minorities) and rural poverty. Indigenous groups have also emerged to demand that

government be responsive to their needs and respectful of their traditions.

A variety of groups have also organized around middle-class and urban issues. In Mexico City, community groups and broader citizen alliances have been active in calling attention to the disastrous levels of air, water, and noise pollution in the capital. Women, with a strong cultural role as caretakers of the home, have begun to mobilize in urban areas around demands for equal pay, legal equality, and opportunities in business traditionally denied them.[21] Religious groups, both Catholic and Protestant, have begun to demand greater government attention to problems of poverty and inequity as well as more government tolerance of religious education and religious practices.

Mexicans demonstrate for better housing in Mexico City's central plaza. *Source:* Freck/Odyssey, Chicago.

In the early 1990s the government's own Solidarity social development program—which many critics claim was a ploy by President Salinas to win back respect for his government after the flawed elections of 1988—helped organize thousands of grassroots organizations and possibly contributed to a trend in broader mobilization independent of the PRI clientelist networks.[22] In 1997 unprecedented numbers of citizens volunteered their time to civic associations that observed the vote to assure, ballot box by ballot box, that the votes were counted accurately. Where this occurred, mostly in urban areas, there were few accusations of fraud.

Civic society in Mexico is becoming more pluralist and less easily controlled. There is broader scope for legitimate protest, opposition, and dissent from government. In predicting change for the future, however, it is important to remember that Mexico has achieved over seventy years of relative stability because its political system offered some channels for representation and participation, despite a high degree of centralization, presidentialism, and PRI domination. It has responded—if reluctantly, slowly, and defensively—to demands for political and policy change and has emphasized compromise, accommodation, and piecemeal distribution of political rewards in order to keep the political peace. Today, Mexicans are engaged in an increasingly open discussion about how to transform the political system rather than how to overthrow it.

Section ❺ Mexican Politics in Transition

Political Challenges and Changing Agendas

When U.S. President Bill Clinton visited Mexico in May 1997, his hosts hoped to show him the richness of Mexican culture and tradition. They brought him two hours outside of Mexico City to a small city called Tlaxcala, in the center of a strongly Nahuátl Indian region. An open-air ceremony had been set up to receive local townspeople so that Clinton could meet everyday citizens face-to-face. Mexican reporters observed the proceedings with some shock even to themselves. There was the expected folklore show for the visitor's benefit, with brightly colored costumes, typical dances, and mariachis, but looking around at the crowd, one could see villagers who came down out of the hills dressed in sparkling white sneakers, impeccable T-shirts with logos, and neatly fitted baseball caps. Any question one would have about the possibility of integrating of these two very different societies was pushed aside—the people already lived it. Posturing by both governments regarding boundaries and nationhood suddenly seemed moot.

This story illustrates a world of increasing interdependence between countries, where nation-states struggle to redefine the meaning of politics. Doubly so, Mexico must confront the evolving nature of its domestic state as well as its international position in terms of relationships with its neighbors. Many Mexicans see NAFTA as the beginning of closer integration with trading partners in Latin America, Asia, and Europe. For all countries, economic integration raises issues of national sovereignty and identity. Mexicans define themselves in part through a set of historical events, symbols, and myths that focus on the country's troubled relationship with the "Colossus of the North." Among numerous national heroes and martyrs are those who distinguished themselves in confrontations with the United States. The myths of the Revolution of 1910 emphasize the uniqueness of the country in terms of its opposition to the capitalists and militarists of the northern country. In the 1970s, Mexicans were encouraged to see themselves as leading Third World countries arguing for increased bargaining positions vis-à-vis the industrialized countries of the north. This view stands in strong contrast to more recent perspectives touting the benefits of an internationally oriented economy, and the undeniable reality of information, culture, money, and people flowing back and forth across borders.

The sense of national identity is affected by international migration. Of particular importance in the Mexican case is labor migration. Every year, large numbers of Mexicans enter the United States as workers to stay for a season, a few years, or settle down permanently. Many return to their towns and villages with new values and new views of the world. Most continue to believe that Mexican culture is preferable to American culture, which they see as excessively materialistic and violent. While they believe that Mexico is a better place to nurture strong family life and values, they are nevertheless strongly influenced by United States mass culture, including popular music, movies, television programs, fast food, and consumer goods.

The future of Mexican politics will be significantly shaped by the ability of the regime to govern the economy. Currently, Mexico's population of 98 million is a young one, with about half under the age of sixteen. The rate of population increase has slowed considerably since the early 1970s and is now growing at less than 2 percent per year. Nevertheless, high birthrates in earlier decades mean that the labor force is growing faster than the population. According to some estimates, 1 million new jobs need to be created every year just to keep up with increasing demand. The demand for jobs for new entrants into the labor market, of course, must be added to existing demand from large numbers of unemployed and underemployed people. Some estimates suggest that as much as one-quarter to one-third of the labor force falls into these categories.

New development policies need to be designed with employment creation in mind. Demand for urban jobs will be particularly strong because of changes in property rights on agricultural lands. In the past, the stipulation that *ejidatarios* could maintain claim to *ejido* plots only if they cultivated them two out of three years kept many of them, even those with the smallest and least productive land, in the countryside. Under legislation introduced by the Salinas administration, many of these peasants are likely to sell or abandon their land and migrate to urban areas in search of jobs.

The inability of the Mexican economy to create enough jobs pushes many Mexicans to seek work in the United States. Extensive migration to the United States has been occurring since the 1880s, when Mexican workers were recruited to help build railroads. In the 1920s and between 1942 and 1964, Mexico and the United States concluded a number of bilateral agreements to provide workers to help the United States meet labor shortages. When such programs ended, a greater proportion of the labor migrants crossed the border into the United States illegally. Differences in wage levels—as high as 13 to 1 during the 1980s—and the jobs lost during the Mexican economic crisis added to the number of workers seeking employment in the United States. The U.S. Congress passed stiff legislation to contain illegal immigration in 1986, but it has been largely ineffective. The difference in wages between the two countries will persist for a long time, which implies that so will migration. In fact, the militarization of the border and the increasing danger of crossing leads more illegal immigrants to settle down permanently in the U.S. rather than risk more trips.

There is disagreement about how to respond to the economic challenges the country faces. Much of the debate surrounds the question of what integration into a competitive international economy really means. For some, it represents the final abandonment of Mexico's sovereignty. For others, it is the basis on which future prosperity must be built. Those who are critical of the market-based, outward-oriented development strategy are concerned about its impact on workers, peasants, and national identities. They argue that the state has abandoned its responsibilities to protect the poor from shortcomings of the market and to provide for their basic needs. They believe that U.S. and Canadian investors have come to Mexico only to find low-wage labor for industrial empires located elsewhere. They see little benefit in further industrial development based on importation of foreign-made parts, their assembly in Mexico, and their export to other markets. This kind of development, they argue, has been prevalent in the *maquiladoras*, or assembly industries, located along the U.S.-Mexico border.

Those who favor closer integration with Canada and the United States acknowledge that some foreign investment does not promote technological advances or move the workforce into higher-paying and more skilled jobs. They emphasize, however, that most investment will occur because the country has a relatively well-educated population, the capacity to absorb modern technology, and a large internal market for industrial goods.

Mexico provides a testing ground for the democratic idea in a state with authoritarian traditions. Although the youth of the population, its increasing education level, and its concentration in urban areas are working against the continued dominance of the PRI, the party continues to have great leverage to set the terms for the interaction of state and civil society. The party has access to extensive resources for buying political support, and its operatives are skilled in the arts of electoral manipulation, even fraud. There is an ongoing struggle for the "soul" of the PRI between those who would like it to become more modern and democratic and those who fear such a path because the party would inevitably lose some of its power.

If the modernizers are successful, their changes will increase the likelihood that the PAN or the PRD will install a president in Los Pinos in the near future. For many party loyalists, this outcome is almost unimaginable. The modernizers retort that the failure to become more democratic will doom the party to loss of legitimacy and push the opposition to violent tactics in an effort to acquire access to power. They believe that the only way the PRI can continue to be relevant to the country's future is to accept more democratic processes and win elections in ways that are accepted as fair by most citizens. It is not yet clear, however, whether their commitment to democracy is strong enough to enable the modernizers to step down from the presidency gracefully should an election go against them. This untested commitment stands in sharp contrast to the commitment of the old guard to hold onto power by whatever means necessary.

More important than internal debate, however, are the large numbers of Mexico's citizens pressuring its political system to become open and democratic, to allow political opposition, and to ensure that public officials can be held accountable for their actions. The democratic ideas of citizen rights to free speech and assembly, free and fair elections, and responsive government are major reasons why the power of the PRI is under attack by so many in Mexico.

The continuing centralization of the Mexican government is one of the critical issues. Countries around the globe increasingly recognize that the solutions to many policy problems lie at regional and local levels. Issues such as how to ensure that children are receiving a high-quality education, how to relieve chronic and massive traffic congestion, how to dispose of garbage in ways that do not threaten public health, and how to reduce air and water pollution require state and municipal governments that have money, authority, and capable public officials—precisely the conditions that only a very few regional and local governments in Mexico have had.

The complexity of contemporary problems and the inability of a single, centralized government to deal with them all at once make the politics of collective identities more important. The pressure for change in Mexico and many other countries is accelerating as modern technology increases the extent to which people in one country are aware of what is occurring in others and the degree to which citizens are able to communicate their concerns and interests among themselves and to the government. However, the ability of citizen groups and opposition parties in Mexico to resist manipulation by the government and to sustain pressure on the regime over an extended period remains untested. The formation of a strong civil society capable of articulating its interests and ensuring that government is responsive to its needs is the other side of political reform.

Human and social development in a country make such a functioning civil society possible. Improving social conditions is an important challenge for Mexico. While elites enjoy the benefits of sumptuous life-styles, education at the best U.S. universities for their children, and luxury travel to the capitals of the world, large numbers of Mexicans remain ill-educated, poorly served with health care, and distant from the security of knowing that their basic needs for food, shelter, and employment can be met. The Chiapas rebellion of 1994 made the social agenda a topic of everyday conversation by reminding Mexicans that some people lived in appalling conditions with little hope for the future. Indeed, the average length of schooling is still under five years nationwide, and only about half of the eligible students are enrolled in secondary school.

What to do about these conditions is debated. As in the United States, some argue that economic growth and expanded employment will resolve the major problems of poverty in the country. They believe that prosperity, tied to Mexico's economic future internationally, will benefit everyone in the long run. For this to occur, however, they insist that education will have to be improved and made more appropriate for developing a well-educated workforce. They also believe that improved education will come about when local communities have more control over schools and curriculum and when parents have more choice between public and private education for their children. From their perspective, the solution to poverty and injustice is fairly clear—more and better jobs and improved education.

For those critical of the development path on which Mexico embarked in the 1980s and 1990s, the problems of poverty and inequity are more complex. Solutions involve understanding the diverse causes of poverty, including not only lack of jobs and poor education but also exploitation, geographical isolation, discriminatory laws and practices, and families disrupted by migration, urbanization, and the tensions of modern life. Citizens must define the role of government in providing social welfare. In the past, Mexicans looked to government for such benefits, but their provision was deeply flawed by inefficiency and political manipulation. The government and the PRI consistently used access to social services as a means to increase their political control and limit the capacity of citizens to demand equitable treatment. Thus, while many continue to believe that it is the responsibility of government to ensure that citizens are well educated, healthy, and able to make the most of their potential, the populace is deeply suspicious of the government's capacity to provide such conditions fairly and effi-

ciently. Decentralization, local control, and active community organizations might provide an answer to how public goods such as social services and basic infrastructure could be provided more effectively.

Mexican Politics in Comparative Perspective

Mexico faces many of the same challenges that beset other countries—creating equitable and effective democratic government, becoming integrated into a global economy, and responding to complex social problems. Indeed, these were precisely the challenges that the United States faced in the 1990s, along with India, Nigeria, China, Japan, Germany, and others. Like these other countries, Mexico confronts these challenges within the context of a unique historical and institutional evolution. The legacies of its past, the tensions of the present, and the innovations of the future will no doubt evolve in ways that continue to be uniquely Mexican.

What will the future bring? How much will the pressures for change and the potential loss of national identity affect the nature of the political system? In 1980 few people could have predicted the extensive economic policy reforms and pressures for democracy that Mexico faced in the next ten years. Many still cannot believe them and are fighting them. But it is important to remember that Mexico has a long tradition of relatively strong institutions. It is not a country that will easily slip into sustained political instability. A tradition of constitutional government, a strong presidency, a political system that has incorporated a wide range of interests, a weak tradition of military involvement in politics, and a strong sense of national identity—these are among the factors that need to be considered in predicting the political consequences of democratization, economic integration, and greater social equality.

Mexico represents a pivotal case for the hemisphere. If it can successfully bridge the gap between its past and its future and move from centralization to effective local governance, from regional vulnerability to global dependability, and from the control of the few to the participation of the many, then the rest of the Americas will surely look to follow in its footsteps. Its success or failure will have serious implications for future patterns of global integration.

Key Terms

mestizos

Amerindian

indigenous groups

maquiladoras

anticlericalism

ejidos

ejidatarios

sexenio

clientelism

corporatist state

state capitalism

import substituting
  industrialization

informal sector

petrodollars

para-statal sector

accommodation

co-optation

Suggested Readings

Baer, M. Delal, and Sidney Weintraub. *The NAFTA Debate: Grappling with Unconventional Trade Issues*. Boulder, Colo.: Lynne Rienner, 1994.

Bailey, John. *Governing Mexico: The Statecraft of Crisis Management*. New York: St. Martin's Press, 1988.

Collier, Ruth Berins. *The Contradictory Alliance: State-Labor Relations and Regime Change in Mexico*. Berkeley: University of California Press, 1992.

Cook, Maria Lorena, Kevin J. Middlebrook, and Juan Molinar, eds. *The Politics of Economic Restructuring in Mexico*. San Diego: Center for U.S.-Mexican Studies, University of California, 1994.

Cornelius, Wayne A. "Nation-Building, Participation, and Distribution: The Politics of Social Reform under Cárdenas." In *Crisis, Choice, and Change: Historical Studies of Political Development*, ed. Gabriel A. Almond, Scott Flanagan, and Robert J. Mundt. Boston: Little, Brown, 1973.

Cornelius, Wayne A., and Philip Martin. *The Uncertain Connection: Free Trade and Mexico-U.S. Migration*. San Diego: Center for U.S.-Mexican Studies, University of California, 1993.

Cornelius, Wayne A., Ann L. Craig, and Jonathan Fox, eds. *Transforming State-Society Relations in Mexico: The National Solidarity Strategy*. San Diego: Center for U.S.-Mexican Studies, University of California, 1994.

Cornelius, Wayne A., Judith Gentleman, and Peter H. Smith, eds. *Mexico's Alternative Political Futures*. San Diego: Center for U.S.-Mexican Studies, University of California, 1989.

Eckstein, Susan, ed. *Power and Popular Protest: Latin American Social Movements*. Berkeley: University of California Press, 1989.

Foweraker, Joe, and Ann L. Craig, eds. *Popular Movements and Political Change in Mexico*. Boulder, Colo.: Lynne Rienner, 1990.

Grindle, Merilee S. *Bureaucrats, Politicians, and Peasants in Mexico: A Case Study in Public Policy*. Berkeley: University of California Press, 1977.

——. *Challenging the State: Crisis and Innovation in Latin America and Africa*. London: Cambridge University Press, 1995.

Hamilton, Nora. *The Limits of State Autonomy: Post-Revolutionary Mexico*. Princeton, N.J.: Princeton University Press, 1982.

Hansen, Roger. *The Politics of Mexican Development*. Baltimore: Johns Hopkins University Press, 1971.

Lustig, Nora. *Mexico: The Remaking of an Economy*. Washington, D.C.: Brookings Institution, 1992.

Meyer, Michael C., and William L. Sherman. *The Course of Mexican History*. 5th ed. New York: Oxford University Press, 1995.

Mumme, Stephen, C. Richard Bath, and Valerie J. Assetto. "Political Development and Environmental Policy in Mexico." *Latin American Research Review* 23, no. 1 (1988).

Paz, Octavio. *The Labyrinth of Solitude: Life and Thought in Mexico*. New York: Grove Press, 1961.

Purcell, Susan Kaufman, and Luis Rubio, eds. *Mexico under Zedillo*. Boulder, Colo.: Lynne Rienner, 1998.

Roett, Riordan, ed. *The Challenge of Institutional Reform in Mexico*. Boulder, Colo.: Lynne Rienner, 1994.

Ronfeldt, David, ed. *The Modern Mexican Military: A Reassessment*. San Diego: Center for U.S.-Mexican Studies, University of California, 1984.

Smith, Peter. *Labyrinths of Power: Political Recruitment in Twentieth-Century Mexico*. Princeton, N.J.: Princeton University Press, 1979.

Suárez-Orozco, Marcelo, ed. *Crossings: Mexican Immigration in Interdisciplinary Perspective*. Cambridge, Mass.: Harvard University Press, 1998.

Womack, John, Jr. *Zapata and the Mexican Revolution*. New York: Vintage Books, 1968.

——. *Rebellion in Chiapas. An Historical Reader*. New York, New Press, 1999.

Endnotes

[1] An excellent history of this event is presented in Wayne A. Cornelius, "Nation-Building, Participation, and Distribution: The Politics of Social Reform under Cárdenas," in *Crisis, Choice and Change: Historical Studies of Political Development*. ed. Gabriel A. Almond, Scott Flanagan, and Robert J. Mundt. (Boston: Little, Brown, 1973).

[2] World Bank, *World Development Report, 1994* (New York: Oxford University Press, 1994).

[3] World Bank, *World Development Report, 1997* (New York: Oxford University Press, 1997).

[4] Merilee S. Grindle, *State and Countryside: Development Policy and Agrarian Politics in Latin America* (Baltimore: Johns Hopkins University Press, 1986), 63, quoting President Avila Camacho (1940–1946).

[5] Kevin J. Middlebrook, ed., *Unions, Workers, and the State in Mexico* (San Diego: Center for U.S.-Mexican Studies, University of California, 1991).

6 Grindle, *State and Countryside*, pp. 79–111.

7 For a description of this process, see Carlos Bazdresch and Santiago Levy, "Populism and Economic Policy in Mexico," in *The Macroeconomics of Populism in Latin America*, ed. Rudiger Dornbusch and Sebastian Edwards (Chicago: University of Chicago Press, 1991), 72.

8 For an assessment of the mounting problems of Mexico City and efforts to deal with them, see Diane E. Davis, *Urban Leviathan: Mexico City in the Twentieth Century* (Philadelphia: Temple University Press, 1994).

9 Joe Foweraker and Ann L. Craig, eds., *Popular Movements and Political Change in Mexico* (Boulder, Colo.: Lynne Rienner, 1989).

10 The Economist Intelligence Unit. Country Profile, Mexico. 1998–1999.

11 Roger Hansen, *The Politics of Mexican Development,* (Baltimore: Johns Hopkins University Press, 1971), 75.

12 Guillermo Trejo and Claudio Jones, "Political Dilemmas of Welfare Reform: Poverty and Inequality in Mexico," in *Mexico under Zedillo*, ed. Susan Kaufman Purcell and Luis Rubio (Boulder, Colo.: Lynne Rienner, 1998), 70.

13 The Economist Intelligence Unit. Country Profile, Mexico. 1998–1999.

14 Frank Brandenburg, *The Making of Modern Mexico* (Englewood Cliffs, N.J.: Prentice Hall, 1964), 141.

15 Daniel Levy and Gabriel Székely, *Mexico: Paradoxes of Stability and Change* (Boulder, Colo.: Westview Press, 1983), 100.

16 United Nations Development Programme, Human Development Report, 1997.

17 *El Norte de Monterrey/Reforma* Opinion Poll on Mexico's Presidential Race, June 1–6, 1994.

18 Wayne A. Cornelius and Ann L. Craig, "Politics in Mexico," in *Comparative Politics Today*, ed. Gabriel Almond and G. Bingham Powell, 5th ed. (Boston: Scott Foresman & Co., 1992), 502.

19 Susan Eckstein, ed., *Power and Popular Protest: Latin American Social Movements* (Berkeley: University of California Press, 1989).

20 Jonathan Fox and Gustavo Gordillo, "Between State and Market: The Campesinos' Quest for Autonomy," in *Mexico's Alternative Political Futures*, ed. Wayne A. Cornelius, Judith Gentleman, and Peter H. Smith (San Diego: Center for U.S.-Mexican Studies, University of California, 1989).

21 Foweraker and Craig, *Popular Movements and Political Change in Mexico.*

22 Wayne A. Cornelius, Ann L. Craig, and Jonathan Fox, eds., *Transforming State-Society Relations in Mexico: The National Solidarity Strategy* (San Diego: Center for U.S.-Mexican Studies, University of California, 1994).

CHAPTER 5

Brazil

Al Montero

Federative Republic of Brazil

Land and Population

Capital	Brasilia
Total Area (square miles)	3,286,500 (slightly smaller than the U.S.)
Population	164 million
Annual Average Population Growth Rate (1990–1997)	1.4%
Urban Population	80%
Ethnic Composition	White 54.4%
	Mulatto and Mestizo 40.1%
	Black and Black/ 4.9%
	Amerindian
	Asian 0.5%
	Amerindian 0.1%
Major Language	Portuguese
Religious Affiliation	Catholic 74.3%
	Protestant 22.5%
	Other 2.3%

Economy

Domestic Currency	Cruzeiro real
Total GNP (US$)	$773.4 billion
GNP per capita (US$)	$4720
GNP per capita at purchasing power parity (US$)	$6240
GNP average annual growth rate (1996–1997)	2.4%
GNP per capita average annual growth rate	1996–1997 1.1%
	1980–1995 –0.4%
	1965–1980 6.3%
Income Gap:	Richest 20% of population
GDP per capita (US$)	$18,563
	Poorest 20% of population
	$578
Structure of Production (% of GDP)	Agriculture 14%
	Industry 37%
	Services 49%
Labor Force Distribution (% of total)	Agriculture 23%
	Industry 23%
	Services 54%
Exports as % of GDP	7%
Imports as % of GDP	8%
Electricity Consumption per capita (kwh)	1954
CO$_2$ Emissions per capita (metric tons)	1.6

Society

Life Expectancy	Female	70.7
	Male	62.8
Doctors per 100,000 people		134
Infant Mortality per 1000 live births		44
Adult Literacy	Female	82.2%
	Male	83.3%
Access to Information and Communications (per 1000 people)	Radios	399
	Televisions	278
	Telephone Lines	75
	Personal Computers	13
Women in Government and Economy		
Seats in Parliament held by Women		6.7%
Women at Ministerial Level		4.0%
Women as % of Total Labor Force		35.0%
Female Business Administrators and Managers		17.0%
Female Professional and Technical Workers		63.0%
1998 Human Development Index ranking (out of 174 countries; 1 = highest)		62

Political Organization

Political System Federal republic, presidential with separation of powers.

Regime History Democratic since 1946 with periods of military authoritarianism, especially 1964–1985.

Administrative Structure Federal, with 26 states plus the Federal District, which also functions as a state. Subnational legislatures are unicameral. State governments have multiple secretariats, the major ones commonly being economy, planning, and infrastructure. The states are divided into municipalities (over 5,000), with mayors and councillors directly elected.

Executive President, vice president, and cabinet. The president and vice president are directly elected by universal suffrage in a two-round runoff election for four-year terms.

Legislature Bicameral: The Senate is made up of three senators from each state and from the Federal District, elected by plurality vote for an eight-year term; the Chamber of Deputies consists of representatives from each state and from the Federal District, elected by proportional vote for a four-year term.

Judiciary Supreme Court, High Tribunal of Justice, regional courts, labor courts, electoral courts, military courts, and state courts. Judiciary has financial and administrative autonomy. Judges are nominated for life.

Party System Multiparty system including several parties of the right, center-left, and left. Elections are by open-list proportional representation. There is no restriction on the creation and merging of political parties.

Politics in Action

In May 1997 thousands of Brazilians gathered outside the stock exchange in Rio de Janeiro while hundreds more collected inside the building. All were waiting for the beginning of an auction of Companhia Vale do Rio Doce (CVRD), the mining conglomerate, and Brazil's largest public firm. The sale of Vale, as the company is known, was the latest in a series of **privatization** moves that began in the early 1990s with the sale of Brazil's steel mills, fertilizer firms, and utilities companies. Fifty-two state enterprises had been sold; now it was Vale's turn. However, for the Brazilians gathered outside the stock exchange, the sale of Vale meant much more: a cherished piece of Brazil's past was being lost to the faceless market. Vale represented memories of the Brazilian economy that blossomed in the post–World War II era with ambitious industrialization projects led by large public firms. Now all of that was under attack by "greedy capitalists" intent on exploiting the patrimony of the Brazilian people for personal gain. For the students, workers, and professionals who joined to protest the sale of the mining giant, it was too much to take. Minutes before the auction gavel fell, tempers flared. The angry crowd pushed against police barricades. Some threw punches, while others were hurled to the floor and trampled. Many would leave with bloodied faces, but the painful defeat was felt by all. The old Brazil was dead.

For those inside the stock exchange, the sale of Vale meant the birth of a new Brazil. By agreeing to privatize one of the most recognizable symbols of Brazilian industry, the country's leaders were embracing the importance of the market in modernizing Brazil. Despite its past successes, the state could no longer guarantee Vale or any industrial firm the resources needed to become competitive in global markets. By putting Vale up for sale, Brazil's political leadership was guaranteeing that the firm would have a future. The new owners of Vale were young Brazilian industrialists and bankers as well as international investors, including U.S. firms such as NationsBank and the financier George Soros. Unlike most Brazilian firms, which are family-owned, the new Vale would be owned by shareholders and operated by professional administrators, much like major U.S. and European multinational firms. Nothing less would befit the world's largest exporter of iron ore. The new Vale was emblematic of the new Brazil: modern, competitive, and linked to global markets.

Although opponents were thwarted in their attempts to stop the sale, the opposition to the auctioning of Vale revealed aspects of the new Brazil. Only a week before the sale, opponents had filed 135 separate lawsuits in state courts to halt the privatization. In response, squads of lawyers for the National Development Bank, the federal agency responsible for organizing the sale of Vale, had traveled to the far corners of Brazil to defeat each and every lawsuit. Yet the absence of a centralized and hierarchical system for adjudicating the dispute highlighted both the weakness of democratic institutions in Brazil and the difficulty of ruling over such a large, decentralized political order. The new Brazil is a relatively young democracy, and like Russia and India, it is big and complicated.

Geographic Setting

Brazil's size is only the most obvious characteristic of this country of 164 million people. In land surface, Brazil is larger than the continental United States and occupies two-thirds of South America. It borders all the other countries of South America except Ecuador and Chile. Because of the expansion of the coffee economy in São Paulo state during the nineteenth century and the growth of an industrial economy during the twentieth century, Brazil's largest cities are concentrated in the southern and southeastern regions. More than 15 million inhabitants live in Greater São Paulo alone. This density contrasts with the northern, sparsely populated rain forest regions of the Amazon. Generally, however, Brazil's 18.2 inhabitants per square kilometer means that the country is more sparsely populated than the United States.

The physical geography of Brazil is impressively diverse, including thick rain forest in the Amazon valley, large lowland swamps known as the *pantanal*

179

Brazil

in the central western states, and vast expanses of badlands known as the *sertão* in the north and northeast. The country is rich in natural resources and arable land. The Amazon has an abundance of tropical fruit and minerals; the central and southern regions provide most of the country's iron ore and coal; off- and onshore sources of petroleum in Rio de Janeiro and the northeast coastline are also significant. Brazil's farmlands are particularly fertile, including large soy-producing areas in the central savannahs called the *cerrados*, coffee areas of the Paraíba Valley near Rio de Janeiro and in São Paulo, and sugar and other agriculture along the narrow stretch off the northeast coast called the *litoral*. While the Amazon's climate is wet and the *sertão* is dry, the agricultural areas of the central, southeastern, and southern regions are temperate.

Centuries of voluntary and involuntary immigration of Europeans and Africans contributed to the emergence of an ethnically mixed society. Combinations of Europeans, Africans, and Indians produced hundreds of distinct colors of people. Although this complexity makes any classification scheme precarious, the National Brazilian Institute of Geography and Statistics (IBGE) claims that 57 percent of the population is white, 37 percent is *pardo* (brown or mulatto), 6 percent is black, and 0.6 percent is Asian.[1] These numbers probably ignore people of mixed race, from indigenous and white parents, who are known as *mestizos* but are sometimes classified erroneously as being white or *pardo*. The indigenous people, who live in the vast Amazon basin and once numbered in the millions, were largely decimated by colonization and modernization. Their number is usually estimated at 250,000, but they occupy over 8.5 million square kilometers, 11 percent of the total area of Brazil.[2] The Asian population is dominated by people of Japanese descent who immigrated to the southeastern states and particularly São Paulo after 1925. Numbering over 2

Critical Junctures in Brazil's Political Development

1822 Dom Pedro I declares himself emperor of Brazil, peacefully ending three hundred years of Portuguese colonial rule.

1824 Constitution drafted.

1888 Abolition of slavery.

1889 Dom Pedro II, who assumed throne in 1840, is forced into exile; landowning elites establish an oligarchical republic.

1891 A new constitution establishes a directly elected president.

1930 Getúlio Vargas gains power after a coup led by military and political leaders. His period of dictatorship (1937–1945) is known as the New State.

1945 Vargas calls for general elections. General Eurico Dutra of the Social Democratic Party wins.

1950 Vargas is elected president. Scandals precipitate his suicide in 1954.

1956 Juscelino Kubitschek becomes president.

1960 Jânio Quadros becomes president.

1961 Quadros resigns. João Goulart gains presidency despite an attempted military coup.

1964 A military coup places power in the hands of successive authoritarian regimes.

1985 *Diretas Já!*, a mass mobilization campaign, calls for direct elections.

1985 Vice presidential candidate José Sarney becomes president upon the sudden death of elected president Tancredo Neves.

1988 A new constitution grants new social and political rights.

1989 Fernando Collor is elected president.

1992 Collor is impeached; vice president Itamar Franco assumes presidency.

1994 Fernando Henrique Cardoso is elected president after his Real Plan controls inflation.

1998 Cardoso is reelected in the midst of a growing financial crisis.

million, São Paulo's community of Japanese descendants is the largest such grouping outside of Japan.

Like other ethnically plural societies such as India, Mexico, Nigeria, Russia, Iran, and the United States, Brazil is a unique blend of distinct cultural influences. Unlike the people of India, Iran, and Nigeria, however, Brazilians are not greatly divided over religious differences. Roman Catholicism was imposed by Portuguese colonial rule, then reinforced by immigration from Catholic Italy, Spain, and Portugal at the end of the nineteenth century. In recent years, evangelical Protestants have made inroads and now compose about 11 percent of the population. Afro-Brazilian religions represent an older, and far more difficult to measure, tendency with religious practices that often mix Catholic and African traditions but are sometimes practiced independently. Indigenous religions and traditions are also part of the cultural landscape. More than religion, the dominance of Portuguese as the language of the land has served to keep this large country united.

Because of its size, large population, large internal market for foreign and domestic industry, and dominance over a majority of the rain forests in the Amazon (the so-called green lung of the planet), Brazil possesses resources that could make it a global superpower. Yet Brazil is also a poor country that struggles to provide for its own people out of its impressive abundance of natural resources. Brazilian governments have often contended with this paradox by entertaining ideas for agrarian reform to break up a very concentrated system of land tenure. All such attempts at distribution have been limited by the priorities of industrial development.

Addressing the immense social problems of this big country requires administering its considerable resources with foresight. Unfortunately, Brazil's potential has often fallen victim to the political baggage from its past.

Critical Junctures

The Brazilian Empire (1822–1889)

Europeans first arrived in Brazil in 1500 with the expedition led by Pedro Alvares Cabral. Unlike the other countries of Latin America, Brazil was a Portuguese colony, not a Spanish one. As a result, Brazil was spared the devastatingly violent wars of independence that afflicted other Latin American states, including Mexico. Violence, however, played a prominent role in Brazil's conquest and development as indigenous peoples and African slaves were mistreated and killed, or died of diseases. Ninety-five percent of the Tupis, the dominant ethnic group of the Atlantic Forest were ravaged in the first decades of the conquest.

In 1808, when Napoleon Bonaparte invaded Spain and Portugal, the Portuguese king, João VI, and his court escaped to Brazil. After the defeat of Napoleon, Dom João returned to Portugal to reclaim his throne. But he left his son, Dom Pedro, behind in Rio de Janeiro as prince regent. In September 1822, Dom Pedro declared Brazil independent and took the new title of Emperor of Brazil. In 1824 a constitution was drafted, making Brazil the only constitutional monarchy in the Americas. In 1840, Dom Pedro I's son, Dom Pedro II, assumed the throne.

The Brazilian empire's chief concern was keeping control of the country's large, mostly unexplored territory. Complicating this task was the divisive issue of slavery, upon which Brazil's plantation economy depended. The solution was to centralize authority in the emperor, who acted as a **moderating power** (*poder moderador*), mediating conflicts among the executive, legislative, and judicial branches of government and powerful landowning elites. This centralization of authority provided a contrast with the other postcolonial Latin American states, which suffered numerous conflicts among territorially dispersed strongmen called *caudillos*. Brazil avoided the rise of figures such as Mexico's arch-strongman, Porfirio Díaz.

The importance of the national slave economy had a direct effect on the centralization of power. In 1819 there were 1.1 million slaves, corresponding to 30 percent of the population. British pressure during mid-century to end the international slave trade led the Brazilian imperial state to take a strong international position in favor of slavery. The regional **oligarchy** was far too fragmented politically and geographically to present a unified front to Britain's influence. Instead, the landed oligarchy relied on the central government to confront international opposition to slavery. This reaffirmed the authority of the central state.

The constitutional empire marked the birth of Brazilian liberal institutions. In contrast with its neighbors, the country enjoyed several features of a functioning representative democracy: regularity of elections, the alternation of parties in power, and scrupulous observation of the constitution. In substance, however, liberal institutions only regulated political competition among the rural, oligarchical elites, reflecting the interests of a privileged minority and not the larger Brazilian population. The social reality of the country was an agrarian and illiterate slave society governed by a cosmopolitan elite that mimicked European civilization.

The Old Republic (1889–1930)

The next critical juncture in Brazilian history occurred in 1889 with the peaceful demise of the empire and the emergence of an oligarchical republic commanded by landowning elites. Many causes led to the end of the empire. The institutions of slavery and the monarchy were topics of heated debate among landowners, politicians, and commercial elites. The international pressures of abolitionists to end slavery resulted in the freeing of slaves over sixty years of age and children of slaves not yet born. Socioeconomic changes also paved the way for abolition. The dynamic coffee economy concentrated in the state of São Paulo had grown impressively since the 1830s. Unlike the plantation sugar economy of the northeast, coffee did not require the use of slave labor, which was prohibitively expensive. Under sustained pressure by the coffee elite, all slaves were freed in 1888. By this time, too, liberal political values in opposition to the centralization of political authority had taken root among the coffee oligarchy.

The Old Republic (1889–1930) consolidated the political rise of the coffee oligarchy and a small urban industrial class and commercial elite linked to the coffee trade. By the end of the nineteenth century, coffee had become the main economic commodity, with Brazil supplying most of the world's demand. Railroads linked coffee growers and markets from the rural areas of São Paulo with the urban commercial elites of Rio de Janeiro and contributed further to the development of the central southern region. These structural changes in the economy accentuated the political influence of coffee elites.

The constitution of 1891, which was inspired by the U.S. model, established a directly elected president as the head of government, guaranteed the separation of church and state, and expanded the franchise to include all literate males (about 3.5 percent of the population before 1930). The **legitimacy** of the republican political system was established on governing principles that, although limited to a privileged few, were no longer determined by the hereditary rights of the emperor. Power was decentralized to the states, which gained greater authority to formulate policy, spend money, levy taxes, and maintain their own militias.

Although the republican elite went further than the empire's elite in expressing liberal ideas in the constitution, to the majority of Brazilians republican liberalism was a sham. Most Brazilians continued to reside in rural areas, where the landed oligarchy vigorously suppressed dissent. As in the southern United States, landed elites manipulated local political activity. The colonels, as these elites were called in Brazil, assumed extensive extralegal authority to gather their poor workers and "vote them" (use their votes to guarantee the election of officials favored by the local colonels). This process became widely known as *coronelismo*.

The ties that developed between the patron (the landowner) and the client (the peasant) during the Old Republic became the basis of modern Brazilian politics. In return for protection and occasional favors, the client did the bidding of the patron. As urbanization and the growth of the state's administrative and bureaucratic agencies proceeded, the process of trading favors and demanding action was transformed and became known as **clientelism**. *Coronelismo* in rural areas and clientelism in urban areas were extended to the politics of the national state. In this way, the state was dominated by **patrimonialism**—the injection of private interests into public policy-making. Pervasive corruption, graft, and outright bribery developed as means of reinforcing patrimonialism.

In contrast to the centralization of power during the empire, the Old Republic consecrated the power of local elites. Perhaps at no time in Brazilian political history was the **politics of the governors** as blatant as it was during the years of the Old Republic. Regional elites, mainly from the coffee and cattle regions, dominated national politics. Three states in particular emerged as key players: São Paulo (coffee), Minas Gerais (coffee and ranching), and Rio Grande do Sul (ranching). These states profoundly influenced economic policy-making and the choice of presidential candidates. The presidency alternated almost on a regular basis between São Paulo and Minas Gerais. The pattern was so obvious that this period of Brazilian political history is popularly referred to as the rule of *café com leite* ("coffee with milk"), reflecting the dominance of the São Paulo coffee and Minas Gerais cattle elites.

Brazilian society became more complex with the arrival of large numbers of European and Asian immigrant laborers after the end of the slave trade in 1851. From 1881 to 1930 almost 4 million Italian, Portuguese, Spanish, and German immigrants entered the country.[3] From 1925 onward, Japan subsidized Japanese immigration. Between 1931 and 1940, the Japanese were the second largest group of immigrants to enter Brazil. Despite the diversity of the immigration experience, immigrants tended to settle in the richer southern half of Brazil. In 1920, 93.4 percent of all foreigners lived in the central, southern, and southeastern regions. Fifty-two percent of all foreign residents in the country lived in the state of São Paulo. European immigrants with socialist and radical trade union backgrounds were the first organizers of the Brazilian labor movement during the Old Republic and often provided leadership in the newly formed trade unions.

The upsurge in European immigration and the beginnings of industrialization paved the way for an expansion of the middle class. Artisans, professionals, politicians, civil servants, and military officers emerged as important actors during the early twentieth century. Their increasing influence in Brazilian politics severely threatened the political monopoly of the rural oligarchy and its clientelistic order.

The 1930 Revolution

The Great Depression of the 1930s upset the economic and political base of the Old Republic. As world demand for coffee plummeted, the coffee and ranch elites faced their worst crisis. Worker demonstrations and a resurgent Brazilian Communist Party

Leaders: *Getúlio Dornelles Vargas*

Getúlio Dornelles Vargas came from a wealthy family in the cattle-rich southernmost state of Rio Grande do Sul. Vargas' youth was marked by political divisions within his family between federalists and republicans, conflicts that separated Brazilians during the Old Republic and particularly in Rio Grande do Sul, which had a strong regional identity. Political violence, which was common in the state's history, also affected Vargas' upbringing. His two brothers were each accused of killing rivals, one at the military school in Minas Gerais that Getúlio attended with one of his older siblings. After a brief stint in the military, Vargas attended law school in Porto Alegre, where he excelled as an orator. Like many in his generation, Vargas' university education was incomplete. He supplemented his studies by reading many foreign books.

After graduating in 1907, he began his political career as a district attorney. Later he served as majority leader in the state senate. In 1923, Vargas was elected federal deputy for Rio Grande do Sul, and in 1924 he became leader of his state's delegation in the Chamber of Deputies. In 1926, Vargas made another political career change when he was named finance minister for the Washington Luis administration (1926–1930). He served for a year before winning the governorship of his home state. Never an ideologue, Vargas embraced a highly pragmatic style of governing that made him one of Brazil's most popular politicians by the end of the 1920s.

Vargas' powerful political position as governor of Rio Grande do Sul catapulted him into national prominence in 1929. The international economic crisis compelled several regional economic oligarchies to unite in opposition to the coffee and financial policies of the government. The states, including the state of São Paulo, divided their support between two candidates for the presidency:

Getúlio Vargas as president in 1952.
Source: Photoworld/FPG.

one, Julio Prestes, supported by President Luis, and the other, Vargas, head of the opposition. The two states of Minas Gerais and Rio Grande do Sul voted as a bloc in favor of Vargas, but he lost the 1930 election. Immediately after this loss, a conspiracy among discontented military and political leaders led to the coup of October 1930, which installed Vargas in power.

No other figure in Brazilian political history affected the country as much as Getúlio Vargas. His New State launched a series of reforms that established the terms on which Brazilian society would be linked to the state for decades. Even today, his political legacy continues in the form of state agencies and laws protecting workers.

Source: For more on Vargas' life, see Robert M. Levine, *Father of the Poor? Vargas and His Era* (New York: Cambridge University Press, 1998).

challenged the legitimacy of the Old Republic. Among the ranks of discontented political elites a figure emerged who would change the shape of Brazilian politics for the rest of the century—Getúlio Vargas.

After a disputed presidential campaign in 1930, Vargas came to power as the head of a new "revolutionary" government. Vargas moved swiftly to crush middle-class and popular dissent. He built a political coalition around a new economic project of industrialization led by the central government and based on central state resources. In contrast to the Old Republic, Vargas insisted on controlling the regional governments by replacing all governors (except in Minas Gerais) with hand-picked allies (**interventores**). Once again, the center of gravity of Brazilian politics swung back to the national state.

Under the Old Republic, calls for rights by workers and middle-class professionals had been treated as issues for the police to resolve with force. By contrast, Vargas believed he could win the support of these groups by answering their demands in a controlled way. They would be allowed to participate in the new political order but only if they mobilized within state-created and state-regulated unions and associations.

This model of government was **state corporatism**. State corporatism refers to a method of organizing societal actors in state-sponsored associations. It rejects the idea of competition among social groups by having the state arbitrate all conflicts. For instance, when workers requested increases in their wages, state agencies would determine to what extent such demands were answered and how business would pay for them.[4]

By 1937, Vargas had achieved a position of virtually uncontested power. From such a vantage point, he implemented a series of reforms whose influence is still felt. During the next eight years, Vargas consolidated his state corporatist paradigm with labor codes, the establishment of public firms to produce strategic commodities such as steel and oil, and paternalistic social policies. Packaged with nationalist fervor, these policies were collectively called the **New State** (*Estado Novo*).

The New State was decidedly authoritarian. Vargas, who was called *pai do povo* ("father of the people"), could not be upstaged by competing political images and organizations. Parties and congressional politicians became mere onlookers. Brazilian society would be linked directly to the state and to Vargas as the state's primary agent. Vargas expressed the illegitimacy of representative bodies this way: "From now on there are to be no middlemen between the president and the people." One of the key thinkers of the New State put it even more clearly: "The new regime can have only one party, namely that of the state, which is at the same time the party of the nation."

Although the New State's constitution had fascist overtones, Vargas' policies were as much inspired by the New Deal of U.S. President Franklin D. Roosevelt as by fascist Italy or Nazi Germany.[5] The new regime expanded the existing rudimentary social insurance and pension programs into a broad welfare and health care system for urban workers. Although unemployment insurance was not envisaged by the new laws, workers were provided with insurance against occupational accidents, illness, and death. Vargas created a Ministry of Labor and labor courts to regulate and solve conflicts between employers and labor.

In the New State, the military became an ever more important institution in Brazilian politics. The armed forces experienced marked improvements in armament production and recruitment. Professional standards of promotion, conduct, and the use of force were codified in the establishment of the Superior War College (*Escola Superior de Guerra*). The military even developed new doctrines to justify the use of public funds to own and operate industries seen as essential to the nation's security. The ideology of the military regimes that dominated Brazil from 1964 to 1985 emerged directly from these earlier experiences.[6]

The Populist Republic (1945–1964)

The ever-growing mobilization of segments of the working and middle classes as well as U.S. diplomatic pressure forced Vargas, in 1943, to call for full democratic elections to be held in December 1945. Three political parties emerged to contest the election: the Social Democratic Party (PSD), the Brazilian Labor Party (PTB), and the National Democratic Union Party (UDN). The PSD was a collection of *Estado Novo* supporters and members of clientelist political machines across the country. The PTB was created by Vargas to mobilize members of the official labor unions. The PSD and the PTB, which operated in alliance, were both dependent upon the state. The UDN, on the other hand, brought together the various regional, anti-Vargas forces, which advocated a return to the liberal constitutionalism of the Old Republic. The UDN continued to support the role of the state in promoting economic development, however. By October 1945, the bitterness of the campaign led the military to force Vargas' resignation, two months before the general election.

The turn to democracy in 1945 fell far short of breaking with the past. The new president, Eurico Dutra of the PSD, was one of the architects of the New State. Although the new 1946 constitution provided for periodic elections, state corporatism continued in full force. The most important economic and social policies of the country were still decided by Brazil's far-flung state bureaucracy, not by the national legislature.

Populism, not democracy, became the defining characteristic of the new political order. In Brazil, the terms *populist* and *populism* refer to politicians, programs, or movements that seek to expand citizenship to previously disenfranchised sectors of society in return for political support. Populist governments tend to grant benefits to guarantee support, but they discourage lower-class groups from creating autonomous organizations. Populist leaders, around whom personality cults often form, were successful in Brazil and other Latin American countries in generating mass support among urban working and middle classes (and sometimes rural groups) through the provision of social insurance, health care, and wage hikes. Yet in no way were these leaders directly representative or accountable to their constituencies.

Populism was Vargas' most important tool after his elected return to the presidency in 1950 with PSD and PTB support. Brazilian workers supported his return because he promised to increase the minimum wage, improve the social insurance system, and provide subsidies for public transportation and basic foodstuffs. However, many of these promises were threatened by economic problems in the early 1950s as inflation increased and wages eroded. Opposition politicians charged that Vargas was no longer able to assure Brazil's development and that, if given a chance, he would impose another dictatorship on the country.[7] Already politically vulnerable, Vargas was soon swept up in a bizarre scandal involving the attempted assassination of a popular journalist. The crisis drove Vargas to take his own life on August 24, 1954.

Under Vargas' democratic successor, Juscelino Kubitschek (1956–1960), the economic picture improved. Brazilian industry expanded tremendously in the 1950s. Kubitschek was a master of political symbolism and **nationalism**. His administration promoted images of a new and bigger Brazil, capable of generating "fifty years of development in five." Chief among these symbols of the new Brazil was Kubitschek's decision to move the country's capital from Rio de Janeiro to a planned city called Brasília. The building of this utopian city served to divert attention from the country's economic and social problems. It also acted as a political symbol to rally support among Brazil's business class for Kubitschek's developmentalist policies.[8]

The weak point in Brazil's political economic order was the country's incoherent party system. After Kubitschek's term ended, a populist anti-party maverick, Jânio Quadros, won the presidency in 1960 because of fragmented party identities and unstable partisan alliances.[9] Economic bad times returned as inflation soared and growth slowed. Then, without much explanation, Quadros resigned, elevating João Goulart, Vargas' former minister of labor and Quadros' acting vice president, to the presidency.

Goulart embarked on an ill-fated campaign for structural reforms, mainly of the educational system and the federal administration, and a progressive agrarian policy. Meanwhile, Brazilian politics were becoming more polarized into right and left. New political actors burst onto the scene: peasant league movements, students, and professional organizations. Protests, strikes, and illegal seizures of land by poor Brazilians heightened ideological tensions. Goulart was severely hindered in responding to these problems by a congress that was almost perpetually stalemated in partisan bickering.[10] Finally industrial and landowning elites came down firmly against Goulart's reforms. Right-wing organizations flooded the streets of the main capital with anti-Goulart demonstrators. Convinced that the situation was out of control and that Goulart would soon resort to extraconstitutional measures, the military intervened in 1964, putting an end to Brazil's experiment with democratic populism.

Brazil's capital, Brasília. The planned city was designed by the world-famous Brazilian architect Oscar Niemeyer.
Source: Georges Holton.

The Rise of Bureaucratic Authoritarianism (1964–1985)

The military government that came to power in 1964 installed what the Argentine sociologist Guillermo O'Donnell has termed **bureaucratic authoritarianism**, or BA.[11] BA regimes are authoritarian regimes that emerge in response to severe economic crises and that are led by the armed forces and key civilian allies, most notably professional economists, engineers, and administrators. Repression in Brazilian BA varied from combinations of mild forms that constricted civil rights and other political freedoms and harsher forms that included wholesale censorship of the press through institutional acts, torture of civilians, and imprisonment without trial. The first and the last two military rulers, Castelo Branco (1964–1967), Ernesto Geisel (1974–1979), and João Figueiredo (1979–1985) presented less violent forms of authori-

tarianism, whereas the rule of Artur Costa e Silva and of Emilio Médici (1968–1974) encompassed the worst forms of physical repression.

Initially the military government envisioned a quick return to civilian rule and even allowed, in a limited form, the continuation of democratic institutions. Although purged in 1964 of perceived enemies of the military, the national congress continued to function afterwards and direct elections for federal legislators (but not the president or state governors) were held at regular intervals. In November 1965 the military abolished all existing political parties and replaced them with only two: the National Alliance for Renovation, or ARENA, and the Brazilian Democratic Movement, or MDB. ARENA was the military government's party, and MDB was the "official" party of the opposition. Although previous party labels were discarded, former members of the three major parties joined one of the two new parties. The most important party affiliations in ARENA belonged to former UDN and PSD members, while many PTB members flocked to MDB. Even though the two parties did not operate until Castelo Branco left office in March 1967, the military hoped that the reform would give the bureaucratic-authoritarian regime a level of democratic legitimacy.[12]

Although these democratic institutions were more than pro forma, their powers were severely limited. The military government used institutional decrees to legislate the most important matters, thereby stopping the congress from having an important say. Few civilian politicians could speak out directly against the military for fear of being removed from office.

In economic policy, the military reinforced the previous pattern of state interventionism. The government actively promoted **state-led development** by creating hundreds of state corporations and investing millions in established public firms such as Vale. Under military leadership, Brazil implemented one of the most successful economic development programs in the Third World. Often called the Brazilian miracle, these programs demonstrated that, like France, Germany, and Japan, a developing country could create its own economic miracle.

The Transition to Democracy and the First Civilian Governments (1974–1998)

After the oil crisis of 1973 set off a wave of inflation around the world, the economy began to falter. Increasing criticism from Brazilian business led Geisel and Figueiredo to embrace a gradual process of democratization.[13] Initially, these leaders envisioned only a liberalizing, or "opening" (*abertura*), of the regime that would allow civilian politicians to contest for political office. As was the case with Gorbachev's *glasnost*, however, control over the process of liberalization gradually slipped from their hands and was captured by organizations within civil society. In 1974 the opposition party, the MDB, stunned the military government by increasing its representation in the Senate from 18 to 30 percent and in the Chamber of Deputies from 22 to 44 percent. These numbers did not give the MDB a majority, but the party did capture a majority in both chambers of the state legislatures in the most important industrialized southern and southeastern states.[14]

Abertura accelerated in the following years. The opposition made successive electoral gains and used them to get concessions from the government. The most important of these concessions was the reestablishment of direct elections for governors in 1982, political amnesty for dissidents, the elimination of the government's power to oust legislators from political office, and the restoration of political rights to those who had previously lost them. The gubernatorial elections of November 1982 sealed the fate of promilitary candidates. Opposition gubernatorial candidates won landslide victories, capturing the most developed states—Minas Gerais, São Paulo, and Rio de Janeiro. The process of liberalizing the authoritarian regime was now irreversible.

The military, which wanted to maintain as much control over the succession process as possible, preferred to have the next president selected within a restricted electoral college. In 1983 mass mobilization campaigns seeking the right to directly elect the next president got off the ground. The *Diretas Já!* ("Direct Elections Now!") movement, which comprised an array of social movements, opposition politicians, and labor unions,[15] expanded in size and influence in 1984. Their rallies exerted tremendous pressure on the military at a moment when the question of who would succeed General Figueiredo was not clear. The military's fight to keep the 1984 elections indirect alienated civilian supporters of the generals, many of whom broke with the regime and backed an alliance (the Liberal Front) with Tancredo Neves, the candidate of the opposition PMDB, or Party of the MDB. Neves' victory in 1984, however, was short-lived. His sudden death on the eve of his inauguration meant that Vice President José Sarney became the first civilian president of Brazil since 1964.

The bizarre sequence of events that led to Sarney's presidency was a keen disappointment to those who had hoped for a clean break with the authoritarian past. Labor unions in particular distrusted Sarney as a former political hack of the military. Such divisions weakened Sarney's government. He became embroiled in conflicts with unions, business organizations, the Catholic church, and international financial institutions. More important, his administration failed to reform the old authoritarian modes of policy-making, including corporatist institutions and military prerogatives over civilian government.

A chance for fundamental change appeared in 1987 when the national Constituent Assembly met to draft a new constitution. Given the earlier success of the opposition governors in 1982, state political machines became important players in the game of constitution writing. The state governments petitioned for the devolution of new authority to tax and spend. Labor groups also exerted influence through their lobbying organization. Workers demanded constitutional protection of their right to strike and called for an extension of the right to public employees who were heretofore prohibited from engaging in such activism. The constitution also granted workers the right to create their own unions without authorization from the Ministry of Labor.[16] As a whole, the constitution guaranteed a rich array of social and political rights, yet it also left vestiges from the corporatist past, including protection of public firms in petroleum and telecommunications from foreign investment and privatization.

The other primary issue of the day was inflation. Soon after Sarney's rise to power, annual rates of inflation began to skyrocket. The government invoked several stabilization plans to stop the explosion of prices but to no avail. By the presidential elections of 1989, the first since the 1960s to be held as direct elections for that post, Brazilian society was calling for a political leader who would remedy runaway inflation and remove corrupt and authoritarian politicians from positions of power.

Rising from political obscurity, an ex-governor from Alagoas, a small state in the poor northeast, Fernando Collor de Mello, became president. Collor and his small party, the Party of National Reconstruction (PRN), had fought a grueling campaign against the popular left-wing labor leader and head of the Workers' Party (*Partido dos Trabalhadores,* or PT), Luiz Inácio "Lula" da Silva. To counteract Lula's appeal among the Brazilian people, Collor's campaign rhetoric appealed to the poor, to the *descamisados* ("shirtless ones"), who were attracted by his attacks against politicians and the social problems caused by bureaucratic inefficiency. As a skillful campaigner on television, Collor convinced Brazilians that he could "kill inflation with one shot" and get rid of the "maharajahs"—corrupt public servants who collected massive salaries but did little.

The Collor presidency was itself a critical juncture as the government's economic team began the privatization of state enterprises, deregulation of the economy, and the reversal of decades of policies that had kept Brazil's markets closed to the world. Yet Collor failed to solve the nagging problem of inflation and, ironically, he was soon accused of bribery and influence peddling and was impeached in September 1992; an ignominious end for the first directly elected president since the 1960s.

Collor's impeachment brought to the presidency Itamar Franco, a well-known politician in Minas Gerais who was less well known at the national level as Collor's vice president. Despite a high level of uncertainty during Franco's first year, including rumors of a military coup that was allegedly in the works, his government provided an important stabilizing role. Perhaps his most important decision was to support his Minister of Finance, Fernando Henrique Cardoso, a sociologist and senator from São Paulo, in a plan to conquer inflation. In July 1994, Cardoso implemented a plan to fight inflation, the Real Plan, which succeeded. Monthly inflation fell from 26 percent to 2.82 percent in October 1994 (see Section 2).

Cardoso rode the success of the Real Plan to the Brazilian presidency, beating out Lula of the PT in 1994 and again in 1998 to become the first Brazilian president in modern times to be reelected. After his inauguration in January 1995, Cardoso proved adept at keeping inflation low and in consolidating some of the structural reforms of the economy, many that had been initiated by Collor. As the tale of Vale suggests, privatization has moved forward. Other reforms, however, remain stuck in congress, including crucial reforms of the pension system. Brazil's budget and trade deficits increased, requiring the government to finance the shortfall with short- and medium-term debt. As in Mexico in 1994, these conditions caused foreign investors to abandon the Brazilian market, leading to billions of dollars in capital flight. Financial crisis in Asia and Russia worsened the crisis in 1998 and 1999. Even Cardoso's reelection in October 1998 could not stop Brazil from becoming the latest casualty in a widening global financial crisis.

Themes and Implications

Historical Junctures and Political Themes

The state has played a central role in the story of modern Brazilian politics. In the world of states, both international and domestic factors have influenced the Brazilian state's structure, capacity, and relations with society. During the days of the empire, international opposition to slavery forced powerful oligarchs to turn to the state for protection. The coffee and ranch economies that provided the material base for the power of the Old Republic were intricately tied to Brazil's economic role in the world. Even the *Estado Novo*, with its drive to organize society, was affected by the events outside Brazil. The defeat of fascism in Europe helped turn the New State's authoritarian project into a populist-democratic one. The return to democracy during the 1980s was also part of a larger, global experience, as authoritarian regimes gave way all over Latin America, eastern Europe, southern Europe, and the Soviet Union.

Within Brazil, the state adjusted to changes in the distribution of power, the rise of new, politically active social classes, and the requirements of development. In the federal state, power shifted regularly between the central and subnational governments. From the centralizing, moderating power of the Brazilian emperor Dom Pedro II and the state corporatist *Estado Novo* of Getúlio Vargas, to the decentralized, power-sharing exchange of *café com leite*, the swings of the pendulum between center and local punctuated many of the critical junctures of Brazilian politics. In recent decades, the pendulum has swung between the centralization of political power required by bureaucratic authoritarianism and the liberalization (and decentralization) of power involved in the transition to democracy.

The inclusion of new political actors such as the working and middle classes reshaped the Brazilian state during the twentieth century. The state corporatism of Vargas' New State provided mechanisms for mobilizing and organizing workers and professionals. Populist democracy later provided these social segments protection from unsafe working environments, the effects of eroding wages, and the prohibitive expense of health care. Public firms such as Vale employed hundreds of thousands of Brazilians and dramatically altered the development possibilities of the country. Now these policies have come under attack by reformists both within the government and in the international financial institutions that believe their reform requires another round of state restructuring, this time with a generous dose of market-oriented criteria. Privatization, deregulation, economic liberalization, and the reform of public employment and pension programs are dramatically altering the role of the Brazilian state and its relations with society.

As for Brazil's distinctive approach to governing the economy, no one should discount the legacies of state-led development in the country's history. During the twentieth century, Brazil was transformed from a predominately agrarian economy into an industrialized economy. To some extent, markets and foreign investment played key roles in this process, but the state also provided crucial financial, technical, and political support that made this great transformation possible. As a result, Brazil's position in the global system of production and exchange was fundamentally guided by politics.

Nonetheless, the growth produced by state-led development was poorly distributed. Social problems that emerged from this unequal model of development are at the heart of the country's ongoing struggles with democracy. For many Brazilians living in poverty, it was not clear what benefits the return to democracy had produced.

Regarding the democratic idea, Brazil certainly has the institutions of a democracy, but in many ways these rules remain incomplete. Decades of patrimonialism, populism, and corporatism have eroded democratic institutions. Brazilian politicians can switch parties with few impediments, for example. As a result, Brazilian political parties are extremely weak. Personal appeals and demagoguery tend to produce positive returns in Brazilian electoral politics. The reign of these **personalist politicians** is exemplified by the initial popularity of Collor. Once in power, Brazilian politicians often ignore the people who elected them. Clientelist relations, favoritism, nepotism, and outright bribery produce rewards for politicians but leave little for constituencies.

Yet even with these enduring shortcomings in democracy, Brazilians continue to prefer this form of government. The appeal of democracy is based, in part, on their negative memories of the repression they suffered under the authoritarian regime and the military's poor management of the economy. More important, Brazilians impute positive values to the improved access to decision-making processes that democracy gives them. Thousands of new political groups, social movements, civic networks, and economic associations have emerged in recent years. The Brazilian state is highly decentralized into twenty-six states, a federal district, and over 5,000 municipalities. Each of these centers of power has become a locus of demand-making by citizens and policy-making by elites. Under these circumstances, centralized rule following the model of the New State or the bureaucratic authoritarian period is impossible today and, in any case, seems undesirable to most Brazilians.

Collective identities remain uncertain in Brazil, even though Brazilians are now more commonly linked through their place in the democratic order. The question Who are the Brazilians? has always been a vexing one, no less so now that Brazil's borders are becoming obsolete in a world of heavy flows of international commerce, finance, and ideas. One common response to the question is that the symbols of the Brazilian nation continue to tie Brazilians together: carnival, soccer, *samba*, and *bossa nova*. Yet even as these symbols have become more prevalent, they have also lost some of their meaning because of commercialization and export as part of a tourist-attracting image of Brazil. Catholicism is a less unifying force today as pentecostalism and evangelism have eaten into the Church's membership. Women have improved both their social position and their political awareness as gender-based organizations have become a more important resource of civil society. Yet even here, Brazil remains an extremely patriarchal society where women are expected to balance motherhood and other traditional roles in the household while they are pressured by economic need to produce additional income.

Perhaps race, more than any other form of identity, remains the most tricky issue in Brazilian politics and society. Racial identity continues to divide Brazilians, but not in the clear-cut manner it does blacks and whites in the United States. These categories are more fluid in Brazil. Racial mixing has been accompanied by ideas of integration, not the segregation that helped to mobilize blacks in the United States during the 1960s. Perhaps it is the fuzziness in Brazilian race relations that undercuts the political mobilization of blacks.

Like race, class continues to separate Brazilians. Economic reforms and the erosion of populist redistribution have only caused social gaps to widen further, making Brazil a highly fragmented society. Although it is one of the world's ten wealthiest economies, with a gross domestic product over US$500 billion, that wealth is poorly distributed. Like India, Brazil's social indicators such as income distribution, infant mortality, and nutrition consistently rank near the bottom in the world of states. Income disparities mirror racial differences as the poor are represented by mostly blacks and mulattoes. The rich are almost invariably white. The poverty of the north and northeast also contrasts with the more industrialized and prosperous southeastern and southern states.

Implications for Comparative Politics

As a large, politically decentralized, and socially fragmented polity, Brazil presents several extraordinary challenges to the study of comparative politics. First, the Brazilian state is an anomaly. It has been both highly centralized and decentralized during different periods of its history. In each of these periods, the state produced lasting political legacies that have both strengthened and weakened its capacity for promoting development, democracy, and social distribution. Although political centralization has been an important factor in making the French state strong, decentralized states such as the U.S. and German federations have also proven to be successful formulas for government. The Brazilian case is a laboratory for evaluating which approach is likely to be more successful in other large, highly decentralized states in the developing world, such as Russia, China, and India.

While the complexity of the Brazilian state represents one problem area, the weakness of the country's democratic institutions suggests another, perhaps more troubling, concern. Along with Russia, Brazil demonstrates how the lack of coherent party systems and electoral institutions can endanger democracy. In contrast to the highly organized polity of Germany and the strength of parties in parliamentary democracies like the United Kingdom and Japan, Brazil's experience highlights how anemic representative institutions can weaken democracy.

Paradoxically, as Brazil developed economically and made its way back to democracy in the 1980s, it also became a more socially unequal country. Established democracies like India and transitional democracies like Mexico and Russia have also experienced the reality that democratization does not improve distribution of wealth. Yet the longest established democracies in our study—the United States, Britain, France, Germany, and Japan—are also the richest and, by and large, the countries where wealth is most equally distributed. Brazil and India, therefore, are a bit of a puzzle: if democracy and social development are intricately linked, shouldn't the distribution of wealth be getting better, not worse, in these two countries?

Finally, the complex divisions afflicting Brazilians' collective identities challenge all attempts to address the country's problems. Yet, even today, Brazilians and outside observers continue to treat the country as a singular unit. In this regard, Brazil presents a puzzle for theories about collective identities: How has such a socially fragmented society remained a coherent whole for so long?

Section ❷ Political Economy and Development

Brazilian politics have always been shaped by the country's quest for economic and social development. Two processes in particular have left enduring legacies: the pattern of state intervention in the domestic market and the effects of external economic change. Historically these two factors have influenced each other. External economic crises—world depressions, fluctuations in the price of exported goods such as coffee, upsurges in the prices of imported goods— have compelled the Brazilian state to intervene in the domestic economy, through protection, subsidies, and even the production of goods that were previously imported. In turn, policies aimed at promoting the industrial growth of the country have made Brazil one of the newly industrialized countries of the world, alongside states such as Mexico, Taiwan, South Korea, and Indonesia.

In order to clarify how political and economic development have been intertwined in Brazil, this section explores the state-led model of development; considers how the domestic effects of the state-led model and its reform generated enormous social costs; and discusses the international capitalist forces that shaped domestic economic policy and society.

State and Economy

Like that of its Latin American neighbors, Brazil's early economic development was based on **export-led growth**, that is, on the export of agricultural products such as sugar, cotton, coffee, and for a short time in the early 1900s, rubber. Throughout most of the nineteenth century, coffee emerged as the engine of growth in the Brazilian economy. By the time of the Old Republic, a strong demand for Brazilian coffee in Europe and North America gave the country a virtual monopoly in the global market. Cotton, sugar, and cereals continued to be important export products, too, but they were secondary to coffee. By 1919 coffee composed 56 percent of Brazil's total exports. Only five years later, that figure had jumped to 75 percent.[17]

The dominance of coffee ensured that the Old Republic would keep Brazil active in the world market. That meant that the state had only a minimal role in promoting the export-led economy, which functioned so well that money generated by coffee provided a reservoir of capital to build railroads, power stations, and other infrastructure. These investments, in turn, spurred the growth of some light industries, mostly in textiles, footwear, and clothing.

The Brazilian state's role in the economy became far more **interventionist** during the 1930s when the Great Depression caused international demand for coffee decline. As exports fell, imports of manufactured goods also declined. The coffee export sector had created demand for these goods among the urban population in the decades before the Great

Depression.[18] Therefore as the coffee economy declined, incentives to boost domestic industrial production to substitute for previously imported manufactures increased.

During the 1930s, Brazil's economy pursued **import substitution industrialization** (ISI), a model of development that promoted domestic industrial production of previously imported manufactured goods. By 1937 this policy, which relied heavily on state intervention, became a major pillar of Vargas' New State. At first, large doses of state intervention were not necessary. The initial phase of ISI—the so-called light, or easy, phase—focused on manufactured products that required little capital or sophisticated technology. Most of these industries, such as textiles and food processing, were labor-intensive and therefore created jobs. Although these conditions did not require large infusions of state capital, the New State provided limited subsidies and tariff protection to nascent ISI sectors.

At the end of World War II, new ideas about Third World development came to be adopted by various international agencies. The new goal was to "deepen" the ISI model by promoting heavy industry and capital-intensive production. In Brazil, as in Argentina, Mexico, and India, a new generation of state **technocrats**—experts in economic development—took an active role in designing new policies. Inspired by the texts of the United Nations Economic Commission for Latin America (ECLA), these technocrats targeted particular industrial sectors as strategic.[19] Then, through the use of industrial policies including planning, subsidies, and financial support, state agencies promoted the quick growth of these sectors.

Brazil was the epitome of ECLA-style **developmentalism**, the ideology and practice of state-sponsored growth, during the 1950s in Latin America. More than any other Latin American state, the Brazilian state was organizationally capable of implementing industrial policies to deepen ISI. New bureaucratic structures, such as a national development bank and national public firms, were created during the first and second Vargas governments. Petrobrás, the state oil firm, quickly became a model of what the Brazilian state wanted to become—a state that could produce as well as regulate. The producer state promoted private investment by extracting and distributing raw materials for domestic industries at prices well below the international market level. These lower prices were in effect subsidies to domestic industry. In this way, subsidized steel and subsidized credit from the national development bank fueled domestic industrialization. Other firms linked to sectors of the economy receiving these supports would benefit in a chain reaction.

Although growth rates achieved impressive levels during the 1950s and early 1960s and even higher levels in the 1970s (see Table 1 below), it was during this period that the first serious contradictions of ISI emerged.[20] Protection fostered noncompetitive, inefficient production because it removed incentives for competition. Although industries grew, they did so by depending too heavily on public subsidies. ISI also became import-intensive. Businesses used subsidized finance to import technology and machinery. The government helped these firms by overvaluing the currency to make import prices cheaper. This overvaluation of the currency hurt export earnings, which were necessary to pay for imports. As a result, the export sector could not supply the state with much-needed revenues to sustain growth, prompting the government to print money, which in turn led to inflation. Under the Goulart government (1961–1964), the economy's capacity to import and export dwindled, and stagnation set in. The economic crisis that soon followed contributed to the coup of 1964 and Goulart's fall.

The rise of the military governments in 1964 did not mean either the end of ISI or its continued deepening. The state retained its role as the main planner

Table 1

GDP Growth Rates, 1940–1997	
Year	GDP Growth Rate
1940–1950	5.6%
1950–1960	6.1
1960–1970	5.4
1970–1980	12.4
1980–1990	1.5
1990–1997	2.1

Source: Brazilian Institute of Geography and Statistics (IBGE), *Anuario Estatístico Brasileiro* (Rio de Janeiro: IBGE, various years).

Table 2

Sector Composition of the GDP, 1970–1990			
Year	Agriculture	Industry	Services
1970	11.55%	35.87%	52.59%
1980	10.16	40.99	48.84
1990	9.26	34.20	56.54

Source: Werner Baer, *The Brazilian Economy: Growth and Development,* 4th ed. (New York: Praeger, 1994), 382–383. Copyright © 1995 by Werner Baer. Reprinted by permission of Greenwood Publishing Group, Inc. All rights reserved.

and coordinator of domestic industry, but its functions and the political structures that would manage developmental policy changed under military rule.

From 1964 to 1985 the state continued to promote industrialization, especially the production of consumer durable goods such as automobiles, televisions, refrigerators, and machinery for the domestic market. Domestic entrepreneurs relied on the transfer of technology from foreign investors, particularly after 1970, when they collaborated with multinational firms to produce pharmaceuticals and later computers. Table 2 highlights the important contribution of industry to the Brazilian GDP.

Para-statals, also known as public or state firms, played an important role in the military's development model. Large-scale projects in shipbuilding, mining, steel, oil, bauxite, and aluminum were financed and managed by bureaucratic agencies and state firms. These projects often operated in conjunction with larger development plans designed to attract domestic and foreign entrepreneurs. Peter Evans, an American political economist, insightfully characterized these complex relations among the state, foreign investors, and domestic capitalists as a "triple alliance."[21] The state, however, remained the dominant partner.

In the 1970s, Brazil's military leaders realized that the deepening of ISI could not rely on domestic capital alone. In order to finance the huge public expenditures of national industrial policy, the military turned to international financial markets, particularly private investment markets in North America and Europe. The military also began to emphasize primary exports such as coffee, iron ore, cereals, and other agricultural products. Policies designed to increase agricultural productivity and technological modernization that had already been implemented in the first years of military rule were expanded. Agriculture began to be integrated with industrial production.

The export of agricultural surplus and the sale of food products in the internal market were facilitated by a growing agribusiness sector. Spurred on by state subsidies, agribusiness supplied new resources and management for inefficient agricultural subsectors. Agricultural production in the agribusiness sector employed heavy machinery and advanced technologies that increased the size of the average yield. One of the most unusual agribusiness ventures occurred in the 1970s when the military government introduced a plan to use sugarcane alcohol as a fuel source. Northeast agribusiness boomed during these years as the sugar economy became tied to the dynamic industrial economy of the southern and southeastern regions.

The Environmental Costs of State-Led Growth

The impressive growth of industry and agriculture was concentrated in the central and southern regions of Brazil. Centers of growth in the states of São Paulo, Minas Gerais, Rio de Janeiro, and Rio Grande do Sul became the locomotives of the country's development and sites of environmental degradation. As capital-intensive industries became more common in Brazil, ecologically destructive technologies were used without much regulation. Before the mid-1970s, Brazilian policymakers were unconcerned with the emission of toxic waste into the ground at major industrial zones, air pollution in overgrown urban areas, or pesticide and chemical fertilizer use in agricultural regions. Industrial growth was simply more important.

The environmental costs of these attitudes became clear in the 1970s. Guanabara Bay and the Paraíba do Sul River basin, both in Rio de Janeiro state, were brought to the brink of biological death. Urban pollution in São Paulo devastated the Tietê River, which runs through the city, making it no better than a toxic waste dump in some areas and threatening the health of millions. By far the worst tragedy was in Cubatão, an industrial city 60 kilometers east of metropolitan São Paulo. There, petrochemical industries and steel mills wreaked havoc on the environment, pumping 1 million kilograms of pollutants into the surrounding ecological system each day. The conditions in the residential area of Cubatão became so bad that by 1981 one city council member reported that he had not seen a star in twenty years.[22] Thousands reported becoming afflicted with tuberculosis, pneumonia, bronchitis, emphysema, asthma, and cancer. Forty of every thousand babies in Cubatão were stillborn.

Big development projects reached the forests of the Amazon River basin in the 1970s with Vale do Rio Doce's Carajás mining work in the Eastern Amazon. This and other industrial projects threatened the tropical forests, as did cattle ranching, timber extraction, and slash and burn agriculture by poor farmers, a practice that allowed frequent rains to leech nutrients from the soil and prevent the return of tropical habitats. By the 1980s it was clear that the primary result of these practices was the deforestation of the Amazon.

Brazil's worsening environmental problems received official attention after 1972, when the United Nations held its Conference on the Human Environment. Soon afterwards, Brazil created an environmental secretariat, and in 1981 the government established a National Environmental Council (CONAMA), which included officials from national and state government and representatives from business, professional, and environmental groups. State governments also established their own environmental agencies and passed important legislation.[23] In 1975, São Paulo passed a comprehensive antipollution law. The cleanup of Cubatão began in 1983.

Partly as a result of the return to democracy in 1984, new environmental movements within and outside of Brazil began to influence official and public opinion on the costs of resource degradation. Much attention was brought to these problems when the Brazilian government successfully persuaded the United Nations to hold its Conference on the Environment, a follow-up to the 1972 conference, in Rio de Janeiro in 1992. Thousands of delegates and hundreds of **nongovernmental organizations** gathered in Rio to discuss global environmental problems that were virtually all present in Brazil. By that time, numerous environmental organizations were already active in Brazilian politics.[24]

Despite the attention the Rio conference brought to the issue, rates of deforestation, pollution, and resource degradation fell only briefly after 1992, and have since returned to historically high levels. Brazilian business has shown only passing interest in the use of clean technologies because of their expense. In the third international UN conference on the environment, held in Kyoto, Japan, in 1997, Brazil was joined by the rest of the developing world in deflecting the finger of blame for ecological problems. However, it did play an important diplomatic role toward the end of the conference by supporting a U.S.-backed clean development fund. Nevertheless, Brazil currently lags behind its neighbor Argentina, which in November 1998 became the first developing country to adopt binding targets for controlling emissions of industrial waste gases.

The Fiscal System

In developed countries such as the United States, Germany, France, and Britain, governments can use tax policy to punish polluters. In Brazil, however, tax collection has been notoriously weak, making this a less useful instrument to regulate business or individuals. Tax evasion has been a chronic problem. The military governments attempted to change that through a constitutional reform in 1967 that created new taxes, made the federal government better able to collect taxes, and centralized fiscal policy and the control of revenues. However, because one of the military's primary objectives was to stimulate private savings and to increase capital formation, the new tax systems allowed for numerous costly exemptions and transfers of budgetary resources to private firms and to the upper and middle classes. As a result, the Brazilian tax system became more regressive by shifting the tax burden onto the middle and working classes.

As the Brazilian economy became more complex, new opportunities for evading taxes emerged. An **informal economy** of small firms, domestic enterprises, street vendors, and unregistered employees proliferated, virtually outside the domain of the taxable economy. In some cases, these enterprises acquired substantial size, accounting for distribution of everything from artisans' goods to professional services. Legally registered companies began to subcontract unregistered professionals to render services beyond the reach of the tax system. Although reliable information is lacking, economists estimate that the informal economy represents close to half of Brazil's GDP (about US$300 billion) and employs about 30–45 million people.

Other problems developed for the tax system after the transition to democracy. The new constitution of 1988 decentralized the fiscal structure by allowing the states and municipalities to expand their collection of taxes and to receive larger transfers of funds from Brasília. Significant gaps emerged in tax collection responsibilities and public spending as a result of these changes. Although the central state spent less than it collected in taxes between 1960 and 1994, Brazil's 5000 municipal governments spent several times more than they collected. Subnational governments also gained more discretion over spending. More than 90 percent of funds transferred from the federal government to the states went unearmarked, so state governments could use these monies for their own purposes.

New reforms during the Collor administration began to reverse some of the adverse effects of fiscal decentralization and the weak tax system. In the 1980s the state governments, which held almost half of Brazil's total debt, continued to roll over their debt with federal outlays and failed to cut expenditures. In the early 1990s federal threats to cut off debt servicing and close down profligate regional banks owned by the state governments put an end to this unsustainable practice. Other reforms shifted some of the tax burden onto business, which helped to increase tax receipts to 25 percent of GDP.[25]

The Cardoso administration had some success in recovering federal tax revenues and reducing the fiscal distortions produced by Brazil's federal structure. Tax evasion declined as the federal tax collection agency was expanded and its surveillance powers enhanced. Legislation in 1994 allowed the federal government to employ more discretion over transfers of funds constitutionally earmarked for the state and municipal governments. That allowed the federal government to exert some leverage on state governments to control their spending. Brasília also shifted more spending responsibilities in health care, housing, and social policy to subnational governments. That has allowed the federal government to reduce its own spending and control how the states spend their resources. Such stopgap measures reined in public spending. Despite these efforts, high levels of capital

flight and the threat by governors opposed to Cardoso's reforms to default on their debt payments to the federal government, led to a widening financial crisis in early 1999. These problems compelled the president to threaten recalcitrant states by freezing their share of federal funds, leading to a serious intergovernmental conflict.

The Problem of Inflation

Inflation deserves special mention in Brazil, for in no other country, with the possible exception of Germany, has this phenomenon had such a lasting impact on a country's politics. In Brazil inflation accompanied state-led development, especially after 1974. Through various types of controls, the Brazilian state, business, and unions all attempted to govern prices, interest rates, and wages. Such manipulation distorted the value of goods and services, and facilitated inflation. With the return to democracy after 1985, successive governments attempted to control inflation. All of these "stabilization" packages proved unable to sustain the fiscal and monetary discipline necessary for their success, leading to an economic deterioration and four-digit inflation. Figure 1 illustrates this terrible track record.

Figure 1

Annual Rates of Inflation, 1989–1996

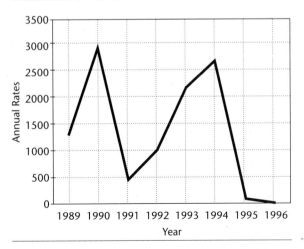

Source: Fundação Getúlio Vargas, *A Economia Brasileira em Gráficos* (Rio de Janeiro: FGV, 1996), 24.

Sarney initially promised to produce "Japanese growth with Swiss inflation." His Cruzado Plan (1986) used a mix of price controls and some fiscal restraint to arrest sharp upsurges in prices for an eight-month period. But inflation eventually returned and became worse. Collor took a more direct approach to the problem. Through another stabilization "shock," the Collor Plan in 1990, the government froze all savings accounts. Inflation fell, but by early 1991 it was back.

The failures of the previous plans prompted the Ministry of Finance under the Itamar Franco government to avoid wage and price freezes or other shock policies. Instead the government attacked inflation through budget cuts, tax increases, curbs on tax evasion, and attempts to stabilize the currency by indexing it to the U.S. dollar, all elements of the *Plano Real* (Real Plan) launched in July 1994. The plan, which successfully curbed inflation, was the brainchild of Franco's Minister of Finance, Fernando Henrique Cardoso, who became president in late 1994.

Like its predecessors, the Real Plan changed the name of the national currency in an attempt to eliminate the memory of inflation. But its most important feature was unique to it. The Real Plan attempted to anchor the real, the new currency, in a unit of real value (URV), which was itself indexed to the U.S. dollar. Unlike a similar plan in Argentina, the Real Plan did not fix the real to the dollar strictly but allowed it to float within bands, thus achieving more flexibility in the exchange rate.

Paradoxically, the Real Plan's formula for success proved to be a source of weakness. Soon after the Mexican peso crisis of December 1994, Central Bank managers in Brasília became convinced that the real was overvalued, just as the peso had been before its crash. Overvaluation made exports more expensive abroad, raised the costs of production, and made imports cheaper. Brazil's trade deficit rose by more than 140 percent after 1995, threatening to scare away foreign investors.[26] Despite dire predictions, though, Brazil's large foreign reserves (US$75 billion in mid-1998) kept investors confident in the economy, although turmoil in Asian financial markets led to the bleeding of these foreign reserves at $1 billion a day during October 1998. Improvements in tax collection, an influx of foreign investment, modest growth, and

repeated attempts by the Cardoso administration to close the trade deficit by limiting imports and removing taxes on exports, helped to keep the real's value stable. Yet high interest rates, escalating public debt, the inability to rein in spending, and monetary instability in Asia and Russia continued to threaten the real's stability. Signs of hope emerged in November 1998 when the IMF negotiated a US$42 billion bailout agreement with Brazil in order to keep the economy from sinking further into financial upheaval. These efforts proved unsuccessful. In January 1999, Itamar Franco, the ex-president and the newly elected governor of Minas Gerais, threatened his former Minister of Finance with a moratorium on the state government's debt to Brasília. The threat led to an upsurge in capital flight (US$6 billion in the first 14 days of 1999) as investors lost confidence in Cardoso's government. Central Bank president, Gustavo Franco, one of the Real Plan's chief defenders, resigned abruptly. The new president, Francisco Lopes announced a "controlled" devaluation of 8 percent. Within just two days, pressures on the real forced the government to abandon the Real Plan's exchange rate regime altogether. The real was forced to float, causing it to decline in value by more than 50 percent against the dollar. The devaluation generated renewed fears of inflation and refocused attention on the need to contain public sector spending.

Society and Economy

Brazil's astounding levels of industrialization during the 1950s, 1960s, and 1970s had lasting effects on the urban population. In 1950, 35 percent of the population lived in urban areas. By 1980 that number had increased to 68 percent. During the same period, employment in industry jumped from 14 percent to 24 percent, while employment in agriculture declined from 60 percent to 30 percent. Import substitution had created these jobs by expanding the domestic market. ISI led to a jump in the size of both the working class and the middle class. Service sector professionals like lawyers, doctors, and private teachers soon found clients as the domestic consumer market grew along with the working class.

Nevertheless, the number of jobs created in the industrial sector did not begin to absorb the huge number of unemployed Brazilians. Many of the new jobs required skilled and semiskilled specialized labor. Metallurgy, automobile production, and mining did not provide many opportunities for the large numbers of unskilled workers in the Brazilian labor market. In the late 1980s and 1990s even skilled workers faced losing their jobs because of intense industrial restructuring. From 1990 to 1996 manufacturing jobs fell by 38.1 percent and unemployment in metropolitan areas rose above 18 percent.[27] Service sector employment increased but not enough to make up for industrial job losses. These jobs also paid less and offered fewer protections from arbitrary dismissal.

Industrialization also failed to eradicate the racial inequalities inherited from slavery. Despite the impressive industrial development of Brazil, Afro-Brazilians continued to make less than their white colleagues and had fewer opportunities for upward mobility. According to one study, nonwhite men and women in Brazil have made real gains in their income because of improvements in education and occupation, but the gap separating nonwhite income from white income remains significant.[28] On average, blacks make 41 percent and mulattoes make 47 percent of what whites make.

Women constitute 28 percent of the economically active population in Brazil and they continue to enter the labor market in record numbers. Working women typically have more years of schooling than men and are better prepared to meet the demands of an increasingly technological economy. Despite such developments, women receive lower salaries than men employed at the same job. Women make 57 percent of what men make. Afro-Brazilian women, who are doubly disadvantaged by race and gender, are in a particularly precarious situation. Many are employed in underpaid and menial jobs, particularly as domestic servants, 90 percent of whom are black women. Mulatto women receive 46 percent of what white men make, and black women take in only 40 percent of what white men make.

The Welfare System

In a country of startling social inequalities, welfare policy plays a remarkably minor role in the lives of most Brazilians. Although welfare and education expenditures currently constitute about 11 percent of the GDP, among the highest levels in the world, the money has not improved Brazil's mediocre welfare state. Unlike the systems in Britain, France, Germany, and Japan, Brazil's welfare system has not reduced the high level of poverty or helped the majority of the poor. Vast sectors of the population, deprived of finance, titles, and jobs, remain totally outside the reach of welfare services.

Brazil supports a public school system as well as a health, retirement, and social assistance system that includes funds for unemployment relief. Salaried workers are entitled to benefits such as health care, workmen's compensation, retirement pensions, paid vacations, and overtime pay. Yet only an estimated 15 percent of the Brazilian population qualify for these benefits. Workers in the informal sector, who are normally undocumented, cannot collect welfare since technically the federal government does not consider them employed. Corruption, clientelism, and outright waste make the welfare system incapable of delivering benefits to the people that need them the most.[29]

Part of the problem is that more people need welfare than actually contribute to the welfare state. Today only half of the 70 million people who are economically active contribute to the welfare system. In the last eleven years, while the population doubled, the number of retired people multiplied elevenfold, adding to the roster of those depending on public welfare spending. In 1995 the welfare system received US$3.5 billion *less* than was needed to pay the retirement pensions of the 15.2 million inactive workers and 3 million new beneficiaries.

During the military period, changes to the welfare system produced additional distortions. Since the days of the New State, workers employed by a firm for ten years or more were guaranteed generous severance benefits. The military replaced these guarantees with a social insurance fund that prorated inferior benefits to the years of employment. The military expanded protection to several sectors of employment that previously had been outside the welfare system: rural workers, domestic workers, and professionals. But the chief beneficiaries of the new system continued to be public employees (including politicians and members of the military). Compared to total benefit payments of US$35.2 billion to 15 million inactive workers in the private sector, inactive public sector workers, who number 404,000, received $10.5 billion during the 1990s. That means that the average retired or unemployed civil servant received $2,188 monthly as compared to an average of $194 for private workers.

As in Margaret Thatcher's Britain, fundamental welfare reform in Brazil came with the rise of a new political figure. Fernando Collor began to dismantle the welfare system soon after his election to the presidency. The funding and quality of welfare services deteriorated to levels never seen in contemporary Brazilian history. Federal funds for health care fell 50 percent. In 1988 the federal welfare system devoted 25 percent of its revenues to health care; in 1990 that number was only 15 percent. In 1993 *no funds* were allocated. At present, the subnational governments have been left to take up the slack, with differing results throughout Brazil.

The combination of distortions in the distribution of welfare benefits and unavoidable social pressure to expand outlays to the poor caused the Cardoso administration to step up efforts to reduce tax evasion and reform the public pension system. Private employers and state companies (among the worst offenders) were increasingly obligated by federal authorities to pay their share of social welfare contributions. As in the United States, France, South America, and Chile, the debate over welfare has begun to revolve around the issue of completely or partly privatizing the system. The experiences these other countries have with such ideas may influence Brazil's choices, but the final response will depend upon whether state agencies and political parties can refrain from employing welfare as a means of clientelism.

Agrarian Reform

The restructuring of the rural economy in the 1960s and 1970s altered the rural social structure. The growing role of agribusiness created jobs for some segments of the rural working class while it crowded out small landowners. After 1964 various state welfare programs were launched in the agricultural sector: retirement policies for low-income producers, pension plans for rural workers, and financial support to community rural associations. These policies played a prominent role in breaking landowners' political and economic control of the rural population. During the 1970s and 1980s rural workers were organized into rural unions that received welfare transfers from the state—medical plans, job security, and protection of wages against inflation.

Land ownership in Brazil remains concentrated in the hands of only 1 percent of the landowning class. The arable land held by this small group of owners (about 58,000) is equal to the size of Venezuela and Colombia combined. Over 3 million other farmers survive on only 2 percent of the country's land. An additional 4.5 million Brazilians are farm laborers or squatters who own no land. In the 1980s and 1990s several landless peasant movements grabbed headlines by sanctioning illegal land invasions and coming to blows with rural landowners and police. Among the most important of these groups, the Landless Workers' Movement (*Movimento dos Sem-Terra*, or MST) attracted the most attention by seizing some 1.38 million acres of land.

The Cardoso administration responded to these problems by expropriating some unproductive estates and settling 186,000 families on them. Substantial sums were set aside to provide financial support and the placement of additional rural families. However, these efforts fell far short of providing a lasting solution to rural poverty. Brazil continues to lack true agrarian reform.

Any serious effort to address rural poverty will affect urban poverty. Through rural to urban migration, the landless poor have swelled the rings of poverty that surround Brazil's major cities. During the 1950s and 1960s the growth of industry in the south and southeast enticed millions to migrate to the states of São Paulo, Minas Gerais, and Rio de Janeiro in the hopes of finding new economic opportunities. The rapidity of rural to urban migration was striking. In the 1960s over 13.8 million people (about 36 percent of the rural population in 1960) migrated to the cities of the south and southeast. In 1970, 17 million (approximately 42.2 percent of the rural population in 1970) moved from the countryside to the city. It took migrations in the United States eight decades to reach the same level of migrants as went from rural to urban areas in Brazil during the 1960s and 1970s. By the early 1980s, 68 percent of Brazil's population was living in urban areas. Between 1960 and 1980 rural to

Favelas in Rio de Janeiro. *Source:* © Marc Valdecantos.

urban migration accounted for 58 percent of urban population growth.

The flood of migrants to urban areas and the growth of urban populations created terrible social problems. The pressures on Brazilian cities for basic services such as sanitation, education, and transportation soon overwhelmed the budgets of municipalities and state governments. Poor people were left to their own devices. Squatters soon took government land, settling on the outskirts of the major cities. Millions of these *descamisados* ("shirtless ones") built "homes" out of cardboard, wood from dumps, and blocks of mortar and brick. Huge shanty towns called *favelas* sprang up around cities like Rio and São Paulo.

Regional disparities in income worsened during this period. The military governments addressed this problem by transferring revenues from the industrialized south and southeast to the poor north and northeast, where many of their supporters were based. The federal government subsidized communication and transportation in the poorer regions and created new state agencies to implement regional developmental projects. These policies had mixed results. The contribution of poor regions to the gross domestic product increased. The growth rate of the central and western regions was spurred on by agribusiness activities, mineral exploration, and financial services. The economic gap between regions narrowed, but social and income disparties within the underdeveloped regions increased.[30] Industrialization in the poorer regions was capital-intensive and therefore labor-saving but not job-creating. Only the most skilled workers in these regions benefited from these changes. Poor agricultural management, ecological destruction, the murder of native Brazilians, and corruption all weakened the distributive effect of these policies.

Today, the northern and northeastern regions remain much poorer than those in the south and southeast. Whereas 15 percent of the population in the southeast subsists under the poverty line, more than 50 percent of the inhabitants of the northeast are below that marker. The life expectancy of a northeasterner—fifty-eight years—is nine years below that of a resident of São Paulo state (sixty-seven years) and fifteen years below that of a resident of Rio Grande do Sul (seventy-three years).[31]

The shrinking labor market for unskilled workers, the rapidity of rural to urban migration, and the regional disparities that add to poverty have all worked against the equalization of income distribution in Brazil. Compared with other developing countries, including Mexico and India, Brazil has the worst structure of income distribution in the world (see Table 3 on p. 345).

Brazil and the International Political Economy

As the financing needs of state-led industrialization outstripped the resources of the national development bank and domestic bankers, the deepening of ISI required Brazil to pursue international sources of credit. During the late 1960s and the 1970s private lenders were eager to provide loans to Brazil and other

Table 3

Brazilian Income Distribution in Comparative Perspective

Country	Year	Percent of Total Income Received by			
		10% Richest	20% Richest	40% Poorest	20% Poorest
Peru	1994	34.3%	50.4%	14.1%	4.9%
China	1995	30.9	47.5	15.3	5.5
United States	1994	28.5	45.2	15.3	4.8
India	1994	25.0	39.3	22.2	4.1
France	1989	24.9	40.1	19.9	7.2
Britain	1986	24.7	39.8	19.9	7.1
Brazil	1995	47.9	64.2	8.2	2.5
Chile	1994	46.1	61.0	10.1	3.5
Mexico	1992	39.2	55.3	11.9	4.1
Germany	1989	22.6	37.1	22.5	9.0
Poland	1992	22.1	36.6	23.1	9.3

Source: World Bank, *World Development Report 1998/99* (Washington, D.C.: World Bank, 1998), 198–199.

fast-growing countries. As a result, Brazil became the largest single debtor country in the developing world. Figure 2 (on p. 346) illustrates the tremendous growth of foreign debt.

External events had a hand in creating and then managing Brazil's external debt. By the end of the 1970s the world economy had been hit with two oil price shocks that sent inflation rates soaring in the United States and other industrialized countries. Many of these countries also held Brazilian debt. As the central banks in Europe and the Federal Reserve in the United States ratcheted interest rates upward to force prices back down, Brazil's interest payments grew precipitously.[32]

After Mexico declared a moratorium on interest payments in 1982, private investors began to shun Brazil and other Latin American debtors. During the 1980s, the so-called Lost Decade of slow growth and debt crisis, the International Monetary Fund and the World Bank became important suppliers of badly needed credit. But only debtors who promised to take concrete steps to reduce inflation, open their domestic markets to foreign competition, promote exports, and privatize state industries were eligible for help.

Brazil, along with Argentina and Peru, rejected these conditions. The Sarney government refused to

implement the free-market policies demanded by the international financial institutions. In 1987 his government took the ultimate gamble in resisting creditors by declaring a moratorium on debt repayment, a move that sent a signal to investors that Brazil would control its own reform agenda on its own terms. The moratorium, however, did not last. It was lifted a few months later under intense pressure from the international financial community. Opposition to the moratorium within the country was also great among the business community, which feared such aggressive action would scare away foreign investors and ruin the country's already tattered credit rating.

Collor reversed course. He agreed to put Brazil on the path of free-market policies—partly in response to pressure from international creditors and partly in recognition that Sarney's alternative policies had failed. The Collor administration invoked both macroeconomic reforms to bring down inflation and reduce balance-of-payments deficits and "structural adjustment" policies to liberalize the domestic market, privatize state enterprises, and deregulate the economy. Although Collor's anti-inflation plans failed, his structural reforms provided a crucial catalyst for freeing up the economy from layers of bureaucratic red tape and inefficiency. These domestic changes were

Figure 2

Growth of Public, External Debt for Select Years, 1973–1996

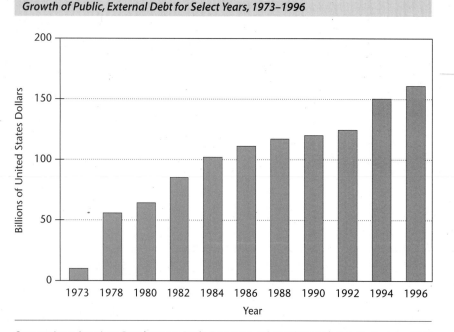

Sources: Inter-American Development Bank, *Economic and Social Progress in Latin America, 1988 Report* (Washington, D.C.: IADB, 1988), 580; *Economic and Social Progress in Latin America, 1997 Report* (Washington, D.C.: IADB, 1997), 256.

reflected externally as Collor began to normalize relations between Brazil and the multilateral agencies, especially the IMF.

The liberalization of markets opened Brazilian industry to higher degrees of foreign competition. As a result, the competitiveness of domestic firms has emerged as a core problem. Brazilian industrial productivity reached its lowest levels in 1992, when, on a list of fifty countries, Brazil was ranked just ahead of Pakistan, which was last. One 1997 study showed that the overall productivity of Brazilian industry runs at only 27 percent of the U.S. level.[33] Although productivity levels improved by 7 percent after 1992, inherent inefficiencies caused by poor infrastructure, untrained labor, and lack of access to technology and capital continue to create obstacles to higher growth. The average Brazilian worker has only six years of schooling, half as much as the average worker in Japan or the United States. These problems undermine the rationale of IMF-style free-market policies, since

they suggest that free markets alone cannot guarantee the country's growth.

How Brazil will fare in an increasingly interconnected and competitive global marketplace will also depend on its external political relations. During the 1980s, Brazil engaged in numerous conflicts with the United States over steel exports (one of Brazil's most export-competitive industries), computer hardware, and patent protection for multinational companies operating in Brazil. Washington threatened to slap protective tariffs on Brazilian products in retaliation. The political climate changed during the Bush and Clinton administrations, when international free-trade accords, such as the North American Free Trade Agreement (NAFTA), received the support of both Washington and most Latin American governments. During the Summit of the Americas in Miami in December 1994, the leaders of the United States, Central America, the Caribbean (except Cuba), and South America agreed to form a Free Trade Area of

Global Connection: *MERCOSUL*

After several years of negotiating the Treaty of Asunción, Brazil, Argentina, Paraguay, and Uruguay inaugurated MERCOSUL, a regional common-market group, in January 1995. Under MERCOSUL (Mercosur in Spanish), Brazil and its trade partners agreed to gradually reduce tariffs on imports from signatories until 2006, when the 10,000 items that make up the tariff listings of all four countries must conform to a common external tariff (CET) regime.

During the negotiations over the Treaty of Asunción between March 26, 1991, and MERCOSUL's inauguration, trade among the partners increased from 8 to 20 percent, making the case for a subhemispheric common market stronger. After a rough start due to the Mexican peso crisis, the signatories reaffirmed their commitment to forge the common market. Efforts to gradually remove tariff protections and nontariff protections such as regulations that slow down the flow of trade, proceeded with few disruptions.

At the center of MERCOSUL's evolution is the long list of products that the CET targets. However, the signatories are allowed to exclude up to 300 items (399 in Paraguay) as exceptions to the CET. The partners also agreed to numerous dispute-resolution mechanisms to avoid conflicts that might threaten the free-trade group.

_____

Source: Lia Valls Pereira, "Tratado de Assunção: Resultados e Perspectivas," in *Mercosul: Perspectivas da Integração*, ed. Antônio Salazar P. Brandão and Lia Valls Pereira (Rio de Janeiro: Fundação Getúlio Vargas, 1996), 11.

MERCOSUL is only the latest in a list of common-market schemes in Latin America. In 1960 the Latin American Association of Free Trade (ALALC) initiated a process for forming a common market in twelve years. Although this goal was unfulfilled because of persistent differences among the group's members, intraregional trade increased from 7.7 percent in 1960 to 13.8 percent in 1980. Subhemispheric common-market groups unconnected to ALALC also emerged as the Andean Group in 1969 (Bolivia, Colombia, Ecuador, and Venezuela) and the Central American Common Market in 1960 (Costa Rica, Guatemala, El Salvador, Honduras, and Nicaragua). ALALC was replaced in 1980 with the Latin American Integration Association (ALADI). Unlike ALALC's mission of forming a common market, ALADI's goal was to foster the formation of preferential trade agreements among subhemispheric groups. These efforts received their most important boost soon after the Bush Administration delivered its Enterprise for the Americas Initiative (EAI) in 1990, a plan of lofty goals for hemispheric economic integration. Soon after the EAI was announced, the existing regional groups and a new wave of other groups formed preferential organizations. Besides MERCOSUL, the most important of these was the North American Free Trade Agreement (NAFTA), initiated on January 1, 1994.

Like its predecessors, MERCOSUL was a product and a cause of increased commercial integration among its signatories. Since its creation, MERCOSUL has contributed to a threefold increase in trade among its signatories.

---

the Americas (FTAA) by the year 2005. At present, Brazil belongs to its own subhemispheric group, the Market of the South (MERCOSUL).

Brazil's degree of commitment to the international free-trade system will depend on the endurance of the country's domestic reform agenda. If inflation threatens to return, Brazil's leaders have already shown that they would be willing to sacrifice MERCOSUL and other commitments to free trade. For example, an attempt to stave off growing trade deficits that threatened the Real Plan in 1995 forced Brazilian policymakers to increase tariffs on imported automobiles from 32 percent to 70 percent, an act that immediately angered Argentina. Although such disagreements are regularly resolved through MERCOSUL's dispute resolution mechanisms, a larger crisis could push Brazil to sacrifice these commitments on the altar of inflation control.

Section ③ Governance and Policy-Making

Organization of the State

The institutions of the Brazilian state have changed significantly since independence. Even so, a number of institutional legacies have endured and continue to shape Brazilian politics today. The most important is the centralization of state authority in the executive. Paradoxically, though, a second legacy is the decentralized federal structure of the Brazilian state. The constitution of 1988 attempted to construct a new democratic order but left these contradictory tendencies in place. The president retained the authority to legislate on social and economic matters, but new powers governing the implementation of these policies were devolved to the state and municipal governments.

As a result, the 1988 constitution was simultaneously the focus of much hope and intense attack. It was to be the governing document for the new democracy, but it became an instrument used to confound political and economic reform. As a product of political horse-trading, it failed to provide a coherent vision of how institutions should be structured and what functions they should have. The separation of powers remains ill-defined in Brazil. Instead, ad hoc and stop-gap arrangements continue to determine the boundaries of official authority, while informal relations and understandings play a major role in the interpretation of law.

Some generalizations about the organization of the Brazilian state can be made. First, the church and state are officially separated. The Catholic Church never controlled any portion of the state apparatus or directly influenced national politics as it did in other Catholic countries, including Spain. This does not mean, however, that the Catholic Church plays no role in Brazilian politics (see Section 4).

Second, Brazil has a presidential system of government. The directly elected president is the head of state, head of government, and commander in chief of the armed forces. The Brazilian state has traditionally placed vast power in the hands of the executive. Although the executive is one of three branches of government (the legislature and the judiciary being the other two), Brazilian presidents have traditionally been less bound by judicial and legislative constraints than their European or North American counterparts. Brazilian constitutions have granted the executive more discretion than the other branches in enforcing laws or in making policy. The legislature and the judiciary historically have played secondary roles.

The Brazilian state does not have the checks and balances of the United States government system. It differs also from the semipresidentialism of France, in which the president, although dominant over the legislature and judiciary, faces broader constraints in the possibility of having to work with a hostile parliamentary majority. Although the French prime minister is appointed by the executive and is not elected by the legislature, as in other parliamentary systems, he or she is chosen from the party with the majority of elected representatives in parliament, which is not necessarily the president's party. Moreover, the French party system is more organized and less fragmented than its counterpart in Brazil, making the legislature more efficient and capable of checking executive actions.

In Brazil the executive and the bureaucracy manage most of the policy-making and implementation functions of government. Both the federal legislature and the state governments look to the presidency and, in economic matters, to the minister of the economy, for leadership on policy. The key agencies of the economic bureaucracy, including the ministers of the economy, planning, the president of the central bank, and the head of the national development bank, have more discretion over the details of policy than the president. Although some Brazilian presidents have delegated less to bureaucratic agencies, recent presidents have had little choice but to delegate, given the growing complexity of economic and social policy. Ultimate authority, however, remains in the hands of the president, who may replace his ministers.

Although the Brazilian president remains the dominant player among the three branches of government, the powers of the legislature and the judiciary are becoming more formidable. After the transition to democratic rule in 1985, these institutions have become critical to democracy. The 1988 constitution gave many oversight functions to the legislature and judiciary so that much presidential discretion in economic and social policy is now subject to approval by either the legislature or the judiciary or both. This gives these branches of government some independence and leverage over the presidency, although this power is not often employed effectively. Centralizing traditions are still strong in Brazil, making the obstacles to the deconcentration of executive power enormous.

A third generalization that may be offered on the Brazilian state is that it is decentralized. Like Germany, India, and the United States, the Brazilian state has a federal structure. The country's twenty-six states are divided into 5000 municipal governments. Most of the country's presidents have relied on subnational bases of power to stay in office. The presidents of the Old Republic and even Getúlio Vargas counted on the support of local clientelist political machines led by self-interested governors and mayors.

With the transition to democracy, these "barons of the federation," as one study calls them, became a crucial source of political support for legislators as well as presidents.[34] By controlling indispensable reservoirs of patronage through their powers of appointment and spending, governors and even some mayors can wield extraordinary influence. In recent years, some of the harsher elements of reform legislation have been jettisoned to mollify this subnational constituency.

Seen as a whole, political decentralization, which was accelerated with the constitution of 1988, has further fragmented the Brazilian polity. At the same time, however, some subnational governments have become an important source of innovative policy-making. Average Brazilian citizens have more access to their municipal and state governments than they do to their federal representatives, which suggests that decentralization may eventually strengthen democracy by making political elites more accountable to their local constituencies.

The Executive

A majority of delegates to the 1987 National Constituent Assembly that drafted the new democratic constitution favored the creation of a parliamentary system. President Sarney, who did not want to see his powers reduced, used his support among the governors to lobby against the parliamentary option.

The best he could do was force the members of the assembly to defer the issue to a plebiscite in 1993. Yet the plebiscite, envisioned by the constitution's framers as the climactic event that would determine Brazil's political structure, ended by giving a stamp of approval to the existing presidential system. With virtually no experience in parliamentary politics, Brazilians opted for presidentialism.

Why is there no parliamentarism in Brazil? For many Brazilians, governmental effectiveness has historically been identified with presidential supremacy. For the poor and for organized sectors such as workers and professionals, the presidency has always been the focus of their demands for improvements in living conditions and wages. As for the armed forces, few generals could imagine being led by a prime minister and a legislature. Although not a constitutional requirement, all Brazilian presidents, and most elected officials, have been men.

In 1993 widespread suspicion of legislative politics was fanned by the argument of the campaign to retain presidentialism that the parliamentary option was little more than a trick to "take the right to vote away from the people." The concept of a parliamentary system that would allow a prime minister to be elected by legislative elites and not directly by the citizenry seemed contrary to what Brazilians had fought for during the long struggle for democracy. Brazilians did not want to lose the ultimate check on the presidency: direct elections by voters every four years. This principle has become even more important as the Cardoso presidency gained the constitutional right to allow the president to run for a second term. Popular elections will now present a crucial test for presidents wishing to pursue their agendas for another four years.

If parliamentary government seemed a far-off goal, rules designed to rein in the power of the federal executive still found their way into the 1988 constitution. In part as a reaction to the extreme centralization of executive authority during military rule, the delegates restored some of the congressional prerogatives that had existed prior to 1964 and granted new ones. The congress gained oversight over economic policy and the right of consultation on executive appointments. Executive decrees—which allowed the president to legislate directly—were abolished. In their place "emergency measures" were established, which preserved the president's power to legislate for thirty days, at the end of which congress can pass or reject the new law. President Collor used emergency measures to install his anti-inflation plans, but they had to survive a two-thirds vote of both houses of the congress. Finally, the 1988 constitution limited the president to a single term, a provision common to Latin American constitutions. In 1997, however, Cardoso succeeded in passing a constitutional amendment through congress that removed the no-reelect rule, allowing him and twenty-two governors to run again in 1998.

Despite these new constraints, Brazilian presidents were still able to use emergency measures with considerable success because of the sad state of the economy. Given such crisis conditions, how could congress deny the president the right to railroad through much-needed reform legislation? Some presidents articulated such arguments with great frequency. Collor, for example, severely abused these powers. In his first year in office, Collor handed down 150 emergency measures. Technically, this meant that the country experienced a crisis situation every forty-eight hours.[35] Worse still, the Supreme Tribunal, the highest court in Brazil, did little to curb this obvious abuse of constitutional authority by the president. The use of presidential discretionary power has only reinforced the powers of the executive to legislate. Over 80 percent of all legislation originates in the executive branch.

The president also retains extremely valuable powers of appointment over the huge Brazilian bureaucracy, particularly at the ministerial level. The Brazilian president retains broad powers to select and dismiss close associates. The president selects ministers for the armed forces according to the merit system prevailing in their respective branches. For most other positions, the president usually appoints ministers from groups of his longtime cronies and collaborators or from any of the existing parties. Although these appointees are not as cohesive a group as the presidential *camarillas* in Mexico, this comparison serves to illustrate the importance of personal ties to the president in Brazil. Under the 1988 constitution, the president must negotiate with congress and some powerful groups (e.g., business associations, labor unions, bar associations) over certain positions in the cabinet,

mainly those responsible for economic policy-making. Even so, the power of appointments in Brazil continues to be a source of great influence.

Among the chief cabinet posts, the ministries of Economy (also called Finance during certain administrations) and Planning have had extraordinary influence. Since the beginning of the military governments, the Ministry of Economy has had more authority than any other executive agency of the state. These powers were heightened as a result of the economic problems of the 1980s and the reform agenda of the 1990s. Thanks to their control of the federal budget and the details of economic policy, recent ministers of the economy have had levels of authority typical of a prime minister in a parliamentary system. The success of Cardoso in the 1994 presidential campaign was due in large part to his effective performance as Itamar Franco's Minister of Economy.

The Bureaucracy: State and Semipublic Firms

Bureaucratic agencies and public firms have played key roles in Brazilian economic and political development during the twentieth century. After 1940 the state created a large number of new agencies and public enterprises. Many of these entities were allowed to accumulate their own debt and plan development projects without undue influence from the central ministries or politicians. Public firms became a key part of the triple alliance of state, foreign, and domestic capital that governed the state-led model of development. Yet it was the state that dominated this alliance. By 1981 ten of the top twenty-five enterprises in Brazil were owned by the federal government and eight others were owned by state governments. Public expenditures as a share of GDP increased from 16 percent in 1947 to more than 32 percent in 1969, far higher than in any other Latin American country, except socialist Cuba.[36]

Much of this spending (and the huge debt that financed it) was concentrated on development projects, many of gigantic proportions. Key examples include the world's largest hydroelectric plant, Itaipú; Petrobrás' petroleum processing centers; steel mills such as the gargantuan National Steel Company in Volta Redonda, Rio de Janeiro; and Vale do Rio Doce, a public firm with interests in sectors as diverse as mining, transport, paper, and textiles. Under the last three military governments (Médici, Geisel, and Figueiredo), dozens of other projects were completed, including the Trans-Amazonian highway, the Tucuruí hydroelectric plants, the Açominas metallurgy park, and the National Nuclear Reactor Program. These and hundreds of other, more modest, projects accounted for much of the country's industrial production. On the eve of the debt crisis in 1982, the top thirty-three projects, including those just listed, absorbed US$88 billion in external debt, employed 1.5 million people, and added $47 billion to the GDP.

Managing the planning and finance of these projects required enormous skill. Several public agencies were responsible, but the National Bank for Economic and Social Development (*Banco Nacional de Desenvolvimento Economico e Social*, or BNDES), stands out as an important coordinator. Founded by Vargas in the early 1950s, the BNDES played a key role in channeling public funds to industrial projects. Among the bank's greatest achievements was the creation of an automobile sector based on subsidized public steel, foreign assemblers such as Ford, General Motors, and Volkswagen, and domestic suppliers of parts and labor. Under President Juscelino Kubitschek, the BNDES implemented an industrial policy in automobiles called the Plan of Goals (*Plano de Metas*), which coordinated domestic and international resources to create the largest automobile industry in Latin America.[37]

The experience of the BNDES demonstrated that despite Brazil's clientelist legacies, the Brazilian bureaucracy could function effectively. Meritocratic advancement and professional recruitment granted these agencies some autonomy from political manipulation. Such agencies were considered islands of efficiency in a state apparatus characterized by patronage and corruption.[38]

Other state and semipublic firms, however, were rife with clientelism. Civilian and military leaders often appointed their supporters as the heads of these enterprises, positions with quite generous salary and retirement packages. Many public firm managers took advantage of their positions to dole out government contracts to associates and even to their own companies in the private sector.

The fiscal crisis of the 1980s had put severe strains on the entire economic bureaucracy, but some things failed to change. The 1988 constitution did not alter significantly the concentration of power in the economic bureaucracy that made developmentalism with clientelism possible. In fact, the new constitution reinforced certain bureaucratic monopolies by codifying them as rights. For example, the state's control over petroleum, natural gas, the exploration of minerals, nuclear energy, and telecommunications was protected constitutionally. These sectors could not be privatized—much less sold to foreign governments or multinational companies.

What the writers of the new constitution did do in response to the fiscal crisis was place new restraints on the activity of state-directed industries. The fiscal independence of state firms was curtailed with restrictions on the amount of debt they could incur. The constitution imposed additional obstacles to the creation of public firms, including the requirement that congress approve any new state enterprises proposed by the executive branch.

Some of the constitutional protections of the public firms lasted only a few years. After his election in 1989, Fernando Collor began a sweeping reform of Brazil's public bureaucracy, beginning with the privatization of large public firms in steel, chemicals, and mining. In 1990 his government launched the National Destatization Program (*Programa Nacional de Destatização*, PND). Under the PND, more than US$20 billion in public firms was sold ($8.5 billion in the steel sector alone). Although the program slowed under the Franco administration, the sell-offs of the steel firms were completed. The Cardoso administration went even further. The government convinced the congress to amend the constitution to remove the public monopoly on petroleum refining, telecommunications, and infrastructure, making these sectors available for auction. Electricity distribution, cellular phone bands, and the octopuslike structure of Vale were put up for privatization. In 1998 much of the public telecommunication sector was privatized, bringing in about $25 billion.

Paradoxically, the agency at the center of the privatization process in Brazil is the BNDES, the agency most responsible for developmentalism. Faced with the fiscal crisis of the 1980s, BNDES' managers adopted a new perspective of the state's role in the economy. Instead of targeting industries and spending large sums to promote them, BNDES' new mission was to provide financing to productivity-enhancing investments such as new technology and labor retraining, outlays that promise to make both soon-to-be-privatized and already-privatized firms more competitive in international markets.[39] As a result, the economic bureaucracy in Brazil continues to play a crucial role in the country's development.

The Military and the Police

The military is another significant arm of the state. Like many other South American militaries, the Brazilian armed forces retain a substantial degree of independence from civilian presidents and legislators. Brazil has suffered numerous coups; those in 1930 and 1964 were critical junctures, while others brought in caretaker governments that eventually ceded to civilian rule. Although the military's grip on power was never as tight as in Nigeria during the Abacha regime, the generals have maintained influence in Brazilian politics, blocking policies they do not like and lobbying on behalf of those they favor.

The military's participation in Brazilian politics became more defined following the transition to democracy. The armed forces were successful in keeping broad prerogatives to "guarantee internal order" and to play a "tutelary role" in civilian government. During the Sarney administration, members of the armed forces retained cabinet-level rank in areas of importance to the military, such as the ministries of the armed forces and the nuclear program. Military officers also kept middle- and lower-level positions in public firms and bureaucratic agencies. Most important, the armed forces were successful in obtaining amnesty for human rights abuses committed during the preceding authoritarian regime.

In an effort to professionalize the armed forces and keep them in the barracks, the Collor government slashed the military budget and replaced the top generals with officers who had few or no connections to the authoritarian regime and were committed to civilian leadership. Collor's reforms were helped by the decline of the country's arms industry, which, during the 1980s, lost key markets for ordinance, tanks, and guns in the Middle East. These industries had previously supplied capital and armaments to the

Brazilian armed forces, keeping them autonomous from civilian control. The collapse and, in some cases, privatization of these military industries gave civilians more control over the generals.[40] The geographic isolation of the Brazilian arms industry in one area of São Paulo state and increasing conflicts over the marketability of expensive weapons systems favored by the armed forces weakened the military's lobbies in Brasília, further eroding the generals' ability to defend their interests.[41]

Police enforcement primarily falls into the domain of the state governments. The state police consists of two forces: the civil police force, which acts as an investigative unit and is not completely uniformed, and the uniformed military police force, which maintains order. The military police are not formally under the command of the military; the constitution stipulates that in the event of a national emergency they can be called to perform active military service. Like the military, the military police are governed by a separate judicial system.

Despite official oversight of police authorities, in practice the military and civil police forces in many cities of the northeast, in São Paulo, and in Rio de Janeiro often act extrajudicially. Cases of arbitrary detention, torture, corruption, and systematic killings by Brazilian police have received much international attention. Human rights investigations have found that off-duty police officers are regularly hired by merchants and assorted thugs to kill street urchins whom they accuse of thievery. One study in Rio de Janeiro between 1993 and 1996 showed that police officers preferred the use of deadly force, shooting to kill rather than to disable.[42] The majority of victims were shot in the shoulders or the head; in 40 of the 697 cases, the victims were shot in the back of the head in gangland, execution style. Most astonishingly, the victims were mostly young black men and boys and had no criminal records whatsoever. Other studies have shown that at least 10 percent of the homicides in Rio de Janeiro are committed by the police. In São Paulo, police violence is just as bad. In 1992 alone, the São Paulo police killed 1,470 people, accounting for one-third of all homicides in the state.[43]

The federal police force is a small unit of approximately 3000 people. It operates as a combined U.S. Federal Bureau of Investigation, Secret Service,

Drug Enforcement Agency, and Immigration and Naturalization Service. Under the authority of the executive the federal police are responsible for providing security to public officials, cracking down on drug rings, administering customs regulations, and investigating federal crimes. The demands placed on this single agency have caused some Brazilian politicians to propose that the federal police be split up into more specialized units, as in the U.S. system.

Other State Institutions

The Judiciary

The Brazilian judiciary is composed of a network of state courts, with jurisdiction over state matters; and a federal court system, not unlike the one in the United States, which maintains jurisdiction over federal crimes. A supreme court (the Supreme Federal Tribunal), similar in jurisdiction to the U.S. Supreme Court but lacking authority over the other branches of government, acts as the final arbiter of court cases. It is composed of eleven justices, each appointed by the president and confirmed by an absolute majority of the Senate. A Superior Court of Justice with thirty-three sitting justices operates under the Supreme Federal Tribunal as an appeals court. Matters requiring interpretation of the constitution go to the Supreme Federal Tribunal. The military maintains its own court system. All judges in the Brazilian judicial system serve for life.

The judiciary is designed to adjudicate political conflicts as well as civil and social conflicts. The Electoral Supreme Tribunal (*Tribunal Supremo Electoral,* TSE) has exclusive responsibility for the organization and oversight of all issues related to voting. The seven-member TSE is composed of three justices elected from the members of the Supreme Federal Tribunal; two from the Superior Court of Justice; and two nominated by the president from a group of six attorneys of notable quality that are selected by the Supreme Federal Tribunal. The seven justices on the TSE have the power to investigate charges of political bias by public employees, to file criminal charges against persons violating electoral laws, and to scrutinize and validate electoral results. In addition to these constitutional provisions, under electoral law and its own regulations the TSE monitors the legal compliance of electoral campaigns and executive neutrality in campaigns. The integrity of the tribunal in the conduct of elections has remained very high, making fraud a relatively rare thing in national elections. The TSE is assisted in this process by a system of regional electoral courts, which oversee local elections.

As in the rest of Latin America, penal codes govern the powers of judges. This makes the judiciary less flexible than its North American counterparts, which operate on case law, but it provides a more effective barrier against "judicial activism"—the tendency of the courts to render broad interpretations of the law.

Since the 1940s the judicial branch of government in Brazil has in theory been highly independent from the executive. In practice, especially under authoritarian rule, the judiciary has been dictated to by the executive branch. President Collor exercised sweeping executive powers without much judicial review. The Supreme Federal Tribunal was viewed as ceding significant extraconstitutional authority by not challenging Collor's rule by fiat. A year after Collor's anti-inflation asset freeze, some of the country's most renowned jurists decided to oppose further blockage of financial assets on the grounds that it was unconstitutional. Although their opposition came late, it began a national debate that continues to this day about the president's "emergency measures." Even so, Cardoso continues to rely heavily upon these discretionary powers.

In recent years, the judiciary has been severely criticized for its perceived unresponsiveness to Brazil's social problems and the persistent corruption in the lower courts. These problems are particularly apparent in rural areas, where impoverished defendants are often denied the right to a fair trial by powerful landowners, who have undue influence over judges and procedures. Children are especially victimized, as courts have refused to hear cases prosecuting those who profit from child prostitution, pornography, and the killing of street urchins.

Prosecuting the police for their misdeeds is exceedingly difficult. In the state of Rio de Janeiro, between January 1996 and July 1997, 68 percent of cases in military court involving the police were retired without a hearing because of insufficient evidence (which is often destroyed by the police) or because of the police's favorite excuse, that the defendant was injured or killed "while resisting arrest." Although federal legislation in 1996 granted civil courts jurisdiction over such matters, paradoxically the power to investigate these crimes was left in the hands of the police.

The Supreme Tribunal's reluctance to act on these matters leaves little hope for change in the short term. Judicial reform has thus far focused upon speeding up the Supreme Tribunal's judicial review functions, avoiding the trickier question of restructuring the judiciary to eliminate corruption.

Restructuring of the judiciary will continue to get attention as the 1988 constitution is revised. Proposals for reform include subjecting judges to external control through periodic elections. Members of the judiciary deeply resent and fear such a prospect. They argue that it would push the institution into the kind of partisanship that has marred policy debates on key social and political issues. Others consider that it is the structure of the judiciary and its approach to interpreting and implementing laws that are the central obstacles to accomplishing policy goals. Like the Brazilian bureaucracy, the judiciary has a complex structure, with multiple jurisdictions at different levels of government. The problems inherent in this complex network of adjudication were made clear during the privatization of Vale when opposition groups in different states and jurisdictions were able to use the local courts to create numerous obstacles to the sale. Attempts to reform the judiciary, most notably in 1997, have been severely limited by jurisdictional conflicts.

Subnational Government

The structure of subnational politics in Brazil is not unlike that of other federal systems throughout the world. Each state government consists of a governor; his chief advisers, who also usually lead key secretariats such as economy and planning; and a unicameral legislature, which is often dominated by the supporters of the governor. Governors are elected to four-year terms and, under the 1997 amendment of the 1988 constitution, they may run for another term.

State and municipal governments wield tremendous influence in Brazilian politics. Since the days of the Old Republic, governors and mayors have been essential sources of support for presidents and federal legislators. This "politics of the governors" expanded with the transition to democracy. The fact that the 1982 elections created the first opportunity since the inauguration of the military regime for Brazilians to elect their governors directly made these subnational politicians crucial standard-bearers of the transition. It lent legitimacy to the governors' campaign to decentralize fiscal resources in the form of taxes and federal transfers. For the "barons of the federation," decentralization was nothing less than part of the democratization process.

The 1988 constitution provided much of what the governors and mayors wanted. First the states and municipalities were promised a larger share of tax revenues. At the same time, however, the governors and mayors were successful in deflecting Brasília's attempts to devolve additional spending responsibilities to subnational government, particularly in the areas of education, health, and infrastructure. The governors also proved successful in protecting state banks from a major overhaul, which was greatly needed given that these financial institutions continued to fund irresponsible subnational spending by accumulating huge debts that the federal government agreed to roll over.

During the Collor administration, the federal government began to regain much of the fiscal authority it had lost to the states and municipalities. The Central Bank made good on its threats to intervene in bankrupt state banks and privatize them. The federal government also refused to roll over state debt without a promise of reform, including the privatization of money-losing utility companies. The Cardoso administration required states and municipalities to finance a larger share of social spending, including education and health care. At the same time, new legislation empowered Brasília to claim more discretionary authority over fiscal transfers and tax revenues that had previously been devolved to subnational governments.

Despite these efforts, Brazilian presidents must continue to negotiate the terms of reform with governors as much as with the congress. Because they can now run for reelection, the governors and their political machines will represent an even more consistent element in national politics. The October 1998 elections proved the staying power of incumbent governors as fifteen of the twenty-two incumbents who ran were reelected, a turnover rate well below the high levels in the legislature (see Section 4).

Although most subnational politics are still preoccupied with the distribution of political favors in return for fiscal rewards, certain governors and mayors have devised innovative solutions to Brazil's social and economic problems. One recent study of the state of Ceará in the poor northern region has demonstrated that even the most underdeveloped subnational governments can produce important policies to promote industrial investment, employment, and social services.[44] Such an example is a useful reminder that not all states and municipalities are the same in a federal system. Much depends on the interests and quality of political and bureaucratic leadership.

The Policy-Making Process

Even though policy-making continues to be fluid and ambiguous in Brazil, certain domains of policy are clearly demarcated. Foreign policy, for example, is exclusively within the purview of the executive branch. Political parties and the congress in general still have only inconsistent power over investment policies. As most legislation originates in the executive branch, bureaucratic agencies have retained command over the details of social and economic policies.

The process of making policy in Brazil can be characterized by one common quality: the tendency of clientelism to inject itself at every stage, from formulation and decision-making to implementation. Even when policies are formulated without the undue influence of societal and political actors, implementation is often obstructed or distorted by clientelism. Again, as noted, exceptions exist, but they are only that—exceptions.[45]

Complex formal and informal networks linking the political executive, key agencies of the bureaucracy, and private interests tend to be the chief players in clientelist circles. One of Cardoso's contributions to sociology before he became involved in Brazilian politics was his characterization of these clientelistic networks as **bureaucratic rings**. For Cardoso, the Brazilian state is highly permeable, fragmented, and therefore easily colonized by private interests that

make alliances with midlevel bureaucratic officers. By shaping public policy to benefit these interests, bureaucrats gain the promise of future employment in the private sector. While in positions of responsibility, bureaucratic rings are ardent defenders of their own interests. Because they are entrenched and well connected throughout the Brazilian bureaucracy, few policies can be implemented without the resources and support of the most powerful bureaucratic rings.

One example of the role of bureaucratic rings is the creation of large development projects. The politics surrounding these decisions were often intense. Governors and mayors wanted lucrative public projects to be placed in their jurisdiction; private contractors yearned for the state's business; and politicians positioned themselves for all the attendant kickbacks, political and pecuniary.[46] Although the days of huge development projects are over, the public sector still formulates policy and allocates resources under the influence of bureaucratic rings.

Among the key sources of influence external to the state is organized business. Unlike business associations in some Asian and West European countries, Brazilian business groups have remained independent of corporatist ties to the state. There is no Brazilian version of the French agricultural association FNSEA or the para-public institutions of the Federal Republic of Germany. Business associations have also remained aloof from political parties. Brazil has nothing akin to Mexico's PAN, a party that claims to represent a large portion of the business class. That does not mean, however, that Brazilian business interests are not organized. Lobbying by Brazilian entrepreneurs is common, and their participation in bureaucratic rings is legendary. Few major economic policies are passed without the input of the Federation of São Paulo Industries (*Federação das Industrias do Estado de São Paulo,* or FIESP). Other business groups, some that have broken off from FIESP, continue to defend their interests energetically as Brazil reforms its economy.

The country's labor confederations and unions have had less consistent access to policy-making. Although unions were once directly organized and manipulated by the corporatist state, they gained autonomy in the late 1970s and the 1980s. From then on they sought leverage over policy-making through outside channels, such as the link between the *Central*

Única dos Trabalhadores (CUT, Workers' Singular Peak Association) and Lula da Silva's Workers' Party. Attempts to bring labor formally into direct negotiations with business and the state have failed. Shortly after assuming power, Sarney initiated talks among business, government, and representatives of the major labor federations. These talks quickly broke down. Widening cleavages within the Brazilian union movement tended to split sectors of organized labor, causing some segments to refuse to be bound by any agreement. Later, during the Collor administration, a second attempt at tripartite negotiation emerged in the form of "sectoral chambers" in the São Paulo automotive sector. These talks produced some noteworthy accords, but the chambers did not last because of opposition from the Ministry of Economy and other agencies. These experiences contrast sharply with the legacy of codetermination in Germany and other formulas for maintaining collective bargaining with state mediation in West European countries.

Policy implementation is also highly politicized. Debate and lobbying do not stop in Brazil once laws are enacted. Policy implementation is a subject of perpetual bargaining. One popular phrase—*o jeito brasileiro* ("the Brazilian way")—captures this aspect of Brazilian politics.[47] The Brazilian way is to scoff at the law and find a way around it. If one wants to get something without really paying for it, one asks for a *jeito*. Paradoxically, *jeito* can be the source of great efficiency in Brazilian society, but it carries a heavy price in that the rule of law is not respected. Therefore, reform of the policy-making process in Brazil will require more than restrictions on clientelism and legislative and judicial oversight of suspected bureaucratic rings. It will require a shift in thinking about the role of law in Brazilian society.

Section ❹ Representation and Participation

Because of urbanization and modernization of the economy, the Brazilian electorate grew impressively after 1945. Improved literacy and efforts by political parties to expand voter registration helped to increase the number of citizens eligible to vote. Voting rights were granted in 1981 to anyone eighteen or older (but not illiterates) and in 1988 to anyone over sixteen. As a result of these changes, the percentage of the total population eligible to vote increased from 16.2 percent in 1945 to 60 percent in 1994. The Brazilian electorate stands at 106 million, 78.5 percent of which turned out for the presidential election in October 1998.

The expansion of the Brazilian electorate coincided with the proliferation of political organizations and movements dedicated to marshaling popular support. Mass appeal became an important element in campaigns and political alliances. With the return to democracy in the 1980s, newly independent labor unions and special-interest organizations emerged, making new alliances in civil society possible.

Nevertheless, the richness of political organization was restrained by the legacies of state-centered structures of social control. Despite the transition to democracy, state corporatism continued to govern important segments of the Brazilian polity. Some political parties and many of the new social movements and political organizations that helped end the military government lacked staying power. Clientelism continued to fragment the legislature and weaken other democratic institutions.

The Legislature

The national legislature (594 members) is bicameral, consisting of an upper house, the Senate, and a lower house, the Chamber of Deputies. Each state and the federal district elects three senators, for a total of eighty-one. Senators are elected by simple majority. Senators serve for eight-year terms and may be reelected without limits. Two-thirds of the Senate is elected at one time and four years later the remaining one-third is elected. For example, in the elections of 1994, two-thirds of the Senate was renewed. In 1998 the remaining one-third was renewed. Senatorial elections are held concurrently with those for the Chamber of Deputies, which places all of its seats up for election after each four-year cycle. Federal deputies may be reelected without limits. The number of members in the Chamber of Deputies is, in theory, proportional to the population of each state and the federal district. Each state is allowed a minimum of eight and a maximum of seventy deputies, regardless of population. In 1998 there were 513 deputies.

Both houses of the legislature have equal authority to make laws. In all cases, one chamber acts as a revisor of legislation passed by the other. Bills go back and forth between houses without going through a conference committee of the two chambers, as is the case in the United States. Once the bill is passed by both houses, the president may sign it into law, reject it as a whole, or reject it in part. The legislature can override a presidential veto with a majority of the vote in both houses during a joint session. Constitutional amendments must survive two three-fifths votes in each house of congress. Amendments may also be passed with an absolute majority in a special unicameral constituent assembly proposed by the president and created by both houses of congress. The Senate retains authority to try the president and other top officials, including the vice president and key ministers and justices, for impeachable offenses. The Senate also has the power to approve appointments to high offices, including justices of the high courts, heads of diplomatic missions, and the directors of the Central Bank.

The formula for determining the proportionality of population to representatives is distorted by complex constitutional rules that favor the most sparsely populated states. As these states are the most numerous in the federal system, they tend to be overrepresented in the legislature. For example, between 1990 and 1994, the northern region had 4.85 percent of the voters but elected 11.33 percent of the deputies, while the southeastern region had 46 percent of the electorate but only 33.59 percent of the seats. Only 40 percent of the population elects a majority of the Chamber of Deputies. The least populated states are also the poorest and most rural in Brazil. Typically, they have been political bases for conservative landowning interests and, more recently, agribusiness. After 1964 the military cultivated support among conservative rural groups by granting statehood to sparsely populated territories in the north and northeast, reinforcing their overrepresentation in the Chamber. These precedents continued into the democratic period and largely explain why conservative landowners and agribusiness elites maintain positions of great influence in the Brazilian congress.

In contrast to the presidency, the Brazilian legislature has rarely played a dominant role in the country's politics. In part, that is due to the ability of the president to impose policy through corporatism and populism. However, the congress must accept some of the blame. Many senators and deputies are more interested in cultivating and dispensing patronage than in representing and being accountable to the voters. As a result, representatives have never organized their parties or large segments of the population in support of national policy. Only the rarest of exceptions exist to this rule of Brazilian congressional politics.

Legislators view their service primarily as a means to enhance their own income with generous public pensions and through kickbacks earned in the dispensing of political favors. Election to the federal legislature is often used as a stepping stone to even more lucrative posts.[48] After the presidency, the governorships of the industrialized states are the most coveted positions. Appointment to head any of the premier ministries and state firms also ranks high, since these are choice positions from which to distribute and receive favors. Although many members of congress are independently wealthy, most come from the middle or upper middle class and therefore have much to gain in the economics of public administration.

The congress has largely failed to use the expanded powers granted by the 1988 constitution. Lack of a quorum to vote is a frequent problem, and recently acquired powers have provided greater opportunities for some legislators to practice corruption and backroom dealing, conditions that have helped to break down party loyalties and reinforce the self-serving nature of congressional politics. The many deficiencies of the Brazilian legislature were magnified in the mid-1990s by several corruption scandals. In the most serious case, a handful of senators and deputies were accused of embezzling from the national treasury.

One response to legislative corruption has been the use of parliamentary commissions of inquiry to review cases of malfeasance by elected officials. Although these temporary committees have demonstrated some influence, most notably the parliamentary commission of inquiry that investigated Collor and recommended his impeachment, they have not always produced results. The temporary committees work alongside sixteen permanent legislative committees that treat issues as diverse as taxation and human rights. These committees, however, are not nearly as strong as the major committees in the U.S. Congress. Due to the self-interested focus of Brazilian politicians and the related weakness of political parties, legislative committees, both temporary and permanent, often fail to get to the end of an investigation or to find solutions to persistent dilemmas in policy.

Public opinion about the federal congress reflects its weakness and irrelevance to the key issues facing Brazil. In a 1996 survey by the JB-Vox Populi organization, the national congress received a mere 17 percent approval rating, the second lowest rank among the thirteen institutions listed in the poll. Only municipal government in the largest cities received a lower score.[49]

Political Parties and the Party System

The Brazilian political party system is one of the most mercurial in the world. Party names, party affiliations, and the structure of party alliances are constantly in flux. This is nothing new in Brazilian political history. Like many of the country's current problems, party instability stretches back to the New State of Getúlio Vargas and the centralization of politics in the Brazilian state. State corporatism and populism were hostile to the development of independent party organizations. Political parties, when they did emerge, were created by state managers. Populist redistribution reinforced these tendencies, as workers and the middle class became accustomed to asking what they would receive from a politician in return for support. Except for members of the Communist Party and other extreme organizations, Brazilian voters did not develop a strong sense of political identity linked to established parties. Personalist loyalties and the distribution of goods and services were more important.

Many of the traditional weaknesses of the party system were reinforced after the transition to democracy, making parties even more anemic. The rules governing the party system made it easier for politicians to switch parties, virtually at will. One of the most important observers of Brazilian democracy, Scott Mainwaring, found that the 559 representatives of the 1987–1991 legislature had belonged to an average of over three parties per politician.[50] Politicians switched parties to increase their access to patronage. Other rules of the electoral system created incentives for politicians to ignore the importance of party labels. Brazil's experience with **proportional representation** (PR), which is used to elect federal and state deputies, is particularly important in this regard.

Brazil's mix of presidentialism and multiparty democracy creates other problems for the country's system of representation. Given the political fragmentation of the legislature and the weakness of the party system, presidents are unable to maintain majority alliances in congress, a requirement for stability in a multiparty system. In parliamentary systems, the party in power has an absolute majority or stands at the head of an alliance of parties that compose a majority. As a result, the ruling party or alliance can implement a programmatic approach to legislation. By contrast, in Brazil, the president has never been able to maintain a supraparty alliance in congress. More often, Brazilian presidents have attempted to govern above parties, dispensing favors to key congressional politicians to get legislation approved. Alternatively, presidents have not been shy about railroading reform through congress by using their discretionary authorities. As Timothy Power, a scholar of presidential authority in Brazil, has noted, "The [presidential] pen is mightier than the congress."[51]

In the midst of Brazil's confusing party system, a number of political organizations have emerged over the last few years. These parties can be defined ideologically, although discrete categories are often not possible. Significant distinctions exist among the country's political parties.

Political parties on the right currently defend neoliberal economic policies designed to shrink the size of the public sector. They support the reduction and partial privatization of the welfare state. A majority advocate a liberal trade policy and MERCOSUL, but a substantial minority press for protectionism and the continuation of subsidies, particularly in agriculture. No party of the right has yet emerged as a solid defender of neoliberal restructuring of the economy. On constitutional reform, right-wing parties are fairly united in favor of curtailing the number and range of social rights protecting welfare entitlements and

Institutional Intricacies: *Proportional Representation*

Proportional representation was first introduced in Brazil in 1932 and was later reaffirmed by the military governments. Unlike Mexico, Britain, and the United States, but like many of the European parliamentary democracies, Brazil is divided into electoral districts that choose more than one representative. The ability to choose more than one representative means that a broader range of voices may be heard in elected offices.

Minority parties can make alliances to pass the threshold of votes needed to achieve representation. Proportional representation may be based on either a closed-list or an open-list system. In a closed-list PR, the party selects the order of politicians, and voters cannot cross party lines. Since voters are effectively choosing the party that best represents them, this system encourages party loyalty among both the electorate and individual politicians. In an open-list PR system, the voters have more discretion and can cross party lines. Brazil's PR system is open-list. Voters cast single ballots either for a party label, which adds to the party's total for determining representation, or for individuals. No names appear on Brazilian ballots, so voters must write in their choices.

Electoral districts for the election of state and federal deputies are entire states in Brazil. In any given election, there may be between six and seventy federal deputies and from twelve to eighty-four state deputies running for office. With few limits on how many individuals and parties may run in the same electoral district, crowded fields discourage party loyalty and emphasize the personal qualities of candidates, who must stand out in the minds of voters. Party affiliations do little to reduce the confusion of the average Brazilian voter as he or she is confronted with dozens of names for each position. Worse still, the open-list PR system creates incentives for politicians to ignore party labels, since voters can cross party lines with ease. That even leads to politicians from the same party running against each other for the same position within a district.

Open-list proportional representation explains why there are so many parties in Brazil. With so much emphasis on the personal qualities of politicians, ambitious individuals can ignore the established party hierarchies while achieving elected office. They need only create their own parties or form alliances to get on the ballot and gain enough votes to qualify for representation. As a result, Brazil has the most fragmented party system in Latin America and one of the most fragmented in the world.

As if the open-list PR system were not distorting enough, Brazilian electoral law also allows incumbents to keep their party affiliation and remain on the ballot for the next election. This provision strips political parties of any control over their members: an incumbent may ignore the party's interests while in office but still must be kept on the ballot during the next contest.

Brazil's electoral system differs from other open-list proportional representation systems in that state, not national, parties select legislative candidates. In most cases, Brazilian governors exert tremendous influence over who can be elected. This further weakens national party leaders, who remain beholden to governors who can reward them with supportive nominees or rivals.

Source: Scott Mainwaring, "Brazil: Weak Parties, Feckless Democracy," in *Building Democratic Institutions: Party Systems in Latin America*, ed. Scott Mainwaring and Timothy R. Scully (Stanford, Calif., Stanford University Press, 1995), 375.

---

workers; they also advocate electoral reform—specifically, the establishment of a majority or mixed, rather than purely proportional, district voting system.

A loose set of conservative parties currently struggles for the mantle of the right. In front of the pack is the PFL (Party of the Liberal Front), the second largest party in the Senate and the largest party in the Chamber. Many wildcard parties, with low to moderate levels of representation in congress, ally themselves with right-wing and center-right parties or advocate right-wing issues: the Brazilian Labor Party (PTB), the Progressive Party (PPB), and the Liberal Party (PL) are examples. Various microparties also compose the right-wing side of the ideological spectrum, including the Party of National Reconstruction (PRN), the neofascist Party of the Reorganization of

Citizen Action: *The Workers' Party*

The creation of the Workers' Party (PT) was a remarkable innovation in Brazilian history. The PT was founded in the early 1980s by workers who had defied the military government and engaged in strikes in São Paulo's metalworking and automobile industries in 1978 and 1979. Although the PT began with a working-class message and leftist platform, its identity broadened during the 1980s and early 1990s. The party and its leader, Luiz Inácio "Lula" da Silva, increasingly campaigned for the support of the middle class, the rural and urban poor, and even segments of business and the upper classes. Unlike previous populist parties in Brazil, the PT aimed both to bring previously excluded groups into the political arena and to change the status quo substantively.

Lula da Silva ran for the presidency three times, in 1989, 1994, and 1998. In 1989 he qualified for, but lost, the runoff to Collor. In 1994 and 1998, he was beaten during the first turn by Cardoso. In 1998, the PT forged an electoral alliance with Leonel Brizola's PDT as well as with the PSB, PC do B, and the PCB. Despite a unified leftist ticket, da Silva captured 31.7 percent of the vote to Fernando Henrique Cardoso's 53.1 percent.

As Margaret Keck, an American scholar of the PT, argues, the Workers' Party was a novel development because it sought to represent the interests of workers and the poor. This had never before been attempted by a political organization that operated independently from the state. The PT also tries to be an internally democratic party. Its leaders respect the views of grassroots organizers and ensure that their voices are heard in the party's decision-making.

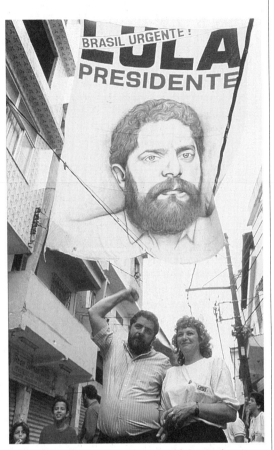

Luiz Inácio "Lula" da Silva, founder of the Workers' Party. *Source:* © Jornal do Brasil, August 19, 1998, Alexandre Sassaki.

*Source: Margaret Keck, *The Workers' Party and Democratization in Brazil*. (New Haven, Conn.: Yale University Press, 1992), 219–220.

the National Order (PRONA), the Christian Social Party (PSC), the Democratic Social Party (PDS—no relation to the Vargas-era PDS; successor to the military's ARENA party), and the Christian Democratic Party (PDC). In 1993 the PDS and PDC merged to form the Reformist Progressive Party (PPR), which joined the Progressive Party (PP) in September 1995 to form the PPB.

The largest party in the Senate and the third largest in the Chamber, PMDB (Party of the Brazilian Democratic Movement—a descendant of the old MDB), and the second largest party in the Chamber and third largest in the Senate, PSDB (the Brazilian Social Democratic Party—originally an offshoot of the PMDB; Cardoso's party through 1999); dominate the center and center-left segment of the ideological spectrum. These two parties are ideologically diverse. Segments of these parties identify with the positions that define the political right or the political left.

Political parties on the left advocate reducing

Table 4

Party Representation in Congress, 1999

Chamber of Deputies		Senate	
Party	Percent of Vote	Party	Percent of Vote
PFL	20%	PMDB	33%
PSDB	19	PFL	23
PMDB	16	PSDB	20
PPB	12	PT	9
PT	12	PDT	5
PTB	6	PPB	4
PDT	5	PSB	4
PSB	4	PTB	1
Other	6	PPS	1

deficits and inflation, but also maintaining the public sector in public hands and improving the welfare state. Left-oriented parties want to expand the state's role in promoting and protecting domestic industry. On constitutional reform, they support the social rights guaranteed by the 1988 constitution.

On the left, the most important party continues to be the Workers' Party (PT). Since 1985 the PT has occupied much of the left's political space, marginalizing already peripheral parties such as the Brazilian Socialist Party (PSB), the Brazilian Communist Party (PCB—renamed the Popular Socialist Party, or PPS, in 1992), the Communist Party of Brazil (PC do B), and the Green Party (PV). The Democratic Labor Party (PDT), a populist organization led by Leonel Brizola, the ex-governor of Rio de Janeiro, advocates Vargas-era nationalism and state-led development. In the elections of October 1998, this party formed an alliance with the PT at the national level. The PPS is led by Ciro Gomes, a former finance minister under the Itamar Franco presidency and a former governor of Ceará. Gomes ran for president in 1998, garnering third place with 10.97 percent of the vote.

As might be expected, the proliferation of political parties has only added to the incoherence of legislative politics. Currently, no party has more than 33 percent of the seats in either house of congress. As Table 4 shows, Cardoso's multiparty alliance of the PSDB-PFL-PTB-PPB controls 57 percent of the vote in the lower house and 48 percent in the upper house. However, because of

party switching and clientelism, the loyalty of these "progovernment" parties to the administration is remarkably soft. Consistency of support is difficult to maintain as turnover in the Chamber is high, with 50–60 percent of the members being replaced with each election. This reality has reinforced the common claim of the executive to be the only source of political order in the Brazilian democratic system.

The results of the October 1998 elections produced mounting recriminations among the leftist parties that a divided opposition was ineffectual. Conservative parties remained suspicious of Cardoso's social reform agenda while center-left forces considered alternatives to right-wing support. Discussions have focused on the possibility of consolidating Brazil's political parties into a three- or four-party left-center-right structure. Brizola has suggested a fusion of the PT and the PDT, which might include an alliance with other parties of the left. The PFL will likely support their leader, Antônio Carlos Magalhães, in his run for the presidency in 2002. Along with alliance partners in the PPB and PTB, this coalition would form a formidable conservative bloc of 209 deputies. The center-left might attempt to make new alliances by rejoining the PMDB with its dissident wing, now the PSDB. A more ambitious plan would be a broader center-left coalition led by PPS leader Ciro Gomes that would unite the PT-PDT merger with the PPS, the PSB, and the most progressive elements of the PMDB and PSDB.

Figure 3

Major Parties in the Chamber of Deputies and Their Percentages of the Vote, 1999 Congress

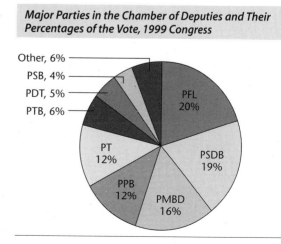

Source: Data from final TSE rally.

Figure 4

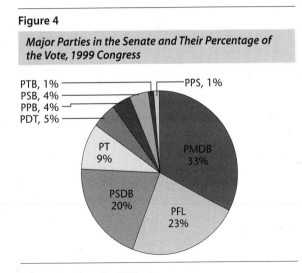

Major Parties in the Senate and Their Percentage of the Vote, 1999 Congress

PTB, 1%
PSB, 4%
PPB, 4%
PDT, 5%
PPS, 1%
PT 9%
PMDB 33%
PSDB 20%
PFL 23%

Source: Data from final TSE rally.

Elections

Contests for public office in Brazil are dominated by the rules of proportional representation (PR). Everything from federal legislative to municipal council positions is distributed on the basis of several mathematical calculations to assure proportionality among political parties. Generally, the number of seats obtained by each party is determined by multiplying the ratio between party and total votes by the total number of seats.

In addition to its effects on the party system, open-list PR rules distort democratic representation in other ways. Given the multiplicity of parties, the unbalanced apportionment of seats among the states, and the sheer size of some electoral districts, candidates often have few incentives to be accountable to their constituency. In states with hundreds of candidates running in oversized electoral districts, the votes obtained by successful candidates are often scattered, limiting the accountability of those elected. In less populated states, there are more seats and parties per voter; the electoral and party quotients are lower. As a result, candidates often alter their legal place of residence immediately before an election in order to run for a safer seat, further compounding the lack of accountability. Electoral laws are highly permissive regarding the candidate's change of residence. For example, ex-president Sarney, realizing that he would

not be eligible to run for a Senate seat in his home state, successfully changed his residence only a few months before the 1990 elections.

As in all modern nations, the media play a key role in Brazilian political campaigns. With the *abertura*, political parties gained the right to air electoral propaganda on radio and television. All radio stations and TV channels are required to broadcast, at no charge, two hours of party programming each day during a campaign season. The parties are entitled to an amount of time on the air proportional to their number of votes in the previous election. Some candidates have no more than a few seconds to present themselves and their platform to the public.

In recent years' elections, particularly presidential contests, have become touchstones of the country's progress in building democracy. Although the president was elected indirectly in 1984 and the eventual president, José Sarney (PMDB and PFL), had not been selected to be president in the first place, this first election set Brazil on the path to democracy. More important was the contest of 1989, which gave Brazilians their first opportunity to elect the president directly. Collor's (PRN) selection became an important precedent that further strengthened Brazilian democracy. Ironically, his impeachment two years later also promoted democracy, because it reinforceed the rule of law and enhanced the oversight functions of the congress. Fernando Henrique Cardoso's election in 1994 and reelection in 1998 repeated and reinforced the 1989 precedent of direct elections for the presidency. Although elections cannot guarantee democracy, recent contests have shown how far Brazilian democracy has come in little over a decade.

Seen from the perspective of average Brazilians, however, the situation is a bit more complex. Although most Brazilians are suspicious of authoritarianism and wary of the return of the military or any other form of dictatorship, they seem to be disappointed with the results of democracy. The weakness of political parties, coupled with the persistence of clientelism, has only discouraged average Brazilians with their country's politics. In one study reported by Scott Mainwaring, Brazilians were asked to classify their interest in politics: 14 percent of the respondents said they had a lot of interest, 22.3 percent said they had moderate interest, 17.8 percent said they had little interest, and 45 percent said they had no interest.[52] Brazilians are increasingly disengaging from electoral politics, and that can only bode ill for the country's democracy.

Political Culture, Citizenship, and Identity

The notion of national identity describes a sense of national community that goes beyond mere allegiance to a state, to a set of economic interests, regional loyalties, or kinship affiliations. The cultivation of a national identity occurs through a process of nation-building during which a set of national symbols, cultural terms and images, and shared myths consolidate around historical experiences that define the loyalties of a group of people.

Several developments made Brazilian nation-building possible. Unlike nation formation in culturally, linguistically, and geographically diverse Western Europe, Africa, and Asia, Brazil enjoyed a homogeneous linguistic and colonial experience. As a result, Brazilian history largely avoided the ethnic conflicts that have become obstacles to nation-building in

Eastern Europe, Nigeria, and India. Immigrants added their ideas and value systems at the turn of the century, but they brought no compelling identities that could substitute for an overarching national consciousness. Regional secessionist movements were scarce in Brazilian history and were short-lived experiences when they did emerge in the twentieth century.

Despite Brazil's rich ethnic makeup, racial identities in Brazil have seldom been the basis for political action. In part, this was the result of the historical myth that the country was racially mixed. Therefore, a singular racial consciousness emerged around the spurious idea that Brazil was a racial democracy. Even in the face of severe economic and political oppression of native peoples, Afro-Brazilians, and Asians, the myth of racial democracy has endured in the national consciousness. As a result, the unique contributions of different ethnic groups were not appreciated.

Brazilian literature, political discourse, and history textbooks reinforced the myth of racial democracy. For example, the famous Brazilian historian Gilberto Freyre in his book *The Masters and the Slaves,* described the evolution of social relations among

Carnival in Brazil, the world's largest floor show, is also an insightful exhibition of allegories and popular myths about the country, its people, and their culture. *Source:* Reuters/Bettmann.

blacks and whites since colonial times, but he treated the underlying reality of racial conflict as an issue of secondary importance.[53] For such intellectuals, miscegenation had diminished racial differences and made conflict unlikely. This thinking buttressed the false belief that prejudice and discrimination were lacking among whites, blacks, Indians, and mulattoes.

Like the myth of racial democracy, the major collective political identities in Brazilian history have sought to hide or negate the real conflicts in society. For example, the symbols and images of political nationalism tended to boost the quasi-utopian visions of the country's future development. Developmentalists under democratic leaders such as Kubitschek and the military governments espoused the optimism that "Brazil is the country of the future." Even in the face of severe fiscal, social, and political problems, Brazilians continue to have faith in their country, even when their confidence in their politicians and democratic institutions has been shaken.

Both the persistence of optimistic myths about the country and an almost angry disengagement from politics are reflections of a weak system of political socialization. Given the dominance of corporatism and populism in twentieth-century Brazilian politics, and the current crisis in these forms of mobilizing popular support, Brazilians lack avenues for becoming more involved in politics. The weakness of political parties is one problem. But an underfunded primary and secondary educational system and the less-than-critical role of the media leave most Brazilians without the resources to become more politically aware. Brazil's illiteracy rate of 16.7 percent remains one of the highest in Latin America and is a key obstacle to mobilizing the electorate. The frenetic nature of political change in Brazil has confused the citizenry, further breaking down whatever continuous political identities might emerge. Perhaps the ultimate reflection of these distressing tendencies is the cynical joke among Brazilians that "Brazil is the country of the future *and will always be.*"

The political sentiments of Brazilian society are actually quite static because most Brazilians feel powerless to change their fates. Brazilians have always considered liberal democratic institutions, particularly individual rights, as artificial or irrelevant. Although this view may appear cynical, it is a deeply ingrained notion in Brazilian political culture. Since the end of the nineteenth century, Brazilians have made a distinction between the "legal" Brazil and the "real" Brazil. The former involves the formal laws of the country; the latter refers to what actually occurs. A prime example was the turn-of-the-century liberal democracy, which concealed the patronage-ridden interior of Brazilian politics. Brazilian intellectuals developed the phrase *para ingles ver* ("for the English to see") to describe the notion that liberal democracy had been implanted to impress foreign observers, hiding the fact that the real politics would be conducted behind the scenes. As Brazil struggles to balance the interests of foreign investors with those of its own people, many Brazilians continue to believe that much of the politics they observe is really "for the English to see."

One of the key outcomes of the sense of powerlessness among the majority of Brazilians was the belief that the state should organize society. This idea helped to justify both the Vargas dictatorship in 1937 and the military rule that followed the coup of 1964. The primacy of the state manifested itself in Brazilian political culture. The notion that the state had a duty to provide for its citizens' welfare placed the state at the center of the Brazilian polity and the president at the center of the state. It should be clear, based on this analysis, that both society and the state in Brazil developed a set of core ideas that favored the establishment of a strong central government with an overbearing presidentialism. These ideas were not just imposed on Brazilians by savvy politicians; they were the product of many decades of social and political conflict.

During the redemocratization process, new trends in Brazilian political culture emerged. Most segments of Brazilian society came to embrace "modernization with democracy," even if they would later raise doubts about its benefits. The Catholic Church played an important role in promoting democracy. During the transition, a number of Catholic political organizations and movements aided by the Church organized popular opposition to the military governments. After the transition, archbishops of the Catholic Church helped assemble testimonials of torture victims. The publication of these depositions in the book *Nunca Mais* (*Never Again*) fueled condemnation of the authoritarian past. In this way, an establishment that had previously been associated with social conservatism and political oppression became a mobilizer of popular opposition to authoritarianism.

Another trend that developed during and after the transition to democracy was the growth of a profound distrust of the state. Brazilians began to doubt the ability of the state to find solutions to the country's economic and social problems. Business groups assailed the failures of state-led development, while labor unions claimed that corporatist management of industrial relations could not satisfy the interests of workers. As a result, Brazilians became increasingly receptive to fringe voices that promised to eradicate the previous economic-political order. By 1989 most Brazilians were willing to trust a little-known politician, Fernando Collor, who told the electorate what they wanted to hear. Collor swore to go to war against indolent state employees, corrupt politicians, and inefficient state enterprises. The results were, at least in part, disastrous. By ceding their authority to an untested figure like Collor, Brazilians failed one of the most important tests of democracy: assuring that elected officials will be accountable to the electorate. In the end, anti-statism proved hostile to democracy.

A third trend in Brazilian political culture can be seen among the most elite segments of society. Soon after the transition to democracy, many journalists, economists, politicians, intellectuals, and entrepreneurs began to embrace the notion that national institutions could be adjusted incrementally to strengthen democracy and promote economic growth. Constitutional, administrative, and economic reform became priorities of politicians such as Fernando Henrique Cardoso.

For average Brazilians, the dynamics of institutional tinkering are virtually unintelligible. The electorate must feel substantial change, primarily in their pocketbooks. Cardoso was able to deliver in 1994 when his Real Plan reduced inflation and increased the buying power of most Brazilians. That success gave Cardoso the popular support he needed to become president and launch an array of institutional reforms. In 1998, facing another presidential contest, Cardoso struggled to convince voters that his government of technocrats had the answers to the country's problems. With his reforms stuck in congress, Cardoso had difficulty backing up his claim to deserve a second term. Economic growth began to stall, raising fears that Cardoso's reforms had run their course

and were beginning to erode. Despite these problems, he was reelected, but he continued to struggle with congress on the reform agenda.

The task of selling even the most complex sets of policies to a population with weak political socialization and poor general education has become central to gaining and maintaining political power in Brazil. That has placed a premium on the adept management of the media, particularly radio and television.

The Brazilian media are free to criticize the government, and most of the broadcast businesses are privately owned. Although there is significant government influence over the resources necessary for media production and the advertising revenue from government campaigns, there is no overt government censorship, and freedom of the press is widely and constitutionally proclaimed. Government officials must engage in a complex dance of symbols and words to attract the attention of the private media and cast the most appealing image to a distrustful electorate.

The largest media organizations are owned by a small group of conglomerates. The Globo network is Brazil's preeminent media empire and one of the five largest television networks in the world. It has been formidable in shaping public opinion; some believe it played a prominent role in Collor's election in 1989. Conglomerates like Globo have played favorites in the past and no doubt will continue to do so. In return, the media giants expect licensing concessions from their political friends.

The media's independence from government interference varies. The print media are generally less restrained than the broadcast media in criticizing politicians and governments. Though television newscasts, which attract millions of viewers, continuously cover events embarrassing to the government or criticize government policies, the majority of viewers hear woefully little information on how and why political decisions are made, why one policy is favored over another, and the ultimate results. Domestic broadcast news coverage in Brazil is often merely the broadcasting of official government versions.

Interests, Social Movements, and Protest

Despite the growing disengagement of most Brazilians from politics and the country's legacy of state corporatism, autonomous collective interests have been able to take positions of importance in the political landscape. The previously mentioned role of business lobbies, rural protest movements, and labor unions, particularly those linked to the Workers' Party, are all examples of how Brazilian civil society has been able to break through the vise of state corporatism and social control.

As noted, the Catholic Church was actively engaged in organizing grassroots movements during and after the transition to democracy. After the profound changes in Catholic doctrine brought about by the Second Vatican Council in the early 1960s, the Church in Brazil became more active in advocating social and political reform. The Brazilian Church, through the National Conference of Brazilian Bishops (CNBB), produced an array of projects to improve literacy, stimulate political awareness, and improve the working and living conditions of the poor. Although some conservative segments of the Brazilian Church reacted violently against the Church's "messing in politics," the CNBB pressed on.

One well-known outcome of these changes was the development of liberation theology, a doctrine which argued that religion had to free people from both their sins and social injustice at the same time. In Brazil this thinking was associated with the Franciscan theologian Leonardo Boff. During the *abertura*, this doctrinal shift sought to relate theology to Brazilian reality by having priests become directly involved in improving the lot of poor Brazilians by defending their social and political needs.[54] By organizing community-based movements to press for improved sanitation, clean water, basic education, and most important, freedom from oppression, Catholic groups mobilized millions of citizens. Among the Brazilian Church's most notable accomplishments was the development of an agrarian reform council in the 1970s, the Pastoral Land Commission. The commission called for the extension of land tenure to poor peasants. The Brazilian Church also created ecclesiastical community movements (CEBs) to improve conditions in the *favelas*.

In the mid-1970s, Brazil witnessed a historic awakening of social and political organization: grassroots popular movements; new forms of trade unionism; neighborhood movements; professional associations of doctors, lawyers, and journalists; entrepreneurial associations; and middle-class organizations. At the same time, a host of nongovernmental organizations (NGOs) became more active in Brazil, for example, Amnesty International, Greenpeace, and native Brazilian rights groups. Domestic groups active in these areas increasingly turned to the NGOs for resources and information, adding an international dimension to what was previously an issue of domestic politics.

Women's organizations played a significant role in popular urban social movements during the 1970s. By the 1980s women were participating in and leading popular initiatives on a wide variety of issues related to employment and the provision of basic services. Many of these organizations enlisted the support of political parties and trade unions in battles over women's wages, birth control, rape, and violence in the home. Although practically absent in employers' organizations, women are highly active in urban unions. Out of the country's 5324 urban unions, 14.8 percent have elected women directors. Fewer women are leaders of rural unions (6.6 percent), but they compose 78 percent of active membership. In recent years, Brazilian women have created over 3000 organizations to address their issues. Included in this total are special police stations (*delegacias de defesa da mulher*, DDMs) dedicated to addressing crimes against women. The DDMs have emerged in major Brazilian cities and particularly in São Paulo, where their performance has been highly rated.

Women's groups have seen their power increase as more women have joined the workforce; 39 percent of women now work outside the home. That figure is higher than in Mexico (22 percent) and Argentina (33 percent). More than 20 percent of Brazilian families are supported exclusively by women. The share of domestic servants in the female workforce has declined from 32 percent to 20 percent over the last ten years, suggesting that traditional roles for women have not absorbed the increase in the female workforce.

Despite women's improved economic and social importance, progress on women's issues is slow. On average, women earn only 57 percent of what men make. Only 7 percent of women with university degrees earn more than twenty times the minimum wage (about $75 per month), as compared to 28 percent of men. Thirty-four percent of illiterate women earn the minimum wage or less, versus 5 percent of illiterate males.

In contrast to the progress of women's movements, a politically significant organization to address racial discrimination has not emerged. This fact is especially surprising because Brazil is one of the world's most racially mixed countries. Only during the 1940s did some public officials and academics acknowledge that prejudice existed against blacks. At that time, the problems of race were equated with the problems of class. Given the absence of legally sanctioned discrimination since the abolition of slavery in 1889, prejudice came to be viewed as class-based, not race-based. Attacking class inequality was thus considered a way to address prejudice against blacks. This belief seemed plausible because most poor Brazilians are either *pardo* (mulatto) or black. But it might be just as logical to suggest that they are poor because they are black. In any case, the relationship between race and class in Brazil is just as ambiguous as it is in the United States and other multiethnic societies.

Some analysts believe that a gradual and peaceful evolution of race relations is possible. Others argue that, as a consequence of white domination, blacks lack the collective identity and political organization necessary to put race relations on the political agenda. Both sides seem to agree, however, that although poverty and color are significantly correlated, overt confrontation among races is uncommon. Ironically, this may explain why no serious national discussion of race relations has ever emerged in Brazil.

On the other hand, the rights of Brazil's indigenous peoples, the Indians of the Amazon, remain at the center of the debate on the country's most pressing social problems. Over the past half century, the development of the Amazon has directly threatened the cultures and lives of Indians. For example, members of the Ianomami, a tribe with one of the largest reserves in Brazil, are frequently murdered by miners so they can gain access to mines in Indian territory. Many such massacres have occurred in territories legally provided by the central state to the Ianomami. During the military government, the national Indian agency,

FUNAI, turned a blind eye to such abuses with its claim that indigenous cultures represented "ethnic cysts to be excised from the body politic."[55] With the *abertura,* many environmental NGOs defended the human rights of indigenous people as part of their campaign to defend the Amazon and its people. The end of military rule and the economic crisis of the 1980s slowed down the exploitation of the Amazon.

The 1988 constitution recognized the rights of indigenous peoples for the first time, creating large reserves for tribes like the Ianomami. Yet these protections were eroded when President Cardoso, under pressure by landowning conservative allies from the northeast, implemented a policy to allow private interests to make claims on over half of all indigenous lands. Miners, loggers, and land developers invade native lands, often with destructive consequences for the ecology and for indigenous people. Allied against these interests are members of the Workers' Party, a coalition of indigenous groups known as COIAB, and church-based missionary organizations. The Kayapó and their resistance to large-scale development projects in the Amazon are a key example of how environmental, labor, and indigenous issues are melding together to form a powerful grassroots campaign. Members of the Kayapó tribe have been successful in politically disrupting damming and mining projects through mass media campaigns.[56] Their struggle continues, but without more federal protection Amazonian Indians will continue to be threatened.

The sprouting of movements, associations, and interest groups may seem impressive, but they represent specific constituencies. Most Brazilians do not bother to participate in parties, movements, and unions because the basic functions of government such as security, justice, education, and health care simply do not reach most Brazilians. When confronted with immediate deprivations, many Brazilians avoid organized and peaceful political action, often taking to the streets in sporadic riots. Such events demonstrate that many Brazilians feel they have only two choices in the face of unresponsive political and state organizations: violent protest or passivity.

Section **5** Brazilian Politics in Transition

Political Challenges and Changing Agendas

As the financial and monetary crisis that began in Asia in late 1997 continued to scare foreign investors throughout the developing world, Fernando Henrique Cardoso appeared on a Cable News Network business show in December. The Brazilian president proclaimed his country a safe place for foreign money, a stable and growth-oriented economy sure to maintain itself immune from the quagmire in Asia. To scholars of Brazil, Cardoso's CNN appearance seemed paradoxical. Here was an avowed social democrat, an old theorist of leftist sociology, pitching his country to international investors. They noted that Cardoso made no mention of his country's worsening social problems, its disparities in income, land tenure, and access to basic social and educational services. For many Brazilians on the left, Cardoso's comments were a ruthless betrayal of shared principles.

From a comparative perspective, we might interpret Cardoso's CNN interview in very different terms. Cardosa's remarks become more understandable when we consider the dilemmas connected to our theme of governing the economy. Much like other leaders of developing countries, Cardoso needs to preserve a stable domestic economy attractive to foreign investors, who are likely to turn to other countries at the first signs of instability. Not surprisingly, then, on CNN the president talked up his economic policy and downplayed the political and social negatives of investing money in Brazil. Rather than a betrayal of his social democratic principles, Cardoso's pitch could be seen as a pragmatic attempt to turn a necessity into a virtue.

At the same time, there are serious costs to Cardoso's strategy of reforming the Brazilian political and economic structure in order to become more competitive in global markets. The Brazilian president has had to embrace the very mechanisms of clientelism that he once so thoroughly criticized to build a political alliance of the center-right. Given a weak party system and constitutional requirements that all amendments survive two majority votes of 60 percent in both houses of congress, clientelism has become

Cardoso's most powerful mechanism for cultivating support. Only with the support of conservative and probusiness groups, who maintain a majority of votes in both houses of congress, does Cardoso believe he will have the wherewithal to implement the constitutional, administrative, and social security reforms needed to restructure the economy.

This strategy has created serious paradoxes for the Brazilian president. Rather than strengthen Brazil's weak political parties and fragmented legislature, Cardoso's tactics have reinforced the factors that make the country's democratic institutions anemic. By kowtowing to clientelistic interests, Cardoso's administration has put on hold reforms to the electoral and party system. In the process, members of his own party, the Brazilian Social Democratic Party (PSDB), have rebuked the president for cultivating support from other parties, particularly the conservative Liberal Front Party (PFL), and sometimes hurting his own social democrats in congressional and gubernatorial contests. By wooing many conservative interests, mostly in the north and northeast regions, Cardoso has strengthened groups that oppose significant agrarian reform, income distribution, and improvements in social services. Most important, his strategy has depended on increased spending, financed with public debt at high interest. The result has been a soaring deficit and public debt. The devaluation of the real in early 1999 will only add to these problems and perhaps bring inflation back.

Despite the heady rhetoric of Cardoso's 1994 presidential campaign and the rising expectations of long-frustrated social democrats inside and outside Brazil, the new president has offered little in the way of changing Brazilian politics for the long haul. Cardoso has made only token progress on the country's persisting social inequalities. The Real Plan reduced the eroding effect of mega-inflation on the incomes of the poor, boosting consumption for millions of Brazilians. But other policies have been less effective. Economic liberalization has caused thousands of Brazilian firms to shave their labor costs, putting hundreds of thousands of Brazilians out of work. As urban unemployment has increased, so has urban violence and crime. The government distributed more land to poor people in rural areas, but these efforts have failed to make a dent in Brazil's concentrated system of land tenure. Education and health reform have received only lip service from the administration.

Both the fiscal and the environmental limits to Brazil's economic development have been stretched almost to their breaking points. Even without a significant downturn in the global economy, the fate of the Brazilian economy is being threatened by the state's burgeoning indebtedness, the inability to cut public spending, and the social and ecological costs of the maldistribution of income and the abuse of natural resources. The tendency to see solutions to Brazil's economic problems in terms of promoting exports and enlarging the economy only deepens these problems. Considering that many of Brazil's exports are still extractive (e.g., iron ore, lumber) these recommendations place ever more pressure on the country's ecology. The quality of life of most Brazilians can only suffer as a result.

The challenges facing Brazil and the way that the country's political leaders have chosen to deal with them are similar to experiences elsewhere. The Brazilian state lacks the resources to promote development as it did during the days of Vargas, Kubitschek, and military rule. As the needs of the Brazilian citizenry grow, the state appears less capable, and political leaders less willing, to respond. With the advent of the Real Plan, the priorities have been to attract foreign capital, boost export earnings, and favor the highest bidders in the privatization of public firms. The developmentalist state lives on only in some BNDES policies. Like former state-led industrializers India, Mexico, and France, Brazil has turned in the neoliberal direction, limiting the state's role in the economy. This shift in the state's organization reminds us of the importance of our theme highlighting critical junctures in state formation.

In contrast to the corporatist and populist role of the state, the moderating power in Brazilian history, the central state has today become a far more passive agent in society. Brazilian workers no longer negotiate labor issues with state mediation, as they still do in Germany. Instead, labor unions, when they are capable, negotiate directly with business. In most cases,

given high urban unemployment, the interests of business usually prevail. Urban workers receive little or no compensation from the state when they suffer layoffs or reductions in their salaries and workplace benefits. Most rural workers, the millions in the informal sector, and minorities are in an even more precarious position as they lack the few benefits and protections enjoyed by salaried, urban workers. The weakness of the judiciary, the abusive use of police authority, and the tendency to vigilantism and class conflict in poor, rural areas reinforce the anemia of a civil society that increasingly discounts its role in politics.

In this context, Brazilian democracy has suffered greatly, the importance of which we highlighted in our theme of the democratic challenge. The poor feel doubly divorced from politics, as they are both socially and politically disenfranchised from a process they view as unresponsive to their needs. Over time, this sense of disengagement has turned into open doubt about the utility of democracy itself. Stories of official corruption and the popular assumption that a politician's priority is his or her own pocketbook reinforce the idea that representatives are unaccountable to their constituencies. The weakness of political party loyalties and the fragmentation of interests compound the problem of accountability. By contrast, much stronger democracies such as Germany, the United States, France, and Britain rely on well-defined rules that force political leaders to be accountable to other branches of government and to their own constituencies. Brazil's example has shown how difficult it is to embrace the democratic idea without these structures.

While some of Brazil's problems are unique, many take the same form they do elsewhere. Like all other major economies in the world, Brazil's is well integrated into the global economy. Despite the country's current problems with monetary stability and debt, Brazil is one of the world's key platforms for agricultural production and manufacturing. Brazil's share of the world market in iron ore, textiles, footwear, steel, machine parts, and autos makes it an important hub in the multinational production of several industrial products. Brazil is a crucial supplier of raw materials as well as a large market for multinational producers. As such, it has advantages few other developing countries enjoy. That also means, however, that Brazilian firms and workers (not to mention the public sector itself) must be able to adapt to greater competition from abroad and the needs of foreign capital. Given the speed with which technology outpaces itself, the pressure to train workers, boost productivity, and enhance research and development has grown tremendously. Brazil is struggling just to keep pace with globalization.

As globalization and democratization have made Brazilian politics less predictable, older questions about what it means to be Brazilian have reemerged. Brazil highlights the point made in the discussion of our theme on political identities in the Introduction that political identities are often reshaped in changed circumstances. What it means to be Brazilian has become a more complex question given the way that Brazil, like the rest of the world, has been bombarded by foreign consumer images. Democracy has given ordinary Brazilians more of a voice, and they have used it to forge their own understandings, but mostly on local issues, not at the national level. Women, nongovernmental organizations, Catholics, pentecostals, blacks, landless peasants, and residents of *favelas* have all organized in recent years around social and cultural issues. On the one hand, these movements have placed additional pressure on an already weakened state to deliver goods and services. On the other hand, these groups have supplied alternatives to the state by providing their own systems of social and cultural support. As the domain of the state in other countries is constrained by the need to compete in the global economy, space is created for nonstate actors to provide goods and services that were previously produced by the state. What is missing in all of this is a sense of the "national question." How are all these disparate groups linked? Do they have a common, national interest? If they are increasingly disconnected, then the proliferation of social movements and organizations is only a symptom of the wider disengagement from the state and political society already being practiced by most Brazilians.

Brazilian Politics in Comparative Perspective

The most important lesson that Brazil offers for the broader study of comparative politics is that frag-

mented polities threaten democracy, social development, and nation-building. The Brazilian political order is fragmented on several levels. The central state is fragmented by conflicts between the executive and the legislature, divided alliances and self-interested politicians in the congress, decentralized government, and an indecisive judiciary with a complicated structure and an uncertain mission. Political parties are fragmented by clientelism and electoral rules that create incentives for politicians and voters to ignore party labels. Finally, civil society itself is fragmented into numerous, often conflictual, organizations, interest groups, professional associations, social movements, churches, and most important, social classes and ethnic identities.

In some societies that are similarly fragmented, such as the United States and India, institutions have proven successful in bridging the gaps between individualistic pursuits and the demand of the people for good government. Rich systems of social organization and reciprocity that are linked to the state through political parties, parliaments, and even informal associations help to strengthen democracy in these countries. Where these systems are faulty, as they are in Brazil, fragmentation reinforces the weakness of the state and the society.

Recent Brazilian politics show that a weak state deepens the citizenry's sense that all politics is corrupt. Although corruption is present in all polities to some degree, it does not by itself produce the angry disengagement from politics that has emerged in Brazil. Much more is wrong with the Brazilian political order. Police brutality, judicial incompetence, and the inability of bureaucratic agencies to respond to social demands have just as powerful an effect in legitimizing civil disengagement.

This only reinforces the importance of creating systems of accountability to reduce the corruption, police abuse, and bureaucratic incompetence that have given rise to these doubts. Unfortunately, the English word *accountability* has no counterpart in either Portuguese or Spanish. Given Brazil's (and Latin America's) long history of oligarchical rule and social exclusion, the notion of making elites accountable to the people is so alien that the languages of the region lack the required vocabulary. Systems of accountability must be built from the ground up; they must be nurtured in local government and in community organizations and then in the governments of states and the central state. The judiciary, political parties, the media, and civil societal organizations must be able to play enforcement and watchdog roles. These are the building blocks of accountability, and the accountability of political elites is the fulcrum of democracy.

Without a system of elite accountability, representation of the citizenry is impossible. The 60 percent of the Brazilian population that is classified as poor or close to that status has few autonomous organizations to pressure government. More than business, labor, or professional groups, the poor depend on their elected officials to find solutions to their problems. Brazilian politicians have shown that through demagoguery and personalism, they can be elected. But being elected is not the same as guaranteeing a constituency its right to be represented. For this to occur, institutions must make political elites accountable to the people that elected them. When that condition is met, genuine representation of citizens' interests becomes possible.

Political fragmentation can also have a virulent effect on a country's sense of national purpose. Collective identities, by definition, require mechanisms that forge mutual understandings among groups of people. Fractured societies turn to age-old ethnic identities that, as the Balkan and Nigerian experiences demonstrate, can produce destructive, internecine conflict. In Brazil such extreme conflict has been avoided, but the divisive effects of a fragmented polity on collective identities are serious nonetheless. Divided by class, poor Brazilians continue to feel that politics hold no solutions for them, so they fail to mobilize for their rights. Blacks, women, and Indians share some of the same interests because they are paid less than white men are for the same kind of work. Yet few national organizations have been able to unite a coalition of interest groups to change business practices in this regard. Finally, all Brazilians should be concerned with the clearing of rain forests, the pollution of rivers and lakes, and the destruction of species, yet the major political parties and the congress seem incapable of addressing these issues on behalf of future generations. Such national concerns continuously take a backseat to the self-interests of politicians in Brazil.

Perhaps the most serious effect of political fragmentation on Brazil has involved the struggle to achieve the country's interests in an increasingly competitive, global marketplace. While globalization forces all countries, and particularly developing countries, to adapt to new technology, ideas, and economic interests, it also lets states take advantage of the opportunity to attract investment. Given the weakness of the Brazilian state, the social dislocation produced by industrial restructuring (e.g., unemployment), and the currently unstable nature of the international investment climate, Brazil maintains only an ambiguous vision of its role in the global capitalist order. Although Brazilian business, some unions, and key political leaders speak of the need to defend Brazil's interests in the international political economy, the country has few coherent strategies. Such questions are inherently complex and politically difficult, perhaps no less so in Brazil than in France. But dealing with these issues requires a somewhat consistent policy created by a political leadership with clear ideas about the interests of the country. In Brazil's fragmented polity, developing such unambiguous strategies is difficult.

Finally, Brazil's experience with economic restructuring and democratization will continue to influence countries undergoing similar transformations in Latin America and the rest of the developing world. As a large and resource-rich country, Brazil presents a useful example for other big developing countries such as Mexico, Russia, India, and China. Brazil's evolving federal structure as well as its efforts to manage its resources while dealing with environmental costs can inform similar processes in these countries.

As a transitional democracy, Brazil can provide insights into which governance systems work better than others. As a negative example, Brazil's ongoing experiment with presidentialism, multiparty democracy, and open-list PR might well confirm the superiority of alternative parliamentary systems in India and Germany or presidentialism in France and the United States. As a positive example, Brazil's experiences with keeping a diverse country united through trying economic times will have much to teach Russia and Nigeria, as these countries are weighed down by the dual challenges of economic reform and nation-building.

Within Latin America, Brazil continues to consolidate its position as the preeminent economy of the region. Through MERCOSUL, Brazil exerts authority on commercial questions, and with its continued dominance of the Amazon basin, the country's political elite retains the world's attention when they speak on environmental issues in the developing world. Brazil's experiences with balancing the exigencies of neoliberal economic adjustment with the sociopolitical realities of poverty will keep it on center stage as the World Bank and the International Monetary Fund and the region's political, economic, and academic leaders discuss the possibilities for a new model of development.

Brazil may not be "the country of the future," but it is a country with a future. None of the maladies of Brazilian politics and social development are immune to improvement. If political reform is consolidated in the next few years, the groundwork will have been laid for transforming Brazil into a country that deserves the respect of the world.

Key Terms

privatization

moderating power

oligarchy

legitimacy

clientelism

patrimonialism

politics of the governors

interventores

state corporatism

New State

populism

nationalism

bureaucratic
    authoritarianism

state-led development

abertura

personalist politicians

export-led growth

interventionist

import substitution
    industrialization

technocrats

developmentalism

para-statals

nongovernmental
    organizations

informal economy

favelas

bureaucratic rings

proportional
    representation

Suggested Readings

Alvarez, Sonia. *Engendering Democracy in Brazil.* Princeton, N.J.: Princeton University Press, 1990.

Baer, Werner, ed. *The Brazilian Economy: Growth and Development.* 4th ed. New York: Praeger, 1995.

Dean, Warren. *With Broadax and Firebrand: The Destruction of the Brazilian Atlantic Forest.* Berkeley: University of California Press, 1995.

Evans, Peter B. *Dependent Development: The Alliance of Multinational, State, and Local Capital in Brazil.* Princeton, N.J.: Princeton University Press, 1979.

Furtado, Celso. *The Economic Growth of Brazil: A Survey from Colonial to Modern Times.* Berkeley: University of California Press, 1963.

Keck, Margaret. *The Workers' Party and Democratization in Brazil.* New Haven, Conn.: Yale University Press, 1992.

Kingstone, Peter R., and Timothy J. Power, eds. *Democratic Brazil: Actors, Institutions, and Processes.* Pittsburgh: University of Pittsburgh Press, 1999.

Lamounier, Bolivar. "Brazil towards Parliamentarism?" In *The Failure of Presidential Democracy,* ed. Juan Linz and Valenzuela Arturo. Baltimore: Johns Hopkins University Press, 1994.

Mainwaring, Scott. "Brazilian Party Underdevelopment in Comparative Perspective." *Political Science Quarterly* 107, no. 4 (1993).

Matta, Roberto da. *Carnivals, Rogues, and Heroes: An Interpretation of the Brazilian Dilemma.* Notre Dame, Ind.: University of Notre Dame Press, 1991.

Roett, Riordan. *Brazil: Politics in a Patrimonial Society.* 4th ed. New York: Praeger, 1992.

Scheper-Hughes, Nancy. *Death Without Weeping: The Violence of Everyday Life in Brazil.* Berkeley: University of California Press, 1992.

Schneider, Ben Ross. *Politics Within the State: Elite Bureaucrats and Industrial Policy in Authoritarian Brazil.* Pittsburgh: University of Pittsburgh Press, 1991.

Skidmore, Thomas E. *Black into White: Race and Nationality in Brazilian Thought.* Durham, N.C.: Duke University Press, 1993.

———. *The Politics of Military Rule in Brazil, 1964–85.* New York: Oxford University Press, 1988.

Stepan, Alfred. *Rethinking Military Politics: Brazil and the Southern Cone.* Princeton, N.J.: Princeton University Press, 1988.

Stepan, Alfred, ed. *Democratizing Brazil: Problems of Transition and Consolidation.* New York: Oxford University Press, 1989.

Tendler, Judith. *Good Government in the Tropics.* Baltimore: Johns Hopkins University Press, 1997.

Viotti, Emilia. *The Brazilian Empire—Myths and Histories.* Chicago: Chicago University Press, 1985.

Von Mettenheim, Kurt. *The Brazilian Voter: Mass Politics in Democratic Transition, 1974–1986.* Pittsburgh: University of Pittsburgh Press, 1995.

Weyland, Kurt. *Democracy Without Equity: Failures of Reform in Brazil.* Pittsburgh: University of Pittsburgh Press, 1996.

Endnotes

[1] IBGE (Instituto Brasileiro de Geografia e Estatística), *PNAD—Síntese do Indicadores da Pesquisa Básica da PNAD de 1981 a 1989* (Rio de Janeiro: IBGE, 1990). For more on Brazil's multiclassification system, see George Reid Andrews, *Blacks and Whites in São Paulo, Brazil, 1888–1988* (Madison: University of Wisconsin Press, 1991).

[2] See Bertha K. Becker and Claudio A. G. Egler, *Brazil: A New Regional Power in the World Economy: A Regional Geography* (New York: Cambridge University Press, 1992), 5, and Terence Turner, "Brazil: Indigenous Rights vs. Neoliberalism," *Dissent* Summer (1996), 67.

[3] For an analysis of immigration during this period, see Douglas Graham and Thomas Merrick, *Population and Economic Development in Brazil—1800 to the Present* (Baltimore: Johns Hopkins University Press, 1979).

[4] For a complete treatment of state corporatism in Brazil during this period, see Ruth Berins Collier and David Collier, *Shaping the Political Arena: Critical Junctures, the Labor Movement, and Regime Dynamics in Latin America* (Princeton, N.J.: Princeton University Press, 1991), 169–195.

[5] Robert M. Levine, *Father of the Poor? Vargas and His Era,* (New York: Cambridge University Press, 1998), 8–9.

[6] For an analysis of this "new professionalism," see Alfred Stepan, *The Military in Politics: Changing Patterns in Brazil* (Princeton, N.J.: Princeton University Press, 1971).

[7] Thomas E. Skidmore, *Politics in Brazil, 1930–1964: An Experiment in Democracy* (New York: Oxford University Press, 1967), 101.

[8] Ibid.

[9] Maria do Carmo Campello de Souza, *Estado e Partidos Políticos no Brasil (1930 a 1964)* (São Paulo: Editora Alfa-Omega, 1975).

[10] Yousseff Cohen, "The Heresthetics of Coup Making," *Comparative Political Studies* 24; no. 3 (October 1991), 348–355.

[11] Guillermo O'Donnell, *Modernization and Bureaucratic-Authoritarianism: Studies in South American Politics* (Berkeley: Institute of International Studies, University of California, 1973).

[12] Thomas E. Skidmore, *The Politics of Military Rule in Brazil 1964–85* (New York: Oxford University Press, 1988), 49.

[13] Leigh A. Payne, *Brazilian Industrialists and Democratic Change* (Baltimore: Johns Hopkins University Press, 1994), Ch. 4.

[14] For an analysis of these critical elections, see Bolivar Lamounier, "Authoritarian Brazil Revisited: The Impact of Elections on the *Abertura,*" in *Democratizing Brazil: Problems of Transition and Consolidation,* ed. Alfred Stepan (New York: Oxford University Press, 1989), and Kurt von Mettenheim, *The Brazilian Voter: Mass Politics in Democratic Transition, 1974–1986* (Pittsburgh: University of Pittsburgh Press, 1995), 101–103.

[15] Margaret Keck, *The Workers' Party and Democratization in Brazil* (New Haven, Conn.: Yale University Press, 1992), 219–220.

[16] Margaret Keck, "The New Unionism in the Brazilian Transition," in *Democratizing Brazil: Problems of Transition and Consolidation,* ed. Alfred Stepan (New York: Oxford University Press, 1989), 284.

[17] See Celso Furtado, *The Economic Growth of Brazil: A Survey from Colonial to Modern Times* (Berkeley: University of California Press, 1963).

[18] For a description of how the coffee export complex created incentives for the substitution of manufactured imports with domestic production, see Bertha K. Becker and Claudio A. G. Egler, *Brazil: A New Regional Power in the World Economy: A Regional Geography,* 45.

[19] For a more complete treatment of how developmentalist ideas cultivated in ECLA affected policy choices in Brazil, see Kathryn Sikkink, *Ideas and Institutions: Developmentalism in Brazil and Argentina* (Ithaca, N.Y.: Cornell University Press, 1991).

[20] More complete treatment of the ISI experience can be found in Albert O. Hirschman, *A Bias for Hope: Essays on Development and Latin America* (New Haven, Conn.: Yale University Press, 1971).

[21] Peter B. Evans, *Dependent Development: The Alliance of Multinational, State, and Local Capital in Brazil* (Princeton, N.J.: Princeton University Press, 1979).

[22] These and other examples of ecological destruction are analyzed in Werner Baer and Charles C. Mueller, "Environmental Aspects of Brazil's Development," in *The Brazilian Economy: Growth and Development,* 4th ed. Werner Baer (New York: Praeger, 1995).

[23] For more on state environmental efforts, see Barry Ames and Margaret E. Keck, "The Politics of Sustainable Development: Environmental Policy Making in Four Brazilian States," *Journal of Interamerican Studies and World Affairs* 39, no. 4 (Winter 1998–99).

[24] Kathryn Hochstetler, "The Evolution of the Brazilian Environmental Movement and Its Political Roles," in *The New Politics of Inequality in Latin America: Rethinking Participation and Representation,* ed. Douglas Chalmers, Carlos M. Vilas, Katherine R. Hite, Scott B. Martin, Kerianne Piester, and Monique Segarra (New York: Oxford University Press, 1997).

[25] Alfred P. Montero, "Devolving Democracy? Political Decentralization and the New Brazilian Federalism," in *Democratic Brazil: Actors, Institutions, and Processes*, ed. Peter R. Kingstone and Timothy J. Power (Pittsburgh: University of Pittsburgh Press, forthcoming).

[26] Alfred P. Montero, "Getting Real About the Brazilian Real Plan," *Hemisphere* (February 1997).

[27] William C. Smith and Nizar Messari, "Democracy and Reform in Cardoso's Brazil: Caught Between Clientelism and Global Markets?" *The North-South Agenda Papers* 33 (September 1998).

[28] Peggy A. Lovell, "Race, Gender, and Development in Brazil," *Latin American Research Review* 29, no. 3 (1994).

[29] Kurt Weyland, *Democracy Without Equity: Failures of Reform in Brazil* (Pittsburgh: University of Pittsburgh Press, 1996).

[30] Wilson Cano, "Concentración, desconcentración y descentralización en Brasil," in *Territorios en Transformación: Análisis y Propuestas*, ed. José Luis Curbelo, Francisco Alburquerque, Carlos A. de Mattos and Juan Ramón Cuadrado (Madrid: Fondo Europeo de Desarrollo Regional, 1994).

[31] Leonardo Guimarães Neto, "Desigualdades Regionais e Federalismo," in *Desigualdades Regionais e Desenvolvimento*, ed. Rui de Britto Álvares Affonso and Pedro Luiz Barros Silva (São Paulo: FUNDAP, 1995).

[32] Jeffry A. Frieden, *Debt, Development, and Democracy: Modern Political Economy and Latin America, 1965–1985* (Princeton, N.J.: Princeton University Press, 1991), 54–65.

[33] Diana Jean Schemo, "The ABC's of Business in Brazil," *New York Times* July 16, 1998, B1, 7.

[34] Fernando Luiz Abrúcio, *Os Barões da Federação: O Poder dos Governadores no Brasil Pós-Autoritário*. Unpublished master's thesis, Universidade de São Paulo, 1994.

[35] Timothy J. Power, "Politicized Democracy: Competition, Institutions, and 'Civic Fatigue' in Brazil," *Journal of Interamerican Studies and World Affairs* 33, no. 3 (Fall 1991).

[36] Thomas J. Trebat, *Brasil's State-Owned Enterprises: A Case Study of the State as Entrepreneur* (New York: Cambridge University Press, 1983).

[37] Helen Shapiro, *Engines of Growth: The State and Transnational Auto Companies in Brazil* (New York: Cambridge University Press, 1994).

[38] Peter B. Evans, "Predatory, Developmental, and Other Apparatuses: A Comparative Political Economy Perspective on the Third World State," *Sociological Forum* 4, no. 4 (1989).

[39] Alfred P. Montero, "State Interests and the New Industrial Policy in Brazil: The Case of the Privatization of Steel, 1990–1994," *Journal of Interamerican Studies and World Affairs* 40, no. 3 (Fall 1998).

[40] Carlos H. Acuña and William C. Smith, "The Politics of Arms Production and the Arms Race among the New Democracies of Argentina, Brazil, and Chile," in *Security, Democracy, and Development in U.S.-Latin American Relations*, ed. Lars Schoultz, William C. Smith, and Augusto Varas (New Brunswick, N. J.: Transaction Publishers, 1994).

[41] Wendy Hunter, *Eroding Military Influence in Brazil: Politicians Against Soldiers* (Chapel Hill: University of North Carolina Press, 1997).

[42] Paulo Sérgio Pinheiro, "Popular Responses to State-Sponsored Violence in Brazil," in *The New Politics of Inequality in Latin America: Rethinking Participation and Representation*, ed. Douglas Chalmers, Carlos M. Vilas, Katherine R. Hite, Scott B. Martin, Kerianne Piester, and Monique Segarra (New York: Oxford University Press, 1997).

[43] Human Rights Watch, *Police Brutality in Urban Brazil* (New York: Human Rights Watch, 1997), 13.

[44] Judith Tendler, *Good Government in the Tropics* (Baltimore: Johns Hopkins University Press, 1997).

[45] For a study of how these exceptions have emerged in Brazil, see Barbara Geddes, *Politician's Dilemma: Building State Capacity in Latin America* (Berkeley: University of California Press, 1994).

[46] Ben Ross Schneider, *Politics Within the State: Elite Bureaucrats and Industrial Policy in Authoritarian Brazil* (Pittsburgh: University of Pittsburgh Press, 1991).

[47] Lívia Neves de H. Barbosa, "The Brazilian Jeitinho: An Exercise in National Identity," in *The Brazilian Puzzle: Culture on the Borderlands of the Western World*, ed. David J. Hess and Roberto A. DaMatta (New York: Columbia University Press, 1995).

[48] Barry Ames, "Electoral Strategy under Open-List Proportional Representation," *American Journal of Political Science* 39, no. 2 (May 1995).

[49] Juan J. Linz and Alfred Stepan, *Problems of Democratic Transition and Consolidation: Southern Europe, South America, and Post-Communist Europe* (Baltimore: Johns Hopkins University Press, 1996), Ch. 11.

[50] Scott Mainwaring, "Brazilian Party Underdevelopment in Comparative Perspective," *Political Science Quarterly* 107 (1993).

[51] Timothy J. Power, "The Pen is Mightier than the Congress: Presidential Decree Power in Brazil," in *Executive Decree Authority: Calling Out the Tanks or Just Filling Out the Forms?*, ed. John M. Carey and Mathew S. Shugart (New York: Cambridge University Press, 1998).

[52] Scott Mainwaring, "Brazilian Party Underdevelopment in Comparative Perspective," 692.

[53] See especially Gilberto Freyre, *The Mansions and the Shanties: The Making of Modern Brazil* (New York: Knopf, 1963), Ch. 12.

[54] Ralph Della Cava, "The 'People's Church,' the Vatican, and *Abertura,"* in *Democratizing Brazil: Problems of Transition and Consolidation,* ed. Alfred Stepan (New York: Oxford University Press, 1989).

[55] Terence Turner, "Brazil: Indigenous Rights vs. Meoliberalism," 67.

[56] William H. Fisher, "Megadevelopment, Environmentalism, and Resistance: The Institutional Context of Kayapó Indigenous Politics in Central Brazil," *Human Organization* 53, no. 3 (1994).

CHAPTER 6

Nigeria

Richard Joseph
Peter Lewis
Darren Kew
Scott Taylor

Federal Republic of Nigeria

Land and Population

Capital   Abuja*

Total Area (square miles)   356,669 (more than twice the size of California)

Population   118 million

Annual Average Population Growth Rate (1990–1997)   2.9%

Age Structure

under 15	45.6%
15–29	25.7%
30–44	15.7%
45–59	8.5%
60–74	3.8%
75 and over	0.7%

Urban Population   41%

Ethno-Linguistic Composition

Hausa-Fulani	32%
Yoruba	21%
Igbo	18%
Ibibio	6%
Various dialects	14%
Other	8%

Official Language   English

Religious Affiliation

Muslim	50%
Christian	40%
Indigenous	10%

Economy

Domestic Currency   Naira

Total GNP (US$) $30.7 billion

GNP *per capita* (US$) $260

GNP *per capita* at purchasing power parity (US$) $880

GNP average annual growth rate (1996–1997)   4.2%

GNP *per capita* average annual growth rate

1996–1997	1.2%
1980–1995	–0.8%
1965–1980	4.2%

Income Gap:
GDP per capita (US$)

Richest 20% of population	$3796
Poorest 20% of population	$308

Structure of Production (% of GDP)

Agriculture	28%
Industry	53%
Services	18%

Labor Force Distribution (% of total)

Agriculture	43%
Industry	7%
Services	50%

Exports as % of GDP   19%

Imports as % of GDP   44%

Society

Life Expectancy   Female 53.0   Male 49.8

Doctors per 100,000 population   21

Infant Mortality per 1000 live births   114

*On 12 December 1991 the capital was officially moved from Lagos to Abuja; many government offices remain in Lagos pending completion of facilities in Abuja

---

Adult Literacy

Female	47.3%
Male	67.3%

Access to Information and Communications (per 1000 population)

Radios	197
Televisions	38
Telephones	4
Personal Computers	*Data Not Available for Nigeria*

Women in Government and Economy

Seats in Parliament held by Women	N/A
Women at Ministerial level	4.0%
Women as % of total labor force	36.0%
Female Business Administrators and Managers	6.0%
Female Professional and Technical Workers	26.0%

1998 Human Development Index ranking (out of 174 countries, 1 = highest)   142

Political Organization

Political System   Military dictatorship (until May 1999)

Regime History   A military regime led by General Abdulsalami Abubakar assumed power after the death of General Sani Abacha in June 1998. This military regime is the fourth since 1983, interrupted only by the 3-month unelected civilian regime of Ernest Shonekan in 1993.

Administrative Structure   Power has been centralized within the military governing body and the Provisional Ruling Council (PRC). However, a system of 36 federal states, plus the Federal Capital Territory (FCT) in Abuja, also exists. Since May 1999, the presidential system resembles that of the U.S.

Executive   Retired General Olusegun Obasanjo was elected president in February 1999 and began a four-year term in May 1999.

Legislature   A bicameral civilian legislature was elected in February 1999. The 109 senators were elected on the basis of equal representation: three from each state, and one from the FCT. The 360 members of the House of Representatives were elected from single-member districts.

Judiciary   The Nigerian judicial system resembles that of the U.S. with a network of local and district courts as well as state-level courts. The state-level judiciaries are subordinate to the Federal Court of Appeal and the Supreme Court of Nigeria, which consists of 15 appointed associate justices and the chief justice. Every state of the federation can also opt to establish a system of Islamic law (*shari'a*) courts for cases involving only Muslims in customary disputes (divorce, property, etc.); the secular courts, however, retain supreme jurisdiction at the federal level if any conflict arises over which system to use. Most Nigerian states feature such courts, which share a Federal *Shari'a* Court of Appeal in Abuja. All levels of the judiciary have been subject to manipulation and corruption by the military regimes.

Party System   Three parties were registered by the Nigerian electoral commission in December 1998: the Alliance for Democracy (AD), All People's Party (APP), and People's Democratic Party (PDP). PDP won the presidency, majorities in both houses of the National Assembly, and control of many of the governorships, state assemblies, and local governments.

Section ❶ The Making of the Modern Nigerian State

Politics in Action

On June 7, 1998, General Sani Abacha, Nigeria's most brutal and corrupt dictator, was poised to have himself declared president. He had orchestrated a three-year sham transition program to mask his own plans to remain in power. In the process, he stalled the economy and stole billions of dollars in oil revenue; murdered, imprisoned, or drove his opponents into exile; and made Nigeria an international pariah.

Then, on June 8, 1998, he suddenly died.

Many southern Nigerians filled the streets of Lagos and other cities to celebrate—until the military announced that another northerner, General Abubakar, was taking charge. Many northerners expressed quiet relief at Abacha's passing but feared a possible backlash from a southern military leader—until Abubakar was sworn in. Although Nigeria has developed well beyond the point in the 1950s when its leaders saw it as a mere geographic expression, the development of national consciousness and character has often progressed *in spite of* the nation's political direction. Many Nigerians intermarry across ethnic and religious lines, share common traditions like chewing kola nuts with friends, work—often their whole lives—and invest in cities outside their ethnic homelands, and unite in support of their national sports teams. Yet when talk turns to politics, southern Nigerians will complain of northern domination of the government, Igbos will claim that Yorubas cannot be trusted for their "betrayal" of Biafra during the civil war, Christians will complain that Muslims want an Islamic fundamentalist state, and so on. Forces of both integration and dissolution are evident throughout the country's independent history, with one or the other being most prevalent at any moment.

Nigeria offers, within a single case, characteristics that identify Africa. These opposing forces are rooted in the constant struggle in Nigeria between **authoritarian** and democratic governance, the push for development and the persistence of underdevelopment, the burden of public corruption and the pressure for accountability. Nigeria, like all African countries, has sought to create a viable nation-state out of the social incoherence created by the borders imposed during the colonial era. Over two hundred and fifty competing nationalities—or ethnic groups, largely defined by language differences—in Nigeria have repeatedly clashed over economic and political resources. All these factors combine to produce the political entity known as Nigeria with a very low level of popular **legitimacy** and **accountability** and an increasing inability to meet the most basic needs of its citizens. The country therefore provides a crucible in which to examine questions of democracy and authoritarianism, the pressures and management of ethnic conflict, and economic underdevelopment brought about both by colonial oppression and independent Nigeria's mismanagement of its vast resources.

Much about Nigeria is controversial. Since gaining independence from British colonial rule in 1960, Nigeria has undergone several political transitions, from democratic governments to autocratic regimes, both military and civilian, and from one military regime to another. After nearly four decades as an independent nation, Nigeria has yet to witness an orderly and constitutional transition from one democratic regime to another. It has experienced six successful coups (most recently in November 1993) and many unsuccessful attempted coups, and it was torn by three years of civil war that claimed over one hundred thousand military, and over a million civilian, casualties. Against this background, Nigeria today remains essentially an **unfinished state** characterized by instabilities and uncertainties.

Another critical turning point was reached in 1999 as a military government transferred power to civilians for the third time. Whether the country is moving toward an increasingly authoritarian future and greater underdevelopment, or toward the achievement of democracy and sustainable growth, remains unresolved.

The saying, "As Nigeria goes, so goes the rest of sub-Saharan Africa" may again be relevant. With a population of 110 million, Nigeria is by far the largest country in Africa and among the ten most populous countries in the world. About one out of every five

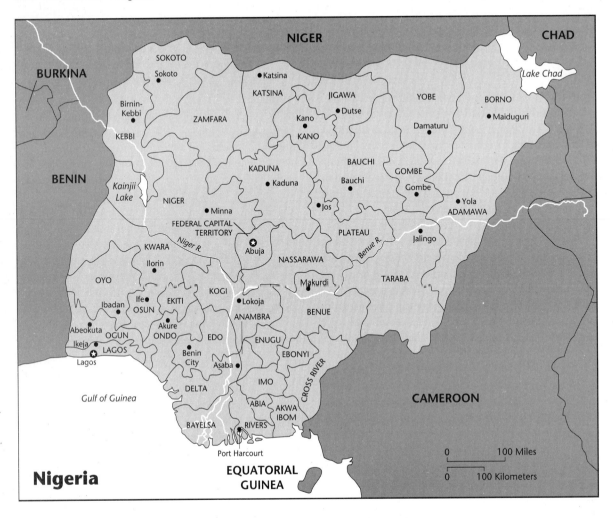

Nigeria

black Africans is a Nigerian. Unlike most other countries on the continent, Nigeria has the human and material resources to overcome the vicious cycle of poverty and **autocracy**. Hopes for this breakthrough for four decades of independent rule have been regularly frustrated, however. If Nigeria, with its vast resources, cannot succeed in breaking this cycle, what does that mean for the rest of sub-Saharan Africa?

Geographic Setting

Nigeria's 110 million people, inhabiting 356,668 square miles, live in the most populous nation in Africa. A center of West African regional trade, culture, and military strength, Nigeria is bordered by four countries: Benin, Niger, Chad, and Cameroon, and by the Gulf of Guinea in the Atlantic Ocean to the south. The modern-day country of Nigeria, however, like nearly all the contemporary states in Africa, is not even a century old.

Nigeria was a British colony from 1914 until its independence on October 1, 1960, although foreign domination of much of the territory had actually begun in the mid-nineteenth century. Britain first ruled northern and southern Nigeria as two separate colonies. Nigeria's identity took its final geographic form (at least in terms of its *external* borders) in 1914 following Britain's amalgamation of its Northern and Southern Protectorates.

Nigeria's location in West Africa, its size, and its oil-producing status have made it a hub of regional activity. In terms of demography and political economy, Nigeria overwhelms the other fifteen countries in West Africa, with a population equivalent to 57 percent of the region's total. Moreover, Nigeria's GNP typically represents more than two-thirds of the total GNP for the entire subregion. Not surprisingly, therefore, Nigeria has been a recipient of migrant labor from the region, and has engaged in recent years in peacekeeping missions, which has involved armed intervention in countries such as Liberia and Sierra Leone. However, Nigerian instability and the succession of military governments have also been a source of instability and uncertainty in the wider region.

Nigeria's ethnic map can be divided into six inexact areas or zones. The northwest (or "core North") is dominated by Nigeria's largest ethnic group, the Hausa-Fulani, two formerly separate groups that over the past century have largely merged. The northeast has minority groups, the largest of which is the Kanuri. Both regions in the north are predominantly Muslim. A large swath of territory stretching across the center of the country, called the Middle Belt, is also home to a wide range of minority groups of both Muslim and Christian identification. The southwest (referred to as the Western Region in the First Republic) is dominated by the country's second largest ethnic group, the Yoruba, who are approximately 40 percent Muslim, 40 percent Christian (primarily Protestant), and 20 percent practitioners of Yoruba indigenous beliefs. The southeast (which formed the hub of the First Republic's Eastern Region) is the homeland of the Igbo, Nigeria's third largest group, who are primarily Roman Catholic, although Protestant evangelical movements have recently been popular. Between the Yoruba and the Igbo regions of the south is the southern minority zone, which stretches across the Niger Delta areas and east along the coast as far as Cameroon.

Critical Junctures

A number of critical junctures helped shape the character of the Nigerian state, and illustrate the difficult path that the country has taken during the past century. This path features influences from the precolonial period, British colonialism, the alternation of military and civilian rule after independence, and the post-1980 economic collapse, precipitated by Nigeria's political corruption and overreliance on its petroleum industry.

The Precolonial Period (800–1860)

State Formation   Much of Nigeria's precolonial history before A.D. 1000 was reconstructed from oral histories because, with few exceptions, a literate culture evolved much later. In contrast to the peoples of the forest belt to the south, the more open terrain in the north, with its need for irrigation, encouraged the early growth of centralized states. Such states from the eighth century included Kanem-Bornu in the northeast and the Hausa states in the west. The more prominent Hausa states that included walled cities were Kano, Katsina, Zazzau (also called Zaria), Rano, Daura, Gobir, and Biram. Still another attempt at state formation led to the emergence of Jukun kingdom; however, by the end of the seventeenth century, the Jukun became a tributary state of the Bornu empire.

A major element that shaped the course of events in the savanna areas of the north was trade across the Sahara Desert with northern Africa. Trade brought material benefits as well as Arabic education and Islam, which gradually replaced traditional, spiritual, political, and social practices in what is now northern Nigeria. In 1808 the Fulani, who came from lands west of modern Nigeria through holy war (**jihad**), established an Islamic empire, the Sokoto Caliphate. Portions of the region to the south, the Middle Belt, were able to repel the jihad and preserve their independence and religious diversity. The Sokoto Caliphate used Islam and a common language, Hausa, to forge unity out of the disparate groups in the north. The Fulani empire held sway until British colonial authority was imposed on northern Nigeria by 1900.

Toward the southern edge of the savanna lived such groups as the Tiv, whose political organizations seldom extended beyond the village level. Within such societies, politics was generally conducted along lineage and kinship lines. Political authority was diffused rather than centralized. Considering their loose political structures, it is not surprising that they were later described by Western contacts as "stateless societies." Under colonialism, these societies escaped

Critical Junctures in Modern Nigeria's Political Development

1960	Independence. Nigeria consists of three regions under a Westminster parliamentary model. **Abubakar Tafawa Balewa**, a northerner, is the first prime minister.
January 1966	Civilian government deposed in coup. **General Aguiyi Ironsi**, an Igbo, becomes head of state.
July 1966	Countercoup led by **General Yakubu Gowon**, an Anga from the Middle Belt, with aid from northern groups.
1967–1970	Biafran civil war.
July 1975	Military coup deposes Gowon; led by **General Murtala Muhammed**, a northerner.
February 1976	Murtala Muhammed assassinated in failed coup led by Middle Belt minorities. Muhammed's second-in-command, **General Olusegun Obasanjo**, a Yoruba, assumes power.
September 1978	New constitution completed, marking the adoption of the U.S. presidential model in a federation with 19 states.
October 1979	Elections held. A majority in both houses is won by NPN, led by Northern/Hausa-Fulani groups. **Alhaji Shehu Shagari** is elected Nigeria's first executive president.
December 1983	Military coup led by **General Muhammadu Buhari**, a northerner.
August 1985	Buhari is overthrown by **General Ibrahim B. Babangida**, a Middle-Belt Muslim, in a palace coup. Babangida promises a return to democracy by 1990, a date he delays five times before being forced from office.

June 12, 1993	**Moshood Abiola** wins presidential elections, but Babangida annuls the election 11 days later.
August 1993	Babangida installs **Ernest Shonekan** as "interim civilian president" until new presidential elections could be held later that autumn.
November 1993	Defense Minister **General Sani Abacha** seizes power in a coup.
July–Sept. 1994	Pro-democracy strike by the major oil union, NUPENG, cuts Nigeria's oil production by an estimated 25 percent. Sympathy strikes ensue, followed by arrests of political and civic leaders.
October 1995	General Abacha announces a three-year transition to civilian rule.
November 1995	Ogoni-rights activists Ken Saro-Wiwa and eight others hung. Nigeria is suspended from the Commonwealth.
June 1998	General Abacha dies; succeeded by **General Abdulsalami Abubakar**, a Middle-Belt Muslim from Babangida's hometown.
July–August 1998	Abubakar releases nearly all political prisoners and installs a new transition program. Parties are allowed to form unhindered.
February 1999	Former head of state **Olusegun Obasanjo** and his party, the PDP, sweep the Presidential and National Assembly elections, adding to their majority control of state and local government seats.
May 1999	Obasanjo sworn in as president; the federation now contains 36 states.

much of the upheaval experienced by the centralized states and retained much of their autonomy.

The development of collective identities was equally complex in what is today southern Nigeria. Groups included the highly centralized empires and kingdoms of Oyo and Ife (now identified with the Yoruba), Benin to the west, the fragmentary, **acephalous societies** to the east (now identified with the Igbo), and the trading city-states of the Niger Delta and its hinterland.

Precolonial Polities and Societies. *Source:* K. Michael Barbour, Julius Oguntoyinbo, J.O.C. Onyemelukwe, and James C. Nwafor, *Nigeria in Maps* (New York: Africana Publishing Company, 1982), 37.

Precolonial Nigeria

Lake Chad

GOBIR
KATSINA
Sokoto   KEBBI   DAURA
KANO
BORNU
YAWURI   ZAZZAU (Zaria)
Bauchi/Plateau Societies
BORGU   Nok   JUKUN   Benue River
NUPE   (Kororofo)
Niger River
OYO   TIV   ADAMAWA
IFE   IGALA   IDOMA
IJEBU
BENIN   IGBO
DELTA   EFIK

.... Approximate limits of Sokoto Caliphate

0   100 Miles
0   100 Kilometers

Contact with Europeans along the coast and the hinterland generated social conflicts and tensions, and provoked the subsequent loss of autonomy for these polities. External factors led to the eventual disintegration of the Oyo empire in the early nineteenth century through attacks from the Dahomey kingdom to the west (now in the neighboring country of Benin) and Islamic jihadists from the Fulani empire to the north.

The Emergence of the Democratic Idea Several precolonial societies had democratic elements that scholars speculate might have led to more open and participatory polities had they not been stymied by colonialism. Among the Yoruba and Igbo communities, in particular, an important feature of governance was the doctrine of *accountability*: rulers could not disregard the views and interests of the governed or they would risk revocation of that consent and loss of their positions. Another element was *representation*, defined less in terms of procedures for selecting leaders than in terms of the representativeness of those who

governed, to ensure that the ruler and ruled adhered to culturally mandated principles and obligations.

Among the shared traits of many precolonial African societies were tales of origin that traced their political communities to a particular god, heaven, or mythical ancestor. The pervasive role of religion in the theory and practice of governance ensured that the use of social power was legitimized by divine and supernatural forces. Thus, many precolonial African political systems were theocratic and absolutist in their demand for loyalty, yet these theocratic elements provided important limits to the exercise of power. These limits were further strengthened by additional social structures such as councils of chiefs, secret societies, warrior bands, and age-grade associations. "Use-of-power" contracts in which the people could invoke ancestral spirits against a ruler who had abused his authority were not uncommon in precolonial societies. Moreover, the rights of both the ruler and the ruled were defined in communal rather than personal terms. The survival of the individual and the ruler therefore depended on the survival of the community. Not surprisingly, crimes against society often received more severe punishment than crimes against the individual.

Modes of participation in decision-making in precolonial societies also reflected aspects of the democratic idea. For example, popular discussions preceded public policy decisions in the acephalous societies of the Middle Belt as well as among the Igbos in the east. The age-based system of rule often meant that popular discussions occurred in councils of elders and similar institutions, thereby conferring on older persons greater powers to influence decisions. The southern empires and kingdoms featured what was essentially a constitutional monarch whose authority depended on the council of chiefs, the deities, and various corporate bodies that could articulate public views.

Among the Islamic communities of the north, political society was highly structured in line with Islamic principles established in the Qur'an. Leadership structures were considerably more hierarchical than those of the south, dominated by a few educated elites in positions of authority. In addition, although some of the pre-Islamic indigenous beliefs showed deference to important women spirit leaders, women were consigned to a subordinate position in systems of governance. The Islamic Fulani empire was a confederation in which the rulers, **emirs**, owed allegiance to the sultan, who was the temporal and spiritual head of the empire. The sultan's powers, in turn, were circumscribed by the obligation to observe the principles of Islam in fulfilling his duties.

Colonial Rule and Its Impact (1860–1960)

Competition for trade and empire drove the European imperial powers into Africa after 1860. During the colonial period Nigeria's resources were extracted, and its people exploited as cheap labor, to further the growth of British society and defray administrative costs of the British Empire. Colonialism left its imprint on all aspects of Nigeria's existence, bequeathing a British political system that was inappropriate in many respects.

Where centralized monarchies existed, particularly in the north, the British ruled indirectly, allowing traditional structures to persist subsidiary to the British governor and a small administrative apparatus.

Where more nearly democratic societies existed, particularly in the Igbo east, the colonialists strengthened the authority of traditional chiefs and kings and appointed **warrant chiefs**, weakening the rulers' accountability to the ruled and restricting or barring indigenous popular participation. Colonial regimes used these policies across Africa, upsetting older traditions that had checked the powers of rulers in many precolonial African polities.

By empowering certain individuals and groups and weakening others, the British left a heritage of harsh authoritarian domination that persists today. They instilled the idea that there were two sets of rules: one for political leaders and another for the citizenry. This dual standard left a conflicted democratic idea: formal democratic institutions dependent upon an authoritarian political culture. Colonialism also contributed to strengthening the collective identities of Nigeria's multiple ethnic groups by fostering competition among them, primarily among the three largest: the Hausa-Fulani, the Yoruba, and the Igbo.

Foundations of Nigeria's Political Economy The colonial experience helped shape the character of the Nigerian state in relation to the international capitalist system. Nigeria first entered the modern international economy as a colonial territory and had to operate within terms designed by more dominant and experienced members of the international system. Nigeria has since found it difficult to overcome its colonial political economy, structured by the British to export primary products.

Moreover, the concept of the state introduced into the colony was a set of administrative, legal, and coercive systems whose overriding purpose was to restructure relationships within and between civil society and public authority in order to subordinate the local economy to European capitalism. The Nigerian colonial state was conceived and fashioned as **interventionist**, in which the state intrudes into the major sectors of the economy and society. It was unhindered in the pursuit of its economic objectives, in contrast to the British state, where political freedoms and market capitalism limited state action.

The principal goals of the colonial enterprise were to maintain tight control over the Nigerian economy and the flow of resources from the colonies to Britain.

Of secondary concern was the creation of an economic environment driven by free markets and private enterprise. Nigeria's interventionist state went deep into the management of the economy, tightly controlling and frequently establishing significant ownership positions in areas as diverse as agriculture, banking, commerce, manufacturing, transportation, mining, education, health, and employment. The problems caused by such massive state intervention in Nigeria have continued to plague it since the pattern was first established in the colonial era.

Impact of Colonialism on Democratic Ideas
Colonialism introduced a cultural dualism—a clash of customs, values, and political systems—between the traditions of precolonial society and the dictates of the West. Traditional cultural traits, which had ensured accountability in society, were partly replaced with the ideas of individualism. The religious beliefs of traditional society, particularly as they pertained to governance and accountability, were also altered by colonialism and its Christian god, who was not directly concerned with issues of daily governance as were the deities of traditional beliefs. The marginalization of traditional norms and rulers early in the colonial regime caused a weakening of the indigenous basis for the accountability of rulers and the social responsibility of the governed as well as of age-old checks on abuse of office.

Colonial rule left Nigeria with the machinery of parliamentary democracy following the Westminster model but socialized the local population to be passive subjects rather than responsive participants. Even as colonial rule sought to implant democracy in principle, in practice it was a form of military rule that bequeathed an authoritarian legacy to independent Nigeria.

This dualism led to the development of two public realms to which individuals belonged: the communal realm, in which people are identified by ethnic or subethnic groups (Igbo, Tiv, Yoruba, etc.) and the civic realm under the colonial administration and its imposed institutions, in which citizenship was universal.[1] Both realms fed on each other, though the communal realm was often stronger in certain respects than the civic realm. For the populace, questions as to how one's citizenship is defined and to which group one owes primary loyalty are unresolved. For those in government, questions persist about whose interests should be served at any given time, the national or the parochial? Because they saw the advent of the colonial civic realm and the colonial state as an alien, exploitative force, Nigerians tend to view its postcolonial successor as the realm from which rights must be extracted and from which duties and taxes must be withheld (see Section 4).

As colonial powers did elsewhere in Africa, Britain had to build a support system of Nigerians to incorporate into the management structure of the colony in order to limit the drain on the empire's overtaxed resources. These individuals were carefully selected from the traditional elite and rulers who were willing to work with the colonial government under a system of governance known as **indirect rule**. An indigenous bureaucracy was trained primarily in the south, where Christianity and Western education penetrated. In the north, where more developed, hierarchical political structures were already present and the British had significantly less penetration, they utilized indigenous structures and left intact the emirate authorities and Islamic institutions of the region.

Colonialism thus had profoundly different effects on the northern and southern regions. The south experienced both the benefits and burdens of colonial occupation. The proximity of Lagos, Calabar, and their regions to the Atlantic Ocean made them important hubs for trade and shipping activity, around which the British built the necessary infrastructure—schools, roads, ports, and the like—and a large African civil service in order to facilitate colonialism. Northern Nigeria, which was administered with less direct contact from British personnel, received few of these benefits. The north was remote from the shipping capitals of the south and possessed fewer resources of interest to the colonialists. Moreover, indirect rule largely preserved the north's traditional administration. A pattern of uneven development resulted, with the south enjoying the basis for a modern economy and exposure to democratic institutions, and the north remaining largely agricultural and monarchical. These disparities between northern and southern Nigeria would haunt the country well after independence.

Nigeria in 1955: Divided into Three Federated Regions. The administrative division of Nigeria into three regions later became the basis for ethnoregional conflicts. (Note: At the time of independence, the southeastern part of the country, which had been governed as a trust territory, opted to become part of independent Cameroon; two northern trust territories opted to become part of independent Nigeria.) *Source:* K. Michael Barbour, Julius Oguntoyinbo, J.O.C. Onyemelukwe, and James C. Nwafor, *Nigeria in Maps* (New York: Africana Publishing Company, 1982), 39.

Ethnic Politics under Colonialism Based on the British example, leaders of the anticolonial movement came to regard control of the state as a means to pursue personal and group interests rather than collective, national interests. Thus the three largest ethnic groups—Hausa-Fulani, Igbo, and Yoruba, which together compose approximately 65 percent of Nigeria's population—have dominated the political process since the British began to prepare Nigeria for independence in the 1940s. Ironically, these group identities did not exist in their contemporary forms in the precolonial era and were clearly delineated only in the context of colonial rule to manage the colony and establish administrative areas. Further, if the indigenous groups were pitted against one another, no unified threat of opposition to British authority would emerge. By providing resources to some groups, such as missionary education and lower-level civil service jobs, while depriving other groups, an environment of envy and mistrust was fostered.

Reinforced by colonial authorities and championed by local educated elites, Nigerian ethnic groups began to propound tales of origin that provided the bases for wider self-definition and a more exclusivist identity and heritage. Indigenous elites were able to rally followers based on notions of common identity. The self-declared representatives for these groups

mobilized popular support, then constantly lobbied and challenged the colonial administration. Extensive attempts were made to develop standardized and written forms of the languages and histories of these groups where few had existed previously.

The early ethnic-based associations were initially concerned with nonpolitical issues: promoting mutual aid for housing and education as well as sponsoring cultural events. With the encouragement of ambitious leaders, however, these groups took on a more political character. As the prospects for independence increased, indigenous elites began to divide along ethnic lines because the appeal to ethnic identities was an effective means of mobilizing support. Pan-ethnic cultural groups formed and subsequently served as the nuclei for two of the parties that succeeded the colonial regime after independence, namely, the Northern People's Congress, or NPC, in the north, and the Action Group, or AG, in the west. In the case of the National Council of Nigeria and the Cameroons (NCNC) in the east, the Igbo State Union took over effective control of the party.

As independence approached, the British began to make provisions to bring Nigerians into the administration of the country, and Nigeria became a federation of three regions in 1954. Each of the federated units soon fell under the domination of one ethnic group and one party. The Northern Region came under the control of the NPC, associated with and dominated by Hausa-Fulani elites. In the southern half of the country, the Western Region was controlled by the AG, which was controlled by the elites of the Yoruba group. The Igbo, the numerically dominant group in the Eastern Region, were closely associated with the NCNC, which became the ruling party there. Thus the distinctive and often divisive ethnic and regional characteristics of modern Nigeria were reinforced during the transition to independence.

In a celebrated statement made in 1947, one of the first generation of Nigerian political leaders, Chief Obafemi Awolowo of the Action Group, argued that "Nigeria is not a nation. It is a mere geographical expression. There are no 'Nigerians' in the same sense as there are 'English,' 'Welsh,' or 'French.' The word 'Nigerian' is merely a distinctive appellation to distinguish those who live within the boundaries of Nigeria from those who do not."[2] Influential leaders like Awolowo helped entrench the belief that Nigeria was a mere "geographical expression" and made the task of governing an independent Nigeria as a unified nation all the more difficult.

The First Republic (1960–1966)

The British handed over Nigeria in 1960 to a civilian parliamentary government. Nigerians adopted the British Westminster model at the federal and regional levels, in which the chief executive—the prime minister—was chosen by the majority party. Northerners came to dominate the federal government by virtue of their greater population, based on the 1952–1953 census. The ruling coalition for the first two years, ostensibly an alliance between the predominantly Igbo NCNC and the Hausa-Fulani-dominated NPC, quickly turned into a northern-only coalition when the NPC achieved an outright majority in the legislature. Having benefited less from the positive economic, educational, and infrastructural aspects of colonialism, the northerners who dominated the First Republic set out to redistribute resources in their own direction. This NPC policy of "northernization" brought them into direct conflict with their southern counterparts, particularly the Yoruba-based Action Group and later with the Igbo-dominated NCNC as well.

When an AG internal conflict led to a political crisis in the Western regional assembly in 1962, the NPC-led national government seized the opportunity to declare a state of emergency in the West. The NPC government used the pretext of the crisis to marginalize AG's leader, Chief Awolowo, eventually trying and convicting him on questionable charges of treason, for which he served a prison sentence from 1962 to 1966. By most accounts, Awolowo's trial and subsequent detention were based more on the desire to silence a political rival than on legal procedures, for which the NPC, with support from the NCNC and an anti-Awolowo faction of the AG, showed little regard. This early lack of respect for the rule of law set a significant precedent for Nigerian politics.

The NPC-led national government was now in a position to subdivide the Western (largely Yoruba) Region into West and Midwest, diluting Yoruba political power. Violence escalated among the Yoruba factions in the West as the NPC-dominated government engaged in other acts of political corruption. A fraudulent census, falsified ballots, and violence against and intimidation of supporters and candidates alike assured the NPC a tarnished victory in 1965.

Rivalries intensified as the NPC sat atop an absolute majority in the federal parliament with no need for its former coalition partner, the NCNC. NCNC leader Nnamdi Azikiwe, who was also president in the First Republic (then a largely symbolic position), and Tafawa Balewa, the NPC prime minister, separately approached the military to ensure that, if it came to conflict, they could count on its loyalty. Thus, "in the struggle for personal survival both men, perhaps inadvertently, made the armed forces aware that they had a political role to play."[3]

Civil War and Military Rule (1966–1979)

Essentially offered by the civilian leaders a chance to settle the political struggle, a group of largely Igbo officers instead seized power in January 1966. Aguiyi Ironsi, also an Igbo, became head of state by dint of being the highest ranking officer rather than a coup plotter. His announced aim was to end violence in the Western Region and to stop political corruption and abuses by the northern-dominated government by centralizing the state apparatus, replacing the federation with a unitary state. Although Ironsi claimed to be multiethnic in his perspective, other Nigerians, particularly northerners, were deeply suspicious of his revocation of federalism and the fact that several northerners were killed in the coup, including Tafawa Balewa and the premier of the Northern Region, Ahmadu Bello. Countercoup plotting began almost immediately. A second coup in July 1966 killed General Ironsi and brought Yakubu Gowon, a Middle Belt Christian, to power as a consensus head of state among the non-Igbo coup plotters.

Because many northern officials had been killed in the initial coup, a tremendous backlash against Igbos throughout Nigeria flared throughout 1966, even after the second coup. Igbo migrant laborers were persecuted in the north, and many fled to their "home" region in the east. By 1967 the predominantly Igbo population of eastern Nigeria attempted to secede and form its own independent nation, called Biafra. The secessionists wanted to break free from Nigeria, believing that the north, by virtue of its greater numbers, would permanently lock the other regions out of power. Moreover, since the northern region was less developed economically and educationally than the East and West, many Igbos feared that the country's progress would continue to be hampered by northern dominance of the federal government. General Gowon built a military-led government of national unity in what remained of Nigeria (the North and West), and after a bloody three-year war of attrition and starvation tactics defeated Biafra by January 1970. The conflict exacted a heavy toll on Nigeria's populace, including an estimated 2 million deaths.

After the war, Gowon presided over national reconciliation with the mostly Igbo separatists, which proceeded fairly smoothly with the aid of growing oil revenues. He also oversaw an increase in the armed forces from about 10,000 men in 1966 to nearly 250,000. Senior officers reaped the benefits of the global oil boom in 1973–1974, and corruption was widespread. Influenced by the unwillingness of the military elite to relinquish power and the spoils of office, Gowon opted to postpone a return to civilian rule, which he had pledged originally to complete by 1976. He was overthrown in 1975 by Murtala Muhammed, who promptly reactivated the transition program.

General Olusegun Obasanjo was the Nigerian head of state who supervised the transition to civilian rule from 1976 to 1979. In 1995 he was arrested and convicted in a secret trial in connection with an alleged attempt to overthrow the regime of General Abacha. After his release, he won the presidency in 1999 as a candidate for the PDP. *Source:* Reuters/Bettmann.

Through its extensive and unrestrained use of the coup d'état, the highly politicized Nigerian military has often justified its takeover and stay in power as a corrective for civilian government corruption. Following the first coup in 1966, the centralized planning of the civil war economy, and federal control of petroleum revenues after the war, the central government became much more powerful than the states. Thus, access to and control of this source of wealth and power spurred even greater corruption in the unaccountable military than among their civilian predecessors. Murtala Muhammed claimed a commitment to the restoration of democracy, but he was assassinated in 1976. General Olusegun Obasanjo, Muhammed's second-in-command who took power after the assassination, peacefully ceded power to an elected civilian government in 1979. After his detention from 1995 to 1998 for allegedly plotting a coup against General Abacha, Obasanjo once again became central in Nigerian politics as victor of the 1999 presidential elections.

The Second and Third Republics, and Military Rule (1979 to the Present)

The president of the Second Republic, Alhaji Shehu Shagari, and his ruling National Party of Nigeria, NPN (the northern successor party to the First Republic's NPC), did little to assuage the mistrust between the various parts of the federation. Shagari's government was perceived as a defender of northern interests, and it failed to stem the increase in bribery, smuggling, and the diversion of government proceeds from petroleum production. The most flagrant acts of corruption in the Second Republic, however, were the methods employed by the NPN to "win" its 1983 reelection bid. Voter registration was falsified, names were added to the register in some constituencies and mysteriously deleted in the south. During the election itself, massive fraud was committed on ballots and in polling stations. When it was over, the NPN had won an implausible thirteen of (then) nineteen state governorships and overwhelming majorities in the House and Senate elections. In a multiple-candidate race, Shagari won reelection with an equally implausible 47 percent of the vote. Led by Major General Muhammadu Buhari, the military seized power just a few months later, in December 1983.

When General Buhari refused to pledge a rapid return to civilian rule, his popular support wavered, and in August 1985 General Ibrahim Babangida seized power. Although Babangida announced a program of transition to democratic rule as one of his first acts as the new head of state, he and his colleagues engaged in an elaborate set of stalling techniques in order to extend their tenure in office. What promised to be the dawn of a Third Republic ended in betrayal

when Babangida annulled the presidential election of June 12, 1993, which should have preceded a full withdrawal of the military from the political scene. In stark contrast to all prior elections since independence, the 1993 election was widely acclaimed as free and fair, apparently won by a southern businessman, Chief Moshood Abiola. The annulment provoked an angry reaction from a population weary of postponed transitions, military rule, and deception. Babangida could not withstand the pressure to resign, but he did manage to handpick his successor, Ernest Shonekan, and a civilian caretaker government.

Following the pattern set by his predecessors, General Sani Abacha seized power in November 1993 from Shonekan. Abacha, who had held top military positions in both the Buhari and Babangida regimes, seized the reins of power from the ineffectual Shonekan. Shonekan's government, never regarded as legitimate after Babangida installed it in August 1993, was vulnerable to increasing agitation from both civilian and military ranks. As head of state, General Abacha prolonged the now established tradition of military dominance and combined increased repression with frequent public commitments to restore constitutional democracy. Like Babangida, Abacha announced a new program of transition to civilian rule and regularly delayed the steps in its implementation. Only Abacha's sudden death in June 1998 saved the country from certain crisis, as his scheme to orchestrate the outcome of the transition to produce his own "election" as president became clearer. General Abdulsalami Abubakar, Abacha's successor, in his first broadcast to the nation, announced his intention to return power to civilians. Within two months, Abubakar had established a new transition program with a prompt handover promised in May 1999 to its election victors, Obasanjo and the People's Democratic Party. Nigeria's penchant for such transitions is discussed in Section 4.

Themes and Implications

Historical Junctures and Political Themes

Nigeria's adoption of a federal arrangement has been a strategy to ensure unity in diversity by building a coherent nation-state out of over two hundred

General Sani Abacha, a prominent member of Nigerian military regimes since December 1983, took over the government in November 1993, disbanded all elective institutions, and suppressed opposition forces. His death in June 1998 was celebrated in the streets; he and his close supporters looted billions of U.S. dollars from the nation's coffers. *Source:* AP/Wide World Photos.

and fifty different nationalities and blending the precolonial, traditional democratic values with modern accountable government. In reality, however, and as a consequence of many years of colonial and military rule, a *unitary* system has emerged in a federal guise; it is a system with an all-powerful center surrounded by weak and economically insolvent states.

Another consequence of military rule, whose roots must be traced to the colonial era, is the relative overdevelopment of the executive arm at all levels of government—federal, state, and local—at the expense of weak legislative and judicial institutions. Executive superiority, a key feature of the colonial era, has been strengthened by each period of military rule. This unchecked executive power has encouraged a web of patron-client networks that sap the economy of vitality, prevent accountability, and undermine the rule of law.

The dominance of the executive has also ensured that the vitality of institutions and processes crucial to a democratic system—elections, electoral institutions, an independent judiciary, and a free press— is in constant jeopardy. The result: a spate of electoral failures

and cycles of civil and political instability culminating in periodic military coups.

Nigeria in the World of States: Oil Dependence and Decline Although Nigeria enjoys economic and military power within the West African region, on a global level Nigeria has become increasingly marginalized. Resource-rich, Nigeria has long been regarded as a potential political and economic giant of Africa. Yet the World Bank lists Nigeria among the poorest 20 percent of the countries of the world, with a GDP per capita of just US$269. Instead of independent growth, today Nigeria depends on dwindling oil revenues, sparse external loans, and aid, a victim of its leaders' bad policies and poor management. Owing to underinvestment in and neglect of agriculture, in the mid-1960s Nigeria moved from self-sufficiency in the production of basic foodstuffs to heavy dependence on imports of those goods less than twenty years later. Nigeria's total reliance on oil as a source of foreign earnings has made it vulnerable to price fluctuations in that market.

Nigerian politicians are infamous for their corruption. In order to win elections, they incur great debts to pay off supporters, so once in office they seek a return on their campaign "investments." With the constant danger of a military coup looming, they also seek to enrich themselves while their time in office remains.
Source: The Guardian (Lagos), August 28, 1998.

Nigeria is increasingly vulnerable and weakened within the world of states. The inclusion of Nigeria on the U.S. government's list of countries making insufficient efforts to combat the illegal drug trade, and the fact that Nigeria is a way station for international drug trafficking to the United States, has intensified its isolation. Nigerian sponsorship of international commercial fraud has also gravely harmed its reputation. Until the arrival of the Abubakar regime in June 1998, Nigeria was a prominent target of international action to curb widespread human rights abuses.

Nigeria's Fragile "Collective" Identity   Given the potential explosiveness of ethnic conflict, efforts by both the Babangida and Abacha regimes to manipulate ethnoregional fears and to set different sections of the country against one another as part of their survival strategies have had tragic consequences. Thus, almost three decades after the Biafran civil war, Nigeria often seems as divided as it was in the prelude to that conflict. Fears of another civil war rose during the mid-1990s.

Nigeria's experience with alternating forms of government indicates that **clientelism**, corruption, and authoritarian governing structures hinder economic potential. Clientelism is the practice by which a particular group receives disproportionate policy benefits or political favors from a political patron, usually at the expense of the larger society. In Nigeria patrons are often linked to clients by ethnic, religious, or other cultural ties, and these ties have generally benefited only a small elite. Clientelism tends to undermine social trust and political stability, which are necessary conditions for economic growth.

Ruling elites, whether military or civilian, have used state power to redistribute wealth in their own favor rather than for the creation of new wealth and investment in productive assets that would benefit the country as a whole. The abuse of state power through corrupt and clientelist actions has perverted federalism into a means to distribute "the national cake" to explicitly ethnic clients rather than using federalism to mitigate conflict. The ethnic basis of political power, compounded by corruption, is inherently unstable, often opening the door for a military seizure of power. The politicization of the military leaves regimes vulnerable to countercoups from within their own ranks; thus the alternation of Nigerian governments continues to be a threat.

Implications for Comparative Politics

Nigeria remains the oldest surviving federation in Africa. At a time when other federations are dissolving, whether peacefully as in the former Czechoslovakia or violently as in the former Yugoslavia, Nigeria manages to maintain its fragile unity. That unity has come under increasing stress, and a major challenge is ensuring that Nigeria does not go the way of Yugoslavia. One fact is certain: Military dominance and northern dependence on revenues generated in the south preclude a peaceful dissolution of the federation. Nigeria's multiethnic, multireligious, multiclass, and multiregional nature make it an especially valuable case for the study of social cleavages in conflict and cooperation.

Nigeria's failure to sustain democracy and economic development also renders it an important case for the study of resource competition and the perils of corruption, and its experience demonstrates the interrelationship between democracy and development. Democracy and development also depend on other factors, including leadership, mass culture, the level of institutional autonomy, and the external economic climate. A long-standing debate among scholars of comparative politics suggests that authoritarian regimes—because they lack legislative opposition and can force uncomfortable changes on society without fear of electoral reaction—are better able to accelerate economic growth and development. More recent research has shown, however, that democracies are no less likely to foster economic development and, in fact, may even establish predictable norms and further respect for property rights, both essential for economic development. The history of independent Nigeria shows that a combination of authoritarian government and widespread corruption have thwarted sustained development. Moreover, the Nigerian experience points to the need to pursue, with conviction, both economic and political liberalization. The latter process would open up society to democratic tendencies, while the former would provide the material bases (across a wider spectrum of society) for democratic consolidation.

At this stage, whether Nigeria will return to the path of autocracy, underdevelopment, and fragmentation, or turn to a course of democratic renewal and vigorous national construction, is uncertain. In the following sections we explore these issues and evaluate how they may shape Nigerian politics in the years ahead.

Section ❷ Political Economy and Development

Politics and economics have become so inseparable in Nigeria one cannot be seriously addressed without discussing the other. Section 2 explores the domestic and international contexts of Nigeria's political economy, and the role of the state and how it has intervened in Nigeria's economy. This active role of the state is consistent with the legacy established by the colonial regime, as discussed in Section 1.

State and Economy

The state plays the central role in Nigeria in making decisions about the extraction, deployment, and regulation of scarce economic resources. As individuals, groups, and communities jostle for control of, or access to, the state, economic and social life has become overpoliticized. The state has evolved beyond being a regulator and licenser, as it is in laissez-faire, less interventionist economies like Hong Kong. Although access to the state and its leaders confers economic advantages in most societies, it does so even more in developing countries. In Nigeria, the state is perceived as the greatest economic resource.

At the international level, the state has remained weak and dependent on Western industrial and financial interests four decades after Nigeria became a full-fledged member of the international community. The country suffers from an increasing debt burden. In addition, Nigeria is dependent on the developed industrial economies for finance capital, production and information technologies, and basic consumer items and raw materials. Nigeria strives to provide leadership at the continental (African) and subregional (West African) levels. Most of its policy and intellectual elites support this self-image.

In the period since independence, state intrusion into the economy and society has been strengthened by the control over **rents** accruing from agricultural, then petroleum, exports. The exigencies of the civil war and the consequences of prolonged military rule contributed to the centralized and intrusive approach to economic affairs. At the same time, the state has become a theater of struggles for ascendancy among groups and interests in civil society. To that extent, the state simultaneously affects and reflects forces in the political economy.

Origins of Economic Decline

In the colonial and immediate postcolonial periods, Nigeria's economy was centered on agricultural production for domestic consumption as well as for export.[4] Peasant producers were "induced" by the colonial state to produce primary export commodities—cocoa in the west, palm oil in the east, and ground nuts and cotton in the north—through direct taxation, forced cultivation, and the presence of European agricultural firms. Despite the emphasis on exports, Nigeria was self-sufficient in food production at the time of independence. Vital to this effort was small-scale local production of sorghum and maize in the north and cassava and yams in the south. Some rice and wheat were also produced. It was not until later in the 1960s that emphasis shifted to the development of nonfood export crops through large-scale enterprises.

Near-exclusive state attention to large-scale, nonfood production meant that small farmers were left out and received scant government support. Predictably, food production suffered, and food imports were stepped up to meet the increasing needs of a burgeoning population. Nevertheless, agriculture was the central component of the national economy. Michael Watts points to a combination of three factors that effectively undermined the Nigerian agricultural sector. The first was the Biafran war (1967–1970), which drastically reduced palm oil production in the east, where the war was concentrated. Second, severe drought in 1969 produced a famine in 1972–1974. Finally, the development of the petroleum industry caused a total shift in economic focus from agriculture (in terms of both labor and capital investment) into petroleum production. In contrast, agricultural export production plummeted from 80 percent of exports in 1960 to just 2 percent by 1980. To compensate for widening food shortfalls, food imports exploded by 700 percent between 1970 and 1978.[5]

With revenue from oil, Nigeria greatly increased its expenditures on education, defense, and infrastructure throughout the 1970s. The university system was expanded, roads and ports were built, and industrial and office buildings were constructed. Imports of capital goods and raw materials required to support this expansion rose by over 700 percent between 1971 and 1979. Similarly, imports of consumer goods also rose dramatically (600 percent) in the same period, as an increasingly wealthy Nigerian elite developed a taste for expensive imported goods.[6] By 1978 the Nigerian government had outspent its revenues and could no longer finance many of its ambitious projects; consequently, the government was forced to borrow money to make up the deficit, causing debt levels to accelerate rapidly.

The acceleration in oil wealth was mirrored by a corresponding increase in graft. Many public officials became very wealthy by setting up joint ventures with foreign oil companies. Other officials simply stole public funds for their own benefit. According to Watts, "Throughout the 1970s, enormous but inestimable amounts of money capital mysteriously appeared in private European bank accounts (estimated to be

Institutional Intricacies: *Corruption in Nigeria*

Corrupt government and private-sector practices occur in all countries. The motivations to do so are as specific as the individuals involved, yet greed and the desire for quick funds are certainly universal. Developing states, however, are particularly susceptible to corruption for a number of reasons. First, political institutions are often weak, which means that they are unable to implement essential national policies that conflict with the interests of specific groups or personal goals. Second, in the absence of strong institutions, personal ties predominate. As a consequence, people may find their immediate interests are better served through their ethnic grouping or religious institution and thus may place the demands of their family, ethnic kin, or religious group above the functioning of the public or private institution within which they work. Loyalty to a public or private institution is thus often subverted by considerations of personal connections and status.

Economic decline also contributes to corruption. In Nigeria, between 1980 and 1998, per capita incomes dropped 75 percent and the value of the naira fell from one naira to almost two U.S. dollars, to ninety naira to one U. S. dollar. Funds for most public works projects and social services such as health and education dried up, and competition for what remained became fierce. Corruption among elites became a way of life, while for poorly paid state employees it became a means of survival.

Consider, for example, that a bureaucrat in the Ministry of Works and Housing has a contract to award to a construction company to build a public housing project. He (or, more recently, she) probably has his immediate family to support, as well as his extended family and friends in his home village expecting him to contribute to household expenses. He hears stories from his friends about the huge sums of money stolen by the heads of state and their immediate subordinates, yet the government has not paid his agency's salaries in over four months—salaries that have not kept pace with the exorbitant rate of inflation. All the firms bidding for the contract promise to inflate the costs to the government for their work by 50 percent or more and pass half of that money secretly back to the bureaucrat for receiving the contract. At the height of postindependence optimism in the 1960s, many Nigerians avoided such temptations. Over time and with the massive influx of profits from the oil boom, however, increasing numbers succumbed to corruption.

When oil revenues began to pour into the country in the early 1970s, massive profits began to flow through the offices of military brass and senior-level bureaucrats. Some of these individuals, each involved in the personal networks described above, diverted a portion of these profits for themselves. When civilians came to power under the Second Republic in 1979, the number of people with access to oil revenues expanded, and a bonanza of inflated contracts, bogus public projects, and other scams proliferated. General Buhari justified his successful coup in 1983 in part to stamp out this massive corruption, and he did so temporarily—at the expense of civil liberties, which he severely curbed. Nonetheless, Buhari and his second-in-command General Idiagbon are still remembered by many Nigerians as the sort of "strong-handed" leaders that Nigeria needs to fight corruption.

Yet the notion that the military was any less corrupt than the civilians was dashed by the unprecedented avarice of Generals Babangida and Abacha. In the shadow of these massively corrupt military strongmen stands the average Nigerian, trying to eke out some semblance of a life in a land of growing poverty. Lacking jobs with adequate salaries or security, Nigeria's large university-educated population tries to emigrate to the United States or Europe, or turns to commercial fraud scams (known as "419"). Some individuals have turned to smuggling heroin, so that by 1998, Nigeria had become the largest transit point for that narcotic into the United States. Most Nigerians, however, never engage in such conduct. They work two or three jobs, sell food or small products by the roadside, carry jugs of fuel for miles on their heads to sell in neighboring countries, or do whatever else they can to sustain their families.

between $5 and $7 billion), and the level of bureaucratic malfeasance was simply staggering."[7] The economic downturn of the 1980s created even greater incentives for government corruption, and the Babangida and later the Abacha administrations became infamous for avarice. By 1992 reporters uncovered World Bank allegations that Babangida had "diverted" at least US$2 billion of a $3 billion windfall during the Gulf crisis of 1990–1991. Two years later, a Nigerian government commission reported that some $12.2 billion had been diverted to "special" accounts between 1988 and 1993.

General Abacha continued this looting spree to the point that he was willing to bring the country to its knees to make a profit. Within three years of seizing power, he allowed all of Nigeria's oil refineries to collapse, forcing this giant oil-exporting country into the absurd situation of having to import refined petroleum. Shamelessly, Abacha's family members and friends, who essentially served as fronts for him, monopolized the contracts to import this fuel in 1997.

In sum, the oil boom was a double-edged sword for Nigeria. On one hand, it has generated tremendous income; on the other, it has become a source of external dependence and has badly skewed the Nigerian economy. Nigeria has relied on oil for over 90 percent of its export earnings since the early 1970s. In that time, the industry has accounted for about three-quarters of *all* government revenues, as shown in Table 1. Frenzied, ill-managed industrial and infrastructural expansion under both military and civilian regimes, combined with the neglect of the agricultural sector during the oil boom years, further weakened the Nigerian economy. As a result, the Nigerian economy was unable to absorb the sharp fall in world oil prices after 1981 and found itself in crisis.

From 1985 to the Present: Deepening Economic Crisis and the Search for Solutions

Structural Adjustment The year 1985 marked a turning point for the Nigerian state and economy. It ushered in Ibrahim Babangida's eight-year rule and revealed the precarious condition of the Nigerian economy. Within a year of wresting power from General Buhari in August 1985, the Babangida regime developed an economic **structural adjustment pro-**

gram (SAP) with the active support of the World Bank and IMF (also referred to as the **international financial institutions**, or IFIs). The decision to embark on SAP was made against a background of increasing economic constraints arising from a combination of factors: the continued dependence of the economy on oil exports, a growing debt burden, **balance of payments** difficulties, and lack of fiscal discipline.

The Nigerian SAP contains provisions that are similar to most economic reform programs that have been instituted in Africa and elsewhere. It had three broad objectives: first, to restructure and diversify the economy to reduce dependence on oil and on various imports; second, to achieve fiscal discipline and balance of payments viability by curtailing government spending to reduce budget deficits and the rising debt; and third, to embark on the **privatization** of state-owned enterprises (para-statals). In the decade since SAPs came into widespread use in Africa, their success has been mixed. The length of time allotted to such programs has usually been extended because of the failure of Africa's economies to respond quickly to the shock treatment.

African governments and their publics in general have resisted SAPs and IFI intervention for two reasons. First, states do not relish the prospect of ceding important aspects of their economic sovereignty to international institutions. Second, the austerity that results from such programs, although intended and predicted to be a short-term consequence, can be destabilizing to governments and populations alike. However, because they are dependent on lenders for continued support, most African governments have complied with the demands of multilateral creditors. Besides, other creditors (including private banks or foreign governments) often will not consent to provide additional monies in the absence of an agreement with the IFIs.

Federal control of earnings from oil and other mining rights enabled the state to increase its involvement in direct production. Beginning in the 1970s, the state created a number of para-statals (state-owned enterprises) and acquired large shares in major banks and other financial institutions, manufacturing, and construction companies. This practice has ensured that the state remains the biggest employer as well as the most important source of revenue, even for the private sector. By the 1980s the public service bureaucracy in Nigeria had swollen to over 3 million employees (most employed by the federal and state governments), representing more than 60 percent of employment in the modern sector of the economy.

The share of the private sector in the economy has actually fallen in recent years. According to one analysis, private-sector investment across the economy was approximately 45 percent during the first national development plan (1962–1968). By contrast, the fifth

Table 1

Oil Sector Statistics, 1970–1998

	Annual Output (million barrels)	Average Price Index	Oil Exports as Percent of Total Exports	Government Oil Revenue (Naira millions)	Percent of Total Revenue
1970	396	37	58	166	26
1971	559	43	74	510	44
1972	643	40	82	767	54
1973	750	39	83	1,016	60
1974	823	162	93	3,726	82
1975	651	109	93	4,271	77
1976	756	115	94	5,365	79
1977	761	115	93	6,081	76
1978	692	100	89	4,556	62
1979	840	237	93	8,881	81
1980	753	220	96	12,353	81
1981	525	225	97	8,563	70
1982	470	212	99	7,814	66
1983	451	200	96	7,253	69
1984	508	190	97	8,268	74
1985	544	180	97	10,915	75
1986	534	75	94	8,107	66
1987	464	90	93	19,027	76
1988	507	60	91	20,934	77
1989	614	87	95	41,334	82
1990	–	125	–	–	–
1991	–	80	–	–	–
1992	714	79	98	164,078	86
1993	720	62	91	162,102	84
1994	733	70	85	160,192	79
1995	705	65	95	244,902	53
1996	783	95	95	266,000	51
1997	803	85	95	250,000[a]	80
1998[a]	700	62	90	248,500	70

[a]Projected.

Sources: Output is from *Petroleum Economist* (1970–1989); price index and exports are from IMF, *International Financial Statistics* (1970–1984) and from Central Bank of Nigeria, *Annual Reports* (1985–1989); revenues are from Central Bank of Nigeria, *Annual Reports* (various years). From Tom Forrest, *Politics and Economic Development in Nigeria*. (Boulder: Westview Press, 1993), 134. 1990s statistics are from the Nigerian Federal Office of Statistics, *Annual Abstract of Statistics: 1997 Edition*, from the 1998 IMF *Annual Report*, and from *Report of the Vision 2010 Committee: Main Report* (Abuja: Federal Government of Nigeria, September 1997). Compilation and some calculations by Darren Kew.

Global Connection: *Structural Adjustment Programs*

The solutions to Nigeria's economic woes depend, in the first instance, on its own people and government, but assistance must also come from outside its borders. In addition to bilateral (country-to-country) assistance, multilateral economic institutions are a key source of loans, grants, and other forms of development aid. Two multilateral institutions that have become familiar players on the African economic scene are the International Monetary Fund (IMF) and the World Bank. These international financial institutions, or IFIs, were established following World War II to provide short-term credit facilities to facilitate growth and expansion of trade and longer-term financing packages, respectively, to rebuild the countries of war-torn Europe. Today, the functions of the IFIs have adapted and expanded to meet contemporary needs, including efforts to stabilize and restructure faltering economies. One area of emphasis by the IFIs, particularly among African countries, is the structural adjustment program (SAP).

Assistance from the World Bank and the IMF comes with many strings attached. These rigorous programs, which are intended to reduce government intervention and to develop free markets, call for immediate austerity measures by recipient governments. SAPs generally begin with currency devaluation and tariff reductions. These actions are followed by measures aimed at reducing budget deficits, restructuring of the public sector (particularly employment practices), privatizing state-owned enterprises, agricultural reform (especially raising producer prices), and the reduction of consumer subsidies on staple foods. The social and economic hardships of these programs, particularly in the short term, can be severe. SAPs result in considerable economic—and frequently social—dislocation; dramatic price increases in foodstuffs and fuel, plus rising unemployment, are seldom popular with the general population.

At Babangida's insistence, Nigeria's SAP was developed and deployed in 1986 independently of the IMF and the World Bank. The program was, however, endorsed by the IFIs, making Nigeria eligible to receive disbursements of funds from the IMF and the Bank and to reschedule US$33 billion of external debt with the Paris and London clubs of lenders. Ironically, Nigeria's SAP was in many regards more rigorous than an initial program designed by the IMF. Like SAPs elsewhere, the Nigerian program was designed to encourage economic liberalism and promote private enterprise in place of a reliance on state-owned enterprises and public intervention. The logic was that competition leads to more efficient products and markets. Recovery among Africa's struggling economies has, however, been limited. Africa's economic problems are deeply entrenched; although an economy may be stabilized relatively quickly, comprehensive *structural* adjustment takes considerably longer. Thus far, Nigeria's SAP—in part because of the popular reaction to austerity measures, continued corruption in its implementation, and the complicating factor of unstable military rule—has failed to revitalize the Nigerian economy. The final years of the Babangida administration (1985–1993) saw a marked slippage in the reform program, and the Abacha regime continued that trend. Abacha did enact a number of liberal economic policies in 1995 and 1996 that lowered inflation, stabilized the exchange rate, and fostered mild GDP growth, but by 1997 these achievements had been squandered. General Abubakar pledged to return to a liberal economic agenda, including the privatization of the major government para-statals.

national development plan (1981–1985) anticipated just a 14 percent contribution from the private sector.[8] That is, funding for the plan was to be provided mainly by the government. Attempts in the 1970s to widen Nigerian participation in business life and reduce the foreign presence enhanced state involvement because government had to take over shares and businesses when local bids proved inadequate.

The stated goal of Nigerian governments since the mid-1980s has been to reduce unproductive investments in the public sector, improve the sector's efficiency, and promote the growth of the private sector. Privatization, one of the most substantial aspects of economic liberalization, means that state-owned businesses would be sold to private (nonstate) investors, either domestic or foreign. The benefits of

Current Challenges: *Vision 2010*

In the early 1990s, concerned with the nation's economic decline, a number of the larger Nigerian businesses and key multinational corporations decided to pursue new initiatives. With the appointment as head of state in August 1993 of Ernest Shonekan, who was the former chairman of West Africa's largest local corporation, UAC, these businesses sensed an opportunity to alter the course of Nigeria's economic policies. With Shonekan's involvement, they arranged the first Economic Summit, a high-profile conference that advocated numerous policies to move Nigeria toward becoming an "emerging market" that could attract foreign investment along the lines of the high-performing states in Asia.

Shortly after the first Economic Summit, however, General Abacha took control and continued the ruinous economic approach of Babangida's later years. The Economic Summit, meanwhile, continued to meet annually. After his flawed 1994 budget sent the Nigerian economy into a tailspin, Abacha was ready to listen to the Summit participants. He accepted several of their recommendations, and by 1996 the economy began to make modest gains. Therefore, when key members of the Summit proposed *Vision 2010,* General Abacha seized the opportunity and endorsed it in September 1996.

Vision 2010 relies on a model of strategic planning that begins with a "visioning" process that identifies key corporate goals and the paths of action to realize these goals. The process brings together key stakeholders and "implementers" who are expected to bring goals to fruition. Malaysia and other developing countries successfully employed this model in the 1980s to devise blueprints for development. As part of the "visioning" process, the government adopts a package of business-promoting economic reforms, while business pledges to work toward certain growth targets consistent with governmental priorities in employment,

taxation, community investment, and the like. General Abacha's estimation of the potential of *Vision 2010* was so great that he quickly increased its scope beyond its initial economic intentions. Committees were set up to develop plans for Nigeria's sports teams, interethnic relations, media development, and even for civil-military relations under the expected democratic rule. Along with government and business leaders, key figures were invited to participate from nearly all sectors of society, including the press, nongovernmental organizations, youth groups, market women's associations, and others. Government-owned media followed *Vision 2010*'s pronouncements with great fanfare, while the private media reviewed them with a healthy dose of skepticism regarding Abacha's intentions and the elitist nature of the exercise.

In September 1997, on schedule, the *Vision 2010* executive committee presented its final report. Its four volumes painted a surprisingly candid picture of where Nigeria stood, and recommended how the country could transform itself into a strong emerging-market democracy by 2010. The recommendations called for, in part: restoring democratic rule, restructuring and professionalizing the military, lowering the population growth rate, rebuilding education, meaningful privatization, diversifying the export base beyond oil, supporting intellectual property rights, and central bank autonomy.

Whatever its merits, *Vision 2010* was imperiled because of its association with Abacha. After Abacha's death in 1998, General Abubakar (who had earlier participated in the formulation of *Vision 2010*) announced that his administration endorsed the *Vision 2010* recommendations. He pledged to implement the initial economic policy reforms, including privatization, before leaving office in May 1999. Business leaders remain generally enthusiastic, but what relationship they will enjoy with the new civilian government, and whether the key proposals of *Vision 2010* will be retained following the resumption of competitive multiparty politics, are uncertain.

Source: *Vision 2010 Final Report*, September 1997.

privatization are threefold: (1) revenue is generated for the state when the enterprise is sold; (2) there is a substantial reduction in state expenditure because the state is no longer financing the operation of money-losing operations; and (3) there is an implicit assumption that the private sector can run businesses more efficiently than the government sector. However, privatization typically results in job loss: a private company cannot afford to maintain a bloated payroll if it hopes to survive. The government is often reluctant to swell the ranks of the unemployed and to confront the consequent political opposition that such actions usually provoke.

Nevertheless, central to Nigeria's economic adjustment program is the commercialization and privatization of state enterprises. Government has successfully divested itself of shares in such areas as banking and finance, but has proceeded slowly regarding most of the key para-statals. Moreover, individuals in public office or with access to the state have been able to invest in privatized companies at insider prices. Much of the Nigerian economy therefore remains as interventionist and centralized as ever.

Expectations that deregulation would encourage investment in manufacturing by both Nigerians and foreign interests have not been fulfilled. The healthy annual growth rate in gross domestic investment of 14.7 percent between 1965 and 1980 dropped precipitously—10.2 percent annually from 1980 to 1990. For potential foreign investors, uncertainties about Nigeria's future have discouraged long-term investment. Meanwhile, new investors are hesitant to risk significant capital in an environment characterized by political and social instability, a weak economic adjustment program, and unpredictable military regimes. On a domestic level, Nigerian entrepreneurs have found that trading and government contracting offer more attractive and quicker yields than manufacturing. The service sector, as a consequence, grew between 1980 and 1990 whereas manufacturing and industry actually declined.

Economic Planning   Beginning in 1946, when the colonial administration announced a ten-year plan for development and welfare, national plans have been prepared by ministries of finance, economic development, and planning. Five-year plans were the norm from 1962 through 1985, when their scope was extended to fifteen years. The national plan, however, has not been an effective management tool. The reason for this disparity is the absence of an effective database for planning as well as a great lack of discipline in plan implementation. The state strives to

control and dictate the pace and direction of economic development but lacks the tools and political will to deliver on its obligations. Nigerian and foreign business leaders revived dialogue on economic direction in 1996 with the *Vision 2010* process. *Vision 2010*, however, was vastly different from past plans in that it was a business-led initiative that government later adopted and contributed to as an equal partner. *Vision 2010* also sought to scale back government's excessive role in the economy, in the hope of increasing market efficiency and reducing competition for control of the state.

Although *Vision 2010* eventually may provide a basis for reform, many problems must still be overcome in the economy: low investment, low capacity utilization, unreliable distribution, stifling corruption, and overregulation. Average annual GDP growth rates have been negative in several years since the early 1980s. Consumption and investment have also recorded negative growth (see Table 2).

Table 2

Selected Economic Indicators, 1980–1998

	Real GDP (Naira billions) (1993 = 100)	GDP (% Growth)	Manufacturing Capacity Utilization (%)[a]	Inflation Rate (%)
1980	96.2	5.5	70.1	9.9
1985	68.9	9.4	37.1	5.5
1990	90.3	8.1	40.3	7.4
1991	94.6	4.8	42.0	13.0
1992	97.4	3.0	41.8	44.6
1993	100.0	2.7	37.2	57.2
1994	101.0	1.3	30.4	57.0
1995	103.5	2.2	29.3	72.8
1996	106.9	3.3	32.5	29.3
1997	111.1	3.9	–	8.5
1998	113.3	2.0	–	9.0
1976–1986		–1.3		
1987–1997		1.6		

[a]Manufacturing capacity utilization is the average (across the economy) percentage of full production capabilities at which manufacturers are producing.

Sources: *Report of the Vision 2010 Committee: Main Report* (Abuja: Federal Government of Nigeria, September 1997); World Bank, "Nigeria at a Glance," 1998 (http://www.worldbank.org/); the 1998 IMF *Annual Report*.

Exacerbating Nigeria's economic decline is its heavy foreign debt. The total amount owed to foreign governments and international commercial banks exceeded US$28 billion by the end of 1996—ten times the total government budget for that year. Total debt service as a percentage of exported goods and services jumped fivefold, from 4.2 percent in 1980 to 37.4 percent in 1996. This means that of every dollar Nigeria earns from its exports, 37 cents must theoretically go to service the national debt. Such a level of debt servicing cannot, obviously, be met with more debt. Nigeria, once considered a country likely to achieve self-sustaining growth, now ranks among the more debt-distressed countries in the developing world. It cannot earn enough from the export of goods to service its foreign debt and also meet the basic needs of the population (see Table 3).

Social Welfare   Given the continued decline in its economic performance since the early 1970s, it is not surprising that Nigeria's social welfare has suffered greatly as well. Since 1986 there has been a marked deterioration in the quantity and quality of social services, complicated by a marked decline in household incomes (see Table 4). The SAP program, with its emphasis on austerity and the reduction of state expenditures, has forced cutbacks in spending on social welfare.

Economic austerity and stagnation have hurt vulnerable groups such as the urban and rural poor, women, the young, and the elderly. Indeed, Nigeria performs poorly in meeting basic needs: life expectancy is barely above fifty years, and infant mortality is estimated at more than 90 deaths per 1000 live births. Nigeria's provision of basic education is also inadequate. Moreover, Nigeria has failed to develop a national social security system, such as that found in the United States and elsewhere. There has also been a general tendency for growth in public social spending to lag behind growth in the economy. Much of the resulting gap has traditionally been filled by culturally based networks of extended families. The scant social spending that does exist is often manipulated for partisan political purposes by both civilian and military governments. Public spending on housing, for example, represents less than 1 percent of the federal budget and is often diverted to meet the needs of the military.

Table 3

Nigeria's Total External Debt (US$ millions; current prices and exchange rates)

1975–1979	1980	1981	1982	1983
3,304	8,934	12,136	12,954	18,540
1984	1985	1986	1987	1988
18,537	19,551	24,043	31,193	31,947
1989	1994	1995	1996	1997
32,832	34,000	35,010	33,442	32,906

Nigeria's Debt Compared to Its Earnings:

	1976	1986	1996	1997
Total Debt/GDP	3.7	109.9	72.0	63.1
Total Debt Service/Exports	3.7	28.4	15.2	15.9
Present Value of Debt/GDP	–	–	63.3	–
Present Value of Debt/Exports	–	–	178.6	–

Sources: UNDP, World Bank, *African Development Indicators* (Washington, D.C.: World Bank, 1992), 159; UNDP, *1998 Human Development Report*; World Bank, "Nigeria at a Glance," 1998 (http://www.worldbank.org/); the 1998 IMF *Annual Report*.

The provision of health care and other social services—water, education, food, and shelter—remain woefully inadequate in both urban and rural areas. Rural areas are doubly burdened by their relative isolation because of poor roads, transportation, telecommunication facilities, and sparse electrical power. In all parts of Nigeria, health care facilities lack equipment, drugs, and doctors. Although the national leadership gives lip service to the importance of social welfare in general, health care has been accorded a low priority in Nigeria's national development plans, especially when compared with expenditure on the military.

Society and Economy

The Nigerian state, and especially the central government, controls access to capital resources. As a result, the state has become the major focus for competition among ethnic, regional, religious, and class groups. In such an environment, elite members of these groups become "conflict generators" rather than "con-

Table 4

Index of Real Household Incomes of Key Groups, 1980/81–1986/87, 1996 (Rural self-employed in 1980/81 = 100)

	1980/81	1981/82	1982/83	1983/84	1984/85	1985/86	1986/87	1996[a]
Rural self-employed	100	103	95	86	73	74	65	27
Rural wage earners	178	160	147	135	92	95	84	48
All rural households	105	107	99	89	74	84	74	28
Urban self-employed	150	124	106	94	69	69	61	41
Urban wage earners	203	177	164	140	101	101	90	55
All urban households	166	142	129	109	80	80	71	45

[a]Estimated, based on 1980/81 figures adjusted for a 73% drop in per capita GDP from 1980 to 1996. The FOS lists annual household incomes for 1996 as US$75 (N 6,349) for urban households and US$57 (N 4,820) for rural households, suggesting that the gap between urban and rural households is actually 19% closer than our estimate.

Sources: National Integrated Survey of Households (NISH), Federal Office of Statistics (FOS) consumer price data, and World Bank estimates. As found in Paul Collier, *An Analysis of the Nigerian Labour Market*, Development Economics Department Discussion Paper (Washington, D.C.: World Bank, 1986). From Tom Forrest, *Politics and Economic Development in Nigeria* (Boulder: Westview Press, 1993), 214. 1996 data from FOS, *Annual Abstract of Statistics: 1997 Edition*, 80.

flict managers."[9] Furthermore, a partial explanation for the failure of economic strategies can be found within Nigerian society itself—a complex mix of contending, often hostile, ethnic, religious, and regional constituencies.

Ethnic and Religious Cleavages

Nigeria's ethnic relations have generated tensions that sap the country's economy of much-needed vitality. Competition among the three largest groups is centered on access to national economic and political resources. The dominance of the Hausa-Fulani, Igbo, and Yoruba in the country's national life, and the conflicts among political elites from these groups, flow over into economic affairs as policy decisions are often made less on their merits and more on how they impact perceptions of group strength.

Religious cleavages have also affected economic and social stability. Some of the federation's states in the far north are populated mainly by Muslims, whereas others, particularly in the middle and eastern parts of the south, are predominantly Christian. The imagery in popular (and often academic) discourse often simplifies the more complex reality by juxtaposing a so-called Christian south with a Muslim north (the Yoruba people in the southwest, for example, are almost equally divided between Muslims and Christians and with many adherents of Yoruba traditional beliefs).

A combination of inept government actions—or outright manipulation—and a worldwide upsurge in Islamic and Christian assertion have heightened conflicts between adherents. Christians have perceived the northern-dominated federal government as being pro-Islam in its management and distribution of scarce resources as well as in its policy decisions. Christians fear that government actions are jeopardizing the secular nature of the state and putting the country on the path to an Islamic theocracy. In response, Muslims have questioned the secular nature of the Nigerian state. Muslims insist that colonial rule, under the tutelage of the church-state of England, created a state more Christian than secular in Nigeria, and one that is unable to provide a positive environment for the observance of Islam. The consequence of these disputes throughout the 1980s and 1990s was a series of clashes along religious lines in various parts of the country, often accompanied by extensive loss of life.

Further complicating matters, the 1980s witnessed an increase in social disturbances associated mainly with the extremist fringes of Islamic groups in some parts of the north. The decline in the Nigerian economy also contributed to the rise of fundamentalism. As elsewhere in the world, Islamic leaders have increasingly blamed secular governments for the rise in poverty and social dislocation. In northern Nigeria, disputes over economic issues have sometimes escalated into physical attacks on Christians and members of southern ethnic groups residing in the north. Occasionally, religious revivalism among some of the various Christian sects has provoked violent protests by Muslims.

Poverty and social dislocation have yet to promote a militant religious movement in the Christian south, but evangelical Christian churches swept across the region in the 1990s. Offering music, dancing, community, and even instant miracles (especially in regard to fertility, relationships, and finances), these churches have sprouted in nearly every neighborhood where Christians are to be found. Although they do have an umbrella national organization, the evangelicals have yet to solidify into a coherent political force. Their social influence, however, has been unmistakable, as nearly every public figure peppers his pronouncements with religious references. The evangelical churches augment the more established denominations, including Anglicans, Roman Catholics, and Methodists.

Based on general perceptions that the south fears "northern political domination—the tyranny of population," while the north fears a "southern tyranny of skills,"[10] it is often argued that the north must continue to control political power at the central government level—through military or civilian means—so as to neutralize the south's perceived advantages. Such attitudes came into the open during the Babangida regime, which was perceived as a northern-dominated administration and willing to manipulate Nigeria's ethnic divisions more than any of his predecessors.

General Abacha's Provisional Ruling Council (PRC) tilted overwhelmingly in favor of northerners, specifically Hausa-Fulani, in its membership. Any appearance of regional representation in the council was shattered in August 1994 when Abacha replaced most of the non-northern senior military staffers. The December 1997 arrest of deputy head of state (nominally the second-highest position of power in the country) General Oladipo Diya for allegedly plotting a coup along with a dozen other generals and senior staff—all but one of whom were Yoruba—confirmed southern fears of a northern bias in the PRC. Meanwhile, numerous attacks were perpetrated against prominent southern civilians, particularly

Yoruba, and many suspected government complicity. The Abacha government also closed universities and detained a number of activists, particularly in the south.

But it is not only Yoruba groups that were adversely affected by Abacha's rule. The Ogoni, Ijaw, and other southern minorities, who are heavily represented among oil industry workers, were brutalized by military and police forces when they protested against the regime. The Ogoni in particular were well-organized through the Movement for the Survival of the Ogoni People (MOSOP), under the leadership of internationally renowned writer and environmentalist Ken Saro-Wiwa. MOSOP effectively blended its claims for **self-determination**, which in this case meant increased local political autonomy and national political representation, with concerns over oil industry pollution in the Niger Delta—primarily on the part of global oil giant Royal Dutch/Shell—as a platform to forge alliances with international environmental and human rights organizations.

This alliance became an active force in 1994, when Saro-Wiwa was arrested on trumped-up charges along with eight other Ogoni activists. Their kangaroo trial by a military tribunal brought pleas for clemency from international human rights organizations, as well as from South African President Nelson Mandela, U.S. President Bill Clinton, and other world leaders. Ignoring such pleas, the government executed Saro-Wiwa and his compatriots in November 1995. International condemnation followed: Nigeria was suspended from the Commonwealth (an international organization composed of former British colonies) within days, and a subsequent UN mission of inquiry in 1996 declared the hangings illegal, not only under international standards of jurisprudence but also under Nigeria's own system of laws.

Rejecting many of the harsher tactics of his predecessors, General Abubakar introduced a transition program in 1998 for a rapid return to democracy, in part to mitigate the intense ethnic and religious tensions. He also partly adjusted the ethnic balance in the PRC to allow greater southern representation. Yet the political space and freedoms restored by Abubakar released the pent-up ethnic tensions aggravated by Abacha and Babangida, a situation that bodes poorly for hopes of ethnic accommodation in the new civilian regime.

In an August 1998 meeting, Yoruba leaders largely agreed to forgo the late M.K.O. Abiola's 1993 presidential mandate and to participate in the Abubakar transition program, but only after a lengthy debate over calls for secession or for a confederal Nigeria. A number of leaders also threatened that the Yoruba would go their own way if Nigeria's next president was not from their region. Key Igbo leaders made similar calls for an Igbo president, while Hausa-Fulani politicians stressed the view that democracy means majoritarianism—meaning that their more numerous population should ensure a president from the north.

Meanwhile, youths from the Niger Delta minorities, primarily the Ijaw, occupied Shell and Chevron facilities in September and October 1998 to protest their group's perceived marginalization. In light of the oil companies' vital importance to the Nigerian government, they have recently become the favorite targets of Delta protests. Their operations were shut down or occupied several times in 1997 and 1998 as Ijaw and Itsekeri youths fought over control of their common local government.

Nigerian political and business elites have also demonstrated a propensity toward accentuating sectional cleavages. Culture or ethnicity is used to fragment rather than to integrate the country, with grave consequences for the economy and society. These divisive practices overshadow certain positive aspects of sectional identities. For example, associations based on ethnic and religious affinities often serve as vehicles for mobilizing savings, investment, and production, such as informal credit associations. In addition, professional associations—composed of lawyers, doctors, journalists, business and trade groups, academics, trade unions, or students' organizations—played a prominent role in the anticolonial struggle. These groups, which form the core of civil society, have continued to provide a vehicle for political expression while also reflecting the divisive pressures of Nigeria's cultural pluralism. It should benoted, however, that the most political of these groups traditionally have been dominated by men. Although women form a vital part of the economic sector, they have only recently begun to emerge as a major social force in Nigeria.

Gender Differences

Although the Land Use Act of 1978 stated that all land in Nigeria is ultimately owned by the government, land tenure in Nigeria is still governed by traditional practice, which is basically patriarchal. Despite the fact that women, especially from the south and Middle Belt areas, have traditionally dominated agricultural production and form the bulk of agricultural producers, they are generally prevented from owning land, which remains the major means of production. Trading, in which women feature prominently, is also controlled in many areas by traditional chiefs and local government councillors, who are overwhelmingly male.

Women have not succeeded in transforming their economic importance into political clout, but important strides are being made in this direction. Their past inability and current struggle to achieve direct access to state power is a reflection of several factors. Women's associations have tended to be elitist, urban-based, and mainly concerned with issues of trade, welfare, and religion. The few that did have a more political orientation have been largely token appendages of the male-dominated political parties or instruments of the government. An example of the latter was the "Better Life Program" directed by the wife of Babangida, and its successor, the "Family Support Program," directed by Abacha's wife. Women are grossly underrepresented at all levels of the governmental system.

Reflecting their historical economic and educational advantages, women's interest organizations sprouted in southern Nigeria earlier than in the north. Although these groups initially focused on generally nonpolitical issues surrounding women's health and children, organizations like Women in Nigeria began to form in the 1980s with explicit political goals, such as getting more women into government and making more money available for education.

By the 1990s northern women had become nearly as active as southerners in founding nongovernmental organizations (NGOs). As in the south, northern women's NGOs at first focused on nonpolitical issues, but by the end of the decade explicitly political organizations such as the 100 Women Groups, which sought to elect one hundred women to every level of government, emerged. Northern groups also showed tremendous creativity in using Islam to support their activities, which was very important considering that tenets of the religion have been regularly used by Nigerian men to justify women's subordinate status. Women's groups in general have been much more dynamic than male-dominated NGOs—nearly all of which are entirely dependent on foreign or government funding—in developing income-generating projects to make their organizations and the women they assist increasingly self-reliant.

Nigeria and the International Political Economy

In the years since independence, Nigeria has been active in the Organization of African Unity (OAU), the Commonwealth, the Nonaligned Movement, and the United Nations. In recent years, Nigeria played a major role in reorienting the focus of the Nonaligned Movement toward issues of economic development and cooperation. In bodies such as the OAU and the UN, Nigeria generally took firm positions to promote decolonization and the development of the Third World, and against the apartheid regime in South Africa. Unfortunately, this international goodwill was largely squandered by the Abacha regime, and, ironically, the democratic government of South Africa became one of its leading critics. President Nelson Mandela, himself a former political prisoner, was prominent among world leaders calling for the immediate release of Moshood Abiola. South Africa was the first country General Abubakar visited shortly after taking office in order to patch the relationships frayed under his predecessor.

Nigeria and the Regional Political Economy

Nigeria has aspired to be a regional leader in Africa. These aspirations have not been dampened by its declining position in the global political economy. Nigeria was a major actor in the formation in 1975 of the **Economic Community of West African States** (ECOWAS) and has carried a disproportionately high financial and administrative burden for keeping that troubled organization afloat. Nigeria has also been the largest contributor of troops to the West African peacekeeping force, the ECOWAS Monitoring Group (known as ECOMOG). Under

Nigerian direction, the ECOWAS countries dispatched ECOMOG troops to Liberia in August 1990 to restore order and to prevent the Liberian civil war from destabilizing the subregion. In July 1997 the election of a national governing committee under the former warlord Charles Taylor was an ambiguous outcome of these efforts. Ironically, despite military dictatorship at home, Nigerian ECOMOG forces invaded Sierra Leone in May 1997 to restore its democratically elected government—a move generally endorsed by the international community. These forces have been drawn more deeply into the conflict as the former Sierra Leonean military junta has formed alliances with rural rebel militias and counterattacked.

Because it is the largest economy in the West African subregion, Nigeria has been a magnet for illegal immigration. At the height of the 1970s oil boom, many West African laborers, most of them from Ghana, migrated to Nigeria in search of employment. When the oil-based expansion ceased and jobs became scarce, Nigeria sought to protect its own workers by expelling thousands of West Africans in 1983 and 1985.

On balance, ECOWAS has not accomplished its goal of economic integration. The region is riven by jealousies and rivalries among French- and English-speaking blocs. Each of these blocs maintains closer ties to its former colonial masters economically and culturally than with each other. As a result, formal-sector trade (that which pays taxes and ends up in GDP calculations, and usually derives from the activity of well-established businesses and manufacturers) within ECOWAS has been disappointing. The informal sector (petty trade, services, and smuggling) across West African borders, however, is estimated to be enormous, with Nigerian traders its driving force. A number of analysts estimate that the Nigerian informal sector can be valued at a figure approximately 20 percent the size of the entire Nigerian GDP—much of which is earned through cross-border trade. That trade is all the more important because it provides income to 70 percent of Nigerians, the poorer majority.

Nigeria and the Political Economy of the West

Nigeria's global influence peaked in the 1970s at the height of the oil boom. Shortly after the 1973–1974 global oil crisis, Nigeria's oil wealth was perceived by the Nigerian elite largely as a source of strength. In 1975, for example, Nigeria was selling about 30 percent of its oil to the United States[11] and was able to apply pressure to the administration of President Gerald Ford in a dispute over Angola. By the 1980s, however, the global oil market had become a buyer's market. Thereafter, it became clear that Nigeria's dependence on oil was a source of weakness, not strength. In addition to its dependence on oil revenues, Nigeria was dependent on Western technology and Western industrial expertise for exploration and extraction of its oil reserves.

Nigeria is listed very close to the bottom of the United Nations' Human Development Index (HDI), 142 out of 174, behind India and Haiti. Gross national product (GDP) per capita in 1996 was US$269, less than 2 percent of which was recorded as public expenditures on education and health. These figures compare unfavorably with the $860 per capita GNP for China and $390 per capita for India. On the basis of its per capita GDP, the Nigerian economy is the nineteenth poorest in the world in a 1997 World Bank ranking. For comparative purposes, the same study ranks Ghana as thirty-first poorest and India twenty-seventh.

The depth of this international weakness became clear with the adoption of structural adjustment in the mid-1980s. Given the enormousness of the economic crisis, Nigeria was compelled to seek IMF/World Bank support to improve its balance of payments and facilitate economic restructuring and debt rescheduling, and had to accept direction from foreign agencies for the first time since gaining independence. The annual budget proposals of the federal government and its various accounts have been subject to scrutiny by these institutions.

The link between internal and external (in this case, Western) factors in Nigeria's political economy is best reflected in the interplay of forces that eventually drove General Babangida from power on August 26, 1993, following his nullification of the June 12 presidential election. Pro-democracy groups were strengthened in their anti-Babangida campaign by the pressure from external donors and creditors, especially the United States, Britain, and the European Union.

Relations with these foreign powers deteriorated steadily after the 1993 election annulment. In July 1993 the United States announced plans to suspend commercial military sales to Nigeria and canceled all but humanitarian aid. In July 1994 the U.S. House of Representatives passed a resolution condemning human rights abuses and advocating the restoration of democracy, and the following year an economic sanctions bill was introduced in the Senate. Germany and Britain issued similar pronouncements. Nigeria nonetheless avoided severe sanctions from the international community because of its size, high-grade petroleum reserves, and the significant presence of foreign oil companies in the country. Pressure on their home governments by U.S. and European multinationals, especially oil companies alongside a group of well-paid Abacha lobbyists, ensured that severe economic sanctions on Nigeria were never imposed.

International pressure is often limited in what it can achieve. Nigeria's global leverage stems directly from oil. It remains a highly visible and powerful member of OPEC, selling on average 2 million barrels of petroleum daily and contributing approximately 8 percent to United States oil imports. Babangida and Abacha presided over an economy in which the leading European countries such as Britain, France, and Germany each had over US$1 billion in investments. Nigeria's oil wealth and its great economic potential have tempered the resolve of Western nations for combating human rights and other abuses, notably during the Abacha period from 1993 to 1998.

The government of General Abacha was far less sensitive to international pressure than its predecessors. Limited economic sanctions and the growing threat of more severe measures had little influence on the regime. Abacha at first decided unilaterally to stop implementing key features of the structural adjustment program. When the economy plummeted in 1994 as a result of this decision, the government instituted minor economic reforms that lowered inflation and increased GDP growth in 1995 and 1996. By 1997, however, these gains were erased as massive official corruption locked the nation in recession. Abacha and his cronies allowed Nigeria's already dysfunctional petroleum refineries to collapse, forcing this oil-exporting OPEC nation to import fuel—through contractors connected to Abacha. Transport prices doubled overnight, as did the price of food and most other goods. Further, in an ostensible effort to

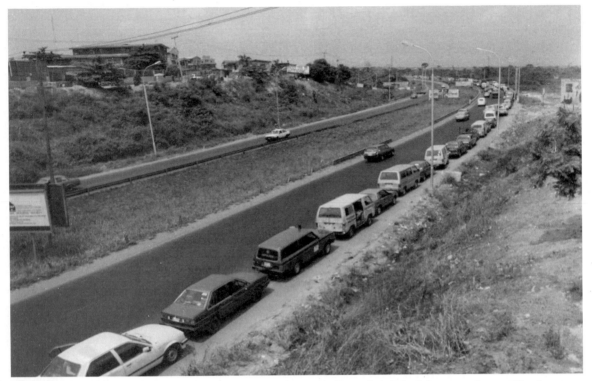

Despite being sub-Saharan Africa's largest crude oil exporter, Nigeria faces chronic fuel shortages. General Abacha allowed the nation's four refineries to collapse, forcing the country into the absurd situation of importing fuel—through middlemen who gave enormous kickbacks to Abacha and his family. *Source:* Jay Oguntuwase-Asope, *The Guardian* (Lagos), August 12, 1998.

combat inflation, but more likely to cover up the billions his cabal was siphoning from the budget, Abacha withheld all appropriations to government agencies, except portions of the military, for the first seven months of 1997. Given the large role of the government in the economy, activity all but ground to a halt.

General Abubakar's release of most political prisoners and his regime's new transition program in 1998 quickly won back much of the international standing lost under Abacha. His promise to implement the economic reforms recommended by the *Vision 2010* committee, much of which President-elect Obasanjo pledged to continue, also won praise from businesses and renewed attention from some international investors.

Section ❸ Governance and Policy-Making

The rough edges of what has been called the unfinished Nigerian state can be seen in its institutions of governance and policy-making. What seemed like an endless political transition under the Babangida and Abacha regimes was rushed through in less than a year by their successor, Abdulsalami Abubakar. A prolonged rambling process, followed over fourteen years, followed by a rushed one, makes it more difficult to characterize the institutions of governance in Nigeria than in other countries. With that in mind, an account is presented of how these institutions functioned in Nigeria historically, how Nigerians hoped they would perform, and how they have operated in practice.

Organization of the State

The National Question and Constitutional Governance

After four decades of independence, Nigerians are still debating the basic political structures of the country, who will rule and how, and even if the country should remain united. They call this fundamental governance issue the "national question": How is the country to be governed given its great diversity? What should be the institutional form of the government? How can all sections of the country work in harmony and none feel excluded or dominated by the others? Nigerian leaders have attempted to answer these questions in various ways. Since the creation of Nigeria by the British, one path has been reliance on the Anglo-American tradition of rule by law rather than by individuals. Another path has been military guidance. None have succeeded, so Nigeria has stumbled along, recently under some hybrid of these two tendencies. As a consequence, Nigeria has produced many constitutions but has yet to entrench constitutionalism.

Since the amalgamation of northern and southern Nigeria in 1914, the country has introduced, or nearly inaugurated, nine constitutions, five under colonial rule (in 1922, 1946, 1951, 1954, and 1960) and four after colonial rule: the 1963 republican constitution, the 1979 constitution of the Second Republic, the 1989 constitution intended for the Third Republic; and a 1995 constitution that will finally be introduced in greatly amended form before power is transferred in 1999. Despite the expenditure of huge sums by both the Babangida and Abacha regimes on constitution-making, Nigeria experienced the anomaly of conducting national elections in 1998–1999 without a settled constitutional document.

In the United States, the U.S. Constitution is perceived as a living document and subject to interpretation. Even though the U.S. Constitution has been interpreted in various ways based on legal precedent and political expedience, the document itself has endured for over two hundred years with just twenty-seven amendments. In contrast, Nigerian constitutions have earned no such respect from military and civilian leaders, who have been unwilling to observe legal/constitutional constraints. Governance and policy-making in this context are conducted within fragile institutions that are often swamped by personal and partisan considerations. Military rule has bolstered these tendencies and personalized governance and policy-making. With this in mind, we discuss key elements of recent periods of military rule, their continued influence in the present, and the institutions projected for the Fourth Republic.

Federalism and State Structure

Nigeria's First Republic experimented with the parliamentary model, in which the executive is chosen directly from the legislative ranks in a manner inspired by the British system. The First Republic was relatively decentralized, with the locus of political power in the three federal units, the Northern, Eastern, and Western Regions. The Second Republic constitution, which went into effect in 1979, adopted a U.S.-style presidential model. The consensus among Nigeria's constitutional planners for the next Republic is that its structure should continue to be a variant of the U.S. model. In this view, democratic Nigeria should possess a presidential system with a strong executive who is constrained by a system of checks and balances on authority; a bicameral legislature; and an independent judicial branch charged with matters of law and constitutional interpretation. In addition, Nigeria should have a federal structure comprising states and local government units empowered to enact their own laws within their individual jurisdictions, but limited in scope by the constitution and federal laws. Together, these units should constitute a single national entity.

Nigeria's federal system thus operates with three levels of government. The first or highest is the national government, and, as in the U.S. federal system, state and local levels of government as well. Like the national government, each of the thirty-six state governments and 774 local governments in Nigeria has an executive branch and a legislative branch, although the legislatures are usually disbanded under military rule. The judicial system also resembles that of the United States, with a network of local and district courts as well as state-level courts.

Under a true federal system, the formal powers of the different levels of government would be clearly delineated, and the relationships among and between them defined. In Nigeria, by contrast, these institutions have been radically altered by military rule. The dominance of central government authority, particularly the executive, has been enhanced to suit the expedience of the junta of the moment. So while Nigerian federalism remains a subject of political and social discourse, in large part because of its ethnic overtones and federal character (see next section), the military is not a unit of governance in the traditional design of a federal structure. The control of oil wealth by this centralized command structure has further cemented economic and political control in the center, resulting in a skewed federalism in which states enjoy nominal powers but in reality are totally dependent on the central government. In other words, Nigeria under military rule has been a federation in name only. In reality, the nation has been governed as a unitary state, with the federal constituent parts acting primarily as administrative appendages of the center.

Federal Character

Numerous attempts have been made to arrive at some form of elite accommodation to moderate some of the more divisive dimensions of cultural pluralism. For example, recruitment of local elements into the army shortly after independence followed a quota system. Through such a system it was hoped the army would reflect the country's complex ethnic makeup. A similar practice, reflecting what Nigerians now refer to as **federal character**, was introduced into the public service and formally codified in Section 14(3) of the 1979 constitution:

> The composition of the Government of the Federation or any of its agencies and the conduct of its affairs shall be carried out in such manner as to reflect the federal character and the need to promote national unity, and also to command national loyalty thereby ensuring that there shall be no predominance of persons from a few states or from a few ethnic or other sectional groups in that government or any of its agencies.

Federal character has also come to be applied in university admissions, and as a requirement for private companies that do business with the government. Many businesses and organizations therefore feature their own hiring programs to promote ethnic balance.

Because federal character is also perceived as a tool of ethnic management, disputes about its application have tended to focus on ethnic representation rather than on representation of state interests. Although this principle was originally regarded as a positive Nigerian contribution to governance in a plural society, its application has tended to intensify rather than reduce intergroup rivalries and conflicts. In recent years there have been calls for the use of merit over federal character in awarding public-sector jobs.

Most of the resistance to federal character has come from southern Nigerians, whose historically higher levels of education and income have left many of them bitter that they have been passed up for job promotion or admission to the best universities in favor of northerners. For many southerners, federal character has become synonymous with "northernization," a presumed strategy of the north to control both the government and the economy. Northern professionals, meanwhile, express frustration that they are often assumed to be incompetent by their southern counterparts.

The Executive

Evolution of Executive Function

In the Second Republic, the earlier parliamentary system was replaced by a presidential system based on the U.S. model. The president was chosen directly by the electorate rather than indirectly by the legislature. The rationale for the change was based on the experience of the First Republic; the instability and ultimate failure of that government, which was less a result of the parliamentary model per se than of underlying societal cleavages, left a bitter legacy. In addition, there was a widespread belief that a popularly elected president, a truly national figure, could serve as a symbol of unity. Finally, the framers of the Second Republic's constitution believed that placing the election of the president in the hands of the electorate rather than parliament would mitigate the effects of a lack of party discipline in the selection of the executive.

Current Challenges: *Nigeria's "Federal Character"*

What is Nigeria's "federal character"? Federal character, in principle, is an affirmative action program to ensure representation of all ethnic and regional groups, particularly in the civil service. Although federal character is regarded as a euphemism for ethnic balancing, in practice it has provoked ethnic instability, rivalry, and conflict. Federal character goes beyond federalism in the traditional Western and territorial sense, although it definitely contains a territorial element. Federalism as a principle of government has a positive connotation (especially in regard to mitigating ethnic conflict); however, federal character elicits unevenness and inequality in Nigerian politics.

The pursuit of ethnic balancing has had numerous ill effects, several of which are identified by Nigerian scholar Peter Ekeh. First, federal character has created benefit-seeking and autonomy-seeking groups in areas where they did not previously exist. Second, federal character and federalism have overloaded the political system in terms of personnel and other costs. Federal character has also "invaded the integrity of the public bureaucracy" by ignoring merit. Finally, the thirty-six states that currently exist in Nigeria are vying for control of the center in order to extract the greatest benefits, using federal character's ethnic quotas as a lever. None of these conditions is likely to change in the near future, whether a military or a civilian government is in power. Federal character, and everything that goes with it, appears

to be a permanent part of Nigeria's political and social landscape.

Despite the methods of its institution and reform, ironically, the federal system has enjoyed wide support within Nigeria historically. With the national question unanswered, however, the federal structure endures increasing strain. At the conclusion of the civil war in 1970, many assumed that the question of national unity had been finally settled. Thus attempts to include clauses on the right to secede into the constitutions of 1979 and 1989 were roundly rejected by the drafting committees. Yet the Abubakar transition period featured a number of public debates about secession, particularly among the Yoruba. Other widely held beliefs are now questioned by some elements in society. For example, will Nigeria continue to be a secular state as outlined in the 1979 constitution and persist as a federation to accommodate the country's ethnic, cultural, and religious heterogeneity? Some northerners have advocated turning Nigeria into an Islamic state, prompting fear among many Christians.

To resolve these issues, some Nigerians have called for a national conference to review the basis of national unity and even to consider the restructuring of Nigeria into a loose confederation of autonomous states, perhaps along the lines of the First Republic. Such calls have been ignored by the military, which refused to permit any debate on the viability of a united Nigeria in the 1994–1995 constitutional conference, thus maintaining the geographic status quo. General Abubakar also ignored renewed calls for a national conference when he initiated his transition program in 1998. Key members of some of the nascent political parties have indicated that they will include such a conference in their platforms.

Source: See Ekeh, "The Structure and Meaning of Federal Character in the Nigerian Political System" in *Federal Character and Federalism in Nigeria*, ed. Peter P. Ekeh and Eghosa E. Osaghae (Ibadan: Heinemann, 1989).

In rejecting British parliamentarism for U.S.-style presidentialism, and a two-term limit, the framers of the 1979 constitution of the Second Republic argued that the new arrangement would lead to a more focused and effective executive. According to them, the U.S. model would also ensure (through the exercise of checks and balances and separation of powers) that no single arm of government would gain so much power as to put the liberties of citizens at risk. It was

argued also that presidentialism would promote political integration, since it authorized the head of the executive branch to appoint individuals from outside the legislature to the cabinet.

The Second Republic's experiment with presidentialism lasted for only four years before it was ended by the 1983 coup. Although political scientists continue to debate the relative merits of parliamentarism versus presidentialism,[12] that coup did not indict the presidential model as such. The return of military rule in 1983 further concentrated power in the hands of the chief executive, the head of state Major-General Muhammadu Buhari, until his removal in a 1985 palace coup. His successor, General Babangida, although obviously unelected, assumed the title of president, the first Nigerian military ruler to do so. After ousting Shonekan in November 1993, Sani Abacha also assumed the title of president.

The Executive under Military Rule and Future Civilian Governments

The styles and leadership approaches among Nigeria's seven military heads of state have varied widely. The military regime of General Gowon (1966–1975) was initially consensual, but as he clung to power for five years after the Biafran war, his authority declined and he increasingly relied on a small group of advisers. Although all have talked of "transitions to democracy," only General Obasanjo as a military ruler (1976–1979) and General Abubakar (1998–1999) have fulfilled the pledge of yielding power to an elected government. Buhari's coup in 1983 was initially welcomed by popular support in the wake of the abuses during the Second Republic. Many Nigerians today look back on the Buhari regime as a brief period during which the government exercised some discipline. He was, however, disliked for his authoritarian methods, the suspension of political liberties and outlawing of political activities, and for the extensive use of security services against political opponents.

After a few years of relatively consensual governance, the Babangida regime (1985–1993) drifted into the repressive policies of the Buhari era. Abacha outdid them all, however, and his harsh authoritarian rule included the 1994 suspension of habeas corpus and the hounding of outspoken Nigerians into exile. General Abubakar began like many of his predecessors, moving quickly to release political prisoners, institute a rapid democratization program, and curb the abuses of the security services. Fortunately for Nigeria, his decision to transfer power within less than a year guaranteed that his regime would not follow the usual pattern of decay, authoritarianism, and corruption.

Under both civilian and military administrations, appointments to most senior positions have been made by the president, or head of state, without seeking legislative approval. Even with the tumultuous events in Nigeria since Babangida stepped aside in August 1993, patron-client relationships remain fundamental to Nigeria's politics. Not surprisingly, therefore, ethnic, religious, and regional constituencies pay close attention to the pattern of appointments to the executive branch. Under the 1989 constitution, the proposed Third Republic would have included an executive similar to the U.S. model with several checks and balances. The U.S. presidential model is the one being followed in the Fourth Republic, although some of the innovations in Abacha's 1995 constitution (which he never formally issued), such as a rotational presidency among sections of the country, have been dropped. Whether the provisions of the eventual constitution of the Fourth Republic will be respected through implementation, however, remains to be seen. Nigeria's political history and recent experience suggest that the country will again experience the unchallenged rule of an executive president and his handpicked cabinet, ineffectually checked by a weak legislature and judiciary, both vulnerable to executive and clientelist pressures.

The Military as Executive Branch

As a result of its long years in power, the military has emerged as a central component of executive authority in Nigeria. As a consequence, the armed forces have been structurally weakened. Unlike their professional counterparts in other countries, Nigeria's military lacks camaraderie, discipline, a clear command structure, and unity of purpose. Since 1966 a distinction has developed between the military-in-government (officers appointed to political posts) and the military-in-barracks, who perform traditional military duties. Senior officers in the latter group have increasingly called for a withdrawal of the armed forces from politics and the restoration of military professionalism.

Coups conducted against military governments have often resulted from intramilitary tension. Several such attempts have failed, followed invariably by the execution or dismissal from the service of individuals implicated or suspected of disloyalty. Keenly aware of this, Babangida protected himself by constantly shuffling military personnel. Command and other major postings were dictated largely by questions of loyalty to his regime, resulting in the rapid advance of northern officers like himself. Increasingly under Babangida and then Abacha, the gulf between junior officers and the inner circle of northern military elites widened. The former were beset by a lack of prestige and inadequate pay, whereas many of the latter, including Abacha himself, profited greatly from their control of state resources.

One major consequence of these developments has been the loss by the Nigerian military of its non-political status. It is no longer considered by many Nigerians as a temporary, politically neutral alternative to civilian rule. As an institution, the military has been transformed from an instrument that guarantees national defense and security into another predatory apparatus similar to, but more powerful than, political parties. Three decades after the first military coup of January 1966, most Nigerians now believe that the country's political and economic development has been profoundly hampered by military domination and misrule. Since the late 1980s civil society groups have insisted that the military's withdrawal from public life is imperative if progress is to be made in virtually all areas of public life.

The Bureaucracy

The bureaucracy is related to and affects all aspects of Nigerian government. Although we referred to the Nigerian bureaucracy in the previous two sections, it is necessary to explain further how the Nigerian bureaucracy came to be bloated, inefficient, and corrupt. The colonial system relied greatly on an expanding bureaucracy to govern Nigeria. As government and society were increasingly "Africanized," the bureaucracy became a way to reward individuals in the patrimonial, prebendalist system. Bureaucratic growth was no longer determined by function and need; increasingly, individuals were appointed on the basis of patronage, ethnic group, and regional origin rather than merit. Administrative departments also became politicized as the government insulated and protected itself by installing civil servants who were loyal to and beholden to it.

Military governments in particular looked for allies in the bureaucracy, whose skills they needed for the complex tasks of governing. As successive military governments since 1967 increased the number of states, while also launching grandiose public projects, the capabilities of the bureaucracy declined, while its size steadily increased. It is conservatively estimated that federal and state government personnel increased from a modest 72,000 at independence to well over 1 million by the mid-1980s.

Para-statals

The largest component of the national bureaucracy in Nigeria is the state-owned enterprises, or **para-statals**, which increased from 75 entities to 500 over the same period. Para-statals in Nigeria are corporate enterprises owned by the state and established to provide specific commercial and social welfare services. They are situated between institutions that engage in traditional government operations, such as customs or the postal service, and those in the private sector that operate primarily for profit. In organizational terms, such para-statals are similar to private enterprises in having their own boards of directors. In principle they are autonomous of the government that established them. In reality, however, such autonomy is limited, since their boards are appointed by, and ultimately answerable to, the government through the supervising government ministry.

In general, para-statals are established for the following reasons. First, they serve as public utilities that provide services which government departments cannot handle effectively but which the government is reluctant to pass on to private businesses. They include ports, waterworks, telecommunications, defense industries, hydroelectric power, and petroleum exploration and extraction. A second rationale for the establishment of para-statals is the need to accelerate economic development by controlling the "commanding heights" of the economy, including steel production, petroleum and natural gas, and certain areas of agriculture. Third, para-statals are intended to provide basic utilities and services (water, electricity, public transportation, agricultural support) to citizens at a low cost. These costs are held below the level of charges for the same services needed by private firms to generate profit.

Finally, there is a nationalist dimension that relates to issues of sovereignty over sectors perceived sensitive for national security. In this regard, para-statals

Institutional Intricacies: *Corporatism*

Corporatism has varying definitions and interpretations, but may be defined broadly as a system of interest-group aggregation whereby interest groups are hierarchically ordered in terms of their relationship with the state and licensed or controlled by the state. European or societal corporatism allows the national government greater access to information about various groups in society. Societal corporatism usually connotes a coherent and efficient state bureaucracy and describes a set of centralized interest organizations that bargain with the state. Many Africanist scholars, however, have argued that the concept of corporatism does not apply in Africa because the state is fragmented. State, local, and national agencies operate at cross-purposes in pursuit of different goals, and lack centralization and coherence. A few, notably Julius Ihonvbere and Tim Shaw, have argued, however, that a state corporatist model can be applied to Nigeria.

The theoretical debate notwithstanding, the Nigerian state has endeavored to institute corporatist-like controls over various societal interest groups, including labor and business, in what might be labeled state corporatism, a variety of corporatism consistent with the authoritarian aspects of military rule. A blatant example of Nigeria's state corporatism was the 1994 attempt to control organized labor by firing the union heads and replacing them with Abacha's cronies. Unlike most environments of societal corporatism in which labor leaders with the support of their consitutents agree to cooperate with government, much of the rank and file of Nigerian labor refused to cooperate with the Abacha regime. His decimation of the union leadership was, however, effective in reducing the threat posed by trade unions to his rule.

Source: Julius Ihonvbere and Tim Shaw, "Corporatism in Nigeria" in *Corporatism in Africa: Comparative Analysis and Practice*, ed. Julius Nyang'oro and Tim Shaw (Boulder, Colo.: Westview Press, 1989).

are intended to provide services in economic areas that the government wishes to keep from the control of foreign capital and expertise. The para-statal structure is seen as a way to reduce dependence on foreign multinational firms in such industries as air transportation, seaport management, steel and petroleum production, power generation, and mass communication.

In Nigeria para-statals such as commodity boards and the Nigerian National Petroleum Corporation (NNPC) have served as major instruments of the interventionist state. They have been used to co-opt and hierarchically order business and societal interests for the purpose of controlling both society and economy —a form of governance usually called **state corporatism**. Because they are not motivated by profit, are protected by the state, and are frequently managed by administrators whose jobs are based on their personal connections rather than on managerial ability, the track record of Nigerian para-statals is littered with inefficiency, cronyism, and corruption. Most para-statal enterprises in Africa, just as in Nigeria, are a tremendous drain on the economy. It is not surprising, therefore, that one of the major requirements of the economic structural adjustment programs (see Section 2) is the privatization of most of these enterprises.

Although laudable in principle, in practice frequently mismanaged privatization programs have led to a continuation of problems. Without concerted and genuine efforts at privatization, Nigerian para-statals will likely continue to fall far short of the original expectations that they would contribute to economic development and efficient provision of services. Moreover, unless they are greatly reduced in number, they will contribute to the politics of patronage and resource allocation conducted along class and ethnic lines.

Other State Institutions

Other institutions of governance and policy-making, including the federal judiciary and subnational governments (incorporating state and local courts), operate within the context of a strong central government dominated by an all-powerful chief executive.

The Judiciary

At one time, the Nigerian judiciary enjoyed relative autonomy from the executive arm of government. Aggrieved individuals and organizations could take the government to court and expect a judgment based on the merits of their case. This situation changed as each successive military government demonstrated a profound disdain for judicial practices, and eventually undermined not only the autonomy but also the very integrity of the judiciary as a third branch of government.

The principal instrument used by the Babangida and Abacha regimes to achieve this outcome was a spate of repressive decrees that contained clauses disallowing judicial review. Such clauses were regularly inserted in government decrees barring any consideration of their legality by the courts as well as any actions taken by government officials under them. Other methods included intimidation by the security services, the creation of parallel special military tribunals that could dispense with various legal procedures and due process, and disrespect for courts of record. Through the executive's power of appointment of judicial officers to the high bench as well as the executive's control of funds required for the running of the judiciary, the government can manipulate and dominate the courts at all levels. Even in more routine civil and criminal actions, the courts are subject to political interference. In addition, what was once regarded as a highly competent judiciary has been undermined severely by declining standards of legal training as well as bribery. Deprived of adequate resources and the protections afforded the judiciary in Western societies, the judiciary has become an instrument of military regimes rather than an independent branch of government.

Any remaining doubts about this development were dispelled on July 22, 1993, when, in what analysts labeled "judicial terrorism," the Supreme Court endorsed a government position that literally placed all actions of the executive beyond the pale of judicial review. In a landmark judgment on a suit that sought judicial review of Babangida's decision to annul the June 12 election, the court ruled that it lacked jurisdiction, thereby bowing to the argument that any decree of a military government cannot be legally challenged. The judiciary in Nigeria has effectively ceased to be the last bastion for the protection of the rights of Nigerian citizens. The prolonged detention and death of Moshood Abiola after he declared himself president in June 1994, combined with the multiple changes in presiding judges hearing challenges to his detention, further eroded public confidence in the judiciary. The detention and hanging of Ken Saro-Wiwa and eight other Ogoni activists in 1995 underscored the politicization and compromised state of judicial system. The military did not even bother to make a legal argument before a court of law. Instead, the military arranged its own court, consisting primarily of military officers, for the nine accused civilians. Not surprisingly, this sham court returned a guilty verdict; within forty-eight hours of the verdict, the nine had been hung, an action that was itself a violation of the automatic review procedure for death penalty decisions under Nigerian law.

State and Local Judiciaries

The judiciaries at the state level are subordinate to the Federal Court of Appeal and the Supreme Court. Some of the states in the northern part of the country with high Muslim populations maintain a parallel court system based on the Islamic *shari'a* (divine law). Similarly, some states in the Middle Belt and southern part of the country have subsidiary courts based on customary law. Each of these, in turn, maintains an appellate division. Otherwise, all courts of record in the country are based on the English common law tradition, and all courts are ultimately bound by decisions handed down by the Supreme Court. As noted earlier, however, the decisions of all courts may be effectively overruled by the military government.

Because it has been a source of continuing debate in Nigerian politics, the subject of *shari'a* deserves mention. For several years, some northern groups have participated in a movement to apply *shari'a* to all of Nigeria, and some even advocated that it be made the supreme law of the land. In 1977 northern groups led a boycott of the Constituent Assembly when it began drafting the Second Republic constitution, demanding stronger emphasis on *shari'a* in that national document. Although the military government of Obasanjo blocked the expansion of *shari'a*, provisions were made that allowed the appointment of several judges qualified in Islamic personal law to the federal Court of Appeal and the Supreme Court. Demands for a broader application of Islamic law were made during the drafting of the 1989 constitution, but these were again thwarted. At present, *shari'a* courts have jurisdiction only in civil proceedings and in questions of Islamic personal law.

The application of *shari'a* has sparked heated debate. On the one hand, Muslims view *shari'a* as a way of life. On the other, southerners and Christians consider the very presence of *shari'a* on a national level threatening to their own interests and beliefs, and another example of northern domination. The attempt under Babangida to alter Nigeria's status from observer to full membership in the Organization of Islamic Conference in 1986 also prompted fears that the secular nature of the state was endangered.

It is hoped that some of the professionalism and dignity engendered by independence will revert to the judiciary in the next Republic. New budgetary arrangements will be needed to protect the institutional interests of the judiciary vis-à-vis the executive. Moreover, the executive will need to be encouraged to respect judicial autonomy as a vital component of democratic governance. Unfortunately, the experience of the judiciary during periods of civilian party politics, although not as devastating as during military rule, does not bode well for the restoration of an autonomous judiciary and respect for the rule of law in the near future.

State and Local Government

Because the creation of new states and local governments opens new channels to the oil wealth accumulated at the federal level, localities are constantly clamoring for more. Sensing opportunities to buy support for their regimes, Babangida and Abacha nearly doubled the number of states and tripled that of local governments (see Table 5 on page 583). Although they touted these moves as answering the national question by increasing opportunities for local self-determination, probably only Lagos and Kano states could survive without federal subsidies.

Debate over the 1995 constitution, therefore, raised the idea of cutting the number of states, but no one wanted to be the first to give up theirs. In response, constitutional planners raised the notion of six zones in Nigeria to correlate roughly with the major ethnic regions in the country—Hausa-Fulani, Igbo, Yoruba, and three minority-dominated areas. The only concrete purpose of the zones that the Abacha administration publicly discussed was to delineate the regions among which the presidency was to rotate. This notion of a rotational presidency was presented as yet another attempt to answer the national question, but was set aside by the Abubakar government in 1999.

Virtually the entire process of constituting and reconstituting this federal arrangement, including the addition of a third level of government, consisting of 774 local governments by 1996, has occurred under either colonial or military rule. The initial motivation to create additional subnational units in the federation was to bring government closer to the people, foster development, and accommodate the demands of minority ethnic groups for their own units. In addition, creating more states addressed the key structural flaw of the First Republic's weak federalist arrangement of three (and in 1963, four) regions: the Northern Region was larger territorially and in population terms than the others combined. Breaking the north into states was intended to blunt its influence on the federal government, although it has subsequently retained a greater number of states than the south.

As mentioned, however, adding more states to the federation was also clearly an intrinsic part of a strategy of state corporatism, designed to keep the many subnational units financially dependent on and beholden to the central government. Such practices were employed by the Babangida and Abacha military regimes to divide and control the Nigerian population rather than to enhance popular participation. In sum, the Nigerian experience has promoted a distributive approach to federalism. The lofty claims for federalism as a way of promoting unity through diversity are lost amid the intense competition among "local communities and elites for access to national patronage in the form of oil revenues which are collected, and then appropriated or redistributed, by the federal administration"[13] through the states (see Table 6 on page 584).

State governments are generally weak and dependent on federally controlled revenues. Most of them

Table 5

Political Divisions, 1963–1996					
1963	*1967*	*1976*	*1987*	*1991*	*1996*
Northern Region	North Central	Kaduna	Kaduna	Kaduna	*(Northwest zone)* Kaduna
			Katsina	Katsina	Katsina
	Kano	Kano	Kano	Kano	Kano
				Jigawa	Jigawa
	North-Western	Sokoto	Sokoto	Sokoto	Sokoto
					Zamfara
				Kebbi	Kebbi
					(North-central zone)
		Niger	Niger	Niger	Niger
	Benue-Plateau	Benue-Plateau	Benue-Plateau	Benue	Benue
				Plateau	Plateau
					Nassarawa
		Abuja	Abuja	FCT (Abuja)[a]	FCT (Abuja)
	West-Central	Kwara	Kwara	Kwara	Kwara
				Kogi[b]	Kogi
					(Northeast zone)
	North-Eastern	Bauchi	Bauchi	Bauchi	Bauchi
					Gombe
		Borno	Borno	Borno	Borno
				Yobe	Yobe
		Gongola	Gongola	Adamawa	Adamawa
				Taraba	Taraba
Eastern Region	East-Central	Anambra	Anambra	Anambra	*(Southeast zone)* Anambra
				Enugu	Enugu
					Ebonyi
		Imo	Imo	Imo	Imo
				Abia	Abia
					(South-south zone)
	South-Eastern	Cross River	Cross River	Cross River	Cross River
			Akwa Ibom	Akwa Ibom	Akwa Ibom
	Rivers	Rivers	Rivers	Rivers	Rivers
					Bayelsa
Mid-West Region	Mid-Western	Bendel	Bendel	Edo	Edo
				Delta	Delta
Western Region	Western	Ogun	Ogun	Ogun	*(Southwest zone)* Ogun
		Ondo	Ondo	Ondo	Ondo
					Ekiti
		Oyo	Oyo	Oyo	Oyo
				Osun	Osun
Lagos[c]	Lagos	Lagos	Lagos	Lagos	Lagos

[a]Abuja replaced Lagos as the federal capital in December 1991, although its boundaries were first delineated in the 1970s.
[b]Kogi state was created by combining parts of Benue and Kwara states.
[c]Lagos was excised from the Western Region in 1954 and became the federal capital. In 1967 it also became capital of the new Lagos state, which included Badagry, Ikeja, and Epe districts from the Western Region.

Source: From *Politics and Economic Development in Nigeria* by Tom Forrest. Copyright © 1993, 1995 by Westview Press Inc. Reprinted by permission of Westview Press, a member of Perseus Books, L. L. C.

Table 6

Percentage Contribution of Different Sources of Government Revenue to Allocated Revenue, 1980–1996

| | Oil Revenue | | Non-Oil Revenue | | |
	Petroleum Profits Tax	Mining Rents and Royalties	Customs and Excise Duties	Other	Total
1980	58.1	25.7	12.3	3.9	100.0
1981	55.5	19.6	20.4	4.5	100.0
1982	44.5	27.3	21.5	6.7	100.0
1983	35.7	33.4	18.9	12.0	100.0
1984	44.8	32.4	15.2	7.6	100.0
1985	47.8	30.0	14.7	7.5	100.0
1986	40.5	25.3	14.6	19.6	100.0
1987	50.6	25.4	14.3	9.7	100.0
1988	46.7	31.5	15.9	5.9	100.0
	Oil Revenue (Combined)		Non-Oil Revenue	Other	Total
1992	86.2		8.4	5.4	100.0
1993	84.0		8.0	8.0	100.0
1994	79.3		9.1	11.6	100.0
1995	53.2		8.1	38.7[a]	100.0
1996	51.1		10.6	38.3[a]	100.0

[a]Beginning in 1995, the Nigerian government began including surplus foreign exchange as federally collected revenue in its accounting.

Sources: Federal Ministry of Finance and Economic Development, Lagos. From Adedotun Phillips, "Managing Fiscal Federalism: Revenue Allocation Issues," *Publius: The Journal of Federalism* 21, no. 4 (Fall 1991), 109. Nigerian Federal Office of Statistics, *Annual Abstract of Statistics: 1997 Edition.*

would be insolvent and unable to sustain themselves without substantial support from the central government, because of the states' weak resource and tax base. In the same way that states depend on federal handouts, local governments have remained dependent on both state and federal governments. This practice has continued despite reforms of the local government system initiated by the Babangida regime in 1988, supposedly to strengthen that level of government. The state and local governments have the constitutional and legal powers to raise funds through taxes. However, Nigerians, especially those in self-employment, trade, and other informal sector activities, share a pronounced unwillingness to pay taxes and fees to a government with such a poor record of delivering basic services. Moreover, experience seems to support the belief that most funds paid to government, at all levels, will be misused or simply stolen. The result is a vicious cycle. Government is sapped of resources and legitimacy, and cannot adequately serve the people. Communities, in turn, are compelled to resort to self-help measures to protect these operations and thus withdraw further from the reach of the state. Because very few individuals and organizations pay taxes, even the most basic government functions cannot be performed (see Table 7 on page 585).

Although intergovernmental relations tend to be less confrontational under military rule because of its unitary command structure, conflict between subnational and national governments is inevitable. During the civilian Second Republic (1979–1983), conflicts developed between the federal and state governments, mostly over access to economic resources. About 90 percent of state incomes were received directly from the federal government, which includes a lump sum based on oil revenues, plus a percentage of oil income based on population. One of the challenges confronting the Fourth Republic is to develop a more effective federal system that would devolve more resources to state and local governments. These governmental units

Table 7

Share of Total Government Expenditure								
	1961	1965	1970	1975	1980	1987	1992	1996
Federal government	49%	53%	73%	72%	66%	75%	72%	74%
State government	51%	47%	27%	28%	34%	25%	28%[a]	26%[a]
Total expenditure (Naira millions)	336	445	1,149	10,916	21,349	29,365	128,476	327,707

[a]Note that 67% of state spending in 1992 and 49% in 1996 came from federal government oil earnings, part of which are allocated annually to all the states roughly in proportion to their population size.

Sources: Central Bank of Nigeria, *Annual Report and Statement of Accounts;* Federal Office of Statistics, *Abstract of Annual Statistics* (Lagos: Federal Government Printer, 1961, 1965, 1970, 1975, 1980, 1987, and 1997). From Izeubuwa Osayimwese and Sunday Iyare, "The Economics of Nigerian Federalism: Selected Issues in Economic Management," *Publius: The Journal of Federalism* 21, no. 4 (Fall 1991), 91. 1990s percentage calculations by Darren Kew.

must, however, generate more resources of their own to increase the efficiency of both their administrations and private economic sectors.

The Policy-Making Process

Nigeria's prolonged experience with military rule has resulted in a policy process based on top-down directives rather than on consultation, political debate, and legislation. Formal powers are concentrated in the military ruler. Much of the policy input process (to the extent it exists) comes to the president and his "cabinet" through informal channels and networks where clientelist practices flourish.

Because of their influence in recruitment and promotions, as well as through their own charisma or political connections, senior officers often develop a network of supporters of the same or lower rank, creating what is referred to as a "loyalty pyramid."[14] Once in power, the men at the top of these pyramids in Nigeria have access to tremendous oil wealth, which is passed on through the lower echelons of the pyramid to reward support. Often these pyramids feature ethnic or religious affiliations (see the discussions of corruption in Section 2 and prebendalism in Section 4), such as the "Kaduna Mafia" of officers from the Middle Belt, but pyramids like the "Babangida Boys" or "Abacha Boys" included a patchwork of officers from beyond the Middle Belt or northern sections of their leaders. In addition, the

well-developed pyramids have allies or personal connections in the bureaucracy, business, or elsewhere in the private sector.

When the military seizes power, divisions within its ranks can become as politicized as those among the political parties in a civilian legislature. Thus a hierarchical institution structured to perform a single function—national security—over time will see its institutional solidarity and identity in constant tension with the politics of loyalty pyramids. As the regime struggles to address Nigeria's mammoth problems, whatever legitimacy the regime first gained in its claim to end corruption or to save the integrity of the state tends to be replaced by a legitimacy based on the tool that lifted it to power in the first place: the gun.

The personal ambitions of loyalty pyramid leaders eclipse the unified corporate mission of the military to "save" the nation. In time, personal ambition is the defining characteristic of the regime, with its only check being another coup. Most civilian leaders, of course, also have strong personal ambition, but if the democratic system is strong, their choices are constrained by the desire to be reelected. In most military regimes, the executive is constrained only by the balance of power among the loyalty pyramids within the armed forces, and the weakness of the overall economic and political systems that existed before the coup. Rather than addressing national problems, military regimes end up spending most of their time trying to solidify their shifting sources of power among the loyalty pyramids, which in Nigeria no leader or coalition of pyramids has been able to sustain indefinitely. Thus, in the end military regimes are no more stable, no less corrupt, no more effective economic managers than the civilians.

In many African countries, a coup signifies the ascension of one particular loyalty pyramid into power, often at the expense of others. Nigeria's first coup in 1966 appeared to signal the rise of a group of Igbo officers under General Ironsi, although he tried to maintain a more nationalist image. General Gowon, on the other hand, helped to establish a collegial (or consensus) model of military governance in which important decisions were made by an ethnically balanced body consisting of the leaders of the major loyalty pyramids. Because of the Biafran civil war, the young Gowon, a Christian from the Middle Belt and without much of a loyalty pyramid of his own, was picked by his senior officers to be a compromise head of state.Using this collegial model, Gowon successfully oversaw the reintegration of Biafra into Nigeria. The Muhammed and Obasanjo regimes also employed this model, as did Buhari and, at first, Babangida.

General Babangida, however, signified the turning point within the military when national concerns became increasingly subsumed by personal ambitions. He was a master at playing the different loyalty pyramids against each other, lavishing the nation's oil wealth on friends and buying the support of opponents he could not crush. Although Babangida's Armed Forces Ruling Council (AFRC) was initially tailored in the collegial fashion to reflect the ethnic and religious balance in the nation, he gradually replaced AFRC members with officers of northern descent who, more important, were his "boys." By the early 1990s the AFRC was quickly becoming a one-man operation with only one agenda: personal aggrandizement and enrichment. Babangida managed to survive two coups (of which the public was aware) but could not withstand the public outcry over his annulment of the June 1993 election, combined with pressure spearheaded by the Abacha faction within the military for him to step aside. Once in power, General Abacha made little pretense of accommodating other factions, ruthlessly centralizing nearly all government decision-making and spreading little of the largesse for which Babangida was famous.

Abacha's personal bonanza with the nation's revenues dispelled the notion that the military was a cohesive, nationalist institution capable of governing Nigeria more efficiently than the civilians. Young people fought for entrance to the military academies as the preferred career path to wealth and power, and private groups sprouted up—with the active support and participation of Abacha supporters in the military—to "demand" that the General stay on as a civilian president. Fearful of the growing tide of resentment within the military, Abacha rarely left the presidential fortress at Aso Rock in Abuja, almost never gave public speeches, and allowed only a cadre of closest supporters to meet with him regularly to make government policy decisions. Officers that showed a shred of independence or professionalism found their names on the next retirement list, were transferred to Liberia and Sierra Leone to fight in ECOMOG, or were even indicted for participating in coup plots that were likely fabricated. A parallel structure of junior officers fiercely loyal to Abacha acted as his gatekeepers, circumventing and humiliating the military's normal chain of command.

General Abubakar took the reins in June 1998 of a military that was a cohesive institution in name alone. The exact course of events has yet to be made public, but a number of senior officers with some remaining professionalism and concern for the integrity of the armed forces, and perhaps for the nation, appear to have rallied behind Abubakar, then chief of defense staff, to be head of state. Although Abubakar was once considered a "Babangida boy" and could not have ascended the height of the military command by being an absolute professional, he seemed intent on restoring the integrity of the military by returning it to the barracks. Within a month he had removed most of the "Abacha boys" from positions of power, instigated internal investigations into the money they had stolen, and reenergized the democratization process. He himself, however, did not appear to have the extensive loyalty pyramids of his predecessors and employed the collegial model to balance those of his current allies. Nonetheless, Abubakar's precarious position was quickly strengthened by the public and international support he won by releasing political prisoners and instituting a rapid transition program, making the likelihood of a countercoup attempt remote.

Yet regardless of whether the professional and pro-democratic inclinations of General Abubakar and his allies were genuine, others in the military clearly yearned for their turn at the top. Younger officers had spent at least fifteen years getting law degrees and Ph.D. degrees, and seeking traditional titles and chieftaincies. They had tasted power as military governors, built their own loyalty pyramids, and seen the lavish living of their predecessors, while still retaining the perspective that civilians are ineffective leaders. These men had made career investments that counted on military rule, and may not give up those ambitions lightly. Furthermore, the civilian government in 1999 inherited huge economic problems and social divisions that were certain to stretch its fragile institutions to the limits. Any chaos that results may offer ample excuses for a military entrepreneur to make his move. The civilian politicians appear well aware of this danger, but whether they will be able to resist by forging a new role with the military, as well as a sustainable coalition of support with civil society groups and public constituencies, remains to be seen.

Section ④ Representation and Participation

Representation and participation are two vital components in modern democracies; however, Nigeria clearly is not yet a democracy. As noted, Nigerian legislative bodies have been ineffectual in practice; fraud, elite manipulation, and military interference have marred the party system and elections. Nevertheless, other modes of participation exist in Nigerian society outside the official structures. An important focus of this section is the unofficial (nongovernmental) methods of representation and participation through the institutions of civil society. Whereas the institutions of political society include such entities as parties, constitutions, and legislatures, those of **civil society** include professional associations, trade unions, religious groups, and various interest groups.

The Nigerian experience described in this section emphasizes the complex nature of the relationship between representation and participation. It shows that formal representation does not necessarily enhance participation. In fact, there are situations in which the most important modes of political participation are found outside of, and in opposition to, the institutional modes such as elections and legislatures.

The Legislature

Not surprisingly, Nigeria's legislature has been a victim of the country's political instability. Legislative structures and processes have not operated free of abuse, neglect, or peremptory suspension by the executive arm for any significant length of time since independence. As a consequence, the legislature has not become a vital component of a democratic system and there is little understanding of the functions and responsibilities of the legislature.

Until the first coup in 1966, Nigeria operated its legislature along the lines of the British model with an elected lower house and a smaller upper house composed of individuals selected by the executive. Then for the next thirteen years under military rule, legislative functions were performed by a supreme military council, which initiated and passed decrees at will. During the second period of civilian rule, 1979–1983, the legislature was similar to the United States system. As in the United States, Nigeria employed a bicameral structure, with both houses (Senate and House of Representatives) consisting of elected members. The Fourth Republic that began on May 29, 1999, maintained a U.S.-inspired legislative system and a separately elected president and vice president.

Beginning with the 1983 coup led by Muhammadu Buhari, Nigeria has witnessed a succession of military councils under different names (the Supreme Military Council; the Armed Forces Ruling Council; the National Defense and Security Council; and most recently, the Provisional Ruling Council, or PRC, under Abacha) that performed the function of approving decrees issued by the military administrations. The roles and powers of these institutions varied. Usually, however, they rubber-stamped decisions made by the head of state as the system became progressively autocratic.

As part of the Babangida regime's transition program, the civilian members of the National Assembly elected in July 1992 actually held meetings until mid-1993. Once seated, however, they were barred by military decree from deliberating on issues other than those dealing with uncontroversial topics. Part of the interim national government arrangement, which only lasted from August to November 1993, was that full powers of legislation would be granted to the Senate and House of Representatives. When Abacha took over, however, he dismissed both houses as well as all other elected officials at the state and local levels.

Only one woman sat among the 91 senators and two among the 593 representatives in the Third Republic, and only eight women were elected in 1999 to sit in the Fourth Republic's National Assembly. This reflects the limited political participation of Nigerian women in formal institutions, as discussed in Section 2. Election to the Senate is on the basis of equal state representation, with three senators from each of the thirty-six states, plus one senator from the federal capital territory, Abuja. The practice of equal representation in the Senate is identical to that of the United States, except that Nigerian states elect three senators instead of two. Another difference is the election of a senator from Abuja Capital Territory, whereas Washington, D.C., has no such representation. Election to the Nigerian House of representatives is also based on state representation but weighted to reflect the relative size of each state's population, again after the U.S. example.

An innovation made in the halting transition to the Third Republic is that local government structures were to be granted greater autonomy from state control. The lessons from Nigeria's past, however, will weigh on future developments: on the whole, the federal executive has dominated the other branches of government. Subordination of the legislature to the executive is partly a consequence of the frequency of military coups. It is standard practice among coup leaders to replace all elected legislatures with ruling councils, handpicked by the military executive. Indeed, General Abacha's first act as head of state in November 1993 was to abolish all political institutions, including the duly elected national and state legislatures. He allowed the local governments elected in 1997 to take office but not the state and national assemblies elected in 1997 and 1998.

To summarize, Nigerian legislatures under military government were either powerless or nonexistent. However, even under elected civil administrations, Nigerian legislatures have been subjected to great pressure by the executive and never assumed their full constitutional role. Because the executive and majority interests in the assembly have belonged to the same party, this influence has been easily exercised through the actions of party machines and by outright bribery. The history of independent Nigeria reveals a subverted national legislature that has never effectively represented the electorate. Underlying all this is a political economy skewed in favor of an executive branch, and the dependence of legislators on the executive for their allowances and the resources to meet the relentless demands from their constituents for jobs, contracts, and other favors.

The Party System and Elections

The unfortunate legacy of the party and electoral system since independence in 1960 was that political parties were associated with certain regions and ethnic groups. This extreme factionalization was further encouraged by the tendency of most Nigerians to perceive politics as a zero-sum (or winner-take-all) struggle for access to scarce state resources. Unlike Mexico and, to some extent, India, Nigeria did not develop an authoritarian de facto single-party system after independence that might have transcended some of these social cleavages. Instead, the multiparty system reinforced and deepened existing social divisions.

Nigeria's use of a "first-past-the-post" plurality electoral system produced legislative majorities for parties with strong ethnic and regional identities. All of the parties of the First and Second Republics were more attentive to the welfare of the regions from which they drew most support than to the development of Nigeria as a whole. Control of the center, or at least access to it, ensures access to substantial financial resources. In a polity as potentially volatile as Nigeria, however, these tendencies intensified political fragmentation and persistent resentment among the losers.

Nigerian parties during the First Republic were dominated by the three largest ethnic groups. During subsequent democratic experiments, many of the more recent parties could trace their roots to their predecessors in the First Republic. Although the name of a given party may have changed, its leadership and the areas from which it drew its strongest support remained fairly consistent. For example, the victorious NPN of the Second Republic, under the leadership of Shehu Shagari, was the political heir of the northern-dominated NPC of the First Republic. Similarly, the runner-up UPN of the Second Republic can be connected to the western-based Action Group of the First Republic. The Second Republic's NPP drew on the legacy of the NCNC of the First Republic, the strongest party of the former Eastern Region. The four-year experiment with a two-party system from 1989 to 1993 and the election of Abiola in 1993 demonstrated the potential within Nigeria to move beyond ethnicity. Abiola won a number of key states in the north, including the hometown of his opponent. Once the election was annulled, however, the more familiar north-south divisions reemerged, fostered by both the regime and Abiola's most determined advocates.

The Two-Party Mandate

In its wavering steps toward the civilian Third Republic, General Babangida's administration in October 1989 announced a landmark decision to establish, by decree, two political parties. The state provided initial start-up funds and wrote the constitutions and manifestos of these parties. According to the government, its decision to form the parties followed the failure of various political associations to satisfy the requirements set by the government for registration as political parties. Based on this controversial decision, the National Republican Convention (NRC) and the Social Democratic Party (SDP) emerged, designed by the government to be "a little to the right and a little to the left," respectively, on the political-ideological spectrum.

The NRC and SDP were the only two parties allowed to operate legally until Abacha seized power in November 1993. Significantly, the NRC and SDP were modeled after their Western counterparts, the Republican and Democratic parties in the United States and the Conservative and Labour Parties in Britain, with two vital differences. First, the U.S. and British party structures emerged after years of voluntary interaction. They were not decreed into existence by the state, as in Nigeria. Second, although two parties dominate the political arena in the United States and Britain, they are not the sole parties, and significantly there are no legal restrictions on the formation of additional parties. In Nigeria the two-party limitation was explicit, and no association other than the two recognized parties could contribute to party funds or election expenses of candidates.

Interestingly, the elections that took place between 1990 and 1992 at local, state, and federal levels indicated that, despite their inauspicious beginnings, the two parties cut across the cleavages of ethnicity, regionalism, and religion in their membership and electoral performance. The election results also suggested that some of the old interethnic factionalism was reappearing, although a substantial measure of interethnic cooperation contributed to the victory of Moshood Abiola, a southern Muslim, in the June 12 presidential election. As shown in Table 8 on pages 590–591, northern-based parties dominated the first and second experiments with civilian rule. Given this historical trend, it is significant that a southerner was able to win the presidency in 1993—the first time in Nigeria's history that a southerner defeated a northerner in elections to lead the nation. Southerners, therefore, perceived the decision by the northern-dominated Babangida regime to annul the June 12 elections as a deliberate attempt by the military and northern interests to maintain their decades-long domination of the highest levels of government.

The annulment, and the regional and ethnic tension that followed it, resuscitated the belief that Nigerian party and electoral processes could not overcome ethnic and cultural cleavages. The SDP was linked in terms of its membership and leadership to a southern-dominated Second Republic alliance of the Unity Party of Nigeria, UPN (mainly Yoruba), and the Nigerian Peoples Party, NPP (mainly Igbo). However, it also attracted splinter elements of the Second Republic's Peoples Redemption Party, PRP (organized and located around Kano city in northern Nigeria), and the Great Nigerian People's Party, GNPP (organized around the Kanuri northeast). Similarly, the NRC was seen as having its roots in northern forces that were the core of the National

Table 8

Federal Election Results in Nigeria, 1959–1999

1959 Federal Parliamentary Elections[a]

	No. of Seats	NPC	NCNC/NEPU Alliance	AG	Others
Total	310	134	89	73	14
Percent	100	43.2	28.7	23.6	4.5

Distribution of Parliamentary Seats after 12/64 and 3/65 Elections[b]

	No. of Seats	NPC	NNDP	NCNC	AG	NPF	Independent
Total	312	162	36	84	21	4	5
Percent	100	51.9	11.6	26.9	6.7	1.3	1.6

1979 General Elections, House of Representatives[c]

	No. of Seats	GNPP	UPN	NPN	PRP	NPP
Total	449	43	111	168	49	78
Percent	100	9.6	24.7	37.4	10.9	17.4

1979 Senate Elections[d]

	GNPP	UPN	NPN	PRP	NPP
Seats won (out of 95)	8	28	36	7	16
Percent	8.4	29.5	37.9	7.3	16.9

1979 Presidential Election[e]

		Ibrahim (GNPP)	Awolowo (UPN)	Shagari (NPN)	Kano (PRP)	Azikiwe (NPP)
Actual vote	16,846,633	1.68 million	4.92 million	5.69 million	1.74 million	2.81 million
Percent	100	10.0	29.2	33.8	10.3	16.7
No. states won	25%	3	6	12	2	3

Requirements for victory: plurality of popular vote, plus at least 25% of the vote in two-thirds (66.66%) of the nineteen states. Note that Shagari reached this level in just twelve of nineteen states (63.16%); however, a favorable ruling by the Federal Elections Commission (FEDECO) ensured his victory.

1983 House of Representatives Elections[f]

	No. of Seats	NAP	GNPP	UPN	NPN	PRP	NPP
Total	450[g]	0	0	33	264	41	48
Percent	100	0	0	7.3	58.7	9.1	10.7

1983 Senate Elections[h]

	NAP	GNPP	UPN	NPN	PRP	NPP
Seats won (out of 96)[i]	0	1	16	61	5	13
Percent	0	1.0	16.7	63.6	5.2	13.5

1983 Presidential Election[j]

		Tunji Braithwaite (NAP)	Waziri Ibrahim (GNPP)	Obafemi Awolowo (UPN)	Shehu Shagari (NPN)	Hassan Yusuf (PRP)	Nnamdi Azikiwe (NPP)
Actual Vote	25,454,967	.289 million	.641 million	7.91 million	12.05 million	1.04 million	3.53 million
Percent	100	1.1	2.5	31.1	47.3	4.1	13.9
No. states won (25%)	–	0	0	7	16	1	4

Requirements for victory: plurality of popular vote, plus at least 25% of the votes in two-thirds of the nineteen states.

Table 8 (*continued*)

Federal Election Results in Nigeria, 1959–1999

1991 State Government Elections[k]

	Total Gubernatorial Seats	Total State House Majorities[l]
SDP	14	17
NRC	16	11

1992 National Assembly and Senate Elections

	Total National Assembly Seats	Total Senate Seats
SDP	276	38
NRC	317	53

1993 Presidential Election (annulled by military)

	Percentage of Popular Vote	States Won (out of 30)
SDP (Abiola)	58	19
NRC (Tofa)	42	11

1998 Local Government Elections[m]

	Total Council Chairs (out of 774)	Total States with Majority (out of 36, plus FCT)
PDP	426	28 (including FCT)
APP	172	2 (one tied with PDP)
AD	95	6
Others	6	0

1999 State Gubernatorial and House of Assembly Elections

	Total Governor Seats (out of 36)	House of Assembly Majorities (out of 36)
PDP	21	23
APP	9	8
AD	6	5

1999 National Assembly Elections[n]

	Senate (out of 109)	House (out of 360)
PDP	59	206
APP	24	74
AD	20	68

1999 Presidential Election

	Percentage of Votes Cast
PDP (Obasanjo)	62.78
APP/AD (Falae)	37.22

[a]Adapted from Richard Sklar, *Nigerian Political Parties: Power in an Emergent African Nation* (New York: NOK Publishers, 1983), 36.

[b]Adapted from Larry Diamond, *Class, Ethnicity and Democracy in Nigeria: The Failure of the First Republic* (Syracuse: Syracuse University Press, 1988), 227.

[c]Figures from Richard A. Joseph, *Democracy and Prebendal Politics in Nigeria* (London: Cambridge University Press, 1987), 126.

[d]Figures from Joseph, 125.

[e]Adapted from Joseph, 127.

[f]Adapted from Toyin Falola and Julius Ihonvbere, *The Rise and Fall of the Second Republic* (London: Zed Books, 1985), 221.

[g]One seat added for FCT.

[h]Adapted from Falola and Ihonvbere, 220.

[i]One seat added for FCT.

[j]Adapted from Falola and Ihonvbere, 220.

[k]All 1991–1993 election results are from Larry Diamond, Anthony Kirk-Greene, and Oyeleye Oyediran, eds., *Transitions Without End: Nigerian Politics and Civil Society under Babangida* (Boulder, Colo.: Lynne Rienner, 1997).

[l]Two of the State Houses of Assembly were evenly split between SDP and NRC.

[m]Preliminary results, *The Guardian* (Lagos), Dcember 9, 1998.

[n]Preliminary results, *The Guardian* (Lagos), February 24, 1999. Six Senate and twelve House seats required by-election runoffs or court rulings.

Table 9

List of Acronyms Used in Table 8	
AD	Alliance for Democracy
AG	Action Group
APP	All People's Party
GNPP	Great Nigerian People's Party
NAP	Nigerian Advance Party
NCNC	National Convention of Nigerian Citizens (formerly, National Council of Nigeria and the Cameroons)
NEPU	Northern Elements Progressive Union
NNDP	Nigerian National Democratic Party
NPC	Northern People's Congress
NPF	Northern Progressive Front
NPN	National Party of Nigeria
NPP	Nigerian People's Party
NRC	National Republican Convention
PDP	People's Democratic Party
PRP	People's Redemption Party
SDP	Social Democratic Party
UPN	Unity Party of Nigeria

Party of Nigeria (NPN), which dominated the central government in the Second Republic under the leadership of Shehu Shagari. Thus, even before the 1993 election debacle, and despite statistics indicating a fairly diverse (especially for Nigeria) support base for each party, the SDP was informally regarded as the "Southern" Democratic Party and the NRC as the "Northern" Republican Convention.

Abacha's Ambition and Abubakar's Promise

Nigerians in general greeted General Abacha's 1993 coup and subsequent banning of the SDP and NRC with expressions of anger, while the response of party members, with a few exceptions, was muted. Southern-based human rights and pro-democracy groups, in alliance with student unions and other organizations, launched street demonstrations, while trade union strikes brought the economy to a halt by mid-1994. With the unions crushed and Abiola in jail by the end of 1994, Abacha started his own transition program. His plan began with a constitutional conference in 1994–1995, a third of whose members were

government appointees while the others were elected in electoral contests largely ignored by the public. To the nation's surprise, the conference passed a motion that the military should relinquish power by January 1996—a resolution orchestrated by retired General Shehu Yar'Adua, who had been General Obasanjo's deputy head of state as well as an SDP presidential contender. The military used bribery and pressure to have the resolution reversed. In March 1995, Yar'Adua found himself accused of plotting a coup with Obasanjo and a score of other Abacha opponents. Unlike Obasanjo, Yar'Adua did not survive his incarceration, as he died in prison in December 1997 under suspicious circumstances.

Without publicizing the constitution produced by the conference, General Abacha announced a new transition timetable in October 1995, which featured a series of elections from the local to the federal levels over the following three years in a manner reminiscent of the Babangida program. The military promptly fell behind this schedule, taking nearly a year before even allowing new parties to form. Once the ban on political associations was lifted, some of the Second Republic party structures resurfaced and applied for accreditation with the election commission. To general surprise, not only was a party favored by northern oligarchs not registered but most of the other parties led by powerful figures were also denied. In late 1996 the Abacha government registered only five parties, most of whose members had no public constituency and little political experience. By the time local government elections were held in January 1997, again behind schedule, the few people who did vote had little idea for whom they were voting; and some of the candidates confessed publicly that they had never even seen their party's manifesto.

During 1997 the five parties, which Chief Bola Ige, Second Republic governor of Oyo state, branded "five fingers of a leprous hand," began to clamor for General Abacha to run for president. Public participation in delayed state assembly elections in December 1997 was abysmal, as each of the parties proclaimed, one after another, that Abacha was their candidate. Despite strong resistance from some of its leaders, the fifth party finally succumbed to pressure and nominated Abacha in April 1998, making the presidential elections scheduled for August 1998 a mere referendum, which received the endorsement of the Chief Justice of the Supreme Court as being legally permissible. The transition process had become a travesty. Throughout the Abacha transition, military influence or active involvement in the parties was common. Key generals in the ruling regime would orchestrate party policies and provide supplementary funding for the already government-funded groups. The government actively disqualified party candidates just days before the casting of ballots, and peremptorily reversed some election results.

In 1996–1997, condemnation of the Abacha government came primarily from Lagos-based human rights and pro-democracy groups, exiles abroad, international nongovernmental organizations, and foreign governments. By April 1998, once Abacha's plan to be proclaimed president became a certainty, domestic opposition increased. A group of former governors and political leaders from the north (many former NPN and PRP members) publicly petitioned Abacha not to run for president. They were later joined by colleagues from the south, forming what they called the Group of 34 (G-34). Human rights and pro-democracy organizations began again to form alliances to organize protests, and critical press coverage recovered some of its former boldness. General Babangida in late May also voiced his opposition to Abacha's continuing as president. Nevertheless, public disenchantment and apathy were so pervasive after years of economic struggle and broken political promises that the only real obstacle to Abacha's plan for "self-succession" was whether the military would allow it.

Rumors of Abacha's ill health had circulated for a year, but his sudden death on June 8, 1998, was still a great surprise. The following day General Abubakar, Chief of Defense Staff, was sworn in as head of state. Shortly thereafter he promised a speedy transition to democracy and began releasing political prisoners. There were immediate calls for Abiola's release and his appointment to head an interim government of national unity. Abiola's death by heart attack on July 7, 1998, removed the last obstacle to the holding of entirely new elections, the preferred option of the Abubakar administration. New parties quickly formed, and even Yoruba political leaders agreed by August to participate, although they insisted that the next president should be a Yoruba to compensate their

people for having been robbed of their first elected presidency.

Once again, political associations centering on well-known personalities emerged around the country, and intense bargaining and mergers among the smaller groups took place. The G-34, the prominent group of civilian leaders who had condemned Abacha's continuation plans, tried to transform itself into a political party. They created the People's Democratic Party (PDP) in late August, minus most of the key Yoruba members of G-34, who joined a primarily Yoruba-based Alliance for Democracy (AD). At least twenty more parties applied for certification to the electoral commission, INEC, many of which were truly grassroots movements, including a transformed human rights organization and a trade union party. The Abubakar administration evidently played no role in party formation, nor did it provide government funds for their functioning, unlike its two predecessors, the Babangida and Abacha regimes.

For the first round of party registration, INEC required that parties have offices in twenty-four of the thirty-six states and pay a 1 million naira registration fee. Nine parties met these qualifications in October 1998, the most prominent of which were PDP, AD, and the All People's Party (APP); the latter included a mixture of groups from the Middle Belt, the southeast, and the far north. The next INEC hurdle required that parties earn at least 5 percent of the votes in two-thirds of the states in the December 1998 local government elections in order to proceed to the state and federal levels. This turned out to be an ingenious way of reducing the number of parties for the most important elections, and also to oblige them to try to broaden their appeal. As a consequence, only three parties competed in the elections for the federal legislature and the presidency in February 1999, with the AD and APP forming an alliance against the PDP for the purpose of the presidential vote.

In comparison to the failed experiments of Babangida and Abacha, the transition process under Abubakar moved ahead peacefully, if problematically. One important exception was the continuing unrest in the southern Niger Delta region. A number of minority groups there, who in some local government areas had engaged in a small-scale civil war since 1997, complained of being excluded from the process. In

September 1998 they seized several production sites from multinational oil corporations and demanded more local government access, development projects, and a greater share of the oil wealth. Bayelsa state elections were disrupted and had to be rescheduled, as were some local government contests in the region. Voter turnout in the Niger Delta region for the presidential and National Assembly elections was abysmal, while the political parties fraudulently inflated the returns.

Most of the registered parties rely on elite-centered structures established during previous civilian governments and transition programs. The PDP includes core members of the northern establishment NPN and the northern progressive PRP of the Second Republic. From the Second Republic, the AD drew key individuals from the Yoruba-dominated UPN, and the APP from the GNPP (a Kanuri–Middle Belt dominated party). The latter also featured southern politicians who had prominent roles in the five Abacha parties. Demonstrating the cross-ethnic alliances that have been forged and reworked despite the political disruptions of a quarter-century, only the AD reflected a specific ethnic configuration. General Obasanjo and other Yoruba leaders joined PDP. In a fiercely contested nomination battle, Obasanjo was chosen as the PDP's presidential nominee, defeating Second Republic Vice President Alex Ekwueme, who is Igbo. Obasanjo then went on to defeat the AD/APP alliance candidate, Chief Olu Falae, in the presidential contest in February 1999.

APP is truly a multiethnic collection, drawing northern politicians of royal lineage, northeastern and Middle Belt minorities, Igbo business moguls, and southern minority leaders. AD appears to be as Yoruba-centric as its Second Republic UPN and First Republic AG predecessors. Yet, like these earlier parties, it has attracted dynamic politicians from other areas, such as Alex Nwankwo, an Igbo. It is important to note the political pragmatism of the Abubakar administration (and the INEC) in registering the AD, despite its ethnoregional base, and allowing it to compete for the presidency in alliance with the APP. It made sense to accommodate rather than alienate the Yoruba people on account of the deep sense of grievance toward the federal government provoked by the 1993 annulment of Abiola's victory and the

subsequent five years of bitter conflict. The rapidity of the Abubakar-supervised electoral process benefited civil and military politicians with access to substantial financial resources. The civil society groups that led much of the struggle against the Abacha dictatorship found themselves at a disadvantage in trying to influence, and participate in, this process. The Obasanjo government will have to find ways to avoid alienating these groups—including trade unions, student associations, pro-democracy/human rights NGOs, and women's organizations—as a disaffected constituency outside the political structures of the Fourth Republic.

Military rule has shown a tendency to exacerbate ethnoregional and clientelist factionalization and has retarded the development of a party and electoral system in Nigeria. As Larry Diamond has argued, progress toward the evolution of multiethnic parties was being made during both the First and the Second Republics. In each case, this progress was terminated by military intervention. The nineteen-state structure and various electoral provisions of the Second Republic requiring broad ethnic representation in parties contributed to these advances, despite the chaotic conflicts among individuals and factions in the various parties.[15] These issues and challenges emerged once again in the 1998–1999 transition. A key question that arises is whether the party and electoral system will have the breathing space to overcome its many deficiencies or whether it will be subjected to so much top-down manipulation that it loses credibility and efficacy once again.

The requirement by the Abubakar government's electoral commission that registered parties win 5 percent of the local government election votes in two-thirds of the states in order to advance to the state level was an example of judicious political engineering. Nigeria still has to get this process right, namely, party formation through bargaining and negotiation nudged along by enabling rules and legislation. At the start of the Fourth Republic, the leadership of the parties essentially comprises arrangements of convenience among powerful individuals who retain their own resource and client bases and lack a common ideology or clear policy agenda. That is, however, how party systems began in many countries that now possess stable two- or three-party systems with periodic alternation in power. An important question, therefore, is whether Nigeria will get beyond the initial disorderly stage of party formation during the Fourth Republic or see it decay once again into confusion.

Political Culture, Citizenship, and Identity

Traditionally, institutions that represent and mobilize society in the political sphere include legislatures, political parties, and trade unions. In the process, they help to shape, organize, and express political culture and identities, thus nurturing qualities of citizenship. For all but ten years since independence in 1960, however, these institutions in Nigeria have been proscribed and disbanded (in the case of legislatures and political parties) or muzzled (in the case of labor unions). Their roles have been largely assumed by other groups and institutions, including ethnic and religious organizations, the mass media, and professional and trade groups.

The basic units of socialization are mainly family, community, and peer groups; thus it is not surprising that ethnic, religious, and educational institutions have assumed a large role in the organization and expression of political attitudes and culture. Although these institutions can be a positive force, they often possess elements that complicate the political process. In many of these circles, the state (federal government) is regarded as an amoral entity. The state's unwillingness or inability to deliver appropriate services to the populace, its rampant corruption, and the frequency of military coups have fostered a political culture of apathy and alienation among many Nigerians, and militant opposition among particular communities and groups.

Modernity Versus Traditionalism

The terrain of political culture, citizenship, and identity is a contested arena within Nigeria. The interaction of modern (colonial, Western) elements with traditional (precolonial, African) practices has created the duality of a modern sociopolitical system that rests uneasily on traditional foundations. In other words, traditional elements have been modernized and modern elements traditionalized, so that individual Nigerians straddle two worlds that are each undergo-

ing constant evolution. On one hand, the strong elements in communal societies that promoted accountability have been weakened by the intrusion of Western culture oriented toward individuality. On the other hand, the modern state has been unable to free itself from rival ethnic claims organized around narrow, exclusivist constituencies.

As a result, exclusivist identities have come to dominate Nigerian political culture and define the nature of citizenship. Individuals tend to identify with their immediate ethnic, regional, and religious (or subethnic, subregional, and subreligious) groups rather than with state institutions, especially during moments of crisis. Nigerians usually seek to extract as many benefits as possible from the state but hesitate when it comes to performing basic civic duties such as paying taxes or taking care of public property. In short, entirely missing from the relationship between state and citizen in Nigeria is a fundamental reciprocity—a working social contract—based on the belief that there is a common interest that binds them.

Religion

Religion has been a persistent basis of conflict in Nigerian history. Islam first began to filter into northeast Nigeria in the eleventh and twelfth centuries, spread to Hausaland by the fifteenth century, and greatly expanded in the early nineteenth century. In the north, Islam first coexisted with, then gradually supplanted, indigenous religions. Christianity arrived later but expanded rapidly through missionary activity in the south dating from the early nineteenth century. The amalgamation of northern and southern Nigeria in 1914 brought together the two regions and their belief systems.

These religious cultures have consistently clashed over political issues, such as during the *shari'a* debate. For most Muslims it represents a way of life and supreme (personal) law that transcends secular and state law; for many Christians it threatens the secular nature of the Nigerian state and their position within it. The pull of religious versus national identity becomes even stronger in times of economic hardship. The Babangida period corresponded with a rise in both Islamic fundamentalist movements and

Current Challenges: *Prebendalism*

Prebendalism, the peculiarly Nigerian version of corruption, is an extreme form of clientelism that refers to the practice of mobilizing cultural and other sectional identities by political aspirants and officeholders for the purpose of corruptly appropriating state resources. Prebendalism is an institutionalized pattern of political behavior that justifies the pursuit of and the use of public office for the personal benefit of the officeholder and his clients. The official public purpose of the office becomes a secondary concern. As with clientelism, the officeholder's "clients" are a specific set of elites to which he is linked, typically by ethnic or religious ties, and this linkage is key to understanding the concept. There are thus two sides involved in prebendalism, the officeholder and the client; and expectation of benefits by the clients (or supporters) perpetuates the prebendalist system. Prebendalism explicitly involves the abuse of the public realm, and therefore its inevitable consequence is the bankrupting of the state's coffers. In the context of prebendalism, a civilian or military officeholder, for example, might award state contracts to clients solely on the basis of their financial support, without regard to merit or due consideration of more qualified proposals. As practiced in the Babangida era, when official corruption occurred on an unprecedented scale, prebendalism deepened sectional cleavages and eroded the resources of the state. It also discouraged genuinely productive activity in civil society and expanded the class of individuals who live off state patronage.

As long as prebendalism remains the norm of Nigerian politics, a stable democracy will be elusive. These practices are now deeply embedded in Nigerian society and therefore are difficult to uproot. The corruption resulting from prebendalist practices is blamed in popular discourse for the enormous flight of internally generated capital into numbered accounts in overseas banking institutions. The lion's share of the US$12.2-billion Gulf War windfall is believed to have been pocketed by Babangida and senior members of his regime and the Central Bank, an example of the magnitude of the systematic pilfering of public resources. General Abacha continued this pattern and is accused of diverting US$4 billion from the Nigerian Central Bank. There are so many officeholders in Nigeria who indulge in these practices, albeit at less gargantuan levels, that Transparency International regularly listed Nigeria during the 1990s among the most corrupt countries.

evangelical Protestantism. Where significant numbers of southern Christians are living in predominantly Muslim states (for example, Kaduna state), many clashes have erupted, with great loss of life and the extensive destruction of churches, mosques, and small businesses.

The Press

The plural nature of Nigerian society, rather than the emergence of a shared political culture, can be seen in virtually all aspects of public life. The Nigerian press, for instance, has long been one of the liveliest and most irreverent in Africa. The Abacha regime moved to stifle its independence, banning several publications and threatening suspension of others. Significantly, most of the Nigerian press has been based in a Lagos-Ibadan axis in the western part of

Nigeria and has frequently been labeled "southern." In 1994, Abacha closed several of the most influential and respected southern Nigerian newspapers and magazines, including the *Guardian*, *Concord* (owned by Abiola), and *Punch*, leaving less critical and more biased publishers intact. In this regard, he was following the nefarious example of his predecessor Babangida, especially during the final and increasingly conflictual years of his rule. A northern paper, the *New Nigerian* published in Kaduna, succumbed at times to overt sectionalism. The fact that the media are sometimes regarded as captives of ethnic and regional constituencies has weakened their capacity to resist attacks on their rights and privileges. More recent developments in Nigeria have been the emergence of independent television and radio stations and the steadily increasing use of the Internet.

Interests, Social Movements, and Protest

Issues relating to political attitudes, political culture, and identities are still dominated and defined largely by elite and male urban-based interests. These interests include ethnic as well as professional and associational groups. The few non-elite groups, such as urban-based market women's associations, often serve as channels for disseminating the decisions and agendas of male-dominated groups. In essence, non-elite and rural elements continue to be marginalized and manipulated by elites and urban groups. Lacking competence in the language of public discourse, namely English, and access to financial networks, non-elites have difficulty confronting, on their own, the decision-making centers of the state and society.

Elite and non-elite Nigerians alike come together in civic organizations and interest groups such as labor unions, and student and business associations. Because the political machinery has usually been in the hands of the military, Nigerian citizens have sought alternative means of representation and protest in an effort to have an impact on political life. Historically, labor has played a significant role in Nigerian politics, as have student groups and various radical and populist organizations. Business groups, on the other hand, have frequently supported and colluded with corrupt civilian and military regimes. In the last year of the Abacha regime, however, the business class through mechanisms like *Vision 2010* called for concrete policies to end such arbitrary rule.

Labor

Continuous military pressure since 1983 has forced a decline in the once independent and powerful role of organized labor in Nigerian politics. The Babangida regime implemented strategies of state corporatism designed to control and co-opt various social forces such as labor. Organized labor, which played an important role in challenging governments during both the colonial and postcolonial eras in several African countries, now has difficulty sustaining such actions in Nigeria. Whenever the leadership of the Nigerian Labour Congress (NLC), to which all unions compulsorily belong, took a vigorous stand against the government (as happened in the strike action against the Abacha regime in summer 1994), the government sacked the leaders and appointed conservative replacements. The Nigerian labor movement has been vulnerable to reprisals by the state and private employers. First, the state has always been the biggest single employer of labor in Nigeria as well as the recognized regulator of industrial relations between employers and employees. Second, ethnic, regional, and religious divisions have often hampered labor solidarity while being deliberately manipulated by the state.

The first attempt to establish a corporatist structure for organized labor was made in 1978 under the military government of Olusegun Obasanjo, which, as mentioned earlier, used a conflict within the labor movement to impose a single central labor organization, the NLC. This policy of centralization and co-optation was carried further under Babangida, who ensured that only candidates endorsed by the government were elected to lead the more powerful unions. The result has been a waning of trade union militancy and a steady decline in the role of labor as a political, ideological, and social force.

If allowed to function without such manipulation and control by the government, however, the labor movement can regain its vitality. That potential was demonstrated during the summer of 1994, when pro-democracy strikes by the National Petroleum Employees Union (NUPENG) and other sympathetic labor groups significantly reduced oil production and nearly brought the country to a halt before the Abacha regime arrested and disbanded its leadership. One of General Abubakar's first reforms was to remove the government-appointed union administrators and allow the unions to elect their own leaders. Labor still claims an estimated 2 million members across Nigeria and remains one of the most potent forces in civil society. It therefore has a great stake in the consolidation of constitutional rule during the Fourth Republic and the protections that would allow it to organize and act freely on behalf of its members and, more broadly, the masses of disadvantaged people in Nigeria.

The Business Community

Associational and professional life has remained vibrant. Nigeria has a long history of entrepreneurialism and business development. Stifling this spirit, however, is its history of capitalism based on the appropriation of state resources. Its business class is often characterized as "pirate capitalists" because of such tendencies and the high level of corrupt practices. Many wealthy individuals have served in the military or civilian governments, or indirectly protect their access to state resources through sponsoring elected officials. Nevertheless, as the economic and political conditions in Nigeria deteriorated, the state offered fewer avenues for businesspeople and could no longer provide even the necessary infrastructure for business development.

Private interests have proved surprisingly resilient as organized groups have emerged to represent the interests of the business class and to promote economic development generally. Increasingly, such efforts occur without direct state sponsorship as groups of enterprising capitalists create interlinked business associations. These associations have proliferated throughout Nigeria and, in many areas, represent diverse groups from butchers, to manufacturers, to car-hire firms. In a number of cases, they have demonstrated social responsibility by building roads, schools, market stalls, and similar infrastructure, all of which reduces demands on government revenue. As discussed in Section 2, business associations in the 1990s emerged as a leading force in promoting economic reform in Nigeria, as well as in raising related issues.

Many local or regional groups are also members of national organizations. National business associations, such as the Nigerian Association of Chambers of Commerce, Industry, Mines, and Agriculture (NACCIMA), the largest in the country, have taken an increasingly political stance by pressing the military leadership to resolve the June 12 crisis and by forging networks with other groups through *Vision 2010*. In their bid to reduce uncertainty, halt economic decline, and protect their economic interests, large business associations increasingly perform what are clearly political roles. It will be interesting to observe if they maintain or step back from such prominent activities during the Fourth Republic.

Other Social Groups

Student activism continues to be an important feature of Nigerian political life. University and other higher-level student groups play an important political role. Along with their teachers, they suffered government harassment, banning, and attempts to engineer divisions in their unions and associations, including countless closings of the universities, during the Babangida and Abacha regimes. By 1996 the military, using the usual tactics of pressure and bribery, succeeded in dividing the students into pro- and anti-government factions in an effort to reduce their effectiveness in the democracy struggle. Professional associations of doctors and lawyers have also become champions of human rights, reflecting a tendency characteristic of societies confronting repressive governments. They often support campaigns conducted by social rights organizations, which have proliferated since the founding of the Civil Liberties Organization (CLO) in 1987.

The activities of these organizations have increased significantly since the introduction of the economic structural adjustment program (SAP). Marginal groups, including women and the young, the urban poor, and people in rural areas, have perceived an imbalance in the distribution of the benefits and burdens generated by the SAP program. Not surprisingly, the flagrant display of wealth by senior members of the military has alienated these groups and encouraged a "culture of rage"[16] among youths, artisans, the urban poor, and the unemployed.

This rage over economic hardship and military oppression led to a sharp increase in the number of human rights groups and other nongovernmental organizations (NGOs) in the 1990s. Greater funding for NGOs from governments and private foundations in Europe and the United States assisted the growth of this sector, most notably in the south but gradually in the north as well. They generally focus on such issues as civil protection, gender law, health care, media access, and public housing. Most are urban-based, although efforts to develop rural networks are under way.

The personality conflicts, ethnic divisions, and intense competition for funding hampered the challenge posed by these civil society organizations to military dictatorship. Pro-democracy efforts by NGOs peaked in the 1993–1994 struggle over the nullification of the June 12 election, when they managed to stage successful stay-home strikes in Lagos and several other southern cities. The Campaign for Democracy in 1993, and then the National Democratic Coalition (NADECO) in 1994, built an antimilitary front among the NGOs that also included students, academics, some labor unions, and other groups. As Abacha moved forward with his "self-succession" campaign in 1997–1998, once again this

sector was able to mount numerous street demonstrations and other protests to counter the regime's orchestration. Nigeria's prospects for building a sustainable democracy during the Fourth Republic will depend, in part, on the willingness of many of these advocacy groups to increase their collaboration and maintain a high level of vigilance and activism.

Section ⑤ Nigerian Politics in Transition

After winning Nigeria's freest and fairest presidential election on June 12, 1993, Moshood Abiola returned to Nigeria to try to negotiate a peaceful transfer of power. He was imprisoned in 1994 and died in 1998, just days before his expected release. On the positive side, the popular success in pressuring military strongman Babangida to step aside in August 1993 underscored the resilience and vitality of Nigeria's democratic forces. Moreover, the failure of Babangida's tactics—which reflect the essence of neopatrimonial rule, or **patrimonialism**, in which "the chief executive maintains authority through personal patronage, rather than through ideology or law"[17]—reveals that patrimonialism does not inevitably succeed in countries like Nigeria. However, the long history of patrimonial rule and prebendal politics in Nigeria does not bode well for economic or democratic political reform. As Goran Hyden has argued, "While patrimonialism may provide stability in the short-run, it tends to block the road to constitutional development and reform. As a result, changes in the system are difficult without resorting to unconstitutional means."[18]

The popular vote on June 12, 1993, provided a radical departure from the sectionalism of the past and offered a refreshing opportunity to develop a more national political agenda. The June 12 vote was as much a protest against the military as a ruling group and against Babangida as a discredited leader as it was an endorsement of Moshood Abiola for president. June 12 was a historical breakthrough, the day the ordinary people of Nigeria rose against the ethnic, religious, and regional prejudices, and the divisive politics with which colonialism and the political class had oppressed them for half a century. In doing this, they took a great step toward making Nigeria a truly

viable and democratic polity. However, this historical opportunity was allowed to slip away on account of the cynical campaign by those who created the political impasse to ethnicize and regionalize it. This campaign by the Abacha regime placed ethnicity, religion, and regionalism firmly back on the agenda. Following the sudden deaths in mid-1998 of both Abacha and the elected president he had imprisoned, Abiola, Nigeria was rushed through a hasty transition in which ethnic and regional issues predominated in the choice of candidates and in the conduct of elections. Nigeria's Fourth Republic must find ways of developing a truly national political process in which mobilization and conflicts along ethnic, regional, and religious lines gradually diminish.

Political Challenges and Changing Agendas

The Nigerian transition has been halting in part because it was planned and directed from above. This approach contrasts sharply with the popular-based movements that unseated autocracies in central and eastern Europe beginning in 1989. Promises of democratic transition have been made periodically during Nigeria's political history as a ploy by the military to stabilize and legitimize their governments. General Abubakar was determined to complete the second such transition in 1999, although ensuring that the military's interests are well-protected under civilian rule. His rapid transition program, however, has produced a tenuous democratic government that faces daunting tasks of restoring key institutions, securing social stability, and reforming the economy.

Nigeria faces enormous political challenges. One must question the peculiar nature of a transition imposed and manipulated, or at best, refereed, from above by military rulers. The continuing strength and influence of collective identities defined on the basis of religion or ethnicity are often more binding than national (that is, all-Nigerian) ones. These identities have previously been used to mobilize support at the local level, and they foster divisive politics at the federal level. The parasitic nature of the Nigerian economy is a further source of instability. Rent-seeking and other unproductive, often corrupt, business activities are accepted norms of wealth accumulation.

Nonetheless, Nigerians are sowing seeds of change in all of these areas. Attitudes toward the military in government have shifted dramatically. The decline in the appeal of military rule can be attributed to the abysmal performances of the Babangida and Abacha regimes in economic policies and governance. Many now recognize that the military, despite its important contributions to national security, is incapable of promoting economic and social progress in Nigeria. In fact, military rule has resulted in the greatest erosion of national cohesion since the civil war in the late 1960s. General Abubakar's handling of the 1998–1999 transition improved the credibility of the military, but as details of Abacha's theft mounted, so also did awareness of the ravages of military rule.

The nature and outcome of the battle against patrimonialism will help to determine the direction of political and economic change in Nigeria. For now, it is enough to note that the political crisis since 1993 provided the opportunity for an embattled people to challenge patrimonial rule by attacking its very lifeline: earnings from oil exports that go directly to the state's coffers.

Foreign pressure played an important role in maintaining the quest for democracy and sustainable development. In recent years major external forces have been more forthright and decisive in supporting civil society and democratization in Nigeria. The United States, Britain, and some member states of the European Union were very visible in exerting pressure on Babangida to leave and in applying modest sanctions in support of democracy. This has been made possible, in part, by a changing international environment, especially the willingness of the major industrial countries and the international financial institutions to support democracy in the Third World in Africa. Nigeria's increasingly weak economy and enormous debt, now estimated at US$32 billion, has made it susceptible to this kind of pressure. It is important to note, however, that although diplomatic pressures were applied to the Abacha regime, economic sanctions were never seriously threatened by the international community, allowing Abacha considerable breathing room.

Western commitment to development and democracy in Africa is not guaranteed. Much of the initiative for Africa's growth, therefore, still needs to emerge from within. In Nigeria, such initiatives will depend on substantial changes in the way Nigerians do business. As Larry Diamond has warned, "If there is to be any basis for self-sustaining growth and peaceful, democratic politics, there must be a transition from pirate capitalism to a more sophisticated and effective nurture capitalism. Nigeria must develop, for the first time, a basis of production and accumulation outside of oil and outside the state."[19] In other words, there must be a gradual replacement of the current political, economic, and social elite that derives its power and resources from state patronage by an elite that derives its economic power from diversified sources and through private initiatives outside the state system. Indeed, as Hyden has indicated, it is becoming increasingly clear that constitutional governance will be difficult to enthrone in much of Africa "without a concomitant rise of a bourgeoisie ready to defend those principles."[20]

In addition, the project of building a coherent nation-state out of competing nationalities remains largely unfinished and under constant siege by resurgent ethnonationalism and religious fundamentalism. The challenge here is to achieve a proper balance between ethnic-based symbols and institutions and those of a transethnic nature. Ethnic consciousness cannot be eliminated from society, but ethnicity should not become the main basis for political competition. Even though the opposition activities by human rights and pro-democracy activists in 1993 and 1994 were remarkable, they never coalesced into a truly national movement. These urban-based efforts did achieve a measure of success in their efforts to link up with mass associations, including some trade unions, market women, artisans, and other guild associations.

And it was the actions of these latter elements that paralyzed the economy after the arrest and detention of Moshood Abiola in June 1994.

Events since the annulment of the June 12, 1993, election demonstrate that civil society is no longer willing to be a passive vehicle for elite intrigue in Nigerian politics. The Babangida regime was unprepared for the widespread condemnation of this action and by the frequent demonstrations and riots. Pressure for a complete transition to democratic rule did not cease when Babangida tapped Ernest Shonekan to lead an interim "civilian" administration before stepping down in August 1993. For the first time in independent Nigeria's history, the elite could not control street-level politics—"people power" had been unleashed and could not be fully suppressed. The Nigerian elite was in disarray and the people filled the void by supporting militant civic and trade union leaders.

Nevertheless, the reach of most civic groups in Nigeria paled in comparison with the obtrusive state security apparatus put in place by Babangida and used effectively by Abacha. Babangida's security forces ensured that Nigerian politics resembled that of several Latin American countries in the 1960s and 1970s with recourse to state terrorism, disappearances, and the penetration of educational, associational, and opposition groups. In the later months of 1994, Nigeria's security services were responsible for an unprecedented wave of political terror as militant trade unionists and pro-democracy activists were harassed and detained, and their properties set on fire.

Although there was renewed optimism after Babangida was forced from office, the Abacha coup reignited grave doubts about whether Nigeria could escape the military's firm hold on power. One question persists: Can an army that has enjoyed the spoils of uncontested power for most of the period of independent nationhood voluntarily relinquish power? The transition supervised by General Abdulsalami Abubakar in 1998 and 1999 gave some grounds for hope, but the role of the military in Nigeria's politics remains an urgent and contested issue.

A review of Nigerian politics up to the fall of the Second Republic lamented that "since a democratic route to nationhood, in the context of Nigeria's social pluralism, is a parlous one, and an authoritarian route has not been seriously attempted, Nigerian society is left to oscillate between the broadening of democratic participation and the freezing of such practices with the reimposition of military rule."[21] That statement was made before Nigerians experienced heightened authoritarianism under Babangida and Abacha.

When the Second Republic collapsed in December 1983, the assumption among Nigerians was that it was unlikely that Nigeria would produce a dictator in the fashion of Togo's Eyadema, Uganda's Idi Amin, the Central African Republic's Bokassa, or Zaire's Mobutu Sese Seko. Although they came very close to that reality under Babangida, Nigerians were forced to confront it under Abacha. Here is a pertinent remark made in 1993 by a Nigerian businessman:

> The silence of an elite too anxious to protect what little gains they have made, caused us to so severely jeopardize the future of our children. . . . We have to pay tribute to the activists, for it could have been worse without them. We must dedicate ourselves to preventing this from happening again. Unless we say never again, we will wake up one day and a psychopath in uniform will usurp authority, use and abuse power to plunder the nation and dare us speak.[22]

As it turned out, Abacha was such a ruler who usurped authority, used and abused power, plundered the nation mercilessly, and punished those who dared speak. Will Nigeria be able, having witnessed the perils of unaccountable government, to prevent such a tragedy from happening again?

As indicated in Section 1, Nigerian politics has been characterized by turmoil and periodic crises since the British relinquished colonial power in 1960. Forty years later, the country still lacks a stable and orderly political system. Its retrogression is evidenced by the stagnation and decline of major productive sectors, infrastructure and institutions, the heightened sociopolitical tension, an increasingly irresponsible elite, and an expanding mass culture of despondency and rage. Although Nigeria completed a series of elections in February 1999, and a handover of power to an elected government on May 29, 1999, it would be premature to classify it as a democratic polity. The person elected president on February 27, 1999, Olusegun Obasanjo, is a former military ruler whose party received extensive financial support from other retired military officers, including the same individual who annulled the 1993 elections, Ibrahim Babangida. Although international observers accepted the results as fair, all the elections of the 1998–1999 transition were marred by irregularities. It is more appropriate to regard Nigeria as having just begun a possible evolution away from a nondemocratic system. Whether this transition will be completed depends on the realization of substantial progress in overcoming deep structural problems.

Two possible scenarios are apparent. Now that General Abubakar has successfully handed over power to an elected civilian government in May 1999, the restored democratic system must manage its internal contradictions sufficiently to govern. Moreover, although it benefited from a military-supervised transition, the Obasanjo government must engineer a thorough transformation of the armed forces into a constitutional and professional entity.

As in the past, issues of governance are certain to be filtered through an intense struggle among the parties for control of the government. Within a short time, the party that comes to power, while addressing the main interests of its members and supporters, will have to utilize the new democratic institutions without abusing them. Opposition parties, meanwhile, will have to accept the procedural limits of democratic institutions while promoting alternative policies in the federal legislature and state-level governments. The military will have to be depoliticized and restored to its constitutional and professional role in a democratic system.

One of the critical issues the new democracy will face is what Nigerians call the national question. There have been insistent calls for a genuine national conference to restructure the federation, rewrite the constitution, and renegotiate control of the oil wealth. Persistent discontent among the Yoruba, along with the low-intensity civil war in the Niger Delta, will likely force the new government to permit debate on the structure of the Nigerian federation, perhaps within narrow parameters. Unlike Nigeria's previous democratic experiments, the new democracy will include the activities of a highly mobilized civil society. Business interests, which have become more vocal and active through the Economic Summits and *Vision 2010*, will continue their efforts to move government economic policy in a free-market direction. Labor unions will regain their independence and most likely

advance alternatives to the business agenda that would include demands for a more active role of the state in addressing the steep decline in the value of wages and in social welfare. Some religious institutions, especially Islamic, will raise challenges, once again, to the avowed secular nature of the Nigerian state. The many advocacy groups in civil society are likely to be much more vigilant and outspoken than during the last period of civilian rule. A vigorous articulation of health, education, human rights, and women's interests can be anticipated, and a concerted attempt to counter the usual emphasis on narrow elite and ethnic concerns.

This optimistic scenario is full of ifs, and is clouded by the continued threat of military intervention. A weak democracy could fall prey to the narrow, parochial interests of individuals in powerful positions who are willing, once again, to foment ethnic and religious divisions. Rather than serving the nation's interest in broad-based economic development, the new leaders may spend most of their time trying to consolidate power within their parties and the government while seeking to siphon government funds for their own uses. The military is no longer a coherent organization, which might permit the new democracy an extended grace period. Generals Abacha and Babangida left the armed forces rife with division and rivalry, and they may be incapable of, resuming power in the near future.

Unlike Nigeria's previous democratic experiments, the new democracy will enjoy the independent participation of a more highly mobilized civil society. Business, well organized and active through the Economic Summits and *Vision 2010*, is certain to continue its efforts to move government economic policy in a free-market direction. Labor unions will regain their independence and most likely resist the business agenda. Religious institutions will seek to debate the secular nature of the Nigerian state, while the media are likely to renew their reputation as the most freewheeling in Africa. NGOs will continue to lobby for their targeted issues (health, local development, human rights, women's rights) and will serve as watchdogs over the government and the military. The strong articulation by civil society of these interests can force the new government to respond in ways that strengthen democratic institutions and move politics away from narrow elite or ethnic concerns.

Nigerian Politics in Comparative Perspective

Theoretical insights from the historical experiences of one country or region are seldom fully applicable to another; and political scientists are wary about stretching concepts so far as to suggest that one polity can be modeled after another. Given this caveat, the study of Nigeria has important implications for the study of African politics and, more broadly, of comparative politics. The Nigerian case embodies a number of key themes and issues that can be generalized to increase social science knowledge, and these themes deserve careful consideration. We can learn much about how democratic regimes are established and achieve stability by understanding the pitfalls Nigeria has encountered. By analyzing the historical dynamics of Nigeria's ethnic conflict, for example, we can identify institutional mechanisms that may be effective in reducing ethnic conflict in other states. We can also learn much about how viable and sustainable economies are developed by contrasting their evolution with Nigeria's. Each of these issues, in turn, offers comparative lessons for the major themes explored in this book: a world of states, governing the economy, the democratic idea, and the politics of collective identities.

A World of States

Nigeria exists in two worlds of states—one in the global political economy and the other within Africa. We have addressed at length Nigeria's position in the world. Economically, Nigeria was thrust into the world economy in a position of weakness, first as a British colony and later as an independent nation. Despite its resources and the potential of oil to provide the investment capital needed to build a modern economy, Nigeria has grown weaker. It has lost much of its international clout and, in place of the respect it once enjoyed in diplomatic circles, Nigeria now gets criticism for persistent human rights abuses. Although calls for stringent sanctions have been loud, these have elicited mainly symbolic actions, such as the denial of visas to government officials.

In a continent that comprises more than 10 percent of the world's population, there remain vast resources (for indigenous consumption and export), large poten-tial markets, and many opportunities to achieve greater prominence in the world of states. This chapter began by quoting the statement, "As Nigeria goes, so goes the rest of sub-Saharan Africa." Instead of leading the continent, Nigeria has been left behind in such respects as national cohesion, state capabilities, economic growth, and democratization.

The future of democracy, political stability, and economic renewal in other parts of Africa, and certainly in West Africa, will be greatly influenced, for good or ill, by unfolding events in Nigeria. Beyond the obvious demonstration effect, the economy of the West African subregion can be revitalized by resumed growth of the Nigerian economy. International political, scholarly, and business attention has shifted steadily to the south of the continent, focusing chiefly on South Africa and its stable neighboring states of Botswana and Namibia. That shift portends a greater danger of marginalization, as Africa becomes divided into a zone of prosperity that attracts investment and a zone of decay.

Governing the Economy

Nigeria provides important insights into the political economy of underdevelopment. At independence in 1960, Nigeria was stronger economically than its Southeast Asian counterparts. Independent Nigeria appeared poised for growth, with a wealth of natural resources, a large population, and the presence of highly entrepreneurial groups in all regions of the country. Today, Nigeria is among the poorest countries in the world in terms of per capita income, while many of its Asian counterparts have joined the ranks of the newly industrializing nations. One critical lesson Nigeria teaches is that a rich endowment of resources is not enough to ensure economic development. In fact, it may encourage rent-seeking behavior that undermines more productive activities.

Other variables are critically important, notably political stability (if not necessarily democracy) and a strong developmentalist ethic. Such a developmentalist ethic, and an institutional structure to enforce it, can set limits to corrupt behavior and constrain the pursuit of short-term personal gain at the expense of national economic growth. Institutions vital for the pursuit of these objectives include a professional civil service, an independent judiciary, and a free press. Nigeria has had each of these, yet they were gradually undermined and corrupted. The public "ethic" that has come to dominate the Nigerian political economy has been prebendalism. Where corruption is unchecked, as in Nigeria, the Philippines under Ferdinand Marcos, or in Latin American countries such as Mexico and Venezuela, economic development suffers accordingly.

Nigeria also demonstrates that sustainable economic development requires sound economic policy. Without export diversification, commodity-exporting countries are buffeted by the price fluctuations of one or two main products. This situation, of course, can be traced back to overreliance on primary commodity-export-oriented policies bequeathed by the British colonial regime. Yet other former colonies, such as Malaysia and Indonesia, have managed to diversify their initial export base. Nigeria, in contrast, has substituted one form of commodity dependence for another; and it has allowed its petroleum industry to overwhelm completely all other sectors of the economy. Nigeria even became a net importer of products (for example, palm oil and palm nuts) for which it was once a leading world producer. In comparative perspective, we can see that natural resource endowments can be tremendously beneficial. The United States, for example, has parlayed its endowments of agricultural, mineral, and energy resources into one of the world's most diversified modern economies. Meanwhile Japan, which is by comparison poorly endowed with natural resources, has one of the strongest economies in the world, achieved in large part through its unique developmental strategies. Each of these examples illustrates the primacy of sound economic policies.

The Democratic Idea

As mentioned earlier, many African countries have experienced transitions from authoritarian rule. With the end of superpower competition in Africa, and the withdrawal of support from the former Soviet Union and the United States for Africa's despots, many African societies experienced a resurgence of popular pressures for greater participation in political life and for more open forms of governance. Decades of authoritarian, single-party, and military rule in Africa

have left a dismal record: arbitrary imprisonment and silenced political opposition; harassment of civic, professional, and religious institutions; stifled public discourse and free speech; and bankrupted treasuries and mismanaged economies. At the same time, a handful of elites have acquired large fortunes through wanton corruption. The examples, sadly, are plentiful. Consider Nigeria's "missing" US$12.2 billion windfall in oil revenues after the Gulf War in 1991; or the fact that Zairian president Mobutu Sese Seko's "personal" wealth was estimated to be several billion dollars, perhaps as much as half the external debt of the entire country. Or that Kenya's president Daniel Arap Moi is considered among the richest men in Africa, a group to which Ibrahim Babangida and the late Sani Abacha of Nigeria belong. The devious ways in which these fortunes were acquired and dispensed make it difficult to give concrete figures. They do, however, suggest that the exercise of postindependence authoritarian rule in Africa has contributed to economic stagnation and decline. The difficulty that such countries as Kenya, Cameroon, Togo, and Zimbabwe have experienced in moving to democratic systems is a reflection, among other factors, of the ruling elites' unwillingness to cede control of the political instruments that made possible their self-enrichment.

Nigeria exemplifies the harsh reality of authoritarian and unaccountable governance. Corruption, fraud, and mismanagement, and the restriction of political liberties, were tolerated in the past by populations numbed into complacency by political repression and the daily struggles for economic survival. Nigerians have endured six military regimes, countless attempted coups, and a bloody civil war that claimed over 1 million lives. They have also seen a once prospering economy reduced to rubble. Today, democracy has become a greater imperative because only such a system provides the mechanisms to limit abuses of power and render governments accountable.

Collective Identities

Nigeria presents an important case in which to study the dangers of ethnically based competition in a society with deep cultural divisions. How can multiethnic countries manage their diversity? What institutional mechanisms can be employed to avert tragedies such as the 1967–1970 civil war, or the continuing conflicts that have brought great suffering to the former Yugoslavia and Rwanda? This chapter has suggested institutional reforms such as proportional representation, decentralization, and a strengthened federal system that can contribute to reducing tensions and minimizing conflict.

Insights from the Nigerian experience may explain why some federations persist and help to identify the factors that can undermine them. Nigeria's complex social situation, and its varied attempts to create a nation out of its highly diverse population, enhance our understanding of the politics of cultural pluralism,[23] and the difficulty of accommodating sectional interests under conditions of political and economic insecurity. As described in this chapter, federal character in Nigeria has been distorted into a form of ethnic and regional favoritism and a tool for dispensing patronage. Yet, the country has benefited in some ways from the attention devoted to creating state and local governments, and from giving people in different regions a sense of being stakeholders in the entity called Nigeria.

The challenges that Nigeria will face in the next century concern not only its people's frustrated hopes for a better life, stable government, and a democratic political order but also the potential contributions that this country and its people could still make to the entire continent, and to the world at large, if only an exit can be found from the cycle of endless woe.

Key Terms

authoritarian
legitimacy
accountability
unfinished state
autocracy
jihad
acephalous societies
emirs
warrant chiefs
interventionist
indirect rule
clientelism
rents
structural adjustment
  program

international financial
  institutions
balance of payments
privatization
self-determination
Economic Community of
  West African States
federal character
para-statals
state corporatism
shari'a
civil society
prebendalism
patrimonialism

Suggested Readings

Achike, Okay. *Public Administration: A Nigerian and Comparative Perspective.* London: Longman, 1978.

Adamolekun, L. *Politics and Administration in Nigeria.* London: Hutchinson, 1986.

Agbaje, Adigun. *The Nigerian Press: Hegemony and the Social Construction of Legitimacy, 1960–1983.* Lewiston, N.Y.: Edwin Mellen Press, 1992.

——. "Twilight of Democracy in Nigeria." *Africa Demos* 3 (no. 3): 5. Atlanta: Carter Center of Emory University, 1994.

Bienen, Henry. *Political Conflict and Economic Change in Nigeria.* London: Frank Cass, 1988.

Crook, Richard, and A.M. Jerve, eds. *Government and Participation: Institutional Development, Decentralization and Democracy in the Third World.* Bergen, Norway: Chr. Michelsen Institute, 1991.

Decalo, Samuel. *Coups and Army Rule in Africa.* 2d ed. New Haven: Yale University Press, 1990.

Diamond, Larry. *Class, Ethnicity and Democracy in Nigeria: The Failure of the First Republic.* London: Macmillan, 1988.

——. "Nigeria's Search for a New Political Order." *Journal of Democracy* 2, no. 2 (Spring 1991): 54.

Ekeh, Peter P., and Eghosa E. Osaghae, eds. *Federal Character and Federalism in Nigeria.* Ibadan: Heinemann, 1989.

Forrest, Tom. *Politics and Economic Development in Nigeria.* Boulder, Colo.: Westview Press, 1993.

Healey, J., and M. Robinson. *Democracy, Governance and Economic Policy: Sub-Saharan Africa in Comparative Perspective.* London: Overseas Development Institute, 1992.

Hodgkin, Thomas. *Nigerian Perspectives.* London: Oxford University Press, 1975.

Horowitz, Donald L. *Ethnic Groups in Conflict.* Berkeley: University of California Press, 1985.

Jackson, Robert H., and Carl G. Rosberg. *Personal Rule in Africa.* Berkeley: University of California Press, 1982.

Joseph, Richard A. *Democracy and Prebendal Politics in Nigeria: The Rise and Fall of the Second Republic.* Cambridge: Cambridge University Press, 1987.

Kew, Darren. "Political Islam in Nigeria's Transition Crisis," *Muslim Politics Report* (Council on Foreign Relations: New York), May–June 1996.

Lewis, Peter M. "Endgame in Nigeria? The Politics of a Failed Democratic Transition." *African Affairs* 93 (1994): 323–340.

Lewis, Peter M., Barnett R. Rubin, and Pearl T. Robinson. *Stabilizing Nigeria: Pressures, Incentives, and Support for Civil Society.* New York: Century Foundation, for the Council on Foreign Relations, 1998.

Nyang'oro, Julius, and Tim Shaw, eds. *Corporatism in Africa: Comparative Analysis and Practice.* Boulder, Colo.: Westview Press, 1989.

Ogwu, U. Joy, and Adebayo Olukoshi, eds. "Special Issue: The Economic Diplomacy of the Nigerian State." *Nigerian Journal of International Affairs* 17, no. 2 (1991).

Onoge, Omafume, ed. *Nigeria: The Way Forward.* Ibadan: Spectrum Books, 1993.

Oyediran, Oyeleye, ed. *Nigerian Government and Politics Under Military Rule.* London: Macmillan, 1979.

Oyovbaire, Sam E. *Federalism in Nigeria: A Study in the Development of the Nigerian State.* London: Macmillan, 1985.

Sklar, Richard L. *Nigerian Political Parties: Power in an Emergent African Nation.* New York: NOK Publishers, 1983.

Turok, Ben, ed. *Alternative Development Strategies for Africa.* Vol. 3: *Debt and Democracy.* London: Institute for African Alternatives, 1991.

Watts, Michael, ed. *State, Oil, and Agriculture in Nigeria.* Berkeley: University of California Press, 1987.

Wunsch, James S., and Dele Olowu, eds. *The Failure of the Centralized State: Institutions and Self-Governance in Africa.* Boulder, Colo.: Westview Press, 1990.

Young, Crawford. *The Rising Tide of Cultural Pluralism: The Nation-State at Bay?* Madison: University of Wisconsin Press, 1993.

Endnotes

[1] Peter Ekeh, "Colonialism and the Two Publics in Africa: A Theoretical Statement," *Comparative Studies in Society and History* 17, no. 1 (January 1975).

[2] Obafemi Awolowo, *Path to Nigerian Freedom* (London: Faber and Faber, 1947), 47–48.

[3] Billy J. Dudley, *An Introduction to Nigerian Government and Politics* (Bloomington: Indiana University Press, 1982), 71.

[4] The following discussion is based on Michael J. Watts, ed., *State, Oil, and Agriculture in Nigeria* (Berkeley: University of California Press, 1987), 61–84.

[5] Watts, 71.

[6] Watts, 66.

[7] Watts, 69.

[8] Dele Olowu, "Centralization, Self-Governance, and Development in Nigeria," in *The Failure of the Centralized State: Institutions and Self-Governance in Africa*, ed. James S. Wunsch and Dele Olowu (Boulder, Colo.: Westview Press, 1990), 211.

[9] Billy J. Dudley, *Instability and Political Order: Politics and Crisis in Nigeria* (Ibadan: Ibadan University Press, 1973), 35.

[10] J. Isawa Elaigwu, "The Nigerian Federation and Future Prospects," in *Nigeria: The Way Forward*, ed. Omafume Onoge (Ibadan: Spectrum Books, 1993), 32–33.

[11] Douglas Rimmer, "External Trade and Payments," in *Nigeria Since 1970: A Political and Economic Outline*, ed. Anthony Kirk-Greene and Douglas Rimmer (London: Hodder and Stoughton, 1981), 136.

[12] See Juan Linz, "The Perils of Presidentialism," *Journal of Democracy* 1, no. 1 (1990): 51–69; and responses in "Debate— Presidents vs. Paliaments," *Journal of Democracy* 1, no. 4 (1990); 73–91.

[13] William D. Graf, *The Nigerian State: Political Economy, State Class and Political System in the Post-Colonial Era* (London: James Currey, 1988), 205.

[14] Samuel Decalo, *Coups and Army Rule in Africa*, 2d ed. (New Haven: Yale University Press, 1990), 18.

[15] Larry Diamond, "Introduction: Roots of Failure, Seeds of Hope," in *Democracy in Developing Countries*, Vol. 2: *Africa*, ed. Diamond et al. (Boulder, Colo.: Lynne Rienner, 1988), 10.

[16] Adigun Agbaje, "Adjusting State and Market in Nigeria: The Paradoxes of Orthodoxy," *Afrika Spectrum* 27, no. 2 (1992): 132.

[17] Michael Bratton and Nicolas van de Walle, "Neopatrimonial Regimes and Political Transitions in Africa," *World Politics*, vol. 46 (July 1994): 453–489.

[18] Goran Hyden, "Reciprocity and Governance in Africa," in *The Failure of the Centralized State: State Institutions and Self-Governance in Africa*, ed. James S. Wunsch and Dele Olowu (Boulder, Colo.: Westview Press, 1990), 265.

[19] Larry Diamond, "Nigeria: Pluralism, Statism and the Struggle for Democracy," in *Democracy in Developing Countries*, Vol. 2: *Africa*, ed. Diamond, Lipset, and Linz (Boulder, Colo.: Lynne Rienner, 1988), 85.

[20] Goran Hyden, "Reciprocity and Governance in Africa," in *The Failure of the Centralized State: State Institutions and Self-Governance in Africa*, ed. James S. Wunsch and Dele Olowu (Boulder, Colo.: Westview Press, 1990), 263.

[21] Richard A. Joseph, *Democracy and Prebendal Politics in Nigeria* (Cambridge: Cambridge University Press, 1987).

[22] *The Guardian*, July 16, 1993, 17.

[23] Crawford Young. *The Politics of Cultural Pluralism* (Madison: University of Wisconsin Press, 1976), and Crawford Young, ed., *The Rising Tide of Cultural Pluralism: The Nation-State at Bay?* (Madison: University of Wisconsin Press, 1993).

CHAPTER 7

Iran

Ervand Abrahamian

Islamic Republic of Iran

Land and Population

Capital	Tehran	
Total Area (square miles)	634,562 (slightly larger than Alaska)	
Population	68.9 million	
Annual Population Growth Rate (1998)	2.04%	
Urban Population	59%	
Ethnic Composition	Persian	51%
	Azerbaijani	24%
	Gilaki and Mazandarani	8%
	Kurd	7%
	Arab	3%
	Other	7%
Major Languages	Farsi (Persian)	58%
	Turkic and Turkic dialects	26%
	Kurdish	9%
	Other	7%
Religious Affiliation	Shi'a Muslim	89%
	Sunni Muslim	10%
	Zoroastrian, Jewish, Christian, and Baha'i	1%

Economy

Domestic Currency	Rial	
Total GNP (US$)	$113.5 billion	
GNP per capita (US$)	$1780	
GNP per capita at purchasing power parity (US$)	$5530	
GNP average annual growth rate (1996–1997)		3.2%
GNP per capita average annual growth rate	1996–1997	1.2%
	1980–1995	–0.2%
	1965–1980	2.9%
Income Gap: GDP per capita (US$)	Data not available for Iran	
Structure of Production (% of GDP)	Agriculture	21%
	Industry	37%
	Services	42%
Labor Force Distribution (% of total)	Agriculture	32%
	Industry	25%
	Services	43%
Exports as % of GDP	21%	
Imports as % of GDP	16%	

Society

Life Expectancy	Female	69.1
	Male	67.9
Doctors per 100,000 people		62.5
Infant Mortality per 1000 live births		33
Adult Literacy	Female	59.3%
	Male	77.7%
Access to Information and Communications (per 1000 people)	Radios	228
	Televisions	134
	Telephone Lines	76
	Personal Computers	
	Data not available for Iran	
Women in Government and Economy		
Seats in parliament held by women		4.9%
Women at ministerial level		3%
Women as % of total labor force		24.0%
Female business administrators and managers		4.0%
Female professional and technical workers		33.0%
1998 Human Development Index ranking (out of 174 countries, 1 = highest)		78

Political Organization

Political System   Theocracy (rule of the clergy) headed by a cleric with the title of Supreme Leader. The clergy rule by divine right.

Regime History   Islamic Republic since the 1979 Islamic Revolution.

Administrative Structure   Centralized administration with 28 provinces. The Interior Minister appoints the provincial governor-generals.

Executive   President and his cabinet. The president is elected by the general electorate every four years. The president chooses his cabinet ministers, but they need to obtain the approval of the *Majles* (parliament).

Legislature   Unicameral. The *Majles,* formed of 270 seats, is elected every four years. It has multiple member districts with the top runners in the elections taking the seats. Bills passed by the *Majles* do not become law unless they have the approval of the clerically dominated Council of Guardians.

Judiciary   A Chief Judge and a Supreme Court independent of the executive and legislature but appointed by the Supreme Leader.

Party System   The ruling clergy restrict all party and organizational activities.

Note: Some of the categories and data used for Iran are different than for other countries in *ICP* because the World Development Report (World Bank) does not gather full statistics for Iran.

Section ❶ The Making of the Modern Iranian State

Politics in Action

In 1997 the Iranian people surprised the world—not to mention their own establishment—by electing as president a relatively unknown liberal cleric named Muhammad Khatami. Khatami was not a senior cleric with the exalted title of Grand Ayatollah ("Sigh of God") or a simple **ayatollah**, but a middle-ranking hojjat al-Islam ("Proof of Islam"). In the election, he had vigorously campaigned on the theme of creating a viable civil society and improving the "sick economy." He had stressed the importance of an open society that would protect individual liberties, freedom of expression, women's rights, political pluralism, and most essential, the rule of law. He had even authored books applauding such liberal thinkers as Locke, Voltaire, and Rousseau. It was as if he were transferring into practical politics principles found in political science textbooks. His electoral campaign had also stressed the need to have a dialogue with the West, especially with the United States. This was a far cry from the early days of the Iranian Revolution, when Grand Ayatollah Ruhollah Khomeini, the leader of that revolution, had denounced the United States as the "Great Satan" and had encouraged a group of university students to take over the U.S. embassy compound. This takeover, which lasted 444 days, involved fifty-two officials and became famous as the "hostage crisis." It prompted a break in U.S.-Iranian diplomatic relations. It also helped terminate Jimmy Carter's presidency.

Khatami's electoral success in 1997 was especially surprising because much of the religious establishment had openly endorsed his conservative rival. Most commentators, both inside and outside the country, had predicted the easy win of the conservative candidate. The conservatives controlled an impressive array of newspapers, radio stations, television programs, state institutions, quasi-state foundations, clerical organizations, and tens of thousands of prayer pulpits. They warned that any opening up of the system could endanger the whole regime and that Khatami could become another Gorbachev, the Soviet leader who had inadvertently presided over the demise of the Soviet Union by initiating political reform. Even the Supreme Leader of the Islamic Republic, Ayatollah Ali Khamenei, had implicitly endorsed the conservative candidate. In the upset election, Khatami won a landslide victory, obtaining 70 percent of the vote in a campaign that drew nearly 80 percent of the electorate. In U.S. presidential elections, by contrast, less than 50 percent of eligible voters vote. Much of Khatami's vote came from women, university students, and youth throughout the country, and from the armed forces. He followed up his victory by liberalizing the press, promising the establishment of political parties, and initiating a "dialogue" with the United States on the Cable News Network (CNN). He even bolstered the case for liberalization by citing *Democracy in America*, the famous book by the nineteenth-century French traveler Alexis de Tocqueville. Khatami further followed up his electoral victory by assuring the West that Iran had no intention of implementing the *fatwa* (religious decree) that Ayatollah Khomeini had placed on Salman Rushdie, the Muslim-born British writer. Khomeini had condemned Rushdie to death on the grounds that his book *Satanic Verses* blasphemed Islam and thus proved that its author was an apostate from Islam—a capital offense according to a very narrow interpretation of the Islamic law.

The 1997 presidential elections vividly illustrated the main dilemmas confronting the Islamic Republic established by Ayatollah Khomeini in the aftermath of the 1979 revolution. The republic is a mixture of **theocracy** and democracy, a political system based on clerical authority as well as on popular sovereignty, on the divine right of the clergy as well as on the rights of the people, on concepts derived from early Islam as well as from Montesquieu's separation of powers. The country has regular elections for the presidency and the *Majles* (Parliament), but a clerically dominated **Guardian Council** determines who can and cannot run in these elections. The president is the formal head of the executive branch of government, but he can be overruled, even dismissed, by the chief cleric known as the **Supreme Leader**. The president appoints the

Iran

Minister of Justice, but the whole judiciary is under the supervision of the Chief Judge, who is appointed directly by the Supreme Leader. The *Majles* is the legislative branch of government, but its bills do not become law unless the Guardian Council deems them compatible with Islam and the Islamic constitution. In short, the political system is built both on vox dei (the voice of God) and on vox populi (the voice of the people).

Geographic Setting

Iran—three times the size of France, slightly larger than Alaska, and much larger than its immediate neighbors—is notable for two geographical features.

The first is that much of its territory is inhospitable to agriculture. A vast arid zone known as the Great Salt Desert covers much of the central plateau from Tehran to Afghanistan and Pakistan. A mountain range known as the Zagros takes up the western third of the country. Another range, the Elborz, stretches across the north. Rain-fed agriculture is confined mostly to the northwest and the Caspian provinces. In the rest of the country, population settlements are located mostly on oases, on the few rare rivers, and on constructed irrigation networks. Only pastoral nomads can survive in the semiarid zones and in the high mountain valleys. Thus 67 percent of the total populaton of 69 million is concentrated in 27 percent of the land—mostly in the Caspian provinces, in the northwest, and in such cities as Tehran, Qom, Isfahan, Shiraz, and Ahwaz. In the past, the inhospitable environment was a major obstacle to economic development. In recent decades, this obstacle has been circumvented by oil revenues. Iran is the second largest oil producer in the Middle East, and the fourth largest in the world. Its oil wells help fuel the West, especially by France, Italy, Germany, and Japan. These oil revenues account for the fact that Iran is now urbanized and partly industrialized, and can be described as a developing rather than a stagnant society. Nearly 60 percent of the population lives in urban centers; 68 percent of the labor force is employed in industry and services; 60–75 percent of adults are literate; life expectancy has reached 68 years; and the majority enjoy a standard of living well above that of populations in Asia and Africa.

Iran's second notable geographical feature is that it lies on the crossroads between Central Asia and Asia Minor, between the Indian subcontinent and the Middle East, between the Arabian Peninsula and the Caucasus Mountains. This has made the region vulnerable to invaders—Indo-Europeans in the distant past (they gave the country the name of Iran, Land of the Aryans); Islamic Arab tribes in the seventh century; and a series of Turkic incursions in the Middle Ages. The present populaton reflects these historic invasions. Some 51 percent of the country speaks Persian (**Farsi**) as a first language—Persian is an Indo-European language; 27 percent speak various dialects of Turkic, mainly Azeri and Turkoman; 8 percent speak Gilaki or Mazandarani, distant Persian dialects; 7 percent speak Kurdish, another Indo-European language; and 1–3 percent speak Arabic. Although Iranians have traditionally called their country Iran and their main language Farsi, Europeans since the Middle Ages have referred to the country as Persia, associating it with the dominant language and the central province of Fars. In 1935, Iran formally asked the international community to cease calling the country Persia.

Critical Junctures

Although modern Iran traces its roots to the ancient Iranian empire of the sixth century B.C. and its Islamic religion to the Arab invasions of the seventh century, its current national identity, geographical boundaries,

Critical Junctions in Modern Iran's Political Development

1921	Colonel Reza Khan's military coup
1925	Establishment of the Pahlavi dynasty
1941–1945	Allied occupation of Iran
1951	Nationalization of the oil industry
1953	Coup against Mosaddeq
1963	White Revolution
1975	Establishment of the Resurgence Party
February 1979	Islamic Revolution
1979–1981	U.S. hostage crisis
December 1979	Referendum on the constitution
January 1980	Bani-Sadr elected president
March 1980	Elections for the First Islamic *Majles*
1980–1988	War with Iraq
June 1981	President Bani-Sadr ousted
October 1981	Khamenei elected president
1984	Elections for the Second Islamic *Majles*
1988	Elections for the Third Islamic *Majles*
1989	Khomeini dies; Khamenei appointed Supreme Leader; Rafsanjani elected president
1992	Elections for the Fourth Islamic *Majles*
1996	Elections for the Fifth Islamic *Majles*
1997	Khatami elected president on reform platform

particular interpretation of Islam—**Shi'ism**—and political system were formed by four more recent critical junctures: the Safavid (1501–1722), Qajar (1794–1925), and Pahlavi (1925–1979) dynasties, and the Islamic Revolution of 1979, which led to establishment of the current Islamic Republic.

The Safavids (1501–1722)

Modern Iran, with its Shi'i Islamic identity and its present-day boundaries, can be traced to the sixteenth century, when the Safavid family conquered the territory with the help of fellow Turkic-speaking tribes and established their dynasty. They revived the ancient Iranian titles of Shah-in-Shah (King of Kings) and Shadow of God on Earth, and proceeded to forcibly

---

Background: **Islam and Shi'ism**

Islam, with some 1 billion adherents, is the second largest religion in the world. Islam means literally "submission to God," and a Muslim is someone who has submitted to God—the same God that Jews and Christians worship. Islam has one central tenet: "There is only one God, and Muhammad is His Prophet." Muslims, in order to consider themselves faithful, need to perform the following four duties to the best of their ability: give to charity; pray every day facing Mecca, where Abraham is believed to have built the first place of worship; make a pilgrimage at least once in a life-time to Mecca which is located in modern Saudi Arabia; and fast during the daytime hours in the month of Ramadan to commemorate God's revelation of the Qur'an (Koran, or Holy Book) to the Prophet Muhammad. These four, together with the central tenet, are known as the Five Pillars of Islam.

From its earliest days, Islam has been divided into two major branches—the Sunnis and the Shi'is. The Sunnis, meaning literally "followers of tradition," are by far in the majority worldwide. The Shi'is, literally "partisans of Ali," constitute less than 10 percent of Muslims worldwide and are concentrated in Iran, southern Iraq, Azerbaijan, and southern Lebanon.

Although both branches accept the Five Pillars, they differ mostly over who should have suceeded the Prophet Muhammad (d. 632). The Sunnis recognized the early dynasties that ruled the Islamic empire with the exalted title of Caliph ("Prophet's Deputy"). The Shi'is, however, argued that as soon as the Prophet died, his authority should have been passed on to Imam Ali, the Prophet's close companion, disciple, and son-in-law. They further argue that Imam Ali passed his authority to his direct male heirs, the third of whom, Imam Husayn, had been martyred fighting the Sunnis in 680, and the twelfth of whom had supposedly gone into hiding in 941. They refer to the latter as the Mahdi, the Hidden Imam, and believe him to be the Messiah who will herald the end of the world. Furthermore, they argue that in his absence the authority to interpret the *shari'a* (religious law) should be in the hands of the senior clerical scholars—the ayatollahs. Thus, from the beginning, the Shi'is harbored ambivalent attitudes toward the state, especially if the rulers were Sunnis or lacked genealogical links to the Twelve Imams. For Sunnis, the *shari'a* is based mostly on the Qur'an and the teachings of the Prophet. For Shi'is, it is also based on the teachings of the Twelve Imams.

---

convert their subjects to Shi'ism. Although small Shi'i communities had existed in this area since the beginning of Islam, the vast majority had adhered to the majority Sunni branch. The Safavid motivation for this drastic conversion was to give their state and population a distinct identity separate from the surrounding Sunni powers—the Ottomans in the west, the Uzbeks in the north, and the Afghans in the east.

By the mid-seventeenth century the Safavids had succeeded in converting nearly 90 percent of their subjects to Shi'ism. Sunnism survived among the peripheral tribal groups—Kurds in the northwest, Turkomans in the northeast, Baluchis in the southeast, and Arabs in the southwest. It should be noted that the Safavids, despite their conquests, failed to capture from the Ottomans the two most holy Shi'i places located in modern Iraq: Karbala, the site of Imam Husayn's martyrdom, and Najaf, the main theological center.

In addition to the Sunni minority, Safavid Iran contained small communities of Jews, Zoroastrians, and Christians (Armenians and Assyrians). These small minorities lived mostly in Isfahan, Shiraz, Kerman, Yazd, and Azerbaijan. Jews had lived in Iran since ancient times, predating the great diaspora prompted by the Roman destruction of Jerusalem. Zoroastrians were descendants of those who retained their old religion after the Arab invasions. The Christians had lived in the northwest long before the advent of Islam. To strengthen their foothold in central Iran, the Safavids transported there some 100,000 Armenians, encouraging them to become craftsmen and merchants, especially in the lucrative silk trade. The Safavids, like most Muslim rulers but unlike medieval Christian kings, tolerated religious minorities as long as they paid special taxes and accepted royal authority. According to Islam, Christians, Jews, and Zoroastrians were to be tolerated as legitimate **People of the Book**. They were respected both because they were mentioned in the Holy **Qur'an** and because they had their own sacred texts—the Bible, the Torah, and the Avesta.

The Safavids established their capital in Isfahan, a Persian-speaking city, and recruited Persian scribes into their court administration. Such families had helped administer the ancient Iranian empires. They proceeded to govern not only through these Persian scribes and Shi'i clerics but also through local magnates—tribal chiefs, large landowners, religious notables, city merchants, guild elders, and urban ward leaders.

The Safavid army was formed mostly of tribal cavalry led by local chieftains. Financial constraints prevented the Safavids from creating a large bureaucracy or an extended standing army. Their revenues came mostly from land taxes levied on the peasantry. In theory, the Safavids claimed absolute power—Europeans labeled them Oriental despots. In reality, their power was limited, since they lacked a central state and had no choice but to seek the cooperation of many semi-independent local leaders. The central government was linked to the general population not so much through coercive institutions as through provincial and hereditary notables. It survived for the most part because the society below was sharply fragmented by lack of communications, geographical barriers (especially mountains), and regional, tribal, communal, and ethnic differences. Moreover, some of the senior clerics resided in Najaf, safely out of royal reach. The monarch did not control society. Rather, he hovered over it, systematically orchestrating its many existing rivalries.

The Qajars (1794–1925)

The Safavid dynasty collapsed in 1722 when Afghan tribesmen invaded the capital. The invasion was followed by a half century of civil war until the Qajars, another Turkic tribe, reconquered much of Iran. The Qajars moved the capital to Tehran and re-created the Safavid system of central manipulation and court administration, including the Persian scribes. They also declared Shi'ism to be the state religion even though they, unlike the Safavids, did not boast of genealogical links to the Twelve Imams. This was to have far-reaching repercussions. Since these new

shahs did not pretend to wear the Imam's mantle, the Shi'i clerical leaders could claim to be the main interpreters of Islam. In addition, many of them safeguarded their independence from the state by continuing to reside in Iraq and collecting religious contributions directly from the faithful in Iran. These contributions came mainly from wealthy merchants.

Qajar rule coincided with the peak of European imperialism. The Russians seized parts of Central Asia and the Caucasus from Iran, and extracted a series of major economic concessions, including a monopoly to fish for sturgeon in the Caspian Sea and exemption from import duties, internal tariffs, and the jurisdiction of local courts. The British Imperial Bank won the monopoly to issue paper money. The Indo-European Telegraph Company got a contract to extend communication lines through the country. A British citizen named D'Arcy bought the exclusive right to drill for oil in the southwest. The later Qajars also borrowed heavily from European banks to meet lavish court expenses. By the end of the century, these loans had become so heavy that the Qajars were obliged to guarantee repayments by placing the country's entire customs service under European supervision. Iranians felt that their whole country had been auctioned off, that their merchants faced unfair competition, and that the shah had given away far too many concessions, or capitulations, as they called them.

These resentments culminated in the constitutional revolution of 1905–1909. The revolution began with shopkeepers and moneylenders demonstrating against the Europeans' being placed in charge of the customs collections. They suspected that the shah would renege on local debts in favor of repaying his foreign loans. They also protested that the government was not doing enough to protect native merchants and local industries. The protests intensified when the government tried to lower sugar prices by publicly whipping two major merchants after sugar prices rose out of control as a result of the disruptions of the 1905 Russian revolution.

The protests peaked in 1906, when some 14,000 took sanctuary inside the gardens of the British legation in Tehran and demanded a written constitution. After weeks of haggling, the shah conceded because the British legation advised compromise and because the unpaid Cossack Brigade, the regime's sole standing army, threatened to join the protesters. Led by Russians and named after the tsar's praetorian guards, the Cossack Brigade was the only force in Iran resembling a disciplined army. A British diplomat commented, "The shah with his unarmed, unpaid, ragged, starving soldiers, what can he do in face of the menace of a general strike and riots?"[1]

The 1906 constitution, modeled after the Belgian one, introduced essential features of modern government into Iran: elections, separation of powers, laws made by a legislative assembly, and the concepts of popular sovereignty and the nation (*mellat*). It also generated a heated debate, with some arguing that democracy was inherently incompatible with Islam and others countering that true Islam could not be practiced unless the government was based on popular support. Some even argued in favor of secularism—complete separation of religion from politics, church from state, clergy from government authority, the affairs of the next world from those of this world.

While retaining the monarchy, the new constitution centered political power in a national assembly called the *Majles*. It hailed this assembly as "the representative of the whole people" and guaranteed two seats to the recognized religious minorities—the Jews, the Zoroastrians, and the Christians. Significantly, no seats were given to the Baha'is, a nineteenth-century offshoot of Shi'ism. The clerical leaders deemed the Baha'is to be apostates from Islam and Baha'i to be a "sinister heresy linked to the imperial powers."

The constitution endowed the *Majles* with extensive authority over all laws, budgets, treaties, loans, concessions, and the composition of the cabinet. The ministers were accountable to the *Majles*, not to the shah. "Sovereignty," declared the constitution, "is a trust confided (as a divine gift) by the people to the person of the shah." The constitution also included a bill of rights guaranteeing citizens equality before the law, protection of life and property, safeguards from arbitrary arrest, and freedom of expression and association.

Although the constitution was modeled on a liberal secular system of government, it made some concessions to Shi'ism. Shi'ism was declared Iran's official religion. Only Shi'is could hold cabinet posts. Clerical courts retained the right to implement the *shari'a* (religious law), especially in family matters. A Guardian Council formed of senior clerics was given

veto authority over parliamentary bills deemed un-Islamic. In short, popular sovereignty was to be restricted by a clerical veto power. In actual fact, this Guardian Council was not convened until the 1979 Islamic Revolution. Divisions within the clerical establishment as well as opposition from parliament prevented the convening of this Guardian Council.

The initial euphoria that greeted the constitutional revolution gave way to deep disillusionment in the subsequent decade. Pressures from the imperial powers continued, and a devastating famine after World War I took some 1 million lives, almost 10 percent of the total population. Internal conflicts polarized the *Majles* into warring liberal and conservative factions. The former, mostly members of the intelligentsia, championed social reforms, especially the replacement of the *shari'a* with a modern law code. The latter, led by landlords, tribal chiefs, and senior clerics, vehemently opposed such reforms, particularly land reform, women's rights, and the granting of full equality to religious minorities.

Meanwhile, the central government, lacking any real army, bureaucracy, or tax-collecting machinery, was unable to administer the provinces, especially the regions inhabited by the Kurds, Turkomans, and Baluchis. Some tribes, equipped with modern breech-loading European rifles, had more firepower than the central government. Moreover, during World War I, Russia and Britain formally carved up Iran into three zones. Russia occupied the north; Britain the south. Iran was left with a small "neutral zone" in the middle.

By 1921, Iran was in complete disarray. The shah was gathering his crown jewels to flee south. The British, in their own words, were hoping to "salvage" some "healthy limbs" in their southern zone. Left-wing rebels, helped by the young communist regime in Russia, had taken over the Caspian province of Gilan and were threatening nearby Azerbaijan, Mazandaran, and Khurason. According to a British diplomat, the propertied classes, fearful of bolshevism, were anxiously seeking a savior on horseback.[2]

The Pahlavis (1925–1979)

The savior appeared in February 1921 in the person of Colonel Reza Khan, the recently appointed commander of the 3000-man Cossack Brigade. Carrying out a typical military coup, he replaced the cabinet and, while paying lip service to the monarch, consolidated power in his own hands, especially the post of commander in chief of the armed forces. Four years later, he emerged from behind the throne, deposed the Qajars, crowned himself Shah-in-Shah in the style of his hero Napoleon, and established his own Pahlavi dynasty, adopting a name associated with the glories of ancient Iran. This was the first nontribal dynasty to rule the whole of Iran. To forestall opposition from Britain and the Soviet Union, he assured both countries that Iran would remain strictly nonaligned. A compliant *Majles* endorsed this transfer of power from the Qajars to the Pahlavis.

Reza Shah ruled with an iron fist until 1941, when the British and the Soviets invaded Iran to forestall Nazi Germany from establishing a foothold there. Reza Shah promptly abdicated in favor of his son, Muhammad Reza Shah, and went into exile, where he soon died. In the first twelve years of his reign, the young shah retained control over the armed forces but had to live with a free press, an independent judiciary, competitive elections, assertive cabinet ministers, and boisterous parliaments. He also had to confront two vigorous political movements: the communist Tudeh (Masses) Party; and the National Front, led by the charismatic Dr. Muhammad Mosaddeq (1882–1967).

The Tudeh drew its support mostly from working-class trade unions. The National Front drew its support mainly from the salaried middle classes and campaigned to nationalize the British-owned oil company that had a monopoly over the drilling, refining, and sale of all petroleum in Iran. Mosaddeq also wanted to sever the Shah's links with the armed forces. He argued that according to the constitution the monarch should reign, not rule, and that the armed forces should be supervised by cabinet ministers responsible to parliament. In 1951, Mosaddeq was elected prime minister and promptly nationalized the oil industry. The period of relative freedom, however, ended abruptly in 1953, when royalist officers overthrew Mosaddeq and installed the shah with absolute power. Since this 1953 coup was financed by the U.S. Central Intelligence Agency (CIA) and the British, it intensified anti-British sentiment and created a deep distrust of the United States. It also made the Shah appear to

be a puppet of the foreign powers. Muhammad Reza Shah began to rule much in the style of his autocratic father until overthrown by the 1979 Islamic Revolution.

During their fifty-four-year rule, the Pahlavis built a highly centralized state, the first in Iran's history. This state rested on three pillars: the armed forces; the bureaucracy; and the extensive patronage system. The armed forces grew from fewer than 40,000 men in 1925 to 124,000 in 1941, and to over 410,000 in 1979. In 1925 the armed forces had been formed of a motley crew of cossacks, city policeman, and gendarmes (rural policemen). By the mid-1930s they had the power to disarm the tribes and impose the will of the state on the provinces. By 1979 they constituted the fifth largest army in the world, the largest navy in the Persian Gulf, the largest air force in western Asia, and one of the best-equipped tank brigades in the Third World. They were supplemented with a pervasive secret police known as SAVAK—the Persian acronym for the Organization to Protect and Gather Information for the State.

The bureaucracy expanded from a haphazard collection of hereditary scribes—some without fixed offices—to twenty-one ministries employing over 300,000 civil servants in 1979. The Interior Ministry (the main bureaucracy) appointed the provincial governors, town mayors, district superintendents, and village headmen. Since it also appointed electoral supervisors, it could rig *Majles* elections and thus provide the Shah with rubber-stamp parliaments. The constitutional laws of 1906–1909 survived, at least in theory. The Education Ministry grew twentyfold and by 1979 administered 26,000 primary schools with some 4 million children, and 1850 secondary schools with 740,000 pupils. Meanwhile, the Ministry of Higher Education administered 750 vocational schools with 227,000 students; and thirteen universities with 154,000 college students.

The Justice Ministry supplanted the *Shari'a* with a European-style civil code and the clerical courts with a modern judicial system. This went from district courts through provincial courts all the way up to a Supreme Court. To practice in these courts, lawyers and judges had to pass government-administered exams based on European jurisprudence. The system was further secularized in the 1960s, when the Shah decreed a controversial Family Protection Law. This contradicted the *shar'ia* on a number of points. It raised the marriage age to twenty for men and eighteen for women. It allowed women to override spousal objections and work outside the home if they got court permission. It restricted polygamy by stipulating that husbands could marry more than one wife only if they first obtained permission from previous wives and the courts. For some, the state had extended its arm to reach into the most intimate area of existence—family life.

Other ministries experienced similar expansion. For example, the Transport Ministry built an impressive array of bridges, ports, highways, and railroads known as the Trans-Iranian Railway. The Ministry of Industries financed the construction of numerous factories specializing in consumer goods. The Agricultural Ministry attained prominence in 1962, when the Shah made land reform the centerpiece of his much-heralded White Revolution. The government bought land from large absentee owners and sold it to small farmers through low-interest long-term mortgages. It also undertook the task of transforming small farmers into modern commercial entrepreneurs by providing them with fertilizers, cooperatives, distribution centers, irrigation canals, dams, and tractor-repair shops. The White Revolution included the extension of the vote to women, the Family Protection Law, and a Literacy Corps to eradicate illiteracy in the countryside. Thus, by 1979, the state had set up a modern system of communications, initiated a minor industrial revolution, and extended its reach into even the most outlying villages.

The state also controlled a number of major institutions: the National and the Central banks; the planning organization in charge of five-year plans; the Industrial and Mining Development Bank, which channeled money to private entrepreneurs; the National Radio-Television network, which monopolized the airwaves—by the 1960s most villages had access to transistor radios; and most important, the National Iranian Oil Company, which grew from a leasing firm in the 1950s to become a large exploring, drilling, refining, and exporting corporation.

The Pahlavi state was further bolstered by court patronage. Reza Shah, the son of a small landowner, used coercion, confiscations, and diversion of irrigation water to make himself one of the largest landowners in the Middle East. In the words of a British diplomat, Reza Shah had an "unholy interest in property," especially other people's property.[3] This wealth transformed the Shah's court into a large military-landed complex providing patronage for the thousands employed in its numerous palaces, hotels, casinos, charities, companies, and beach resorts. This patronage system further grew under Muhammad Reza Shah, especially after he established his tax-exempt Pahlavi Foundation. By the 1970s the Pahlavi Foundation controlled 207 large companies active in tourism, insurance, banking, agribusiness, mining, construction, and manufacturing. The network was handy for rewarding friends and penalizing adversaries.

Although the Pahlavi state looked impressive, it lacked solid foundations. The drive for secularization, centralization, industrialization, and social development won some favor from the urban propertied classes. But arbitrary rule, especially the 1953 coup, the disregard for constitutional liberties, and the stifling of independent newspapers, political parties, and professional associations, produced widespread resentment, particularly among the clergy, the intelligentsia, and the urban masses. In short, this state was strong in the sense that it controlled new instruments of coercion and administration. But it was weak in terms of its failure to link the new state institutions to the country's social structure. The Pahlavi state, like the Safavids and the Qajars, hovered over, rather than embedded itself into, the society. What is more, much of the civil society that had existed in traditional Iran had now been swamped by the modern state.

As if the Pahlavi state did not control enough of society, in 1975 the Shah announced the formation of the Resurgence Party. He declared Iran to be a one-party state and threatened those refusing to join the party with exile and imprisonment. In heralding the new order, the Shah replaced the traditional Islamic calendar with a new royalist one, jumping from the Muslim year 1355 to the royalist year 2535; 2500 years were allocated to the monarchy in general and 35 years for the Shah's own reign. The King of Kings and the Shadow of God also accrued two new titles: Guide to the New Great Civilization and Light of the Aryans (*Aryamehr*).

Leaders: **Ayatollah Ruhollah Khomeini**

Ruhollah Khomeini was born in 1902 into a landed clerical family well known in central Iran. During the 1920s he studied in the famous Fayzieh Seminary in Qom with the leading theologians of the day, most of whom were scrupulously apolitical. He taught at the seminary from the 1930s through the 1950s, avoiding politics even during the mass campaign to nationalize the British-owned oil company. His entry into politics did not come until 1962, when he, along with most other clerical leaders, denounced Muhammad Reza Shah's White Revolution. Forced into exile, Khomeini taught at the Shi'i center of Najaf in Iraq from 1964 until 1978. During these years, he developed his own version of Shi'i populism by incorporating

socioeconomic grievances into his sermons and denouncing not just the Shah but the whole ruling class. Returning home triumphant in the midst of the Iranian Revolution, he was declared the Supreme Leader, the Founder of the Islamic Republic, the Guide for the Oppressed Masses, and Imam of the Muslim community. In the past, Iranian Shi'is, unlike the Arab Sunnis, had reserved the special term *Imam* only for Imam Ali and his Twelve direct heirs, whom they deemed to be semidivine and thereby infallible. For many Iranians in 1979, Khomeini was charismatic in the true sense of the word—a man with a special gift from God. Khomeini ruled as Imam and Supreme Leader of the Islamic Republic until his death in 1989.

The Resurgence Party was designed to create yet another organizational link with the population, especially with the **bazaars** (traditional marketplaces), which unlike the rest of society, had managed to retain their guilds and thus escape direct government control. The Resurgence Party promptly established bazaar guilds as well as newspapers, women's organizations, professional associations, and labor unions. It also prepared to create a Religious Corps, modeled on the Literacy Corps, to go into the countryside to teach the peasants "true Islam." The state was venturing into areas in which previous rulers had feared to tread.

The Resurgence Party promised to establish an "organic relationship between rulers and ruled"; "synthesize the best of capitalism and socialism"; and chart the way toward the New Great Civilization. It also praised the Shah for curbing the power of the "medieval clergy," eradicating vestiges of class warfare, and having the authority of a "spiritual guide" as well as a world-renowned statesman. For his part, the Shah told an English-language newspaper that the party's philosophy was "based on the dialectical principles of the White Revolution" and that nowhere in the world was there such a close relationship between a ruler and his people. "No other nation has given its commander such a carte-blanche [blank check]."[4] The terminology, as well as the boast, revealed much about the Shah at the height of his power.

The Islamic Revolution (1979)

On the eve of the revolution, an Iranian paper published in Paris printed a long denunciation of the Pahlavis entitled "Fifty Indictments of Treason During Fifty Years of Treason."[5] It charged the Pahlavis with establishing a military dictatorship with the help of the CIA; trampling over the constitution; creating SAVAK; rigging parliamentary elections; organizing a fascistic one-party state; taking over the religious establishment; and undermining national identity by disseminating Western culture. It also accused the regime of inducing millions of landless peasants to migrate into urban shantytowns; widening the gap between rich and poor; funneling money away from the small bourgeoisie into the pockets of the wealthy comprador bourgeoisie (the entrepreneurs linked to foreign companies and multinational corporations); wasting resources on bloated military budgets; and granting new capitulations to the West—the most controversial being the extension of diplomatic immunity to U.S. military advisers.

These grievances were given greater articulation when Ayatollah Ruhollah Khomeini began to formulate a new version of Shi'ism from his exile in Iraq. Khomeini's version of Shi'ism has often been labeled Islamic **fundamentalism**, but would be better described as Shi'i populism or political Islam. The term *fundamentalism*, derived from American Protestantism, implies religious dogmatism, intellectual inflexibility and purity, political traditionalism, social conservatism, rejection of the modern world, and the literal interpretation of scriptural texts. Khomeini, however, was less concerned about literal interpretations of the Qur'an than about fanning grievances against the elite and resentment against the United States. By 1979 he was more of a political revolutionary than a social conservative.

Khomeini began to denounce monarchies in general and the Pahlavis in particular as part and parcel of the corrupt elite exploiting the oppressed masses. The oppressors, he said, comprised large landowners, high-ranking military officers, corrupt courtiers, wealthy foreign-connected capitalists, and millionaire palace dwellers. The oppressed, on the other hand, were the masses, especially the landless peasants, the wage earners, the shantytown poor, and the self-employed in the bazaars. His proclamations often echoed the promise of the Bible and the Qur'an that "the poor (meek) shall inherit the earth."

In calling for the overthrow of the Pahlavi monarchy, Khomeini injected a radically new meaning into the old Shi'i term *velayat-e faqih* (**jurist's guardianship**). He argued that jurist's guardianship gave the senior clergy all-encompassing authority over the whole community, not just over widows, minors, and the retarded, as had been the interpretation previously. He insisted that only the senior clerics had the competence to understand the *shari'a;* that the divine authority given to the Prophet and the Imams had been passed on to their spiritual heirs, the clergy; and that throughout history the clergy had championed the rights of the people against bad government and foreign powers. He further insisted that the clergy were the people's true representatives, since they lived among them, listened to their problems, and shared their everyday joys and pains. He also claimed that the Shah intended to confiscate religious endowments, replace Islamic values with "cultural imperialism," and force women to go unveiled and thus "naked" into the streets. In fact, the last Shah had merely encouraged women to unveil; he had never outlawed the veil nor banned the full covering known as the chador. These pronouncements added fuel to an already explosive situation.

Iran now needed a few sparks to ignite the revolution. These came in the form of minor economic difficulties and pressure from international human rights organizations to curb SAVAK. In 1977–1978 the Shah tried to deal with a 20 percent rise in consumer prices and a 10 percent decline in oil revenues by cutting construction projects and declaring war against "profiteers," "hoarders," and "price gougers." Not surprisingly, shopkeepers felt that the Shah was diverting attention from court corruption and planning to replace them with government-run department stores, and that he was intending to destroy the bazaar, which some felt was the "the real pillar of Iranian society."

The pressure to curb SAVAK came from Amnesty International, the United Nations, and the Western press as well as from the recently elected Carter administration in the United States. In 1977, after meeting with the International Commission of Jurists, the Shah permitted Red Cross officials to visit prisons and allowed defense attorneys to attend political trials. In the words of Khomeini's first prime minister, Mehdi Bazargan, this international pressure allowed the opposition to breathe again after decades of suffocation.[6]

This slight loosening of the reins, coming in the midst of the economic recession, sealed the fate of the Shah. Political parties, labor organizations, and professional associations—especially lawyers, writers, and university professors—regrouped after years of being banned. Bazaar guilds regained their independence from the government party. College, high school, and seminary students, especially in the religious center of Qom, took to the streets to protest the quarter century of repression. On September 8, 1978, known as Bloody Friday, troops in Tehran fired into a crowded square, killing hundreds of unarmed demonstrators. By late 1978 a general strike brought the whole economy to a halt, paralyzing not only the oil industry, the factories, the banks, and the transport system but also the civil service, the media, the bazaars, and the whole educational establishment. The oil workers vowed that they would not export any petroleum until they had exported the "Shah and his forty thieves."[7]

Meanwhile, in the urban centers, local committees attached to the **mosques** (Muslim places of worship) and financed by the bazaars were distributing food to the needy, organizing militias known as the *pasdaran* (revolutionary guards), and setting up ad hoc courts to retain some semblance of law and order, since the whole judicial structure and the police had melted away. Equally significant, the antiregime rallies were now attracting as many as 2 million protesters. The largest of them was held in Tehran in December 1978 on the day commemorating the martyrdom of Imam Husayn at Karbala in 680. Protesters demanded the abolition of the monarchy, the return of Khomeini, and the establishment of a republic that would preserve national independence from imperialism and give workers and peasants social justice in the form of decent wages, land, and a proper standard of living.[8] Some soon forgot these economic demands, claiming that the Islamic Revolution was made by fundamentalists.

Although these rallies were led by pro-Khomeini clerics, they had valuable support from a broad spectrum of organizations: the National Front; the Tudeh; the Fedayin, a Marxist guerrilla group; the Mojahedin, a Muslim guerrilla group formed of religious but lay radicals; university and high school students; lawyers, writers, and women's organizations; and many well-financed bazaar merchants and guilds. A secret Revolutionary Committee set up by the pro-Khomeini clerics in Tehran tried to coordinate the strikes and protests that erupted, mostly spontaneously, in the provincial cities. The Revolutionary Committee was in daily phone contact with Khomeini in exile and disseminated his speeches through clandestine tape cassettes. This was a revolution made in the streets and moved along by audiotapes.

After a series of such mass rallies in late 1978, the *Washington Post* concluded that the "disciplined and well-organized marches lent considerable weight to the opposition's claim of being an alternative government."[9] Similarly, the *Christian Science Monitor* stated that the "giant wave of humanity sweeping through the capital declared louder than any bullet or bomb could the clear message, 'The Shah must go.'"[10] Confronted by this opposition and aware that increasing numbers of soldiers were deserting to the opposition, the Shah decided to leave Iran. A year later, when in exile he was dying of cancer, there was much speculation, especially in the United States, whether he could have mastered the upheavals if he had been healthier, possessed a stronger personality, and received full support from the United States. But even

a healthy man with an iron will and full foreign backing would not have been able to deal with 2 million demonstrators, a massive general strike, and defections from his own army rank-and-file.

On February 11—three weeks after the Shah's departure and ten days after Khomeini's return—armed groups, especially of the Fedayin and the Mojahedin supported by air force cadets, broke into the main army barracks in Tehran, distributed arms, and then assaulted the main police stations, the jails, and eventually the national radio-television station. That same evening, the radio station made the historic announcement: "This is the voice of Iran, the voice of true Iran, the voice of the Islamic Revolution." A few hours of street fighting had completed the destruction of the fifty-four-year-old dynasty that claimed a 2500-year-old heritage.

The Islamic Republic (1979 to the Present)

Seven weeks after the February revolution a nationwide referendum replaced the monarchy with an Islamic Republic. Of the 21 million eligible voters, 20 million—97 percent—endorsed the change. Liberal and lay supporters of Khomeini, including Mehdi Bazargan, his first prime minister, had hoped to offer the electorate a third choice—that of a Democratic Islamic Republic. But Khomeini overruled them on the grounds that the term *democratic* was redundant because Islam itself was democratic. The structure of this new republic was implicitly left to Khomeini, who was now hailed not only as a Grand Ayatollah but also as the Leader of the Revolution, the Founder of the Islamic Republic, the Guide for the Oppressed Masses, the Commander of the Armed Forces, and most potent, the **Imam** ("Infallible Leader") of the Muslim community.

The constitution itself was drawn up in late 1979 by a constituent body named the Assembly of Religious Experts (*Majles-e Khebregan*). Although this seventy-three-man assembly was elected by the general public, almost all secular organizations as well as clerics opposed to Khomeini boycotted the elections on the grounds that the state media were controlled, independent papers had been banned, and voters were being intimidated by club-wielding vigilantes known as the **Hezbollahis** ("Partisans of God").

The Shah's statue on the ground, February 1979.
Source: © Abbas/Magnum Photos.

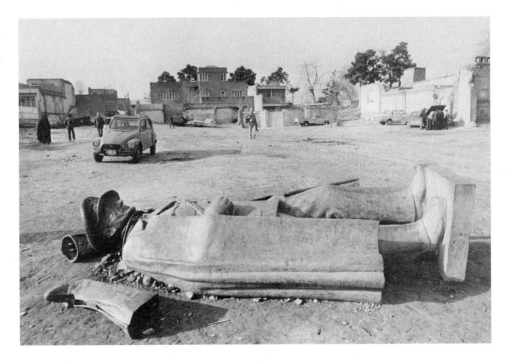

The vast majority of those elected, including forty hojjat al-Islams and fifteen ayatollahs, were pro-Khomeini clerics. They proceeded to draft a highly theocratic constitution vesting much authority in the hands of Khomeini in particular and the clergy in general—all this over the strong objections of Prime Minister Bazargan, who wanted a French-style presidential republic that would be Islamic in name but democratic in structure.

Khomeini submitted this clerical constitution to a national referendum in December 1979, at the height of the American hostage crisis. In fact, some suspected that the whole crisis had been engineered to undercut the Bazargan government which favored keeping cordial ties with the United States. As soon as Bazargan threatened to submit his own secular constitution to the public, the state television network—controlled by the clerics—showed him shaking hands with U.S. policymakers. Meanwhile Khomeini declared that the U.S embassy—the "den of spies"— was plotting a repeat performance of the l953 coup. A month after the embassy break-in and Bazargan's resignation, Khomeini submitted the theocratic constitution to the public, insisting that all had the duty to endorse it—99 percent of those voting endorsed it. The turnout, however, was not so impressive. Of the 21 million eligible voters, only 16 million participated despite the concerted efforts of all the authorities, including the mass media, the local mosques, and the revolutionary guards. The clerics had won their constitution but at the cost of eroding the republic's broad consensus.

In the first decade after the revolution, the clerics were able to further consolidate power for the following reasons. Few could afford to challenge Khomeini's overwhelming charisma. The Iraqi invasion in 1980—prompted by Sadaam Hussein's ambition to obtain vital border regions—rallied most of the population behind the regime; after all, the homeland had been violated by a foreign invader. The price of petroleum on the world market shot up, providing ample oil revenues. Thus, despite war and revolution, the new regime was able to continue the social programs launched by the previous one. In fact, in the 1980s modern amenities, especially electricity, indoor plumbing, televisions, telephones, refrigerators, motorcycles, and medical clinics, made their first significant appearance in the countryside.

The second decade after the revolution, however, brought the clerics serious challenges. Khomeini's death in June 1989 removed his decisive presence. His successor as Supreme Leader, Khamenei, lacked not only his popularity and political experience but also his scholastic credentials. Khamenei had been considered a mere **hojjat al-Islam** until the government-controlled press elevated him to the rank of ayatollah just before his appointment as Supreme Leader. Few senior ayatollahs deemed him their equal. The UN-brokered Iraqi cease-fire in 1988 ended the immediacy of the foreign danger. The drastic fall in world oil prices after 1984 strained state finances and placed a sharp brake on social and economic development. What is more, some clerics within the system began to call for liberalization, revitalization, and opening up of Iran to the West.

Themes and Implications

Historical Junctures and Political Themes

These historical junctures have shaped contemporary Iran, the way it grapples with the democratic idea, Iran's role in the world of states, its attempts to govern the economy and meet rising expectations as well as its aspiration to overcome internal division with a sense of a collective Shi'i Iranian identity.

By far the most important challenge facing the republic is that of reconciling Islam with democracy. Iran has been Muslim since the seventh century and Shi'i Muslim since the sixteenth century. It has also aspired to attain democracy, mass participation, and popular sovereignty since the 1905 constitutional revolution. The dual sentiments for Islam and for democracy culminated in the 1979 Islamic Revolution and appeared to be reconcilable as long as the vast majority supported Khomeini and accepted his notion of the jurist's guardianship. Rights of Man did not seem to contradict the Divine Right of the Clergy. As Khomeini liked to repeat, there was no contradiction between Islam and democracy because the vast majority supported the clerics, had faith in them, respected them as the true interpreters of the *shari'a*, and wanted them to oversee the activities of all state officials. Islam and democracy, however, now appear less reconcilable because the public has lost its enthusiasm

for the clergy, especially since the death of Khomeini. Thus some of his followers have continued to give priority to his concept of theocracy while others have begun to emphasize the need for democracy. In other words, Khomeinism has divided into two divergent branches—political liberalism and clerical conservatism.

The issue of democracy is compounded by the very nature of the *shari'a*. Democracy is based on the two principles that all are equal, especially before the law, and that all individuals have inalienable natural rights, including the right to choose their own religion. The *shari'a*, as conventionally interpreted, rejects both. Formulated in the seventh century, the *shari'a* is based on the principle of inequality, especially between men and women, between Muslims and non-Muslims, between legitimate minorities, known as the People of the Book, and illegitimate ones, known as unbelievers and idol-worshipers. In addition, the *shari'a*, like all religious law, considers rights to be derived from God rather than nature and deems the individual to be subordinate to the religious community. This is of special concern for Muslims who lose their faith or join another religion, since the *shari'a* can condemn them to death as apostates. This is no mere technicality; over 250 Baha'is and over 400 leftist political prisoners have been executed on the grounds of being religious apostates. The latter were hanged after admitting that they did not believe in God, the Resurrection, and the divinity of the Qur'an. But there are plenty of moderate clerics who want to reform the *shari'a* to make it compatible with the modern concepts of individual freedom and human rights. They also favor treating nonbelievers in the traditional fashion: "don't ask, don't tell."

The Islamic Republic is determined to remain the dominant power in the Persian Gulf, even though it attained this position under the Shah mainly thanks to U.S. assistance. In his last years, the Shah had been known as the American policeman in the Persian Gulf. By denouncing the United States as an "arrogant imperialist," by canceling military agreements with the West, and by condoning the taking of U.S. diplomats as hostages, Khomeini carried out a diplomatic revolution in the Middle East. This prompted Saddam Hussein to launch the Iraq-Iranian War. When ministers suggested referring to the Persian Gulf as the

Muslim Gulf to improve relations with Arab countries, all of whom call it the Arab Gulf, Khomeini responded that it should remain what it had always been—the Persian Gulf. Khomeini was as much an Iranian nationalist as a revolutionary Muslim.

Before dying, Khomeini initiated policies that have made it difficult for his successors to improve relations with the West, especially the United States. He called for revolutions throughout the Muslim world, denouncing Arab rulers in the region, particularly in Saudi Arabia, as the "corrupt puppets of American imperialism." He strengthened the navy, buying nuclear submarines from Russia. He launched a research program to build medium-range missiles and nuclear weapons. He denounced the proposals for Arab-Israeli negotiations over Palestine. He sent money as well as arms to Muslim dissidents abroad, particularly Shi'i groups in Lebanon, Iraq, and Afghanistan. He permitted the intelligence services to assassinate some one hundred exiled opposition leaders living in Western Europe. And most important, he issued a *fatwa* against the British writer Salman Rushdie. These policies helped isolate Iran not only from the United States but also from the European Community, human rights organizations and the United Nations. Khomeini's heirs have had to grapple with this heritage, especially since these acts have direct bearing on economic development and the prospects for obtaining foreign investment.

The Islamic Republic began with the conviction that it could rapidly develop the economy if it relied less on oil exports and more on agriculture and manufacturing. It blamed the Shah for the one-export economy, the migration of peasants into the towns, the increasing gap in incomes, the continued high illiteracy rate, the lack of medical and educational facilities, and, in general, the low standard of living. It also blamed the former regime for failing to make Iran self-sufficient and instead making it vulnerable to the vagaries of the world economy by building assembly plants rather than factories that would produce industrial goods.

The new regime soon discovered that although it was relatively easy to narrow the gap between town and country, the underlying problems of developing the economy were formidable. The state remains heavily dependent on oil and thus on the fluctuations of the international petroleum market. Peasants continue to migrate because of geographical pressures, notably the lack of agricultural land and water for irrigation. Industry remains limited because of the lack of capital. Real per capita income has fallen due to forces outside the control of the state. The real price of oil has plummeted; by 1999 it was less than it had been before the dramatic quadrupling of prices in 1974. Meanwhile, the population has grown to almost 69 million. In other words, the population has doubled since the revolution while oil income has stagnated. Not surprisingly, the republic continues to struggle with such financial problems as inflation, high unemployment, and capital shortages. Some decision-makers advocate conventional state-interventionist strategies: price controls, five year plans, and further redistribution of wealth through high taxation and social investment. Others advocate equally conventional laissez-faire strategies: open markets, removal of state controls, more business incentives, and the wooing of foreign capital. Some clerics now openly admit that religion does not have answers to such problems as inflation, unemployment, and the volatility of oil prices. This is a sharp contrast to the early days of the revolution, when Khomeini had confidently declared that Islam had all the solutions and that economics was a subject worthy of donkeys.

Finally, the Islamic Republic began with a broad collective identity, since 99 percent of Iran's population is Muslim. But this major asset was squandered somewhat in the two decades after the revolution. The stress on Shi'ism naturally alienated the Sunnis, who constitute some 9 percent of the population. The triumph in neighboring Afghanistan of the ultraconservative Sunni organization the Taliban further complicated the situation. The Taliban has been supporting Sunni dissidents in Iran; Iran, in turn, has been arming Shi'i dissidents inside Afghanistan. Moreover, the regime's insistence on building the constitution around Khomeini's notion of theocratic government has antagonized many of the top clerics, who rejected this theory of government, as well as lay secular Muslims, who lead most of the political parties. Similarly, the inadvertent association of Shi'ism with the central Persian-speaking regions carries with it the potential danger of eventually alienating the important Turkic minority in Azerbaijan. Thus the Iranian regime, like most developing states, has to solve the problem of how to allocate scarce economic resources without exacerbating ethnic, regional, and sectarian differences.

Implications for Comparative Politics

The Iranian Revolution, the emergence of Islam in Middle Eastern politics, and the collapse of the Soviet Union convinced many Americans that a new specter was haunting the West—Islamic fundamentalism. By the mid-1990s some experts on international relations were predicting that a new "clash of civilizations" would replace the Cold War; that the fault lines in world politics would no longer be over economics and ideology but over religion and culture; and that the main clash would be between the West and the Islamic world, headed by the Islamic Republic of Iran. Islam was deemed a major threat not only because of its size but also because it was "inherently bellicose," and "militant," and bore a historic grudge against the West.

These dire predictions turned out to be gross exaggerations. It is true that the Islamic Republic began denouncing the United States, arming militants in other parts of the Middle East, and calling for a struggle, sometimes termed a *jihad* (crusade), against the West. But these rhetorical denunciations became muted as time passed—the election of Khatami indicates this. The call for Muslim unity fell on deaf ears, especially in Sunni countries. The external assistance was limited to Shi'is in Afghanistan, Iraq, and southern Lebanon. Islam proved to be not a monolith; the Muslim international turned out to be, at most, a Shi'i international. What is more, Iranians themselves, including the clerics, divide sharply into ultraconservatives, conservatives, liberals, and radicals. They even use the Western terms left, right, and center to describe themselves. Iran shows that the notion of Muslim politics has as little meaning as that of Christian politics. In the same way that one does not study the Bible to understand modern Europe, one does not need the Qur'an to analyze Middle Eastern politics.

It is true that Iran is a major power in the Middle East. It has the region's second largest army, a large land mass, human resources, a respectable GNP, and oil production. It has the largest navy in the Persian Gulf. In the days of the Shah, this navy safeguarded the flow of oil to the West. It now poses a threat to the same flow of oil. It also has plans, predating the Islamic Revolution, to build nuclear weapons. But it is also true that Iran is in many ways a much weakened power. It has the GNP of New Jersey, hardly a replacement of the Soviet threat to the United States. Its armed forces are a mere shadow of their former selves. The eight-year conflict with Iraq has made them war-weary. The officer ranks have been decimated by constant purges. Their hardware has been depleted by war, use, and obsolescence, and the regime has difficulty financing arms purchases. In the last years of the Shah, military purchases accounted for 17 percent of the gross domestic product. They now take less than 2 percent. Moreover, a U.S. fleet cruises the Persian Gulf, counterbalancing the Iranian navy, and plans to build nuclear weapons are bogged down in financial, technical, and logistical problems. Iran is unlikely to obtain nuclear weapons—not to mention nuclear capabilities—in the forseeable future.

It is true that Iran has viewed itself as the vanguard of the Islamic world. But that world turned out to be as illusory for its champions as for its detractors. It is formed not of one unitary bloc but of many rival states, each with its own national self-interest as defined by its own local elites. In theory, these rulers stress the importance of unity and solidarity. In reality, they pursue traditional power politics. They give priority to the protection of their own states, even if this involves allying with non-Muslim states against rival Muslims ones. For example, at the height of the American hostage crisis, Iran obtained military equipment from Israel and the United States to pursue the war against Iraq. Similarly, in recent years, Iran has sided with India against Pakistan; Armenia against Azerbaijan; Russia against Chechnya. It has also actively opposed the Afghan Taliban, mainly because the latter is backed by Pakistan and Saudi Arabia, Iran's regional rivals. Those who see the future as a clash of civilizations and a replay of the medieval Christian-Muslim wars forget that the crusaders themselves, both Muslim and Christian, were often divided, with some siding against their own co-religionists. One Muslim world exists no more now than it did in the days of the medieval crusaders.

Section ❷ Political Economy and Development

State and Economy

In 1993 billboards appeared in Tehran announcing the return of Coca-Cola after a fourteen-year absence. In its initial enthusiasm for economic self-sufficiency, the Islamic Republic had ousted Coca-Cola and many other multinational corporations. Although some leaders continued to warn against Western consumerism and cultural imperialism, the regime as a whole was now eager to market this and other hallmarks of international capitalism. Iran, despite its anti-Western stance, was being reintegrated into the world economy.

The Economy in the Nineteenth Century

The integration of Iran into the world system began in a modest way in the latter half of the nineteenth century. Before then, commercial contact with the outside world had been limited to a few luxury goods and the famous medieval silk route to China. A number of factors account for this nineteenth-century integration: the economic concessions granted to the European powers; the opening up of the Suez Canal and the building of the Trans-Caspian and the Batum-Baku railways; the laying of telegraph lines across Iran to link India with Britain; the outflow of capital from Europe after 1870; and, most important, the Industrial Revolution in Europe and the subsequent export of manufactured goods to the rest of the world.

In the course of the nineteenth century, Iran's foreign trade increased tenfold. Over 83 percent of this trade was with Russia and Britain; 10 percent with Germany, France, Italy, and Belgium; and less than 7

Coca-Cola being sold in Iran. *Source:* Rad Eslami/Gamma Liaison.

percent with countries in the Middle East. Exports were confined to carpets and agricultural products, including silk, raw cotton, opium, dried fruits, rice, and tobacco. Imports were mostly tea, sugar, kerosene, and such industrial products as textiles, glassware, guns, and other metal goods. Also in this period, modest foreign investment flowed into banking, fishing, carpet weaving, transport, and telegraph communications.

Contact with the West had far-reaching repercussions. It produced what later became known as economic dependency: the overreliance of the underdeveloped world on the developed; the vulnerability of poor countries to sudden fluctuations in rich economies; and the export of raw materials, whose prices often stagnated or declined, in return for the import of finished products, whose value invariably increased. Some claim that this dependency lies at the root of present-day economic underdevelopment in much of Africa, Latin America, and Asia (including the Middle East).

The nineteenth-century influx of mass-manufactured goods devastated some traditional handicrafts, especially cotton textiles. According to a tax collector in Isfahan, the import of cheap, colorful cotton goods damaged not only the local weavers, dyers, and carders but also the thousands of housewives who in the past had supplemented their family incomes with cottage industries and home spindles.[11] They naturally blamed foreign imports for their plight. Carpet manufacturers, however, benefited, since they found a ready market in Europe and North America.

Moreover, the introduction of cash crops, especially cotton, tobacco, and opium, reduced the acreage available for wheat and other cereals. Many landowners ceased growing food and turned to commercial export crops. This paved the way for a series of disastrous famines in 1860, 1869–1872, 1880, and 1918–1920. Opium cultivation was particularly encouraged by British merchants eager to meet the ever-rising demands of the Chinese market brought about by the notorious Opium Wars.

Furthermore, the competition from foreign merchants, together with the introduction of the telegraph and the postal systems, brought the many local merchants, shopkeepers, and workshop owners together into a national middle class aware for the first time of their common statewide interests against both the central government and the foreign powers. In short, the bazaars were transformed into a propertied middle class conscious of its national grievances. This awareness played an important role in the constitutional revolution.

The Oil Economy

The real integration of Iran into the world system came in the twentieth century. Its main engine was oil. British prospectors struck oil in Khuzistan in 1908, and the British government in 1912 decided to fuel its navy with petroleum rather than coal. It also decided to buy most of its fuel from the Anglo-Iranian Oil Company, in which it was a major shareholder. Iran's oil revenues increased modestly in the next four decades, reaching US$16 million in 1951. After the nationalization of the oil industry in 1951 and the agreement with a consortium of U.S. and British companies in 1955, oil revenues rose steadily, from $34 million in 1955 to $5 billion in 1973, and after the quadrupling of oil prices in 1974, to over $20 billion in 1975 and $23 billion in 1976. Between 1953 and 1978, the cumulative oil income came to over $100 billion.

Oil became known as Iran's black gold. It financed over 90 percent of imports and 80 percent of the annual budget, and far surpassed total tax revenues. In contrast, domestic taxation provides the Japanese government with over 75 percent of its revenues. Oil also enabled Iran not to worry about feeding its population, a problem confronting many poor countries. Instead it could undertake ambitious development programs that other states implemented only if they could squeeze scarce resources from their populations. In fact, oil revenues created what is known as a **rentier state**, a state obtaining a lucrative income by exporting raw materials or leasing out oil wells. Iran as well as Iraq, Algeria, and the Gulf states received enough money from their wells to be able to disregard their internal tax bases. The state became relatively independent of society. The society, in turn, had few inputs into the state. Little taxation meant little representation. It also meant that the state was totally reliant on one commodity whose price was determined by the world market.

Muhammad Reza Shah tried to diminish the dependency on oil by encouraging other exports and attracting foreign investment into nonoil ventures. Neither policy succeeded. Despite some increase in carpet and pistachio exports, oil continued to dominate. On the eve of the 1979 revolution, it still provided 97 percent of the country's foreign exchange. The new nonoil industries faced difficulties finding export markets. Furthermore, Iran failed to draw external capital despite the much-publicized 1955 Law for the Attraction and Protection of Foreign Investments. Even after the oil boom, foreign firms, mostly U.S., European, and Japanese, invested no more than US$1 billion. Much of this was not in industry but in banking, trade, and insurance. In Iran, as in the rest of the Middle East, Western companies grew weary of investing large fixed assets, because of government corruption, high labor costs, the limitations of the internal market, and the fear of potential instability and outright confiscations. Apparently, the companies did not share their governments' confidence that Iran was an island of stability.

Oil revenues financed Muhammad Reza Shah's development projects. It is true—as the opposition liked to publicize—that some revenue was squandered on palaces, royal extravagances, bureaucratic waste, outright corruption, ambitious nuclear projects, and ultrasophisticated weapons too expensive even for many NATO countries. But it is also true that significant sums were channeled into socioeconomic development. Gross national product (GNP) grew at the average rate of 9.6 percent every year from 1960 to 1977, making Iran one of the fastest developing countries in the Third World at that time. The land reform project—the linchpin of the White Revolution—created over 644,000 moderately prosperous farms (see Table 1). The number of modern factories tripled from fewer than 320 to over 980 (see Table 2). Enrollment in primary schools grew from less than 750,000 to over 4 million; in secondary schools from 121,000 to nearly 740,000; in vocational schools from 2500 to nearly 230,000; and in universities from under 14,000 to more than 154,000. The Trans-Iranian Railway was completed, linking Tehran with Tabriz, Meshed, Isfahan, and the Gulf. Roads were built connecting most villages with the provincial cities.

The expansion in health services was equally impressive. Between 1963 and 1977 the number of hospital beds increased from 24,126 to 48,000;

Table 1

Land Ownership in 1977

Size (hectares)	No. of Owners
200+	1300
51–200	44,000
11–50	600,000
3–10	1,200,000
Landless	700,000

Note: 1 hectare is equal to approximately 2.47 acres.

Source: E. Abrahamian, "Structural Causes of the Iranian Revolution," *Middle East Research and Information Project*, no. 87 (May 1980), 23.

Table 2

Number of Factories

Size	1953	1977
Small (10–40 workers)	Fewer than 1000	More than 7000
Medium (50–500 workers)	300	830
Large (over 500 workers)	19	159

Source: E. Abrahamian, "Structural Causes of the Iranian Revolution," *Middle East Research and Information Project*, no. 87 (May 1980), 22.

Table 3

Industrial Production

Product	1953	1977
Coal (tons)	200,000	900,000
Iron ore (tons)	5000	930,000
Steel (tons)	—	275,000
Cement (tons)	53,000	4,300,000
Sugar (tons)	70,000	527,000
Tractors (no.)	—	7700
Motor vehicles (no.)	—	109,000

Source: E. Abrahamian, "Structural Causes of the Iranian Revolution," *Middle East Research and Information Project*, no. 87 (May 1980), 22.

medical clinics from 700 to 2800; nurses from 1969 to 4105; and doctors from 4500 to 12,750. These improvements, together with the elimination of epidemics and famines—mainly due to food imports—lowered infant mortality and led to a population explosion. In the two decades prior to the 1979 revolution, the overall population doubled from 18 million to nearly 36 million. This explosion gave the country a predominantly youthful age structure. By the mid-1970s half the populaton was under sixteen years of age. This was to have repercussions in the street politics of 1977–1979.

Society and Economy

Socioeconomic development, however, did not necessarily make the Shah popular. On the contrary, the way this development was implemented tended to increase his unpopularity. The Industrial and Mining Development Bank channeled over US$50 billion of low-interest loans to court-connected entrepreneurs, industrialists, and agribusinessmen. The Shah, like most conservative economists, believed that if enough benefits were extended to the rich, some of them would gradually trickle down into the lower levels of society. But in Iran, as elsewhere, the benefits got stuck at the top. By the mid-1970s, Iran had one of the worst income distributions in the world.[12] Similarly, land reform, despite high expectations, created a small stratum of prosperous farmers but left the vast majority of peasants landless or nearly landless; over 1.2 million received less than 10 hectares (approximately 24.7 acres), not enough to survive as independent farmers (see Table 1). Not surprisingly, many flocked to the urban shantytowns in search of work.

The factories drew much criticism on the grounds that they were assembly plants and poor substitutes for real industrial development (see Table 3 on page 626). The medical programs still left Iran with one of the worst doctor-patient ratios and child mortality rates in the Middle East. The educational expansion created one place for every five university applicants; failed to provide primary schools for 60 percent of children; and had no impact on 68 percent of illiterates. In fact, the total number of illiterates rose because of the population explosion. The priority given to the capital by the regime increased the dis-parities between Tehran and the provinces. By the mid-1970s, Tehran contained half the country's doctors and manufacturing plants. According to one comparative study, the per capita regional product in the richest provinces was ten times more than in the poorest ones. Iran—after Brazil—had the highest regional disparity in the developing world.[13] According to another study, the ratio of urban to rural incomes was 5 to 1—again, making it one of the worst in the world.[14]

These inequalities created a **dual society**. On one side was the modern sector, headed by the elites with close ties to the oil state. On the other side was the traditional sector comprising the clergy, the bazaar middle class, and the rural masses. Each sector, in turn, was sharply stratified into unequal classes. Thus, Iranian society was divided vertically into the modern and the traditional, and horizontally into a number of urban as well as rural classes (see Figure 1 on page 628).

The upper class—the Pahlavi family, the court-connected entrepreneurs, the military officers, and the senior civil servants—constituted less than 0.01 percent of the population. In the modern sector, the middle class—namely, professionals, civil servants, salaried personnel, and college students—formed about 10 percent of the population. The bottom of the modern sector—the urban working class, which included factory workers, construction laborers, peddlers, and unemployed—constituted over 32 percent. In the traditional sector, the middle class—bazaar merchants, small retailers, shopkeepers, workshop owners, and well-to-do family farmers—made up 13 percent. The rural masses—landless and near-landless peasants, nomads, and village construction workers—made up about 45 percent of the population.

Government statistics show the rising inequality between classes and between regions. In 1972 the richest 20 percent of urban households accounted for 47.1 percent of total urban family expenditures; by 1977 it accounted for 55.5 percent. In 1972 the poorest 40 percent accounted for 16.7 percent of urban family expenditures; by 1977 it accounted for 11.7 percent (see Table 4).

These inequalities fueled resentments against the ruling elite, which, however, were expressed more in cultural and religious terms than in economic and class terms. Articulating these resentments was a

The society was divided sharply not only into horizontal classes, but also into vertical sectors—the modern and the transitional, the urban and the rural. This is known as a dual society.

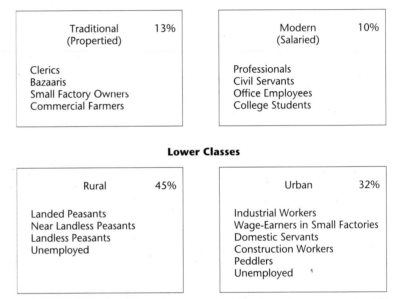

Figure 1

Iran's Class Structure in the Mid-1970s

Upper Class

Pahlavi Family; Court-Connected Entrepreneurs; Senior Civil Servants and Military Officers	0.1%

Middle Class

Traditional (Propertied)	13%	Modern (Salaried)	10%
Clerics Bazaaris Small Factory Owners Commercial Farmers		Professionals Civil Servants Office Employees College Students	

Lower Classes

Rural	45%	Urban	32%
Landed Peasants Near Landless Peasants Landless Peasants Unemployed		Industrial Workers Wage-Earners in Small Factories Domestic Servants Construction Workers Peddlers Unemployed	

gadfly writer named Jalal Al-e-Ahmad (1923–1969). A former communist who had rediscovered his Shi'i roots in the 1960s, Al-e-Ahmad shook his contempo-

Table 4

Measures of Inequality of Urban Household Consumption Expenditures

	Percentage Share in Total Expenditures		
Year	Poorest 40%	Middle 40%	Richest 20%
1972	16.7	36.2	47.1
1977	11.7	32.8	55.5

Source: V. Nowshirvani and P. Clawson, "The State and Social Equity in Postrevolutionary Iran," in *The Politics of Social Transformation in Afghanistan, Iran, and Pakistan*, ed. M. Weiner and A. Banuazizi (Syracuse, N.Y.: Syracuse University Press, 1994), 248.

raries by publishing a polemical pamphlet entitled *Gharbzadegi* (*The Plague from the West*). He argued that the ruling class was destroying Iran by blindly imitating the West, neglecting the peasantry, showing contempt for popular religion, worshipping mechanization, regimentation, and industrialization, and flooding the country with foreign ideas, tastes, luxury items, and mass-consumption goods. He stressed that Third World countries such as Iran could survive this "plague" of Western imperialism only by returning to their cultural roots and developing a self-reliant society, especially a fully independent economy. Al-e-Ahmad inspired the long search for cultural authenticity and economic self-sufficiency.

These themes were developed further by another young intellectual, Ali Shariati (1933–1977). Studying in Paris during the turbulent 1960s, Shariati was influenced by Marxist sociology, Catholic liberation theology, the Algerian revolution, and most important, Frantz Fanon's theory of Third World revolutions as laid out in his famous book, *Wretched of the Earth*. Shariati returned home with what can be called a fresh and revolutionary interpretation of Shi'ism, echoes of which would later appear in Khomeini's writings.

Shariati argued that history was a continuous struggle between oppressors and oppressed. Each class had its own interests, its own interpretations of religion, and its own sense of right and wrong, justice and injustice, morality and immorality. To help the oppressed, Shariati believed, God periodically sent down prophets, such as Abraham, Moses, Jesus, and Muhammad. In fact, Muhammad had come to launch a dynamic community in "permanent revolution" toward the ultimate utopia—a perfectly classless society in this world.

Although Muhammad's goal had been betrayed by his illegitimate successors, the Caliphs, his radical message had been preserved for posterity by the Shi'i Imams, especially by Imam Husayn who had died to show future generations that human beings had the moral duty to fight oppression in all places at all times. Shariati equated Imam Husayn with Che Guevara, the famous Latin American guerrilla killed in Bolivia in 1967. According to Shariati, the contemporary oppressors were the imperialists, the feudalists, the corrupt capitalists, and their hangers-on, especially the "tie-wearers" and "the palace dwellers," the carriers of the "Western plague." He also criticized the conservative clerics who had tried to transform revolutionary religion into an apolitical public opiate. Shariati died on the eve of the 1979 revolution, but his prolific works were so widely read and so influential that many felt that he rather than Khomeini was the true theorist of the Islamic Revolution.

Iran and the International Political Economy

Iran under the Shahs

The oil boom in the 1970s gave the Shah the opportunity to play a significant role in international politics. As the second most important member of the Organization of Petroleum Exporting Countries (**OPEC**), Iran could cast decisive votes for raising or moderating oil prices. At times, the Shah curried Western favor by moderating prices. At other times, he pushed for higher prices to finance his ambitious projects and military purchases. These purchases rapidly escalated once President Richard Nixon began to encourage U.S. allies, such as the Shah, to take greater responsibility in policing their regions. Moreover, Nixon's secretary of state, Henry Kissinger, openly argued that the United States should finance its ever-increasing oil imports—most of them from the Persian Gulf—by exporting more military hardware. The Shah was now able to buy from the United States almost any ultrasophisticated weapon he desired. Arms dealers began to jest that the Shah read their technical manuals in the same way that some other men read *Playboy*. The Shah's arms buying from the United States jumped from US$135 million in 1970 to a peak of $5.7 billion in 1977. Between 1955 and 1978, Iran spent more than $20.7 billion on U.S. arms alone.

This military might gave the Shah a reach well beyond his immediate boundaries. He invaded and occupied three small but strategically located Arab islands in the Straits of Hormuz, thus controlling the oil lifeline through the Persian Gulf. He talked of establishing a presence well beyond the Gulf on the grounds that Iran's national interests reached into the Indian Ocean. "Iran's military expenditures," according to a 1979 U.S. congressional report, "surpassed those of the most powerful Indian Ocean states, including Australia, Indonesia, Pakistan, South Africa, and India."[15]

In the mid-1970s the Shah dispatched troops to Oman to help the local sultan fight rebels. He offered Afghanistan US$2 billion to break its ties with the Soviet Union, a move that probably prompted the Soviets to intervene militarily in that country. The Shah, after supporting Kurdish rebels in Iraq, forced Baghdad to concede to Iran vital territory on the Shatt al-Arab estuary. This had been a bone of contention between the two countries ever since Iraq had come into existence after World War I. A U.S. congressional report summed up Iran's overall strategic position: "Iran in the 1970s was widely regarded as a significant regional, if not global, power. The United

States relied on it, implicitly if not explicitly, to ensure the security and stability of the Persian Gulf sector and the flow of oil from the region to the industrialized Western world of Japan, Europe, and the United States, as well as to lesser powers elsewhere."[16]

These vast military expenditures, as well as the oil exports, tied Iran closely to the industrial countries of the West, and to Japan. Iran was now importing millions of dollars' worth of rice, industrial tools, construction equipment, pharmaceuticals, tractors, pumps, and spare parts. The bulk of the rice and wheat, and a substantial portion of the tractors, medicines, and construction equipment, came from the United States. Trade with neighboring and other Third World countries was insignificant. In the words of the Department of Commerce in Washington, "Iran's rapid economic growth [provided America with] excellent business opportunities."[17]

The oil revenues thus had major consequences for Iran's political economy, all of which paved the way for the Islamic Revolution. They allowed the Shah to pursue ambitious programs that inadvertently widened class and regional divisions within the dual society. They drastically raised public expectations without necessarily meeting them. They made the rentier state independent of society. They also made the state highly dependent on oil prices and imported products. Iran was no longer a simple rentier state, but an oil-addicted one, vulnerable to the vagaries of the world petroleum market. Economic slowdowns in the industrial countries could lead to a decline in their oil demands, which, in turn, could diminish Iran's ability to buy such essential goods as food, medicine, and industrial spare parts. One of the major promises made by the Islamic Revolution was to end this economic dependency on oil and the West.

The Islamic Republic

The Islamic Republic began with high hopes of rapidly developing the economy, and at the same time becoming fully independent of oil and the West. The results have been mixed, illustrating the constraints the political economy places on society. The Pahlavi monarch and the Islamic Republic may have differed in many respects, but they governed the same economy and therefore faced similar financial problems.

The main problem plaguing the Islamic Republic has been instability in the world oil market. This instability has occurred despite the efforts of OPEC to preserve prices by limiting production and setting quotas for its members. The price of a barrel of oil—which had quadrupled from US$5 to $20 in 1974— peaked to $40 in 1980, but plummeted thereafter, reaching $18 in 1985, hovering around $12–$14 in the late 1980s and 1990s, and descending to a new low of $10 in 1999. This meant that Iran's oil revenues—which continued to provide the state with 80 percent of its hard currency and 75 percent of its total revenues—fell from $20 billion in 1978 to $13 billion in the late 1980s. In 1998 they hit a new low of $10.5 billion. Iran is still a rentier state and remains vulnerable to the vagaries of the international petroleum market. Oil, which had brought considerable riches before the revolution, produced relative deprivation in the 1980s and 1990s.

The decline in the world price of oil was due to a number of factors outside Iran's control: the slackening of the demand in the industrialized countries (especially with the recession in the late 1990s); the glutting of the international market by the entry of non-OPEC producers, such as Britain and Mexico; and the tendency of some OPEC members to preserve their revenues by cheating on their production quotas. Iran's oil revenues were also affected by the Iraqi war and the failure of the national oil company to raise production. In some years, Iran was not able to meet even its OPEC quotas. To raise production, Iran needs an influx of capital and new deep-drilling technology, both of which can be found only in the West.

This oil crisis has been compounded by the population explosion, the Iraqi war, and the flight of some 3 million Iranians. The annual population growth rate which had hit 2.5 percent in the late 1970s, jumped to nearly 4 percent by the late 1980s, mainly because the new regime initially encouraged large families. This was the highest rate in the world, causing a major strain on government resources, especially on social services and food imports. The Iraqi war not only hurt the oil industry but also wrought as much as US$600 billion in property damage—whole border cities were flattened. It also caused half a million Iranian casualties. The revolution itself frightened many professionals and highly skilled technicians as well as wealthy entrepreneurs and industrialists into fleeing to the West. Of course, they took their portable assets.

The overall result was a twenty-year economic crisis. Gross national product fell 50 percent. Per capita income declined 45 percent. Inflation hovered around 20–30 percent every year. The value of real incomes, including salaries and pensions, went down as much as 60 percent. Unemployment hit 20 percent—over two-thirds of entrants into the labor force could not find jobs. The absolute number of illiterates increased. Peasants continued to flock to the urban shantytowns. Tehran grew from 4.5 million to 12 million people. The total number of families living below the poverty level increased. By the late 1990s over 9 million urban dwellers lived below the official poverty line.[18] Shortages in foreign exchange curtailed vital imports, even of essential manufactured goods. The value of the currency plummeted: the rial, which had been worth 1.3 cents in 1979, was no more than 0.016 cents on the black market in 1998. What is more, the regime that came to power advocating self-sufficiency is now heavily indebted to foreign banks. Its external debt has jumped from zero to over US$30 billion, forcing it to constantly renegotiate foreign loans.

Despite this on-going economic crisis, the regime scored some notable successes, especially after the Iraqi war ended. The Reconstruction Ministry, established mainly for the rural population, built 30,000 miles of paved roads, 40,000 schools, and 7,000 libraries. It also brought electricity and running water to more than half of the country's 50,000 villages. The five-year plan organization continued to build more dams and irrigation canals. The Agricultural Ministry gave farmers more favorable prices, especially for wheat. Thus by the late 1990s most independent farmers had such consumer goods as radios, televisions, refrigerators, and pickup trucks. The extension of social services also narrowed the gap between town and country, and between the urban poor and the middle classes. The literacy rate rose from 50 percent to nearly 66 percent. The infant mortality rate fell from 104 per 1000 in the mid-1970s to 25 per 1000 in the late 1990s. Life expectancy climbed from 55 to 68 years, one of the best in the Middle East. On the whole, the poor are better off now than their parents were.

The Islamic Republic regime has also made major strides toward population control. At first, it closed down birth control clinics, claiming that Islam approved of large families and that Iran needed workers. But it reversed direction once the ministries responsible for social services felt the full impact of this growth. The regime also realized that only food imports could meet the rising demands. In 1989 the regime declared that Islam favored healthy rather than large families and that one literate citizen was better than ten illiterate ones. It reopened birth control clinics, cut subsidies to large families, and announced that the ideal family should consist of no more than two children. It even took away social benefits to those having more. By 1994 the regime boasted that it had reduced annual rate of population growth to 1.8 percent—the true figure was probably closer to 2.8 percent. Whatever the figure, it is an impressive accomplishment. It is also a sign that the regime is highly pragmatic when it comes to economic issues.

Section ❸ Governance and Policy-Making

Iran is unique in the contemporary world. Its system of government is not presidential, parliamentary, military, monarchical, or a one-party dictatorship. Instead, it is a theocracy with some concessions to democracy. It is a theocracy for the simple reason that the clergy—in other words, the theocrats or the theologians—control most of the important positions. The system nevertheless contains an element of democracy, since some high officials, including the president, are elected directly by the public. Although this combination is unprecedented, similar ones are likely to emerge in other parts of the Middle East if more Islamic countries have similar mass revolutions. So far the others that label themselves Islamic republics are products of either guerrilla wars, like Afghanistan, or of military coups, like Pakistan and Sudan.

Leaders: ***Ayatollah Ali Khamenei***

Ali Khamenei succeeded Khomeini as Supreme Leader in 1989. He was born in 1939 in Meshed into a minor clerical family originally from Azerbaijan. He studied theology with Khomeini in Qom and was briefly imprisoned in 1962. Active in the opposition movement in 1978, he was given a series of influential positions immediately after the revolution even though he held only the middle-level clerical rank of hojjat al-Islam. He became Friday prayer leader of Tehran, head of the revolutionary guards, and in the last years of Khomeini's life, president of the republic. After Khomeini's death, he was elevated to the rank of Supreme Leader even though he was neither a Grand Ayatollah nor a recognized senior expert on Islamic law. He had not even published a theological treatise. The government-controlled media, however, began to refer to him as an ayatollah. Some ardent followers even referred to him as a Grand Ayatollah qualified to guide the world's whole Shi'i community. After his elevation he built a constituency among the regime's more die-hard elements—traditionalist judges, conservative war veterans, and antiliberal ideologues. Before 1989 he often smoked a pipe in public—a mark of an intellectual—but put away the habit when he became Supreme Leader.

Organization of the State

The Iranian state rests on the Islamic Constitution designed by the Assembly of Religious Experts immediately after the 1979 revolution. It was amended in April–June 1989 during the very last months of Khomeini's life by a Council for the Revision of the Constitution handpicked by Khomeini himself. These amendments, in turn, were ratified by a nationwide referendum in July 1989, immediately after Khomeini's death. The final document, totaling 175 clauses and some forty amendments, is a highly complex mixture of theocracy and democracy.

The preamble of the 1979 constitution affirmed faith in God, Divine Justice, the Qur'an, the Resurrection, the Prophet Muhammad, the Twelve Imams, the eventual return of the Hidden Imam (the Mahdi), and of course Khomeini's doctrine of jurist's guardianship. All laws, institutions, and state organizations were to be based on these "divine principles."

The Supreme Leader

The constitution named Khomeini to be the Supreme Leader for life on the grounds that the public overwhelmingly respected him as the "most just, pious, informed, brave, and enterprising" of the most senior clerics. It further described him as the Leader of the Revolution, the Founder of the Islamic Republic, and most important, the Imam of the whole community. It stipulated that if no single Supreme Leader emerged after his death, then all his authority would be passed on to a leadership council of two or three senior clerics. After Khomeini's death, however, his followers so distrusted the other senior clerics that they did not set up such a council. Instead, they elected one of their own, Ali Khamenei, a middle-ranking cleric, to be the new Supreme Leader. All of Khomeini's titles, with the exception of Imam, were bestowed on Khamenei. The Islamic Republic has often been described as the regime of the ayatollahs (high-ranking clerics). It would be more aptly described as the regime of the hojjat al-Islams (middle-ranking clerics), since few senior clerics want to be associated with it. None of the grand ayatollahs and few of the ordinary ayatollahs ever subscribed to Khomeini's novel notion of jurist's guardianship. On the contrary, most disliked his radical populism and political activism.

The constitution gives wide-ranging authority to the Supreme Leader. Described as the link between the branches of government, he mediates between the legislature, the executive, and the judiciary. He "determines the interests of Islam," "supervises the implementation of general policy," and "sets political guidelines for the Islamic Republic." He can eliminate presidential candidates as well as dismiss the duly elected president. He can also grant amnesty. As commander in chief, he can mobilize the armed forces, declare war and peace, and convene the Supreme Military Council. He appoints and dismisses the commanders of the army, navy, air force, and revolutionary guards.

The Supreme Leader can nominate and remove the Chief Judge, the chief prosecutor, and the revolutionary tribunals. He can also remove lower court judges. Even more important, he nominates six clerics to the powerful twelve-man Guardian Council. This council can veto parliamentary bills. It has also obtained (through separate legislation) the right to review all candidates for elected office, including the presidency and the *Majles*. The other six on the Guardian Council are jurists nominated by the Chief Judge and approved by the *Majles*.

The Supreme Leader is also authorized to fill a number of important nongovernment posts: the preachers (**Imam Jum'ehs**) of the main mosques, the director of the National Radio-Television network, and the heads of the main religious foundations, especially the **Foundation of the Oppressed**, much larger than the old Pahlavi Foundation. The Foundation of the Oppressed administers most of the assets of the former Pahlavi Foundation as well as some of the real estate confiscated from the old elite. The Supreme Leader has obtained more constitutional powers than the Shah had ever dreamed of.

The later constitutional amendments expanded and transformed the Assembly of Religious Experts into a permanent eighty-six-man house. Packed by clerics, the assembly not only elected Khamenei as Khomeini's successor but also reserved the right to dismiss him if it found him "mentally incapable of fulfilling his arduous duties." In effect, the Assembly of Religious Experts has become an upper chamber to the Islamic *Majles*. It is elected every four years, and its members are required to have a seminary degree equivalent to an M.A. degree. Figure 2 on the following page illustrates the hierarchy established by the constitution.

The general public elects the *Majles*, the president, and the Assembly of Religious Experts. But the Supreme Leader and the cleric-dominated Guardian Council decide who can compete in these elections.

Since the whole constitution is based on Khomeini's theory of jurist's guardianship, it gives wide-ranging judicial powers to the Supreme Leader in particular and to the clerical strata in general. Laws are supposed to conform to the *shari'a*, and the clergy, particularly the senior jurists, are regarded as

The Shah turning into Khomeini, from an émigré newspaper. *Source:* Courtesy *Nashriyeh.*

the ultimate interpreters of the *shari'a*. In fact, the constitution makes the judicial system the central pillar of the state, overshadowing the executive and the legislature. Bills passed by the Islamic *Majles* are reviewed by the Guardian Council to ensure that they conform to the *shari'a*. All twelve members of this Guardian Council are either clerics or lay jurists

The general public elects the *Majles,* the president, and the Assembly of Religious Experts. But the Supreme Leader and the cleric-dominated Guardian Council decide who can compete in these elections.

Figure 2

The Islamic Constitution

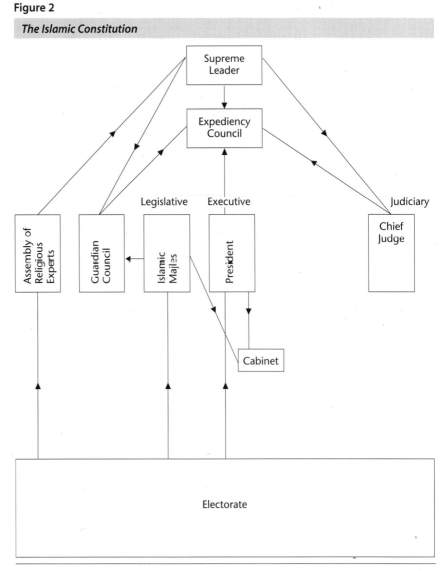

knowledgeable in the *shari'a.* The justice minister is chosen by the president but needs the approval of both the *Majles* and the Chief Judge. The judicial system itself has been Islamized all the way down to the district courts, with seminary-trained jurists replacing university-educated judges. The Pahlavis purged the clergy from the judicial system; the Islamic Republic purged the university-educated from the same judiciary.

The Executive

The President and the Cabinet

The constitution—particularly after the amendments—concentrates a considerable amount of power in the presidency. The president is described as the chief executive and the highest state official after the Supreme Leader. He is chosen every four years through a national election. He must be a pious Shi'i and faithful to the principles of the Islamic Republic. He cannot be elected to more than two terms. He draws up the annual budget and supervises economic matters by chairing the planning and budget organization. He can propose legislation to the *Majles*. He conducts the country's internal and external policies. He signs all international treaties, laws, and agreements. He chairs the National Security Council, which is responsible for all defense matters. He selects the cabinet, whose ministers have increased to twenty-two. The new members head the ministries of Reconstruction, Intelligence, Heavy Industries, and Culture and Islamic Guidance. The president can also select an indefinite number of vice presidents.

The president, moreover, appoints most of the senior officials, including the provincial governors-general, regional governors, town mayors, and ambassadors. Furthermore, as head of the executive, he names the directors of the many large public organizations—the National Iranian Oil Company, the National Electricity Board, and the main banks, airlines, mines, insurance companies, and shipping firms, most of which were nationalized immediately after the revolution.

Although during the revolution Khomeini often promised that trained officials would run the executive, in fact clerics have dominated the presidency. Of the four presidents since the revolution, three have been clerics: Khamenei, Rafsanjani, and Khatami. The exception, Abol-Hasan Bani-Sadr, was ousted in 1981 precisely because he described the regime as "a dictatorship of the mullahtariat" modeled on the communist "dictatorship of the proletariat."

The Bureaucracy

The president, as the chief of the executive branch, heads a huge bureaucracy. In fact, this bureaucracy continued to proliferate after the revolution even though Khomeini had often taken the Shah to task for having a bloated government. It expanded, for the most part, to provide jobs for the many college and high school graduates. On the eve of the revolution, the ministries had 300,000 civil servants and 1 million employees. By the early 1990s they had over 600,000 civil servants and 1.5 million employees. The Iranian

revolution, like many others, ended up creating a bigger bureaucracy.

Of the new ministries, Culture and Islamic Guidance censors the media and enforces "proper conduct" in public life; Intelligence has replaced SAVAK as the main security organization; Heavy Industries manages the recently nationalized factories; and Reconstruction has the dual task of expanding social services and taking "true Islam" into the countryside. Its mission is to build bridges, roads, schools, libraries, and mosques in the villages so that the peasantry will learn the basic principles of Islam. "The peasants," declared one cleric, "are so ignorant of true Islam that they even sleep next to their unclean sheep."[19]

The clergy dominate the bureaucracy as they do the presidency. They have monopolized the most sensitive ministries, Intelligence, Interior, Justice, and Culture and Islamic Guidance, and have given posts in other ministries to their relatives and protégés. These ministers appear to be highly trained technocrats, sometimes with higher degrees from the West, but in fact are powerless individuals chosen by, trusted by, and related to, the ruling clergy.

Semipublic Institutions

The Islamic Republic has set up a number of semipublic institutions. They include the Foundation for the Oppressed, the Alavi Foundation (named after Imam Ali); the Martyrs Foundation; the Pilgrimage Foundation; the Housing Foundation; the Foundation for the Publication of Imam Khomeini's Works; and the Fifteenth of Khordad Foundation, which commemorates Khomeini's 1963 denunciation of the White Revolution. Although these organizations are supposedly autonomous, their directors are clerics appointed personally by the Supreme Leader. According to some estimates, their annual income may be as much as half of the government's budget.[20] All are exempt from paying state taxes and can buy foreign currencies, especially U.S. dollars, at highly favorable exchange rates subsidized by the oil revenues. A large part of their assets is property confiscated from the old elite.

The largest of these institutions, the Foundation for the Oppressed, administers 140 factories, 120 mines, 470 agribusinesses, 100 construction companies, and over 2700 urban real estate properties. Many of these businesses previously belonged to entrepreneurs, senior bureaucrats, and high-ranking officers who either fled the country after the revolution or were judged by the clerical courts to be "active counterrevolutionaries." The foundation also owns the country's two leading newspapers, *Ettela'at* and *Kayhan. The Guardian* (London) estimated that in 1993 the foundation employed some 65,000 and had an annual budget of US$10 billion.[21] According to an Iranian economist, this was as much as 10 percent of the government budget.[22] Its present director is the former head of the *pasdaran*. During the revolution, he served as Khomeini's chauffeur.

The Alavi Foundation, based in Meshed, is the next largest. As the direct heir to the Pahlavi Foundation, it administers the vast assets that belonged to the Shah. The Martyrs Foundation, in charge of helping war veterans, controls property of the old elite that was confiscated in 1979 but not handed over to the Foundation for the Oppressed. It also receives an annual subsidy from the government. These three foundations together own some 20 percent of the country's private assets, employ over 150,000, and administer vast economic empires including 7800 hectares of farmland, 270 orchards, 230 commercial companies, and 90 cinemas. They can be described as states within a state, but with the important caveat that the same clerical elite that controls the state also controls these foundations.

Other State Institutions

The Military

The clergy have taken special measures to control the military. The Supreme Leader has the constitutional authority to appoint the joint chiefs of staff and the leading commanders. Khomeini and Khamenei filled the post of Defense Minister with their own confidants, who reported directly to them, bypassing the president and the cabinet. Moreover, the regime placed chaplains in military units to watch over the officers as well as to minister to the spiritual needs of the troops. They resemble the network of ideological officers, known as commissars, established in communist-bloc countries to forestall military coups.

Furthermore, the regime has built a new army, the *pasdaran* (revolutionary guards). Created as a voluntary militia in 1979, the revolutionary guards expanded rapidly during the Iraq war to parallel the existing armed forces. They obtained their own officers, uniforms, budgets, munitions factories, recruitment centers, and draftees. According to the constitution, the regular army defends the borders, while the revolutionary guards protect the republic. The Defense Minister, who is in charge of both, comes from the revolutionary guards. Most senior field officers are volunteers raised from the ranks because of their ideological commitment. The revolutionary guards are supplemented with a militia of underage and overage volunteers known as the Basej-e Mostazafin ("Mobilization of the Oppressed"). It is estimated that the regular army contains some 200,000 men; the *pasdaran* another 200,000; and the **basej** some 3 million.

The Judiciary

The Islamic Republic regime Islamized the judiciary by enacting a penal law based on an extremely narrow reading of the *shari'a*, so narrow that it prompted many modern-educated lawyers to resign in disgust, charging that it contradicted the UN Charter on Human Rights. It permitted injured families to demand blood money on the biblical and Qur'anic principle of "an eye for an eye, a tooth for a tooth, a life for a life." It mandated the death penalty for a long list of "moral transgressions," including adultery, homosexuality, apostasy, drug trafficking, and habitual drinking. It sanctioned stoning, live burials, and finger amputations. It divided the population into male and female, Muslims and non-Muslims, and treated them unequally. For example, in court, the evidence of one male Muslim is equal to that of two female Muslims. The regime also passed a "law on banking without usury" to implement the *shari'a* ban on all forms of interest-taking and interest-giving.

Although the law was Islamized, the modern centralized judicial system was not dismantled. For years, Khomeini argued that in a truly Islamic society the local *shari'a* judges would pronounce final verdicts without the intervention of the central authorities. Their verdicts would be swift and decisive. This, he insisted, was the true spirit of the *shari'a*. After the revolution, however, he discovered that the central state needed to retain ultimate control over the justice system, especially over life and death. Thus, the new regime retained the appeals system, the hierarchy of state courts, and the power to appoint and dismiss all judges. State interests took priority over the spirit of the *shari'a*.

Practical experience also led the regime to gradually broaden the narrow interpretation of the *shari'a*. To permit the giving and taking of interest, without which modern economies would not function, the regime allowed banks to offer attractive rates as long as they avoided the taboo term *usury*. To meet public sensitivities as well as international objections, the courts rarely implemented the harsh corporal punishments stipulated by the *shari'a*. They adopted the modern method of punishment, imprisonment, rather than the traditional one of corporal public punishments. By the early 1990s those found guilty of breaking the law were treated much as they would be in the West, fined or imprisoned rather than flogged in the public square.

Although the Islamic Republic is a theocracy, some regime supporters argue that it is compatible with democracy. According to the constitution, the government represents the general electorate. The Supreme Leader is chosen by the Assembly of Religious Experts, who, in turn, are elected by the general population. This is viewed as a two-stage popular election. The legislature also has a considerable constitutional role (see Section 4). According to Hojjat al-Islam Rafsanjani, one of the architects of the constitution, the *Majles* is the centerpiece of the Islamic constitution. It has many prerogatives, including that of enacting or changing ordinary laws (with the approval of the Guardian Council), investigating and supervising all affairs of state, and approving or ousting the cabinet ministers."[23] Some add that the public, by voting with their feet in the mass demonstrations of 1978–1979, implicitly favored a type of democracy that would be confined within the boundaries of Islam. Another architect of the constitution has argued that the Iranian people, by carrying out an Islamic Revolution, had determined for future generations that democracy in Iran should be placed within the rubric of jurist's guardianship.[24] Yet another declared that if he had to choose between the people and jurist's guardianship, he would not hesitate to choose the latter, since it came directly from God.[25] On

the eve of the initial referendum for the constitution, Khomeini himself insisted that democracy and jurist's guardianship in no way contradicted each other: "This constitution, which the people will ratify, is in no way a contradiction with democracy. Since the people love the clergy, have faith in the clergy, want to be guided by the clergy, it is right that the supreme religious authority oversee the work of the prime minister or of the president, to make sure that they don't make mistakes or go against the law: that is the Qur'an."[26]

Subnational Government

Although Iran is a highly centralized state, it is divided into provinces, districts, subdistricts, townships, and villages. Provinces are headed by governors-general, districts by governors, subdistricts by lieutenant governors, towns by mayors, and villages by headmen.

The Islamic constitution promised elected councils on each level of administration. The constitution declares that the management of local affairs in every village, town, subdistrict, district, and province would be under the supervision of councils whose members would be elected by the people of the locality. It also declares that governors-general, governors, mayors, and other local officials appointed by the government have an obligation to abide by the decisions of the local councils. These clauses were incorporated because of mass demonstrations organized in late 1979 by the left—notably the Mojahedin and the Fedayin—demanding the formation of elected councils.

Despite the promises, no steps were taken to hold elections for such councils until 1999. Thus local government was left in the hands of government officials. Although these officials did not have to contend with elected councils, they did have to oblige local notables, especially officers of the revolutionary guards, court judges, and Imam Jum'ehs with their mosque pulpits. Each gave them considerable headaches. In 1999 the newly elected president took concrete measures to hold elections for these local councils.

The Policy-Making Process

The policy-making system is highly complex in part because of the complex constitution and in part

The clerical regime and its two stilts—the sword and the oil wells. *Source:* Courtesy *Mojahed* (in exile).

because factional conflicts within the ruling clergy have added more amendments over the years, making the original constitution even more cumbersome. Decisions originate in diverse places. They are modified by pressures coming from diverse directions. And they can be blocked by a number of diverse state institutions. In short, the decision-making process is highly fluid and diffuse, often reflecting the regime's factional divisions.

The clerics who destroyed the old order remained united while building the new one. They were convinced that they alone had the divine mandate to govern. They formed a distinct social stratum as well as a cohesive political group. They followed the same leader, admired the same texts, cited the same potent symbols, remembered the same real and imaginary

indignations under the Shah, and most important, shared the same vested interest in preserving the Islamic Republic. Moreover, most had studied at the same seminaries and came from the same lower-middle-class backgrounds. Some were even related to each other through marriage and blood ties.

But once the constitution was in place, the same clerics drifted into two loose but identifiable blocs: the Society (*Majmu'eh*) of the Militant Clergy, and the Association (*Jam'eh*) of the Militant Clergy. The former can be described as populists, radicals, or statists; the latter as conservatives or supporters of laissez-faire. The statists hoped to consolidate lower-class support by redistributing wealth, eradicating unemployment, raising wages, nationalizing enterprises, confiscating large estates, implementing ambitious social programs, rationing and subsidizing essential goods, and placing price ceilings on many consumer commodities. In short, they espoused the creation of a comprehensive welfare state. The conservatives hoped to retain middle-class support, especially in the bazaars, by removing price controls, lowering business taxes, cutting red tape, encouraging private entrepreneurs, opening up the market, and balancing the budget, even at the cost of sacrificing subsidies and social programs.

The conservative free-marketers were labeled middle-roaders and traditionalists. The statists were labeled progressives, fast-walkers, seekers of new ideas, clergy favoring the oppressed, and followers of the Imam's line. The free-marketers often denounced their rivals as extremists, leftists, and pro-Soviet Muslims. The statists countered by denouncing the free-marketers as medievalists, rightists, capitalist jurists, mafia bazaaris, and pro-American Muslims. Both could bolster their arguments with apt quotes from Khomeini and the Qur'an.

This polarization created a major constitutional gridlock, since the Islamic *Majles* was dominated by the radical clerics while the Guardian Council was controlled by the conservative clerics. Khomeini had appointed conservatives to the Guardian Council to preserve his links with the bazaars and to build bridges to the grand ayatollahs, who distrusted his whole revolutionary movement. Between 1981 and 1987 over one hundred bills passed by the *Majles* were vetoed by the Guardian Council on the grounds that they violated the *shari'a*, especially the sanctity of private property. The vetoed legislation included a labor law, land reform, nationalization of foreign trade, progressive income tax, control over urban real estate transactions, and confiscation of the property of émigrés whom the courts had not yet found guilty of counter-revolutionary activities. Introduced by individual deputies or cabinet ministers, these bills had received quick passage because the radical statists controlled the crucial *Majles* committees and held a comfortable majority on the *Majles* floor. Some ultraconservatives had countered by encouraging the faithful not to pay taxes and instead to contribute to the grand ayatollahs of their choice. After all, one could find no mention of income tax anywhere in the *shari'a*.

Both sides cited the Islamic constitution to support their positions. The free-marketers referred to the long list of clauses protecting private property, promising balanced budgets, and placing agriculture, small industry, and retail trade in the private sector. The statists referred to an even longer list promising education, medicine, jobs, low-income housing, unemployment benefits, disability pay, interest-free loans, and the predominance of the public sector in the economy.

To break the constitutional gridlock, Khomeini boldly introduced into Shi'ism the Sunni concept of ***maslahat***—"public interest" and "reasons of state." In the past, Shi'i clerics had denounced this as a Sunni notion designed to bolster the illegitimate Caliphs. Khomeini now claimed that a truly Islamic state could safeguard the public interest by suspending important religious rulings, even over prayer, fasting, and the pilgrimage to Mecca. He declared public interest to be a primary ruling; the others mere secondary rulings. In other words, the state could overrule the highest-ranking clerics and their interpretations of the sacred law. It could destroy a mosque in the name of public interest. It could confiscate private property in the name of public interest. It could cancel religious contracts in the name of public interest. It could nationalize and raise income taxes in the name of

public interest. Khomeini also argued that the Islamic state had absolute authority, since the Prophet Muhammad had exercised absolute (*motalaq*) power, this power had passed to the Imams, and the Islamic Republic now represented the Hidden Imam. Never before had a Shi'i religious leader claimed such powers for the state, especially at the expense of fellow clerics.

As a follow-up, Khomeini set up a special Expediency Council for Determining the Public Interest of the Islamic Order. It is known simply as the Expediency Council. Khomeini himself remained above the fray so as not to be too closely identified with his radical or his conservative followers. He gave this Expediency Council the task of resolving the conflicts between the Islamic *Majles* and the Guardian Council. He packed the council with thirteen clerics, including the president, the Chief Judge, the speaker of the *Majles*, and six jurists from the Guardian Council. The Expediency Council soon passed many of the more moderate bills favored by the statists. These included a new income tax, banking legislation, and a much-disputed labor law providing workers in large factories with a minimum wage and some semblance of job security.

After Khomeini's death, the constitutional amendments institutionalized this Expediency Council. The new Supreme Leader was authorized not only to name all its members but also to determine its size, tenure, and jurisdiction. Khamenei expanded it to twenty-six members, packed it with eight of his own clerical supporters (none of them prominent ayatollahs), and allowed it to hold meetings in secret. He also extended its jurisdiction, allowing it to initiate entirely new laws and not restrict itself to resolving the existing differences between the *Majles* and the Guardian Council. In effect, the Expediency Council is now a secretive supraconstitutional body accountable only to the Supreme Leader. In this sense, it has become a powerful body rivaling the Islamic *Majles*. Laws can now originate in the Expediency Council as well as in the *Majles*.

Section ❹ Representation and Participation

The Legislature

The Islamic Republic's constitution is undoubtedly a theocratic document. Nevertheless, in recognizing the importance of democracy and popular participation, it leaves some space for civil society and organizations outside government control. The constitution stipulates direct elections for the presidency, for the Assembly of Religious Experts, and most important, for the Islamic *Majles*, which is defined by the constitution as the legislative branch. In describing this branch of government, the constitution uses the term *qanun* (statutes) rather than *shari'a* (divine law) so as to gloss over the fundamental question of whether law is derived from God or the people. The rationale is that the divine law (*shari'a*) comes from God, but statutes (*qanuns*) are made by the people's elected representatives.

The Islamic *Majles*, described by the constitution as "representing the nation," contains 270 deputies elected every four years through secret and direct balloting. All adults over the age of fifteen, including women, can vote. The *Majles* has considerable authority. It can pass *qanun* as long as the Guardian Council deems it compatible with the *shari'a* and the Islamic constitution. It can interpret legislation as long as these interpretations do not contradict the judicial authorities. It chooses six of the twelve-representatives on the Guardian Council, but it is limited to a list drawn up by the Chief Judge.

It can investigate at will cabinet ministers, affairs of state, and public complaints against the executive and the judiciary. It can remove cabinet members—with the exception of the president—through a parliamentary vote of no confidence. It can withhold approval for government budgets, foreign loans, international treaties, and cabinet appointments. It can hold closed debates, provide its members with immunity from arrest, and regulate its own internal workings, especially the committee system.

Although the 1989 constitutional amendments weakened the *Majles* vis-à-vis the presidency and the Expediency Council, the *Majles* nevertheless remains highly important. In recent years, the *Majles* has revamped the annual budget, criticized government policies, modified development plans, and forced the president to replace his cabinet ministers as well as the director of the National Radio-Television network. In 1992, 217 deputies circulated an open letter that explicitly emphasized the prerogatives of the *Majles* and thereby implicitly downplayed those of the Supreme Leader. The latter's supporters promptly issued a counterblast reminding the *Majles* that the Islamic Republic was based on Khomeini's concept of jurist's guardianship.

The powers as well as the limitations of the *Majles* can be seen in how bills are passed into legislation. They can be drawn up by the Expediency Council or introduced in the *Majles* by a deputy, a cabinet minister, or a parliamentary committee. Bills passed by the *Majles* need the approval of the Guardian Council. In addition, all bills, whether originating in the Expediency Council or the Islamic *Majles*, need the Supreme Leader's final approval.

Political Parties

Political parties cannot function in Iran without a license from the Interior Ministry, even though the constitution guarantees the freedom to organize, and the *Majles* in 1980 approved a bill recognizing the right of political parties to function. This bill was shelved by the Guardian Council. By 1999 only one party had obtained a license—the Servants of Reconstruction, formed by associates of former president Rafsanjani. Two others, the Islamic Labor Party and the Islamic Iran Participation Front, both formed in 1999 by associates of President Khatami, had applied for licenses. The following parties function in exile, especially in Europe.

- **The Liberation Movement.** Established in 1961 by Mehdi Bazargan, who became Khomeini's first premier in 1979, the Liberation Movement is a moderate Islamic party similar in some ways to the Western European Christian Democrats. Since 1981 the regime has tightly controlled its activities because it opposed continuation of the war with

Iraq, criticized the arbitrary confiscation of private property, and denounced the clergy for interfering in politics. The Liberation Movement, despite its religiosity, advocates secularism and the strict separation of mosque and state.

- **The Mojahedin.** Formed in 1971 as a guerrilla organization to fight the old regime, the Mojahedin tried to synthesize Marxism and Islam. It interpreted Shi'i Islam to be a radical religion favoring equality, social justice, martyrdom, and redistribution of wealth. Immediately after the revolution, the Mojahedin attracted a large following among college and high school students, especially when it began to denounce the clergy for establishing a new dictatorship. The regime retaliated with mass executions and forced the Mojahedin to move their base of operations into Iraq. Not unexpectedly, the Mojahedin became associated with the national enemy and thereby lost much of its appeal within Iran.
- **The Fedayin.** Formed in 1971, the Fedayin modeled itself after the Marxist guerrilla movements of the 1960s in Latin America, especially those inspired by Che Guevara and the Cuban revolution. Losing more fighters than any other organization in the guerrilla war against the Shah, the Fedayin came out of the revolution with much revolutionary mystique and popular urban support. But it soon lost much of its strength because of massive government repression and a series of internal splits.
- **The Tudeh.** Established in 1941, the Tudeh is the mainstream communist party of Iran, fully supporting the policies of the former Soviet Union. Although the Tudeh supported the Islamic Republic as a "popular anti-imperialist state," it was banned, and most of its organizers were executed during the period 1983–1989. It survives mostly in Europe.

Elections

The constitution promises that all elections, including those for the Islamic *Majles*, will be free. In practice, however, *Majles* elections have become increasingly more regulated, manipulated, and controlled. The Guardian Council routinely eliminates candidates on the grounds that they are not sufficiently committed to the principles of the Islamic Republic. For example, in 1996 the Guardian Council excluded over 44 percent of some 5000 parliamentary candidates by questioning their loyalty to the concept of jurist's guardianship. The National Radio-Television network, the main source of information for the vast majority of people, favors some candidates, ignores others, and denounces yet others. The Interior Ministry bans dissident organizations, especially their newspapers and meetings, with the claim that they are anti-Islamic and antirevolutionary. Ballot boxes are placed in mosques, and the revolutionary guards supervise voting. Neighborhood clerics are on hand to help illiterates complete their ballots. Club-wielding gangs, the Hezbollahis, assault critics of the regime. By-elections are timed to coincide with high religious holidays. The Supreme Leader inevitably denounces those tempted to abstain as "secret agents of the devil." The electoral law, based on a winner-take-all majority system rather than on proportional representation, which guarantees some seats to any party that wins a certain percentage of the vote, was designed to minimize the voice of the opposition, particularly in the early days of the republic, when there was an opposition.

The Islamic Republic has had five *Majles* elections so far: 1980, 1984, 1988, 1992, and 1996. These elections have gone from being relatively free to being completely controlled. If the 1997 presidential campaign is an indication, the next *Majles* elections, due in 2000, may turn out to be more free.

The First *Majles*

In the election for the First *Majles* in 1980, there were over 4400 candidates, over forty parties, over two hundred dailies and weeklies, and thousands of workplace organizations in the bazaars, campuses, high schools, factories, and offices. The parties represented the whole range of the political spectrum from the far right, through the center, to the extreme left. The revolution had shattered the state, liberating scores of social and political groups. It was as if, after years of silence, every professional and occupational association, every political party and ideological viewpoint, and every interest and pressure group rushed into the open to air its views, print its newspapers and broadsheets, and field its parliamentary candidates.

On the right was the Islamic Republican Party (IRP). It was founded immediately after the revolution by Khomeini's closest disciples. The IRP had the support of two highly conservative religious groups that had survived the old regime: the Fedayan-e Islam and the Hojjatieh Society. It also had the support of the Islamic Association of Bazaar Guilds, the Islamic Association of Teachers, the Islamic Association of University Students, the Association of Seminary Teachers of Qom, and most important, the Association of the Militant Clergy in Tehran. The Islamic Republican Party championed Khomeini's notion that the clergy had the divine mandate to rule.

At the center was the Liberation Movement, headed by Mehdi Bazargan. Bazargan had been appointed prime minister in February 1979 by Khomeini himself but had resigned in disgust ten months later when the revolutionary guards had permitted students to take over the U.S. embassy. The Liberation Movement favored free markets, limited government, nonalignment without bellicose attacks on the United States, and a pluralistic political system in which all parties—religious and nonreligious, right and left—would be able to function and compete in fair and open elections. The Liberation Movement also favored a regime built on its own liberal interpretation of Islam, one in which the clergy would guide and advise rather than rule. Bazargan was a former member of Mosaddeq's National Front, the organization instrumental in nationalizing the oil industry in 1951. But Bazargan, unlike Mosaddeq, liked to sprinkle his speeches and bolster his ideas, concepts, and arguments with quotations from the Qur'an, the Prophet, and the Twelve Imams.

Closely allied with the Liberation Movement was the National Front, a mere shadow of its former self, and its offshoots, the National Party and the Democratic National Front. These parties, like the Liberation Movement, favored liberal democracy and were led by Western-educated, middle-aged professionals and technocrats. But unlike the Liberation Movement, they avoided making political use of Islam. Like their deceased mentor Mosaddeq, they preferred to separate politics from religion and to treat the latter as primarily a private matter. The Liberation Movement can be defined as a liberal Muslim party, and the National Front and its offshoots as liberal secular parties.

The left was fragmented even more into religious and nonreligious groups. The religious included such Muslim yet anticlerical ones as the People's Mojahedin, the Movement of Militant Muslims, and the Movement for the Liberation of the Iranian People. The nonreligious included a number of Marxist and ethnic parties: the Tudeh, the Majority and Minority Fedayin, the Kurdish Democratic Party, and at least a dozen small Marxist-Leninist parties. To complicate matters further, Bani-Sadr, who had been elected president in January 1980, was distancing himself from the Islamic Republican Party by fielding a number of his own candidates.

Many of these political parties had their own student, labor, professional, and women's organizations. For example, in the early years of the revolution, there were over a dozen women's organizations in Tehran alone. Among them were the Society of Militant Women, the Islamic Association of Women, the Union of National Women, the Union of Women Lawyers, the Union of Democratic Women, the Women for Justice, and the Society of Islamic Revolutionary Women. Each was affiliated with one of the larger political parties.

Not surprisingly, the elections for this First *Majles* were extremely lively, even though the IRP manipulated the state machinery, especially the Interior Ministry and the National Radio-Television network. On the eve of the voting, the Minister of the Interior forthrightly declared that all were free to run but that only "true Muslims" would have their credentials accepted in the forthcoming parliament.[27] Some 80 percent of the electorate participated in the first round.

The main contestants were, on the one hand, the IRP and its clerical and bazaar affiliates and, on the other hand, President Bani-Sadr, the Mojahedin, and their secular-leftist allies. The competition was so intense in some constituencies, particularly Kurdistan, Kermanshah, West Azerbaijan, and the Caspian provinces, that the Interior Ministry stepped in, impounded the ballot boxes, harassed candidates, and postponed the second round indefinitely. The second round was not held until late 1981. By then, the regime had cracked down on the opposition, forcing Bani-Sadr into exile, banning many leftist parties, and executing hundreds of Mojahedin organizers.

Of the 216 deputies elected in 1980, 120 were

supporters of the IRP, 33 of Bani-Sadr, and 20 of the Liberation Movement, while 33 described themselves as independent. The independents included two Kurdish Democrats and five National Front leaders. The latter had their parliamentary credentials promptly rejected on the grounds that documents found in the recently occupied U.S. Embassy "proved" them to be U.S. spies. The IRP had won only 35 percent of the popular vote but had collected over 60 percent of the filled seats. The Mojahedin, on the other hand, had won 25 percent of the popular vote but had not obtained a single seat. The electoral law based on majority rather than proportional representation had paid off for Khomeini.

Once the IRP carried out the second round and replaced the purged members, including Bani-Sadr's supporters, it gained a solid majority. This included 105 clerics—more than 38 percent of the *Majles*—making it by far the highest clerical representation in Iran's parliamentary history. Most were medium-ranking clerics serving as court judges and town preachers (Imam Jum'ehs). The others were white-collar employees and high school teachers, some of whom were seminary graduates. Over 90 percent came from the propertied middle class. Their fathers had been clerics, bazaar merchants, guild elders, or small farmers.

The Second Majles

The elections for the Second *Majles* in 1984 were carried out under very different circumstances. The "spring of the Iranian Revolution" was over. The opposition—including the Liberation Movement—was now banned. The IRP monopolized the political scene, manipulating the state and controlling a vast array of organizations, including large foundations, local mosques, revolutionary guards, and thousands of town preachers. Not surprisingly, it won a landslide victory, leaving a few seats to independent-minded clerics with their own local followings. Also not surprisingly, voter participation fell sharply to less than 60 percent, even though the voting age was reduced from sixteen to fifteen and even though Khomeini declared that abstaining was tantamount to betraying Islam.

Over 54 percent of the 270 deputies were clerics, almost all middle-ranking. Most of the nonclerics had Ph.D.'s, M.A.'s, B.A.'s, associate degrees, or high school diplomas. Only eleven had not completed high school. Twenty-seven of the lay members had at one time or another attended a seminary. As before, most were in their late thirties or early forties.

In 1987, Khomeini dissolved the IRP in preparation for the Third *Majles*. No reason was given, but the decision was probably prompted by the conflict between the statists and the free-marketers. The party's central committee was divided sharply into radicals demanding land reform, progressive taxation, and more nationalization, on the one hand, and conservatives favoring the bazaar, the industrial employers, and the reduction of state expenditures, on the other. One radical deputy claimed that "the party had been infiltrated by opportunistic time-servers pretending to be devout followers of the Imam's Line."[28] In the *Majles*, the radicals could muster 120 votes; the conservatives some 90; the remainder moved back and forth between these poles.

Moreover, the IRP's monopoly of power had aroused concern. Some drew parallels with the Resurgence Party and remembered how the clergy had unanimously denounced the Shah's totalitarian drive to take over the whole society. Furthermore, provincial clerics with their own power bases lobbied Khomeini against the IRP. They feared the party not only for its economic radicalism but also for its drive to centralize power. Finally, as far as Khomeini himself was concerned, the IRP had accomplished its main purpose: eliminating the Mojahedin, the National Front, the Tudeh, and the Liberation Movement.

In dissolving the IRP, Khomeini declared the clergy to be free to establish two competing organizations as long as both remained diligent against imperialism, advocated neither communism nor capitalism, and agreed to preserve Islam, the Islamic Revolution, the Islamic Republic, and jurist's guardianship. "Political differences," he commented, "are natural. Throughout history our religious authorities have differed among themselves. . . . Besides Iranians should be free to express themselves."[29] He could have added, "within reason and within the context of Islam as defined by myself."

In preparation for the Third *Majles* elections in 1988, the radicals left the Association of the Militant Clergy to form their own Society of the Militant

Clergy. From then on, there were two rival clerical organizations: on one side, the statists with their association and five major newspapers, including the two largest national papers, *Kayhan* and *Ettela'at*; on the other side, the conservative free-marketers with their society and a newspaper called *Resalat* (*Message*). Both had adherents in the seminaries and among the local Imam Jum'ehs. This was political pluralism, but a pluralism limited to the Khomeinist clerics and their protégés, who subscribed fully to their interpretation of Shi'ism. This theocracy resembles an oligarchy, the rule of numerous notables, more than a totalitarian state headed by a one-party dictatorship.

The Third, Fourth, and Fifth Majleses

The radicals won the lackluster elections for the Third *Majles*. In the new parliament, there were eighty-six clerics—a 23 percent decline from the previous assembly. This, however, did not signify the demise of clerical power. Some prominent clerics had gone on to higher positions, especially to the Assembly of Religious Experts. Many of the new lay deputies were young protégés of the clerics recruited into their fold from the students who had taken over the U.S. Embassy. The conservative clerics who did not run in these elections went on to occupy other influential positions as heads of religious foundations, preachers in the city mosques, and editors of mass newspapers.

Although the radical clerics began the Third *Majles* with a clear majority, their influence soon ebbed because of Khomeini's death in 1989 and because Khamenei and Rafsanjani, the new Supreme Leader and president, respectively, began to adopt free-market policies as soon as the war with Iraq ended. During the war, these two had been vocal advocates of price controls, rationing, high taxes, nationalization, and large government budgets. Now, with the ceasefire, they argued that the only way to revive the war-torn economy was to encourage private enterprise, open up the market, and cut government expenditures.

Rafsanjani launched the new course in giving his eulogy for Khomeini.[30] He played down Khomeini's role as a charismatic revolutionary who had led the downtrodden. Indeed, the word *oppressed* was hardly mentioned. Instead, he praised Khomeini as a world-famous statesman who had restored Iran's national sovereignty. He also praised him as a highly reputable scholar-theologian who had intellectually "awakened the moribund seminaries" from their "medieval graves." This ran counter to the prevailing notion that Shi'i Islam was by definition a revolutionary creed against all forms of despotism and exploitation.

In the following months, Rafsanjani—and to a lesser extent Khamenei—stressed that the revolution had been "guilty of excesses." They asked their followers to put away "childish slogans." They talked increasingly of realism, stability, efficiency, managerial skills, work discipline, expertise, individual self-reliance, modern technology, entrepreneurship, and business incentives. They warned that the worst mistake a state could make was to spend more than it earned. Rafsanjani declared, "Some people claim that God will provide. They forget that God provides only for those willing to work." Khamenei sermonized on how Imam Ali, the founder of Shi'i Islam, had taken great pride in his plantations. Khomeini had often depicted Imam Ali as a humble water carrier; Khamenei now depicted him as an entrepreneurial plantation owner.

To ensure that the change of economic course would go smoothly, Khamenei handed over the two main newspapers, *Kayhan* and *Ettela'at*, to the conservative free-marketers and authorized the Guardian Council to monitor the 1992 *Majles* elections. The Guardian Council announced that all candidates had to prove their "practical commitment to the Supreme Leader and the Islamic Republic." The Guardian Council further restricted the campaign to one week, permitting candidates to speak in mosques and run newspaper advertisements but not to debate each other in open forums. The head of the Guardian Council announced that he would use pesticides to cleanse parliament of anyone with "difficult attitudes." Seventy-five radical candidates withdrew. Forty were disqualified by the Guardian Council. Only a handful of radicals were allowed to be elected. Voter participation dropped to a new low. In Tehran less than 55 percent of the eligible voters bothered to cast ballots despite Khamenei's pronouncement that it was the "religious obligation of everyone to participate."

Ayatollah Khalkhali, a vocal radical, was barred from running on the grounds that he did not have appropriate theological training. Yet the same Khalkhali had been considered qualified enough from 1978 to 1987 to sit as a high court judge dispatching hundreds of political prisoners to their deaths. Khalkhali retorted that his candidacy had been rejected by rightists who had sat out the revolution but were now weaseling their way into the Guardian Council. He warned that "true servants of the revolution," like himself, had been subjected to a political purge as a prelude to a future physical purge. Another disqualified candidate, who had earlier dismissed any talk of human rights as a "foreign conspiracy," now complained that the Guardian Council had grossly violated the UN Charter on Human Rights. It had failed to inform him of the charges brought against him; it had given him insufficient time to respond; and it had denied him the right to defend himself in a proper court of law.

The Guardian Council responded that its decisions had been kept out of the mass media in order to protect state secrets and the public reputations of the unqualified. The purged were expected to be grateful for this sensitivity. It also argued that it had followed precedent, reminding the radicals that they themselves had used similar procedures to keep out "undesirables" from the previous three parliaments—undesirables such as the Mojahedin, the Fedayin, the Tudeh, the National Front, the Liberation Movement, and the "pseudo-clerics," who did not believe in jurist's guardianship.

The purge was relatively easy to carry out. For one thing, the extensive powers entrusted to the Supreme Leader by the Islamic constitution left the radicals vulnerable. As Hojjat al-Islam Mohtashami, a leading radical, complained, the institution of jurist's guardianship was now being used to clobber revolutionary heads. When radicals complained that they were being slandered as traitors for merely questioning free-market economics, their opponents countered that disobedience to the Supreme Leader was tantamount to disobedience to God. They argued that only proponents of "American Islam" would dare question the decisions of the Supreme Leader. They also reminded them that the new oath of office required parliamentary deputies to obey the Supreme Leader as "the Vice Regent of the Hidden Twelfth Imam." Khamenei may not have inherited Khomeini's title of Imam, but he had obtained the new exalted position of the Hidden Imam's Spokesman.

What is more, the conservatives effectively used populist rhetoric against the radicals. They described them as the "newly moneyed class" and the "Mercedes-Benz clerics." They accused them of misusing official positions to line their own pockets, open slush funds and secret foreign accounts, give lucrative contracts to their friends, sell contraband, and deceive the masses with unrealistic promises. "They," exclaimed one conservative, "act like a giant octopus, giving with one tentacle but taking away with the others." They also placed the responsibility for the country's economic malaise squarely on the shoulders of the radicals. They argued that a decade of statist policies had further increased poverty, illiteracy, inflation, unemployment, and slum housing. Before the revolution, these problems were blamed on the Pahlavis. Now they were blamed on the "extremist pseudo-clerical radicals."

The purge was so decisive that the radicals suspended the activities of their Society of the Militant Clergy soon after the elections for the Fourth *Majles*. Some went to head foundations and libraries. Some took up seminary positions. Others began to write for newspapers, occasionally arguing that the public should choose its Supreme Leader and that the Guardian Council should stay out of the whole electoral process. Yet others remained politically active, mildly criticizing the regime and quietly awaiting a better day.

This expectation was not far-fetched, for the majority in the Fourth *Majles* divided into two blocs once it had implemented a series of probusiness reforms. These reforms included relaxation of price controls, liberalization of imports, trimming of the ration list, disbanding of courts that penalized hoarders and price gougers, return of some confiscated real estate, withdrawal of all bills associated with land reform, income redistribution, and nationalization of foreign trade, and setting up a stock exchange in Tehran and free-trade zones in the Persian Gulf.

One bloc, named after the newspaper *Resalat*, supported highly conservative cultural policies as well as laissez-faire economics. It favored strict control over the media, the silencing of liberal intellectuals, and the rigid implementation of the dress code for women. It was also reluctant to challenge the financial privileges of the large foundations or open up the economy to international and émigré capital—foreign competition was seen as a threat to the bazaar economy. These conservatives could muster some 170 votes in the *Majles*. The other bloc, while also advocating laissez-faire, favored more active wooing of foreign capital and greater cultural liberalization. It was also eager to balance the budget by downsizing the large clerical foundations and by cutting state expenditures, especially for food and fuel subsidies. This bloc could muster some 40 votes. The remaining 60 members were independent deputies from the provinces. They sometimes voted with the majority, sometimes with the minority.

The first bloc, which can be described as the cultural conservatives, enjoyed the support of Khamenei, the Supreme Leader. The second bloc, the cultural liberals, had the backing of president Rafsanjani. To get a working majority, Rafsanjani had no choice but to water down his own preferences. He had to remove his own brother from the directorship of the National Radio-Television network. He could take no more than modest measures to privatize some five hundred large enterprises, trim the foreign-exchange privileges of the huge clerical foundations, and cut the social subsidies that absorbed much of the oil revenue. Moreover, he was unable to increase business taxes—all the taxes raised by the bazaar guilds together still constitute less than 9 percent of the government's annual tax income. Rafsanjani had to shelve his daring bill designed to attract foreign investment. This bill would have raised the share that foreign interests could own in Iranian enterprises from 49 percent to 100 percent. It would have been a total policy reversal, since the revolutionaries had relished accusing the Shah of selling the country to foreign capitalists. Rafsanjani now argued that he could not jump-start the ailing economy without the injection of massive foreign capital. The bill, however, met stiff resistance from conservatives fearful that foreign capital would swamp the bazaars.

Not surprisingly, Rafsanjani's supporters entered the Fifth *Majles* elections with their own party, Servants of Reconstruction. It was endorsed by ten cabinet ministers, four vice presidents, the governor of the Central Bank, and even more important, the mayor of Tehran. The latter was highly popular because he had made the city into a livable place by building highways, libraries, and parks, often from gardens confiscated from the former elite. Supported by the radical clerics, the Servants of Reconstruction won over 80 seats. Some 140 seats went to the conservatives, many endorsed by the Association of the Militant Clergy. The Fifth *Majles* turned out to be a repeat performance of the lackluster Fourth *Majles*.

Political Culture, Citizenship, and Identity

In theory, the Islamic Republic should be a highly viable state. After all, Shi'ism is the religion of both the state and the vast majority of the population. It can be described as the central component of popular culture. The Islamic constitution guarantees basic rights to religious minorities as well as to individual citizens. All citizens, regardless of race, color, language, or religion, are promised the rights of expression, worship, and organization. They are guaranteed freedom from arbitrary arrest, torture, and police surveillance. In short, the Islamic constitution incorporates the concept of individual rights as developed in the West; according to the constitution, civil society is not a foreign notion in twentieth-century Iran.

The constitution gives specific guarantees to the recognized religious minorities. Although Christians (Armenians and Assyrians), Jews, and Zoroastrians form 1 percent of the total population, they are allocated five *Majles* seats. They are permitted their own places of worship, their own community organizations, including schools, and their own marriage, divorce, and inheritance laws. The constitution, however, is ominously silent about the Baha'is and the Sunnis. The former are deemed apostates; the latter, fellow Muslims theoretically equal in rights to the Shi'i Muslims.

The constitution also gives guarantees to non-Persian speakers. Although 83 percent of the population understands Persian, thanks to the educational system, over 50 percent continue to speak non-Persian languages at home, languages such as Azeri, Kurdish, Turkic, Gilaki, Mazandarani, Arabic, and Baluchi. The constitution promises them rights unprecedented in Iranian history. It declares that "local and native languages can be used in the press, media, and schools." It also declares that local populations have the right to elect provincial, town, and village councils. These councils can watch over the governors-general and the town mayors as well as their educational, cultural, and social programs. They cannot be dismissed by the central government.

These generous promises are honored more in theory than in fact. The local councils—the chief institutional safeguard for the provincial minorities—were not convened until mid-1999. Subsidies to non-Persian publications and radio stations are meager. Jews have been so harassed as "pro-Israeli Zionists" that more than half—40,000 out of 80,000—have left the country. Armenian Christians have had to accept Muslim principals in their schools, end coeducational classes, adopt the government curriculum, abide by Muslim dress codes, including the veil, and close their community clubs to Muslims. Christians, on the whole, are viewed as "contaminated" with Western culture. The Christian population has declined from over 300,000 to less than 200,000.

The Baha'is, however, have borne the brunt of religious persecution. Their leaders have been executed as "apostates" and "imperialist spies." Adherents have been fired from their jobs, had their property confiscated, and been imprisoned and tortured to pressure them to convert to Islam. Their schools have been closed, their community property expropriated, and their shrines and cemeteries bulldozed. It is estimated that since the revolution one-third of the 300,000 Baha'is have left Iran. The Baha'is, like the Jews and Armenians, have migrated mostly to Canada and the United States, especially New York and California.

The much larger Sunni population, which forms as much as 9 percent of the total, has its own reasons for being alienated from the regime. The state religion is Shi'ism. High officials have to be Shi'i. Citizens have to subscribe to Khomeini's concept of government—a notion derived from Shi'ism. Few institutions cater to Sunni needs. There is not a single Sunni mosque in the whole of Tehran. And the regime tends to overlook the existence of Sunnis among the Kurds, Turkomans, Arabs, and Baluchis. It is no accident that in the period 1979–1981 the newborn regime faced its most serious challenges in precisely these areas—among the Sunni Kurds, Turkomans, Arabs, and Baluchis. It succeeded in crushing their revolts by rushing in tens of thousands of revolutionary guards from the Persian Shi'i heartland of Isfahan, Shiraz, and Qom.

Thus one can generalize that the Islamic Republic has its strongest cultural roots in the Persian Shi'i heartland. Its weakest roots are among the non-Shi'is—the Sunnis, Baha'is, Jews, Christians, and Zoroastrians. Its base among the Azeris, who are Shi'i but not Persian speakers, remains to be tested. In the past, the Azeris, who form 24 percent of the population and dwarf the other minorities, have not posed an ethnic problem. They are part and parcel of the Shi'i community. They have prominent figures, such as Khamenei, in the Shi'i hierarchy. Many Azeri merchants, professionals, and workers live throughout the regions of Iran. In short, Azeris can be considered well integrated into Iran. But the 1991 creation of the Republic of Azerbaijan out of the Soviet Union has raised new concerns, since some Azeris on both sides of the border have begun to talk of establishing a larger unified Azerbaijan. It is no accident that in the recent war between Azerbaijan and Armenia, Iran favored the latter. So far, the concept of a unified Azerbaijan has little appeal among Iranian Azeris.

Interests, Social Movements, and Protest

The regime has also violated most of the constitution's clauses promising to respect individual rights and civil liberties. It has closed down newspapers, professional associations, labor unions, and political parties. It has banned demonstrations and public meetings. It has incarcerated tens of thousands without due process. It has systematically tortured prisoners to extract false confessions and public recantations. And it has executed some 25,000 political prisoners, most of them without due process of law. The United Nations, Amnesty International, and Human Rights Watch have all strongly criticized Iran for violating the UN Charter on Human Rights as well as the Islamic constitution itself. Most of the victims have been Kurds, military officers from the old regime, and leftists, especially members of the Mojahedin and Fedayin. The Islamic Revolution, like some others, has devoured its own children.

Although the violation of individual liberties has affected the whole population, it arouses special resentment among the modern middle class, the traditionally minded Shi'is, women, and minorities. The modern middle class, which forms as much as 10 percent of the total population, has been secular and even anticlerical ever since the 1905 revolution. Little love is lost between it and the Islamic Republic. Not surprisingly, most of those executed have been teachers, engineers, professionals, and college students. Members of the intelligentsia who join the regime are regarded by their colleagues as betrayers of their class.

The traditionally minded Shi'is had difficulty accepting Khomeini's populist version of Islam, including his concept of jurist's guardianship. At the time of the revolution, none of the grand ayatollahs subscribed to this theory of government. After the revolution, few of them were willing to be associated with the Islamic Republic. And after Khomeini's death, even fewer were willing to give his successor a helping hand. The grand ayatollahs—some residing in Iraq, others in Iran—could still influence large numbers of pious Muslims, especially from the older generation. Just because the state is Shi'i does not automatically mean it enjoys the allegiance of all Shi'is. The new theocracy is haunted by the old Shi'i distrust of the state.

Finally, some women harbor grievances against the Islamic Republic, especially against the conservative clerics who control the *Majles* and the judiciary. Although the Western press has dwelled on the veil, Iranian women consider the veil one of their lesser problems. Given a choice, many would most likely continue to wear the veil, since they consider it practical and customary. More important to women are their work-related grievances. They have been purged from some offices and occupations. They are the last hired and the first fired. They are discriminated against in pay scales. They are encouraged to stay home, raise children, and do housework. To add insult to injury, the law treats them as wards of their male relatives, requiring them to have legal guidance from their fathers, husbands, or brothers. Even adult women are not allowed to travel without written permission from their male relatives.

Women have countered by publishing newspapers, forming organizations, and waging parliamentary campaigns. They have managed to raise the marriage age to fifteen, implicitly contradicting the *shari'a*. After the Islamic Revolution, the marriage age for women had been abolished. They have persuaded President Rafsanjani to establish a parliamentary Women's Commission.They have tried to restrict polygamy by encouraging the signing of marriage contracts in which the husband gives up the right to have multiple wives. These contracts can also give wives the right to divorce their husbands. Women have persuaded universities to reopen fields closed to them immediately after the revolution, such as geol-ogy, architecture, agriculture, veterinary medicine, and law. They have lobbied to get women back into the judiciary, but so far they have succeeded only in family courts. They have also persuaded the expediency Council that divorced women should be entitled to half the family property accumulated during the marriage. Immediately after the revolution, women's share in the labor force fell from 13 to 8 percent. By the mid-1990s it had rebounded to 13 percent. Even more impressive, women now constitute over 40 percent of university students, 45 percent of medical doctors, and 25 percent of the government labor force. Some observers have started to talk of the emergence of Islamic feminism and even of fundamentalist feminism.

These social pressures—together with the fact that the constitution recognized individual rights, that mass participation made the revolution, and that the concept of democracy made inroads into Iran from the beginning of the twentieth century—have forced the ruling clergy to make important concessions. By the late 1990s the government had recognized the existence of some one hundred organizations. These licensed oganizations include clubs belonging to the recognized minorities, bazaar guilds and chambers of commerce, the Islamic Association of Students, the Islamic Women's Association, and the Workers' House, a center in Tehran for factory employees who support the regime. Most of these organizations are controlled by clerics; all accept the legitimacy of the regime. Other state-approved organizations include the Teachers of the Qom Seminaries, the Society of the Militant Clergy, and the Association of the Militant Clergy. At most, less than 1 percent of the population belongs to these organizations. The increasing distrust of the public is reflected in the official stamps issued to commemorate the revolution. In the early 1980s the commemorative stamps were full of energy and depicted demonstrators realistically. By the late 1980s the commemorative stamp designs were highly abstract and stylized. The crowds have become stylized as well as regimented and controlled.

Society has managed to preserve some semblance of independence from the state because the country's 200,000 clerics are sharply divided. They are divided not only into the conservative Association of the Militant Clergy and the radical Society of the Militant Clergy but also into many informal groups, some supporting ultraconservative ayatollahs, some supporting radical ones, and many keeping their distance from all politics. They prefer to do what clerics have done throughout the ages—preach, teach, study, tend the sick, and bury the dead. This division has given society a breathing space. Conservatives have tried to woo financial and electoral support from bazaar guilds, chambers of commerce, and farmers' associations. Radicals have tried to win over the Islamic Association of Students, the Islamic Association of Teachers, the Islamic Women's Association, and the Workers' House.

The extent, as well as the limitations, of these interest group politics can be seen in the passage of the labor law, which took a full eleven years. Immediately after the revolution, the labor minister, who was a free-market conservative, drafted a bill proposing that almost all labor issues be resolved by employers and employees themselves. His attitude was that the state should not be involved in private contracts and that good Muslim employers did not need government regulations to tell them how to treat their employees. Besides, a society that had the Qur'an, the *shari'a*, and jurist's guardianship did not require a Western-style labor law. He even proposed to do away with child labor restrictions, the minimum wage, mandatory holidays, and the weekly day of rest. This bill caused such outrage that it had to be withdrawn. Most of the outrage came from the radical clerics in parliament and their friends outside, especially the Workers' House and the Islamic Workers' Association. The head of the Workers' House warned that such a backward bill would drive factory employees into the arms of the Marxist parties.

The radical clerics came up with their own fairly comprehensive labor law, which guaranteed pensions, disability pay, health insurance, annual holidays, maximum work hours, a minimum wage, job security, and government arbitration. The bill, however, made no mention of independent labor unions. The Workers' House helped pass the bill through the *Majles* in 1986 by holding a series of mass rallies, especially on May Day, the international workers' day. The bill was promptly vetoed by the Guardian Council on the grounds that it was un-Islamic and violated the sanctity of private property. It was precisely this veto that prompted Khomeini to create the Expediency Council in 1987. The labor minister who had drafted this bill later admitted that the Expediency Council eventually endorsed the legislation in 1989 because of the direct intervention of Hojjat al-Islam Ahmad Khomeini, the Imam's son.[31] The regime that claims to represent the oppressed masses had taken a full decade to enact a fairly mild labor law. But the fact that it had been enacted against the opposition of the employers and the bazaars was a clear indication that interest group politics had taken root in the Islamic Republic.

Section ❺ Iranian Politics in Transition

Political Challenges and Changing Agendas

On the eve of the 1997 presidential elections, *The Economist* (London) published a special survey on Iran predicting the certain victory of Hojjat al-Islam Ali-Akbar Nateq-Nuri, the Speaker of the *Majles*.[32] The journal was confident of this prediction because Nateq-Nuri was overwhelmingly favored by the religious establishment. The detailed survey provided much information on the regime's leading personalities but did not mention Khatami, who proved to be the victor. The survey, as well as the whole election, illustrates the pitfalls of making predictions about a regime that is based on two inherently contradictory principles—theocracy and democracy.

Before the elections, the Guardian Council did what it had habitually done. It weeded out the candidates, leaving only two serious ones: Nateq-Nuri and

Leaders: **Sayyid Muhammad Khatami**

Muhammad Khatami was elected president of the Islamic Republic in 1997. He was born in 1944 into a prominent clerical family in central Iran. His father, an ayatollah, was a close friend of Khomeini. His mother came from a prosperous landed family. He studied theology in Qom and philosophy at Isfahan University. At the outbreak of the revolution, he was in charge of a Shi'i mosque in Germany. After the revolution, he first headed a state publishing house, then sat in the *Majles,* and then served as Minister of Culture and Islamic Guidance. Arousing the wrath of the conservatives, he resigned from the last post in 1992 and took up the teaching of philosophy at Tehran University. He uses the title sayyid and wears a black turban to indicate that he is a male descendant of the Prophet. Although a cleric by appearance and training, he seems to many more like a university professor interested in political philosophy.

Khatami. In weeding out the candidates, the Guardian Council made sure it eliminated all secular and lay liberal voices. The Council was confident that in a two-man race Nateq-Nuri would win. He was well known, having served in a number of parliaments. He had been close to Khomeini, who had at one time named him Minister of Interior. He had presided over a number of revolutionary tribunals. Moreover, he was backed by an impressive array of clerical organizations, interest groups, and newspapers: the Association of the Militant Clergy; the Foundation of the Oppressed; the National Radio-Television network; the newspapers *Resalat, Kayhan,* and *Ettela'at;* the Chamber of Commerce; the Chamber of Bazaar Guilds; the Association of Farmers; and of course, his own conservative bloc in the *Majles.* Furthermore, he was endorsed by most of the Imam Jum'ehs and members of the Guardian Council. Many also felt that he had been implicitly endorsed by the Supreme Leader himself.

In contrast, Khatami had the support only of the Servants of Reconstruction; their newspaper *Hamshahri (Fellow Townsman);* the revived Society of the Militant Clergy and its paper *Salam (Greetings);* the Islamic Association of Students; the Islamic Women's Association and its paper *Zanan (Women);* and the Workers' House and its paper *Kar va Kargar (Work and Worker).* The popular mayor of Tehran served as the chairman of his electoral campaign. Khatami also received the support of a number of small but independent intellectual journals.

Khatami pitched his campaign at youth, women, middle-class professionals, and the urban working class. He appeared at bus stops, supermarkets, and schools. He drove around in his own small car. He was photographed using the Internet and playing table tennis, his favorite sport after soccer. He gave interviews to *Zanan,* whereas his opponent considered such behavior too demeaning. When asked by *Zanan* if his wife drove a car, he confessed that he wished she did since he would like to do less driving himself. His speeches stressed the importance of the rule of law, civil society, political pluralism, toleration, greater openness, and fewer social restrictions. In an appeal to the radical clerics, the urban poor, and the organized working class, he stressed economic justice, job creation, and welfare programs.

His intellectual supporters were more explicit in their criticisms of the conservatives. For example, Abdol-Karim Soroush, a popular lecturer who at Khomeini's behest had helped purge the universities, now stressed the importance of human rights, popular will, and intellectual freedom. He argued that religion and politics should be kept separate for the benefit of both. Politics debased religion into a false ideology. And religion in the hands of a political elite inevitably became a tool of oppression. He also argued that conservatives had used the issue of "cultural imperialism" to silence new voices, that innovative ideas had come not from the seminaries but from such intellectuals as Shariati and Bazargan, and that Iran should become a full-fledged democracy in which Islam would be recognized as the religion of the majority. In other words, Iran should become secular in structure but Islamic in name, just as Bazargan had advocated years earlier. Not surprisingly, Hezbollahis often disrupted his public lectures.

Khatami's electoral themes struck the right note. Whereas 16.4 million voters had participated in the 1989 presidential election and 16.7 million in the election of 1993, over 29 million voted in 1997. Almost 70 percent supported Khatami. This was a resounding yes for him, and, at the same time, a resounding no to the whole establishment. According to journalists, the main concerns for the youth that flocked to the polls were jobs, education, university places, household goods, and freedom in everyday life—freedom from the vigilante Hezbollahis and the *basej*. They also wanted the freedom to go to parties, dance, date, listen to music, watch videos, and own satellite-television dishes. According to the same journalists, most of the revolutionary guards also voted for Khatami. The generation raised after the revolution has had enough of social control and religious guidance. In other words, youth find the clerical revolution to be middle-aged.

Khatami followed up his victory with a number of liberal measures. He placed his own supporters and those of Rafsanjani in charge of the important ministries of Interior, Culture and Islamic Guidance, Labor, and Foreign Affairs. He licensed the Servants of Reconstruction, stressed the importance of political parties, and promised to enact the long-awaited law legalizing political parties. He scheduled elections for local councils—elections that should have been held two decades ago. He encouraged his *Majles* supporters to draft a bill stripping the Guardian Council of the power to vet electoral candidates. He eased the censorship on books, newspapers, films, and television. He criticized fellow believers for the tendency to place their hopes on the Hidden Imam. He declared that the "sick economy" needed social as well as financial reforms. He removed the prison system from the control of die-hard conservatives. He warned Hezbollahis not to disrupt meetings. He freed from house imprisonment a number of grand ayatollahs. He moved the *basej* from the wealthier suburbs of northern Tehran. He permitted the launching of a number of liberal newspapers—one, *Jam'eh* (*Society*) grew overnight to a circulation of over 100,000, outselling the established papers. In addition, he used the cable television station CNN to appeal directly to the West, especially to the U.S. public. He expressed admiration for the United States, especially for its tradition of religious toleration. He also expressed "pity" over the hostage-taking "tragedy." He was clearly trying to break the ice in order to persuade the United States to lift its embargo and allow U.S. oil companies to return to Iran.

This new course did not have smooth sailing. Despite the landslide victory, the president's constitutional powers were sharply limited from all sides—by the Supreme Leader, the judiciary, and the *Majles*. Khamenei undermined the rapprochement with the West by continually denouncing the United States as well as the Israeli-Palestinian peace process. He also removed the jurisdiction of the national police from the Interior Ministry. One of the clerical foundations upped the bounty it had offered to anyone killing Salman Rushdie. The judiciary banned licensed newspapers and arrested associates of Khatami and Rafsanjani. For example, the popular mayor of Tehran was hauled to court on trumped-up corruption charges. The *Majles* forced Khatami to place conservatives in charge of the ministries of Justice, Intelligence, and Defense. It also forced the resignation of Khatami's Interior Minister and drafted a new electoral law raising the voting age from fifteen to sixteen. Meanwhile, Hezbollahis assaulted a number of Khatami supporters, including ministers and venerable Imam Jum'ehs. One of the injured was the Supreme Leader's brother, who was Khatami's close friend. To top it all, a group of assassins, probably organized by the Intelligence Ministry, killed four prominent lay intellectuals. By early 1999 it was clear that Khatami could not pursue his liberal agenda unless he won the *Majles* elections scheduled for 2000. To do that he would need to strip the Guardian Council of the power to vet parliamentary candidates, but for that he would need a parliamentary majority. In other words, Khatami reached a constitutional dead end. So far the theocratic features of the constitution have proved to be stronger than the democratic ones.

Iranian Politics in Comparative Perspective

Iran is both like and unlike the rest of the Third World. Unlike most Third World countries, it is an old state with institutions that go back to the ancient world. Unlike most others, it is not a newly independent country since it was never formally taken over by the imperial powers. It remained officially independent,

---

Leaders: **Hojjat al-Islam Ali-Akbar Hashemi Rafsanjani**

Ali-Akbar Rafsanjani was born in 1934 into a fairly prosperous business and farming family in the heartland of the Shi'i and Persian-speaking provinces. He studied in Qom with Khomeini, found himself in prison four times during the 1960s, set up a number of commercial companies, including one that exported pistachios, and wrote a book praising a nineteenth-century prime minister who had made an aborted attempt to industrialize the country. Nevertheless, Rafsanjani remained active enough in clerical circles to be considered a hojjat al-Islam. After the revolution, he became a close confidant of Khomeini and attained a number of cabinet posts, culminating with the presidency in 1989. After serving two four-year terms, the maximum allowed by the constitution, he was given the chairmanship of the powerful Expediency Council. In some ways, his institutional power rivals that of President Khatami, but not, of course, that of Supreme Leader Khamenei.

---

even at the height of European imperialism. Unlike some others, it has a religion that links the elite with the masses, the cities with the villages, the state with the citizenry. Shi'ism, as well as Iranian identity, serves as social cement, giving the population a collective identity. Unlike most Third World countries, it possesses rich oil resources and thus has the potential for rapid economic development. And unlike most others, it has produced two popular upheavals in the twentieth century: the constitutional and the Islamic revolutions. In both, the citizenry actively intervened in politics, overthrowing the old regime and shaping the new. The Islamic Republic and the 1905 constitution were authentic home products, not foreign imports.

Yet Iran shares some problems with other Third World countries. It has failed to establish a full-fledged democracy. Its economy remains underdeveloped, highly reliant on one commodity, and unable to meet rising expectations. Its collective identity is strained by internal fault lines, especially those of class, ethnicity, and interclerical conflicts. And its ambition to enter the world of states as an important player has been thwarted by international as well as internal and regional realities. In fact, this ambition has helped to undermine democracy and economic development in Iran.

Democracy has been constricted by theocracy. Some argue that Islam made this inevitable. But Islam, like Christianity and the other major religions, can be interpreted in ways that either support or oppose democracy. Islam, as interpreted by some Muslims, stresses the importance of justice, equality, and consultation. It has a tradition of tolerating other religions. Its *shari'a* explicitly protects life, property, and honor. In practice, it has often separated politics from religion, statutes from holy laws, spiritual affairs from worldly matters, and the state from the clerical establishment.

Moreover, the theocracy in Iran originates not in Islam but in jurist's guardianship, a new concept developed by Khomeini. On the whole, Sunni Islam considers clerics to be theological scholars, not a special stratum. This helps explain why the Iranian regime has found it difficult to export the revolution to the rest of the Muslim world. The failure of democracy in Iran should be attributed less to Islam than to the confluence of crises in 1979–1981 that allowed a small group of clerics to seize power. Whether they remain in power into the twenty-first century depends not so much on Islam but on how they handle the opposition, their own differences, and most important, the country's economic problems.

The Islamic Republic is sharply divided on how to manage an economy beset by rising demands, falling petroleum revenues, and the nightmarish prospect that in the next two generations the oil wells will run dry. Most clerics favor the conventional capitalist road to development, hoping to liberalize the market, privatize industry, attract foreign capital, and encourage the propertied classes to invest. Others envisage an equally conventional statist road to development, favoring central planning, government industries, price controls, high taxes, state subsidies, national self-reliance, and ambitious programs to eliminate poverty, illiteracy, slums, and unemployment. Khatami has charted a third road, combining elements of state intervention with free enterprise. This is strikingly similar to the social democracy favored in other parts of the world.

As the clock ticks, the population grows, oil revenues stagnate, and the per capita national income falls. The economic problems that undermined the monarchy could well undermine the Islamic Republic. Only time will tell whether social discontent will be expressed through apolitical channels, such as drug addiction, emigration, and quietist religion; through radical clerics remaining within the regime; through insurrectionary organizations, through ethnic-based movements, or through reformist movements such as Khatami's electoral campaign.

Iran's collective identity has come under great strain in recent years. The emphasis on Shi'ism has antagonized Sunnis as well as non-Muslims. The emphasis on clerical Shi'ism has further alienated all secularists, including lay liberals, radical leftists, and moderate nationalists. Furthermore, the emphasis on Khomeini's brand of Shi'ism has alienated Shi'is who reject the whole notion of jurist's guardianship. And the elevation of Khamenei as the Supreme Leader has antagonized many early proponents of jurist's guardianship. In short, the regime has used slicing tactics on itself, gradually reducing its social base to a bare minimum. It is, however, possible that reformist movements such as that of Khatami could help rebuild the collective national identity.

Finally, the Islamic Republic's attempt to enter the international arena as a militant force has been counterproductive. It has diverted scarce resources to the military, especially the revolutionary guards. It has frightened Saudi Arabia and the Gulf sheikhdoms into the arms of the United States. It has prompted the United States to isolate Iran, discouraging investment and preventing international organizations from extending economic assistance. It has also frightened the neighboring secular states such as Turkey, Tadzhikistan, and Azerbaijan. It has strained relations with some other Third World countries. Moreover, Iran has discovered that its brand of Islam is not exportable to the Sunni world. The West may perceive Iran as the vanguard of the Islamic radicalism that is spreading throughout the Middle East and North Africa. But the Sunni world sees Iran much more as a unique Shi'i phenomenon. Only the future will show whether the 1979 Islamic Revolution can be repeated elsewhere.

Key Terms

ayatollah	mosques
fatwa	*pasdaran*
theocracy	Imam
Majles	Hezbollahis
Guardian Council	hojjat al-Islam
Supreme Leader	*jihad*
Farsi	rentier state
Shi'ism	dual society
People of the Book	OPEC
Qur'an	Imam Jum'ehs
shari'a	Foundation of the
bazaars	Oppressed
fundamentalism	*basej*
jurist's guardianship	*maslahat*

Suggested Readings

Abrahamian, E. *Iran Between Two Revolutions*. Princeton, N.J.: Princeton University Press, 1982.

———. *Khomeinism*. Berkeley: University of California Press, 1993.

———. *Tortured Confessions: Prisons and Public Recantations in Modern Iran*. Berkeley: University of California Press, 1999.

Akhavi, S. *Religion and Politics in Contemporary Iran*. Albany: State University of New York Press, 1980.

Bakhash, S. *Reign of the Ayatollahs*. New York: Basic Books, 1984.

Baktiari, B. *Parliamentary Politics in Revolutionary Iran*. Gainesville: University Press of Florida, 1966.

Bill, J. *The Eagle and the Lion*. New Haven, Conn.: Yale University Press, 1988.

Chehabi, H. *Iranian Politics and Religious Modernism*. Ithaca, N.Y.: Cornell University Press, 1990.

Cottam, R. *Nationalism in Iran*. Pittsburgh: University of Pittsburgh Press, 1964.

Dabashi, H. *Theology of Discontent: The Ideological Foundation of the Islamic Revolution in Iran*. New York: New York University Press, 1993.

Esposito, J. *The Iranian Revolution: Its Global Impact*. Miami: University Press of Florida, 1990.

Fischer, M. *Iran: From Religious Dispute to Revolution*. Cambridge, Mass.: Harvard University Press, 1980.

Foran, J. *Fragile Resistance: Social Transformation in Iran from 1500 to the Revolution*. Boulder, Colo.: Westview Press, 1993.

——. *A Century of Revolution: Social Movements in Iran.* Minneapolis: University of Minnesota Press, 1994.

Green, J. *Revolution in Iran.* New York: Praeger, 1982.

Halliday, F. *Iran: Dictatorship and Development.* London: Penguin, 1979.

Heiss, M. *Empire and Nationhood: The United States, Great Britain, and Iranian Oil, 1950–1954.* New York: Columbia University Press, 1997.

Huntington, Samuel P., *The Clash of Civilizations and the Remaking of the World Order.* New York: Simon & Schuster, 1996.

Kazemi, F. "Civil Society and Iranian Politics." In *Civil Society in the Middle East,* ed. A. Norton. Vol. 2. Leiden: Brill, 1996.

Keddie, N. *Roots of Revolution.* New Haven, Conn.: Yale University Press, 1981.

——. *Iran and the Muslim World.* London: Macmillan, 1995.

Mackey, S. *The Iranians: Persia, Islam, and the Soul of a Nation.* New York: Penguin, 1996.

Milani, M. *The Making of Iran's Islamic Revolution.* Boulder, Colo.: Westview Press, 1994.

Mottahedeh, R. *The Mantle of the Prophet.* New York: Simon and Schuster, 1985.

Najmabadi, A. *The Story of the Daughters of Quchan.* Syracuse, N.Y.: Syracuse University Press, 1998.

Paidar, P. *Women and the Political Process in Twentieth-Century Iran.* Cambridge: Cambridge University Press, 1995.

Rahema, A., and S. Behnab. *Iran after the Revolution.* London: Tauris, 1995.

Ramazani, R. *Revolutionary Iran.* Baltimore: Johns Hopkins University Press, 1986.

Schirazi, A. *The Constitution of Iran.* London: Tauris, 1997.

Weiner, M., and A. Banuazizi, eds. *The Politics of Social Transformation in Afghanistan, Iran, and Pakistan.* Syracuse, N.Y.: Syracuse University Press, 1994.

Endnotes

[1] Quoted in E. Browne, *The Persian Revolution* (New York: Barnes and Noble, 1966), 137.

[2] British Financial Adviser to the Foreign Office in Tehran, *Documents on British Foreign Policy, 1919–39* (London: Government Printing Office, 1963), First Series, XIII, 720, 735.

[3] British Minister to the Foreign Office, *Report on the Seizure of Lands,* Foreign Office 371/Persia 1932/File 34-16007.

[4] *Kayhan International,* November 10, 1976.

[5] Editorial, "Fifty Indictments of Treason During Fifty Years of Treason," *Khabarnameh,* no. 46 (April 1976).

[6] M. Bazargan, "Letter to the Editor," *Ettela'at,* February 7, 1980.

[7] *Iran Times,* January 12, 1979.

[8] "Text of the Mass Rally of Ashura," *Khabarnameh,* December 15, 1978.

[9] *Washington Post,* December 12, 1978.

[10] *Christian Science Monitor,* December 12, 1978.

[11] Mirza Hosayn Khan Tahvildar-e Isfahan, *Jukhrafiha-ye Isfahan* (*The Geography of Isfahan*) (Tehran: Tehran University Press, 1963), 100–101.

[12] International Labor Organization, "Employment and Income Policies for Iran" (Unpublished report, Geneva, 1972), Appendix C, 6.

[13] A. Sharbatoghilie, *Urbanization and Regional Disparity in Post-Revolutionary Iran* (Boulder, Colo.: Westview Press, 1991), 4.

[14] *Wall Street Journal,* November 4, 1977.

[15] U.S. Congress, *Economic Consequences of the Revolution in Iran* (Washington, D.C.: U.S. Government Printing Office, 1979), 184.

[16] U.S. Congress, *Economic Consequences of the Revolution in Iran,* 5.

[17] U.S. Department of Commerce, *Iran: A Survey of U.S. Business Opportunities* (Washington, D.C.: U.S. Government Printing Office, 1977), 1–2.

[18] Cited in H. Amirahmadi, *Revolution and Economic Transition* (Albany: State University of New York Press, 1960), p. 201.

[19] Cited in *Iran Times,* July 9, 1993.

[20] J. Amuzegar, *Iran's Economy Under the Islamic Republic* (London: Taurus Press, 1994), 100.

[21] Cited in *Iran Times,* July 9, 1993.

[22] Amuzegar, *Iran's Economy,* 101.

[23] A. Rafsanjani, "The Islamic Consultative Assembly," *Kayhan,* May 23, 1987.

[24] S. Saffari, "The Legitimation of the Clergy's Right to Rule in the Iranian Constitution of 1979," in *British Journal of Middle Eastern Studies* 20, no. 1 (1993): 64–81.

[25] Ayatollah Montazeri, *Ettela'at,* October 8, 1979.

[26] O. Fallaci, "Interview with Khomeini," *New York Times Magazine,* October 7, 1979.

[27] *Kayhan,* March 6, 1980.

[28] *Kayhan,* April 21, 1987.

[29] *Kayhan-e Hava'i,* November 16, 1988.

[30] A. Rafsanjani, Friday sermon, *Kayhan,* November 4, 1989.

[31] Interview with the former Labor Minister, *Salam,* January 9–25, 1993.

[32] "Survey of Iran," *The Economist,* January 18, 1997.

Glossary*

abertura (*apertura* in Spanish)   in Brazil, refers to the period of authoritarian liberalization begun in 1974 when the military allowed civilian politicians to contest for political office in the context of a more open political society. (See **glasnost.**)

accommodation   an informal agreement or settlement between the government and important interest groups that is responsive to the interest groups' concerns for policy or program benefits.

accountability   a government's responsibility to its population, usually by periodic popular elections and (in **parliamentary systems**) by parliament having the power to dismiss the government by passing a motion of no-confidence. In a political system characterized by accountability, the major actions taken by government must be known and understood by the citizenry. (See **democracy.**)

acephalous societies   literally "headless" societies. A number of traditional Nigerian societies, such as the Igbo in the precolonial period, lacked executive rulership as we have come to conceive of it. Instead, the villages and clans were governed by committee or consensus.

Amerindian   original peoples of North and South America; indigenous people.

anticlericalism   opposition to the power of churches or clergy in politics. In some countries, for example, France and Mexico, this opposition has focused on the role of the Catholic church in politics.

authoritarian   (See **authoritarianism.**)

authoritarianism   a system of rule in which power does not depend on popular legitimacy but rather on the coercive force of the political authorities. Hence there are few personal and group freedoms. It is also characterized by near absolute power in the executive branch, and little if any legislative and judicial controls. (See **autocracy, fascism, patrimonialism.**)

autocracy   a government in which one or a few rulers has absolute power, thus, a **dictatorship.** Similar to **authoritarianism.**

---

*Note: Boldface terms *within* a definition can be found as separate entries in the Glossary.

autonomous region   in the People's Republic of China, a territorial unit equivalent to a province that contains a large concentration of ethnic minorities. These regions have some autonomy in the cultural sphere but in most policy matters are strictly subordinate to the central government.

Ayatollah   literally, God's symbol. High-ranking clerics in Iran. The most senior ones—often no more than half a dozen—are known as Grand Ayatollahs.

balance of payments   an indicator of international flow of funds, it shows the excess or deficit in total payments of all kinds between or among countries. Included in the calculation are exports and imports, grants, and international debt payments.

basej   Persian word for mobilization used to describe the volunteer army of young and old men formed in Iran to help the regular army and revolutionary guards in the war against Iraq.

bazaar   an urban marketplace where shops, workshops, small businessmen, and even export-importers are located.

Brahmin(s)   highest caste in the Hindu caste system, who traditionally dominated the Hindu society of India.

bureaucracy   an organization structured hierarchically, in which lower-level officials are charged with administering regulations codified in rules which specify impersonal, objective guidelines for making decisions. In the modern world, many large organizations, especially business firms and the executives of developed states, are organized along bureaucratic lines.

bureaucratic authoritarianism   a term developed by the Argentine sociologist, Guillermo O'Donnell, to interpret the common characteristics of military-led authoritarian regimes in Brazil, Argentina, Chile, and Uruguay in the 1960s and 1970s. According to O'Donnell, bureaucratic authoritarian regimes led by the armed forces and key civilian allies emerged in these countries in response to severe economic crises. Repression in these regimes varied from the relatively mild forms that constricted civil rights and other political freedoms in Brazil, to the much harsher policy of forced detention, mass exile, and widespread killing that characterized the military regimes of Argentina (1976–1983) and Chile (1973–1989).

A1

bureaucratic rings a term first developed by the Brazilian sociologist and president Fernando Henrique Cardoso that refers to the highly permeable and fragmented structure of the state bureaucracy which allows private interests to make alliances with mid-level bureaucratic officers. By shaping public policy to benefit these interests, bureaucrats gain the promise of future employment in the private sector. While in positions of responsibility, bureaucratic rings are ardent defenders of their own interests.

cabinet the ministers who direct executive departments. In **parliamentary systems,** the cabinet and high-ranking subcabinet ministers (also known as the government) are considered collectively responsible to parliament.

cadre a person who occupies a position of authority in a **communist party-state;** cadres may or may not be communist party members.

caste system India's Hindu society is divided into castes. According to the Hindu religion, membership in a given caste is determined at birth. Castes form a rough social and economic hierarchy. (See **Brahmins, untouchables.**)

central planning (See **command economy.**)

charisma the ability of a leader to attract an intensely devoted following because of personal characteristics that supporters believe endows the charismatic leader with extraordinary and heroic qualities.

civil society refers to the space occupied by voluntary associations *outside* the state, for example, professional associations (lawyers, doctors, teachers), trade unions, student and women's groups and religious bodies, and other voluntary association groups. The term is similar to **society,** although civil society implies a degree of organization absent from the more inclusive term *society.*

clientelism (or **patron-client relations**) an informal aspect of policy-making in which a powerful patron (for example, a traditional local boss, government agency, or dominant party) offers resources such as land, contracts, protection, or jobs in return for the support and services (such as labor or votes) of lower status and less powerful clients; corruption, preferential treatment, and inequality are characteristic of clientelist politics. (See **partimonialism, prebendalism.**)

Cold War the term designates the hostile relations that prevailed between the United States and the USSR from the late 1940s until the demise of the Soviet Union in 1991. Although an actual (hot) war never directly occurred between the two superpowers, they clashed indirectly by supporting rival forces in many wars occurring in the Third World.

collectivization a process undertaken in China under Mao in the 1950s, by which agricultural land was removed from private ownership and organized into large state and collective farms.

command economy a form of **socialism** in which government decisions ("commands") rather than market mechanisms (such as supply and demand) are the major influences in determining the nation's economic direction; also called **central planning.**

communism a system of social organization based on the common ownership and coordination of production; according to Marxism (the theory of German philosopher Karl Marx, 1818–1883), communism is a culminating stage of history, following **capitalism** and **socialism.** In historical practice, leaders of China, the Soviet Union, and other states who have proclaimed themselves seeking to achieve communism have ruled through a single party, the communist party, which has controlled the state and society in an authoritarian manner, and have applied **Marxism-Leninism** to justify their rule.

communist (See **communism.**)

communist party-state a type of **nation-state** in which the communist party attempts to exercise a complete monopoly on political power and controls all important state institutions. (See **communism.**)

comparative politics the study of the domestic politics, political institutions, and conflicts of countries. Often involves comparisons among countries and through time within single countries, emphasizing key patterns of similarity and difference.

comparativists political scientists who study the similarities and differences in the domestic politics of various countries (see **comparative politics**).

Confucianism a social philosophy based on the teachings of the Chinese sage, Confucius (c. 551–479 B.C.) that emphasizes social harmony, righteous behavior toward others, and deference to one's superiors. Confucianism remains a major source of cultural values in the countries of East Asia, including China and Japan.

cooptation incorporating activists into the system while accommodating some of their concerns.

corporatism a pattern of organizing interests and influencing public policy in which the state gives favored status to certain **interest groups;** typically involves tripartite (three-way) consultations among representatives of business, labor, and government over economic policy. Corporatism can occur in both **democratic** and **authoritarian**

settings. However, it is usually criticized for the fact that it limits open debate and representative processes. (See **neo-corporatism, state corporatism.**)

corporatist philosophy   (See **corporatism.**)

danwei   a Chinese term that means "unit" and is the basic level of social organization and a major means of political control in China's **communist party-state.** A person's *danwei* is most often his or her workplace, such as a factory or an office.

decentralization   policies that aim to transfer some decision-making power from higher to lower levels of government, typically, from the central government to subnational governments.

détente   a relaxation of tensions between formerly hostile nations that moves them toward more normal diplomatic relations. Often used to describe a thaw in the **Cold War** beginning in the 1960s.

developmental state   a **nation-state** in which the government carries out policies that effectively promote national economic growth.

developmentalism   an ideology and practice in Latin America during the 1950s in which the state played a leading role in seeking to foster economic development, through sponsoring vigorous **industrial policy.** [See **import substituting industrialization (ISI).**]

dictatorship   (See **autocracy, authoritarianism, totalitarianism.**)

distributive policies   transfer resources from one group to another in the society.

dual economy   an economy that is sharply divided into a modern and a traditional sector.

dual rule   a system of administration used in China (adapted from the Soviet Union) that places a government body under the authority of both a higher level government organization and a communist party organization.

dual-structure system   a structure of an industrial economy characterized by a sharp division between a modern corporate sector composed of large and powerful enterprises on the one hand and a traditional small-business sector, on the other. The latter tend to be dependent on and often controlled by the former. The pre–World War II Japanese economy was characterized by such a structure.

Economic Community of West African States (ECOWAS)   the organization established in 1975 among the sixteen governments in West Africa. The goals of ECOWAS are to strengthen and broaden the economies in the region through the removal of trade barriers among its members (such as import quotas and domestic content laws) and freedom of movement for their citizens and monetary cooperation.

economic liberalization   attempts to dismantle government controls on the economy.

ejidatario   recipient of *ejido* land grant in Mexico.

ejido   land granted by Mexican government to organized group of peasants.

Emergency (1975–1977)   the period when Indian Prime Minister Indira Gandhi suspended many formal democratic rights and ruled in an **authoritarian** manner.

emir   traditional Islamic ruler. The emir presides over an "emirate," or kingdom, in Northern Nigeria.

executive   the agencies of government which implement or execute policy. The highest levels of the executive in most countries is a president or prime minister and cabinet. The top executive officeholders supervise the work of administrative departments and bureaux.

export-led growth   economic growth generated by the export of a country's commodities. Export-led growth can occur at an early stage of economic development, in which case it involves primary products, such as the country's mineral resources, timber, and agricultural products; or at a later stage, when industrial goods and services are exported.

Farsi   Persian word for the Persian language. Fars is a province in central Iran.

fatwa   Islamic term for religious decree.

favelas   in Brazil, huge shanty towns of homes made out of cardboard, wood from dumps, and blocks of mortar and brick. These shanty towns create rings of extreme poverty around cities like Rio de Janeiro and São Paulo. Similar shanty towns can be found in other Latin American cities, although terms to describe them may vary by country. In Peru, for example, these shanty towns are called *barriadas.*

federal character   Nigeria's version of "affirmative action," applied to the civil service and all government agencies to ensure representation of all ethnic and regional groups and to prevent the dominance of any one group. In practice, federal character has tended to promote the employment of northern Nigerians at the expense of southerners.

Foundation of the Oppressed   a clerically controlled foundation set up after the revolution in Iran. It owns much of the confiscated assets of the old elite. Its profits are supposed to go to charity and education.

fundamentalism a term recently popularized to describe radical religious movements throughout the world. It is widely believed that these movements interpret the fundamental texts of their religion literally and intend to recreate their religion's early societies. Iranian leader Khomeini hardly fits this definition of fundamentalism.

gender social division based on the cultural and political significance ascribed to sexual difference.

globalization the intensification of world-wide interconnectedness associated with the increased speed and magnitude of cross-border flows of trade, investment and finance, and processes of migration, cultural diffusion, and communication.

Great Leap Forward a movement launched by Mao Zedong in 1958 to industrialize China very rapidly and thereby propel it toward **communism.** The Leap ended in economic disaster in 1960, causing one of the worst famines in human history.

Great Proletarian Cultural Revolution the political campaign launched in 1966 by Chairman Mao Zedong to stop what he saw as China's drift away from socialism and towards capitalism. The campaign led to massive purges in the Chinese Communist Party, the widespread persecution of China's intellectuals, and the destruction of invaluable cultural objects. The Cultural Revolution officially ended in 1979 after Mao's death and the arrest of some of his most radical followers.

green revolution a strategy for increasing agricultural (especially food) production, involving improved seeds, irrigation, and abundant use of fertilizers.

guanxi a Chinese term that means "connections" or "relationships," and describes personal ties between individuals based on such things as common birthplace or mutual acquaintances. *Guanxi* are an important factor in China's political and economic life.

Guardian Council a committee of twelve jurists created by the Iranian constitution. It has the authority to veto any parlimentary bill it considers to be un-Islamic and against the constitution.

guerrilla warfare a military strategy based on small bands of soldiers (the guerrillas) who use hit-and-run tactics to attack a numerically superior and better-armed enemy.

hegemonic power a state that can control the pattern of alliances and terms of the international order, and often shapes domestic political developments in countries throughout the world.

Hezbollahis literally means the partisans of God. The term is used in Iran to describe religious vigilantes. In Lebanon, it is used to describe the Shi'i militia.

Hindus India's main religion is Hinduism, and its adherents are called Hindus.

hojjat al-Islams literally, the proof of Islam. Medium-ranking clerics in Iran.

household responsibility system the system put into practice in China beginning in the late 1970s in which the major decisions about agricultural production are made by individual farm families based on profit motive rather than by a **people's commune** or the government.

Imam leader. Iranians traditionally used this title only for the twelve early Infallible Leaders of Shi'ism. During the Islamic Revolution, this title was used for Khomeini to elevate him above the other Grand Ayatollahs.

Imam Jum'ehs prayer-leaders in Iran's main urban mosques on Fridays. Appointed by the clerical hiearchy in Qom, these prayer-leaders enjoy considerable authority in the provinces of Iran.

import substituting industrialization (ISI) strategy for industrialization based on domestic manufacture of previously imported goods to satisfy domestic market demands. (See **developmentalism.**)

Indian Administrative Service (IAS) India's civil service, a highly professional and talented group of administrators who run the Indian government on a day-to-day basis.

indigenous groups population of Amerindian heritage in Mexico.

indirect rule a term used to describe the British style of colonialism in Nigeria in which local traditional rulers and political structures were used to help support the colonial governing structure.

informal sector (economy) an underground economy.

insider privatization a term used in relation to Russia to refer to the transformation of formerly state-owned enterprises into **joint-stock companies** or private enterprises in which majority control of the enterprise is in the hands of employees and/or managers of that enterprise.

International Financial Institutions (IFIs) generally refers to the International Bank for Reconstruction and Development (The World Bank) and the International Monetary Fund (IMF), but can also include other international lending institutions. [See **structural adjustment program (SAP).**]

interventionist   an interventionist state acts vigorously to shape the performance of major sectors of the economy.

interventores   in Brazil, allies of Getúlio Vargas picked by the dictator during his first period of rulership to replace opposition governors in all the Brazilian states except Minas Gerais. The *interventores* represented a shift of power from subnational government to the central state. (See **politics of the governors.**)

iron rice bowl   a feature of China's socialist economy that provided guarantees of lifetime employment, income, and basic cradle-to-grave benefits to most urban and rural workers. Economic reforms beginning in the 1980s aimed at improving efficiency and work motivation sought to smash the iron rice bowl and link employment and income more directly to individual effort.

jihad   Islamic "holy war" against nonbelievers. One of the fundamental duties required of Muslims, although its interpretation varies widely.

jurist's guardianship   Khomeini's concept that the Iranian clergy should rule on the grounds that they are the divinely appointed guardians of both the law and the people. He developed this concept in the 1970s.

land reform   the process of reducing gross inequalities in the ownership of farm land by either confiscating or buying it from large owners and redistributing it to those who have little or no land.

legitimacy   a belief by powerful groups and the broad citizenry that a state exercises "rightful" authority. In the contemporary world, a state is said to possess legitimacy when it enjoys consent of the governed, which usually involves democratic procedures and the attempt to achieve a satisfactory level of development and equitable distribution of resources. (See **democracy.**)

Lok Sabha   the lower house of parliament in India where all major legislation must pass before becoming law.

luan   a Chinese term meaning "chaos." It conveys the fear of China's leaders and many of its people that without strong central leadership the country would collaspe into **anarchy.**

Maharajas   India's traditional rulers—monarchs—who retained their positions under British tutelage during the colonial period but who were removed from power when the Indian **republic** was established.

Majles   Arabic term for assembly used in Iran to refer to the parliament.

Manifest Destiny   the public philosophy in the late 19th century that the United States was not only entitled, but destined to occupy all of the territory from the Atlantic to the Pacific.

maquiladora   factories that produce goods for export, often located along the U.S.-Mexican border.

market reform   a strategy of economic transformation embraced by the Deng Xiaoping government in China that involves reducing the role of the state in managing the economy and increasing the role of market forces. In China, market reform has been carried out under the leadership of the Chinese Communist Party and involves less extensive privatization.

maslahat   Arabic term for advisable or prudent. It is now used in Iran to refer to reasons of state or what is best for the Islamic Republic.

mestizo   a person of mixed white, indigenous (Amerindian), and sometimes African descent.

middle-level theory   seeks to explain phenomena in a limited range of cases, in particular, a specific set of countries with particular characteristics, such as parliamentary regimes, or a particular type of political institution (such as political parties) or activity (such as protest).

moderating power   (*poder moderador*)   a term used in Brazilian politics to refer to the situation following the 1824 constitution in which the monarchy was supposed to act as a moderating power, among the executive, legislative, and judicial branches of government, arbitrating party conflicts, and fulfilling governmental responsibilities when non-royal agents failed.

mosque   Muslim place of worship, equivalent to church, temple, or synagogue.

Muslim(s)   followers of Islam.

nationalism   an ideology that seeks to create a **nation-state** for a particular community; a group identity associated with membership is such a political community. Nationalists often proclaim that their **state** and **nation** are superior to others.

nationalization   the take-over by the government of privately owned business firms.

nation-state   distinct, politically defined territory with its own **state,** relatively coherent culture, economy, and ethnic and other social identities. (See **country.**)

New State   (*Estado Novo*)   in Brazil, an authoritarian government led by Getúlio Vargas in 1937 that legitimized its rule through **state corporatism,** massive public sector investment through **para-statals,** and paternalistic social policies.

nomenklatura   a system of personnel selection utilized in the Soviet Union and China under which the Communist Party maintains control over the appointment of important officials in all spheres of social, economic, and political life. The term is also used to describe individuals chosen through this system and thus refers more broadly to the privileged circles in the Soviet Union and China.

nonaligned bloc   a group of countries that refused to ally with either the United States or the USSR during the **Cold War** years.

nongovernmental organization (NGO)   a private group that seeks to influence public policy and deal with certain problems that it believes are not being adequately addressed by governments; examples include Amnesty International (human rights), Oxfam (famine relief), and Greenpeace (the environment).

oligarchy   narrowly based, undemocratic government, often by traditional elites. (See **autocracy, authoritarianism.**)

OPEC   Organization of Oil Exporting Countries. Iran is one of its leading members.

panchayats   the lowest level of local government in India.

para-statals   state-owned, or at least state-controlled, corporations, created to undertake a broad range of activities, from control and marketing of agricultural production to provision of banking services, operating airlines, and other transportation facilities and public utilities. (See **interventionist.**)

pasdaran   Persian term for guards used to refer to the army of revolutionary guards formed during Iran's Islamic Revolution.

patrimonialism (or **neopatrimonialism**)   a system of governance in which a single ruler treats the state as personal property (patrimony). Appointments to public office are made on the basis of unswerving loyalty to the ruler. In turn, state officials exercise wide authority in other domains, such as the economy, often for their personal benefit and that of the ruler, to the detriment of the general population. (See **authoritarianism, autocracy, prebendalism.**)

patrimonial state   (See **patrimonialism.**)

patron-client relations (or **network**)   (See **clientelism.**)

People of the Book   the Muslim term for recognized religious minorities such as Christians, Jews, and Zoroastrians.

people's communes   large-scale rural communities that were in charge of nearly all aspects of political, social, and economic life in the Chinese countryside from the late 1950s until the early 1980s when they were disbanded and replaced by a system of household and village-based agricultural production.

personalist politicians   demagogic political leaders who use their personal charisma to mobilize their constituency.

petrodollars   revenue earned from the sale from petroleum, often circulating internationally as US dollars.

political culture   the attitudes, beliefs, and symbols that influence political behavior; often defined in terms of specific national political-cultural orientations.

political development   the stages of change producing more modern and effective political institutions.

political economy   the study of the interaction between the state and the economy, that is, how the state and political processes affect the organization of production and exchange (the economy), and how the organization of the economy affects political processes.

political institutions   the formal rules, structured relationships, and organizations within the state, and, more broadly, within the political sphere. Some key examples are the executive, legislature, judiciary, military, and political parties.

politics of the governors   in Brazil, refers to periods of history in which state governors acquire extraordinary powers over domains of policy that were previously claimed by the federal government. The term refers most commonly to the Old Republic and the current state of Brazilian federalism. (See **federalism.**)

populism   gaining the support of popular sectors. When used in Latin American politics, this support is often achieved by manipulation and demagogic appeals.

prebendalism   patterns of political behavior that rest on the justification that official state offices should be competed for, and then utilized for the personal benefit of office holders as well as of their support group or clients. Thus, prebendal politics is sustained by the existence of **patron-client networks.** (See **patrimonialism, clientelism.**)

privatization   the sale of state-owned enterprises to private companies or investors. Those who support the policy claim that private ownership is superior to government ownership because for-profit entities promote greater efficiency. Privatization is a central component of **structural adjustment programs (SAPs)** to curtail the losses associated with these enterprises and generate state revenue when they are sold. For Russia, see **spontaneous privatization.**

proletariat   the industrial working class which, according to Marxism-Leninism, is destined to seize power and replace capitalism with socialism.

proportional representation (PR)   a system of political representation in which seats are allocated to parties within multimember constituencies, roughly in proportion to the votes each party receives. PR usually encourages the election to parliament of more political parties than single-member district winner-take-all systems.

Qur'an   the Muslim Bible.

Rayja Sabha   India's upper house of parliament; considerably less significant politically than the *Lok Sabha.*

rentier state   a country that obtains much of its revenue from the export of oil.

rents   above-market returns to a factor of production. Pursuit of economic rents (or "rent-seeking") is profit-seeking that takes the form of nonproductive economic activity.

republic   in contemporary usage, a political regime in which leaders are not chosen on the basis of their inherited background (as in a monarchy). A republic may but need not be **democratic.** For Russia, see **autonomous republic.**

reservations   jobs or admissions to colleges reserved by the government of India for specific social groups, particularly underprivileged groups.

scheduled castes   the lowest caste groups in India, also known as the untouchables.

self-determination   the right of a sovereign state or an ethnic or other group that shares cultural and historical ties to live together in a given territory and in a manner they desire. It is often the basis of the claim by a state or group for political independence and cultural autonomy.

sexenio   six-year administration of Mexican presidents.

shari'a   Islamic law derived mostly from the Qur'an and the examples set by the Prophet Mohammad, but more broadly, the totality of **Muslim** belief and practice; the legal foundation of Islamic theocracy.

Shi'ism   a branch of Islam. It literally means the followers or partisans of Ali. The other main branch of Islam is known as Sunnism, or the followers of tradition.

Sikh(s)   an important religious minority group in India.

social class   common membership in a group whose boundaries are based on a common economic location, notably, occupation and income. Members of the same social class often share similar political attitudes.

socialism   in a socialist regime, the state plays a leading role in organizing the economy and most business firms are publicly owned. A socialist regime, unlike a **communist party-state,** may allow the private sector to play an important role in the economy and be committed to political plu-

ralism. In **Marxism-Leninism,** socialism refers to an early stage in development of **communism.** Socialist regimes can be organized in a **democratic** manner, in that those who control the state may be chosen according to democratic procedures (see **social democracy, democratic socialism**). They may also be governed in an undemocratic manner, when a single party, not chosen in free competitive elections, controls the state and society.

socialist democracy   the term used by the Chinese Communist Party to describe the political system of the People's Republic of China. Also called the people's democratic dictatorship. The official view is that this type of system, under the leadership of the Communist Party, provides democracy for the overwhelming majority of people and suppresses (or exercises dictatorship over) only the enemies of the people. Socialist democracy is contrasted to bourgeois (or capitalist) democracy, which puts power in the hands of the rich and oppresses the poor.

state   a unified political entity; the state comprises a country's key political institutions that are responsible for making, implementing, enforcing, and adjudicating important policies in that country. States have also been defined as those institutions within a country that claim the right to control force within the territory comprising the country and to make binding rules (laws) which citizens of that country must obey. (See **civil society, society.**)

state capitalism   strategy in which government guides industrial and agricultural development and sets political conditions for its success.

state corporatism   an **authoritarian regime** in which the **state** requires all members of a particular economic sector to join an officially designated **interest group.** Such interest groups thus attain public status and they participate in national policy-making. The result is that the state has great control over the groups, and groups have great control over their members. (See **corporatism, neocorporatism.**)

state formation   the historical development of a **state,** often marked by major stages, key events, or turning points (critical junctures) which influence the contemporary character of the state.

state-led economic development   the process of promoting economic development via the use of governmental machinery.

structural adjustment program (SAP)   medium-term, generally 3–5 year, programs (which include both action plans and disbursement of funds) established by the World Bank intended to alter and reform the economic structures of highly indebted, **Third World** countries as a condition for receiving international loans. SAPs often involve the necessity for **privatization,** trade **liberalization,** and fiscal restraint. [See **International Financial Institutions (IFIs).**]

Supreme Leader   the head of the Islamic Republic of Iran.

technocrats   career-minded bureaucrats who administer public policy according to a technical rather than a political rationale. In Mexico and Brazil, these are known as the *técnicos* (for contrasting concepts, see **clientelism, patrimonial state, prebendalism**).

theocracy   a state dominated by the clergy who rule on the grounds that they are the only interpreters of God's will and law.

totalitarianism   a political system in which the state attempts to exercise total control over all aspects of public and private life, including the economy, culture, education, and social organizations, through an integrated system of ideological, economic, and political control. The term has been applied both to **communist party-states** and **fascist** regimes such as Nazi Germany.

township and village enterprises (TVEs)   non-agricultural businesses and factories owned and run by local governments and private entrepreneurs in China's rural areas. TVEs operate largely according the market forces and outside of the state plan.

unfinished state   a **state** characterized by instabilities and uncertainties that may render it susceptible to collaspe as a coherent entity.

untouchables   the lowest caste in India's **caste system,** whose members are among the poorest and most disadvantaged Indians.

warrant chiefs   employed by British colonial regime in Nigeria: A system in which "chiefs" were selected by the British to oversee certain legal matters and assist the colonial enterprise in governance and law enforcement in local areas.

zamindars   landlords who acquired private property rights during British rule of India and retained their property in the modern period.

About the Editors and Contributors

Ervand Abrahamian is Professor of History at Baruch College and the Graduate Center of the City University of New York. His recent publications include *Khomeinism: Essays on the Islamic Republic* (University of California Press, 1993), and *Tortured Confessions: Prisons and Public Recantations in Modern Iran* (University of California Press, 1999).

Merilee S. Grindle is Edward S. Mason Professor of International Development at the John F. Kennedy School of Government, Harvard University. She is a specialist on the comparative analysis of policy-making, implementation, and public management in developing countries and has written extensively on Mexico. Her most recent book is *Challenging the State: Crisis and Innovation in Latin America and Africa* (Cambridge University Press, 1996).

Richard A. Joseph is Asa G. Candler Professor of Political Science at Emory University. He has written extensively on Nigerian politics and governance in sub-Saharan Africa in general. He is the author of *Democracy and Prebendal Politics in Nigeria: The Rise and Fall of the Second Republic* (Cambridge University Press, 1987), and editor of *State, Conflict, and Democracy in Africa* (Lynne Rienner, 1999).

William A. Joseph is Professor of Political Science at Wellesley College and an Associate of the Fairbank Center for East Asian Research at Harvard University. His research focuses on contemporary Chinese politics and ideology. He is co-editor of *New Perspectives on the Cultural Revolution* (Harvard University Press, 1991), and contributing editor of *The Oxford Companion to Politics of the World* (Oxford University Press, 1993) and the Asia Society's China Briefing series.

Mark Kesselman is Professor of Political Science at Columbia University. A specialist on the French and European political economy, his recent publications include contributions to *The Mitterand Era: Policy Alternatives and Political Mobilization in France* (Macmillan, 1995), and *Mitterand's Legacy, Chirac's Challenge* (St. Martin's, 1996). He is the co-author of *A Century of Organized Labor in France* (St. Martin's, 1997).

Darren Kew is a Ph.D. candidate at the Fletcher School of Law and Diplomacy at Tufts University. In 1996–1997 he taught at the Universities of Lagos and Kano (Bayero) in Nigeria on a Fulbright grant. His dissertation focuses on the role of civil society in democratization and conflict resolution in Nigeria.

Atul Kohli is Professor of Politics and International Affairs at Princeton University. His principal research interest is the comparative political economy of developing countries, especially India. He is the author of *Democracy and Discontent: India's Growing Crisis of Governability* (Cambridge University Press, 1990). His current research involves a comparative analysis of industrialization in South Korea, Brazil, India, and Nigeria.

Joel Krieger is Norma Wilentz Hess Professor of Political Science at Wellesley College. His publications include *British Politics in the Global Age: Can Social Democracy Survive?* (Polity, 1999), and *Reagan, Thatcher, and the Politics of Decline* (Oxford University Press, 1986). He was also editor-in-chief of *The Oxford Companion to Politics of the World* (Oxford University Press, 1993).

Peter Lewis is Associate Professor at the School of International Service, American University. He has written extensively on Nigerian political economy, as well as on broader regional issues of participation, democratic transition, and economic adjustment in Africa. He is currently working on a study of the comparative political economies of Indonesia and Nigeria.

Alfred P. Montero is Assistant Professor of Political Science at Carleton College. His recent publications include contributions to *Democratic Brazil: Actors, Institutions, and Processes* (University of Pittsburgh Press, 1999), and articles in the *Journal of Interamerican Studies and World Affairs, Current History,* and *Hemisphere*. He is currently writing a book on subnational industrial policy in Brazil and Spain.

Scott Taylor is Gwendolen M. Carter Lecturer in African Politics at Smith College. His writings focus on African political economy and business-government relations. He is currently writing a book entitled *Business and the State in Southern Africa*.

Index*

*Numbers in boldface indicate the page where a key term is defined.